VIDEO SURVEILLANCE

Edited by **Weiyao Lin**

Video Surveillance
Edited by Weiyao Lin

Published by InTech
Janeza Trdine 9, 51000 Rijeka, Croatia

Publishing Process Manager Ivana Lorkovic

Technical Editor Teodora Smiljanic

Cover Designer InTech Design Team

Additional hard copies can be obtained from orders@intechopen.com

Video Surveillance, Edited by Weiyao Lin
p. cm.
ISBN 978-953-307-436-8

For EU product safety concerns:
IN TECH d.o.o., Prolaz Marije Krucifikse Kozulić 3, 51000 Rijeka, Croatia,
info@intechopen.com or visit our website at intechopen.com.

Meet the editor

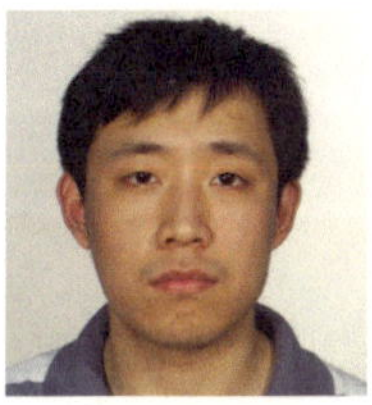

Weiyao Lin received the B.Eng. and M.Eng. degrees from Shanghai Jiao Tong University, Shanghai, China, in 2003 and 2005, respectively, and the Ph.D. degree from the University of Washington, Seattle, USA in 2010, all in electrical engineering. During 2006 to 2010, he worked as research interns at Motorola Labs, San Diego, USA, RealNetworks, Seattle, USA, and Thomson Technology, Princeton, USA. Since 2010, he has been an assistant professor at the Department of Electronic Engineering, Institute of Image Communication and Information Processing, Shanghai Jiao Tong University, Shanghai, China. He has authored and coauthored over 30 technical papers. He holds two 2 issued US patents and has 1 under-review US patent. His research interests include video surveillance, video content analysis, machine learning, computer vision, video coding and transmission. Dr. Lin is a member of IEEE and a member of IEEE Multimedia Communications Technical Committee (MMTC). He has served as a co-chair of the SJTU-HYU joint workshop in 2010, a guest editor of special issue for the Journal of Visual Communication and Image Representation, a technical program committee member of IEEE ICME and VCIP, and a reviewer for multiple journals and conferences.

Contents

Preface

Video surveillance is becoming increasingly important in many applications, including traffic control, urban surveillance, home security, environmental monitoring, and healthcare. With the rapid growth of demand for ubiquitous sensing and security, great challenges have been raised for designing, transmitting, and processing over video surveillance systems. As such, evolution is changing from the tedious manual surveillance to the efficient automatic and intelligent surveillance. And this evolution, in turn, is issuing new challenges in front of us, including system designing, data analysis and processing, resource scheduling, and data streaming. This requires better understanding of the implications of communication, compression, data mining, content-based video retrieval, machine learning, and pattern recognition.

The goal of this book is to consolidate and highlight the latest achievements and developments in the field of video surveillance. The papers selected for this book comprise a cross-section of topics that reflect a variety of perspectives and disciplinary backgrounds. Besides the introduction of new achievements in video surveillance, this book also presents some good overviews of the state-of-the-art technologies as well as some interesting advanced topics related to video surveillance. I believe the 25 chapters presented in this book can provide a clear picture of the current research status in the area of video surveillance.

This book contains a total of five major parts that cover the following directions: overview of the current developments in video surveillance; new designs and frameworks for video surveillance systems; novel algorithms for object extraction and tracking; new methods for video content analysis and event detection; and some advanced topics related to video surveillance.

The brief outline of the book is as follows:

Part I presents tutorials, surveys and comparative studies of several new trends and developments in video surveillance. Chapter 1 is a tutorial on video analysis and information management techniques used for video surveillance applications. These two parts are normally indentified as the key factors for future intelligent video surveillance systems. Chapter 2 gives an overview of the techniques about performance evaluation in distributed video surveillance systems. By discussing the evaluation metrics for various parts including data acquisition, system intelligence, system architecture, user-interface, and user-oriented functionality, this chapter also provides a clear view on where and how to improve the efficiency of a video surveillance system. Chapter 3 describes the legal and policy issues for surveillance applications. While surveillance applications are often weighed against the civil rights of individuals being observed, this chapter gives a very good discussion on this complex rights-and-security balance issue. Thus, it can serve as a good reference during the practical usage of surveillance systems.

Part II comprising six chapters is devoted to the design of video surveillance systems, frameworks, and structures. Here the readers can find a wide variety of surveillance systems and frameworks for different applications. Chapter 4 provides a walkthrough to the ONVIF (Open Network Video Interface Forum) video surveillance system, from the camera through analysis and storage right up to display and export. In addition, this chapter also illustrates the general trend towards processing increasing amounts of data in real-time automatically by avoiding completely the task of decoding the video prior analysis. Chapter 5 describes a real experience of a wireless video-surveillance system, illustrating the overall architecture and the structure of each component block. Specifically, video sources use rate-control to emit a constant bit-rate flow, while the access network is a WMN (Wireless Mesh Networks) implementing a multipath routing algorithm to minimize delay and intrusions. Furthermore, analysis is also carried out against the emission bit rate, and quality perceived at destination is evaluated with an objective parameter. Chapter 6 discusses the QKD (Quantum Key Distribution) protocol and its potential to secure video surveillance applications. This chapter shows examples of a QKD implementation along with reference to other implementations as well as some innovations that can reduce QKD costs, limit some of the side channel attacks and provide hardware support to off load CPU processing. In addition it also touched on the need for integration with existing network infrastructure, providing services necessary for deployment and an on-going standards effort that is needed by both customers and developers. Chapter 7 discusses the data abstraction hierarchy and the system configuration of the next-generation surveillance systems. A conclusion has been made that each camera should be embedded with content analysis ability to become a smart camera instead of just an IP camera. Furthermore, two examples of cooperative surveillance systems are also provided for different scenarios. Chapter 8 describes a video analysis engine called SuperVision system that can analyze video streams from different types of camera, in particular omnidirectional, and to set alarms when preconfigured events are detected. The types of events detected are numerous, and can be composed according to the context and needs of applications. Chapter 9 proposes a multi-stage video analysis framework which is a flexible and efficient solution for automatic analysis of camera images in the monitoring systems.

Part III comprises six chapters and deals with new methods and techniques for object segmentation, detection, and tracking in videos. Chapter 10 summarizes the existing techniques for background subtraction and its application in lane occupancy analysis. By comparing different background subtraction methods, this chapter provides a good insight into the usability and effectiveness for various background subtraction algorithms. Chapter 11 presents a combined shape and feature-based object tracking method. The proposed method adaptively generates background, which serves as a fundamental building block for robust tracking by resolving inherent problems of existing block-matching algorithm. After generating background, the shape tracking module in the proposed algorithm determines object's moving region based on shape control points. Experimental results demonstrate the effeictiveness of the this method.

Chapter 12 presents an extended perceptual curve tracking algorithm using both color and gradient properties. The system can track edge traces and extract semantic curve features at same time. The enhanced tracker provides a more robust and effective solution for edge detection, curve feature extraction with real-time performance. Chapter 13 first summarizes the two major categories for object tracking in the crowd scenario: the blob-based methods and the point-based methods. Then a new point-based tracking method is proposed in this chapter which shows its effectiveness over the existing tracking methods. Chapter 14 introduces a statistical method for measuring human traffic flow. Unlike previous methods that tried to count individuals by detection and tracking, the statistical method estimates the size of human traffic by applying the feature-based regression in a spatiotemporal domain. Since it is a statistical method which does not include time consuming detection and tracking, it requires much smaller computation while achieving similar or higher accuracy compared with the previous methods. Chapter 15 proposes an agent-based architecture in context of a distributed vision based tracking system. The objective of the system is the tracking of objects over a wide area scene by using a high level multi-sensor management strategy. This work concerns the capacity of management of multi-camera systems for surveillance including both overlapping cameras fields of view and distant cameras configuration.

Part IV comprises six chapters and focuses on the problem of content analysis and event detection which is one of the most important parts in video surveillance systems. Chapter 16 reviews and exploits developments and general strategies of stages involved in video surveillance. It also analyzes the challenges and feasibility for combining object tracking, motion analysis, behavior analysis, and biometrics for standoff human subject identification and behavior understanding. It is a very good survey and summary for behavior analysis in videos. Chapter 17 proposes a new framework for unexpected event detection in dense areas. The method cuts the problem of dense area detection into two: the movement characterization, and the learning and classifying procedure. By solving these two issues, the proposed method can provide an efficient solution for this difficult scenario. Chapter 18 presents a new graphical-based method for automatic scenario recognition in videos. The method combines graphical probabilistic techniques in a flexible manner in order to manage decision uncertainties efficiently. The recognition system takes the advantage of an active perception strategy by focusing on the awaited scenarios with respect to the scene behavior. The partial recognition strategy brings efficient predictive capabilities for the high level scenario agent in order prepare the activation of its future awaited events. Chapter 19 introduces a novel system for the real-time summarization of the high resolution surveillance videos under the supervision of an surveillance operator. The system employs an eyegaze tracker that returns the focus points of the surveillance operator. The resulting video summary is an integration of the actions observed in the surveillance video and the video sections where the operator pays most attention or overlooks. The unique combination of the eye-gaze positions with the non-linear video summaries results in a number of important advantages. Chapter 20 focuses on a very important scenario of fall detection. After a detailed overview of different fall detection algorithms, this chapter describes a new system for fall detection which shows its effectiveness in the experimental results over large data. Chapter 21 proposes a new generic video understanding approach able to extract and learn valuable information from noisy video scenes for real-time applications. This approach is able to estimate the reliability of the information associated to the objects tracked in the scene, in order to properly control the uncertainty of data due to noisy videos and many other difficulties present in video applications.

Finally, Part V comprising four chapters discusses some interesting advanced topics related to video surveillance. Chapter 22 discusses an interesting interdisciplinary problem: the relationships between animal eyes and relevant human engineering (HE), in the context of video surveillance. It purposely use engineering language rather than biologic one in order to make those relationships more familiar to video imagery scientists and engineers. Based the detailed discussion of this relationship, some interesting conclusions are also highlighted. Chapter 23 summarizes another interesting problem of fire detection using video surveillance. While discussing the state-of-the-art fire detection approaches and methods, this chapter also points out future directions and discusses first steps which are now being taken to improve the vision-based detection of smoke and flames. Chapter 24 develops a novel tool for placement of cameras for surveillance applications. Apart from camera location, the tool provides optimum pan-tilt angles and zoom level. As the tool is based on extended field of view, it avoids redundancy in sensor placement. Unlike other placement methods, the proposed method calculates the optimum zoom level which improves the quality of service of the vision system. Chapter 25 addresses the issue of stereo disparity map extraction from multi-view videos. It proposes a new method which introduces sparse samples to reduce raster size while keeping the same the spatial resolution of stereo matching. The effectiveness of the algorithm is demonstrated in the experimental results.

Summing up the wide range of issues presented in the book, it can be addressed to a quite broad audience, including both academic researchers and practitioners in halls of industries interested in scheduling theory and its applications. I sincerely hope you will find the chapters as useful and interesting as I did. I am looking forward to seeing another technological breakthrough in this area in the near future.

January 2011

Weiyao Lin
Shanghai Jiao Tong University
Department of Electronic Engineering
Shanghai, P.R. China

Part 1

Overview

1

Information Management and Video Analytics: the Future of Intelligent Video Surveillance

Bennie Coetzer, Jaco van der Merwe and Bradley Josephs
Protoclea Advanced Image Engineering, South Africa

1. Introduction

The need to monitor exists for many reasons. We use it as a mechanism to protect ourselves and our property, we use it to manage large numbers such as traffic information, we use it to monitor behaviour as in crowd surveillance, we use it to monitor production lines and operations and so on. While recognition of events or alarms may assist in reacting to it, a major objective of systems should be to be proactive, in other words, to prevent events.

Video Surveillance has been with us for a long time. Traditionally it was used to display images on monitors, manned by guards or operators. This allowed us to view a number of places using less people and we could also perform patrolling duties from the safety of a control room. It satisfied the goals of safe patrolling and reducing manpower while performing the role of watchdog or guard. When video recording was introduced we found that we could create evidence of events that would be useful in prosecution, analysis, etc. As it became less expensive, more cameras were placed and of course more monitors. We could watch more areas with less people but very soon it became apparent that human beings have limitations. We also found that recording is an expensive exercise as video information is vast. At this point machine intelligence was introduced to assist with detection and also to reduce recording to be event driven, which of course made it less expensive. Initial techniques were crude with many false alarms but image analysis grew and became more sophisticated, resulting in better detection and even object recognition. Image quality improved, storage cost went down, less compression could be used and overall efficiency in terms of human intervention and prosecution success improved.

This article will limit its scope to Information Management as it pertains to the security and traffic arenas, although much of this is clearly applicable in other areas as well. The chapter concentrates on the use of Video Analytics to achieve the various objectives as defined, but, as will be seen in the paragraph on Intelligent Information management, Video Analytics is merely a part of the complete system.

2. Video analytics

2.1 Basics of video analytics

The role of Video Analytics can be described in a number of ways and consist primarily of the following:

2.1.1 Video enhancement
In this role images are manipulated automatically or by user intervention to assist a human or machine to detect or identify objects better. The processes involved could range from noise reduction, image sharpening, edge detection or various others. Such functionality should be part of any system that uses humans to interpret images.

2.1.2 Video reconstruction
In many instances sensors deliver distorted images. This could be because of poor quality lenses, atmospheric distortion, reflections or moving (vibrating) cameras or subjects. Video reconstruction tools such as stabilisation, anti-blurring and so on could be used to reduce such noise to assist users (humans and machines) to 'see better. These techniques could also be applied during post-event analysis and could assist in reconstruction of distorted images due to tape stretching, very high compression ratios and so on.

2.1.3 Video analysis
Video analysis has primarily to do with intelligence extraction from the visual scene and the rest of this chapter will concentrate on this aspect. This is not to downplay the importance of the other aspects but merely to serve the title of the chapter which is about information management.

2.2 Event detection
The initial objective of current systems is to recognise an event. This could of course mean many things. It could be detection of movement or detection of presence or absence of an object.
The basic mechanism employed is difference detection between prior and current views.

2.2.1 Motion detection and tracking
We have heard a lot about motion detection in the past, but it was usually very expensive and the results were not very accurate. With some further developments in the processing capabilities of modern processors, more advanced techniques could be used to give better motion detection results. It is now not only possible to monitor regions of images, but the entire image on a per pixel basis, and since each pixel can be monitored, a tracking algorithm can be applied to mark and follow the moving pixels in an image. Moving pixels of objects are usually grouped together into what some in the image processing community refer to as blobs.
The basic principle behind the detection of motion is to simply detect changes/differences between consecutive frames in an image sequence. Many detection algorithms are based on the subtraction of a "learnt" background model/image from the current image and applying a threshold value to separate the apparent "moving" foreground from the "static" background. This process of separation is also known as segmentation.
The definition of "background" may differ greatly depending on the application; i.e. average human traffic at an airport might be considered as background if we were detecting unattended baggage, or periodic motion, like swaying trees on a windy morning versus completely still trees on a windless afternoon. This very difference in definition and the pure randomness found in the statistical data of video makes modelling an accurate background

very tricky. Therefore a good motion detection system should get this right in order to do accurate detection with as little false positives or negatives as possible.
We will briefly look at a few current theoretical and practical methods in use and some of their advantages and disadvantages.

Modelling the background using a codebook [1]

This method "learns" a background model by monitoring each pixel in a scene over a set period and listing all values "captured" during that time as a list of "background" pixel values. Each new video frame is compared to these values and all pixel values that fall outside the codebook values are considered to be foreground/movement.
With this method it is possible to "train" the system to recognise swaying trees, for instance, as moving background. This however requires the monitored scene to be free of "foreground" movement during the training process, which is usually difficult in real world applications. This method would however be well suited in an indoors environment where light changes are minimal and some movement, such as a moving fan or a moving escalator, is present.
Since calculation consists of only simple value comparisons after the codebook has been learnt, this method is computationally speaking, very inexpensive and therefore requires very little processing power.

Mixture of Gaussians Background Modelling [2]

This algorithm uses an adaptive background; this simply means that the background model is continuously updated to allow slow background changes (such as gradual light condition changes or slow moving shadows cast by the sun) to be factored in, by updating the background model gradually as the scene background changes. Each pixel in the background is modelled by a mixture of K Gaussian probability distributions (where K is a number between 3 and 5), each representing different colour occurrences. The background is then modelled as the top X highest probable colours. Probable colours are the ones which stay longer and more static. In order to keep this model "adapting" each new value is compared and matched to the existing model and if no match is found a new Gaussian component is added and reordered with the existing components to create an updated background model.
This method is very resilient to periodic motion such as swaying trees and gets "better" with age. It can also be tuned to be very sensitive to minute colour changes, thus allowing the algorithm to be used on other image types such as thermal imagers. Another addition to this algorithm is the ability to distinguish shadows cast by moving objects versus static objects by comparing both the chromatic and brightness differences of each new pixel and the current background model to some thresholds.
Even though this model does seem to work well for most indoors and outdoors cases it is still sometimes difficult to balance the predefined threshold perfectly. Clouds passing before the sun in an outdoors scene, does change the total brightness values of the scene, causing the sudden colour change to be detected as movement. This can however be "handled" by monitoring the total scene brightness and adjusting the model parameters accordingly.
In general this detection algorithm does really well when very accurate detection is necessary, and performs well in both colour and monochrome video. False positives (objects detected as foreground that was supposed to be background) do occur rather frequently if

the parameters for the specific scene aren't set properly, which makes this algorithm rather difficult to set up for a generic scene. But in certain detection situations, more false positives can be tolerated for the sake of accuracy of detection.

Foreground Object Detection from Videos Containing Complex Background

This algorithm, developed by Liyuan Li et al. [3], deals with the detection of movement in scenes with complex backgrounds; both stationary and moving background objects, and undergoes both gradual and sudden "once-off" changes. In many shopping malls you have the situation where there are flickering screens, opening/revolving doors, indoor water fountains, high gloss reflective floors, switching lights and so on causing plenty false positive detections. One option is to simply mask these areas as non-detection areas but in doing this you have created a detection black spot. This algorithm is able to deal with scenarios of this kind with much success without "hiding" possible detection areas.
The algorithm employs a Bayes decision rule formulated to classify background and foreground using selected feature vectors. The stationary background object is described by the colour feature, and the moving background object is represented by the colour co-occurrence feature. Foreground objects are extracted by fusing the classification results from both stationary and moving pixels.
The author presented the following block diagram to explain the slightly more complex algorithm:

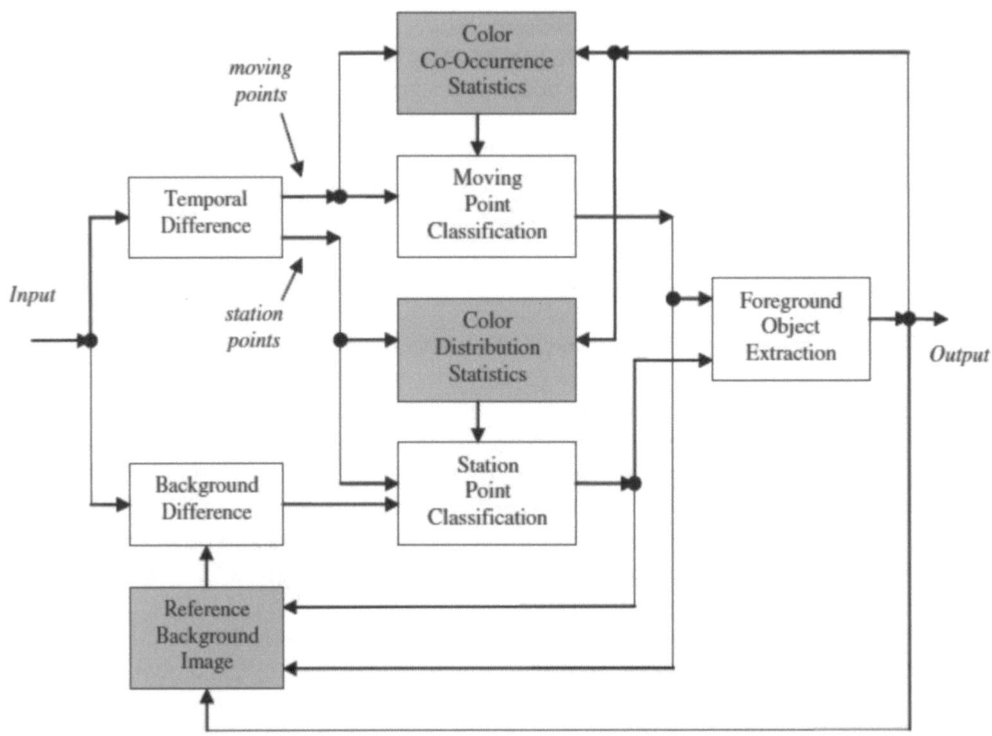

Fig. 1. Algorithm block diagram for the Foreground Object Detection from Videos Containing Complex Background

The algorithm consists of four parts: change detection, change classification, foreground object segmentation, and background learning and maintenance. A block diagram of the Liyuan Li et al. [3] algorithm is shown in Fig. 1. The light blocks from left to right illustrate the first three steps, and the grey blocks illustrate the adaptive background modelling step. In the first step, non-change pixels in the image stream are filtered out by using simple background and temporal differencing (i.e. subtracting two sequential frames). The detected changes are then separated as pixels belonging to stationary and moving objects according to inter-frame changes. In the second step, the pixels associated with stationary or moving objects are further classified as background or foreground based on the learned statistics of colours and colour co-occurrences respectively by using the Bayes decision rule. In the third step, foreground objects are segmented by combining the classification results from both stationary and moving parts. In the fourth and final step, the background models are updated. Gradual and "once-off" learning strategies are applied to learn the statistics of the feature vectors. At each step a reference background image is maintained to make the background difference accurate and adaptive to the changing background. The detail of the algorithm can be obtained from [3].

This algorithm performs well under varying backgrounds with very little false positives, it does however suffer quite a bit from false-negative detections (i.e. not detecting objects it should have) especially in monochrome video such a thermal images. But used in a less critical general monitoring environment this algorithm performs very well with constant detection results.

Fig. 2. Video sequence containing a few tracked objects

In comparison the Mixture of Gaussian Modelling and the Complex background both have good merits for use and are even combined in some instances to achieve user specific requirements. However just motion detection is not enough for a good events detection system. The objects detected have to be tracked to allow for further intelligence extraction. The following paragraph will discuss foreground object tracking.

Tracking

Tracking is the process of following the movement of an object over time. In video analysis this would translate to the following of a detected object in between successive frames in video or in more advanced instances between different videos.

Before we jump into an explanation of how tracking works let us look at an example; Fig. 2 shows a sequence of images containing some tracked objects. The images are a few frames taken from video sequence, showing orange ovals drawn around the moving "objects", each with a tracking number attached to it.

In order to track an object it should first be detected as an object of interest of some nature. In the case of movement detection this would be "foreground" objects detected using any of the previously mentioned motion detectors. The generic output of these methods/algorithms is a series of masks showing groups (blobs) of moving pixels in each frame. Many methods exist to track blobs but the basic principle stays the same; first, detect the "tracking blob" and assign some identifier to it, then detect its position in the next frame and the following ones until it has left the scene or cannot be found anymore.

We have developed our own novel method of tracking blobs based on their contours; to detect a blob, a small buffer of newly untracked blobs is kept and updated with each new frame. If a blob satisfies certain "tracking" criteria, such as size, speed and direction it is added to the list of tracked blobs. A matching blob is then searched for in each new frame. The simplest matching algorithm simply checks whether any of the new blobs found overlaps a currently tracked blob; this however is not always as effective as some blobs may move so fast that they don't overlap in two consecutive frames. In this instance the historical "track" information of the object is used to predict where the object "should" be and then searches for it in within the predicted parameters. This method is fast and able to track large number of multiples objects in real time (i.e. several individuals entering a building during rush hour). To even further enhance the tracking the object shape can be utilised, this allows us to track objects that may be temporarily occluded or partly hidden from view.

The information from these trackers can be fed in real time from the processing unit to any device or service that can make use of the information. Furthermore, a sub-image of each of these tracked objects can be used in an object recognition algorithm to determine the type of object. This is a valuable capability, since it's now possible to "see" what it is, where it's heading, and possibly also what it's doing, all automatically and in real time. The amount of intelligence information that can be gathered in a relatively short space of time is enormous. [4]

2.2.2 Intelligence extraction

Once an event has been detected it has to be analysed to determine whether the event is benign or a threat. Traditionally this task was left to humans but, modern video analytic tools promise automation of this. The event is thus analysed such that benign movement such as scene clutter, movement outside regions of interest (ROI), moving trees, busy roads, etc. are ignored and those movements or events that matter are considered.

Fig. 3. Examples of man-made object detection

Intelligence from Typed Text

A very common form of "object" recognition is optical character recognition (OCR), currently widely used in license plate recognition systems. These systems has accuracies of nearly 100% just showing how much this technology have matured. The technology is also harnessed in other situations such as reading shipping crates and ship identification numbers. Wherever characters are written in a typed font this technology can be utilised.

Fig. 4. Examples of object recognition from a video sequence (Face Recognition)

Intelligence from recognising and detecting objects

Object detection and recognition sounds like something reserved for academic research papers, but the truth is that this technology is gaining rapid popularity and the accuracy of detection and recognition is getting better at an ever increasing rate.

One kind of detection that is rather common in the military and rural security applications is the detection of man-made objects. The examples in Fig. 3 shows how a very simple algorithm that uses texture and edge information can be used to detect man-made "regions" in an image. This at a first glance does not look very useful but imagine having to go through many images or video trying to find scenes containing only farmhouses? This technology could certainly speed up the process if the most likely images could be filtered.

Finally there is also object recognition. The images in Fig. 4 present the recognition of a human- face "object" in a video sequence. This was done in real time, which show that the speed at which this can be done has increased dramatically. In a similar fashion to which the face "object" was recognised, any rigid or regular feature object can be recognised by training the algorithm with the features of the object to be recognised. Objects could be the frontal or side view of a vehicle, or the shape of a certain building, or even different weapon kinds and makes. The possibilities are vast and certainly possible.

3. Information management

While we are convinced that Video Analytics will play the dominant role in intelligence extraction, as described above, this is only a part of the overall requirement as seen in figure 5. From this point onward data analysis plays the major role and databases and analysis techniques are dominant.

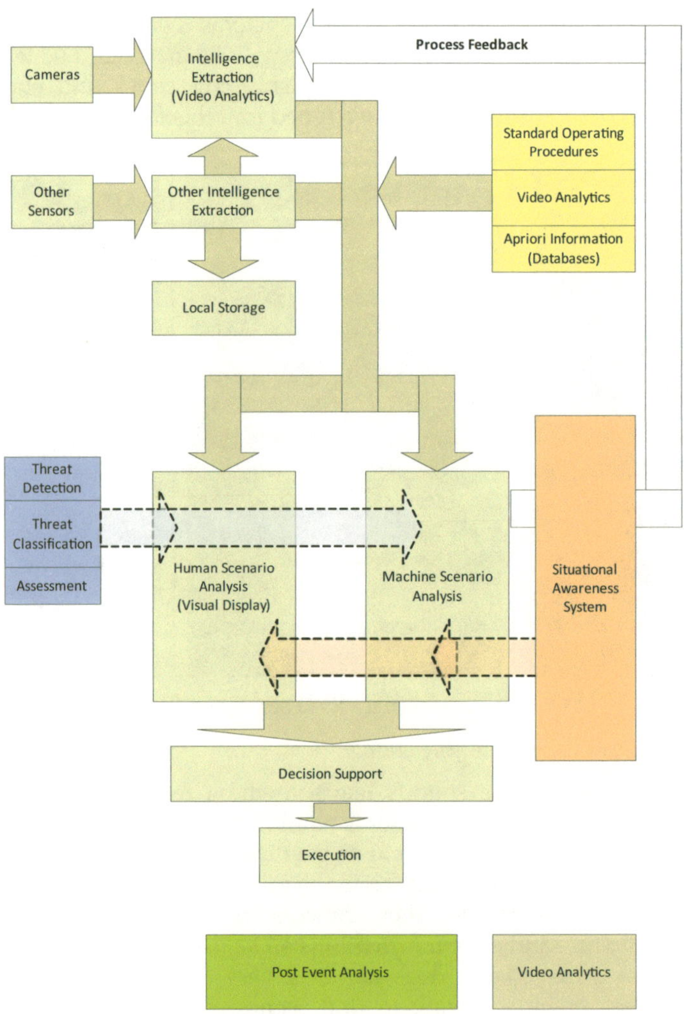

Fig. 5. Information Management Process

Up to this point video analytics played a pivotal role and, improvement in analytic techniques will assist in this. However, the solution to our original problem does not lie solely in our awareness of what is happening around us but also on our ability to recognise the intent of the object, classifying its potential and to be able to put counter effects in motion to prevent unacceptable events. For this we need to add intelligence or predictive ability to the solution.

3.1 Threat detection

After isolating relevant events (intelligence) these need to be classified. At this point the analysis takes a different tack and changes from detection to recognition. A threat could be identified by comparison to a set of known threats, which would be the initial task. This process could be done by **content analysis.**

In addition to recognising threats, a major output of the video analytic system is the ability to provide 'tracks' or a history of the path that an object has taken. This task is achieved by tracking algorithms.

In identifying a threat, a number of parameters are important. Naturally the first would be to identify the object but classifying it as a threat involves more than simply recognising it. Parameters such as direction of movement, speed of movement, linearity (meandering vs purposeful) are important as well. The detection of this is fraught with difficulties such as what to do with multiple objects, ie multiple tracks. Unlike radar images the reality of low angle vision virtually guarantees that objects will pass behind one another (occlusion) resulting in difficulties to attach the track to a specific object. Special algorithms, predictive and otherwise are needed to be able to manage such tracks.

In addition to this, the difficulty of reducing false alarms while at the same time maintaining a high probability of detection is increased dramatically. It is also clear that human intervention at this level will probably always form part of any solution but it is our view that Video Analytic solutions will continually improve and replace human decision making, wherever possible.

Motion-image intelligence extraction

Extraction of intelligence from moving images/video gets a lot more interesting. Once objects can be detected and recognized in each frame, aspects like their movement and behaviour can be analysed which brings a whole new set of automatically extracted information to the table to work with. Following an object's current location can not only give you current behaviour information, but also allow the ability to predict. Behavioural information can be matched up with archived patterns to provide early warning of possible behavioural threats. Proactive decisions, such as pointing a camera, or sending security personnel to the right location in time, can be made, saving precious minutes or even seconds that could just give the upper hand.

With the advancement of computing technology, the speed at which these processes can be performed can be increased considerably, and by adding "machine learning" to regular intelligence questions this extraction can be automated to provide immediate decision support. Imagine deploying several UAV's or autonomous ground vehicles into a disaster or emergency situation and having immediate intelligence information streaming directly back to security and safety headquarters. Intelligence information that can range from something as simple as the number of humans in danger, to a complete situational analysis. A complete situational analysis that could contain a comprehensive breakdown, from type of vehicle, their number plates, their drivers, the identified criminals, the weapons they are wielding to specific threat identification such as fire, explosion hazards and other dangerous situations. Yes, it does sound like something from a science fiction novel, but why not? The technology is there, we should harness it. [4]

3.2 Intelligent analysis

For this context a limited definition of intelligence is the ability to learn about, learn from, understand, and interact with the environment. This general ability consists of a number of specific abilities, which include the following:

- Adaptability to a new environment or to changes in the current environment
- Capacity for knowledge and the ability to acquire it
- Capacity for reason
- Ability to comprehend relationships
- Ability to evaluate and judge

Environment in this definition includes the immediate surroundings, including all objects, reactive capacities and other effects that may influence the judgement.

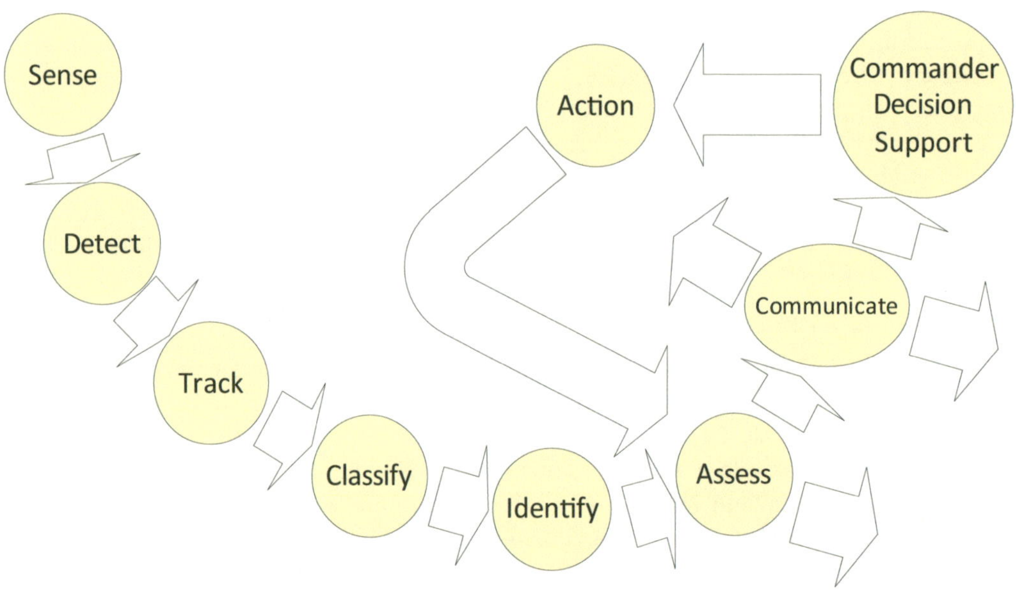

Fig. 6. Decision making process

3.2.1 Intelligence sources

The sources for this information would obviously be the real time sources such as the video information from the cameras. But it should also include other real time sources such as perimeter alarms, information from guards, the news, etc. as well as historical information such as previously recorded footage, faces of suspects and so on.

3.3 Detection of intent

A very important parameter to determine in our problem is the detection of the intent of the identified threat. While any person may be walking in an area, it is the one with malicious intent that is the threat, even though he does not differ physically from the one with benign intent.

A number of algorithms have been demonstrated that attempt to identify this. In this regard algorithms to detect behaviour, especially human behaviour would be those that can contribute most. These algorithms would include relative easy ones such as detection of running, loitering but more sophisticated algorithms can identify aggressive behaviour and possibly recognise specific weapons such as handguns.

The major benefit will come when an object's movement tracks are identified and prediction algorithms are applied to such movement. Thus someone walking along a fence and suddenly turning towards the fence could be identified as having a different intent, possibly a threat.

3.4 Context analysis

Naturally, the analysis of intent is dependent on a clear picture of the current situation, or situational awareness. This aspect would consider not only recognition of and predicting movements but also estimating the threat level and the possible response to such threats. Such decisions clearly require the ability to understand one's own ability to respond and the available options. While we are far from having this kind of engine, at least in practical applications, one can go far by using adequate automatic Standard Operating Procedures (SOP). In this regard analysis of event, behaviour and intent could be a process of applying the pre-determined procedure.

The increasingly sophisticated nature of crime demands a comprehensive approach to solve the problem. Some intelligent video surveillance platforms typically stem from the expansion of Building Management or Access Control systems. What is required is a unified front end that sees and controls all systems on a single user interface. The system should provide a platform that fully integrates DVR's / NVR's, Video Analytics, access control, perimeter alarm systems, fire systems, time and attendance systems and other components. The future has to be **Intelligent Information Management**.

3.5 Data fusion

Proper contextual or scenario analysis requires the ability to evaluate information from different sources. This effort is maintained by a Data Fusion system which generally provides the following functions.

The main functions of the system would include the ability to

- Filter information for relevant intelligence
- Classify the intelligence in the context of the situation
- Be able to predict activity
- Be able to present potential solutions

and finally

DECISION SUPPORT

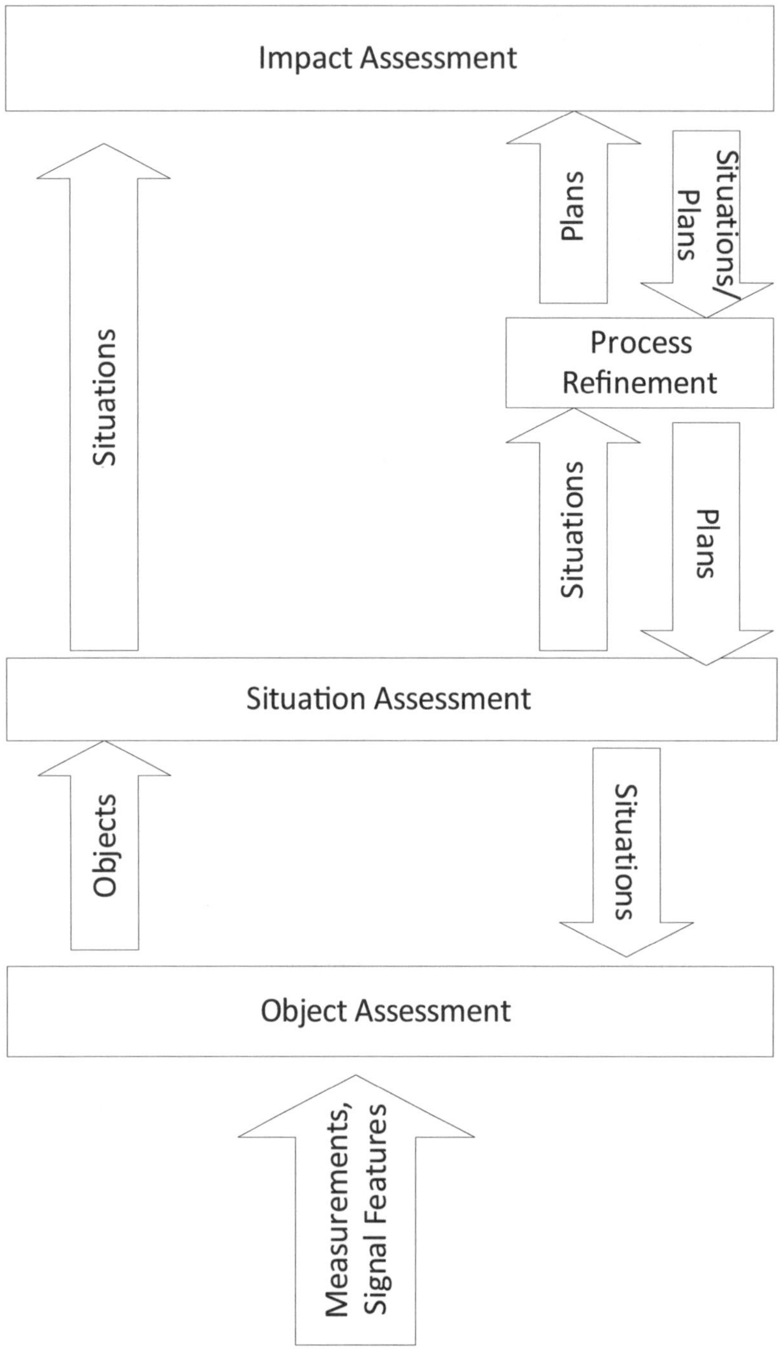

Fig. 7. Data Fusion Process

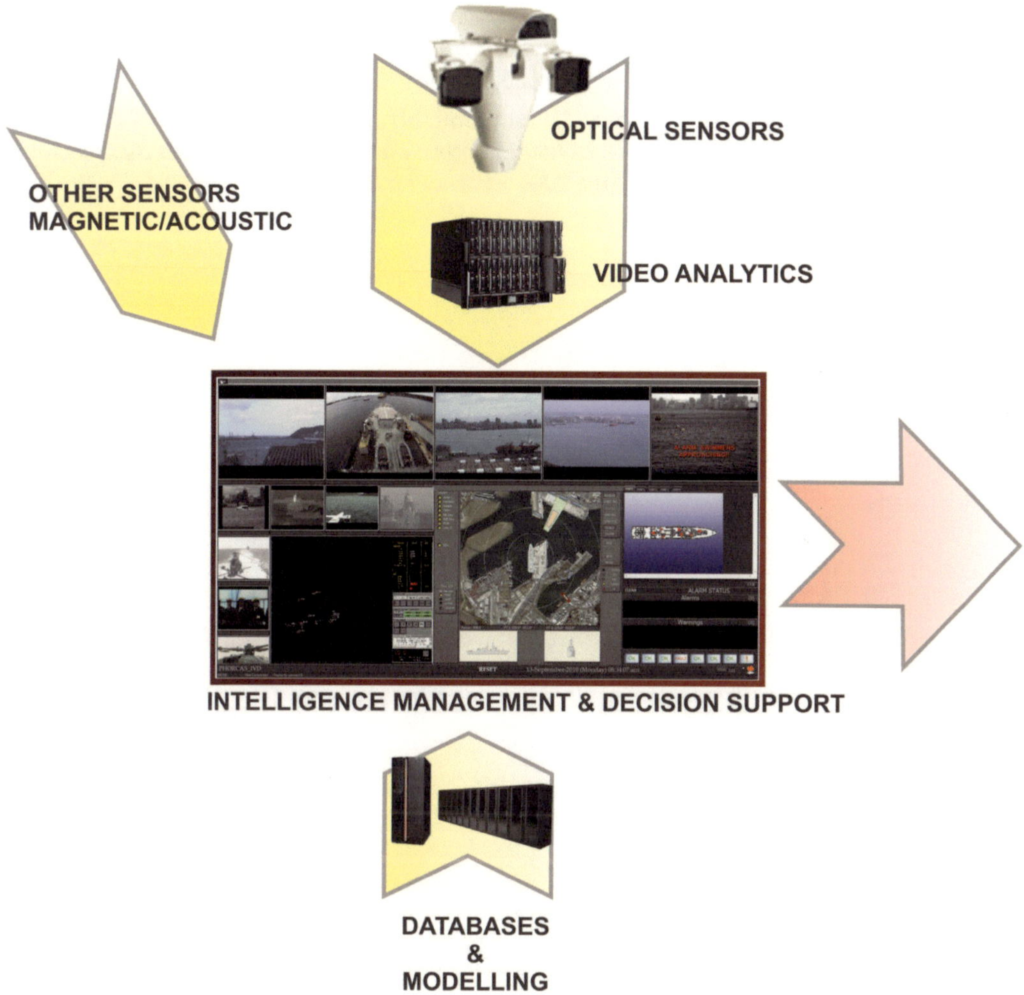

Fig. 8. Unified Decision Support User Interface

4. Conclusion

Simplistic approaches to security are just not good enough. This chapter identifies sophisticated detection (Video analytics) and Intelligent analysis as the key factors for future Video Surveillance.

5. References

[1] G. Bradski, A. Koehler, *Learning OPENCV*, Sebastopol, CA: O'Reilly Media, 2008.

[2] P. KaewTraKulPong, R. Bowden, "An Improved Adaptive Background Mixture Model for Realtime Tracking with Shadow Detection," *Proceedings of the 2nd European Workshop on Advanced Video Based Surveillance Systems*, AVBS01. Sept, 2001

[3] L. Li, W. Huang, I. Y. Gu, Q. Tian,."Foreground object detection from videos containing complex background," *Proceedings of the Eleventh ACM international Conference on Multimedia*, MULTIMEDIA '03. ACM, Nov 2003.

[4] B.H. Coetzer, J.S. van der Merwe, "Interoperability in Visual Command & Control Systems" *Proceedings of the 4th Military Information and Communications Symposium of South Africa*, MICSSA 2009, July, 2009

2

Efficient Video Surveillance: Performance Evaluation in Distributed Video Surveillance Systems

Aleksandra Karimaa
Turku University (Teleste Corp.)
Finland

1. Introduction

The ultimate aim of performance evaluation is to improve the system efficiency. Overall efficiency of the system is a combination of three factors: system functionality, performance and cost. Whereas system functionality improvement and cost optimisation are usually well understood and implemented the third factor of system performance is usually under prioritized. The development and improvements on system functionality are naturally driven by market requirements such as new features, compliance to common standards and adaptation of new technologies. The evaluation of system functionality is available by features benchmarking, etc. The evaluation of cost might be more complex due to the fact of different criteria of system pricing and various methods of following the costs of system and system maintenance. However, the cost of the system is also usually quite well evaluated and optimised - it is naturally driven by market economics. The task of performance evaluation followed with measurements and tests are usually performed only when certain performance problems appear in a system. Additionally, the methodologies to measure and evaluate system performance are not well known and understood. We believe that this approach should be changed. The factors describing system efficiency are interleaved - the performance can affect the cost of the system (usually long term maintenance costs) also the general system functionality depends upon system performance, a system of poor performance may not be able to accommodate new functionality or expand without difficult structural changes.

2. System performance evaluation approach

Evaluation of system performance is a difficult task: there are many different factors to consider, these factors may be (and usually are) interdependent. Moreover, they belong to different categories (see technical vs. business) which make them difficult to compare. There are various approaches on how to evaluate overall system performance. Our approach is to extract performance critical areas in the system and analyse what factors play the most important role in terms of performance. The combination of these factors will be a measure of overall system performance. The performance-critical system areas include: (a) data acquisition and system intelligence, (b) system architecture, (c) user-interface and user-oriented functionality. We try to analyse performance measurements methodologies and review available methods, rules, techniques or tools. Where applicable, we address methodology accuracy, results stability and analyse errors that may affect the quality of the measurements. We aim to provide the description of performance measurement process expended with collection of ideas, theories and concepts related to performance evaluation.

3. Data acquisition and system intelligence

A well performing and intelligent surveillance system will optimize the overall performance of the system by applying variety of intelligent tools. An intelligent system is able to perform initial filtering of the data based on its relevancy before any further processing is applied. It is able to combine the data in an efficient way to optimize a system for various criteria. Some level of intelligence might exist already on the data acquisition level (on the sensor) but intelligent cooperation between system and system's sensors is essential due to the fact the sensors have limited processing power (comparing to distributed system). The analysis of data acquisition performance also involves analysis of low-level detection and processing algorithms that allows a level of filtering of incoming data. Usually, at the level of data collection, data fusion analysis is not applied. The exceptions are the situations where the node posses mutli-sensor capabilities e.g. audio activated camera and the node is able to perform some pre-filtering. Intelligent systems are able to apply automation mechanisms and they also should have learning capabilities.

3.1 Data acquisition

In context of video surveillance systems data acquisition refers to processes of gathering relevant data. In most surveillance systems data is retrieved from multiple sources of different types, such as: (a) video and image content sensors, (b) HW sensors, (c) other sensors, such as audio, or bio-metrics. Despite the fact that in many cases the identification of relevant data is rather subjective, there are good metrics available allowing the evaluation of data acquisition processes. The methodologies evaluating data acquisition systems can be divided into multiple categories. The most applicable are the mapping procedures comparing data to ground truth plus other various ways of comparing data of many different systems. Additionally, the importance of context testing should be discussed. Mapping refers to the mapping of system results against the results gathered from either reference system or ground truth data. The term ground truth refers to information that is collected "on location" and that exists "in reality". The mapping procedure is used to map the results data to ground truth data. In terms of data acquisition for surveillance system ground truth data is the data indentified manually as the relevant and interesting one. Methods relying on ground truth comparison are very well understood. They can be used for many types of sensors but they are especially efficient and commonly used for evaluation of video and image analysis. One of the reasons is the fact that ground truth data can be prepared manually with good quality as the visual information is easier to identify and classify for humans. It is the preferred method to evaluate the quality of single video or image data acquisition system despite the fact the process of identifying the data relevancy may be subjective and the process of preparing ground truth data is laborious and slow. In order to evaluate the system using these methods, the benchmarking data is usually provided together with ground data (see example (PETS, 2010)) or even with ground data and automatic tools for generating scores. Various metrics can be used to compare the output of tested data acquisition systems to ground truth data. The most common metrics include: (a) precision, (b) recall, and (c) f-measure. The system of excellent performance is characterized by high values of precicion, recall and f-measure. The precision describes amount of relevant data within all the data retrieved. The precision can be measured as a rate (see Equation 1). It can be interpreted as probability of that (randomly selected) retrieved data is relevant.

$$Precision = \frac{\{\text{retrieved relevant data}\}}{\{\text{all retrieved data}\}} \tag{1}$$

The recall describes the amount of relevant data that has been retrieved within all the existing relevant data. The recall can be measured as a rate (see Equation 2). It can be interpreted as probability of that (randomly selected) relevant data is retrieved.

$$Recall = \frac{\{\text{retrieved relevant data}\}}{\{\text{all relevant data}\}} \quad (2)$$

The performance of data acquisition systems can be described by these two measures by use of so called precision-recall curves. Other metrics are usually combining either recall or precision and provide either a more precision-oriented or recall- oriented approach. We will briefly present the most popular metrics which could be applied for measuring data acquisition in surveillance. If single score comparison is required, then the metric of F-measure can be used. F-measure (called also F1 score or F score) measures data retrieval accuracy by combining both measures of precision and recall (see Equation 3). F-measure itself can be weighted to be more recall or more precision- centred.

$$F = 2 * \frac{\{\text{Precision}\} * \{\text{Recall}\}}{\{\text{Precision}\} + \{\text{Recall}\}} \quad (3)$$

Additionally, (Kasturi et al., 2009) lists other metrics which are applicable for data acquisition in surveillance. We consider one to be very useful - SFDA (Sequence Frame Detection Accuracy). It was developed for VACE (US Government Video Analysis and Content Extraction) program. In addition to combining of precision and recall- type of measure the metric displays spatial distance between system output object and ground-data object. The other two metrics that we considered interesting in context of data acquisition for surveillance are: MODA (Multiple Object Detection Accuracy) and MODP (Multiple Object Detection Precision). All metrics proposed by (Kasturi et al., 2009) are available as a part of CLEAR program evaluation system (see (CLEAR, 2007)). The methods listed above provide a good base for evaluation of data acquisition systems in general but might not offer a definite answer as to whether system A performs better than system B in a given context - different systems performs well using different types of benchmark data. The benchmark data should reflect the usage scenario of the system.

The benchmark data for different testing context is widely available (see (Russell et al., 2008) and (Martin, 2001)). As all data acquisition methods rely on benchmarking data - test cases should be selected carefully. (Pavlopoulou et al., 2009) proposes the criteria to identify the test cases that should be used when comparing the systems. The comparison between the two solutions should be undertaken by further testing the areas of the biggest differences between algorithms. It will allows identification the weak and strong points of given solution. The results of this research can be applied to evaluation procedures in surveillance system.

3.2 System intelligence

The performance of system intelligence is very important performance factor for all systems where intelligent decision mechanisms exist. In particular, it concerns all the surveillance systems where video content analysis is applied. The primary function of video content analysis tools is to improve the time (speed), reliability and quality of access to relevant material. The secondary function is to provide system automation to improve user quality of work. Video content analysis tools provide various system functionalities, such as: predefined scenario alerting, forensic search capabilities, statistical analysis, traffic flow control and more. Video content analysis is widely deployed in surveillance applications for urban environments, high security objects (usually for access control purposes) and commercial areas. Adding intelligent system tools should have an immediate positive effect on system performance. The system should increase probability of detection. However, the final result of applying intelligent system tools might be also negative. The system intelligence applications operations are scenario- specific, dependent on data context and their efficiency relies on configuration efforts. (Desurmont et al., 2004) reviews the challenges of video content analysis deployment, (Ashani, 2009) evaluates the deployment cases of video content analysis for urban environment applications, (Finn, 2004) addresses the problems related to intelligent surveillance in public transport, and (Lipton et al., 2004) presents video content analysis tools deployment for forensics application. Despite of the fact the video content analysis is well popularized and widely researched, the deployment of the video analytics is considered as one of the most risky areas in surveillance business. It is worth to mention that video content analysis tools should not only have positive impact on system performance but also should have minimum impact on remaining system efficiency factors - cost level and general system features. These facts are major motivations towards introducing pre-deployment performance evaluation. The performance of system intelligence mechanisms in general level can be measured by the same metrics and methodologies as the ones proposed for data acquisition systems. In context of intelligent systems one also can use other metrics (combining the same values as precision and recall): (a) the frequency bias, (b) the proportion of correct, (c) probability of detection and (d) false alarm ratio. Especially two last ones are commonly used to describe overall system performance when it comes to the process of identifying the relevant data. The performance is good for systems with high POD -probability of detection (see Equation 4) also known as a hit rate (HR) and low ratio of false alarms (FAR) (see Equation 5). Both metrics could be calculated as follows:

$$POD = \frac{\{\text{identified relevant data}\}}{\{\text{all relevant data}\}} \tag{4}$$

$$FAR = \frac{\{\text{data misinterpreted as relevant}\}}{\{\text{all identified data}\}} \tag{5}$$

One should be treating with caution the interpretation of the results of system performance as they depend on the context of the captured data. A good example of such interpretation is precision and recall values. In general, the highest are the scores the better is the performance. However, achieving high scores for both precision and recall can be problematic and not always optimum from system performance point of view. There are several situations, where low precision is better (refer to (Menzies, 2007)): (a) when the cost of missing the target is expensive (mission critical applications), (b) when only a small fraction of the data is retrieved (selective sensors), (c) where there is little or no cost in checking false alarms. They should be considered when interpreting the performance measures for surveillance systems.

4. Evaluation of architectural performance

The evaluation of architectural performance is crucial for all surveillance systems. The architectural design defines a systems ability to grow, scale and accommodate new functionality . Architecture defines the basic structure of the distribution of live and recorded media or data streams, communication patterns within the system and its components, etc. It should handle challenges, such as heterogeneous inputs, encoding, distribution and storage. Architectural performance can be evaluated from different perspectives. Evaluation of HW and computation architecture allows improvements in system efficiency aspects, such as: usage of energy and system resources. Evaluation of SW and communication architecture aims to provide system support for scalability, as well as functional and physical development of the surveillance system. It has a big impact on system efficiency by providing the base for expansion and development.

4.1 HW and computation architecture

The design of HW and computational architecture is extremely important for performance of all real-time systems. The topic is well reviewed by international research. The majority of the research concerns topics, such as power consumption optimization for embedded platforms or the techniques for utilization of processing power. The ultimate goal is to provide the rules and evaluation tools to design energy-efficient architecture, applications, and processing. In the case of surveillance systems, the problem of HW architecture performance mainly concerns camera site sensors (cameras, encoders and others). IP cameras, encoders and other camera site devices are critical components of a surveillance system. The performance of camera site devices defines system support for performance-exhausting functions such as video compression or content processing. Moreover, it also defines structure of the system in terms of an applicable intelligent solution. The more intelligence that can be applied on camera site, the more efficient the system is in terms of transmission, energy usage or resource management. Special attention should be given to the design of intelligent heterogeneous sensors where multiple sensing functions are interconnected to intelligently deliver relevant data into the system, e.g. IP cameras with audio, video, IR imaging, PTZ data functions. Fortunately, the task of performance evaluation is currently an integral part of embedded systems design. It is also well supported by developer tools for performance evaluation. The metrics for the performance are well known and cover a wide selection of parameters related to: (a) processing speed (latency and throughput), (b) power consumption parameters, (c) quality and type of output data. (Northern at al., 2007), (Lieverse et al., 2001) and (Lefftz et al., 2010) present the methodologies and metrics for performance analysis of signal processing devices and (Zrida et al., 2009) describes evaluation framework for H.264 multiprocessor video encoders. Above reviews provide a good database of methods applicable for evaluation of camera site embedded devices. When considering HW and computational performance for large scale surveillance system we have identified also other potentially problematic areas of which the evaluation should not be omitted: (a) storage solutions (b) export of data from the system. (Ruwart, 2000) reviews the evaluation methods for variety of storage technologies. (Gang et al., 2000) proposes evaluation methods for storage of network attached disks. (Widmann & Baumann, 1999) reviews multiple performance evaluation methods available for database systems. (Tyagi at al., 2008) addresses the challenges efficient data transfer in distributed systems and presents the examples of how to measure their performance. It is worth to underline here that the context of performance evaluation has a major importance. Therefore, hardware (HW) and software (SW) are usually evaluated together.

4.2 SW and communication architecture

Software performance depends on the architecture and software implementation- a poorly designed SW architecture may be unable to support the future development of the SW whilst supporting the required quality and performance. The same can be stated about communication architecture. The communication architecture determines the basic structure of communication between SW components. If the communication patterns are not well thought in terms of system scalability they will affect greatly the performance of the system when future expansion is required.

The SW (architecture) quality can be described in terms of reliability, scalability, modifiability, absence of SW bugs, or fault tolerance. (Olabiyisi et al., 2010), (Sharma et al., 2005), and also (Jun-Tao & Xiao-Yuan, 2009), (Hauck et al., 2009), and (Woodside at al., 2007) provide a good review of the methods for general analysis of the software quality. The main performance metrics to be considered in context of SW architecture assessment are: throughput, response time and resource utilization (refer to (Olabiyisi et al., 2010)). In general, the evaluation of SW architecture performance should respond to questions, such as: how the expansion of the system affects particular performance metrics (e.g. system response time and throughput when increasing the number of clients) and what are the system limits and bottlenecks; how to allocate SW components within the structure of HW architecture; how to scale the system up and also down (see (Sharma et al., 2005)) The usual motivations towards introducing the performance assesment in the process of creating SW are related to various software performance issues in a system. However, the earlier the assessment is performed in the software life cycle the less expensive and faster it is to identify potential risks and apply solutions to reduce or eliminate these risks. (Williams &Smith, 1998) discusses the advantages of early performance assessment and gives the examples of methods of performance assessments applicable for distributed systems.

(Woodside at al., 2007) distincts two approaches for SW performance evaluation: (a) an early-cycle predictive model-based, and (b) late-cycle measurement-based. It is recommended to combine these approaches to maintain the target performance within entire development cycle.

Typically, the first step towards SW architecture evaluation is architecture modelling. It allows simplifying the complexity of SW by splitting the SW into multiple functional layers. Classical approach to modelling of architecture to is represented by e.g. (Sharma et al., 2005) and (Jun-Tao & Xiao-Yuan, 2009). (Sharma et al., 2005) presents layered approach to evaluating the performance architecture where performance of analysis can be generalized to following steps: (a) layered model for system architecture is proposed, (b) environment is modelled (e.g. queuing network models parameters), (c) the limitations are modelled (e.g. thread limitations), (d) performance model solution and its outputs are proposed (performance factors). (Jun-Tao & Xiao-Yuan, 2009) proposes performance evaluation models, based on UML collaboration and sequence diagram. Additionally, (Inverardi et al., 1998) uses a method which automatically derives a performance evaluation model from a software architecture specification. The approach, is interesting but cannot be applied to surveillance systems.

(Hauck et al., 2009) challenges the evaluation methods based by architectural modelling. The modelling methods (especially for early evaluation) have tendency to be one-dimensional as their main purpose is to avoid implementing systems with poor quality. The current modelling methods do not reflect complexity and multi-dimensionality of environments, e.g. complexity of operating systems and virtual machines (being a base of SW component applications). (Hauck et al., 2009) presents extension to âĂIJmonolithic architecture modelâĂİ to enable accurate performance modelling and prediction for systems in modern complex environments which use disk arrays, virtual machines, and application servers. (Olabiyisi et al., 2010) proposes multiple evaluation models to approach different aspects of performance evaluation.

Both studies are well applicable in context of modern surveillance systems.

(Woodside at al., 2007) and (Olabiyisi et al., 2010) provide an excellent review of current state and future trends of software performance engineering. They conclude the human factors, such as end users demands and customer requirements have growing impact on SW development, whereas they are usually omitted at the model level. The topic of human impact on system performance is elaborated in next chapter.

5. Human factors in evaluation of system performance

We claim that system performance is not only a set of measurable and comparable performance metrics describing technical measures of hardware, SW applications, communication networks, etc. The performance of each system is greatly affected by multiple human factors, such as development decisions or user requirements. Moreover, the evaluation process itself has an ultimate target of providing a system value towards client, end users and customers. The assessment showing the impact of human factors on system performance is rather reactive than proactive- the performance evaluation is usually performed when the system, application or certain process needs to be adjusted to reflect the certain needs or problem.

Different perspectives of human impact on systems and software are investigated in various publications, such as: (Olabiyisi et al., 2010), (Chen et al., 2007), (Duis & Johnson, 1990) and others.

The estimation of impact of human factors on system performance is difficult to quantify. They have rather qualitative than quantitative value, which make them difficult or impossible to measure and compare. However, , we can analyse the impact of human factors on system performance by identifying the important performance objectives and identifying the performance metrics which are or might be meaningful in the context. Some performance indicators and objectives (such as system responsiveness) have an impact on user satisfaction and perceived system quality.

(Olabiyisi et al., 2010) presents a good review of the problem and identifies a need to develop performance modelling techniques that are capable of capturing human- related variables. (Chen et al., 2007) provides a survey of human performance issues and suggests some mitigation solutions.

We have identified multiple major areas, where objective related to human factors are important and therefore have major (however indirect) impact on overall system performance. They are: (a) software development process, (b) user interface design and system support of user work flow.

5.1 Software development process

The problem of human impact on system performance is visible at all stages of the system development. The topic has been well described by (Olabiyisi et al., 2010). It identified multiple decision variables having an impact on the final shape of system development. They include items such as: commitment of the staff, IT literacy level of operations staff, adequacy of user requirement specification and representation, communication between users and software developers, technical knowhow and the level of system training for operators, etc. (Olabiyisi et al., 2010) identified the problem with current system architecture modelling phase claiming they are machine-driven. The general solution for above problem would be creating a model which incorporates different decision variables (with the focus upon system user). It would complement the existing performance evaluation methods and make performance evaluation more user oriented.

5.2 Performance of user interface

The performance of user interface is one of the most important factors in every surveillance system.

The user interface is a system presentation layer. A well designed and well performing interface can provide the user with a good experience of the system whereas a poor performing user interface might discourage user from using the system. Additionally, the end-users role has an impact on the user interface performance, by making performance evaluation more user oriented with the introduction of the valued end-user local knowledge element. (Nielsen, 1993) discuss the importance of end user knowledge by proposing user testing based approach to performance evaluation of user interface quality. The case studies revealed great improvement of user interface quality when redesign of user interfaces was driven by user testing. (Chen et al., 2007) reviews the end users impact of performance problems , such as: insufficient bandwidth, time lags, etc. It proposes user interface improvements to address these problems, including multimodal interfaces, and various predicative and decision support systems.

Multiple metrics can be applied to measure the system performance in context of end-user interface. The most important are interface responsiveness and system (and user interface) support for users workflow.
(Duis & Johnson, 1990) discusses the value of the user interface responsiveness in context of system performance and proposes the techniques for improving it by means of parallel processing, adaptive resource allocation and pre-computing solutions.
The performance of the user interface can be also measured by its ability to support user workflow. This type of performance evaluation is very important in scenarios where the surveillance system is integrated with other systems, such as telephony and intercom systems, access control systems, traffic control systems, security systems, and others.
Almost all modern surveillance systems are workflow systems where the user interface requirements are highly tailored. The general idea for the evaluation of user work flow system support is to evaluate how well the system is supporting the user in performing individual tasks and consecutive actions in terms of user ergonomics, intuitiveness of interface and system response parameters (accuracy and speed) . The performance evaluation of such system is addressed by multiple publications, such as (Zuoxian et al., 2009), (Tay & Cockburn., 1996) and (Kwang-Hoon & Dong-Soo, 2001). However, it should be stressed that the applicability of performance evaluation methods proposed in above articles is very individual and should not be generalized - they should serve as examples of performance evaluation.
(Zuoxian et al., 2009) discusses the time performance metrics for workflow systems and proposes concepts of active transition and active pattern, these were proposed to estimate time performance and build efficient performance analysis algorithm. Same metrics can be used in the process of evaluation of modern surveillance systems.
(Kwang-Hoon & Dong-Soo, 2001) proposes performance analysis model for distributed system based on server-client architecture. It makes the research findings applicable for video surveillance systems. It addresses the typical problems of such systems such as complexity of the development affected by various decisions and requirements

6. Summary

This work addresses the problem of improving general efficiency of the system by evaluating and improving its performance. Whereas a majority most of current research concerns the performance characteristics of individual system components or system functionality, our aim is to analyse overall system performance by identifying the most critical areas. We review different perspectives of performance starting from technical aspects, such as; performance of data retrieval, analysis and fusion, ending with more subjective, such as quality of user interface. We focus on distributed, heterogeneous and multi-sensor systems where the primary function is video surveillance. We believe in the case of these systems the effect of performance optimisation will be visible due to the fact the optimisation techniques are not usually applied. We define areas critical for improved system performance and for each of these areas we review techniques and methodologies for measuring the performance and propose the most applicable. We identify types of systems where given performance-critical areas are important. The study is highly important for future video system development, design and deployment as it addresses the efficiency problems of modern complex video networks.

7. Acknowledgements

The author gratefully acknowledges the contribution of Pete Ward. It should nevertheless be stressed that the views in this paper are authors own and do not necessarily represent the views of Teleste

8.References

Ashani, Z. (2009). Architectural Considerations for Video Content Analysis in Urban Surveillance, *Proceedings of the 6th IEEE International Conference on Signal Based Surveillance*, pp. 289 - 289, ISBN 978-1-4244-4755-8

Chen, J.Y.C.; Haas, E.C & Barnes, M.J. (2007). Human Performance Issues and User Interface Design for Teleoperated Robots, *IEEE Transactions on Systems, Man,and Cybernetics, Part C: Applications and Reviews*, pp. 1231-1245, ISSN: 1094-6977

Desurmont, X.; Chaudy, C; Bastide, A.; Delaigle, J.F. & Macq, B. (2004). A seamless modular image analysis architecture for surveillance systems, *IEE on Intelligent Distributed Surveillane Systems*, pp. 66-70, ISBN 0-86341-392-7

Duis, D. & Johnson, J. (1990). Improving user-interface responsiveness despite performance limitations, *Digest of Papers. Thirty-Fifth IEEE Computer Society International Conference on Intellectual Leverage, compcon Spring' 90*, pp. 380-386, ISBN 0-8186-2028-5

Finn, B.M. (2004). Keeping an eye on transit, *IEE on Intelligent Distributed Surveillane Systems*, pp. 12-16, ISBN 0-86341-392-7

Gang, Ma; Khaleel, A.& Reddy, A.L.N. (2000). Performance evaluation of storage systems based on network-attached disks, *IEEE Transactions on Parallel and Distributed Systems*, Vol. 11, No. 9, pp. 956-968, ISSN 1045-9219

Hauck, M.; Kuperberg, M.; Krogmann, K.& Reussner, R.(2009). Modelling Layered Component Execution Environments for Performance Prediction, *Proceedings of the 12th International Symposium on Component-Based Software Engineering*, pp. 191-208, ISBN: 978-3-642-02413-9

Inverardi, P.; Mangano, C.; Russo, F. & Balsamo, S. (2009). Performance evaluation of a software architecture: a case study, *Proceedings of the 9th International Workshop on Software Specification and Design*, pp. 116-125, ISBN: 0-8186-8439-9

Jun-Tao, L. & Xiao-Yuan, J. (2009). An Approach to Performance Evaluation of Software Architecture, *Proceedings of the First International Workshop on Education Technology and Computer Science*, pp. 853-856, ISBN: 978-1-4244-3581-4

Kasturi, R.; Goldgof, D; Soundararajan, P.; Manohar, V; Garofolo, J.; Boonstra, M.; Korzhova, V. & Zhang, J. (2009). Framework for Performance Evaluation of Vace, Text and Vehicle Detection and Tracking in Video: Data, Metrics and Protocol, *IEEE Transactions on Pattern Analysis and Machine Intelligence*, Vol. 31, No. 2, pp. 319 - 336, ISBN 0162-8828

Kwang-Hoon, K & Dong-Soo, H. (2001). Performance and scalability analysis on client-server workflow architecture, *Proceedings of the Eighth International Conference on Parallel and Distributed Systems*, pp. 179 - 186, ISBN 0-7695-1153-8

Lefftz, V.; Bertrand, J.; Casse, H.; Client, C.; Coussy, P.; Maillet-Contoz, L.;Mercier, P; Moreau, P.; Pierre, L. & Vaumorin, E. (2010). A design flow for critical embedded systems, *Proceedings of International Symposium on Industrial Embedded Systems*, pp.229-233, ISBN 978-1-4244-5839-4

Lieverse, P.; Van Der Wolf, P.; Deprettere, E. & Vissers, K. (1999). A methodology for architecture exploration of heterogeneous signal processing systems, *The Journal of VLSI Signal Processing*, Vol. 29, No. 3, pp. 197 - 207

Lipton, A.J.; Clark, J.I; Brewer, P.; Venetiane, P.L.& Chosak, A.J. (2004). ObjectVideo forensics: activity-based video indexing and retrieval for physical security applications, *IEE on Intelligent Distributed Surveillance Systems*, pp. 56-60, ISBN 0-86341-392-7

Martin, D.; Fowlkes, C.; Tal, D.; Malik, J. (2001). A database of human segmented natural images and its application to evaluating segmentation algorithms and measuring ecological statistics, *Proceedings of the 8th IEEE International Conference on Computer Vision*, Vol.2., pp. 416-423, ISBN 0-7695-1143-0

Menzies, T.; Dekhtyar, A; Distefano, J.; Greenwald, J. (2007). Problems with Precision: A Response to "Comments on 'Data Mining Static Code Attributes to Learn Defect Predictors'", *IEEE TRansactions on Software Engineering*, Vol. 33, No. 9, pp.637-640, ISBN 0098-5589

Nielsen, J. (1993). Iterative user-interface design, *IEEE Computer*, Vol. 26, No. 11, pp. 32-41, ISSN 0018-9162

Northern, J.& Ribeiro, M. (2007). GENIE: A Genetic Algorithm Model Based Integrated Simulation Framework for Design of Embedded Systems , *IEEE Proceedings of Region 5 Technical Conference*, pp.223-227, ISBN 978-1-4244-1280-8

Olabiyisi, S.O; Omidiora, E.O; Uzoka, F.M.E; Mbarika, V.; Akinnuwesi B.A. (2010). A Survey of Performance Evaluation Models for Distributed Software System Architecture,*Proceedings of the World Congress on Engineering and Computer Science*, Vol. 1, ISBN: 978-988-17012-0-6

Pavlopoudou, C.; Martin, D; Yu, S.& Jiang, H. (2009). Learning from disagreements: Discriminative Performance Evaluation, *Proceedings of the 11th IEEE International Workshop on PETS*, pp. 1-8, ISBN 978-07049-1501-4

Russelli, B.C.; Torralba, A; Murphy, K.P. & Freeman, W.T. (2008). LabelMe: a database and web-based tool for image annotation, *International Journal of Computer Vision*, Vol. 77, No. 1-3, pp.157 - 173, ISBN 0920-5691

Ruwart, T.M. (2000). Disk Subsystem Performance Evaluation: From Disk Drives to Storage Area Networks, *Proceedings of 17th IEEE Symposium on Mass Storage Systems*, pp.1-24

Sharma, V.S; Trivedi, K.S. (2005). Quantifying software performance, reliability and security: An architecture-based approach, *Journal of Systems and Software*, Vol. 80, No. 4, pp. 493-509, ISSN 0164-1212

Tay, A. & Cockburn, A. (1996). User interfaces for workflow systems: designing for end-user tailorability, *Proceedings of 6th Australian Conference on Computer-Human Interaction*, pp. 302-303, ISBN: 0-8186-7525-X

Tyagi, V.; Gupta, C. (2008). Optimizing iSCSI storage network: A direct data transfer scheme using connection migration, *Proceedings of 16th International Conference on Networks*, pp.1-6, ISBN 978-1-4244-3805-1

Widmann, N. & Baumann, P. (1999). Performance evaluation of multidimensional array storage techniques in databases, *Proceedings of International Symposium on Database Engineering and Applications*, pp.385-389, ISBN 90-7695-0265-2

Williams, L.G.& Smith, C.U. (1998). Performance Evaluation of Software Architectures,*Proceedings of the First International Workshop on Software and Performance*, Performance Engineering Services and Software Engineering Research, Colorado, USA

Woodside M.; Franks G.& Petriu D.C (2007). The Future of Software Performance Engineering, *IEEE Proceeding of Future of Software Performance Engineering*, pp.171-187, ISBN 0-7695-2829-5

Zrida, H.K.; Ammari, A.C,;Jemai, A.; Abid, M. (2009). System-level performance evaluation of a H.264/AVC encoder targeting multiprocessors architectures, *Proceedings of International conference on Microelectronics*, pp.169-172, ISBN 978-1-4244-5814-1

Zuoxian, N.; Xin-hua, J.; Jian-cheng, L. & Shen, J. (2009). Performance analysis of workflow instances, *Proceedings of 6th International conference on Service Systems and Service Management*, pp.865-869, ISBN 978-1-4244-3661-3

PETS 2010, Benchmark data, *13th IEEE International Workshop on Performance Evaluation of Tracking and Surveillance*, Boston, USA

CLEAR 2007, The Evaluation, *Evalaution and Workshop on Classfication of Events, Activities and Relationship*, Baltimore MD, USA

3

Federalism, Privacy Rights, and Intergovernmental Management of Surveillance: Legal and Policy Issues

Michael W. Hail
Morehead State University,
United States of America

1. Introduction

The legal and policy issues involved with surveillance require recognition of the complexity of governance in United States intergovernmental system. With over 83,000 units of government, the U.S. intergovernmental system is complex and fragmented. And even within levels, much less across them, the United States system of federalism is one of limited government combined with an interdependent system of checks and balances. Rights are guaranteed by constitutions and court systems at two levels, operating concurrently. Additionally, the executive agencies across all levels are increasing engaged in collecting data on individuals. The myriad systems of data collection and management require a careful review for those developing, marketing, servicing, or using surveillance technologies.

2. Federalism and public policy

The legal rights of those operating surveillance systems are weighed against the civil rights of individuals being observed. This complex balance of rights exists in a multi-level grid of policymaking at the federal, state, and local levels of government in the United States (Hail, 2009). In addition to federalism distributing policy across levels of government, the U.S. constitutional system has always taken a sectoral approach to the regulation of privacy and a common law approach to privacy jurisprudence (Paruchuri et al., 2009).
In considering legal and regulatory issues in the United States, one must remember that to develop a comprehensive understanding of privacy not only must the federal judiciary be examined, but also the 50 states treatment of privacy issues related to technology and surveillance. This would include the dimensions of constitutional roles, bureaucratic organization, and policy authorities and the principal regulatory infrastructure for Third Party Federalism (Hail, 2004). The state government role is more significant for identification of individuals and the overall content of privacy concerns is more substantial at the sub-national level. As a recent article discussing state policy among state CIOs noted, "States' role in E-Authentication is greater than at the federal level" (Sternstein, 2005). These sub-national governments are primarily responsible for implementation of domestic

homeland security response and are the governments of "first responders". The use of technology by these governments involves intergovernmental finance instruments and the complex network of federalism policymakers.

Protection of privacy in video surveillance addresses privacy requirements for civil liberties protection at the multiple levels of government. It should be noted that over half of the States have an enumerated right to privacy protection in their constitutions or statutes that extends or exceeds the federal right to privacy. Additionally, legal concerns are thereby addressed for broad adoption of the privacy protecting technology and its effective use by government for homeland security and law enforcement.

This assessment of the public management issues for surveillance and data management for multi-jurisdictional environments provides important considerations for both public officials and scientists. The origins of political rights under constitutional government systems resulted in non-uniformity of political rights and legal and regulatory requirements (Hail and Lange, 2010). Surveillance technology requires a regulatory balance for the protection of individuals and the commercialization of technology. The research results indicate political culture for innovation and new technology development has a positive correlation with governance systems of federalism.

3. Recent survey research findings

Protection of privacy in video surveillance addresses constitutional and civil liberties protections across the institutions of federalism. In addition to the federally protected rights in the 1st, 4th, 5th, and 9th Amendments, it must be noted that over half of the States have an enumerated right to privacy protection in their constitutions or statutes that extends or exceeds the federal right to privacy. Additionally, legal concerns are thereby addressed for broad adoption of the privacy protecting technology and its effective use by government for homeland security and law enforcement. To assess these issues in the general population as well as among homeland security and law enforcement agencies, a surveys were conducted, as well as focus groups and interviews.

In the general population survey, citizens across demographic groups were comfortable with expansion of government video surveillance if it protected privacy rights. The survey research was conducted utilizing a modified list-assisted Waksberg-Mitofsky random-digit dialing procedure for sampling and the population surveyed was non-institutionalized Kentuckians eighteen years of age and older.[i] The margin of error is +/- 3.3 percent at the 95 percent confidence interval. SRC response rate was 31.1% and CASRO rate was 38.1%. Total N=3243 with 904 completes.

The respondents were asked, "Do you have a video security system that is used routinely?" The results reflected that 55% of employed Kentuckians have an operative video surveillance system at their workplace. We then asked of those employed, "Would you be interested in a video surveillance system at work if you knew it could protect an individual's privacy?" The solid majority of 60% expressed that they were interested in privacy protecting video surveillance. There was clear recognition that video surveillance has become a regular feature of public and private workplace environments.

Urban residents, those in higher income levels, and those with advanced education attainment all were more disposed to privacy protecting video technology.

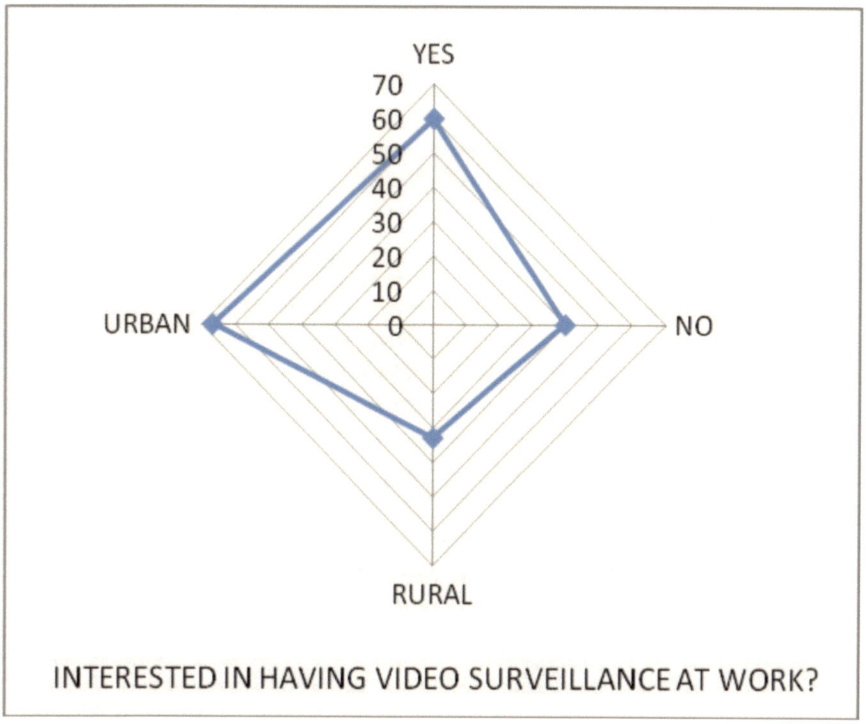

Fig. 1. Urban and Rural Views of Workplace Video Security

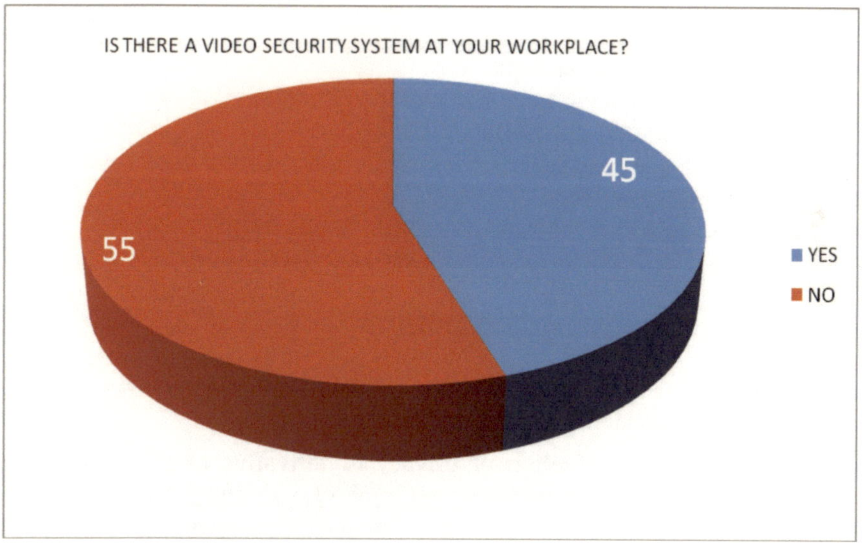

Fig. 2. Video Security at the Workplace

Additionally, focus groups of law enforcement, first responders, hospitals, and public infrastructure managers have reflected strong interest in privacy protecting video technology. Contact was made with 25 critical infrastructure officials from across Kentucky and site visits conducted with six critical infrastructure locations. Two focus groups were held and nineteen participants from 8 local, state, and federal agencies attended. The focus groups were asked a series of questions to evaluate their knowledge of civil liberties with regard to privacy protection and the use of video evidence. They were also asked, "Would you be interested in a video surveillance system that could protect an individual's privacy?" 100% of the attendees responded favorably and several expressed interest in implementation of privacy protecting video surveillance at their infrastructure facilities.

4. Judicial policy and intergovernmental management

There have been several important court rulings that establish the judicial policy framework for privacy and surveillance. In all cases, state courts must defer to the establishment of civil liberties by federal courts under the constitution's supremacy clause. As such, the analysis of judicial policy focuses upon federal policy parameters.

MAJOR FEDERAL PRIVACY RULINGS
Olmstead v. United States (1928)
Bartnicki v. Vopper (2001)
Brendlin v. California (2006)
Georgia v. Randolph (2006)
Hudson v. Michigan (2006)
Cutter v. Wilkinson (2005)
Davenpeck v. Alford (2004)
San Diego v. Roe (2004)
Boy Scouts of America v. Dale (2000)
Lawrence and Garner v. Texas (2003)
Bowers v. Hardwick (1986)
Waller v. Georgia (1984)
Katz v. United States (1967)
Stanley v. Georgia (1969)
Wilson v. Layne (1999)
Los Angeles County, California v. Max Rettele (2007)
Goodridge v. Department of Public Health (2003)
Troxel v. Granville (2000)
Planned Parenthood v. Casey (1992)

Table 1. Major Federal Judicial Rulings on Privacy

The American legal conceptualization of privacy is derivative of a tradition of privacy theory reaching from Plato and Aristotle through John Locke and John Stuart Mill. But the American legal jurisprudence for privacy rights has a central focus on the work of Samuel Warren and Louis Brandeis in their 1890 Harvard Law Review article (Warren and Brandeis, 1890). Warren and Brandeis developed a federal jurisprudence for privacy based upon the implied powers of the constitutions derivative of the Bill of Rights. They stated, "the right to privacy does not prohibit the communication of any matter, though in its nature private, when the publication is made under circumstances which would render it a privileged communication according to the law of slander and libel," and that "the law would probably not grant any redress for the invasion of privacy by oral publication in the absence of special damage," and they conclude that the right to privacy is to "protect the privacy of private life" (Warren and Brandeis, 1890). The right to privacy was in these terms understood as a tort where redress was a matter of civil concern rather than criminal. The rapid development of technology in the twentieth century created circumstances where the courts were challenged to apply this legal reasoning well after the technology had reached a broad application in society.

The state courts, like state governments across all areas of public policy, have generally been more advanced in dealing with judicial policy than their federal counterparts. In 1905, in *Pavesich v. New England Life Insurance Co.*, the Georgia Supreme Court created a common law right of privacy when the New England Life used the Pavesich 's name and picture, without consent, to advertise insurance services. The Georgia Court followed Warren and Brandeis, interpreted "the right to be let alone" in their ruling. This was followed in 1928 by U.S. Supreme Court case of *Olmstead v. United States.*, which established the first major federal court ruling. In *Olmstead*, federal law enforcement agents installed wiretaps in the basement of Olmstead's building as well as the streets near his home without obtaining a warrant and the evidence resulted in Olmstead being convicted. The Court held that neither the Fourth nor Fifth Amendment rights of the recorded parties were violated. The use of wiretapped conversations as incriminating evidence did not violate their Fifth Amendment protection against self incrimination because they were not forcibly or illegally made to conduct those conversations. Instead, the conversations were voluntarily made between the parties and their associates. The Fourth Amendment rights were not infringed because mere wiretapping does not constitute a search and seizure under the meaning of the Fourth Amendment. These terms refer to an actual physical examination of one's person, papers, tangible material effects, or home but not their conversations. *Olmstead* was overturned in 1967 by *Katz v. United States.* In *Katz v. United States*, the Supreme Court redefined a search. Recognizing that the Fourth Amendment protects "people, not places," the Court said that a search occurs whenever the government intrudes into a person's reasonable expectation of privacy. This is a complete change from the *Olmstead* Court which in essence said that there was no expectation of privacy in conversations.

The Fourth Amendment to the U.S. Constitution has become a fertile ground for privacy litigation. The Fourth Amendment prohibits unreasonable searches and seizures by the government. This is combined with the protections not enumerated in the Ninth Amendment where the residual rights not addressed in the constitution are reserved to the people. The Fourth Amendment does not prohibit all searches, only ones considered unreasonable. The Supreme Court has made this inquiry simple. Any search made without a warrant is per se unreasonable, unless it can be justified by one of several narrowly defined exceptions to the warrant requirement.

The case law has been supplemented by several Congressional Acts over the last 50 years. Some of the major acts include the Federal Wiretap Act in 1968 (FWA), Electronic Communications Privacy Act of 1986 (ECPA), The Foreign Intelligence Surveillance Act of 1978 (FISA), and the Patriot Act of 2002 (PAT).

In order for surveillance data to be admitted in a judicial trial, the technology behind the video must stand up to judicial scrutiny as well. The history of scientific evidence admitted in court starts in 1923 with the case of *Frye v. United States.* This was a case from the Court of Appeals of the District of Columbia which held that evidence could be admitted in court only if "the thing from which the deduction is made" is "sufficiently established to have

MAJOR FEDERAL VIDEO & WIRED RECORDING RULINGS

Bartnicki v. Vopper, 121 S. Ct. 1753 (2001)

Baugh v. CBS, 828 F. Supp. 745 (N.D. Cal. June 22, 1993)

Boehner v. McDermott, 22 Fed. Appx. 16 (D.C. Cir. 2001)

Copeland v. Hubbard Broadcasting, Inc., 526 N.W.2d 402 (Minn. Ct. App. Jan. 24, 1995)

Desnick v. ABC, 44 F.3d 1345 (7th Cir. 1995)

Food Lion Inc. v. Capital Cities/ABC Inc., 194 F.3d 505 (4th Cir. 1999)

Hornberger v. American Broadcasting Company, Inc., 799 A.2d 566 (N.J. App. 2002)

Krauss v. Globe International, No. 18008-92 (N.Y. Sup. Ct. Sept. 11, 1995)

Medical Laboratory Management Consultants v. American Broadcasting Company, Inc., 306 F.2d 806 (9th Cir. 2002)

Oregon v. Knobel, 777 P.2d 985 (Or. 1989), acquitted on retrial, No. 86-545 (Ore. Dist. Ct. Josephine Cty. Jan. 9, 1991)

Pennsylvania v. Duncan, CR78-92 (Pa. 11th Jud. Dist., charges dismissed, March 26, 1992)

PETA v. Bobby Berosini, Ltd., 895 P.2d 1269 (Nev. 1995)

Sussman v. American Broadcasting Cos., Inc., 186 F.3d 1200 (9th Cir. 1999)

In the matter of Entercom New Orleans License, LLC, FCC File No. EB-01-IH-0099 (2002)

In the Matter of Use of Recording Devices in Connection with Telephone Service, 2 FCC Rcd 502 (1987)

Broadcast of Telephone Conversations, 47 C.F.R. §73.1206 (1989)

P.L. 99-508 (The Electronic Communications Privacy Act of 1986), amending 18 U.S.C. §§ 2510 et seq.

Table 2. Major Federal Judicial Rulings on Recording Technologies

gained general acceptance in the particular field in which it belongs. "*Frye* dealt with a systolic blood pressure deception test, which was the forerunner of the polygraph test. In 1923, this blood pressure test was not widely accepted among scientists, and so the *Frye* court ruled it could not be used in court.

However, in 1993, the United States Supreme Court changed the long-standing law of admissibility of scientific expert evidence by rejecting the Frye test as inconsistent with the Federal Rules of Evidence in the case of *Daubert v. Merrell Dow Pharmaceuticals*. The Court held that the Federal Rules of Evidence and not *Frye* were the standard for determining admissibility of expert scientific testimony. *Frye's* "general acceptance" test was superseded by the Federal Rules' adoption. Rule 702 is the appropriate standard to assess the admissibility of scientific evidence. The Court derived a reliability test from Rule 702.

Under *Daubert*, the admissibility of expert testimony is to be more rigorously scrutinized by the trial judge to determine whether it meets the requirements of Fed. R. Evid. 702, which provides "If scientific, technical, or other specialized knowledge will assist the trier of fact to understand the evidence or to determine a fact in issue, a witness qualified as a expert by knowledge, skill, experience, training or education, may testify thereto in the form of an opinion or otherwise." In order to qualify as scientific knowledge, an inference or assertion must be derived by the scientific method and any proffered testimony must be supported by appropriate validation. In short, the requirement that an expert's testimony pertaining to scientific knowledge establish a standard of evidentiary reliability is the requirement for admissibility. The Supreme Court later clarified the expert testimony could not be highly focussed or developed for the case in question, but performed research independent of the litigation. Now, any expert must provide verifiable evidence that the expert's testimony is based on scientifically valid principles with possible objective sources of such verification include learned treatises, the policy statement of a professional association, and published articles in reputable scientific journals.

These complex judicial policies for the use of surveillance technology and its admissability make the work of executive branch agencies and bureaucratic managers ever more challenging. Not only the bargaining of juridictional issues and inter-agency politics, but the legal requirements for compliance make these use of surveillance technology ever more specialized and politically complex.

5. The interdependence of devolution of policy in American federalism and intergovernmental management of technology and data

In the U.S., federalism distributes sovereignty between the national government and those of the States. The intergovernmental system of policy making ensures cooperation and conflict within and between levels of government. Against this complex political system, one must understand the constitutional parameters placed upon these governments by the constitution. The implementation of any major surveillance technology requires regulation of the use of that technology by multiple governments protecting the rights of commerce in the market for that technology and the civil liberties of those it might be used upon.

The Bill of Rights remains central to the federal jurisprudence for privacy rights. The Founding Fathers were divided as to whether there should be a "bill of rights." In fact, the Philadelphia Convention of 1787 completed its work without including any such explication of rights, though they had considered and subsequently rejected enumeration of rights. "George Mason almost as an afterthought in the last days of the convention brought the issue up, …[and subsequently] it was defeated by every state"(Wood, 1969). Even as the ratification debates produced a compromise between leading federalists and anti-federalists that included such prominent founders as James Madison, other federalists such as Roger Sherman, the author of the Connecticut Compromise that created modern American federalism, remained opposed to a "bill of rights" as unnecessary. Even after the Constitution is ratified and the first ten amendments added, it should be remembered that it was a natural rights understanding of "rights" that informed the Founding Fathers view of the Constitution. As James Burnham phrased it, "these rights, in short, are limits, not powers" (Burnham, 1959). Thus, the constitutional theory of the Founding Fathers was premised upon limitations to the national powers as reflected in the amendments in the Bill of Rights. These limitations on government are unevenly applied to other entities and individuals in society, and the exponential growth of technology has made this moreso.

As Elazar and other federalism scholars have noted, the States serve as a laboratory for policy experimentation and for addressing the often unique, heterogeneous needs resulting from local and regional diversity (Elazar, 1987). Even after a century of nationalizing policy authority, the States play a significant, meaningful, and constitutionally guaranteed role in the intergovernmental policy process that both affirms and extends the rights and limitations that serve as guarantees of liberty in the Bill of Rights and the constitution. The enduring challenge of public administration and policy makers is how to preserve this constitutional framework in the face of accelerated technology applications that challenge civil liberties. The management of growing volumes of data by government agencies and regulation of surveillance technologies in an integrated legal challenge for constitutional governments and at the center of both remains the right of privacy.

6. References

Burnham, James (1959). Congress and the American Tradition. Regnery Publishing. Washington, DC:

Elazar, Daniel J. (1987). Exploring Federalism. University of Alabama Press. Tuscaloosa.

Hail, Michael W. (2009). "Bush's New Nationalism: The Life and Death of New Federalism." Perspectives on the Legacy of George W. Bush. Michael Orlov Grossman and Ronald Eric Matthews Jr., Editors. Cambridge Scholars Publishing. Newcastle upon Tyne.

Hail, Michael W. (2004). "Measuring Devolution Through Third Party Federalism." Proceedings of the 2004 meeting of the Mid-West Political Science Association.

Hail, Michael., and Lange, Stephen. (2010). Federalism and Representation in the Theory of the Founding Fathers: A Comparative Study of U.S. and Canadian Constitutional Thought. *Publius: The Journal of Federalism*, Special Issue (February 25), 1-24.

Paruchuri, Jithendra K., Sen-ching S. Cheung, and Michael W. Hail. (2009). "Video Data Hiding for Managing Privacy Information in Surveillance Systems." *EURASIP Journal on Information Security*. Volume 2009 (2009), Article ID 236139, 18 pages.

Sternstein, Aliya. (2005). "NASCIO faces authentication." Jan. 7, 2005. http://fcw.com/geb/articles/2005/0103/web-privacy-01-07-05.asp.

Warren, Samuel D. and Louis D. Brandeis (1890). "The Right of Privacy", 4 Harvard Law Review. 193. Boston, Massachusetts.

Wood, Gordon. (1969). The Creation of the American Republic 1776-1787. W.W. Norton & Co. New York.

---

[i] The survey was a cooperative effort through the University of Kentucky annual Kentucky Survey and the research was sponsored by a grant from the US Department of Homeland Security through the National Institute for Hometown Security.

Part 2

Video Surveillance Systems, Frameworks, and Structures

4

Video Surveillance of Today: Compressed Domain Object Detection, ONVIF Web Services Based System Component Communication and Standardized Data Storage and Export using VSAF – a Walkthrough

Houari Sabirin[1] and Gero Bäse[2]
[1]*Bandung Institute of Technology,*
[2]*Siemens AG - Corporate Technology,*
[1]*Indonesia*
[2]*Germany*

1. Introduction

The growing trend for surveillance systems performing multiple functions (video surveillance, access control, response co-ordination) driven by technology integration and interoperability is emerging because organizations increasingly viewing integrated security systems as inevitable and necessity. In this paper we focus on the interoperability aspect for video surveillance systems.

An open standard has been developed by the Open Network Video Interface Forum (ONVIF) to facilitate the interoperability between networked surveillance video components. The ONVIF specification defines the network layer of IP security devices including automatic device discovery, video streaming and intelligent metadata. It is IP-based, makes use of web services and provides a formal conformance process. By employing the specification, interoperability is assured between products regardless of brand. End-users are enabled to compose the most suitable combination of products for their specific needs regardless of vendor and integration costs are reduced significantly. Conformance of products to the ONVIF specification is based on vendor self-declaration and applying test tools available for ONVIF members.

With the latest advance in compression technology such as MPEG-4 AVC|H.264, a joint standard from ISO/IEC (ISO/IEC 14496-10:2009) and ITU-T (ITU-T Recommendation H.264 (03/10)), the surveillance system provides better video quality and larger video resolution, while not stressing the network bandwidth further. Moreover, a novel export format fostering interoperability not only between different installations but also close cooperation with legal authorities "MPEG-A Part 10 Video surveillance application format" has been published by the Moving Picture Experts Group (MPEG). It specifies the use of MPEG-4 AVC|H.264 along with content description metadata e.g. object identification and other particularly surveillance related information neatly arranged.

The mission for this book chapter is to raise awareness for the specifications provided by standardization that ensure the interoperability of surveillance system as well as to introduce the surveillance system that combines low computational cost for video content analysis with cost-effective and flexible communication protocols for networked video. This chapter provides a walkthrough to the ONVIF video surveillance system, from the camera through analysis and storage right up to display and export. In addition and serving as key example for modern analytics a novel algorithm for object detection in compressed video data will be presented. It illustrates the general trend towards processing increasing amounts of data in real-time automatically by avoiding completely the task of decoding the video prior analysis.

2. Camera and web services

A camera is called NVT (Network Video Transmitter) in the ONVIF eco-system. It is left open how many (different) video streams a camera may generate. Therefore, also implementations combining video encoding for several analog cameras in one box are supported as NVT maintaining backward compatibility to legacy systems.

As can be seen from the available configuration entities listed below a NVT is much more than just a camera. Edge devices in a network are being equipped with ever increasing processing power. Thus, complexity of algorithms being executable on board of the device is growing also. ONVIF supports for example analytic algorithms at the camera as well as parallel processing of video data of different source areas of a megapixel-camera.

A wide range of Pan, Tilt and Zoom (PTZ) features are supported. Differentiation between absolute, relative and continuous move operations is also enabled as is a range of coordinate systems and settings for home positions and presets.

Picture data compression
For the encoding of video JPEG is the only required standardized format to be supported by every NVT. The ONVIF group did acknowledge the growing acceptance of MPEG-4 AVC | H.264 in the market by supporting it as video compression standard but has chosen JPEG as minimal conformance requirement.

Configuration of a NVT is condensed in a structure called "Media Profile". A Media Profile can be regarded as a box of building bricks, combining the input of one configuration entity with the output of another, e.g. a video encoder configuration and the appropriate video source configuration.

Every NVT has to provide at least one Media Profile. The number of supported Media Profiles is limited by available on-board resources only.

Configuration entities may be generated once and reused in different profiles. Signaling is in place if changing attempts for a particular configuration entity may affect other profiles as well. Configuration entities are only present, if the respective device supports this capability. E.g. it is not required for each and every NVT to support audio decoding capabilities.

Depending on available computational and memory resources configurations may be dynamically made available for usage in media profiles by a NVT. Particularly the number of supported video encoder instances may change dynamically depending on the requested frame rate, resolution and compression format of profiles already in use.

In order to support users in the creation process of a Media Profile NVT's provide information about compatible configurations to existing profiles, available options for configuration entities but may refuse adding an output configuration entity to a Media Profile if no appropriate source configuration entity has been added previously.

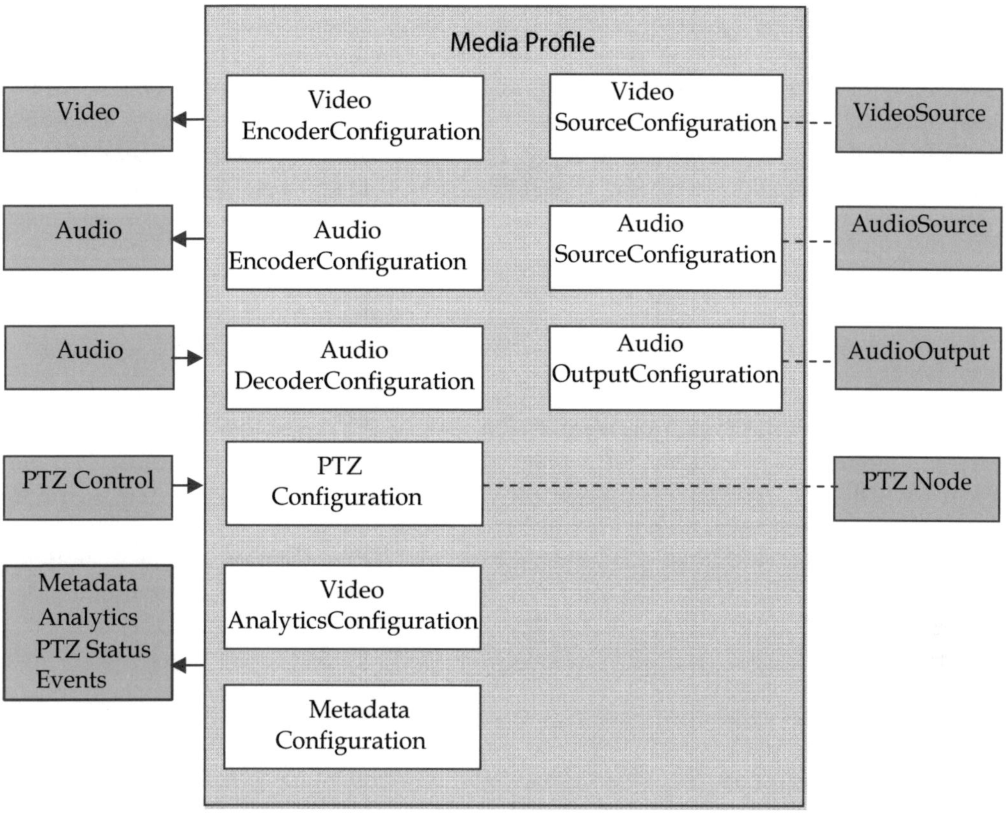

Fig. 1. Media Profile (source ONVIF)

Each and every Media Profile provides a URI where media data processed according to the settings in the profile can be requested as live media stream.

All configuration services defined in the ONVIF standards are expressed as web services operations, which in turn are based on the Organization for the Advancement of Structured Information Standards (OASIS) web service standards framework, representing a basic design principle of ONVIF standards: to make use of already existing standards wherever possible. Web services allow for fast integration in different platforms.

Web services

Web services are providing the main components for client server operation: finding, binding and data exchange. Web services are intended for automated data exchange with or function calling on remote machines. The usage of web services provides for open and distributed architectures independent of platforms, programming languages and protocols. All devices in ONVIF are taking on the role of a web service provider. On top of HTTP (Hypertext Transfer Protocol) as transport mechanism, keeping firewall traversal issues as small as possible, SOAP (Simple Object Access Protocol) message exchange protocol is used for the communication between web service requester and provider. Integration on client side (web service requester) is simplified by providing WSDL (Web Services Description Language) files, which are normative in ONVIF. There are WSDL compiler tools available to generate platform specific code on a variety of platforms.

ONVIF relies on WS-Discovery standard techniques as common way to discover service providers. An exception here is the discovery proxy definition. ONVIF provides an alternative definition to allow for remote discovery in network architectures not fully supported by WS-Discovery. A discovery proxy is particularly necessary if service requester and provider do not reside in the same administrative domain of a network.
Security is of major concern for any installation using web services. ONVIF makes use of WS-Security framework for message level security. In order to allow for mutually authenticated transport session as well as preserving the confidentiality and the integrity at transport level usage of Transport Layer Security (TLS) protocols is recommended in addition.
All web services defined in ONVIF follow the Web Services Interoperability Organization (WS-I) basic profile 2.0 recommendations to assure best practice.

Every device in the ONVIF eco-system has to implement the *Device (web-) Service*. It allows a service requester to get an URL entry point of the NVT where all the necessary product specific WSDL and schema definitions can be retrieved. Furthermore, device specific parameter can be retrieved and set.
Embedded storage of a NVT may be utilized in an ONVIF conformant way by operating it under *Recording Service* (see paragraph 4) control. Here, the media profile is used as data source description. In case of network failure this mechanism may be used as temporary storage.

3. Data analysis

Thoroughly inspection of the video sometimes requires more processing power than available for analysis in a NVT. Additionally, analysis across video data originating in different NVT's, potentially at different instances of time, has to be performed server-based, also known as central or host-based analytics.

3.1 Analytics device and notification

In ONVIF the *Analytics Device Service* provides for the configuration and set-up of such dedicated devices and the *Analytics Service* is being used to configure analytic algorithms. Furthermore, compilation of rules by provisioning of a rule description language is supported. Such a device is being referred to as NVA (Network Video Analytics). If the analytic part of the NVA is composed of different vendor modules it can be encapsulate with the *Analytics Device Service*.
Input for a NVA is mainly video data in different configurations. Also, audio and metadata may be used for analytic purposes and can be input to a NVA if algorithms handling such kind of data have been installed. Provisioning exists for additional informative data to be conveyed to and used by analytic algorithms. On the other hand, different sets of parameter controlling the analytic algorithms can be used to enable e.g. day-night switching.
Composition of analytic algorithm modules into analytic engines is enabled. Single analytic engines may be composed to an analytics application. In a control instance for the *Analytics Device Service* all necessary information for such an application is condensed.
In addition, the state of a particular control instance can be inquired. The expandable structure allows for also conveying state information for substructures like analytic engines or even single analytic algorithm modules.

Generally speaking, analysis in ONVIF provides two different kinds of results. Events may be sent out addressing subscribers and a more comprehensive scene description may be generated. A XML schema has been defined covering basic scene elements and providing for easy extension of almost every single element to enable vendor specific data provisioning.


```
<?xml version="1.0" encoding="UTF-8"?>
<tt:MetaDataStream xmlns:tt="...www.onvif.org/...">
 <tt:VideoAnalytics>
  <tt:Frame UtcTime="2008-10-10T12:24:57.321">
   ...
  </tt:Frame>
  <tt:Frame UtcTime="2008-10-10T12:24:57.621">
   ...
  </tt:Frame>
 </tt:VideoAnalytics>
</tt:MetaDataStream>
```

```
<?xml version="1.0" encoding="UTF-8"?>
<tt:MetaDataStream xmlns:tt="...www.onvif.org/...">
 <tt:Event>
  <wsnt:NotficationMessage>
   <wsnt:Message>
    <tt:Message UtcTime= "2008-10-10T12:24:57.628">
     ...
    </tt:Message>
   </wsnt:Message>
  </wsnt:NotficationMessage>
 </tt:Event>
</tt:MetaDataStream>
```


Fig. 2. Scene description and event XML stream structure example (source ONVIF)

In order to receive an event a requester has to subscribe to it on the interface of the device generating that particular event. The interface is provided by the *Event Service* which is mandatory to be supported by all devices. It is based on OASIS WS-BaseNotification and WS-Topics specifications. The device acts as notification producer and topic expressions are being used as filter. Topic expressions may be created as expression tree. By subscribing to a particular topic expression automatically all notifications for leaves expressions further down the tree are being subscribed to. Events may be streamed over RTP or transmitted as message in the web service environment. Here, also a real-time pull point interface is specified providing for a firewall friendly solution.

The notification messaging framework defined in WS-BaseNotification is being exploited. The message element of a NotificationMessage as defined in the ONVIF schema is composed of "Source", "Key" and "Data". A unique identification of the device's component detecting the event should be indicated by "Source". "Data" should contain detailed information about the detected event.

A categorization of events is provided by the usage of topics. A collection of root topics is being provided in the ONVIF namespace. It is easily expandable for event specific topics according to vendor needs.

If the topic refers to a property "Key" is used in order to make the property unique, i.e. distinguishing different qualities of objects in the scenery. Properties can be "initialized", "changed" and "deleted", in this way keeping track of what has been observed over the lifetime of a property.

```
<wstop:TopicNamespace name="ONVIF" targetNamespace="...www.onvif.org/..." >
 <wstop:Topic name="Device"/>
 <wstop:Topic name="VideoSource"/>
 <wstop:Topic name="VideoEncoder"/>
 <wstop:Topic name="VideoAnalytics"/>
 <wstop:Topic name="RuleEngine"/>
 <wstop:Topic name="PTZController"/>
 <wstop:Topic name="AudioSource"/>
 <wstop:Topic name="AudioEncoder"/>
 <wstop:Topic name="UserAlarm"/>
 <wstop:Topic name="MediaControl"/>
 <wstop:Topic name="RecordingConfig"/>
 <wstop:Topic name="RecordingHistory"/>
 <wstop:Topic name="VideoOutput"/>
 <wstop:Topic name="AudioOutput"/>
 <wstop:Topic name="VideoDecoder"/>
 <wstop:Topic name="AudioDecoder"/>
 <wstop:Topic name="Receiver"/>
</wstop:TopicNamespace>
```

Fig. 3. ONVIF root topics (source ONVIF)

It should be noted, the synchronization of subscribed properties between device and client by requesting a SynchronizationPoint (see paragraph 4) corresponds to tuning in to an existing session. All properties are set to "Initialized" starting their lifetime for that particular client from beginning.

"Source", "Key" and "Data" each consists of a set of simple name value pairs or structured information. A device can describe the items contained separately for each topic using the Message Content Description Language provided by ONVIF.

Each and every device is required to provide URI locations to schemata being used in the description as well as URI locations to topic expression dialects and message content filter dialects supported.

Support of the Concrete Topic Expressions defined in the [WS-Topics] specification and its ONVIF extension referred to as ConcreteSet is mandatory. The extension allows e.g. for usage of "OR" operations providing for general subscriptions to topics generated by different sources at once.

Also required is support for a subset of XPath 1.0 syntax allowing for more detailed message content filtering for client subscriptions.

Figure 4 provides an overview of all ONVIF defined interfaces and services required to be implemented for a NVA. The NVA device can be managed using the *Device Service* and functionally configured using the *Analytics Device Service*. In addition the *Analytics Service* is used for the configuration of single analytics algorithms (not shown). The *Receiver Service* provides necessary information in order to fetch media data using the data streaming interface. Notification is provided using the *Event Service* and metadata of a scene description may be streamed out.

3.2 Compressed domain video analysis

The video data stream arriving at the NVA is compressed in e.g. MPEG-4 AVC|H.264 format. In order to analyze the picture data the stream needs to be decompressed first. If compressed domain analysis is being performed the decompression stage can be avoided, thus reducing required computationally complexity.

We propose a method to perform object detection in MPEG-4 AVC|H.264 bitstream by taking into account motion and residue information. It is performed in two steps: First, a

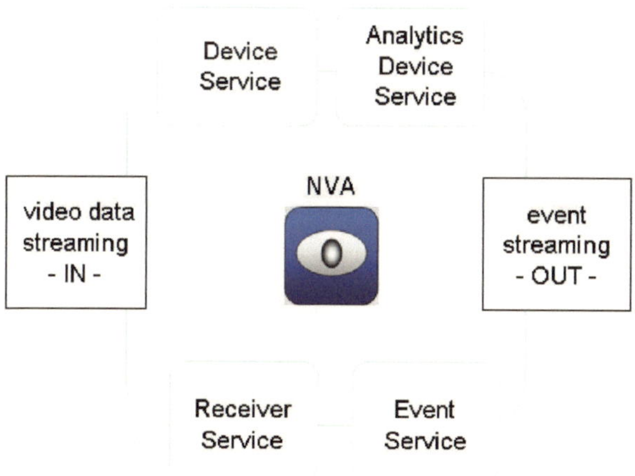

Fig. 4. Network Video Analytics device required services/interfaces

simple segmentation process using temporal filtering is performed over each motion vectors and coefficients to segment the moving object from background. The filtering process is performed by observing the smoothness of a frame, denoted by the number of macroblock having nonzero motion vectors and nonzero dequantized coefficients (a "qualified" macroblock to represent moving objects); second, an automatic clustering is performed to classify groups of block partition into clusters representing the candidate of object. In this process we define searching windows with respect to camera position to group adjacent blocks into the same cluster without determining the number of cluster and initial cluster center. Using appropriate searching window scheme we can ensure that even small objects can be correctly recognize by the algorithm.

The algorithm first parses the MPEG-4 AVC|H.264 bitstream and defines the data into "block partition data" and "residue data". Block partition data is the data that are uniform within a 4x4 block partition, that is, all 16 pixels in that block has the same value. Residue data is the data that is unique for each pixel, in which a 4x4 block partition may have different values in its 16 pixels. Therefore, in one macroblock there are 16 partitions of block partition data and 256 partitions of residue data. The reason to categorize the data into these categories is to simplify and increase the accuracy filtering frame from noise. Fig. 3 shows the block diagram of the algorithm.

3.2.1 Data definitions

In MPEG-4 AVC|H.264 luminance component of a macroblock can have various combinations of block partitions due to tree structured motion compensation that enables a macroblock partitioned into 16x16, 16x8, 8x16, 8x8, 8x4, 4x8 and 4x4 partition types (ISO/IEC 14496-10:2009). Therefore, a macroblock may have motion vectors only in several block partitions, leave some other partitions have no motion vectors and can be assumed as partition that is not belong to moving object. By adjusting the partition of macroblock we can further remove 4x4 block partitions that are actually not belong to moving object by observing the distribution of residue data in that macroblock. Thus we may keep our process only for the partitions with motion vectors. For block partition data, if the original macroblock partition is larger than 4x4, we adjust the block partition to have the same motion vectors for each of its 4x4-partition member.

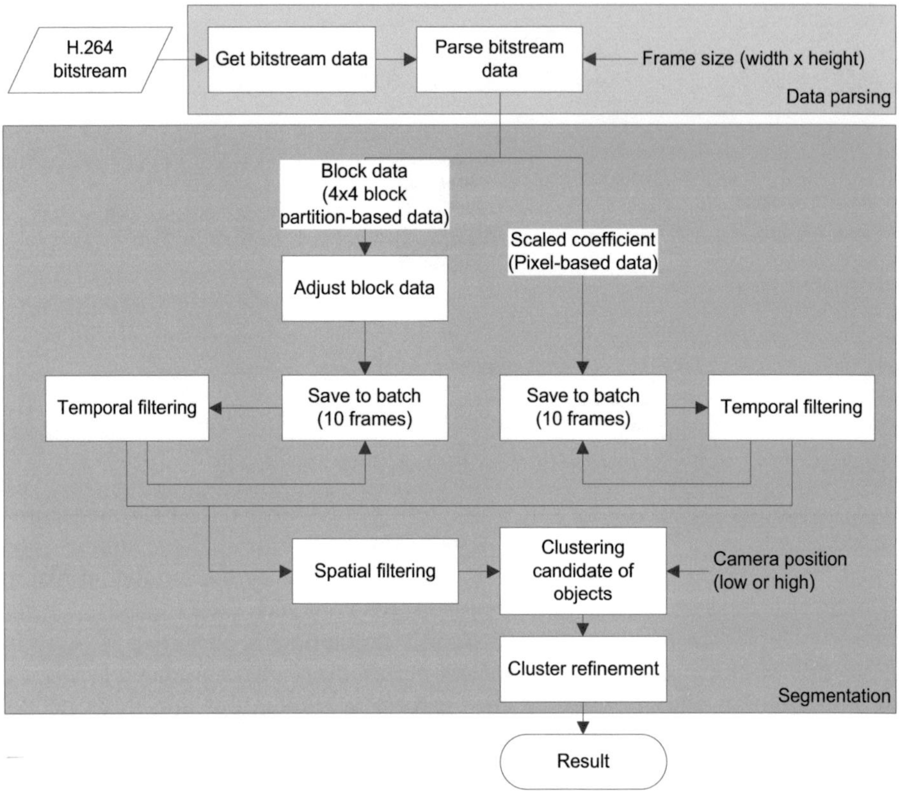

Fig. 5. Block diagram of object detection algorithm

After adjusting the distribution of values in block partition data, the segmentation process continues by first removing noise that may lead to incorrect object detection using temporal filtering. Here noise is defined as data that appears inconsistently along the series of consecutive frames. In the temporal filtering, series of ten frames as one batch are set. Within the batch, the consistency of a macroblock containing block partition data and residue data appears are observed. For this purpose we must take the subset of block partition data and residue data in a frame from one macroblock.

First, define block partition data B_{ij} as a 4x4 block partition data in location *{i,j}* and R_{mn} is residual data of a pixel in location *{m,n}* in a frame. The index *{i,j}* is in 4x4 block-unit and *{m,n}* is in pixel unit. Therefore, in a CIF frame, for example, there are 25,344 block partitions structured into 88 rows and 72 columns of block partitions and up to 352x288 residue data.

Next, define M_k as an arbitrary *k*-th macroblock in frame *f* composed of non-null block partition B_{ij} and nonzero residue data R_{mn}, respectively. Macroblocks with non-null block partition and nonzero residue data is defined as "qualified macroblocks".

The segmentation process continues by removing noise that may lead to incorrect object detection using temporal filtering. Here we define noise as data that appears inconsistently along the series of consecutive frames. In our temporal filtering, we set series of ten frames as one batch. Within the batch, we observe how consistent a macroblock containing block partition data and residue data appears. For this purpose we must take the subset of block partition data and residue data in a frame from one macroblock.

3.2.2 Block filtering

Threshold values are set to determine the degree of inconsistency in terms of number of frames in a batch to filter the noise macroblock. These values are adjusted based on how much motion vectors and residual data are produced in the encoded bitstreams. In the experiments the consistency of qualified macroblocks along the sequence are observed by adjusting the number of frames in which the macroblocks that are inconsistent are allowed to be kept.

Camera position is also used to determine the threshold value. In video taken from camera located in high position such as outdoor surveillance where camera is located in a pole at the side of a street, it is expected to have small moving object, therefore an object may be represented by few number of block partitions. On the other hand, if the camera is located in low position such as indoor surveillance where camera is located in the ceiling of a room, we expect to have large moving object which represented by many block partitions.

By adjusting the threshold value for several sequences with value from 2 (i.e. remove a macroblock if it inconsistently appear in less than 2 frames within the batch) to 8, our observations yield the optimum threshold value for block partition data ρ_B=5 for high camera position and ρ_B =4 for low camera position. Similarly we determine threshold value for residue data ρ_R =4 for both camera positions.

Finally, let h be the number of frame in a series of consecutive 10 frames, the data is filtered for every macroblock M_k within the 10 frames by keeping the blocks B_{ij} if $h>\rho_B$ and keeping residue data R_{mn} if $h>\rho_R$, otherwise the blocks and residue data are removed.

Up to this process, we already remove the noise and segment the frame into foreground: the block partition data and residue data that expected to be part of moving object; and background: the data that are not part of moving object. To keep the relation of block partition data and residue data in a single representation, we define both data types into single unit of 4x4 block partition size.

We define C_{ij} as the i-th block partition data in frame f called "candidate of cluster" composed of B_{ij} and R_{ij}. R_{ij} is composed of 16 residue data of R_{mn} where *{m,n}* is the location of 16 pixel inside block *{i,j}*. C_{ij} is constrained by having non-null block partition data and at least one nonzero residue data exist in a block partition. Therefore any block partition composed by either only B_{ij} or only R_{ij} will be omitted in the next process.

In temporal filtering, we removed any data that are inconsistent during series of frame. However, we may also find consistent data (according to the threshold parameters) which are actually noise. Such data occurred as isolated data, i.e. the data comprises of only few number of block partition (usually less than four blocks), or block partitions that "dangled" from group of blocks. The spatial filtering process aims to remove such noise.

Based on the aforementioned problem, the spatial filtering is quite simple: keep C_{ij} if it has more than four adjacent neighbors, otherwise, it is removed. The adjacent neighbor is defined as 8-connectivity neighbor is the direct adjacent block of C_{ij} from top-left, top, top-right, right, left, bottom-left, bottom and bottom-right order, respectively.

After the noises are removed, the blocks are then grouped into clusters where each cluster represents the blocks of actual detected moving object.

3.2.3 Automatic clustering

Clustering aims for collecting groups of block partitions, the candidate of cluster, into single representation of object to be tracked. A cluster is defined as group of block partitions in a frame that adjacent to each other. A group may contain at most four block partitions and consistently appears in several frames of ten consecutive frames based on the threshold of temporal filtering and at least has four neighbors based on spatial filtering process.

Clustering process can be seen as mapping block partition into clusters in subjective and non-injective case, that is, one block partition shall be mapped to exactly one cluster while one cluster may be mapped from one or more block partition, and there is no null cluster (a cluster without any block partitions mapped to it).

Here we perform automatic clustering of the block partitions because we don't know how many clusters can be generated from group of blocks and we cannot initiate random cluster center. It is a greedy algorithm that scans all block partitions in a frame in progressive order and search for its adjacent neighbor using specified searching window then recursively find for block partition and its adjacent neighbor inside the window.

Define a cluster O_p consists of groups of candidate of cluster blocks where p denotes the index of cluster. A cluster may consist of a finite number of block partitions, where one cluster may contain any arbitrary adjacent C_{ij}s. To lower the computational complexity in implementation the maximum number of clusters to be recognized is set to ten objects.

We use searching window to find adjacent blocks of a block partition. The searching window determines how far we must search for adjacent blocks to be grouped into the same cluster as the initial block partition from which the search is started. Two searching windows are defined, as shown in Fig. 6, with respect to the position of the camera used to take the video: 4-connectivity neighborhood window ("4w" window) for high camera and 20-connectivity neighborhood window ("20w" window) for low camera. We omit the adjacent blocks at the corner of the searching window to avoid the blocks that are actually not part of another object be clustered in the same cluster of an object.

In video taken with camera located in high position the searching window is limited to the four adjacent neighboring blocks. On the other hand, if the camera is located in low position, with the possibility that one object may have several group of block partitions, the searching area is extended to the adjacent twenty neighboring blocks. Since the position of camera usually unchanged during the use of the camera, implementation of searching window can be appropriately chosen once for one camera.

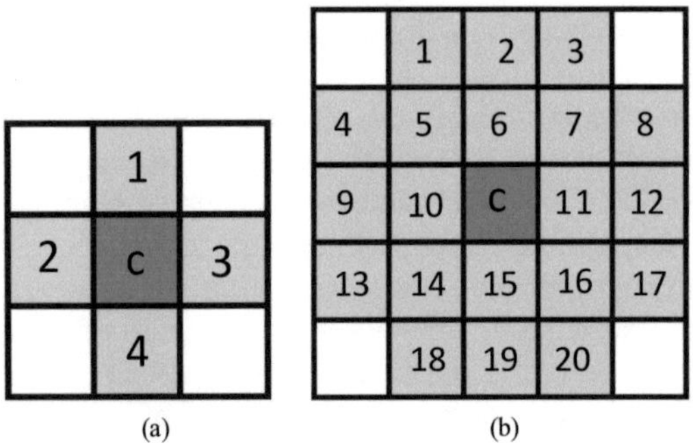

Fig. 6. Searching window (a) 4-connectivity neighborhood window and (b) 20-connectivity neighborhood window; c is the block partition to be searched for neighbor

Due to incorrect motion estimation or very small differences of two frames, sometimes the moving object cannot be detected by looking at the availability of blocks with non-zero motion vectors or residual data. In the end, the clustering method will be failed to cluster any object. In this case, a temporal refinement is performed to restore missing clusters.

In the temporal refinement, we project the clusters that inconsistently disappear in series of frames. A cluster may be projected when there is missing clusters in a frame, by taking the

average value of static parameters of clusters in a series of five frames so the interpolated cluster will have average value of position, direction and energy. From filtering and projection process we expect to have consistent clusters (the candidate of objects).
The examples of segmented clusters are shown in Fig. 7, where clusters are distinguished with different colors for visualization.

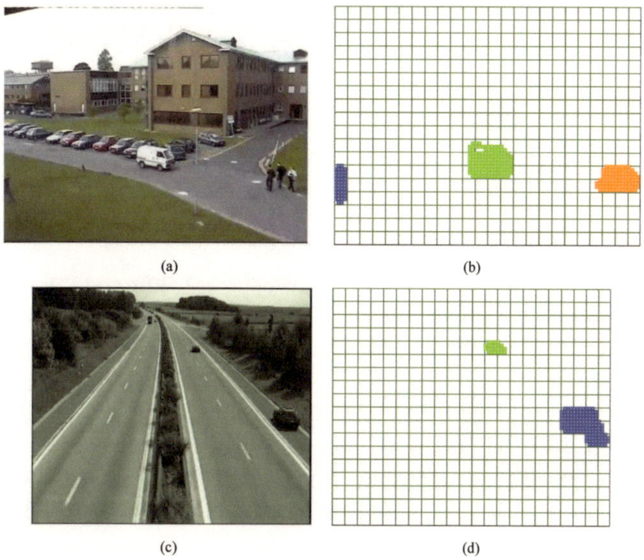

Fig. 7. Block partitions already labeled into different clusters (shown with different colors) in (a),(c) original frame and (b),(d) clusters generated from the 428th frame of *PETS2001* sequence and the 51st frame of *Speedway* sequence, respectively.

The result of video analysis discussed in this section can be annotated in a structured description using XML metadata instantiation. The annotation may describe pertinent information such as the time and frame number when the objects are detected, the actual time information of the scene, the description of the location of detected object, the identity of the detected object and the information about the networked camera used to detect the object. These descriptions will be stored in a structured file format together with the actual video data through the network video storage device.

4. Storage device and data streaming

Media data provided by NVT's and associated metadata generated by NVA's have to be recorded in order to be used for later re-viewing and further forensic analysis. In ONVIF appropriate interfaces for a Network Video Storage (NVS) device have been defined providing for recording of streamed media and metadata as well as for structured access by clients.
The logical structure chosen is comprised of a container denoted as recording holding any number of tracks. Tracks can be of the type video, audio and metadata containing appropriate data at certain times. The minimum configuration, three tracks - one of each video, audio and metadata, might be extended by creating additional tracks for e.g. audio backchannel recording. The creation of new recording container and new tracks respectively is supported only if signalled as particular capability of the NVS.

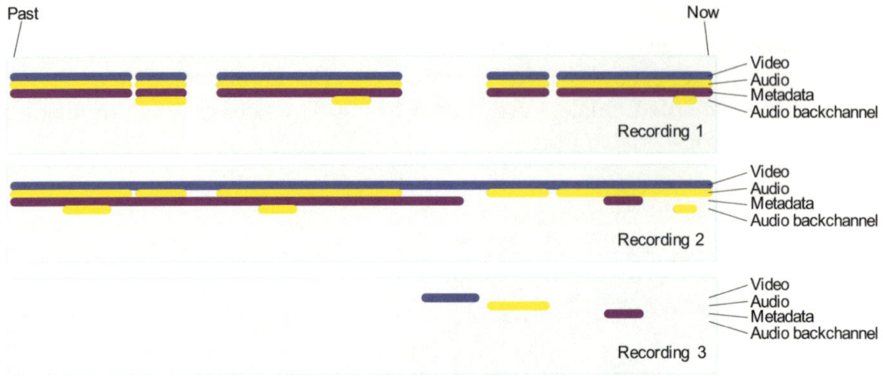

Fig. 8. Example of recordings and tracks structure (source ONVIF)

A parameter has been defined determining the maximum time data of a recording shall be stored. Retention time can be set to infinite but the device may automatically free up any required storage space for new recordings. A mechanism to lock ranges of data has not been defined by ONVIF.

To save data to a recording a RecordingJob as control instance is needed pulling data from one or more sources into the tracks of the recording. Required structures can be pre-configured providing means to implement e.g. alarm recording. Here, changing the mode of RecordingJob between idle and active is the only action required to start and stop recording.

The NVS relies on the *Receiver Service* in order to receive media data from other devices.

Receiving streamed data in ONVIF is unified and consolidated in the *Receiver (Configuration) Service*. Every device able to receive media streams implements this service. It is the client's responsibility configuring the receiver object to contain the operative stream URI, information how to setup the stream and the mode of the receiver. Modes are defined for the receiver attempting to maintain a persistent connection as well as to connect on demand. There is no actual media data transfer necessary because the receiver serves as RTSP client endpoint. Appropriate keep-alive methods may be used to obtain persistence. Tagging mechanisms are being used by the services calling the receiver to distinguish between tracks of the same type within a RTSP stream.

Receivers are to be used non-exclusively reducing the number of parallel connections a device may be required to maintain.

A particular point of failure has been identified in dangling RecordingJobs and receivers not properly connected to each other or not deleted completely. Therefore, a mechanism has been defined to automatically create a new receiver and attach it to a recording job. However this mechanism only works for receivers used with a single recording job. If the RecordingJob does not use the receiver any more it should be deleted automatically.

Data streaming

Transportation of media and metadata between endpoints in the ONVIF eco-system is being performed as streaming over IP-networks. Here, usage of the Real-time Transport Protocol (RTP) is required. It defines a packet based delivery of data providing support for detecting unordered arrival of packets. It has to be used together with the User Datagram Protocol (UDP).

Additionally, support is required for media transfer using RTP/RTSP/HTTP/TCP in order to traverse firewalls. Here, conformance to QuickTime available form Apple Inc. has to be assured for the tunneling while also the Embedded [Interleaved] Binary Data specification for RTSP shall be obeyed. The latter requires for Base64 encoding of RTCP feedback as well as backchannel packets.
For the initiation of sessions as well as for playback control RTSP over TCP has to be used and the Session Description Protocol (SDP) for information provisioning about media types, formats and associated properties.
In order to keep RTSP sessions alive the client side is expected to send receiver reports or to call the RTSP server using any method. All devices are expected to support RTCP sender reports for media synchronization.
Error classification for RTP and HTTP respectively follows the standard status code definitions.
For metadata streams particular definitions have been made concerning several RTP header elements. For example, if the RTP marker bit is set to "1" it signals completion of the XML document transmitted.
Raising the level of efficiency a particular syntax has been chosen for the transmission of JPEG data over RTP. ONVIF uses RFC 2435 in which an RTP header extension is defined omitting JPEG frame header, JPEG scan header as well as quantization and Huffman coding table transmission in the payload bitstream.
Particular attention has to be paid to the backchannel connection handling. Here, functionality extensions to RTSP have been defined which can not be understood by regular server implementations. A Require tag is introduced to the RTSP header and clients use it in the DESCRIBE message to signal a bidirectional connection request. The enabled server includes an attribute in the SDP media description section indicating the direction media data will be send.

Not all in ONVIF required data streaming protocols guaranty for data delivery, e.g. packet loss may occur. In order to define a payload coding format independent mechanism to indicate a request for synchronization the Picture Loss Indication (PLI) message has been chosen. It is a RTSP feedback message providing for statistically more immediate feedback to the sender. If receiver implementations have access to the web service interface of the transmitter the synchronization point mechanism as defined in ONVIF may be applied instead. Through this mechanism the NVT is enforced to insert an INTRA coded picture in the video stream as soon as possible. Also, event properties or PTZ status information may be synchronized by this means.
The *Event Service* is being used to provide notification about creation, configuration changes and deletion of tracks and recordings. For those events particular Topics and message payload have been defined.
In general, it is left to the vendor of a NVS to provide information about data recorded, structures, timelines of recordings, etc. Assistance on how to convey this information in an ONVIF conformant way has been introduced with the concept of historical events represented also as notification messages. Here, events are being generated by the device itself and recorded. The *Recording Search Service* has been designed to have access to that type of events. Two events for the RecordingHistory root topic are required to be provided. That is, the state of a recording (signaling start/stop of a recording) and presence of data for a track (signaling substantial content).

In order to retrieve recordings and events associated with recordings a NVS hast to provide a search interface. It is session based (identified by a token) and realized as coupled find and fetch results operations. Results may be fetched all at once or in increments as defined by the requester. The search can be performed backwards and forward in time from a chosen starting point.
The search space can be limited with a set of parameters e.g. recording tokens and filters to be provided by the requester. Here, a restricted XPath dialect is being used to navigate around a tree representation of the XML data and selecting nodes based on search criteria. Also other metadata and PTZ positions may be addressed by the search interface.
In addition to providing access to historical events generated by the device itself or inserted by a client a NVS may be required to generate virtual events in order to communicate the original state of property events. If a requester indicates desire to be informed about the status of properties at the start point of the search such virtual events needs to be created on the fly.

5. Display device and data export

A Network Video Display (NVD) device provides processing for the decoding of media streams and configuration options on where and how to output it for human observer.
A NVD provides outputs and potentially also sources for media data in case the backchannel mechanism is supported. Configuration of these entities requires *DeviceIO Service* to be supported.
After configuring the physical in- and outputs of the NVD a client can define a layout for each output. A layout defines the arrangement of display areas on a monitor, e.g. single view or split screen. During the session set-up a NVD signals if a certain set of predefined layouts is available.
Areas on a physical display being addressable and configurable are called pane. A layout assigns the area of the display and the pane configuration. The order of the panes in the layout also determines the order of the panes on the monitor if overlapping panes (windows) are supported by the device. The first pane on the list is displayed in the foreground at start.
Audio and video data for a particular NVT media profile are combined in one pane configuration. If a NVT has a microphone attached and supports audio encoding, audio data may be transmitted and listened to at the NVD. If a NVT has loudspeakers attached and supports audio decoding, audio data may be transmitted from the NVD and output at the NVT. The latter is enabled by the backchannel mechanism defined in ONVIF.
The NVD is required to decode JPEG data and if it supports audio also G.711µLaw - exactly the same codecs that are mandatory for the NVT.
The NVD also has to support the *Event Service*. Particular events have been defined to signal if unsupported data formats are being received or packet loss occurred.
The NVD also makes use of the *Receiver Service* in order to pull the data. Data may be received from NVS or NVT directly. The pane configuration holds a reference to the appropriate receiver object containing the URI from where to fetch data.
If data are being received from a NVS the *Replay Service* will provide it. Every NVS has to implement the *Replay Service* defined by ONVIF. It defines extension to the RTSP protocol in order to support e.g. timing and track referencing.
A RTP header extension is being defined containing monotonically increasing NTP timestamps, indicating absolute UTC time associated with the access unit. An additional Rate-control header field is introduced distinguishing between server and client side based playback speed control. If not present the server will be in control, providing support for modest client implementations.

Several features are supported in order to make replay convenient and provide for surveillance typical requirements. One of it is reverse replay. In that case transmitted data are segmented into chunks always starting with an INTRA coded picture. These chunks are sent in reverse order while the packets inside the chunk are being sent in regular order. For single stepping the client is expected to cache a chunks data. Depending on the Rate-control header field setting the RTP timestamps take on different values (decreasing or increasing within a chunk) which has to be taken into account presenting the pictures to an observer as well as for saving it to file.

The *Replay Service* is in ONVIF also used to provide for data export. The client can download the required data in order to process and safe it to an appropriate exchange format.

5.1 Video surveillance exchange format

Data access and distribution within the ONVIF system has been described above. For the cooperation with governmental authorities as well as between different forces of legislation and execution data might to be taken out of the ONVIF system. A standardized data exchange format is necessary at this point enabling data exchange without any loss or damage and to reduce costs for further analysis and viewing equipment. In the following such an exchange format is described purposefully designed for the application in the surveillance domain.

The MPEG-A Multimedia Application Format (MAF) is MPEG standard that has the aim of providing the standardized package format of audiovisual contents, content description metadata and intellectual property management and protection (IPMP) metadata and rights expression language (REL) metadata etc. for specific application domains. The MAF defines not only the file structure based on ISO base Media File Format, but also the components of resources and metadata to be included. The MAF may consist of MPEG and non-MPEG standard technologies, upon requirements for specific industry applications. The VSAF standard is Part 10 of MPEG-A (ISO/IEC 23000-10:2009) which specifies the storage format for video surveillance recording and its corresponding metadata which adopts MPEG-4 AVC|H.264 as the video resource and a set of MPEG-7 Multimedia Description Scheme (MDS) tools (ISO/IEC 15938-5:2003) and Visual descriptors (ISO/IEC 15938-3:2002). Its purpose is to enable interoperability for various video surveillance systems as well as to provide the description about the file structure and visual contents.

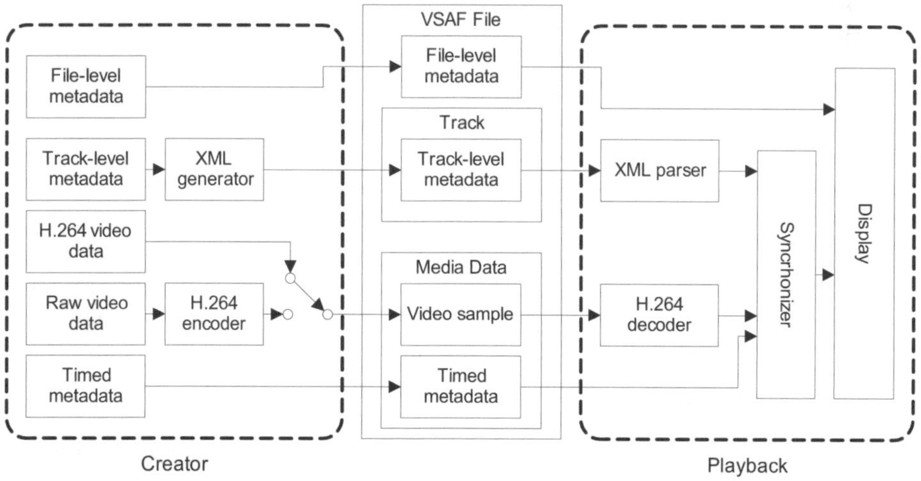

Fig. 9. Creating and using VSAF file format

Fig. 9 shows the conceptual illustration of creating and using VSAF file format for video surveillance data and metadata in a single file. Generally there are two types of data used to create VSAF file: video data and metadata. VSAF specification requires at least one track of video data type encoded using MPEG-4 AVC|H.264 Baseline profile (up to level 3.1). If the source camera does not provide such bitstream then the video shall be first encoded conform to the specification. In addition, different video track, contain the same or different content with the main AVC video track, encoded with other coding technology is also permitted. The metadata stored in VSAF file comprises of binary metadata and textual metadata. Binary metadata is stored in binary format according to the VSAF file structure while textual metadata is stored as XML instantiation of MPEG-7, thus an XML generator shall be needed to create the instantiation.

The structure of VSAF file format in brief is as follow. The file is composed of structure called box, an object-oriented structure in which the data is stored according to specified syntax and semantics. The actual video data is stored in a box called media data box in which the data is usually partitioned into samples called chunks. To enable playback of these chunks, synchronization information such as time stamp, data offset (location) and data size are stored in binary timed metadata box within the media data box. The bitstreams specific information such as profiles and levels for codec types, bitrates, frame rates and screen size are also needed for decoding the bitstreams. This information is stored in boxes within another box called track box where one box corresponds to one video data. In VSAF file format, the track box also contains a box that stores textual metadata and, in addition to ISO base file format, a box for binary metadata is also specified in root (file-level) box. VSAF file structure also enables movie fragments to support the playback of the surveillance video while the data is still being recording. With this structure, features such as instant replay or live metadata generation can be enabled.

It is not uncommon for surveillance video to have long time period of recording while on the other hand the storage or transmission device may have provided limited space or bandwidth. To overcome this problem, the VSAF specification enables the VSAF to be stored in so-called VSAF fragments where each fragment covers a limited amount of time and can be connected to other VSAF fragment. The connection between VSAF fragments is determined by linking their universal unique identifier (UUID). Each VSAF fragment is linked to a predecessor and successor fragment via UUID. A current VSAF fragment is set when the fragment does not have any predecessor or successor fragments. By doing so, a long-time surveillance recording can be fragmented into several linked VSAF fragments (i.e. VSAF files).

Playing VSAF file is performed by first parsing the file format for the metadata and video data. In order to playback the video, it shall be first decoded from MPEG-4 AVC | H.264 bitstream and synchronized with timed metadata. The XML metadata shall be first parsed using XML parser and synchronized with the video to show the appropriate scene description. Obtaining information such as querying specific object using a color as cue or finding the record of object's trajectory can be easily performed because the XML instantiation provides specific location (timestamp information) of the queried object in the video data.

VSAF specification enables the use of metadata to describe information about the content and the file video itself. Two formats of metadata are used to describe the video: binary and textual metadata. Binary metadata are used to store information about the time stamp of video sample (timed metadata) and to store the information of identification and creation time of VSAF file (file-level metadata). This metadata is stored in VSAF as binary data according to VSAF file format specification. The timed metadata is used to describe the timestamp information of the video stored in the file in which every video sample has it own time information. The file-level metadata is used to describe the information regarding the identification and creation time of a VSAF file and the textual annotation about the contents within the VSAF. It also allows for the use of classification scheme to describe the content. The metadata should be located in the top level of the VSAF file in order to enable easy access for identification information of the VSAF file. In the file structure hierarchy of VSAF, this metadata is located in the file level, hence being called the file level metadata.

On the other hand, the textual metadata is used to describe the information regarding the content of the VSAF. It is specified by selecting some parts of MPEG-7 MDS tools and Visual descriptors for the VSAF. It describes the track identification information, camera equipment, timing information for each track, text annotation to describe the event, decomposition of frames, locations of the objects as ROI's in the frame, color appearance of the objects, and identification of the object. The specification of VSAF has a limited set of MPEG-7 Visual descriptors such as the dominant color and scalable color descriptors. Since the track-level metadata describes the video content, the metadata with the MPEG-7 dominant color and scalable color descriptor values are located inside the respective track boxes of VSAF, hence being called the track level metadata.

Metadata structures defined in MPEG-7 can be utilized to capture results of the object detection described in Section 3. More specifically, time information, location information and object's identity can be described using MPEG-7 MDS while visual information such as the location of the detected object in the frame and its trajectory can be described in MPEG-7 Visual. VSAF also enables embedding other metadata formats such as from ONVIF without any change to the VSAF file structure by merely adding an additional metadata element in the textual metadata.

6. Conclusion

In this chapter we provided an overview of modern surveillance system composition exploiting available standardized technology supporting recent trends in the surveillance domain: networked cameras and web services, host-based automated data analysis as well as interoperable media formats for data streaming, storage and export.

7. References

OASIS Organization for the Advancement of Structured Information Standards; www.oasis-open.org

ONVIF Open Network Video Interface Forum; Core Specification; Version 2.0; www.onvif.org

ISO/IEC 23000-10:2009, Information technology – Multimedia application format (MPEG-A) – Part 10: Video surveillance application format, http://www.iso.org/iso/iso_catalogue/catalogue_tc/catalogue_detail.htm?csnumber=50554

ISO/IEC 15938-3:2002, Information technology -- Multimedia content description interface – Part 3: Visual http://www.iso.org/iso/iso_catalogue/catalogue_tc/catalogue_detail.htm?csnumber=34230

ISO/IEC 15938-5:2003, Information technology -- Multimedia content description interface -- Part 5: Multimedia description schemes http://www.iso.org/iso/iso_catalogue/catalogue_tc/catalogue_detail.htm?csnumber=34232

ISO/IEC 14496-10:2009, Information technology -- Coding of audio-visual objects -- Part 10: Advanced Video Coding http://www.iso.org/iso/iso_catalogue/catalogue_tc/catalogue_detail.htm?csnumber=52974

ITU-T Recommendation H.264 (03/10): Advanced video coding for generic audiovisual services http://www.itu.int/rec/T-REC-H.264-201003-I/en

5

Realizing Video-Surveillance on Wireless Mesh Networks: Implementation Issues and Performance Evaluation

Giovanni Schembra
DIIT – University of Catania, Italy

1. Introduction

Video-surveillance systems are currently undergoing a transition from traditional analog solutions to digital ones. This paradigm shift has been triggered by technological advances as well as increased awareness of the need for heightened security in particular vertical markets such as government and transportation. Compared with traditional analog video-surveillance systems, digital video-surveillance offers much greater flexibility in video content processing and transmission. At the same time, it can also easily implement advanced features such as motion detection, facial recognition and object tracking. Many commercial companies now offer IP-based surveillance solutions.

This chapter starts from an experience of deployment of a prototype of a large-scale distributed video-surveillance system that the authors' research group has realized as a common testbed for many research projects. It consists of sixty video cameras distributed over the campus of the University of Catania, transmitting live video streams to a central location for processing and monitoring.

Deployment and maintenance of large-scale distributed video-surveillance systems is often very expensive, mainly due to the installation and maintenance of physical wires. The solution chosen in order to significantly reduce the overall system costs, while increasing deployability, scalability, and performance is the use of wireless interconnections (Collins et al., 2001); (Chiasserini & Magli, 2002).

With this in mind, the basis idea is to apply multi-hop wireless mesh networks (WMN) (Akyildiz et al., 2005); (Karrer et al., 2003); (Bhagwaty et al., 2003); (Tropos) as the interconnection backbone of a wireless video-surveillance network (WVSN). The proposed architecture is shown in Fig. 1. As we will see in Section 2, it fits in well with the structure of a WMN (Draves et al., 2004), where traffic sources are networked digital video cameras, while the nodes of the WVSN are fixed and wirelessly interconnected to provide video sources with connections towards a video proxy with processing and filtering capabilities. Video proxies are typically located in the wired network.

Nevertheless, implementing an intelligent, scalable and massively distributed video-surveillance system over wireless networks remains a research problem and leads to at least the following important issues, some of which have been raised in (Feng et al., 2001):

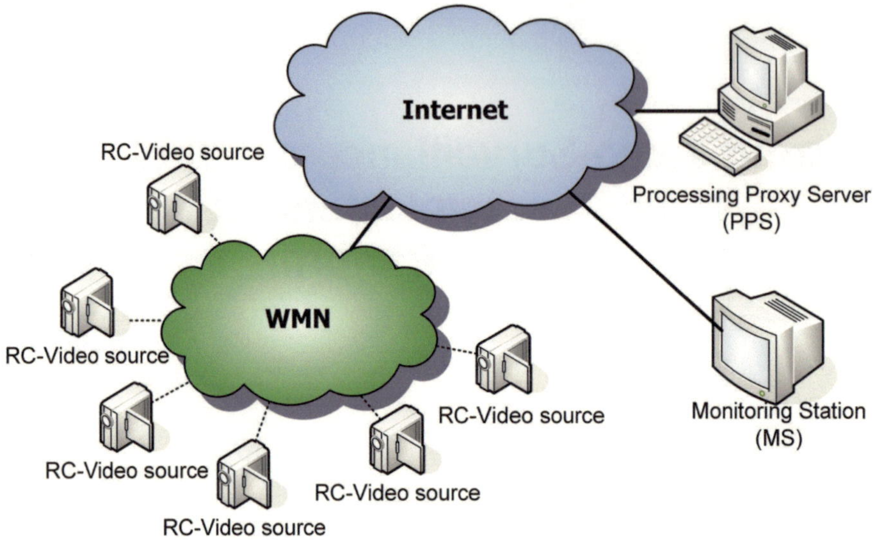

Fig. 1. WVSN Architecture

- transmission bandwidth and transmission power are scarce resources in wireless environments;
- wireless links are more vulnerable to interceptions and external attacks;
- the high loss percentage of wireless links requires sophisticated techniques for channel encoding that often increase transmission delays.

On the contrary, a video-surveillance system presents the following features:

- commonly used computer vision algorithms in a video-surveillance environment perform better when video is encoded with high PSNR and temporal quality. However, increasing video quality causes an increase in both the required transmission bandwidth and transmission power;
- interceptions and external attacks are a serious problem in video-surveillance applications;
- delay and delay jitter are very harmful, and therefore must be kept below a given acceptable threshold.

So, the target of this work is twofold: 1) describing a real experience based on a new WVSN architecture, defined by the authors, which is based on a wireless mesh network as the interconnection backbone; 2) analyzing its performance in order to evaluate some protocol and implementation issues, and provide some insights into the choice of design parameters that will optimize the quality of video received at destination by the Processing Proxy Server. This can be achieved by trying to obtain the best trade-off between video encoding quality and the network traffic generated at the source side, and using suitable routing algorithms in the wireless mesh network. The video quality at destination is evaluated through an objective quality parameter which is able to simultaneously account for packet losses in the network (impacting the received frame rate) and encoding quality (impacting the PSNR of the decoded frames).

The chapter is structured as follows. Section 2 introduces the related work. Sections 3 and 4 present the considered system and describe the proposed architecture. Section 5 discusses the achieved performance. Finally, Section 6 concludes the chapter.

2. Related work

Analog video-surveillance systems (e.g. CCTV) are increasingly being replaced by more advanced digital video surveillance (DVS) solutions, often utilizing IP technologies and networked architectures. Besides the ever-increasing demand for security, the low cost of cameras and networking devices has contributed to the spread of *digital distributed multimedia surveillance systems*. This now constitutes an emerging field that includes signal and image processing, computer vision, communications, and hardware.

The automated analysis and processing of video surveillance is a central area of study for the computer vision and pattern recognition research community. IBM Research's PeopleVision project (PeopleVision), for example, has focused on the concept of *Smart Surveillance* (Hampapur et al., 2003), or the application of automated analysis of surveillance video to reduce the tedious, time-consuming task of viewing video feeds from a large number of security cameras. There have been a number of famous visual surveillance systems. The real-time visual surveillance system W4 (Haritaoglu et al., 2000) employs a combination of shape analysis and tracking, and constructs models of people's appearances in order to detect and track groups of people as well as monitor their behaviors even in the presence of occlusion and in outdoor environments. This system uses a single camera and grayscale sensor. The VIEWS system (Tan et al., 1998) is a 3D-model-based vehicle tracking system. The Pfinder system (Wren et al., 1997) is used to recover a 3-D description of a person in a large room. It tracks a single non-occluded person in complex scenes, and has been used in many applications. The system at CMU (Lipton et al., 1998) can monitor activities over a large area using multiple cameras that are connected into a network.

As far as hardware for video-surveillance is concerned, companies like Sony and Intel have designed equipments suitable for visual surveillance, e.g., active cameras, smart cameras (Kemeny et al., 1997), omni-directional cameras (Boult, 1998); (Basu & Southwell, 1995), and so on. Networking devices for video surveillance are the Intelligent Wireless Video Systems proposed by Cisco® with the 3200 Series Wireless and Mobile Routers. Cisco Systems offer for example an outdoor and mobile wireless router with intelligent video functions, addressing public safety and transportation customer needs for highly secure, cost-efficient, and standards-based video surveillance applications (Cisco).

Another important focus of research into video surveillance systems is on communications between networked cameras and video processing servers. This is the field of this chapter.

The classical approach to digital video surveillance systems is based on wired connections with existing Ethernet and ATM dedicated-medium networks (Telindus, 2002). Another wired-based approach is proposed in (Chandramohan et al., 2002), where IEEE 1394b FireWire is investigated as a shared medium protocol for ad hoc, economical installation of video cameras in wireless sensor networks (WSNs). However, they are the cost and performance bottleneck to further deployment of large-scale video surveillance systems with highly intelligent cameras (Feng et al., 2001). A hybrid routing protocol for future arbitrary topology WSNs is presented. It uses distributed location servers which maintain the route-attribute-location knowledge for routing in WSNs.

The latest step in the evolution of video surveillance systems, aimed at increasing the scalability of large video surveillance systems, is the migration to wireless interconnection networks. Many solutions have been proposed in this context, by both industries and research institutions. Firetide Inc., a developer of wireless multi-service mesh technology, and Axis Communications, a company working on network video solutions, have announced a strategic partnership to deliver high-quality video over wireless mesh networks, which are being used by a number of cities to provide wireless video surveillance. In Massachusetts, for example, the Haverhill Police Department selected these technologies for its own video surveillance system (Firetide, 2006). Initially installed in a small, high-crime area downtown, the solution consists of Firetide HotPort outdoor and indoor wireless mesh nodes and AXIS 214 PTZ (pan-tilt-zoom) and AXIS 211 fixed cameras.

A great amount of work has been done to reduce power consumption in wireless video surveillance networks. (Doblander et al., 2005) defines some QoS-parameters in video surveillance, like video data quality and its distortions in network transmission (jitter). Further parameters include quality metrics such as image size, data rate or the number of frames per second (fps). The work in (Chiasserini & Magli, 2002) investigates the trade-off between image quality and power consumption in wireless video surveillance networks. However, existing implementations lack comprehensive handling of these three correlating parameters. In (Zhang & Chakrabarty, 2003), an adaptive checkpointing algorithm is proposed that also minimizes energy consumption.

Another important issue to be considered from the communications point of view is routing. A very large amount of research has been carried out regarding routing in ad-hoc wireless networks. Now we have to take into account that the network environment we are considering in this chapter is a wireless mesh network, which is a particular case of wireless ad-hoc networks. In addition, as we will illustrate in the following section, we will apply multipath routing, given that multiple paths can provide load balancing, fault-tolerance, and higher aggregate bandwidth (Mueller & Ghosal, 2004). Load balancing can be achieved by spreading the traffic along multiple routes. This can alleviate congestion and bottlenecks. From a fault tolerance perspective, multipath routing can provide route resilience. Since bandwidth may be limited in a wireless network, routing along a single path may not provide enough bandwidth for a connection. However, if multiple paths are used simultaneously to route data, the aggregate bandwidth of the paths can satisfy the bandwidth requirement of the application. Also, since there is more bandwidth available, a smaller end-to-end delay can be achieved.

Many multipath routing protocols have been defined in the past literature for ad-hoc wireless networks. The Multipath On-demand Routing (MOR) protocol (Biagioni & Chen, 2004) was defined to connect nodes in wireless sensor networks. Other important routing protocols for ad-hoc networks are DSR (Johnson et al., 1999), TORA (Park & Corson, 1997) and AODV (Perkings et al., 2003). DSR is an on-demand routing protocol which works on a source routing basis. Each transmitted packet is routed carrying the complete route in its header. TORA is an adaptive on-demand routing protocol designed to provide multiple loop-free routes to a destination, thus minimizing reaction to topological changes. The protocol belongs to the link reversal algorithm family. AODV is an on-demand distance-vector routing protocol, based on hop-by-hop routing. It is a modified DSR protocol incorporating some features presented in the DSDV protocol, such as the use of hop-by-hop routing, sequence numbers and periodic beacon messages.

However, all the above protocols are reactive, or on-demand, meaning that they establish routes as needed. The advantage of this approach is obvious if only a few routes are required, since the routing overhead is less than in the proactive approach of establishing routes whether or not they are needed. The disadvantage of on-demand establishment of routes is that connections take more time if the route needs to be established. However, given that the wireless mesh networks considered in this chapter have stable topologies because nodes are fixed and powered, the proactive approach works better. For this reason we propose to use the distance-vector multipath network-balancing routing algorithm (Vutukury & Garcia-Luna-Aceves, 2001), which is a proactive routing algorithm.

3. Description of the WVSN system

In this section we describe the video-surveillance platform considered in the rest of the chapter. The system topology is shown in Fig. 2. It is made of an access network and a core network. In order to monitor six different areas of the campus, the access network comprises six edge nodes. Each edge node is equipped with one omni-directional antenna to allow wireless access to video cameras. Both edge and core nodes are routers wirelessly connected to the other nodes by high gain directional antennas to minimize interferences, and so to avoid network capacity degradation. All the links of the mesh network are IEEE 802.11b wireless connections at 11 Mbps. More specifically, the following antennas have been used:

- Omnidirectional antenna installed in each edge node for connection of wireless cameras: Pacific wireless 2.4GHz PAWOD24-12, with a gain of 12dBi, a frequency range of 2400-2485 MHz, and a vertical Beam Width of 7 degrees;

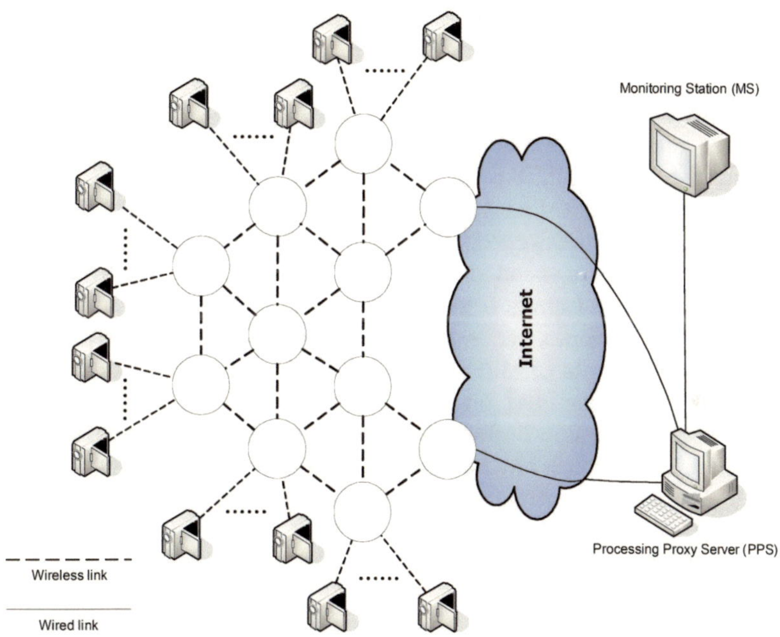

Fig. 2. WVSN topology

- Unidirectional antenna installed in each node (both edge and core) for point-to-point connection with the other nodes: Pacific wireless 2.4GHz Yagi PAWVA24-16, with a gain of 16dBi, a frequency range of 2400-2485 MHz, and a Beam Width of 25 degrees.

Radio frequencies have been designed in such a way that different radio interfaces on the same node use different radio channels.

The wireless mesh network is connected to the Internet through the gateway nodes. We have chosen a number of two gateway nodes to distribute network load and guarantee path diversity towards the proxy server.

Video sources are networked digital video cameras connected to the edge nodes through IEEE 802.11b wireless connections at 11 Mbps. Specifically, ten wireless video cameras are connected to each edge node. Video cameras are set to encode video with a 352 × 288 CIF format, using a standard MPEG-4 encoder at a bit-rate settable in the range between 100 kbps and 600 kbit/s, and a frame rate of 12 fps. Each frame is encoded as an I-frame.

4. WVSN architecture

The distributed architecture defined for the video-surveillance system is sketched in Fig. 1. It consists of a number of wireless networked rate-controlled video cameras (*RC-Video sources*) which, thanks to the WMN, access the Internet and continuously transmit their video flows to a *Processing Proxy Server* (PPS) for processing and filtering. The PPS is directly, or again through the Internet, connected to one or more *Monitoring Stations* (MS). Not every video streams that are sent to the PPS for processing is shown to the end user at the MS. In fact, the PPS analyzes all the received video flows, and alerts the MS only if a suspicious event is detected. The focus of this chapter is concentrated on the RC-video sources (and video stream destination at the PPS) and the wireless mesh network. They will be described in Sections 4.1 and 4.2. The Processing Proxy Server will be briefly described in Section 4.3, even though the internal algorithms are beyond the scope of this chapter.

4.1 RC-Video source

The logical architecture of the RC video system is sketched in Fig. 3. It is an adaptive-rate MPEG video source over a UDP/IP protocol suite. The video stream generated by the video source is encoded by the *MPEG Encoder* according to the MPEG-4 video standard (ISO, 1992 - a); (ISO, 1992 - b). In the MPEG encoding standard, each frame, corresponding to a single picture in a video sequence, is encoded according to one of three possible encoding modes: intra frames (I), predictive frames (P), and interpolative frames (B). Typically, *I*-frames require more bits than *P*-frames, while *B*-frames have the lowest bandwidth requirement. For this reason the output rate of MPEG video sources needs to be controlled, especially if the generated flow is transmitted on the network. Thus, as usual, a Rate Controller combined with the Transmission Buffer has been introduced in the video encoding system. It works according to a feedback law by appropriately choosing the so-called *Quantizer Scale Parameter* (QSP) in such a way that the output rate of the MPEG Encoder results as much constant as possible. The *MPEG Encoder* output is packetized in the *Packetizer* according to the UDP/IP protocol suite and sent to the *Transmission Buffer* for transmission.

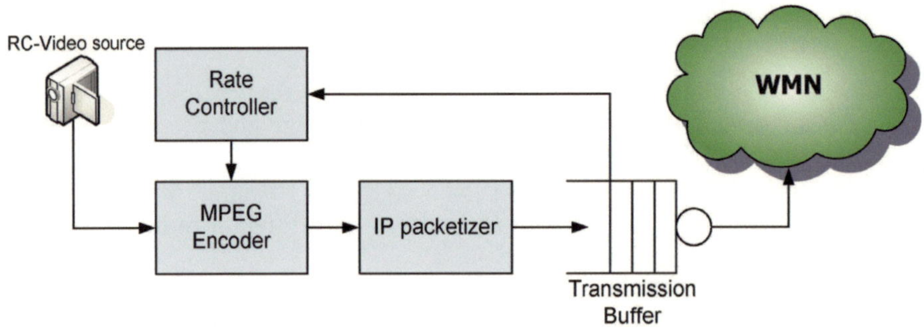

Fig. 3. RC-Video source architecture

The QSP value can range within the set $[1.31]$: 1 being the value giving the best encoding quality but requiring the maximum number of bits to encode the frame, and 31 the value giving the worst encoding quality, but requiring the minimum number of bits. However let us note that it is not possible to encode all the frames with the same number of bits at least for the following three reasons: 1) quantizer scale is chosen a-priori before encoding, and this choice is only based on long-term video statistics, and not on the particular frame to be encoded; 2) quantizer scale parameter can assume 31 values only, and therefore granularity is not so high to obtain any value desired for the number of bits of the encoded frame; 3) sometimes, for example when scene activity is too high or too low, the desired number of bits cannot be obtained for none of the 31 quantizer scale parameter values. Taking into account this, the Transmission Buffer role is necessary to eliminate residual output rate variability. In fact, the Transmission Buffer is served with a constant rate, and therefore its output is perfectly constant, except for the cases when it empties. Of course, the Transmission Buffer queue should not saturate because high delays and losses should be avoided, and therefore the Rate Controller presence is fundamental to maintain the queue around a given threshold, avoiding both empty queue and saturation states.

So the Rate Controller is necessary to make the output rate of the MPEG video source constant, avoiding losses in the Transmission Buffer, and maximizing encoding quality and stability. As said so far, it works according to a given feedback law. This law depends on the activity of the frame being encoded and the current number of packets in the Transmission Buffer. More specifically, in order to keep the output rate as constant as possible, a frame-based feedback law is used (Lombardo & Schembra, 2003). According to this law, the target is to maintain the of the Transmission Buffer very close to a given threshold, θ_F. This is based on the statistics of the video flow, expressed in terms of rate and distortion curves (Chang & Wang, 1997); (Cernuto et al., 2002).

The rate curves, $R_{a,j}(q)$, give the expected number of bits which will be emitted when the *j*-th frame in the GoP has to be encoded, if its activity value is *a*, and is encoded with a QSP value *q*. The distortion curves, $F^{(j)}(q)$, give the expected encoding PSNR for each value of the QSP (Ding & Liu, 1996). The rate and distortion curves for the implemented video-surveillance system are shown in Fig. 4.

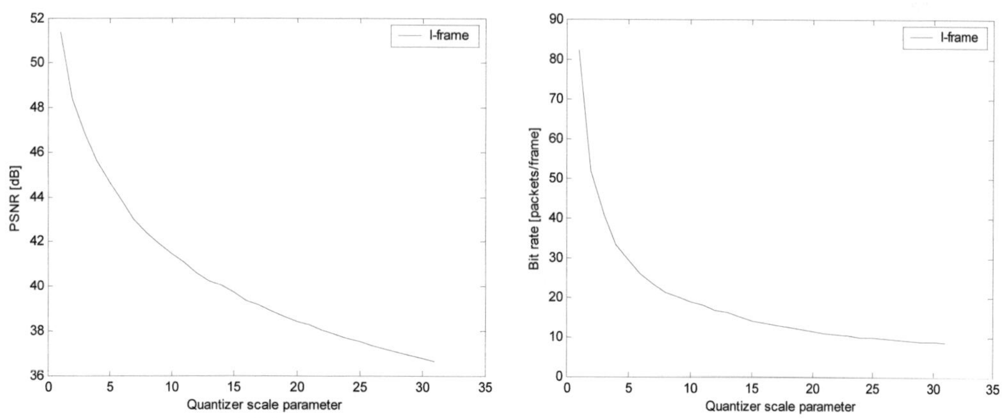

(a) Distortion curve (b) Rate curve

Fig. 4. Rate-distortion curves

As said so far, the aim of the Rate Controller is to maintain the Transmission Buffer queue length lower than, and very close to θ_F at the end of each frame encoding interval. Indicating the frame to be encoded as *j*, its activity as *a*, and the number of data units in the transmission buffer queue before encoding as s_Q, the expected number of packets to encode can be calculated from the rate curve, $R_{a,j}(q)$. So, the frame-based feedback law works by choosing the QSP as follows:

$$q = \Phi\left(s_Q, a, j\right) = min_{\overline{q} \in [1,31]}\left(\overline{q} : s_Q + R_{a,j}(\overline{q}) \le \theta_F\right) \qquad (1)$$

4.2 Processing Proxy Server (PPS)

The logical architecture of the PPS is sketched in Fig. 5. Its main task is to process the video signals in order to detect an intrusion in the controlled area and to send the relative video to the MS.

The RC-Video receiver block receives the video flows from the distributed video-surveillance network through the Internet. It is made up by three fundamental blocks: a *Packet reordering buffer* and a *Jitter compensator buffer*, with the aim of eliminating loss of packet order and delay variations introduced by the network, and an *MPEG Decoder block* to decode the received video flow.

The decoded video streams are processed by the *Video processor and alarm trigger* block. When an intrusion is detected by the Video processor, the trigger system sends the relative video images to the *Video Mosaic Multiplexer* block which makes a spatial composition of the videos. Finally, the multiplexer output video is sent to the Monitoring Station (MS) for visualization by the final user.

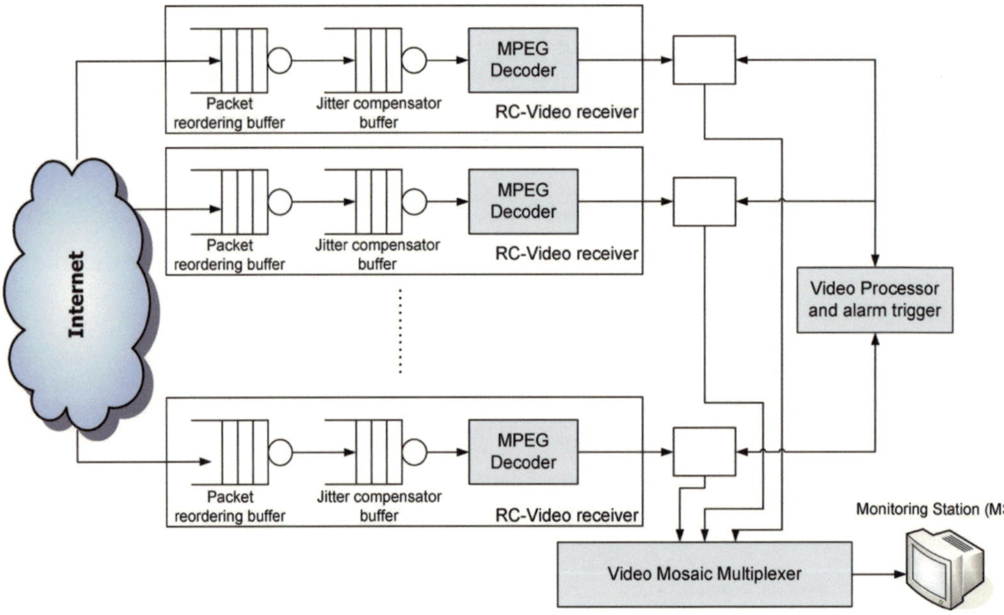

Fig. 5. Processing Proxy Server architecture

4.3 Wireless Mesh Network (WMN)

The WMN constitutes the infrastructure interconnection network for the wireless video-surveillance system. It comprises a number of edge nodes, a number of core nodes and a number of gateway nodes, all interconnected through wireless links. It is a multihop wireless network which, unlike mobile ad-hoc networks (MANET), is constituted by fixed nodes. RC-Video sources are connected to edge nodes, while the WMN is connected to the Internet through the Gateway nodes. The number and location of the edge nodes have to be chosen in such a way as to allow the connection of all the networked wireless cameras.

An important role in this architecture is played by the routing algorithm. Given that the WMN is stable in time because nodes are powered and fixed, a proactive discovery of paths is the best solution since it provides reduced packet delays (deleterious for video-surveillance applications) (Yuan et al., 2003). On the other hand, additional packet latency due to on-demand route discovery, typical in reactive routing strategies, is not acceptable.

Bearing in mind the above-mentioned issues, we have used a distance-vector multipath network-balancing routing algorithm (Vutukury & Garcia-Luna-Aceves, 2001). According to this algorithm each node, thanks to a distance-vector algorithm knows the distance from the Internet through each path in the Mesh network, and forwards packets, in a round-robin fashion, through all the paths having the same minimum cost to reach the Internet, whatever the destination Gateway node. The distance-vector multipath network-balancing routing algorithm is used for two reasons: first it is able to reduce delay (Vutukury & Garcia-Luna-Aceves, 2001); (Vutukury & Garcia-Luna-Aceves, 1999 - a); (Vutukury & Garcia-Luna-Aceves, 1999 - b); secondly, thanks to its multipath peculiarity, it increases the robustness of the architecture to external attacks and interceptions. In fact, if a path is (maliciously or not) shielded, or its quality is temporally degraded, all the packets flowing through it are lost; however, the application of the multipath network-balancing routing algorithm guarantees that a high percentage of packets are able to reach the Video Decoder block, and therefore frames can be decoded, by applying an error concealment video decoding algorithm (Lee et al., 2002); (Pei & Chou, 2004); (Tsekeridou & Pitas, 2000).

Mesh nodes are implemented as software routers running on low-cost computers with the Click Modular Router (Click); (Morris et al., 1999) on a Linux Platform. Hardware of each node is realized by using the Soekris Engineering net4801 single board computer, chosen as a good trade-off between costs and performance.

Click is a software architecture for building flexible and configurable routers. A Click router is assembled from packet processing modules called elements. Individual elements implement simple router functions like packet classification, queueing, scheduling, and interfacing with network devices. A router configuration is a directed graph with elements at the vertices; packets flow along the edges of the graph. A standards-compliant Click IP router has sixteen elements on its forwarding path. Click configurations are modular and easy to extend. The Click Modular Router configuration we have designed and implemented for Mesh nodes is shown in Fig. 6. The *AOMDV* element implements the multipath routing algorithm by communicating with the other network nodes through the network interfaces, represented as eth0 and eth1 in Fig. 6. Then it elaborate information and manages the IP Routing Table, which is read by *the LookupIPRoute* element.

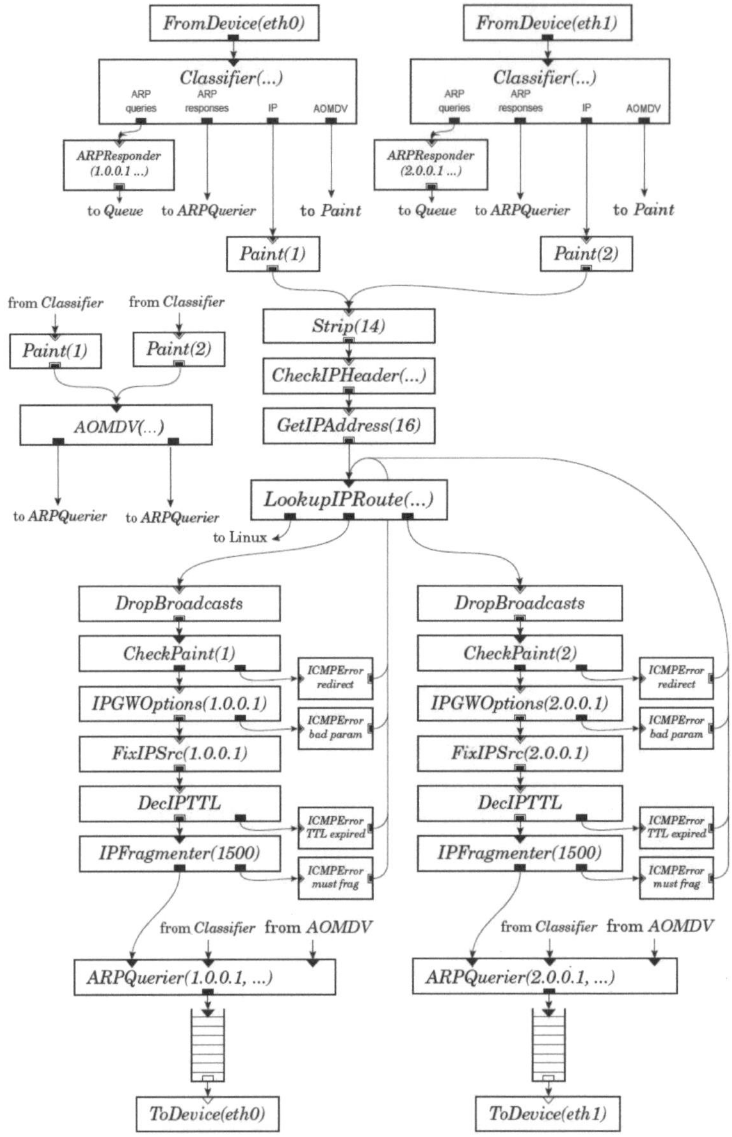

Fig. 6. Edge and Core node implementation

5. Numerical results

In this section we will analyze the performance of the wireless video-surveillance system described so far, and the Quality of Service (QoS) perceived at the PPS Video processor block, which is crucial for the detection of suspicious events.
More specifically, we will discuss the following two main issues:

- Delay analysis for jitter compensation buffer dimensioning;
- Quality of service (QoS) perceived at destination by the PPS, and in particular by its Video Processor block, which is crucial for the detection of suspicious events.

Both analyses are carried out by comparing the distance-vector multipath network-balancing routing algorithm proposed for this system with classic single path Minimum Hop Count routing, in order to evaluate the advantages and disadvantages of the proposed approach.

The analysis has been carried out versus the encoding rate imposed by the Rate Controller to each video source. This rate was changed in the range [200, 600] kbps, given that greater rates cannot be supported by the four bottleneck links connecting the mesh network to the Gateway nodes, because each link has a maximum transmission rate of 11 Mbps.

As regards the delay analysis, we considered both the end-to-end average delay and the delay jitter, represented by the standard deviation of the delay distribution (Lombardo & Schembra, 2003).

The Quality of Service (QoS) perceived at destination by the PPS Video Processor block depends on both the encoding quality at the source and losses occurring in the network and the jitter compensation buffer. More specifically, the encoding quality is decided by setting the quantizer scale parameter, q, as described in Section 4.1. Losses in both the network and the jitter compensation buffer cause an additional degradation of the quality of the decoded frames at destination, given that some frames will never arrive at destination, while other frames will arrive corrupted because not all their packets are available to the decoder at the right time. In this case an error concealment technique is used at destination to efficiently reconstruct corrupted and missing frames and thus improve the quality of the decoded video.

Given that the concealment technique used is beyond the scope of this chapter, in order to achieve results independently of it, we assumed that all frames which have registered a loss percentage greater than a given threshold, here set to $\tau = 20\%$, are not decodable; instead, frames with fewer lost packets are reconstructed, with a quality depending on the percentage of arrived packets.

To summarize, losses in the network and the jitter compensation buffer cause both a reduction in the quality of decoded frames, and a frame rate reduction due to non-decodable and non-arrived frames.

The quality of decoded frames at destination is described by the peak signal-to-noise ratio (PSNR), defined as the ratio between the maximum possible power of a signal and the power of corrupting noise that affects the fidelity of its representation. The PSNR is most easily defined via the mean squared error (MSE). For two $m \times n$ monochrome images I and K, where I is the original image before encoding, and K is the reconstructed image at destination, MSE is defined as:

$$MSE = \frac{1}{m \cdot n} \sum_{i=0}^{m-1} \sum_{j=0}^{n-1} \left\| I(i,j) - K(i,j) \right\|^2 \tag{2}$$

Then the PSNR is defined as:

$$PSNR = 20 log_{10} \left(\frac{MAX_I^2}{MSE} \right) \tag{3}$$

where MAX_I is the maximum pixel value of the image. Since pixels are represented using 8 bits per sample, this is 255. More generally, when samples are represented using linear PCM with B bits per sample, MAX_I is $2^B - 1$. PSNR is usually expressed in terms of the logarithmic decibel scale because many signals have a very wide dynamic range.

In order to account for the frame rate reduction as well, we used the objective quality parameter Q proposed in (Telindus, 2002), defined as:

$$Q = 0.45 \cdot psnr + (fr - 5)/10 - 17.9 \quad (4)$$

where *psnr* is the PSNR value measured at the destination, after error concealment processing, while *fr* is the frame rate of the video sequence perceived at destination, counting decoded frames only. The constant coefficients in (4) were calculated in (Telindus, 2002) by evaluating the data set obtained in a survey, and assuming a minimum acceptable frame rate of 5 frame/s. According to the above definition, the greater the PSNR and the frame rate at destination, the greater the Q parameter.

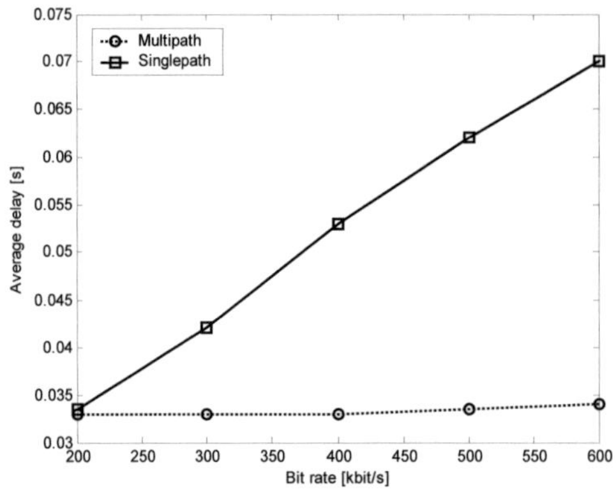

Fig. 7. End-to-end average delay

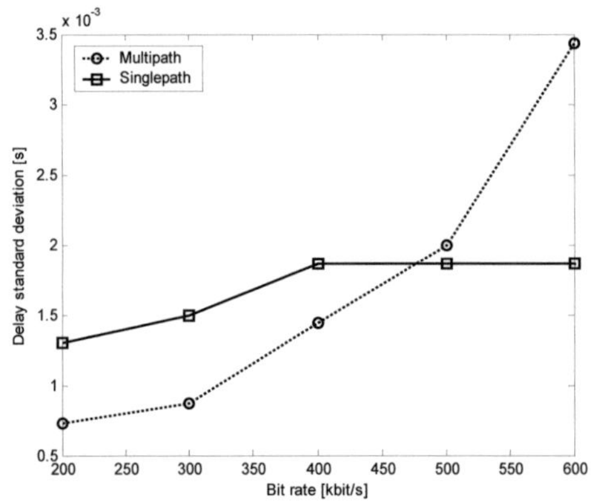

Fig. 8. End-to-end delay standard deviation

Given that the WMN is made up of wireless lossy links, usually constituting bottlenecks due to their low transmission capacity, the Internet is considered as lossless, jitter and losses being introduced by the WMN only.

Figs. 7 and 8 show the average value and the measured standard deviation of the end-to-end delay, respectively. We can see that multipath routing allows a lower average delay to be achieved, as compared to single path routing; however it introduces a larger delay jitter, due to the fact that packets follow different paths, and therefore may experience different delays.

Jitter has to be compensated by the Jitter compensator buffer at the PPS. To this end, delay distributions can be used to choose the value of the threshold σ_J leaving on its right a negligible portion of probability, representing the percentage of packets that are lost if the Jitter compensator buffer equalizes delays to the chosen threshold σ_J. Of course, the greater the value of σ_J, the less the loss percentage introduced by the Jitter compensation buffer, but the higher the equalization delay. In our system we chose σ_J such that 0.1% of packets suffer a delay greater than σ_J, and are therefore discarded.

In order to evaluate the QoS perceived at destination, we first calculated:

- the average PSNR, measured at the destination side as specified in (2) and (3) on the frames fully or partially arrived and decoded (Fig. 11);

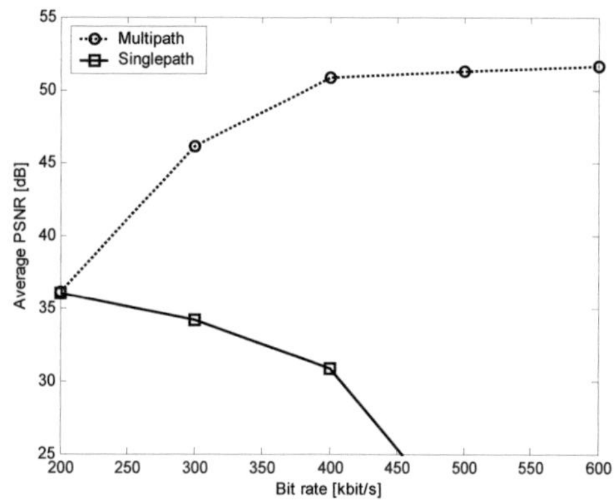

Fig. 11. Average PSNR

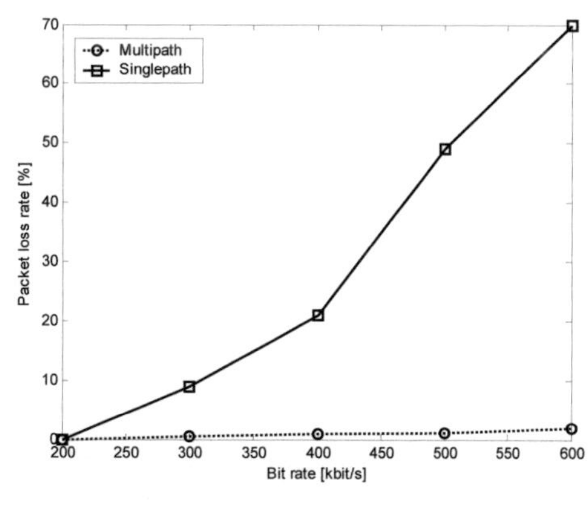

Fig. 12. Packet loss rate

- the packet loss rate in the WMN network (Fig. 12);
- the video frame corruption percentage (Fig. 13), and the consequent effective frame rate, *fr*, measured at destination (Fig. 14), obtained as the ratio of the number of frames that have been decoded (also thanks to the application of the error concealment decoding technique) over the measurement period.

Fig. 11 shows the *psnr* term, defined in (4) as the PSNR calculated at the destination, after error concealment processing. We can observe that the *psnr* obtained with multipath routing

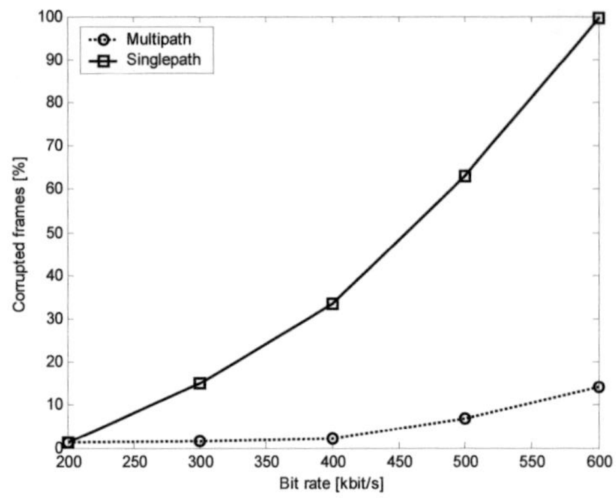

Fig. 13. Video frame corruption percentage

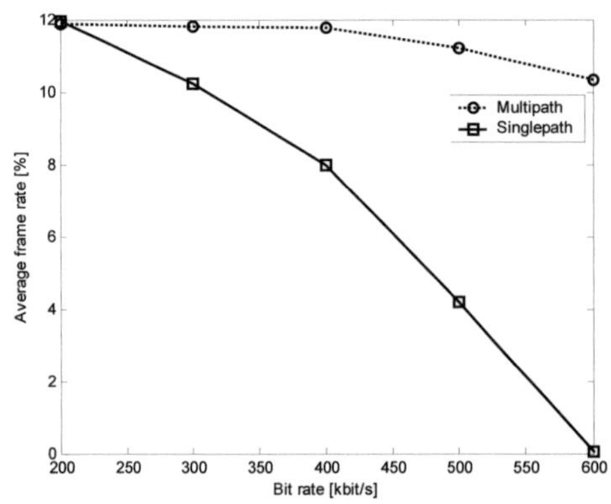

Fig. 14. Average video frame rate, *fr*

is higher than that obtained with single path routing. In this case, in fact, the reduced packet loss rate in the network allows the error concealment algorithm run at destination to work better, therefore providing frames with a better quality, more similar to the original ones. However, when the encoding bit rate is too high (over 400 kbit/s), the PSNR increase at the source side corresponds to PSNR degradation due to network losses, and the PSNR therefore exhibits a flat trend. Of course, with encoding bit rate values higher than 600 kbit/s, not shown here because unrealistic due to the enormous loss rate, the curve would have exhibited a decreasing trend. On the other hand, the huge number of losses encountered with single-path routing, which increase with the encoding bit rate, cause a decreasing PSNR trend, although the PSNR at the source increases.

Figs. 12 and 13 present the packet loss rate in the WMN network, and the consequent video frame corruption percentage. From these figures we can notice that when the output bit rate increases, the destination frame rate achieved with single-path routing soon becomes too low, while multipath routing allows the source to encode at a high rate while maintaining a high destination frame rate: losses remain low up to 400 kbps.

As shown in Fig. 13, with low bit-rate values, we can reduce packet losses by decreasing the video source transmission bit rate. In fact, by decreasing it, the probability of a packet being discarded decreases, and the received video quality grows.

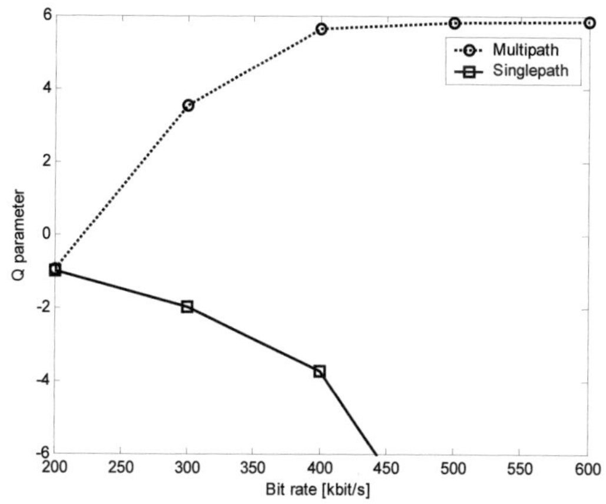

Fig. 15. Objective parameter Q

Finally, Fig. 15 summarizes the QoS perceived at destination by showing the overall objective quality parameter Q defined in (4), and demonstrates the power of multipath routing in guaranteeing a perceived QoS greater than that achieved by single-path routing with any video source output rate. The behavior of this parameter is determined by both the *psnr* parameter shown in Fig. 11, and the *fr* parameter shown in Fig. 14. We can observe that, when single-path routing is used, the overall quality decreases with increasing encoding bit rates, and the best quality is achieved with the minimum considered encoding bit rate, equal to 200 kbit/s. On the contrary, using multipath routing allows us to encode at a higher bit rate, the best being between 500 and 600 kbit/s.

To summarize, taking into account that multipath routing, besides robustness to external attacks and interceptions, provides a higher decoding quality and less delay than single-path routing, it is the best solution for the proposed video-surveillance system. The only problem of multipath routing is that delay jitter is higher, but this can be compensated for by a compensation buffer at destination.

6. Conclusions

This chapter describes a real experience of a wireless video-surveillance system, illustrating the overall architecture and the structure of each component block. Specifically, video sources use rate-control to emit a constant bit-rate flow, while the access network is a WMN implementing a multipath routing algorithm to minimize delay and intrusions. However this causes jitter, which is not acceptable for video-surveillance applications but can be compensated at destination if delay statistics are known. Analysis is carried out against the emission bit rate, and quality perceived at destination is evaluated with an objective parameter. Numerical results have demonstrated that multipath routing guarantees less delay and the best quality at destination. So it is the best solution for the proposed video-surveillance system with any encoding bit rate.

7. Acknowledgments

This work was partially supported by the Italian Ministry of University and Research through the PRIN project "Sorpasso".

8. References

Collins, R. T., Lipton, A. J., Fujiyoshi, H. & Kanade T. (2001), "Algorithms for Cooperative Multisensor Surveillance," *Proceedings of the IEEE*, Vol. 89, No. 10, Oct. 2001, pp. 1456–77.

Chiasserini, C. F. & Magli, E. (2002), "Energy Consumption and Image Quality in Wireless Video-Surveillance Networks," *Proceedings of the 13th IEEE International Symposium on Personal, Indoor and Mobile Radio Communications*, 2002.

Akyildiz, I. F., Wang, X. & Wang, W. (2005), "Wireless Mesh Networks: A Survey," *Computer Networks Journal, Elsevier*, March 2005.

Karrer, R., Sabharwal, A. & Knightly, E. (2003), "Enabling Large-scale Wireless Broadband: The Case for TAPs," *Proceedings of the HotNets '03.*

Bhagwaty, P., Ramanz, B. & Sanghi, D. (2003), "Turning 802.11 Inside-Out," *Proceedings of HotNets '03.*

Tropos Networks, http://www.tropos.com.

Draves, R., Padhye, J. & Zill B. (2004), "Routing in Multi-radio, Multi-hop Wireless Mesh Networks," *Proceedings of ACM MobiCom 2004*, Philadelphia, PA, September 2004.

Feng, W., Walpole, J., Feng, W. & Pu, C. (2001) "Moving towards massively scalable video-based sensor networks," *Proceedings of the Workshop on New Visions for Large-Scale Networks: Research and Applications*, Washington, DC, USA, March 2001, pp. 12–14.

PeopleVision Project, IBM Research, http://www.research.ibm.com/peoplevision.

Hampapur, A., Connell, J., Pankanti, S., Senior, A. & Tian, Y. (2003) "Smart Surveillance: Applications, Technologies and Implications," *Proceedings of IEEE Pacific-Rim Conference On Multimedia*, Singapore, 2003.

Haritaoglu, I., Harwood, D. & Davis L. S. (2000) "W: Real-time surveillance of people and their activities," *IEEE Transactions on Pattern Anal. Machine Intell.*, Vol. 22, pp. 809–830, Aug. 2000.

Tan, T. N., Sullivan, G. D. & Baker, K. D. (1998) "Model-based localization and recognition of road vehicles," *International Journal on Computer Vision*, Vol. 29, No. 1, pp. 22–25, 1998.

Wren, C. R., Azarbayejani, A., Darrell, T., & Pentland A. P. (1997) "Pfinder: real-time tracking of the human body," *IEEE Trans. Pattern Anal. Machine Intell.*, Vol. 19, July 1997, pp. 780–785.

Lipton, A. J., Fujiyoshi, H. & Patil, R. S. (1998) "Moving target classification and tracking from real-time video," in *Proc. IEEE Workshop Applications of Computer Vision*, 1998, pp. 8–14.

Kemeny, S. E., Panicacci, R., Pain, B., Matthies, L. & Fossum, E. R. (1997) "Multi-resolution image sensor," *IEEE Trans. Circuits Syst. Video Technol.*, Vol. 7, No. Aug., 1997, pp. 575–583.

Boult, T. (1998) "Frame-rate multi-body tracking for surveillance," *Proceedings of DARPA Image Understanding Workshop*, Monterey, CA, Nov. 1998, pp. 305–308.

Basu, A. & Southwell, D. (1995) "Omni-directional sensors for pipe inspection," *Proceedings of IEEE Int. Conf. Systems, Man and Cybernetics*, Vol. 4, 1995, pp. 3107–3112.

Cisco Systems® documentation, "Intelligent Wireless Video Surveillance Solutions," available at *http://www.cisco.com/en/US/products/hw/routers/ps272/prod_brochure0900aecd804a8cad.html.*

Telindus (2002) "People-Mover Project Brings 21st Century Surveillance System to Dallas Airport," Telindus, 2002, available at *http://www.cellstack.com/news_info/case_dallas_airprt.pdf.*

Chandramohan, V. & Christensen, K. J. (2002) "A First Look at Wired Sensor Networks for Video Surveillance Systems," *Proceedings of 27th Annual IEEE Conference on Local Computer Networks (LCN 2002)*, Tampa, FL, USA, 6-8 November 2002, pp. 728-729.

"Firetide, Axis Partner to Deliver Wireless Video Surveillance," *Telematics Journal*, September 25, 2006, available at *http://www.telematicsjournal.com/content/newsfeed/8344.html.*

Doblander, A., Maier, A. & Rinner, B. (2005) "Increasing Service Availability in Intelligent Video Surveillance Systems by Fault Detection and Dynamic Reconfiguration," *Proc. of the Telecommunications and Mobile Computing Workshop on Wearable and Pervasive Computing (TCMC'05)*. Graz, Austria, March 2005.

Zhang, Y. & Chakrabarty, K. (2003) "Energy-Aware Adaptive Checkpointing in Embedded Real-Time Systems," *Proceedings of the Design, Automation and Test in Europe Conference and Exhibition* (DATE'03), 2003.

Mueller, S., Ghosal, D. (2004) "Multipath Routing in Mobile Ad Hoc Networks: Issues and Challenges," *Invited paper in Lecture Notes in Computer Science*, edited by Maria Carla Calzarossa and Erol Gelenbe, 2004.

Biagioni, E. & Chen, S. H. (2004) "A Reliability Layer for Ad-Hoc Wireless Sensor Network Routing," *Proceedings of the 37th Hawaii International Conference on System Sciences*, Big Island, HI, USA, January 2004.

Johnson, D. B., Maltz, D. A. & Broch, J. (1999) "DSR: The dynamic source routing protocol for multi-hop wireless Ad Hoc networks", 1999.

Park, V. D. & Corson, M. S. (1997) "A highly adaptive distributed routing algorithm for mobile wireless networks," University of Maryland, College Park, MD (USA), 1997.

Perkings, C. E., Belding-Royer, E. & Das, S. R. (2003) "Ad Hoc on-demand distance vector routing". RFC 3561, 2003.

Vutukury, S. & Garcia-Luna-Aceves, J. J. (2001) "MDVA: A Distance-Vector Multipath Routing Protocol," *Proceedings of Infocom 2001*, Anchorage, Alaska, USA, 22-26 April 2001.

ISO, (1992 - a), Coded Representation of Picture and Audio Information. International Standard ISOIEC/JTC1/ Sc29/WG11, MPEG Test Model 2. July 1992.

ISO, (1992 - b), Coding of Moving Pictures and Associated Audio for Digital Storage Media up to 1.5 Mbit/s Part 2, Video. International Standard ISO-IEC/JTC1/SC29/WG11, DIS11172-1. March 1992.

Lombardo, A. & Schembra G., (2003) "Performance evaluation of an Adaptive-Rate MPEG encoder matching IntServ Traffic Constraints," *IEEE Transactions on Networking*, Vol. 11, No. 1, February 2003, pp. 47-65.

Chang, C.F. & Wang, J. S. (1997) "A Stable Buffer Control Strategy for MPEG Coding," *IEEE Transactions on Circuits and Systems for Video Technology*, Vol. 7, No. 6. December 1997.

Cernuto, A., Cocimano, F., Lombardo, A. & Schembra, G. (2002) "A Queueing System Model for the Design of Feedback Laws in Rate-Controlled MPEG Video Encoders," *IEEE Transactions on Circuits and Systems for Video Technology*, Vol. 12, No. 4, April 2002, pp. 238-255.

Ding W. & Liu, B. (1996) "Rate control of MPEG video coding and recording by rate-quantization modeling," *IEEE Transaction on Circuits and Systems for Video Technology*, vol. 6, no. 1, pp. 12--19, 1996.

Yuan, X. *et al.*, (2003) "A Distributed Visual Surveillance System," AVSS 2003, Miami, FL, July 21-22, 2003.

Vutukury, S. & Garcia-Luna-Aceves, J. J. (1999 - a) "A Simple Approximation to Minimum-Delay Routing," *Proceedings of SIGCOMM'99*, Cambridge, Massachusetts, USA, September 1999.

Vutukury, S. & Garcia-Luna-Aceves, J. J. (1999 - b) "A Practical Framework for Minimum-Delay Routing in Computer Networks," *Journal of High Speed Networks*, Vol. 8, No. 4, Wiley, 1999, pp. 241-263.

Lee, Y.-C., Altunbasak, Y. & Mersereau, R. M. (2002) "Multiframe error concealment for MPEG-coded video delivery over error-prone networks," *IEEE Transactions on Image Processing*, Vol. 11, No. 11, November 2002, pp. 1314 - 1331.

Pei, S.-C., & Chou Y.-Z. (2004) "Novel error concealment method with adaptive prediction to the abrupt and gradual scene changes, " *IEEE Transactions on Multimedia*, Vol. 6, No. 1, February 2004, pp 158 - 173.

Tsekeridou, S. & Pitas, I., (2000) "MPEG-2 error concealment based on block-matching principles," *IEEE Transactions on Circuits and Systems for Video Technology*, Vol. 10, No. 4, June 2000, pp. 646 - 658.

The Click Modular Router Project: http://pdos.csail.mit.edu/click/.

Morris, R., Kohler, E., Jannotti, J. & Kaashoek, M. F. (1999) "The Click modular router," *Proceedings of the 17th ACM Symposium on Operating Systems Principles (SOSP '99)*, Kiawah Island, South Carolina, December 1999, pp. 217--231.

6

An Application of Quantum Networks for Secure Video Surveillance

Alan Mink, Lijun Ma, Barry Hershman and Xiao Tang
National Institute of Standards and Technology, USA

1. Introduction

Security is an increasingly growing concern for network communications and video is an emerging segment of network traffic that uses large amounts of bandwidth. Streaming video, vs. downloading a video for later viewing, requires a continuous, high data rate. The data rate will vary depending on the quality of the video. Video surveillance is a streaming video application that in addition may require securing the data stream to prevent others from viewing it as well as prevent any tampering of that video stream.

There are two parts to secure communication, key distribution and ciphers. A cipher requires a secret key that is used to encrypt data (plaintext), transforming it into an unreadable form (ciphertext) and then to decrypt it back into its original form. Key distribution is the method used to exchange the secret key between the desired end users and no one else. Current block ciphers are relatively slow compared to existing bandwidth because they require a substantial amount of processing that must compete for CPU cycles with the video encoding and compression processing. Frequently changing keys is thought to increase security, but the public key exchange method requires even more processing than the cipher. Cipher and key exchange processing can be off-loaded from the CPU, when the communication end point is the other end of the link, by using dedicated hardware called a link encryptor.

Current classical security algorithms are based on the perceived computational complexity of certain mathematical functions and have not been proved secure. The public key algorithm is at risk from future quantum computers, whereas block ciphers are only weakened and an easy fix is to double the length of the key. Both are constantly at risk from a potential break through algorithm. Communications channels that exploit properties unique to quantum systems have been shown to enable functionality that cannot be achieved by classical means. If a high level of security is deemed necessary for the video stream, one might consider the use of a One-Time-Pad cipher [Wikipedia 2010], the only provably secure cipher, along with Quantum Key Distribution (QKD), also a provably secure method of exchanging the secret keys used by a cipher.

QKD is a protocol based on the quantum laws of physics and is provably information theoretically secure to accomplish key distribution [Gisin, et al., 2002]. QKD keys, when used with a One-Time-Pad cipher, can provide secure communications. A One-Time-Pad cipher algorithm performs an Exclusive OR (XOR) on a random secret key and the message. This is a simple operation that incurs little overhead compared to the more common computationally intensive ciphers, but it requires the key to be the same length as the message and discarded once used. For video, that requires a continuous stream of random secret keys, which is one of the features of QKD. Because of that feature, QKD is considered to have a long-term security perspective because of its "perfect forward security" attribute. The term perfect forward security means that any compromised keys cannot be used to determine other keys, either past or future. Since QKD keys are random strings and are not produced by a mathematical function, any compromised keys cannot be used to determine other keys.

QKD is still a technology under development even though a few commercial systems are available [Ouellette, 2004]. Some of the limitations of QKD are speed, distance and cost. Distance is a major concern, since without a break-through in developing a quantum repeater the quantum signal is limited to a few 100 km at best. Amplification is not possible since the quantum "no cloning law" specifies that a quantum state cannot be copied. If trusted, intermediate nodes are acceptable, then longer distances are possible via a multi-hop propagation of the key over multiple QKD links. This is not always acceptable and for these situations a quantum repeater would be required. It is currently under development, but none have yet been demonstrated. Speed, the ability to produce secure keys at a high rate is important to cope with the large amount of communication traffic over high-speed connections and hardware implementations that off-load the CPU have been demonstrated. Cost is an ever-present constraint and designs that use lower cost components and share rather than replicate components reduce the cost. In some cases, designs that share rather than duplicate components help to reduce concerns of side channel attacks upon engineered components (vs theoretical ones), but usually at the detriment of speed.

This chapter includes a short summary of the BB84 QKD protocol and its various stages. We then present a section on the configuration of a QKD system targeted for short distances and how a number of innovations lowered the cost and evolved that core design for longer distance communication and current infrastructure use. Another section will discuss hardware support for the data handling necessary to implement high-speed QKD. Extending QKD point-to-point systems to form QKD networks makes it even more attractive for applications such as video surveillance and we will discuss early networking demonstrations. In closing, we will discuss initial QKD standards efforts currently being conducted

2. BB84 protocol

The basic QKD protocol is known as BB84 [Bennet & Brassard, 1984] and has evolved into a family of protocols as researchers experiment with various approaches within a common framework. The BB84 protocol consists of four stages, see Fig 1. The first stage is the transmission of a randomly encoded quantum information stream between Alice (the initiator) and Bob (the responder) through an unsecured public link (called the quantum channel) to establish the raw key. The quantum information stream consists of quantum bits, called "qubits". Photons are used for qbits because light travels well over distances while atoms are better for storage, as in quantum memory, because they are easier to hold in one place. This is the most technically challenging stage of the protocol and has inspired many variations. Horizontal-vertical and diagonal states of photon polarization are a pair of quantum states that cannot be precisely measured simultaneously and are common candidates for QKD. For example, Alice sends each photon set in one of the four linear polarization states: horizontal-vertical (belonging to the horizontal-vertical basis) or +/- 45 degree diagonal (belonging to the diagonal basis). One of the polarization states in each basis represents a "0" bit value and the other a "1". Alice keeps a temporary database of the state of all photons sent. Bob randomly chooses to measure each photon in either the horizontal-vertical or diagonal basis. Since there is only a single photon, Bob can only do a single measurement. If Bob chooses correctly, the value he measures will be correct. If he chooses incorrectly, the value he measures will be random.

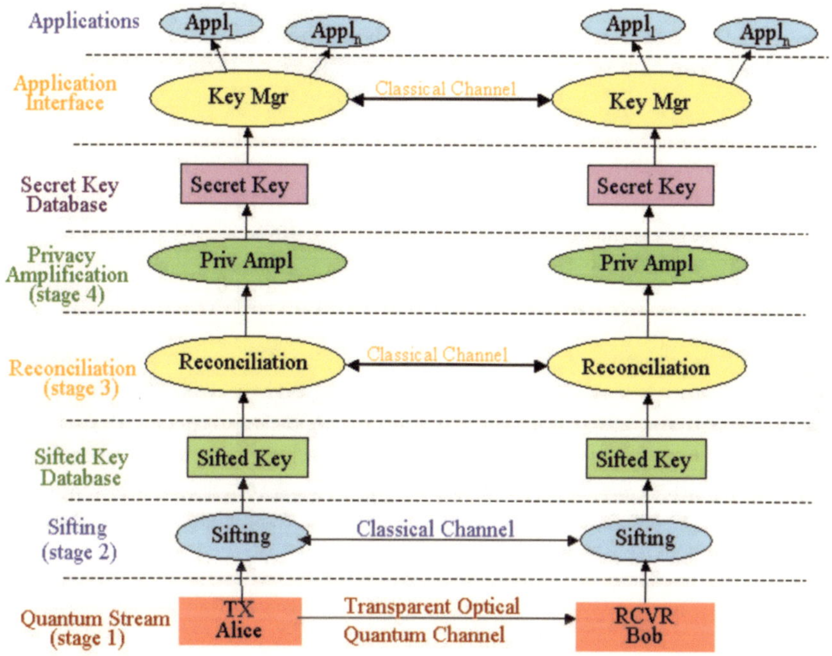

Fig. 1. QKD protocol flow with a Key Manager Application Interface

The remaining stages of the protocol are conducted over an unsecured public link, called the classical channel (this can be any conventional communications channel). The classical channel may be implemented as multiple physical and/or logical channels (e.g., multiple IP sockets for the different protocol stages). The QKD messages sent over them must be authenticated (integrity protected) to prevent tampering, although encryption is not needed since secrecy is unnecessary. The second stage is sifting, where Bob sends a list to Alice of photons detected and how they were measured (basis), but not their measured value. Alice retrieves, from her temporary database, only those entries measured by Bob in the correct basis and sends this list back to Bob (without their values), informing Bob which of his measurements were correct. Bob only keeps those entries on Alice's list. Alice and Bob now have a list of ordered random bits called sifted-keys. These two lists are the same length and, in theory should be identical. However, in practice the lists have some errors between them called quantum bit errors. The quantum bit error rate (QBER) may be caused by ordinary communication noise, but may also be a potential indication of eavesdropping. The eavesdropper is commonly called Eve. If the QBER is low enough, the protocol proceeds to the next stage. If the QBER gets too high the protocol cannot be sure that Eve's information is limited and the current group of sifted-key is discarded.

The third stage is reconciliation to correct these errors. Cascade [Nakassis, et al., 2004], and its variants, is the predominant reconciliation algorithm that exchanges parity and error correcting codes to reconcile errors without exposing the key values. This process requires a number of communications between Bob and Alice and results in a list smaller than the sifted list, since some of the keys are discarded to reduce any information Eve may glean from these exchanges. Niagara [Elliot, et al., 2005] is another algorithm that is based on a low-density parity check method and requires a single exchange between Bob and Alice.

The fourth stage is privacy amplification, which computes a new (even smaller) set of bits from the reconciled set of bits using a hashing algorithm and requires no communication between Alice and Bob. The purpose of privacy amplification is to significantly reduce any information that Eve may have acquired from this protocol. Unless Eve knows all or most of the original bits, she will not be able to compute the new set.

A simplified version of BB84 that reduces complexity, called B92 [Bennett, 1992], uses only two nonorthogonal quantum states, but is considered less secure and is used mostly in R&D to evaluate different QKD implementations and only focuses on stage 1 and 2 of the protocol.

A conventional threat model assumes Eve intercepts the photons, measures them and generates new photons based on those measurements, which are sent to Bob. From this attack, Eve will introduce on average a 25% QBER in the raw key that Bob recovers. Even using other more complex attacks that involve entanglement, Eve still cannot eavesdrop successfully to obtain the keys without introducing a detectable QBER in the raw key. Furthermore, privacy amplification can be strengthened to compensate for these attacks when the QBER is within acceptable bounds. Attacks that focus on side channels and the reality of engineered (vs theoretical) components [Scarani & Kurtsiefer, 2009; Xu, et al., 2010] are a concern for all security measures.

3. A high speed QKD system

We present, as an example, our design of a high speed QKD system. This system was designed for high-speed, short distance communication (< 10 km) and (relatively) low cost. It can operate over a free-space or fiber optic quantum channel. This system uses Vertical-Cavity Surface-Emitting Lasers (VCSELs) for attenuated photon sources, silicon avalanche photo diodes (Si-APDs) for detectors and a pair of custom printed circuit boards (PCBs) [Mink, et al., 2006] to process the QKD protocol data at a continuous high data rate to create a shared sifted-key. A fiber based QKD design is shown in Fig. 2. This system operates the quantum channel at 850 nm and the classical channel in the standard 1550 nm telecommunication range. Both channels operate at the same synchronized 1.25 GHz rate.

Si-APDs are relatively low cost single photon detectors that operate at room temperature in a free running mode with a relatively high quantum efficiency (QE) of about 70% for the optimal wavelength. We chose 850 nm for the quantum channel because it's one of the (older) standard telecommunication wavelengths and thus has commercially available components, even though it's not the optimal wavelength for QE. Also 850 nm is a good short-range wavelength for both free-space and fiber optic transmission. We also chose polarization as the quantum property to encode information on single photons. This is common in QKD. In free-space, the polarization of light doesn't change, although it does in fiber optics and that requires additional handling to compensate for externally caused distortion.

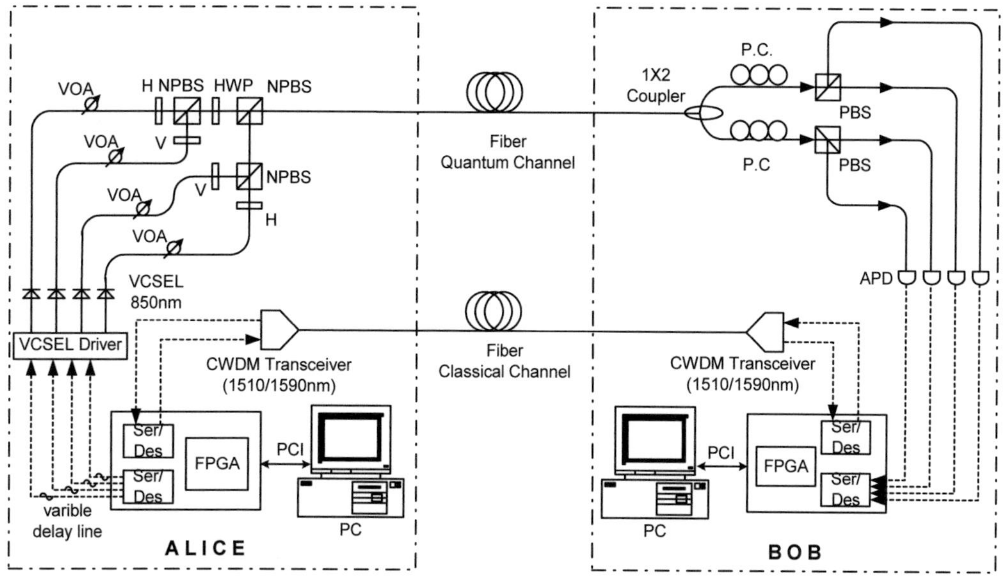

Fig. 2. Schematic diagram of our BB84 fiber-based QKD system; VCSEL: vertical-cavity surface-emitting lasers; Pol.: polarizer; VOA: variable optical attenuator; NPBS, non-polarizing beam splitter; P.C.: polarization controller; FPGA: custom printed circuit board controlled by a field-programmable gate array; PCI: PCI bus; PBS: polarizing beam splitter; Solid line: optical fiber; Dotted line: electric cable

Two commercial 1.25 Gb/s course wavelength division multiplexing transceivers form the bi-directional classical communication channel operating at 1510 nm and 1590 nm. Bob's PCB recovers Alice's clock from the classical channel, allowing it to synchronize with Alice. The clock frequency dictates the resolution of a detection event time bin. Synchronized, aligned time bins are important because the QKD protocol requires Alice and Bob to communicate about specific photons and a way to identify them is by labeling their occurrence in time. The concept is to treat each detector output as a serial data stream and search it for a rising edge (a 0-to-1 transition) indicating a single photon detection event. The bit position in that data stream is the time bin. These time bins can be aligned between Alice and Bob by correlating events in the classical channel to events in the quantum channel.

Alice's PCB generates an 800 ps electrical pulse every 1600 ps (625 MHz) on the randomly selected quantum output. Each of the four outputs drives a 10 Gbit/s 850 nm VCSEL that generates a laser pulse. The intensity of the laser pulse is then attenuated by variable optical attenuators (VOA) to the single photon level. A linear polarizer and a half-wave plate (HWP) sets the polarization orientation, -45°, +45 °, 0° or 90 °, that corresponds to the output path. These four output streams are combined into a single stream by non-polarizing beam-splitters (NPBSs) and sent to Bob over the quantum channel. The mean photon number, μ, at Alice's output is set to 0.1, therefore on average, Alice emits one photon every ten pulses.

At Bob, a 1 x 2 non-polarizing single-mode fiber coupler performs a random choice of polarization basis measurement. After the coupler, a polarization compensation module recovers the photon's polarization state and a polarizing beam-splitter (PBS) separates the photons by their polarization directing them to a Si-APD that feeds Bob's PCB. This process separates the photons into four paths, corresponding to the four BB84 encoding states. A photon measured in the wrong basis would be randomly detected as a "0" or "1".

Polarization compensation is needed continuously for a fiber-based system. Initially, and periodically, Bob cooperates with Alice to recover the photon's polarization state that may change during transmission through the fiber. We developed two types of active polarization controllers [Franson and Jacobs, 1995] for a polarization recovery and auto-compensation subsystem [Ma, et al, 2006], since it avoids back-scattering issues of passive polarization controllers [Stucki, et al., 2002]. One type uses liquid crystal retarders (LCR) and the other type uses Piezo Polarization Controllers (PZ), see Fig 3. We chose the PZ controller over the LCR because the PZ is faster (30 μs vs 100 ms), it doesn't need to be aligned with the PBS, it's fiber based with virtually no insertion loss and it can achieve an arbitrary transformation. The disadvantages of the PZ controller are it may drift slowly and it exhibits poor repeatability that results in additional search time.

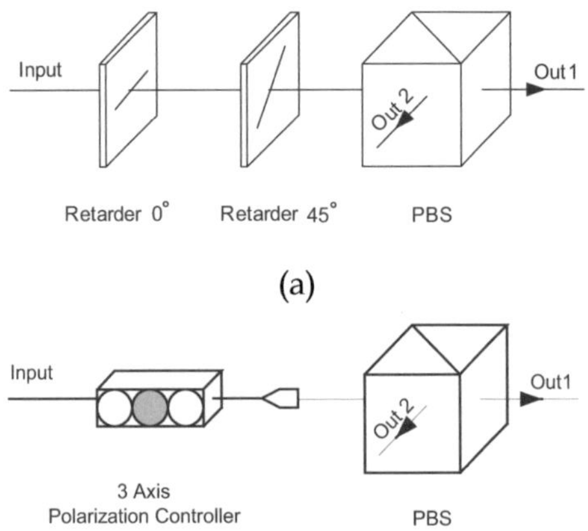

(b)

Fig. 3. Two active polarization recovery and auto-compensation (PRAC) subsystem: (a) Liquid Crystal Retardance and (b) Piezo Polarization Controllers.

These controllers maximize the polarization extinction ratio, which is the ratio of the correct photon counts to the incorrect counts in a compatible measurement basis. For example, the ratio between the counts of the two output ports of the PBS when a photon stream of all the same polarization is sent. The algorithm that controls these subsystems does a coarse-step search to find the optimal area and then a fine-step search in that area to find the optimal point. This procedure is run at startup and then invoked periodically or when the QBER increases.

A practical QKD system must be able to use existing fiber infrastructure. We have devised a technique that allows 850 nm single photons to share standard telecom fiber, SMF-28, with telecom traffic. Since the cutoff wavelength of SMF-28 fiber is much longer than 850 nm, some higher order transverse modes (LP_{11} mode) exist in the fiber and travel slightly slower than the fundamental mode (2.3 ns/km delay). Also its polarization state is different than the fundamental mode. At high data rates, when the detection time bin is small this higher order pulse can occur in an adjacent time bin, see Fig. 4(a), and be erroneously detected causing an increase in the QBER. Fusion splicing a short piece of HI780 fiber to the end of the SMF-28 fiber functions as a spatial filter and partially filters the higher order mode pulse [Townsend, 1998; Gordon, et al., 2004], see Fig. 4(b), allowing the 850 nm quantum channel to successfully coexist with 1550 nm traffic on standard telecom fiber.

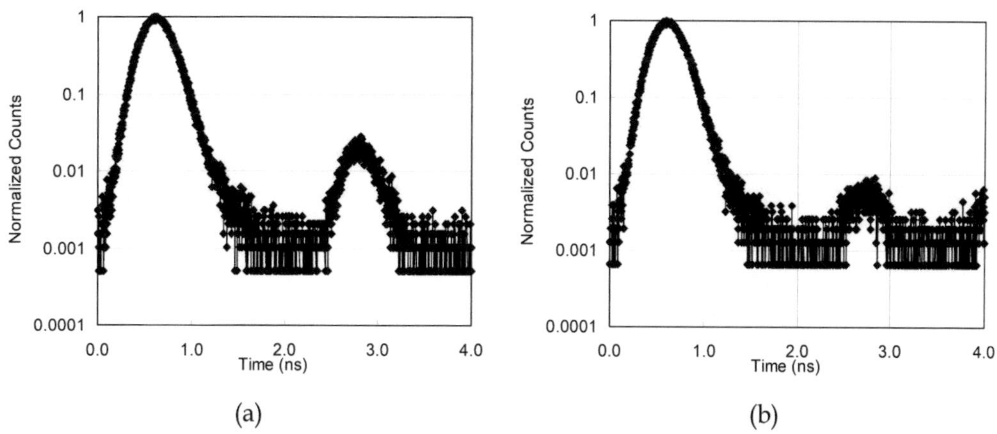

Fig. 4. A photon detection histogram of our 850 nm quantum channel over 1 km of 1550 nm single-mode fiber (SMF28): (a) no splice and (b) ≈40 cm of HI780 fusion-spliced at fiber end.

The quantum channel has a high loss. It is common to only detect a few photons for each 1000 attempts to generate them. Because attenuated sources generate photons based on a Poisson distribution and the intention is to minimize any multi-photon generation, a typical mean photon number, μ, of 0.1 is used. These results in nothing generated ≈89% of the time, one photon generated ≈10% and more than 1 photon generated ≈1%. Thus there is a ≈90% loss right at the source. Normal attenuation applies to the photons in the transmission medium and additional loss is encountered at detectors. In addition to the detector QE, which indicates the percent of photons detected vs. the number that actually arrive, there is also the detector dead time. After an APD detects a photon, the avalanche process generates an electrical output signal. The device then needs a certain amount of time (dead time) to recover to its initial operational state for detection of the next photon. During this dead time, the bias voltage across the p-n junction of the APD is below the breakdown level and no photon can be detected [Ghioni, et al., 2003]. Our Si-APD has a QE of ≈45% at 850 nm, InGaAs APDs (another common QKD detector) tend to have a QE of ≈10% while other types of detectors can have a QE as low as ≈1%.

Two important performance metrics of a QKD system are the secure key generation rate and QBER. Sifted-key rate is related to secure key rate and is a common metric used to evaluate the first two stages of a QKD system. Fig. 5 shows the measured sifted-key rate and the QBER at two quantum transmission rates, 625 Mbit/s and 312.5 Mbit/s, and two fiber lengths, 1 km and 4 km. Demonstrating this system can provide more than 4 Mbit/s of sifted-key over a 1 km of fiber with a mean photon number of 0.1. However, due to the relative high attenuation of 850 nm light in optical fiber, the sifted-key rate decreases quickly (logarithmically linear) as the distance increases, to about 1 Mbit/s at 4 km.

Environmental QBER in our system is mainly caused by the following factors: (1) Si-APD dark count rate and light leakage, (2) cross-talk caused by an imperfect polarization extinction ratio, (3) timing jitter and (4) high order mode noise. Dark counts are caused by a thermo-initiated avalanche process in the APD and unexpected photon detection. They are independent of the transmission rate and for our system are on the order of 200 per second. With proper light sealing and filtering, the counts can be reduced to a few tens per second. Compared to our Mbits/s detection rate, this factor is negligible. The polarization extinction ratio was measured to be between 23 dB to 28 dB, resulting in a contribution of about 1/3 of the QBER and is independent of the transmission rate. Timing jitter also limits the transmission rate. Timing jitter is mostly caused by the original optical pulse width, its jitter and the timing jitter of the APD. Our optical pulse width is 800 ps (FWHM), and the jitter of the APDs is measured at about 180 ps (FWHM). We also observed APD count-dependent jitter [Gordon, et al., 2005] and VCSEL data-dependent jitter [Guenter & Tatum, 1998] during transmission of randomly encoded photons. Because of this jitter, our detection window is limited to 1.6 ns. Narrowing our detection window results in a higher QBER. High order mode noise contributes about 1/3 of the QBER after filtering. All of these factors yield a QBER for our QKD system of about 2% to 3%. High order mode noise and photon attenuation do slightly increase the QBER at 4 km compared to 1 km.

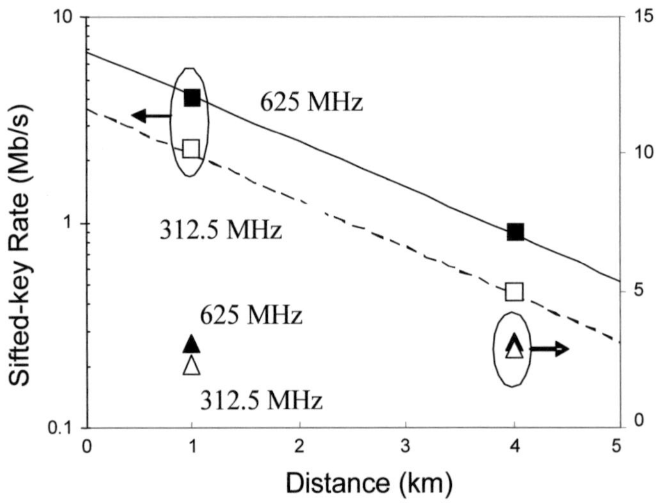

Fig. 5. The system performance of our 850 nm QKD system at 625 MHz and 312.5 MHz.

There are other variations for BB84 implementations that we briefly mention here. "One-way weak coherent pulse" QKD [Gisin , et al., 2002] uses polarization (as we've shown above) or phase encoding of quantum information on single photons sent from Alice to Bob. Plug-and-play QKD [Muller, et al., 1997] is where Bob sends a relatively strong, orthogonally-polarized pair of light pulses to Alice, who modulates their relative phase, attenuates them to single-photon levels, and reflects them back to Bob. The relative phase of the amplitude pulses carries the quantum information to Bob. Using free-space [Bienfang, et al., 2004] as the medium (vs. fiber) eliminates the need for polarization control, but adds the need for the acquisition, pointing, and tracking of the photon path between moving platforms, Alice and Bob. Even stationary buildings are moving due to vibration, wind and thermal expansion but optical communication telescopes exist to handle these problems. Satellites are the ultimate targets. The generation of two or more photons in a pulse used in a quantum link poses an opportunity for information to be obtained by an eavesdropper. On-going work continues to build a source that will generate single photons on demand [Granger, et al., 2004]. Using a source to generate entangled photon pairs [Ling, et al., 2008], one sent to Alice and one to Bob, is another approach that both eliminates multi-photon concerns and the need for a random number generator, since each entangled pair produced is randomly encoded and independent from each other. Currently, generating entangled photon pairs is a relatively slow process. Continuous variable QKD [Fossier, 2009] encodes small deviations of the phase, amplitude, or polarization of a bright optical pulse. The difficulty is in measuring the received data and determining a state when the variance is comparable with the shot noise limit.

3.1 Reducing the number of detectors

Our high speed 850 nm QKD system uses four Si-APDs, which is the most expensive device in the QKD systems. To reduce the cost and reduce potential side channel attacks of our QKD system, we introduce a detection-time-bin-shift (DTBS) scheme [Breguet, et al., 1994] that projects the measurements into separate time-bins, rather than separate detectors. The disadvantage is the quantum transmission rate is reduced, resulting in proportionately reduced key rates. DTBS schemes can also eliminate side channel concerns caused by self-synchronizing detectors and variations between detector efficiencies. However, when gated mode detectors are used in DTBS schemes, a time-bin-shift (TBS) intercept-resend attack might exploit a side channel and countermeasures should be adopted.
The original DTBS scheme, Fig. 6(a), uses two couplers, each adding a 3 dB loss. In the enhanced scheme, Fig. 6(b), we replace the second coupler with a PBS. A passive coupler performs a random choice of measuring polarization and projects the results onto a short (0° basis) or long (45° basis) delay path resulting in the photon arriving in one of two adjacent time bins. In the short path, the polarization state of the photon is unchanged and is recorded in the first time bin. In the long path, the photon is delayed by one time bin and the polarization state of the photon is rotated by 45° and is recorded in the second time bin. The photons on these two paths are combined using a PBS, thus avoiding a 3 dB loss from a second coupler, and then fed to a single detector. Our scheme of Fig. 6(b) can be further extended to handle all four BB84 states as shown in Fig. 6(c), whereas the original scheme of Fig. 6(a) cannot. By adding another PBS and another pair of paths as well as changing the initial delay to a two time bin delay, we now can map the photon state to one of four time bins. Thus we need to reduce the photon transmission rate by four. The upper path is now a two time bin delay, and thus a photon traversing that path will be detected in time bin two or three, depending on the path it follows in the second pair of paths. The lower path is still a zero time bin delay and thus a photon traversing that path will be detected in time bin zero or one depending on the path it follows in the second pair of paths. Using a DTBS scheme requires only one quantum stream to be aligned to the classical channel, rather than multiple ones. Also during sifting, Bob and Alice must use the transmission clock windows to identify photons, not the DTBS time bins, otherwise the QKD protocol remains unchanged.
Self synchronizing sequences can occur when dead time makes detectors temporarily unavailable, which can result in repeating detector firing order, for example, using two detectors for "0" and "1", respectively. Once one detector has been fired, it becomes unavailable for the duration of its dead time. In a high photon transmission rate system there is a high probability that the other detector will fire before the first detector recovers. If this sequence of one detector being dead while the other detector fires continues, it results in strings of 1010... . Runs of such strings reduce the randomness of the keys and degrade the security of the QKD system. In our QKD system with 50 ns dead time and a transmission rate of 1.25 GHz, there are 62 (800 ps) time bins for a photon to arrive at the other detector while the first is in its dead time. Because of the quantum channel losses, the 10% emission rate, μ=0.1, of the sources and the QE=45% of the detector, the expected number of photons

arriving in this duration is three. BB84, 4-detector systems suffer from the same problem [Rogers, et al., 2007]. One solution is to disable all detectors once one detector has fired until the dead time has passed and all detectors are available again.

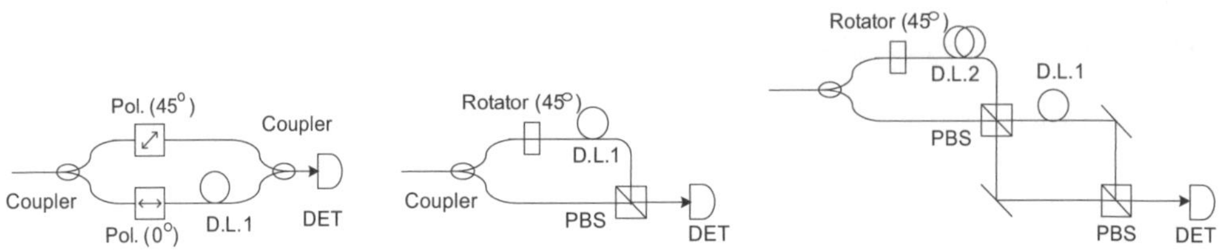

(a) (b) (c)

Fig. 6. Schematic diagram of DTBS schemes: (a) original scheme, (b) enhanced scheme and (c) enhanced scheme for BB84. Coupler: passive fiber coupler; D.L.1: one time-bin delay; D.L.2: two time-bin delay Line; PBS: polarizing beam splitter; DET: single photon detector.

When separate photon detectors are used for different photon values it's difficult to build all photon detectors with identical efficiency. A detector with higher efficiency would fire more frequently than one with lower efficiency. This unbalanced characteristic would cause key values to skew more towards one of the values and undermine the randomness of keys. Using the single detector DTBS scheme of Fig. 6(c), avoids all these problems. Futhermore, some DTBS schemes are also vulnerable to the TBS intercept-resend attack [Xu, et al., 2006] when single photon detectors operate in a gated mode. Some single photon detectors, such as InGaAs APDs, can only work in a gated mode, where photons can only be detected in specified time windows. DTBS systems with single photon detectors operating in free-running mode, such as Si-APD, are not susceptible to this attack.

3.2 Frequency up-conversion for distance

For QKD systems beyond 10 km, the wavelength of the quantum signal needs be in the 1310 nm or 1550 nm bands, where the telecom fiber loss is lowest. WDM and erbium-doped fiber amplifier (EDFA) technology are widely used in current optical communication links and the noise they induce in the 1550 nm band is too high to allow single photon transmission in that band on the same fiber. This leaves the 1310 nm band as a compromise for single photon transmission that can share (WDM) a fiber with existing 1550 telcom traffic.

Among the single photon detectors available for the 1310 nm band, InGaAs APDs [Yuan , et al., 2007], superconducting single-photon detectors (SSPDs) [Hadfield, et al., 2007] and up-conversion detectors using Si-APDs [Langrock, et al., 2005] are used to implement high-speed QKD systems. Recently, a self-difference technique was developed for InGaAs APDs that suppresses the afterpulse noise, and it has been successfully applied to a GHz QKD system [Yuan, et al., 2008]. The InGaAs APD has about 10% detection efficiency, but it still has about 6% afterpulse probability, which would contribute an extra 3% to the QBER of a QKD system. SSPDs can operate in the free-running mode and their response time can be less than 100 ps. However, SSPDs are expensive and need to be operated at 4° K. Si-APDs are low cost, operate at room temperature and have the highest detection efficiency among these detectors, but they don't operate at wavelengths longer than 1000 nm. To alleviate this limitation we implemented an up-conversion detector that transforms 1310 nm single photons into 710 nm photons for detection by Si-APDs.

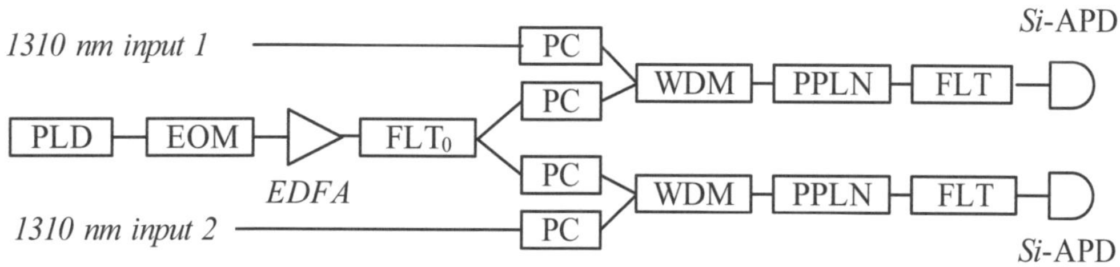

Fig. 7. Configuration of our up-conversion detectors. PLD: laser diode; EOM: Eelectric-optic modulator (LiNbO3); EDFA: erbium-doped fiber amplifier; FLT: optical filter; PC: polarization controller; WDM: wavelength-division multiplexer for 1310 nm and 1550 nm; PPLN: periodically-poled LiNbO3 waveguide module.

Our up-conversion detector [Ma, et al., 2009] structure, based on nonlinear optical sum frequency generation, is shown in Fig. 7. A 1557 nm CW laser diode (PLD) output is modulated to a pulse stream and amplified using an EDFA. A 7 nm (FWHM) optical filter (FLT_0) is used to suppress the EDFA optical noise between 1000 nm and 1300 nm that can induce a large amount of dark counts. After the FLT_0, the 1557 nm pulse is divided into two streams by a 50:50 coupler to function as a pump for two QKD quantum streams at 1306 nm. After polarization control is applied, the 1306 nm QKD signals and the 1557 nm pump are combined by the WDMs and sent to the periodically-poled LiNbO3 (PPLN) waveguide modules where they are up-converted to 710 nm. The output of the PPLN is coupled to a 700 nm single mode fiber, which cuts off the strong 1550 nm pump light, and is passed to the FLT, which contains a 20 nm band-pass filter and a short-wavelength-pass filter, and then finally detected by a Si-APD. This combination of filters helps to attenuate the light between 730 nm to 1000 nm by more than 80 dB. The internal quantum conversion efficiency of the PPLNs is almost 100%, while the overall efficiency of this up-conversion detector is about 20%. The coupling loss is significantly larger than those in [Langrock, et al., 2005] and degrades the overall detection efficiency. PPLN up-conversion is polarization sensitive and can be used as a polarizer, saving a 1 dB loss that a separate polarizer would add.

By using pulsed light at 1557 nm to pump our 1310 nm signal we reduced the noise and the dark counts of our up-conversion detector. The anti-Stokes noise at 1310 is much less than the Stokes noise from a pump whose wavelength is longer than our signal wavelength. Also a pulsed pump can use the same average power as a continuous one while achieving a higher peak power.

The QKD system performance using our up-conversion detector is shown in Fig. 8. During our measurements, the pump power was fixed at 40 mW. The sifted-key rate is 2.5 Mbit/s for a back-to-back connection, 1 Mbit/s at 10 km, and 60 kbit/s at 50 km. The QBER is approximately 3% back-to-back, remains below 4% up to 20 km, and reaches 8% at 50 km. The modulator extinction ratio and system timing jitter induces a background QBER of approximately 2.5% and the rest is from dark counts generated by both the pump light and the classical channel. We set the pump power close to the maximum up-conversion efficiency and the QBER remains small until 20 km due to the low dark count rate of the 1550 nm up-conversion detector.

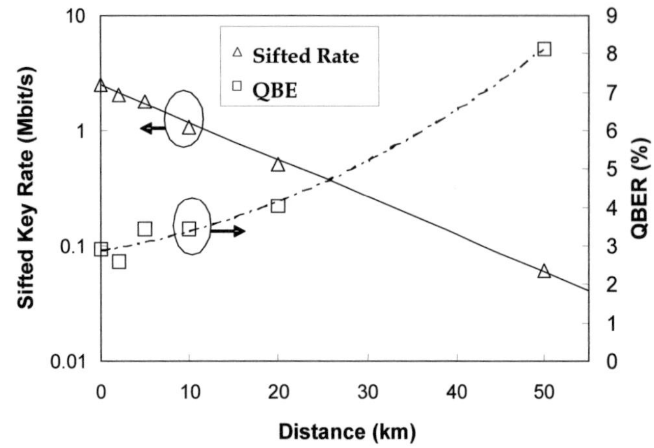

Fig. 8. The performance of our 1310 nm QKD system using up-conversion detectors.

4. Programmable hardware and gigahertz signalling

Because secure video surveillance and other such applications require high speed QKD to generate sufficient secure key, this section will discuss the time tagging, synchronization and data handling necessary to achieve high speed QKD. We focus on an implementation that uses dedicated field programmable gate arrays (FPGAs) and synchronization techniques that enable transmission rates above 1 GHz and avoid some of the data-handling bottlenecks that can limit performance. Research has demonstrated that both the throughput and the signal to noise ratio on the quantum channel of these systems can be improved by operating at high repetition rates and with strong temporal synchronization and gating [Gordon, et al., 2005]. It is well known that the benefits of this approach are ultimately limited by the temporal resolution of the single-photon detectors [Bienfang, et al., 2006]. Available single-photon detector resolution can be below 100 ps (FWHM) [Ghioni, et al., 2007] and can therefore resolve transmission rates well into the gigahertz regime.

For QKD systems operating over kilometer-scale links, synchronization with picosecond accuracy is most commonly achieved with either clock-distribution techniques [Bienfang, et al., 2006], in which synchronization is continuously enforced with active phase-locked-loops (PLLs), or with stable Rubidium oscillators, in which occasional resynchronization processes ensure accurate and synchronous local clocks [Ling, et al., 2008]. The hardware support we discuss in this section focuses on clock-distribution and recovery techniques, mainly because PLL systems are commonly incorporated into commercially available data-processing chips.

With stable synchronization established over the link, detection events can be time tagged by identifying where the detector signal's rising edge occurs with respect to the clock. We view the detector signal as if it were a synchronous serial data stream and implement time tagging by identifying in which bit period the detector signal makes a transition (e.g. 0 to 1). In this approach the serial data rate of the receiver defines the temporal resolution of our time-tagging system; for example, a 1.25 Gb/s serial data rate defines 800 ps time bins. An additional advantage of time tagging with a serial data receiver is that the system operates continuously with no reset time.

Our approach is to use existing chips with transceivers for these tasks to capture serial signals above a GHz and move into the parallel realm for processing at reduced frequencies.

Even at these reduced frequencies, however, feeding the parallel signals into a computer for software processing is not a viable option. Software is a sequential set of operations that requires a certain number of computer-clock cycles for each set of parallel signals. Even with a program designed to operate in the required time period, memory allocations and background applications controlled by the operating system may make it impossible to guarantee that the necessary amount of processing time would be available for continuous signal acquisitions. A 1.25 Gb/s serial signal (800 ps time bins) can be demultiplexed into a synchronous 16 bit parallel word stream at 78.125 MHz. Software that seeks to identify detection events in such a signal would need to execute every 12.8 ns, and complete before the next 12.8 ns time interval. This is challenging even for dedicated real-time computers. A 10 Gb/s signal (100 ps time bins) would generate a synchronous 32 bit parallel signal at 312.5 MHz, leaving only 3.2 ns for processing. And there is the additional difficulty of developing a hardware interface to continuously load the parallel data into the computer at that rate. For such systems, an FPGA board is a flexible approach that can be optimized for a given application and connected to a computer via standard high speed interfaces.

FPGAs can include standard programmable-logic elements, both combinatorial (e.g. AND, OR, NOT) and sequential (e.g. Flip-flop), as well as dedicated specialized devices, such as memory, digital signal processors (DSPs), and high-speed transceivers. FPGAs allow a user to build custom logic sequences that process data acquired from input pins, store the data in internal memory and output the data. Detectors and other devices can be connected directly to FPGA pins and computers can interface with FPGAs using a variety of standard interfaces. FPGA programming is similar to writing a program for a computer, but an FPGA allows the user to control both the data size and operations within each clock cycle, whereas in a computer the operating system and processor make these choices. Controlling the timing sequence becomes an additional "dimension" in programming. Even when the FPGA clock rate is low compared to a given computer, operations can be arranged in parallel and sequenced into tight groups without interruption to compensate for the lower clock rate and achieve comparable or even superior performance.

FPGAs can be programmed to adjust their level of parallelism, but they do not operate at gigahertz rates (yet) and therefore cannot directly process a serial input with sub-nanosecond time bins. Below 1 ns some degree of parallelization is necessary. As discussed above, the faster the input detection stream is sampled by the receiver, the smaller the detection time bins become and the greater the necessary parallelization. Organizing the processing into a pipeline sequence, like an assembly line in which each operation is performed in parallel and a new item can be placed on the assembly line each cycle, allows processing times to exceed the time-bin limit. Current FPGAs can operate with a clock rate up to about 0.5 GHz, though they typically realize only about 1/3 of that rate for all but elementary operations. It is worthwhile to point out that with each new generation of FPGA there has been an increase in operational clock rate of about 10%. Fortunately, data input and output are typically supported at the maximum specified clock rate, and with dual data rate (DDR) capabilities (operating on both the rising and falling clock edges) input and output can operate at speeds up to twice the FPGA's clock rate. By converting a TTL or CMOS signal from a single-photon detector to a differential signal, an FPGA could directly sample the detector signal with resolution down to about 1 ns.

Below 1 ns, front-end circuitry is necessary that will sample the signal and present parallel data to the FPGA at a lower rate. Using existing gigahertz transceivers, or their fundamental core the SerDes (serializer/deserializer), is an attractive choice because they are commonly available chips and they are included in some FPGAs as internal devices. For input data, a SerDes uses a clock and data recovery (CDR) circuit to sample a serial data stream and recover the clock and data. The SerDes then collects a sequence of the serial bits (in a shift register) and then outputs that group of bits in parallel (to a holding register) along with the recovered clock divided down to the parallel rate. For example, a 1.25 GHz serial input data stream is converted by a SerDes to 10-bit parallel data accompanied by a 125 MHz clock. 125 MHz is much more suited to FPGA processing rates and each parallel data item can be processed in a pipelined manner to maintain a continuous flow of time-tagging data.

One drawback to this approach is that the input serial data stream to a SerDes must be continuous and have sufficient data transitions (balanced) for the internal PLLs to recover the embedded clock. Most single-photon detector signals are random and sparse, with no guaranteed transition interval. For this application, we use additional circuitry to piggyback the single-photon-detector signal onto the known classical channel signal by an exclusive-OR (XOR) before the SerDes as shown in Fig. 9. A similar XOR operation is performed a second time, inside the FPGA, to recover the original detector signal. Thus the balanced classical channel signal provides the timing for the detection stream. It is the rising edge of the detector signal that indicates the arrival time of a photon (the pulse can be given a conveniently long duration provided it does not limit the maximum count rate of the detector). It is the bit period of the classical channel that determines the resolution of the time tags recorded for each single-photon detection event. Finally, time tagging requires a mutual reference event between source and destination that can be used to identify common time bins. This configuration allows such events to be sent over the classical channel, as a predetermined measage.

This approach assumes synchronous signals that are stable when sampled during each clock period. All synchronous electronic devices specify setup (time before the clock edge) and hold (time after the clock edge) times relative to the clock edge when the data must be stable. When the signal is not stable during that period, the output is not deterministic and could result in a metastable [On-Semi, 2007; Unger, 1995; Kleeman & Cantoni, 1987] or undetermined state. This can result in the rising edge being assigned to either of the adjacent time bins somewhat randomly and could add to the overall timing jitter of the system resulting in an increased QBER, and hence fewer usable keys. For this reason the detection time bin should be chosen to be larger than the maximum detector jitter.

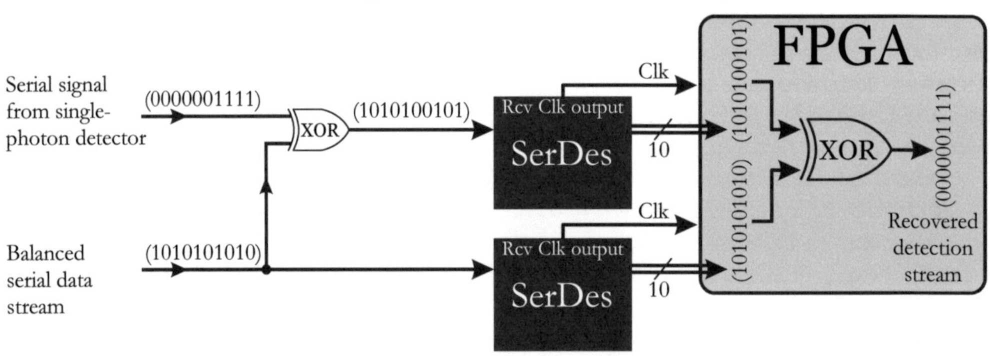

Fig. 9. Piggybacking the sparse signal from a single-photon detector on top of a balanced serial data stream allows the SerDes receiving the single-photon detection events to synchronize to the clock of the balanced data stream. The data and the received clock (Rcv clk) are passed to the FPGA, where the piggybacking signal is removed from the detection signal in a parallel format.

We developed a pair of custom PCB for our GHz-rate QKD system [Mink, et al., 2006], the more complex Bob board shown in Fig. 10. Alice's board is similar, but since its quantum channel is all transmit outputs, it doesn't need the additional front-end receiver logic. To implement the BB84 QKD protocol, we require interfaces for four single-photons detectors. The piggybacking scheme of Fig. 9 is used to sample the detector signal at gigahertz rates and bring it into an FPGA for processing. However, applying Fig. 9 directly results in unstable operation because the jitter in the detector signal can cause transitions at non-regular intervals of the clock. The resulting signal can violate setup and hold times of the SerDes sampling circuit, as discussed above, and potentially cause an unrecoverable metastable condition in the sampling circuit. To avoid this situation we use additional circuitry to stabilize the detector signal, as shown in Fig. 10: two flip-flops (FFs) triggered by the clock recovered from our classical channel. The second FF is necessary because the detector signal can cause instability in the first FF, though it will recover by the next clock edge. We also use two programmable delays: the first aligns the detector signal to the FF clock to minimize the instability in the first FF, the second compensates for the phase difference between the FF output and the clock of the classical stream entering the XOR. Although the clocks driving the FFs are frequency synchronized to the classical stream, they are out of phase due to signal propagation delays on the PCB.

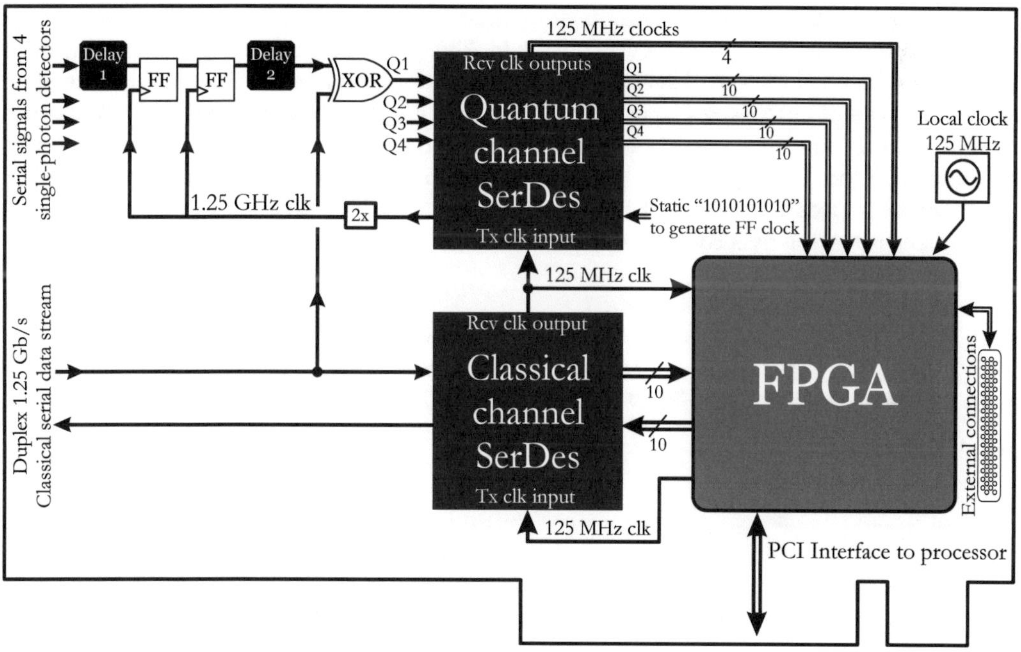

Fig. 10. Schematic of a custom PCB used for QKD experiments. Four single-photon detector channels are recovered using the piggybacking scheme in Fig. 9. Metastability due to detector jitter is avoided with the synchronizing components before the XOR. All four single-photon detector inputs are treated in this manner; only one circuit is illustrated.

The SerDes chip used in this system can support four duplex channels. Each SerDes has one input clock (Tx clk) for all four of its transmit streams, and a separate recovered clock for each receive stream. The two main clocks used by the FPGA are its local clock and the clock recovered from the classical channel. Although these two clocks are nominally 125 MHz, they are only accurate to within 10^{-4} and are asynchronous to each other. The local clock drives the classical channel transmit stream while the recovered clock from the classical channel is fed to both the FPGA and the quantum channel SerDes. The quantum SerDes uses the classical channel recovered clock to transmit the static 10-bit pattern "1010101010," thus producing a 625 MHz clock. We then double this clock to 1.25 GHz to trigger the FFs synchronously with the classical data stream. Each parallel receive stream from the quantum channel SerDes is fed to the FPGA, along with its own recovered 125 MHz clock, mesochronous to each other and the classical channel. In the FPGA each recovered clock is used to store its associated incoming parallel data stream into dual ported first-in first-outs (FIFOs) that use separate clocks for input and output and can be asynchronous to each other. The FIFOs are capable of synchronizing the data between these two clock domains.

We have built systems using SerDes that are external components connected to the FPGA via PCB traces (c.f. Fig. 10), and more recent implementations [Mink 2007] in which the SerDes are internal to the FPGA package. Internal SerDes saves board space, but in either implementation the interface between the SerDes and the FPGA logic is similar. In most FPGAs the user can configure the operational parameters of internal SerDes. For example, we can change the serial speed of the SerDes to a few predefined points in the range from 1.25 GHz to 6.25 GHz by reprogramming the FPGA.

In addition to timing, the classical channel carries messages to implement the sifting process, where Bob sends its detection events to Alice and Alice returns only the valid ones to Bob. At 1.25 GHz (800 ps detector time-bin resolution) we have achieved a performance of over 4 Mb/s of sifted-key [Tang, et al., 2006], see Fig. 8. Electrical tests have shown the PCBs to have a capacity in excess of 40 Mb/s, though our detectors cannot currently support this rate. This processing reduces the data stream from Gb/s to Mb/s and the resulting sifted-key data stream has no real-time processing constraints; attributes that are attractive for further processing by a computer.

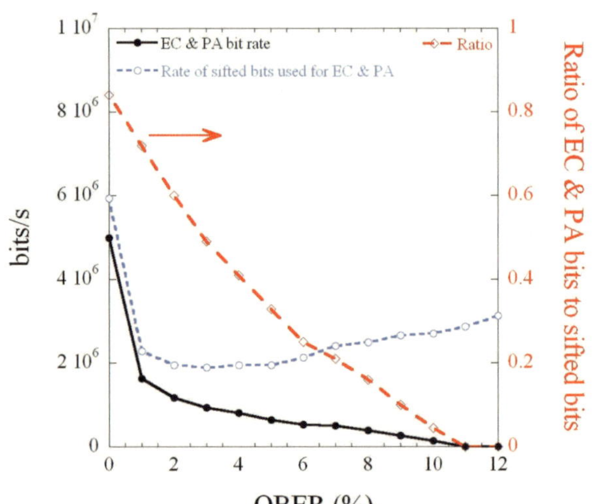

Fig. 11. The maximum processing rate of our EC & PA software implementation (black) as a function of the QBER. For this test the algorithms are running on a typical desktop processor, and sifted bits (blue) are provided as fast as the algorithm can process them (i.e. the output is not limited by the input rate).

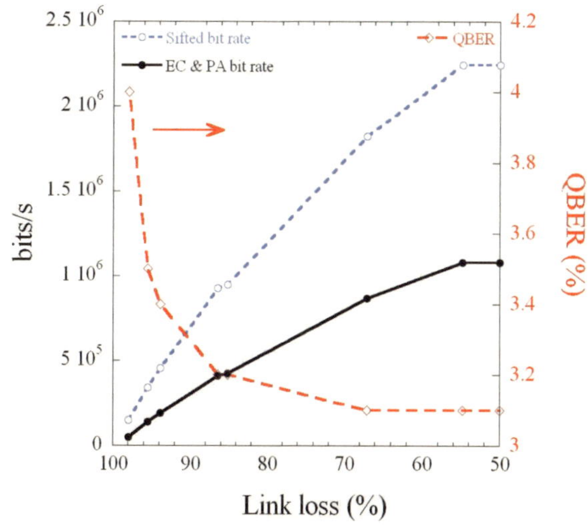

Fig. 12. Performance of our 1.25 GHz free-space QKD system, with the custom PCBs shown in Fig. 10, as a function of link loss. As the optical link losses decrease the high throughput rises until the EC & PA algorithms saturate at about 55% loss.

Once the sifting process has been carried out, subsequent reconciliation and privacy amplification (EC & PA) can be implemented in software or hardware. Reconciliation also requires a classical channel, but it doesn't need to be the same one used by the lower two QKD protocol stages. The processing rate of our software implementation is strongly dependant on computer speed. Fig. 11 shows the maximum output rate of our software EC & PA implementation, as a function of the QBER, when running on a standard desktop system. Our current QKD system can saturate this software implementation. Fig. 12 shows the results from a QKD free-space experiment with a quantum channel transmission rate of 1.25 GHz at 850 nm using Si-APDs. As the link loss is reduced, the sifted-key rate and the EC & PA rates increase and the QBER decreases. At 55% loss and below, rather than continuing to increase, the EC & PA rate reaches a constant value just over 1 Mb/s due to the saturation of our software EC & PA, which in this case is running on a dual-processor machine. The saturation causes the transmit board to wait until space is available before resuming transmission in the quantum channel, resulting in a relatively constant sifted-key rate below 55% link loss. The QBER is not affected. Newer FPGAs now in use are large enough to include our EC & PA algorithms on the chip, but require extensive programming to implement them. The FPGA programming is too extensive to discuss here. On this system, with 1% QBER we have achieved EC & PA secure key rate in excess of 12 Mb/s, significantly greater than the ≈1 Mb/s of our computer software version. To sustain that rate requires a sifted-key rate of ≈15 Mb/s. Our current QKD systems are not able to reach the capacity of this hardware implementation. A further benefit of this hardware implementation is that it removes the significant processing required by the EC & PA algorithms from the CPU and opens those cycles to applications, such as surveillance video.

There are a number of standard high-speed interfaces available for transferring data from an FPGA to a computer. As with FPGA processing one can not expect to achieve the rated throughput; 1/3 to 1/2 of the maximum rated speed is typical. Implementing sifting on the PCB significantly reduces the data rate between PCB and computer, which for us is less than

10 Mb/s. Our QKD board supports a Gb/s PCI interface and a 480 Mb/s USB computer interface. The PCI interface is a 32-bit parallel data interface that runs at 33 MHz. The USB is a high-speed serial interface and an external USB chip on the PCB provides the serial-to-parallel interface and interacts with the FPGA at 33 MHz with 16-bit parallel data. The QKD boards also have an external 65-bit interface (64 data bits plus a clock bit) that allows multi-Gb/s of random number data to be streamed to the FPGA. Operating at 16 MHz, this interface can supply the PCB at a Gb/s. Operating at 160 MHz, this interface can supply the PCB at 10 Gb/s, but at this rate signal integrity may become a concern.

We have found these PCBs to provide a stable and reconfigurable platform for QKD as well as other single-photon experiments. The gigahertz sampling interfaces, the synchronization between source and detector, and the re-programmability of the controlling FPGA, has allowed us to reconfigure these boards for various QKD implementations as well as correlated-photon measurement experiments.

5. Quantum networks and a surveillance video application

Video surveillance usually encompasses more than a single site, but the QKD protocol was designed for a point-to-point implementation. Extending this technology to form quantum (or QKD) networks makes it more attractive to such applications. A QKD network is an embedded sub-network within a conventional communication network for the purpose of developing shared secrets, not transporting secure messages. The secure messages are transported on the conventional communication network. The quantum and classical channels may be dedicated or they can share (via WDM) the existing physical network links of the conventional network, but the quantum channels must have an end-to-end transparent optical path between each QKD node. Building QKD networks and integrating them into conventional networks that support traditional security protocols, and other applications, and use existing network infrastructure is an important step towards the practical deployment of these systems. For deployable systems additional services are required, such as network management and key management with an application interface.

There are two types of QKD networks, passive and active. Passive networks use passive optical components (e.g. the optical coupler) to implement multi-user connectivity. Passive networks can realize multi-terminal communications simultaneously, or "broadcast" from one node to multiple nodes. Several groups have successfully demonstrated a passive QKD network [Phoenix, et al., 1995; Townsend, et al., 1994; Fernandez, et al., 2007]. However, in a passive network, the photons are split by couplers according to their coupling ratio and distributed proportionally to each node, resulting in a proportionally reduced key rate between each node. The second type adopts active optical components, such as optical switches, to dynamically control the communication path. This type is similar to current switched optical communication networks, and establishes a reconfigurable QKD link. Switching time and QKD link initialization are the main overhead factors. Optical switches have been investigated in QKD systems [Toliver, et al., 2003], and demonstrated by BBN Technologies [Elliott, et al., 2005] and NIST [Ma, et al., 2007] but only the NIST system is fast enough to support a one-time pad cipher for video.

A potential solution to extend QKD over longer distances is to chain together a number of QKD links. This approach requires that all intermediate nodes be trusted and secure because the key must be one-time pad transported, in multiple hops, across each additional QKD link to the communication end point, exposing the key at each node. In some cases this may be acceptable, it depends on the security requirements. For example, this may be acceptable in a corporate application where each node resides within a secure corporate controlled location. This is also applicable to quantum networks where each node cannot be directly connected to each other, such as in a mesh network vs. a star configuration. This also allows the use of non-switched quantum networks where the QKD links are static, such as in the SECOQC network [Peev, et al., 2009]. An example of this multi-hop approach is shown in Fig. 13. There are three QKD links, A-B, C-D and E-F, in a quantum network that connect nodes 1, 2, 3 and 4. QKD link ends B and C are co-located in the same node as are D and E. If we want to send a message from node 1 to node 4, encrypted with QKD key(a), then we need to get key(a) to node 4, but it exists only on Nodes 1 and 2. So node 2 gets key(c) from QKD link C-D and One-Time Pad encrypts key(a) with key(c) and then sends that encrypted key(ac) as a message to node 3. Node 3 decrypts it using key(c), extracting the original key(a). Node 3 then gets key(e) from QKD link E-F and One-Time Pad encrypts key(a) with key(e) and then sends that encrypted key(ae) as a message to node 4. Node 4 decrypts it using key(e), extracting the original key(a).

QKD systems produce a database of ordered secure bits at each end of a QKD link. A key manager, as shown in Fig. 1, is needed to demultiplex and synchronize these QKD bits for various applications, including conventional network security applications such as IPSec and TLS. Demultiplexing divides up the bits in the database into multiple independent key streams for each application. Synchronization makes sure that the same bits, in the same order, are allocated to the same demultiplexed stream on both sides of the network connection. Key management is easier for point-to-point QKD links, but becomes more complex for networks with trusted intermediate nodes since all node combinations must be accommodated. Key management also requires a mechanism to detect and recover from loss of synchronization. The key management application interface, operating within the security perimeter of each local node, would require its peers, as well as applications and their peers, to share a common, unique ID in order to retrieve the proper corresponding key. An application can have as many IDs as desired so it can implement virtual, independent key streams. For example, one for outgoing messages and another for incoming messages.

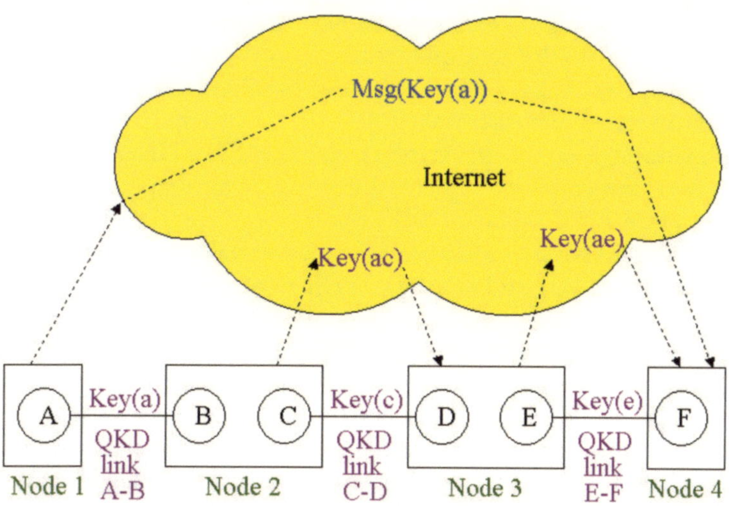

Fig. 13. Example of QKD multi-hop mechanism across 3 QKD links, A-B, C-D, and E-F

Since duplicate secret keys are kept at the respective ends of the channel, there is always a concern that some bits may be dropped or corrupted. A few corrupted bits will ruin a key, but future keys will not be affected. A few dropped bits, however, can be disastrous. Since the keys exist as an ordered set of random bits duplicated at each end of the link, if any bits are dropped at one end and not the other then all future key streams will differ at their respective ends and all future encrypted messages will be undecodeable.

Recovery from a few corrupted bits can be accomplished by discarding that key and obtaining a new key. Preventing such an occurrence can be accomplished by exchanging an error detection hash code for each group of keys transferred at QKD stages. For example, when 1 Mbit of key is transferred from the reconciliation stage to the privacy amplification stage a 64-bit hash code is exchanged to verify their equivalence. If the codes don't match, then that entire group of keys will be discarded. The key manager can take similar actions. At each QKD stage, steps are taken to prevent loss of key synchronization. If high error rates are detected, then the QKD link is reset and restarted. This detects and corrects both corrupted and dropped bits. The secure keys can be labeled by their ordered bit position in the secure key database and the key manager can exchange that information to keep its reserved and multiplexed bit groups synchronized for the applications.

Quantum network management features include controlling the switches, handling routing and verifying that the referenced node does have a currently operational QKD link that can be reached from the current node. Complications arise when switching (vs. static links) is required, because QKD uses circuit switching that requires 10s of seconds to switch, initialize and produce usable keys. Furthermore, periodic adjustments of the quantum channel may be necessary that would cause temporary interruption of the QKD link.

Fig. 14 shows the NIST active, switched quantum network. It has 3 nodes (Alice, Bob1 and Bob2) in a star configuration and uses commercial MEMS optical switches for the quantum and classical channels. The system operates at a 1.25 Gbps clock rate and can provide more than 1 Mb/s sifted-key rate over 1 km of optical fiber. As part of this QKD network, we have developed a quantum network manager and a key manager with an application interface similar to that discussed above. To demonstrate the speed of this QKD system, we have developed a video surveillance application, see Fig. 14, that is secured by a one-time pad cipher using keys generated by this quantum network and transmitted over standard internet IP channels. Two Bobs, at two different locations, are each equipped with a monitoring video camera, and are linked to Alice, who resides at the surveillance monitoring station, through this switched quantum network and the internet. A benefit of a one-time pad cipher is the simple encryption/decryption algorithm that adds little overhead to an application, since it's a bit-by-bit XOR operation of the data stream with the key stream. This, and the QKD hardware support, allows the available CPU cycles to be focused on video surveillance processing and not key and cipher processing.

Our surveillance application uses commercial webcams and an open source media encoder and player, all of which run on standard Windows based PCs. Each webcam output is processed by the media encoder and sends a UDP video data stream to its attached Bob (Linux) machine. Only one Bob (i.e., Bob1 or Bob2) at a time is active and connected to Alice through the switch. Our encryption application, running on the active Bob, receives the video stream as well as a stream of secure keys from its local QKD key manager, see Fig. 1, and performs a one-time pad encryption on the video stream. The now encrypted video stream is sent over the internet to Alice, also a Linux machine. Our decryption application,

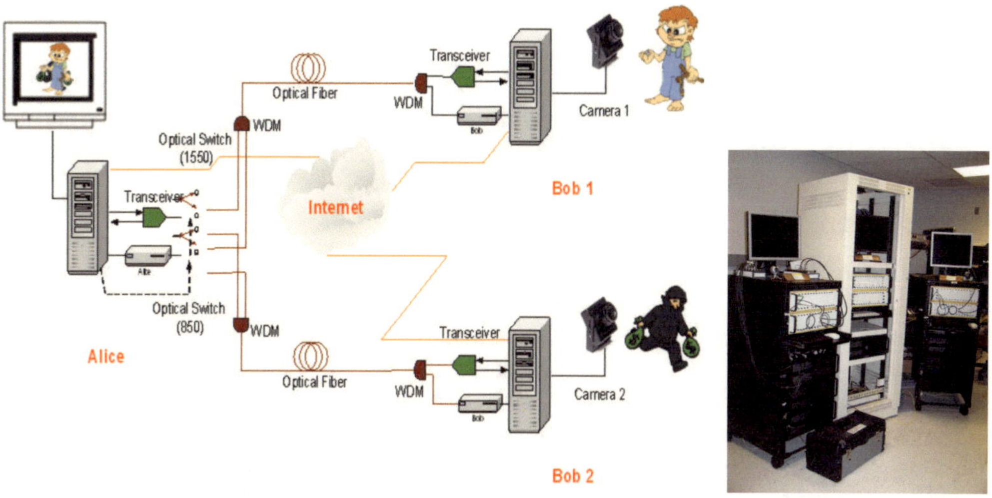

Fig. 14. A Video Surveillance application secured by the NIST QKD network and a one-time pad cipher. Network diagram (left) and actual nodes (right).

running on Alice, receives the encrypted TCP video stream as well as the matching synchronized stream of secure keys from its local QKD key manager. It then uses the key stream to decrypt the video stream and sends the clear text video as a UDP stream to its attached Windows based PC, which is running the media player that displays the video on the PC monitor. The result is continuous video displayed from the webcam, although delayed by a few seconds. Each Windows/Linux machine pair is within a local security perimeter and can be replaced by a single machine by porting the necessary software. When a user at Alice's monitor chooses to switch the video between Bob1 and Bob2, the QKD protocol flow to the active Bob is terminated and his secure key pool is conserved for when we switch back to him. The inactive Bob's QKD protocol flow is started up. The inactive Bob will start to send encrypted video to Alice using any conserved secure keys in its database, otherwise it will stall until its QKD starts to generate keys. An alternative approach to a secure video application would be to integrate the QKD key manager with a conventional network security application, such as IPsec, TLS or a link encryptor. The benefits being a vetted security application and greater portability for the surveillance application.

6. Standards activities

For any significant QKD commercial market penetration, standards are necessary for consumer understanding and verification, and for manufacturers' requirements. Because the QKD community is small, in comparison with the Internet community, only a single initial standards effort could be supported. That effort has been undertaken by the European Technology Standards Institute (ETSI) [Laenger & Lenhart, 2009] with worldwide participation. Delegates come from academia, research centers and industry. The intent of these standards is far reaching. They will need to include definitions and characterization of components (e.g., sources, detectors, random number generators, etc.) as well as the overall system. They will also need to include the metrology necessary to verify component and system operation, and testing to verify conformance to operational and security specifications. Furthermore, standard interfaces are necessary to integrate and interoperate with existing infrastructure, components and applications. The job is a big one and this standards group is mapping out this complex space. The group was started at the end of 2008 and to complete the underlying work necessary to support these standards and the time to develop the standards will easily take a number of years and will require significant effort from all the member organizations.

7. Conclusion

In this chapter we have discussed the QKD protocol and its potential to secure video surveillance applications. We have shown examples of a QKD implementation along with references to other implementations. We have also shown some innovations that can reduce QKD costs, limit some of the side channel attacks and provide hardware support to off load CPU processing. In addition, we have discussed the expansion of QKD into quantum networks and the concern and complexities associated with trusted intermediate nodes. We also touched on the need for integration with existing network infrastructure, providing services necessary for deployment and an on-going standards effort that is needed by both customers and developers. QKD is an attractive technology that holds significant promise but requires substantial research to bring it to fruition. QKD may not develop into a viable widely deployable technology, but with on-going research at least niche applications have potential.

8. References

Bienfang, J.; Gross, A.; Mink, A.; Hershman, B.; Nakassis, A.; Tang, X.; Lu, R.; Su, D.; Clark, C.; Williams, C.; Hagley, E.; Wen, J. (2004). "Quantum key distribution with 1.25 Gbps clock synchronization", *Optics Express*. Vol. 12, No. 9 (May 2004), pp. 2011-2016 <http://www.antd.nist.gov/pubs/Optics%20Express%20Submiss-1_4_6_04.pdf>

Bennett, C. & Brassard, G. (1984). "Quantum cryptography: Public key distribution and coin tossing", *Proc. of the IEEE Int. Conf. on Computers, Systems & Signal Processing*, pp. 175-179, Bangalore, India, Dec. 1984. <http://www.cs.ucsb.edu/~chong/290N-W06/BB84.pdf>

Bennett, C. (1992). "Quantum cryptography using any two nonorthogonal states", *Phys. Rev. Lett.*, Vol. 68, No. 21 (May 1992), pp. 3121-3124 <http://prl.aps.org/toc/PRL/v68/i21>

Breguet, J.; Muller, A. & Gisin, N. (1994) "Quantum Cryptography with Polarized Photons in Optical Fibres Experiment and Practical Limits", *J. of Modern Optics*, Vol. 41, No. 12 (Dec. 1994), pp. 2405-2412 http://dx.doi.org/10.1080/09500349414552251

Elliott, C.; Colvin, A.; Pearson, D.; Pikalo, O.; Schlafer, J. & Yeh, H. (2005). "Current status of the DARPA Quantum Network", BBN Technologies, Mar. 2005 <http://arxiv.org/ftp/quant-ph/papers/0503/0503058.pdf>

Fernandez, V.; Collins, R.; Gordon, K.; Paul, P. & Buller, G. (2007). "Passive Optical Network Approach to GigaHertz-Clocked Multiuser Quantum Key Distribution", *J. IEEE J. of Quantum Electronics*, Vol. 43, No. 2 (Feb. 2007), pp. 1-9 <http://arxiv.org/ftp/quant-ph/papers/0612/0612130.pdf>

Fossier, S.; Diamanti, E.; Debuisschert, T.; Villing, A.; Tualle-Brouri, R. & Grangier, P. (2009). "Field test of a continuous-variable quantum key distribution prototype", *New Journal of Physics*,Vol. 11, No. 4 (Apr. 2009), 045023, pp. 1-14 <http://iopscience.iop.org/1367-2630/11/4/045023>

Franson, J. & Jacobs, B. (1995). "Operational system for quantum cryptography", *Electronics Letters*, Vol. 31, No. 3 (Feb. 1995) pp. 232-234 <http://ieeexplore.ieee.org/stamp/stamp.jsp?arnumber=00362616>

Ghioni, M.; Giudicem, A.; Cova, S. & Zappa, F. (2003). "High-rate quantum key distribution at short wavelength: performance analysis and evaluation of silicon single photon avalanche diodes", *J. of Modern Optics*, Vol. 50, No. 14 (2003), pp. 2251–2269, ISSN: 1362-3044 <http://dx.doi.org/10.1080/09500340308234577>

Ghioni, M.; Gulinatti, A.; Rech, I.; Zappa, F. & Cova, S. (2007). "Progress in silicon single-photon avalanche diodes", *IEEE J. of Select Topics in Quantum Electron.,* Vol. 13, No. 4 (July 2007), pp 852-862

Gisin, N.; Ribordy, G.; Tittel, W.; & Zbinden, H.; (2002). "Quantum cryptography", Rev. Mod. Phys. Vol. 74, No. 1 (Jan 2002), pp. 145~195, ISSN 0034-6861 <http://rmp.aps.org/pdf/RMP/v74/i1/p145_1>

Gordon, K.; Fernandez, V.; Townsend, P. & Buller, G. (2004). "A Short Wavelength GigaHertz Clocked Fiber-Optic Quantum Key Distribution System", *IEEE J. of Quantum Electron*, Vol. 40, No. 7 (July 2004), pp. 900-908, ISSN: 0018-9197

Gordon, K.; Fernandez, V.; Buller, G.; Rech, I.; Cova, S. & Townsend, P. (2005). "Quantum key distribution system clocked at 2 GHz", *Opt. Express*, Vol. 13, No. 8, pp. 3015-3020 (Apr. 2005) <http://www.opticsinfobase.org/oe/abstract.cfm?uri=OE-13-8-3015>

Granger, P., et al. (2004). "Focus on Single Photons on Demand", *New Journal of Physics*, Vol. 6, No. 1 (July 2004) <http://iopscience.iop.org/1367-2630/6/1/E04>

Guenter, J. & Tatum, J. (1998). "Modulating VCSELs", *Honeywell Application Sheet*, Honeywell Inc., Feb. 1998 <http://www.imedea.uib.es/~salvador/coms_optiques/addicional/app_notes/honeywell_1.pdf>.

Hadfield, R.; Schlafer, J.; Ma, L.; Mink, A.; Tang, X. & Nam, S. (2007) "Quantum key distribution with high-speed superconducting single-photon detectors", *Proc. of CLEO 07 QML4*, Balt., MD, May 2007 <http://www.antd.nist.gov/pubs/892-papers/High-speed superconducting single photon detectors.pdf>

Kleeman, L & Cantoni, A. (1987). "Metastable behaviour in digital systems", *IEEE Design & Test of Computers,* Vol. 4, No. 6 (Nov. 1987), pp 4-19, ISSN: 0740-7475

Laenger, T. & Lenhart, G. (2009). "Standardization of quantum key distribution and the ETSI standardization initiative ISG-QKD", *New Journal of Physics*, Vol. 11, No. 055051 (May 2009), pp 1-16 <http://iopscience.iop.org/1367-2630/11/5/055051>

Langrock, C.; Diamanti, E.; Roussev, R.; Yamamoto, Y.; Fejer, M. & Takesue, H. (2005). "Highly efficient single-photon detection at communication wavelengths by use of upconversion in reverse-proton-exchanged periodically poled LiNbO3 waveguides", *Opt. Lett.*, Vol. 30, No. 13 (July 2005), pp. 1725-1727 <http://www.opticsinfobase.org/abstract.cfm?URI=ol-30-13-1725>

Ling, A.; Peloso, M.; Marcikic, I.; Scarani, V.; Lamas-Linares, A. & Kurtsiefer, C. (2008). "Experimental quantum key distribution based on a Bell test", *Phys. Rev.* A, Vol. 78 (Aug 2008), 020301 <http://arxiv.org/abs/0805.3629>

Ma, L.; Xu, H. & Tang, X. (2006) "Polarization recovery and auto-compensation in Quantum Key Distribution network", *Proc. of SPIE Optics & Photonics: Quantum Communications and Quantum Imaging IV*, Vol. 6305, 630513, San Diego, CA, Aug. 2006, SPIE <http://w3.antd.nist.gov/pubs/2007/Polarization recovery and auto-compensation.pdf>

Ma, L.; Chang, T.; Mink, A.; Slattery, O.; Hershman, B. & Tang, X. (2007). "Experimental demonstration of an active quantum key distribution network with over Gbps clock synchronization", *IEEE Communications Letters*, Vol. 11, No. 12 (Dec. 2007), pp. 1019 <http://w3.antd.nist.gov/pubs/892-papers/Quantum Key Distribution Network.pdf>

Ma, L; Slattery, O.; Mink, A. & Tang, X. (2009). "Low noise up-conversion single photon detector and its applications in quantum information systems", *Proc. of SPIE: Quantum Communications and Quantum Imaging VII*, Vol. 7465, pp. 74650W, San Diego, CA, Aug. 2009, SPIE <http://scitation.aip.org/getpdf/servlet/GetPDFServlet?filetype=pdf&id=PSISDG0074650 0000174650W000001&idtype=cvips&prog=normal>

Mink, A.; Tang, X.; Ma, L.; Nakassis, T.; Hershman, B.; Bienfang, J.; Su, D.; Boisvert, R.; Clark, C. & Williams, C. (2006). "High Speed Quantum Key Distribution System Supports One-Time Pad Encryption of Real-Time Video", *Proc. of SPIE Defense and Security Symposium: Quantum Information and Computation IV*, Vol. 6244, pp. 62440M 1-7, Orlando, Fla., Apr. 2006, SPIE <http://w3.antd.nist.gov/pubs/Mink-SPIE-One-Time-Pad-6244_22.pdf>

Mink, A. (2007). "Custom hardware to eliminate bottlenecks in QKD throughput performance", *Proc. of SPIE Optics East:Quantum Communications Realized*, Vol. 6780, pp. 678014 1-6, Boston, MA, Sept. 2007, SPIE <http://w3.antd.nist.gov/pubs/Next_gen_Paper_5_07.doc>

Muller, A.; Herzog, T.; Huttner, B.; Tittel, W.; Zbinden, H. & Gisin, N. (1997). "Plug & play systems for quantum cryptography", *Applied Physics Letters,* Vol. 70, No. 7 (Feb. 1997), pp. 793–795 <http://www.gap-optique.unige.ch/Publications/PDF/APL00793.pdf>

Nakassis, A.; Bienfang, J. & Williams, C. (2004). "Expeditious reconciliation for practical quantum key distribution", *Proc. of SPIE: Quantum Information and Computation II,*

Vol. 5436, Orlando, FL, Apr. 2004 <http://w3.antd.nist.gov/pubs/orlando.pdf>

Ouellette, J. (2004) "Quantum Key Distribution", *The Industrial Physicist*, Dec 2004, <http://www.aip.org/tip>

ON Semiconductor Corp. (2007). "Metastability and the ECLinPS family", *Application Note AN1504/D* <http://www.onsemi.com/pub_link/Collateral/AN1504-D.PDF>

Peev, M.; et al. (2009). "The SECOQC quantum key distribution network in Vienna", *New Journal of Physics*, Vol. 11, No. 075001 (July 2009) <http://iopscience.iop.org/1367-2630/11/7/075001>

Phoenix, S.; Barnett, S.; Townsend, P. & Blow, K. (1995). "Multi-user quantum cryptography on optical networks", *J. of modern optics*, Vol. 42, No. 6 (June 1995), pp. 1155-1163

Rogers, D.; Bienfang, J.; Nakassis, A.; Xu, H. & Clark, C. (2007) "Detector dead-time effects and paralyzability in high-speed quantum key distribution", *New Journal of Physics*, Vol. 9, No. 319 (Sept. 2007), pp 1-13 <http://iopscience.iop.org/1367-2630/9/9/319/pdf/1367-2630_9_9_319.pdf>

Scarani, V. & Kurtsiefer, C. (2009). "The black paper of quantum cryptography: real implementation problems", arXiv:0906.4547v1, quant-ph, June 2009, <http://arxiv.org/abs/0906.4547>

Stucki, D.; Gisin, N.; Guinnard, O.; Ribordy, G. & Zbinden, H. (2002). "Quantum key distribution over 67 km with a plug&play system", *New Journal of Physics* ,Vol. 4, No. 41, (July 2002) pp. 41.1-41.8 <http://iopscience.iop.org/1367-2630/4/1/341>

Tang, X.; Ma, L.; Mink, A.; Nakassis, T.; Xu, H.; Hershman, B.; Bienfang, J.; Su, D.; Boisvert, R.; Clark, C. & Williams, C. (2006) "Quantum key distribution system operating at sifted-key rate over 4 Mbit/s", *Proc. of SPIE: Quantum Information and Computation IV: Proc. SPIE Defense & Security Symposium,* Vol 6244, pp. 62440P 1-8, Orlando, FL, April 2006, SPIE <http://w3.antd.nist.gov/pubs/Xiao-SPIE-QKD-4mMbps-6244_25.pdf>

Toliver, P.; Runser, R.; Chapuran, T.; Jackel, J.; Banwell, T.; GoodMan, M.; Hughes, R.; Peterson, C.; Derkacs, D.; Nordholt, J.; Mercer, L.; McNown, S.; Goldman, A. & Blake, J. (2003). "Experimental investigation of quantum key distribution through transparent optical switch elements", *IEEE Photon. Technol. Lett.*, Vol. 15, No. 11 (Nov. 2003), pp. 1669-1671

Townsend, P.; Phonenix, S.; Blow, K. & Barnett, S. (1994). "Design of quantum cryptography systems for passive optical networks", *IEEE Electronics Letters*, Vol. 30, No. 22 (Oct. 1994), pp. 1875-1877

Townsend, P. (1998). "Experimental investigation of the performance limits for first telecommunication-window quantum cryptography system", *IEEE Photon. Technol. Lett.* , Vol. 10, No. 7 (July 1998), pp. 1048-1050, ISSN: 1041-1135

Unger, S. (1995). "Hazards, critical races, and metastability", *IEEE Trans. on Computers,* Vol. 44, No. 6 (June 1995), pp 754-768

Wikipedia. (2010). http://en.wikipedia.org/wiki/One-time_pad, last modified July 2010, last accessed July 2010

Xu, F.; Qi B. & Lo H. (2010). "Experimental demonstration of phase-remapping attack in a practical quantum key distribution system", arXiv:1005.2376v1 [quant-ph] May 2010, < http://arxiv.org/abs/1005.2376>

Xu, H.; Ma, L.; Bienfang, J. & Tang, X. (2006) "Influence of the dead time of avalanche photodiode on high-speed quantum-key distribution system", *Proc. of CLEO/QELS Photonic Applications Systems Technologies*, Technical Digest (CD) paper: JTuH3, Long Beach, CA, May 2006, Optical Society of America <http://www.opticsinfobase.org/abstract.cfm?URI=QELS-2006-JTuH3>

Yuan Z.; Kardynal, B.; Sharpe, A. & Shields, A. (2007). "High speed single photon detection in the near infrared", *Applied Physics Letters*, Vol. 91, No. 4, #041114 (July 2007) <http://arxiv.org/PS_cache/arxiv/pdf/0707/0707.4307v1.pdf>

Yuan, Z.; Dixon, A.; Dynes, J.; Sharpe, A. & Shields, A. (2008). " Gigahertz quantum key distribution with InGaAs avalanche photodiodes", *Applied Physics Letters*, Vol. 92, No. 20, #201104 (May 2008) <http://arxiv.org/PS_cache/arxiv/pdf/0805/0805.3414v1.pdf>

7

Cooperative Visual Surveillance Network with Embedded Content Analysis Engine

Shao-Yi Chien and Wei-Kai Chan
Media IC and System Lab, Graduate Institute of Electronics Engineering and Department of Electrical Engineering, National Taiwan University
Taiwan

1. Introduction

Visual surveillance plays an important role in security systems of digital home and enterprise Regazzoni et al. (2001). Evolving from CCTV video surveillance, the IP camera surveillance system with Internet as the connection backbone is a trend in recent years. A typical IP camera surveillance system is shown in Fig. 1. IP camera systems have the advantages of easy setup and universal access ability; however, several issues in network transmission are introduced Foresti & Regazzoni (2001), which become more and more important when the number of camera grows. Since the surveillance systems share the same network with other applications and devices of digital home and enterprise, the congestion of network caused by transmission of large surveillance contents may degrade the service quality of the these applications, including the surveillance application itself. Besides, the control server can only afford the content storage from a limited number of video channels, which limits the system extension in camera number.

Further evolving from IP camera systems, the maturity of visual content analysis technology makes it feasible to be integrated into the next-generation surveillance systems to achieve intelligent visual surveillance network Mozef et al. (2001) Hu et al. (2004) Stauffer & Grimson (1999) Elgammal et al. (2000) Comaniciu et al. (2003) Cavallaro et al. (2005) Maggio et al. (2007), where high-level events can be automatically detected, and multiple cameras can cooperate with each other, including different types of fixed cameras and mobile cameras hold by robots, as shown in Fig. 1.

In the next-generation system in Fig. 1, namely cooperative visual surveillance network, new design challenges are introduced. First of all, the system configuration should be carefully designed since the distribution of the computations for these analysis functions will significantly affect the performances of these visual content analysis algorithms, and it will also affect the utilization efficiency of network resources. Moreover, the large computation of content analysis algorithms will increase the loading of servers, which will further limit the scale of camera number. Thanks to the advanced silicon manufacturing technology, which makes the transistor count in single chip increase dramatically, more and more functions can be considered to be integrated as a System-on-a-Chip (SoC) to cover more and more tasks for

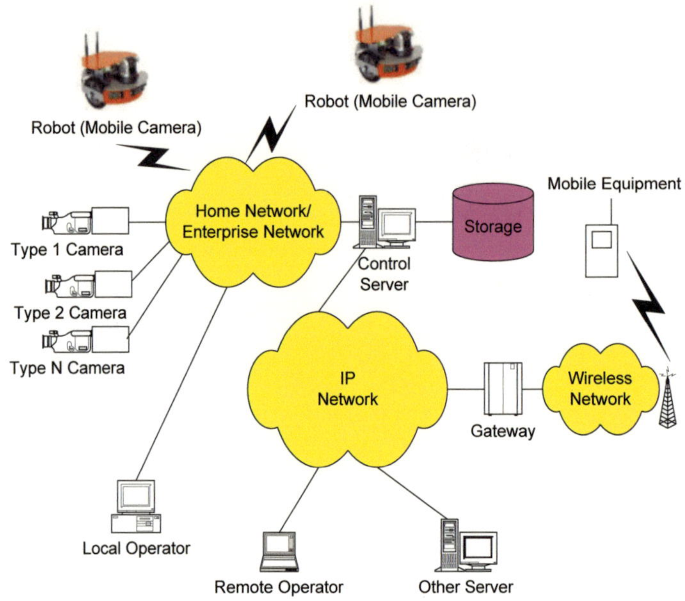

Fig. 1. Illustration of a cooperative video surveillance network.

surveillance applications Wolf et al. (2002). An efficient smart camera SoC is required to help reducing the deployment space and cost and solving the above issues.

This chapter is organized as follows. In Section 2, the issues in conventional IP camera surveillance systems are discussed, and our solution for the next-generation surveillance system is introduced. The surveillance system pipeline in system level, and an five-layered surveillance visual content abstraction hierarchy are presented. In Section 3, the proposed algorithms to be embedded in each surveillance camera are introduced, including video segmentation in complex and dynamic background, user-friendly video object description, efficient multiple video object tracking with split- and merge-handling, and efficient face detection and scoring. Next, in Section 4, our proposed visual content analysis hardware engine is introduced, where the proposed content analysis algorithms are implemented, and the overall hardware architecture for smart camera SoC is also provided. Two design examples are then demonstrated. The first one is a multi-fixed-camera surveillance system, which will be shown in Section 5; the second one is a surveillance network with several fixed cameras, one robot (mobile camera), and in-door localization system using Zigbee, which will be shown in Section 6. Finally, we will conclude this chapter and introduce some future directions in Section 7.

2. Proposed system configuration and data abstraction hierarchy

In this section, the system configuration of the next-generation surveillance systems are discussed with considering the issues mentioned previously, and a better system configuration is analyzed based on the surveillance pipeline model shown in Fig. 2. After that, the new ability of abstraction hierarchy of the next-generation surveillance systems is introduced as shown in Fig. 3. With content analysis ability, the scalability in IP camera surveillance systems can be extended across all of the five layers according to

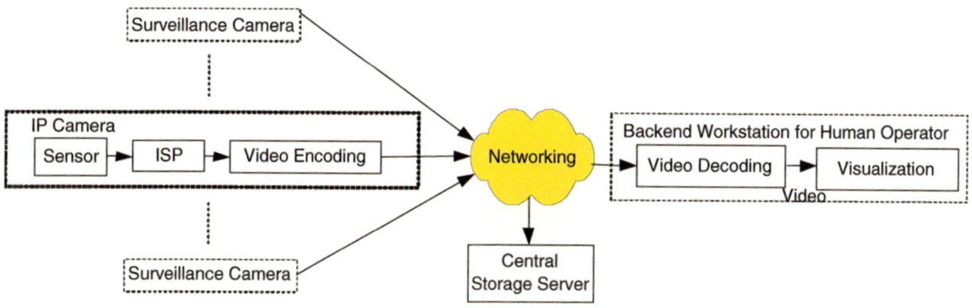

Fig. 2. Surveillance pipeline model of the conventional IP camera surveillance system.

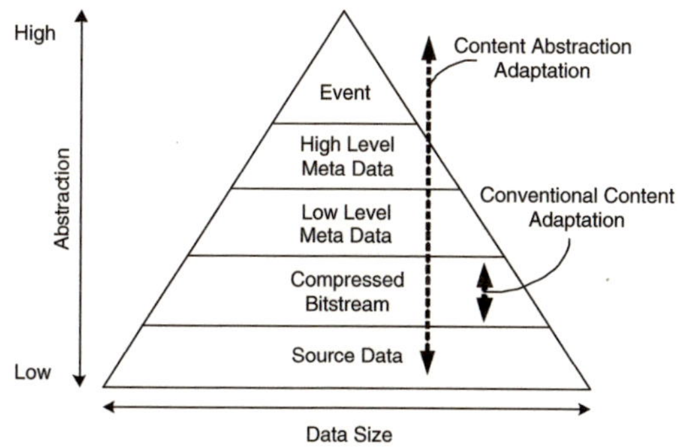

Fig. 3. Abstraction hierarchy of visual content in a surveillance network.

operation conditions, network conditions, and storage space conditions. The most important information in semantics will be transmitted under restricted communication and storage resources.

A conventional IP cameras surveillance system is modeled with the pipeline in Fig. 2. In this pipeline, there are seven important tasks: Video Sensing (*Sensor*), *Image Signal Processing (ISP)*, *Video Encoding*, *Network*, *Video Decoding*, *Content Storage*, and *Visualization*. In the *Back-end Workstation*, which is placed at the other side of the *Network* from the *IP camera*, the transmitted video stream is decoded in *Video Decoding*. The video data is then displayed with *Visualization* for the human operators. The coded video data is also received and stored in the *Central Storage Server*, and the *Back-end Workstation* and *Central Storage Server* can be integrated in the same machine in some cases. Note that the detailed tasks in *Network* are ignored in the pipeline since they are beyond the scope of this chapter. From Fig. 2, we can see that all of the compressed bitstreams from every IP camera should be transmitted through *Network* for inspection by the human operators. When the number of cameras increases, a network congestion problem will occur, and the surveillance system's performance will degrade significantly.

2.1 Content abstraction hierarchy

When visual content analysis tools are employed in surveillance systems, the essential change is the introduction of a content abstraction hierarchy, which is described in the first place before the system configuration discussion. As shown in Fig. 3, there are five different layers to represent the visual surveillance contents: *Source Data Layer*, *Compressed Bitstream Layer*, *Low Level Meta Data Layer*, *High Level Meta Data Layer*, and *Event Layer*. The *Low Level Meta*

Data represents the low-level features of the source video, such as color and shape features, and the *High Level Meta Data* is obtained through further analysis of the *Low Level Meta Data*, where the concept of "object" is considered, such as face locations, object trajectories, poses, and the gaits of human objects. *Event* represents the results of an event detection, where the event is defined in advance according to different application scenarios. In a conventional IP camera surveillance system, the content scalability only occurs in the *Compressed Bitstream Layer* to adjust the coding bitrate according to different network conditions or storage space conditions, which is indicated as the *Conventional Content Adaptation* in Fig. 3. With content analysis ability, the scalability in IP camera surveillance systems can be extended across all of the five layers in Fig. 3 according to operation conditions (results from event detection...etc), network conditions (network congestion...etc), and storage space conditions. That is, the most important information in semantics will be transmitted under restricted communication and storage resources.

2.2 System configuration discussion

In order to discuss the system configuration, surveillance pipeline models similar to the one in Fig. 2 are employed. Three representative surveillance pipelines are provided in Fig. 4. In these pipelines, *Content Analysis* tasks are added. With the minimum modification to the conventional surveillance pipeline in Fig. 2, the *Back-End Content Analysis* task in Fig. 4(a) utilizes visual content analysis tools in the back-end workstation after the video bitstream is received from the network and decoded. In such a surveillance pipeline, the delay of event detection due to network transmission delay could be expected. Moreover, the coding process and the packet loss in transmission may also degrade the video quality for analysis. Besides, when the number of IP cameras becomes large, more *Back-End Workstations* are required to provide sufficient computing power, which will dramatically increase the system cost and deployment space. In addition, the *Central Storage Server* cannot afford to perform all the storage tasks for all the surveillance cameras, and the network loading also increases for the purpose of storage. To deal with the above-mentioned problems, the *Back-End Content Analysis* can be moved to the front-end as distributed *Front-End Content Analysis Workstations*, and distributed *Local Storage* can be used to replace the *Central Storage Server*. The resultant pipeline from these two modification is shown in Fig. 4(b). In this pipeline, the network congestion problem can be solved by using a content abstraction hierarchy to transmit only the semantically meaningful information for visualization, while the *Local Storage* stores the complete video bitstream for off-line historical inspection and review. However, the number of *Front-End Content Analysis Workstations* will still increase as the number of cameras increases, which leads to large cost and deployment space. Consequently, a choice is made to replace the *Front-End Content Analysis Workstation* with a smart camera SoC with visual content analysis functions. For the issues mentioned here, the surveillance pipeline that features distributed local storage and smart camera SoCs in Fig. 4(c) is our chosen solution. It is the best solution among these three pipelines in terms of system cost, deployment space, network loading, and system scalability. The comparisons among these three pipelines are summarized in Table 1.

2.3 Proposed visulization strategy

A visualization strategy is also proposed with the five-layered visual content abstraction scalability in Fig. 3 and the selected pipeline in Fig. 4(c), where human objects is the focus in our system. This strategy consists of three condition levels: normal level, alert level,

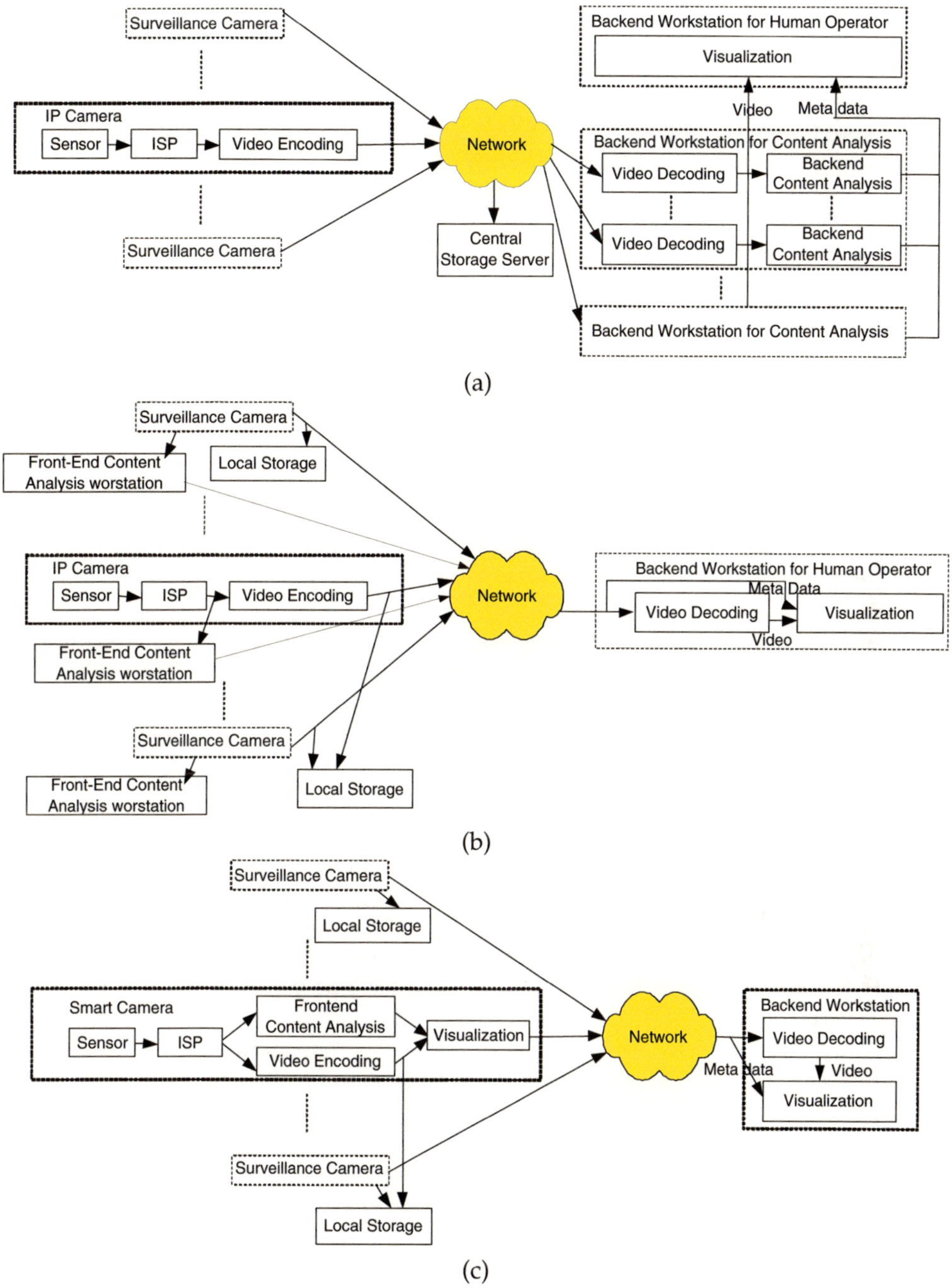

Fig. 4. Surveillance pipelines with different configurations. (a) Surveillance pipeline with a central storage server and back-end content analysis. (b) Surveillance pipeline with local storage servers and front-end content analysis workstations. (c) Next-generation surveillance pipeline with local storage servers and front-end content analysis in a smart camera SoC.

Surveillance Pipeline	Fig. 4(a)	Fig. 4(b)	Fig. 4(c)
Network Congestion[1]	More possible	Less possible	Less possible
Limitation from Storage Space[2]	More limited	Less limited	Less limited
Video Quality for Analysis[3]	Low	High	High
Event Detection Delay[4]	More possible	Less possible	Less possible
Deployment Space and Cost[5]	High	High	Low
System Scalability[6]	Lower	Middle	Highest

Table 1. Comparison between Surveillance Pipelines in Fig. 4

1. In Fig. 4(a), the video bitstreams should be transmitted to the back-end workstation through network for analysis. This will cause network congestion problem more frequently.
2. In Fig. 4(a), one central storage server can not afford the storage of video from all of the cameras.
3. The quality of the video for analysis in Fig. 4(a) may be degraded due to network transmission loss, such as packet loss, and video coding distortion.
4. The event detection delay in Fig. 4(a) is due to the delay of video streaming.
5. The deployment space and cost are largely reduced with smart camera SoCs in Fig. 4(c) .
6. The highest system scalability in Fig. 4(c) is due to its lowest requirements on the network bandwidth, the processing capacity of a single storage server, and the system deployment space and cost.

and operator interaction level. In the normal level, only the data in event layer and meta data layers in Fig. 3 will be transmitted to the back-end workstations for human operators. Meta data here includes a clear, representative face for each human object, and all objects' current positions and their color features. Once an event has been detected at a front-end smart camera, the current condition level will be switched to alert level. Note that the event definition can be defined according to different application scenarios by human operators. In alert level, a small-sized video stream from the cameras that detect this event will be sent to human operators along with the meta data. The human operators can judge the true condition by inspecting the small-sized video and all the meta data. Once the human operators want to see what happens clearly, the current condition level can be switched to operator interaction level on human operators' commands at any time. In operator interaction level, the upper four layers of data, which includes a large-sized video, will be transmitted to the back-end for further checking.

Two examples are described here to show the data-size-reduction ability of the proposed visualization strategy. The sizes of the data to be transmitted for each frame are measured and compared with those of conventional IP camera surveillance systems. In the first example, the sequence Hall Monitor is tested, and the required data sizes to be transmitted are shown in Fig. 5(a). For the proposed visualization strategy, the condition level will be switched to alert level if there is any object appearing from the left door in the scene. At the begging, only the meta-data is transmitted, and almost no data needs to be transmitted. At frame number 20, these is a human object appeared from left door, so the alert level is triggered. The video of size 176x144 is transmitted to the operator. At frame number 132, when the human operator finds that the man is putting something near the wall, he requires the corresponding camera to transmit the large-sized video in 352x288 frame size for detailed inspection. On the other hand, for a conventional IP camera surveillance system, the video with frame size 352x288 is always transmitted over the network even when there is no event of interests. As shown by the dashed curve in Fig. 5(a), it is obvious that the size of transmitted data is larger. In the

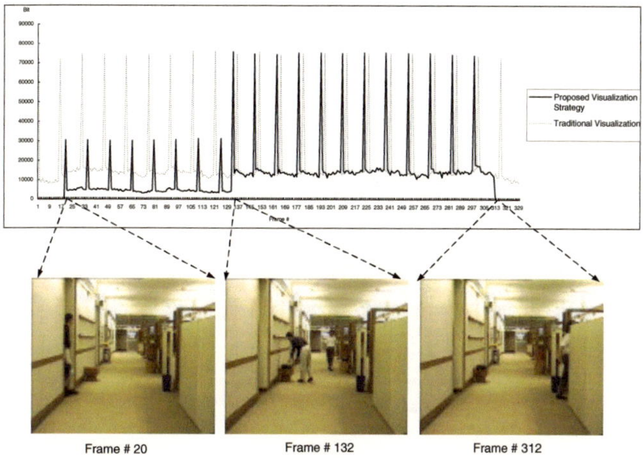

(a)

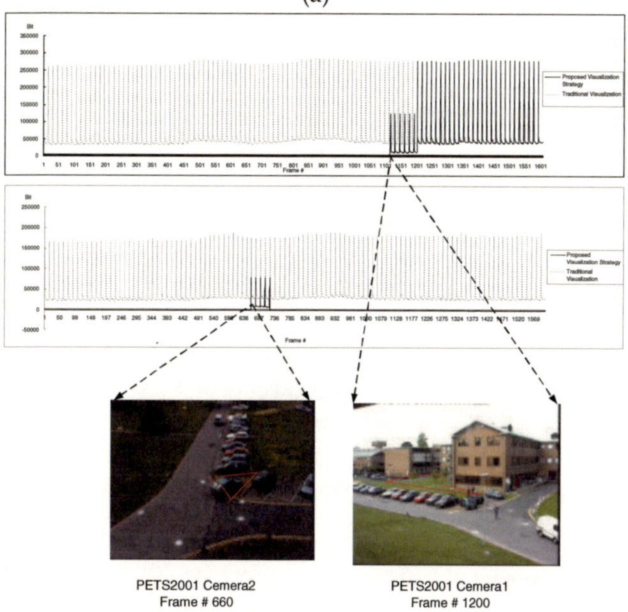

(b)

Fig. 5. Comparisons of data size to be transmitted.

second example, the PETS2001 multi-camera sequences PETS (2007) are tested as shown in Fig. 5(b). In this case, there are two cameras monitoring the same area. We set that camera 1 is used to detect illegal treading on grass, and camera 2 is used to detect illegal parking. At frame number 660, an illegal parking event is detected. At frame number 1116, a treading on grass event is detected. It can be seen that compared with conventional approach, the data size is greatly reduced in Fig. 5(b) with our proposed visualization strategy because only the semantically meaningful information for visualization is transmitted, which will greatly relief the network loading.

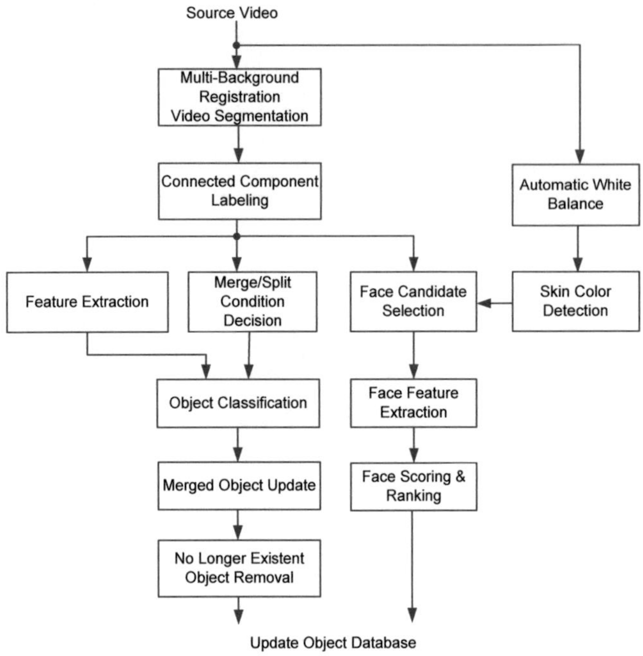

Fig. 6. The block diagram of the proposed front-end content analysis algorithm in a single smart camera.

3. Single camera operation

In this section, the algorithms proposed to be embedded in each smart camera in the next-generation surveillance pipeline for the front-end content analysis are introduced. The proposed algorithms can be shown with the block diagram in Fig. 6. There are three major components, which are video object segmentation Chan & Chien (2007), video object description and tracking Chien, Chan, Cherng & Chang (2006), and face detection and scoring Chen et al. (2007). These three components are described as follows.

3.1 Video object segmentation

As shown in Fig. 6, the video object segmentation is the first step. The segmentation algorithm employs a multiple layer background modeling technique named Multi-Background Registration. It models the background with N layers of images to contain up to N possible values of the background at every pixel Chan & Chien (2007). The object mask is produced with comparing the current frame with these background images (background subtraction), while the thresholds are decided with our threshold decision technique Chien et al. (2004). The object mask is further de-noised with morphological operations.

3.2 Video object description and tracking

In this subsection, the video object description and tracking component of our algorithm is introduced. We designed this component with the considerations below. First, the style of video object description should be close to what people are used to describe video objects, since the users would like such a description style for their inspection convenience. Second, the tracking algorithm should be capable of tracking multiple video objects with mutual merging and splitting. Finally, since there are usually similar operations in segmentation, description, and tracking, these operations should be further combined as a single system without redundant computations.

This component is based on Chien, Chan, Cherng & Chang (2006) combined with a mechanism to handle the object merging and splitting Kumar et al. (2006). As shown in Fig. 6, this component is a segmentation-and-description based video object tracking algorithm. It receives the segmentation results from our proposed *Multi-Background Registration Video Segmentation* introduced in the previous subsection. The *Connected Component Labeling* step in Fig. 6 is used to give each blob on the object mask a unique label. After that, several features/descriptors are extracted for each blob, which corresponds to the *Feature Extraction* step in Fig. 6. Our proposed Human Color Structure Descriptor (HCSD) Chien, Chan, Cherng & Chang (2006) is used as one of the descriptors to be extracted. The HCSD requires a skeletonization process to decompose the blobs. A decomposition example is shown in Fig. 7. We can see that the human object's blob is decomposed into a Body part and Limbs part in Figs. 7(d) and (e), respectively. After skeletonization decomposition, we can easily extract the color features in each individual part. Especially for human objects, they can be described in terms of their shirt color and pants color, which is usually how people describe strangers. Beside HCSD, four other features are also extracted. These are the overlapped area sizes of the blobs in the current frame with the video objects in the previous frame (Object- Blob Overlapped Area), the area of each blob (Blob Area), the center of each blob (Blob Center), and the color histogram of each blob in YUV color space (Blob Color Histogram).

On the other hand, the merging and splitting conditions are judged in *Merge/Split Condition Decision* step in Fig. 6 in advance before *Object Classification*, where the correspondences between the blobs on the object mask and the video objects in the history database will be built. Here we use the reasoning method based on blob-object overlapping condition Kumar et al. (2006) to judge the merging and splitting conditions. However, we do not use the Kalman filter to predict video objects' motions Kumar et al. (2006). The overlapping conditions between the blobs in the current frame and the video objects in the history are employed instead considering that Kalman filter may fail to predict random motions.

After *Feature Extraction* and *Merge/Split Condition Decision*, the correspondences between the blobs and the video objects in the history database are built in *Object Classification*. The correspondences involved with merging objects or splitting objects are built according to the merging or splitting conditions obtained from the *Merge/Split Condition Decision* step, while the correspondences involved with only single objects (non-merging and non-splitting) are built with selecting the closest object in the history database for each blob. The closest object here is obtained with the comparison based on the four features extracted previously.

In *Merged Object Update* step, the single objects split from some merged objects (judged with the *Merge/Split Condition Decision* step) can be removed from the merged object lists. Meanwhile, objects that are no longer observed for a predefined length of time will be removed from the object list for object-blob matching in the *No Longer Existing Object Removal* step.

3.3 Face detection and scoring

The face detection and scoring algorithm is based on segmentation and feature based face scoring Chen et al. (2007). Firstly, as shown in Fig. 6, the algorithm detects skin color regions Chai & Ngan (1999) on the surveillance video after automatic white balance Ramanath et al.

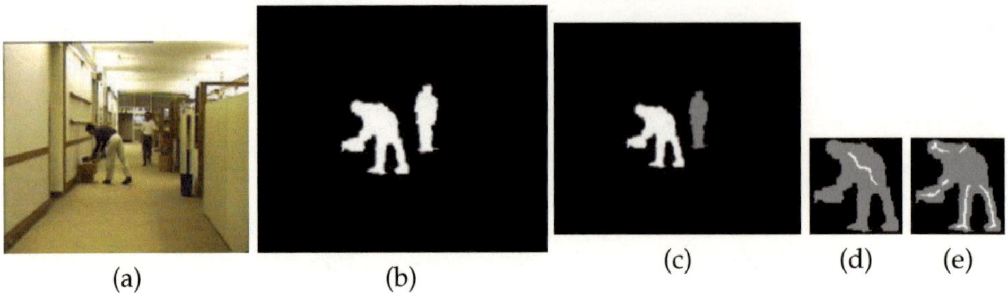

Fig. 7. An example from segmentation step to skeletonization step, where the test sequence is *Hall Monitor*. (a) Original sequence of *Hall Monitor*; (b) result after segmentation; (c) result after connected component labeling; (d) result after skeletonization: Body part; (e) result after skeletonization: Limb part.

(2005). Then, in *Face Candidate Selection* step, the possible locations of faces on the overlapped area between the skin color regions and the foreground regions in the object mask are found via a mean shift process Comaniciu et al. (2003). After finding the possible locations of faces, these face candidates are scored with four face feature scores, which are Skin Color Coverage Score, Luminance Variation Score, Circularity Measurement Score, and Eye-pixel Histogram Score Chen et al. (2007). These four scores are linearly combined to form the final score function. A neural network is employed to train the weighting of each score based on Least-mean-square (LMS) delta rule. The faces with higher final scores are better ranked and are selected as the detected faces.

4. Smart camera hardware architecture with embedded content analysis engine

Before hardware architecture design and mapping, the whole content analysis algorithm is first analyzed with execution time profiling and data flow graph. We find that there are three computationally intensive operations that dominate the computation time, which are multi-background registration video segmentation, morphological operations (to de-noise the object mask), and the connected component labeling. Based on this analysis result, the hardware architecture of the smart camera SoC is proposed as shown in Fig. 8(a). We can see that there are three hardware accelerators, *Segmentation Hardware Accelerator*, *Morphology Coprocessor*, *CCL Hardware Accelerator* in the proposed *Visual Content Analysis Hardware Engine*. These three accelerators are used to accelerate the processing of the three computation intensive operations in our profiling.

There are several design issues for these hardware content analysis accelerators. First, the operations involved in a single camera have very different requirements. For example, some of the algorithms should be implemented to have high throughput, and dedicated hardware accelerators may be a better solution for this case. Some of the algorithms are adaptive according to different situations, and programmable hardware accelerators could be used. In addition, morphology operations Serra (1982) are widely used in the proposed content analysis algorithms. Hardware sharing between different algorithms should be considered. Moreover, most of the operations involved are basically frame-level operations, which means that the next operation can be executed only when the whole frame is completely scanned or processed by the current operation. To achieve high throughput for such operations, frame-level pipeline technique should be employed, and a frame buffer is required. For

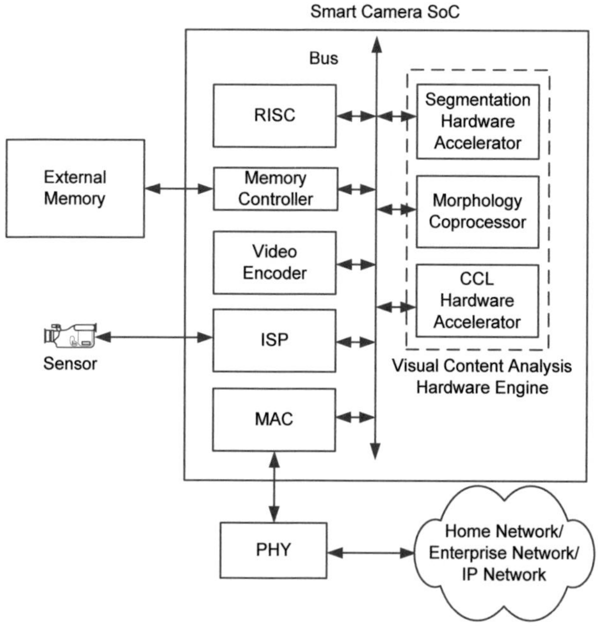

(a)

Process	TSMC $0.13\mu m$	
Working Frequency		
CPU (ARM926EJ-S)	266MHz	
Visual Content Analysis Hardware Engine	62.5MHz	
System Bus (64-bit)	133MHz	
Hardware Cost		
	Gate Count	On-Chip Memory (Kb)
Segmentation	23,216	10.00
CCL	6,111	15.63
Morphology Coprocessor	276,480	30.00
Total Hardware Cost	305,807	55.63
Processing Speed	30 640x480 frames/s	

(b)

Fig. 8. (a) Block diagram of smart camera SoC hardware architecture with heterogeneous content analysis hardware engine. (b) System specifications and implementation results.

the requirement of large frame size, the frame buffer is not feasible to be implemented on-chip and should be located in the off-chip memory, which will introduce high memory bandwidth requirement. Furthermore, when these hardware accelerators are integrated in an SoC, bit-width mismatch may sometimes lower the performance of the hardware. That is, for the various algorithms, the data formats are quite different. Some are 8-bit, some are binary, and some are 16-bit; however, the bit-width of the system bus is fixed, which is decided to be 64-bit in this paper after system analysis. To efficiently utilize the system bus bandwidth, the hardware should be carefully designed.
For the above reasons, firstly, the visual content analysis hardware engine is proposed to be designed with heterogeneous processing units, which includes CPU, dedicated and programmable hardware accelerators here. Besides, these algorithms can be separated into special operations and morphological operations. Therefore, in our proposed visual content analysis hardware engine, there are three modules: *Segmentation Hardware Accelerator*, *Connected Component Labeling (CCL) hardware accelerator*, and *Morphology Co-Processor*. The *Segmentation Hardware Accelerator* and *CCL Hardware Accelerator* are dedicated hardware accelerators for video object segmentation and connected component labeling operation, respectively. The major design techniques employed are delay-line and partial-result-reuse technique Chien, Hsieh, Huang, Ma & Chen (2006). The *Morphology Co-Processor* is a programmable hardware accelerator for binary morphology operations, which can be used to accelerate the processes of Video Segmentation, Skeletonization, and Face Detection and Scoring Hartenstein (2001) Chan & Chien (2006a) Serra (1982). As for the bit-width mismatch problem, the design concept of subword level parallelism (SLP) Chan & Chien (2006b) is considered in our design to efficiently utilize the system bus bandwidth.
The implementation results are shown in Fig. 8(b), which demonstrates a nice trade-off between hardware cost and performance. It can achieve the processing speed of 30 VGA frames/s with a reasonable hardware cost.

5. Case study I: Surveillance system with multiple fixed cameras

The first case study is a surveillance system with multiple fixed cameras. We will introduce two key techniques for the spatial consistency labeling in multi-camera surveillance systems: homography transformation Semple & Kneebone (1979) and earth movers distance (EMD) Rubner et al. (1998). The PETS2001 multi-camera sequences PETS (2007) are employed as the test sequences.
Spatial consistency labeling (SCL) algorithm is used to find the object correspondences between different camera views Chang et al. (2008). With the assumption that the views should have a common ground plane, the algorithm for SCL is based on ground plane homography transformation Semple & Kneebone (1979) Bradshaw et al. (1997). The homography transformation matrix is defined as follows.

$$\begin{bmatrix} \lambda_i X_i \\ \lambda_i Y_i \\ \lambda_i \end{bmatrix} = \begin{bmatrix} M_{11} & M_{12} & M_{13} \\ M_{21} & M_{22} & M_{23} \\ M_{31} & M_{32} & 1 \end{bmatrix} \begin{bmatrix} x_i \\ y_i \\ 1 \end{bmatrix} \tag{1}$$

In this equation, **M** is the ground plane warping matrix between two views. (X_i, Y_i) and (x_i, y_i) represent the corresponding ground plane positions. Homography transformation converts the coordinates of a ground point in one view to the coordinates in the other view. An example is shown in Fig. 9. Given four or more matching pairs, the ground plane warping matrix can be derived with least square errors.

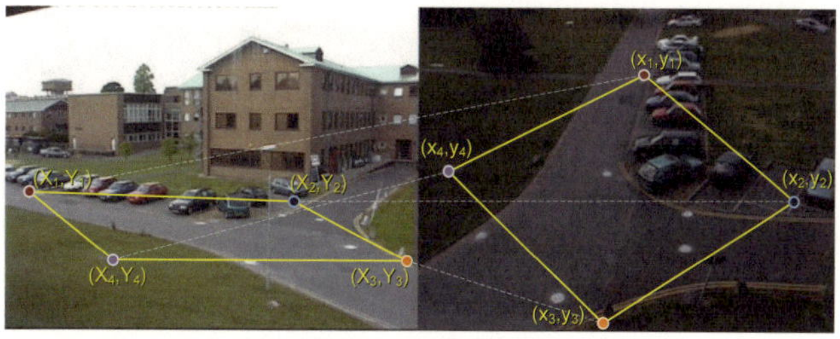

Fig. 9. Warping a ground plane from one view to another using homography transformation.

The bottom center of a bounding box of a mask is assumed to be the object ground point. However, for a mask of a person, the shadow in the mask may shift the ground point from the true position, and for a mask of a vehicle, the same object in different views may have totally different ground points. For instance, for the same car, the left rear tire is regarded as its ground point in one view, and the right rear tire may be regarded as its ground point in another view. For this issue, two concepts, earth mover's distance (EMD) Rubner et al. (1998) and trusting-former-pairs-more, are employed to prevent the generation of wrong matching pairs in this type of case.

EMD is originally used as a difference measure between two distributions. The distance measurement is modeled as a transportation problem, where a flow of goods with minimum transportation cost from suppliers to customers is required to be found and the minimum transportation cost per unit of good flow is defined as the earth mover's distance. In our matching approach, let $P = \{(\mathbf{p}_1, w_{\mathbf{p}_1}), ..., (\mathbf{p}_m, w_{\mathbf{p}_m})\}$ be the ground-point distribution with m converted coordinates of points from the first view to the second view with homography transform, where $\mathbf{p}_i$ is the converted coordinate of a point and $w_{\mathbf{p}_i}$ is the weighting of the point. Here we set the weighting to 1 since each point needs to be paired to only one point at most in the other view. Then let $Q = \{(\mathbf{q}_1, w_{\mathbf{q}_1}), ..., (\mathbf{q}_n, w_{\mathbf{q}_n})\}$ be the ground-point distribution with n points in the second view. We also let $\mathbf{D} = \{d_{ij}\}$ be the distance matrix where d_{ij} is the distance between $\mathbf{p}_i$ and $\mathbf{q}_j$. $\mathbf{F} = \{f_{ij}\}$ is the flow matrix where f_{ij} is 1 if and only if $\mathbf{p}_i$ and $\mathbf{q}_j$ are considered as a pair otherwise f_{ij} would be 0. Fig. 10 shows an example of notation representation. The objective is finding an $\mathbf{F}$ that will minimize the total cost function $C(P, Q, \mathbf{F})$

$$C(P, Q, \mathbf{F}) = \sum_{i=1}^{m} \sum_{j=1}^{n} d_{ij} f_{ij}, \tag{2}$$

and then the EMD(P, Q) is calculated as

$$\mathrm{EMD}(P, Q) = \frac{C(P, Q, \mathbf{F})}{\sum_{i}^{m} \sum_{j}^{n} f_{ij}}. \tag{3}$$

EMD tries to find the matching pairs that will minimize the overall cost. It means that if some ground point deviations exist, EMD still works correctly because it finds pairs with a minimum global cost but does not pursue a minimum matching distance one point by one point.

The other concept, trusting-former-pairs-more, is performed for stable and reliable consistency labeling. To work with satisfactory performance, we have to make an assumption that a new incoming object should keep its distance from other objects at the start. In this case,

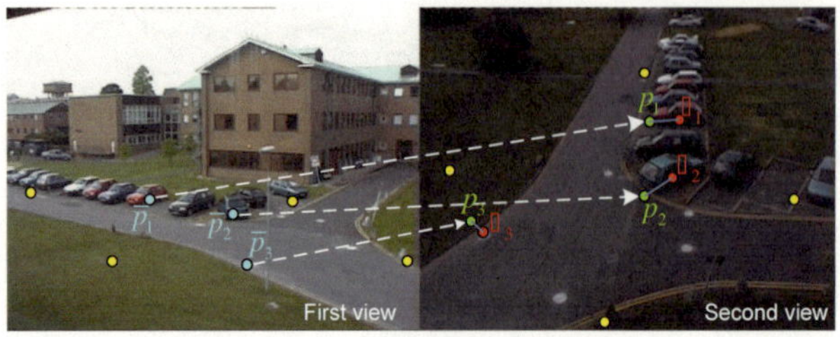

Fig. 10. Illustration of earth mover's distance. The ground point addresses $\bar{p}_i$ in the first view are converted to the addresses $\mathbf{p}_i$ in the second view. $\mathbf{q}_j$ are the ground point addresses in the second view. Yellow points are referenced points for generating a homography transformation matrix.

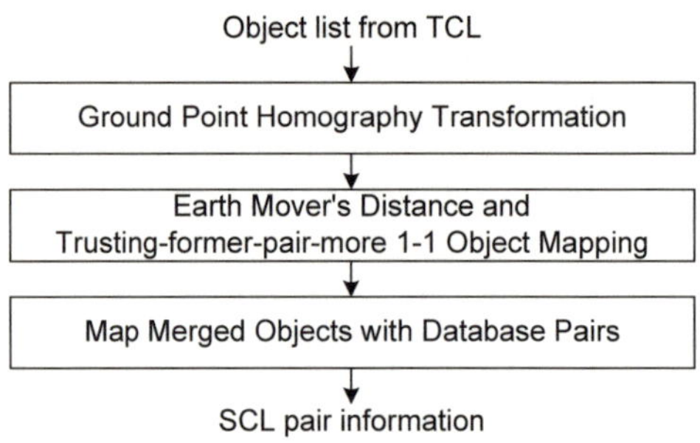

Fig. 11. Spatial consistency labeling flow.

if a new mask starts to appear in two cameras, the corresponding mask found at this time has higher confidence than the other corresponding masks found in the future, since the mask has relatively less occluding problems, less interactions with other masks, and fewer matching choices. Therefore, even if it has a large ground point deviation, the matching algorithm can still produce a correct pair. The pair still has chances to be renewed if the absolute point distance goes too far. The large absolute point distance reveals that a wrong pair has been generated, and the pair should be discarded from the database.

The overall flow of SCL is shown in Fig. 11. The database generated by single camera tracking, named as Temporal Consistent Labeling (TCL), is used as the input for SCL. The database provides the ground point information of single objects to EMD object matching. The concept of trusting-former-pairs-more is realized in the *one-to-one object mapping*. Note that the merged object masks are not matching in this stage because the ground point of a merged object is meaningless. Finally, the merged objects get the pair information from every single object before they are merged. This stage depends totally on the pairs in the history database.

One SCL result is shown in Fig. 12. Blue, green, red, and yellow grid points in two views are the given match points for homography matrix generation. The bounding boxes of objects with same color indicate they are matched pairs. A merged object will present alternately all color tags come from single objects paired before they are merged. Fig. 13 shows two cases that the pairs are renewed when their distances are larger than the predefined outlier distance. Fig. 13(a) shows that a man is leaving a car, which lead to an object splitting case. Fig. 13(b) shows that a car enters the left view but it is merged with the bike at the boundary. These errors are fixed at the SCL stage. In order to present the objective results of SCL, the concepts in multi-object tracking evaluation Smith et al. (2005) are employed and modified for SCL here. We define the ratio of the false pair number to the total ground true pair number in

Fig. 12. Spatial consistency labeling result. The merged object in left view contains green, red, and blue tag which represents the driver, the green car, and the dark blue car in turn. If an object in the left view is a single object, its transformed ground point is shown in the right view.

(a) (b)

Fig. 13. Fig. 13(a) shows that a man is leaving a car. The system has no prior information about the man in the car and the car is considered as a single object. Due to the warping point deviation, the car in the left view matches the man in the right view. Later, the distance between them is large enough for fixing their pairs. Fig. 13(b) shows that a car enters the left view but it is merged with the bike at the boundary. That mask is considered as same objects before and after the switching during object tracking stage. The error is fixed at the SCL stage.

an entire sequence as the averaged falsely identified pair ($\overline{FIP}$). The $\overline{FIP}$ of the PETS2001 sequence is 0.22, which means that there are 0.22 false pair per ground true pair. Most errors are generated from bad foreground masks and the situation when objects enter the view but occluded by others.

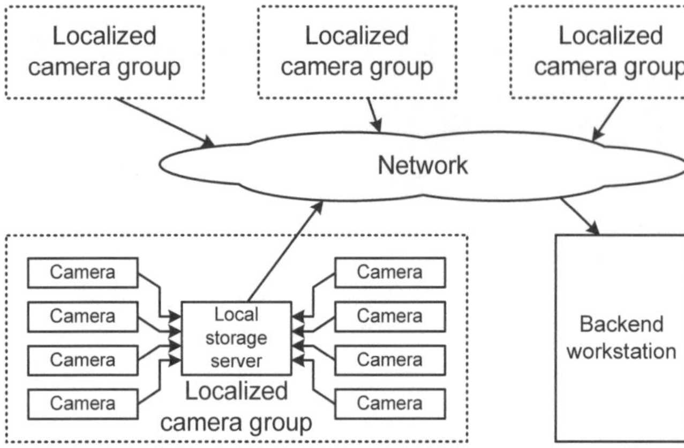

Fig. 14. Hierarchical surveillance system. In a localized area, bitstreams and object coordinates generated by each camera should be transmitted to a local storage server.

Running with on an Intel Core 2 Duo processor at 2.8 GHz, the SCL processing speed is about 4,638 fps per one pair of CIF-sized video channels. To carry out SCL, object positions from different cameras are needed to be transmitted to a server. Besides, all recorded bitstreams in a localized area should be stored for future inspection. These two reasons make the hierarchical surveillance system shown in Fig. 14 become reasonable. The local storage server stores all the data in this area, and the proposed low-complexity SCL makes it easy to be realized in this server.

6. Case study II: Cooperative surveillance system with fixed camera localization and mobile robot target tracking

The second case study is a cooperative surveillance system with fixed-camera localization and mobile-robot target tracking Chia et al. (2009). As shown in Fig. 15, the fixed cameras detect the objects with background subtraction and locate the objects on a map with homography transform with the techniques described in Section 3 and 5. At the same time, the information of the target to track, including the position and the appearance, is transmitted to the mobile robot. After breadth-first search in a map of boolean array, the mobile robot finds the target in its view by use of a stochastic scheme with the given information, then it will track the target and keep it in the robot's view wherever the intruder goes. With this system, the dead spot problem in typical surveillance systems with only fixed cameras is considered and resolved.

6.1 Motivation and introduction to the cooperative system

Recent approaches in surveillance systems typically include the use of static cameras along with the content analysis algorithms Regazzoni et al. (2001) Stauffer & Grimson (1999). The drawback is that blind spots cannot be covered, and intruders can try to avoid the fixed camera's sight, which results in less robustness for the surveillance systems. Systems employing pan-tilt-zoom (PTZ) cameras or omni-directional camera system can increase the covering range Micheloni et al. (2005) Foresti et al. (2005) Iwata et al. (2006). However, there may still exist blind spots and the covering area still depends on the cameras' positions decided in the deployment phase. Besides, several object tracking algorithms that are capable of tracking targets with a mobile camera are developed in recent years Maggio et al. (2007)

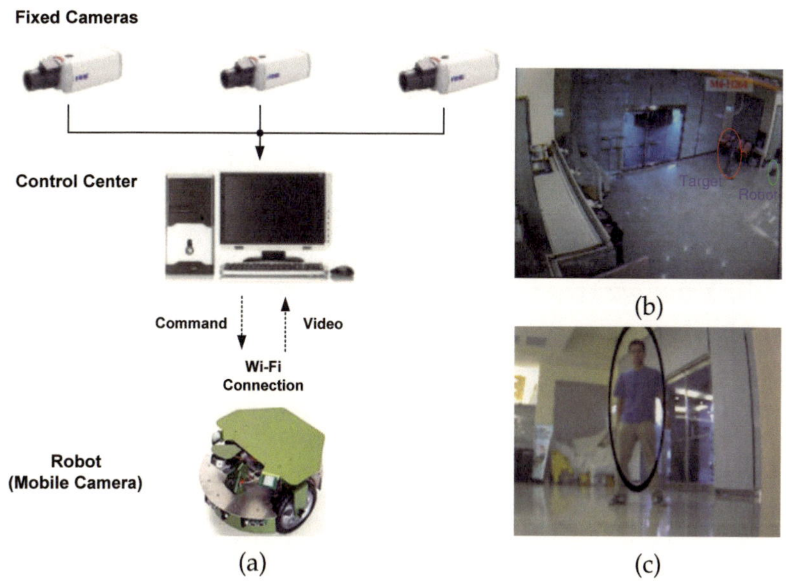

Fig. 15. (a) The proposed cooperative surveillance system. (b) Video captured by one fixed camera. (c) Video captured by the mobile robot.

Comaniciu et al. (2003). The critical issue in the use of these algorithms is the initialization of the tracker, which is usually manually selected without automatic initialization scheme.
We now introduce a prototype system which consists of fixed cameras and a mobile robot as shown in Fig. 15 and the overall operation flowchart is shown in Fig. 16. In this system, we propose a cooperation scheme between ZigBee localization system, fixed cameras and a mobile robot. The fixed cameras can do object detection and feature extraction automatically as described in Section 3. Then the object is localized on a map of the environment via homographic relations Bradshaw et al. (1997) between the fixed cameras and a global map, which is constructed in the camera calibration phase. After these fixed camera operations, the information of the object's location in the map and its appearance are provided to the mobile robot, in which a target finding algorithm and a target tracking algorithm are implemented. The robot will follow the target throughout the entire environment and keep it in the center of the robot's view.

6.2 Intruder detection and localization

In this section, the *Target Detection and Localization* subsystem in Fig. 16 is introduced. This subsystem integrates two localization mechanisms: *ZigBee Localization* and *Vision Localization*.

6.2.1 ZigBee localization

ZigBee is a specification for a suite of high level communication protocols using small, low-power digital radios based on the IEEE 802.15.4 standard for wireless personal area networks (WPANs). It is generally targeted at radio-frequency applications that require a low data rate, long battery life, and secure networking.
Being widely deployed in wireless monitoring applications with high-reliability and larger range, ZigBee transmitters are spread around the environment. We assume that all authorized in-comers should wear a ZigBee receiver so that their locations can always be monitored. The

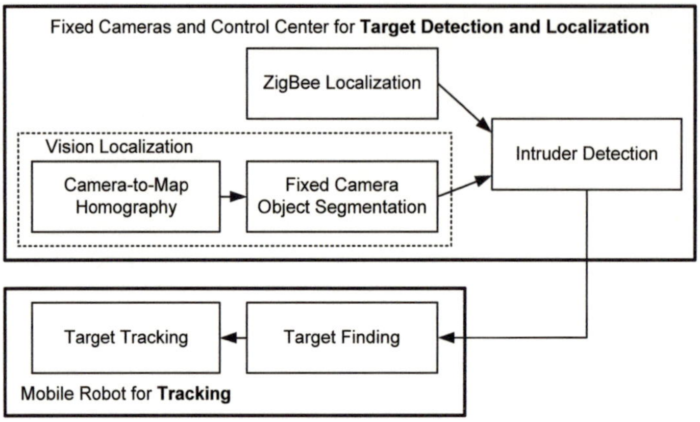

(a)

Fig. 16. the proposed cooperation scheme.

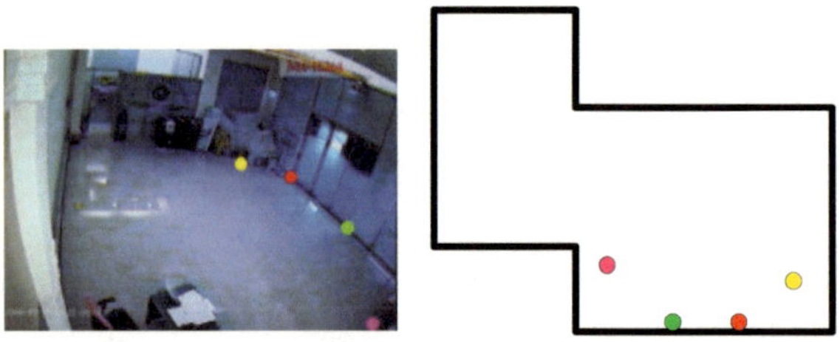

(a) (b)

Fig. 17. (a) Shot of the test environment taken by one of the fixed cameras and (b) a simple global map. The colored points are the four corresponding pairs of points chosen.

control center can receive information about the number of authorized visitors and their rough locations Lorincz & Welsh (2005).

6.2.2 Vision localization

Vision Localization is based on homography transform Bradshaw et al. (1997). After background subtraction and appropriate denoising, the segmentation result can be used to detect and localize the objects in the view of each fixed camera. Here, as described in Section 5, the bottom-centroid of each segmented object blob is treated as the object's location in the view of each fixed camera. In order to localize the object in a global coordinate system, a homography transform is employed to build the correspondences between the coordinates of fixed camera views and the coordinate of a global map, as shown in Fig. 17(b). The vision localization gives location information about all objects, including authorized and unauthorized, when they are detected with background subtraction.

6.2.3 Integration for identification

Identification (Intruder detection) can be easily done by comparing the results from *ZigBee Localization* in Section 6.2.1 and those from *Vision Localization* in Section 6.2.2. From the *ZigBee Localization*, the system receives information about the number of authorized visitors and their rough locations. At the same time, fixed cameras can find the objects (people), including authorized and unauthorized, and locate them in terms of global coordinates. Intruders, who have no authority to come in, are then detected by comparing the object information from the fixed cameras with those from the ZigBee system.

6.3 Mobile robot for tracking

From Section 6.2, the coordinate of the intruder can be inferred. A template of the intruder can also be obtained from the segmentation results in fixed cameras. Information about the object's location and appearance will then be transmitted immediately to the mobile robot to start tracking. In this section, we will introduce our *Tracking* subsystem in Fig. 16.

6.3.1 Target modeling and similarity measurement

Since the camera on the robot may be different from the fixed cameras, specific camera calibration techniques, including those for cameras with different lighting conditions and orientations, are useful for the processing and analysis Haralick & Shapiro (1992). The template of the intruder will be modeled with a color histogram, which is a viewing-angle-invariant feature. The object is represented by an ellipse. The sample points (pixels) of the model image are denoted by x_i and $h(x_i)$, where x_i is the 2D coordinates and $h(x_i)$ is the corresponding color bin index of the histogram. The number of color bin indexes used is denoted as β. The object's color histogram is constructed as follows.

$$p(u_j) = \sum_{i=1}^{I} k(\|\frac{x_i - c}{\sigma}\|)\delta[h(x_i) - u_j], 0 \leq j \leq \beta \tag{4}$$

where I is the number of pixels in the region, u_j is the color bin index in the histogram. σ is the bandwidth in the spatial space and c is the center of this object. δ is the Kronecker delta function. To increase the reliability of the color distribution, smaller weights are assigned to pixels farther away from the center (denoted as c), which are more likely to belong to the background. The chosen weighting function here is the Epanechnikov kernel : $k(u) = \frac{3}{4}(1 - u^2), |u| \leq 1$.

Here Bhattacharyya coefficient is adopted to measure the distribution similarity as shown with the following equations Comaniciu et al. (2003).

$$B(I_x, I_y) = \sqrt{1 - \rho(p_x p_y)} \tag{5}$$

where function ρ is defined as

$$\rho(p_x, p_y) = \int \sqrt{p_x(u) p_y(u)} du \tag{6}$$

6.3.2 Target finding with mobile robot

The mobile robot then receives information about the intruder, including its coordinate and appearance (color distribution). The initial location and the initial direction of the robot can be decided according to different environments in advance with respect to any target location. The mobile robot can go to any location, including the initial location, by breadth-first search with a 2D boolean array, in which the array element stores 1 or 0 indicating whether the location is reachable or not Cormen et al. (2001). After arriving at the initial location and turning to the initial direction with the help of a compass module, the robot finds the target within its view with a stochastic scheme. First, different hypotheses are made randomly about the target's location and size. Each hypothesis is again represented by an ellipse, with randomly chosen center, and the ratio of the two axis is fixed into 3.5:1 (which approximately stands for a person's ratio in height and width). The Bhattacharyya distance between the color histogram of each hypothesis and that of the target model is then calculated, and those hyposthsis with smaller disntances will be selected. Finally, the estimated target's location and size can be derived with the average of these selected hypothesis.

6.3.3 Target tracking with mobile robot

Particle filter with color-based features is employed for target tracking with mobile robot. Particle filter, also known as Sequence Monte Carlo method or Sampling-Importance-Resampling (SIR) filter, is a state estimation technique based on simulation Ristic et al. (2004) Nummiaro et al. (2003). Here, the state of target is described by the center of the ellipse and a scaling factor representing the length of axis, since the ratio of the two axes is fixed.

The idea of particle filter is to evaluate the probability of all the particles and thus estimate the location of our target. We use a particle sample set $S = \{s^{(n)} | n = 1 \dots N\}$, each sample s is a hypothetical state of the target.

After successfully locating the target according to Section 6.3.2, we can construct a sample set with all the samples equivalent to the target just found and then start evolution. Evolution of the particles is described by propagating each particle according to a Gaussian noise added to its center. Note that, many previous approaches propagated the particles according to a system model including moving direction and speed; however, it is not considered in our case since the tracker robot is also moving

After the particle propagation, weighting of the sample set can be computed by estimating the Bhattacharyya coefficients. We would give larger weights to samples whose color distributions are more similar to the target model. The weighting of each sample is given as follows:

$$\pi'^{(n)} = \frac{1}{\sqrt{2\pi}\sigma} e^{-\frac{1-\rho(p_{(n)},q)}{2\sigma^2}} \tag{7}$$

Normalizing $\pi'^{(n)}$ with the following equation, we obtain $\pi^{(n)}$.

$$\pi^{(n)} = \pi'^{(n)} / \sum \pi'^{(n)} \tag{8}$$

We can then estimate the location of our target as:

$$E[S] = \sum_{n=1}^{N} \pi^{(n)} s^{(n)} \tag{9}$$

In the last step, namely resampling, samples with higher weights will be reproduced more times than the samples with lower weights Ristic et al. (2004). When the next frame comes, the whole process can be repeated again to continue tracking.

After locating the target in each frame, the robot will judge if the target is in the left-side or the right-side of its view in order to decide which way it should turn. At the same time, it make a decision on going forward or backward according to the change in the target's scale, for example, going forward if the target's scale becomes smaller and going backward if the target's scale becomes bigger.

(a) (b)

Fig. 18. (a) Dr.Robot X80; (b) Vivotek WLAN Network Camera IP7137.

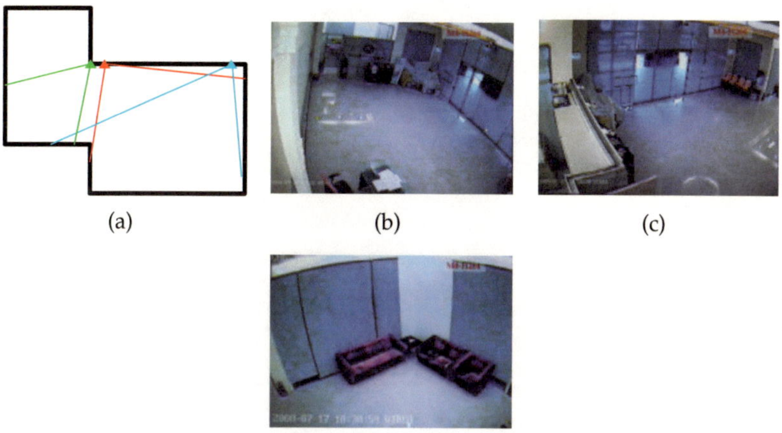

(a) (b) (c)

(d)

Fig. 19. The environment of Ming-Da Building: (a) A simple map of the environment with the three fixed cameras and their view range marked; (b) the image of camera colored in red; (c) the image of camera colored in blue; (d) the image of camera colored in green.

6.4 System implementation and experiment

6.4.1 System implementation

The control center is a PC with an Intel Core 2 Quad 2.4GHz CPU (1066MHz FSB), and all of the processing tasks are implemented with C♯ in Visual Studio 2005. The mobile robot we used is Dr.Robot X80. Instead of the using the built-in camera of the robot, Vivotek Network Camera IP 7137, a wireless camera with video streaming function, is equiped on the robot to provides the high-qulity video for analysis. The robot and the camera are shown in Fig.18. The overall system can track the target with the robot at 3–5 fps while the code is not optimized. Our test environment is the Technology Exhibition Center at the Ming-Da Building 1st floor of our university with three fixed cameras. The respective views of these three cameras are shown in Fig.19.

6.4.2 Experimental result

In this section, we present some results of this cooperative surveillance system. In the first place, two different scenarios are setup for testing this system. The first one (Fig.20) is that an intruder comes in and goes into the blind spots that fixed cameras cannot cover. The second scenario (Fig.21) is that an intruder is going out of the building, where the fixed

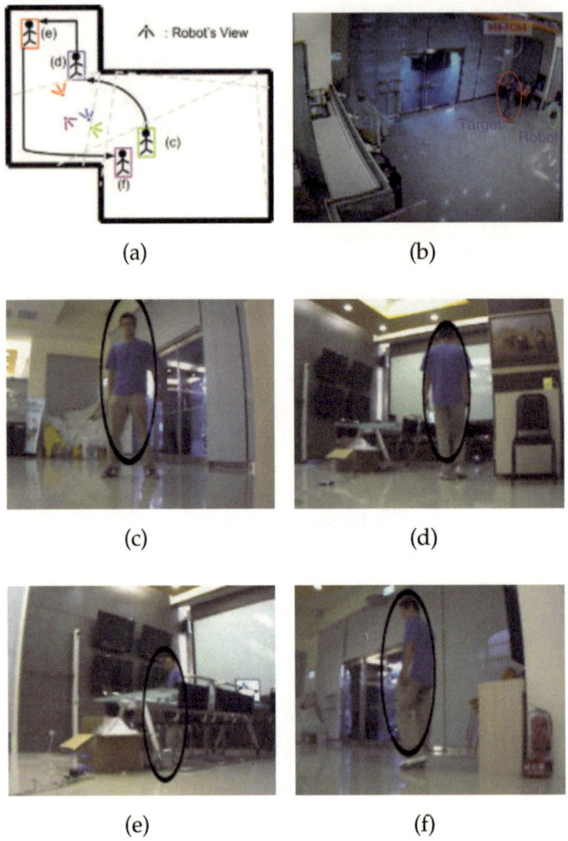

Fig. 20. Scenario one — blind spot experiment: in image (d) and (e), the intruder goes into a blind spot where the fixed cameras cannot see.

camera obviously cannot cover. In these two scenarios, our system have shown robustness in successfully locating and tracking the intruder.

In Fig.20 and Fig.21, each figure contains one map with four images. The map shows the intruder and the robot's route, where the small black man represents the intruder and a mark (viewpoint) represents the robot and its viewing direction. The four images are taken from the moving camera (i.e. the robot's view), and in each image, the target being tracked is shown with an ellipse surrounding it. In the map, the position of the green mark (robot) and the green-framed small man (target) shows where the first image is taken, while blue for the second image, red for the third image, and purple for the last image.

7. Conclusion

In this chapter, we discuss the data abstraction hierarchy and the system configuration of the next-generation surveillance systems. A conclusion has been made that each camera should be embedded with content analysis ability to become a smart camera instead of just an IP camera. The requirements of network condition, data storage, deployment space and cost are largely reduced, and even the content analysis accuracy can be enhanced with better input video quality. A simple example of smart camera SoC for the smart surveillance camera has

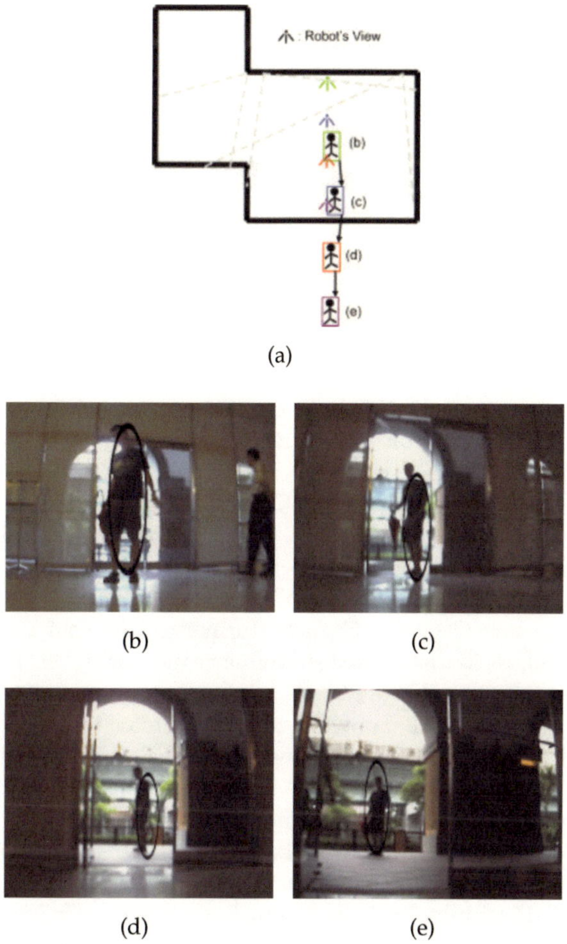

Fig. 21. Scenario two — out of building experiment, in image (d) and (e), the intruder escaped out of the door where the fixed camera cannot continue tracking.

been shown as well to show the feasiblity of the proposed concept. Finally, we provide two examples of cooperative surveillance systems, one is composed of multiple fixed cameras to jointly track objects across different camera views, and the other example is a cooperative surveillance system composed of fixed cameras and a mobile robot to resolve the blind-spot problem and the track initialization problem.

To construct robust and efficient next-generation smart surveillance systems, it is suggested that more robust content analysis algorithms should be developed. The hard conditions, such as occlusions and bad lighting conditions, should be considered and handled. Real-time performance is critical for visual surveillance camera network. More flexible programmable hardware accelerators should be designed and proposed in the future, especially for supporting more complex algorithms, such as particle filter for object tracking. Moreover, the cooperations between different cameras and even between different modalities, such as video, audio and wireless localization, should be a good way to further enhanced the performance and ability of futher systems. All the above-mentioned issues or topics would be interesting research directions for the researchers in this area.

8. Acknowledgements

The authors would like to thank Prof. Liang-Gee Chen, Dr. Jing-Ying Chang, and Dr. Tse-Wei Chen in National Taiwan University for discussion and information sharing. This work is partially supported by National Science Council, Taiwan (R.O.C.) under Grant NSC97-2220-E-002-012 and NSC97-2221-E-002-243-MY3. This work is also partially supported by VIVOTEK Inc. EDA tools are supported by Chip Implementation Center (CIC).

9. References

Bradshaw, K., Reid, I. & Murray, D. (1997). The active recovery of 3d motion trajectories and their use in prediction, *IEEE Transactions on Pattern Analysis and Machine Intelligence* 19(3): 219–234.

Cavallaro, A., Steiger, O. & Ebrahimi, T. (2005). Tracking video objects in cluttered background, *IEEE Trans. Circuits Syst. Video Technol.* 15(4): 575–584.

Chai, D. & Ngan, K. N. (1999). Face segmentation using skin-color map in videophone applications, *IEEE Trans. Circuits Syst. Video Technol.* 9(4).

Chan, W.-K. & Chien, S.-Y. (2006a). High performance low cost video analysis core for smart camera chips in distributed surveillance network, *Proc. IEEE Multimedia Signal Processing Workshop*, pp. 170 – 175.

Chan, W.-K. & Chien, S.-Y. (2006b). Subword parallel architecture for connected component labeling and morphological operations, *Proc. IEEE Asia Pacific Conference on Circuits and Systems*, pp. 936 – 939.

Chan, W.-K. & Chien, S.-Y. (2007). Real-time memory-efficient video object segmentation in dynamic background with multi-background registration technique, *Proc. IEEE Multimedia Signal Processing Workshop*.

Chang, J.-Y., Wang, T.-H., Chien, S.-Y. & Chen, L.-G. (2008). Spatial-temporal consistent labeling for multi-camera multi-object surveillance systems, *Proc. IEEE International Symposium on Circuits and Systems(ISCAS'08)*, pp. 3530–3533.

Chen, T.-W., Chan, W.-K. & Chien, S.-Y. (2007). Efficient face detection with segmentation and feature-based face scoring in surveillance systems, *Proc. IEEE Multimedia Signal Processing Workshop*.

Chia, C.-C., Chan, W.-K. & Chien, S.-Y. (2009). Cooperative surveillance system with fixed camera object localization and mobile robot target tracking, *Proc. Pacific Rim Symposium on Advances in Image and Video Technology*, pp. 886–897.

Chien, S.-Y., Chan, W.-K., Cherng, D.-C. & Chang, J.-Y. (2006). human object tracking algorithm with human color structure descriptor for video surveillance systems, *Proc. IEEE International Conference on Multimedia and Expo*, pp. 2097 – 2100.

Chien, S.-Y., Hsieh, B.-Y., Huang, Y.-W., Ma, S.-Y. & Chen, L.-G. (2006). Hybrid morphology processing unit architecture for moving object segmentation systems, *Journal of VLSI Signal Processing* 42(3): 241-255.

Chien, S.-Y., Huang, Y.-W., Hsieh, B.-Y., Ma, S.-Y. & Chen, L.-G. (2004). Fast video segmentation algorithm with shadow cancellation, global motion compensation, and adaptive threshold techniques, *IEEE Trans. Multimedia* 6(5): 732–748.

Comaniciu, D., Ramesh, V. & Meer, P. (2003). Kernel-based object tracking, *IEEE Trans. Pattern Anal. Machine Intell.* 25(5): 564–577.

Cormen, T. H., Leiserson, C. E., Rivest, R. L. & Stein, C. (2001). *Introduction to Algorithms, 2nd Ed.*, McGraw Hill/The MIT Press.

Elgammal, A., Harwood, D. & Davis, L. (2000). Non-parametric model for background subtraction, *Proc. European Conference on Computer Vision*, pp. 751–767.

Foresti, G. L. & Regazzoni, C. S. (2001). Video processing and communications in real-time surveillance systems, *J. Real-Time Imaging* 7(3).

Foresti, G., Micheloni, C., Snidaro, L., Remagnino, P. & Ellis, T. (2005). Active video-based surveillance systems: the low-level image and video processing techniques needed for implementation, *IEEE Signal Processing Mag.* 22(2): 25–37.

Haralick, R. M. & Shapiro, L. G. (1992). *Computer and Robot Vision*, Addison Wesley, Reading, MA.

Hartenstein, R. (2001). Coarse grain reconfigurable architectures, *Proc. Asia and South Pacific Design Automation Conference*, pp. 564–569.

Hu, W., Tan, T., Wang, L. & Maybank, S. (2004). A survey on visual surveillance of object motion and behaviors, *IEEE Trans. Syst., Man, Cybern.* 34(3): 334 – 352.

Iwata, K., Satoh, Y., Yoda, I. & Sakaue, K. (2006). Hybrid camera surveillance system by using stereo omni-directional system and robust human detection, *Lecture Notes in Computer Science, Advances in Image and Video Technology, IEEE Pacific-Rim Symposium on Image and Video Technology (PSIVT'06)*.

Kumar, P., Ranganath, S., Sengupta, K. & Huang, W. (2006). Cooperative multi-target tracking with efficient split and merge handling, *IEEE Trans. Circuits Syst. Video Technol.* 16(12): 1477–1490.

Lorincz, K. & Welsh, M. (2005). MoteTrack: A robust, decentralized approach to RF-based location tracking, *Proceedings of the International Workshop on Location and Context-Awareness (LoCA 2005) at Pervasive*.

Maggio, E., Smerladi, F. & Cavallaro, A. (2007a). Adaptive multifeature tracking in a particle filtering framework, *IEEE Trans. Circuits Syst. Video Technol.* 17(10): 1348–1359.

Micheloni, C., Foresti, G. & Snidaro, L. (2005). A network of cooperative cameras for visual-surveillance, *IEE Proc. on Visual, Image and Signal Processing* 152(2): 205–212.

Mozef, E., Weber, S., Jaber, J. & Tisserand, E. (2001). Urban surveillance systems: From the laboratory to the commercial world, *Proc. IEEE* 89(10).

Nummiaro, K., Koller-Meier, E. & Gool, L. V. (2003). An adaptive color-based particle filter, *Image and Vision Computing* 21(1): 99–110.

PETS (2007). PETS: Performance evaluation of tracking and surveillance. URL: *http://www.cvg.cs.rdg.ac.uk/slides/pets.html*

Ramanath, R., Snyder, W. E., Yoo, Y. & Drew, M. S. (2005). Color image processing pipeline: a general survey of digital still camera processing, *IEEE Signal Processing Mag.* 22(1): 34–43.

Regazzoni, C., Ramesh, V. & Foresti, G. L. (2001b). Special issue on video communications, processing, and understanding for third generation surveillance systems, *Proc. IEEE* 89(10): 1355–1367.

Ristic, B., Arulampalam, S. & Gordon, N. (2004). *Beyond the Kalman Filter: Particle Filters for Tracking Applications*, Artech House.

Rubner, Y., Tomasi, C. & Guibas, L. J. (1998). The earth mover's distance as a metric for image retrieval, *Technical Report STAN-CS-TN-98-86*, Stanford University, CA.

Semple, J. G. & Kneebone, G. T. (1979). *Algebraic Projective Geometry*, Oxford University Press.
Serra, J. (1982). *Image Analysis and Mathematical Morphology*, London: Academic Press.
Smith, K., Gatica-Perez, D., Odobez, J.-M. & Ba, S. (2005). Evaluating multi-object tracking, *Proc. IEEE Computer Society Conference on Computer Vision and Pattern Recognition*, pp. 36–43.
Stauffer, C. & Grimson, W. E. L. (1999). Adaptive background mixture models for real-time tracking, *Proc. IEEE International Conference on Computer Vision and Pattern Recognition*, p. 246ąV252.
Wolf, W., Ozer, B. & Lv, T. (2002). Smart cameras as embedded systems, *IEEE Computer* 35(9): 48–53.

8

SuperVision: Video Content Analysis Engine for Videosurveillance Applications

Lisa Usai, Francesco Pantisano,
Leonardo G. Vaccaro and Franco Selvaggi
Elsag Datamat S.p.A.,
Italy

1. Introduction

Greater challenges in the security area and declining cost of technology have promoted the development of ever more sophisticated video surveillance systems. Such systems are widely employed both in the public sector, to support police activities for example, and in the private sector, in banks, shopping centres security, etc, working 24 hours a day, 7 days a week.
Beside security applications, video surveillance is successfully employed in other fields, such as monitoring traffic or studying people's behaviour or consumer's preferences.
The increasing extent of the areas to be monitored requires the use of a large number of cameras. Video-streams flow to central control room and are displayed in real time to operators. The large amount of data makes the task of security staff demanding but also very tedious. Although security operators are trained, it's impossible they maintain high levels of attention when confronted with multiple inputs for more than a few minutes, (also because most of the time video streams show ordinary behaviour). Furthermore sociological researches (McCahill & Norris, 2003; Smith, 2004) have proven that often it is the operator who decides on which camera to focus his attention, basing the decision on the appearance rather than the behaviour of people in the scene.
Video content analysis represents a solution to these problems. Its main purpose is to analyze video streams and alert the operator only when relevant events are detected. This will help solve the problem of operators discontinuous attention.
Even the European community is paying close attention to these issues and in recent years several funded projects were launched to develop the most appropriate technologies to solve specific problems. The main goal of ISCAPS, for example, has been to reinforce security for European citizens and to try to reduce terrorist threats. The aim of SAMURAI is to develop and integrate an innovative intelligent surveillance system to monitor people and vehicle activities in critical public infrastructures and their surrounding areas. SUBITO addresses the problem of automated real time detection of abandoned luggage, fast identification of the owner and his/her subsequent path and current location.
The organization of intelligent video surveillance systems is hierarchical and generally starts with object detection, estimates the position of the detected object over time (object tracking) and describes what happens in the scene (event recognition).

The Elsag Datamat SuperVision system (SV) is a set of software technologies, whose aim is to support video surveillance systems development. It consists of a set of modules:

- A server that includes scene analysis, scene interpretation and alarm generation (it is the core of the system);
- A client that allows interaction with the user through streams viewer;
- A digital recorder of video streams, alarms and metadata.

The core algorithm of the SuperVision system uses Video Content Analysis technologies to describe the scene symbolically and to produce alarms when potentially hazardous actions occur: for example unattended baggage or crossing of not allowed areas are detected. The SV exploits special cameras, like the omnidirectional with fisheye or catadioptric optics and can drive a Pan/Tilt/Zoom (PTZ) camera to follow specific targets in the monitored area and it is capable of providing the operator with high resolution images of the area of interest.

The scene is described in world coordinates that consider the actual size of the monitored area and of the detected objects.

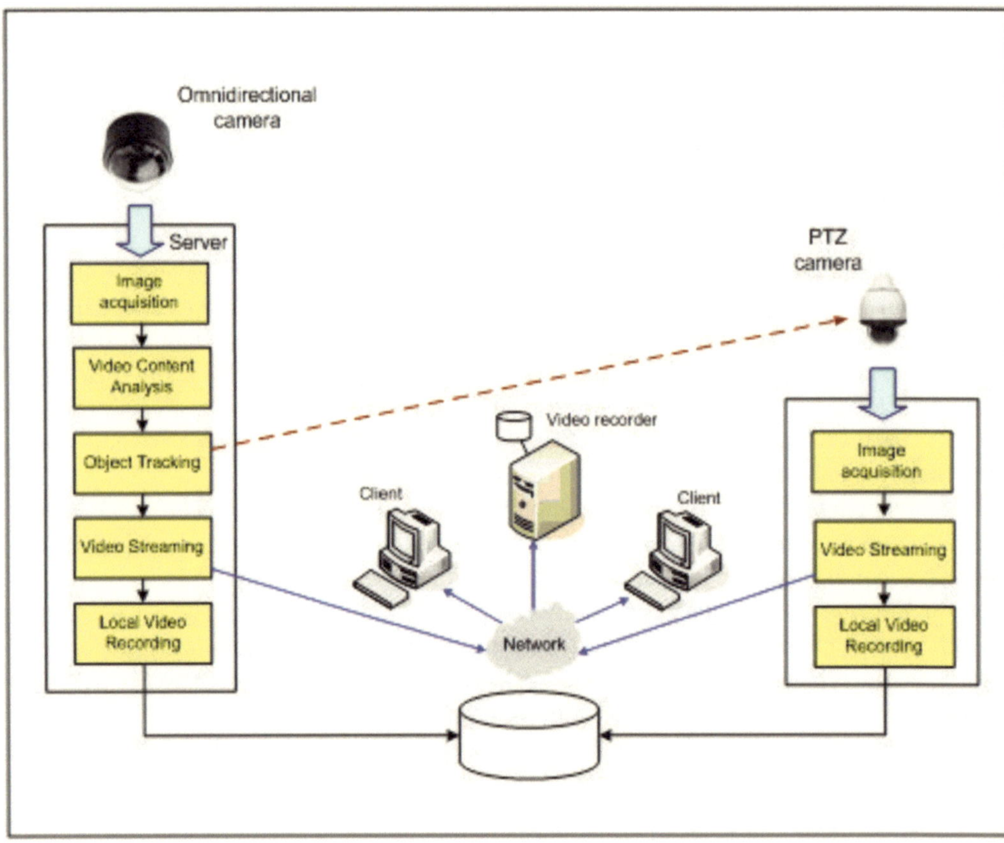

Fig. 1. Process flow

2. Features of SuperVision

The SuperVision system includes many video analysis functions that can be grouped into the following classes:

1. *General Video Content Analysis*. To extract synthetic information from video streams and describe moving objects in the scene. For each detected target, position, dimensions, type (person, vehicle, baggage), trajectory and radiometric features (intensity, colour) are extracted. (This information is called "metadata" and is collated to the video stream).
2. *Video Analytics*. Used, together with the analysis of metadata, to recognize preconfigured dynamic events and to report them as warnings or alarms. Typical filters are tripwire, unattended baggage, loitering, speed, abnormal direction detection. Video analytic applications are expected to grow meeting new requirements.
3. *Graphic Features*. Graphic features modify, with suitable transformations, images that are presented to the operator. The most common transformations are projection on the ground and correction of panoramic images (cylindrical projection and virtual PTZ).
4. *Support Features*. To help set up the operating environment. They include camera calibration (required for the system precision) and diagnostic functions (required to guarantee continuous operations).
5. *Automatic drive of PTZ camera*. It can be useful to capture high resolution images in the most interesting areas of the scene, although it isn't properly a video content analysis feature. Typically the PTZ is controlled automatically by the video analytic applications output, but it can also be controlled by Video Content Analysis metadata.

3. Omnidirectional optics

The omnidirectional optics can capture the scene with a 360° horizontal angle. Several (correlated) traditional cameras would be necessary to obtain an equivalent view. Common used optics are fisheye and catadioptric optics. The choice depends on applications. The former cover the half plane from the vertical to the horizon and are suited for fixed and dominant positions (high above the ground). The latter can look over the horizon but have a blind zone and they are suited for mobile applications and low height. The SuperVision system can manage both. In other words it's capable to convert their image coordinates in world coordinates (camera calibration is required).

3.1 Fisheye optics

The field of view of the fisheye optics is from 0° to about 95°. They cover the half plane from the vertical up to the horizon and thus they don't have a central blind zone. Their drawback is that the angular resolution goes down rapidly when moving away from the optical centre. The fisheye lens projects the image on the sensor with a transformation:

$$r = f \cdot \theta \tag{1}$$

Where r is the distance on the sensor from the optical centre, expressed in pixel, θ is the paraxial angle expressed in radiant and f is the focal length (in pixels) of the fisheye.

Fig. 2. Fisheye optic. On the left the optic's schema, on the right a fisheye lens.

3.2 Catadioptric optics

The catadioptric optics is formed coupling refractive lenses and reflective surfaces. In this way it is possible to achieve a field of view that extends above the horizon. The drawback of these types of optics is the presence of a blind zone at the optical centre that corresponds to the minimum tilt angle visible by the mirror. In other words the field of view is a ring that covers 360 degrees horizontally but only about from -10° to + 10° degrees vertically.

A convex mirror coupled with a traditional lens is the simplest configuration of catadioptric optics. The constraint is that the axis of symmetry of the mirror must coincide with the optical axis of the camera. This way the centre of projection is unique (Baker & Nayar, 1999) and it is quite simple to rectify the distortion due to the mirror and to produce geometrically correct planar prospective images. The profile of the mirror is typically hyperbolic because it's the only shape capable of removing the astigmatism, achieving a homocentric system. Unfortunately this solution has a strong drawback: it considerably reduces the resolution. In other words it's impossible to bring into focus the entire image.

Fig. 3. Single mirror catadioptric optic. On the left the optic's schema, on the right a catadioptric lens.

An alternative consists of two mirrors, one convex and one concave, coupled with a traditional lens. The profiles of the mirrors are (in general) parabolic and thus the system is homocentric. The presence of the two mirrors increases the degrees of freedom, attaining a partial correction of the curvature.

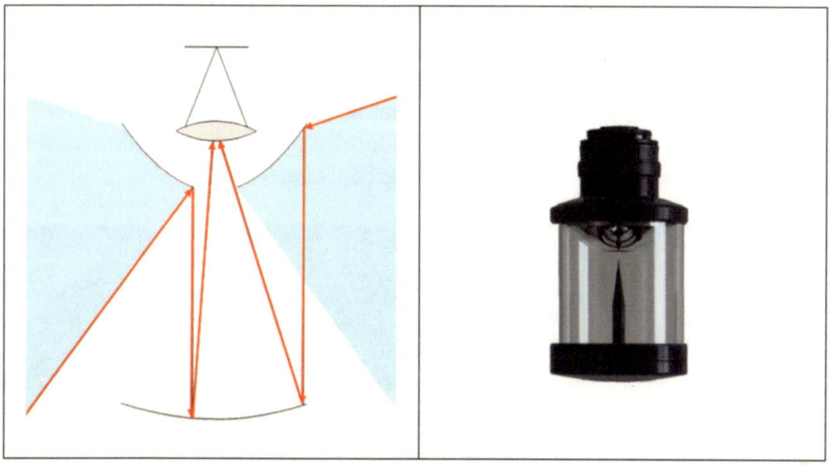

Fig. 4. Double mirror catadioptric optics. On the left the optics design principle, on the right an example of catadioptric lens.

A third solution, more expensive to realize, is a special refractive surface coupled with two reflective surfaces and a traditional lens. The refractive surface and the reflective one are realized with a single piece of optical glass and the reflection occurs inside the glass. The refractive surface is homocentric and its profile is described with a forth order polynomial. One of the reflective surfaces has a concave elliptical profile and the other a convex parabolic profile. Thus the whole system is homocentric. In addition the three surfaces increase the degrees of freedom and it is possible to accurately correct the curvature.

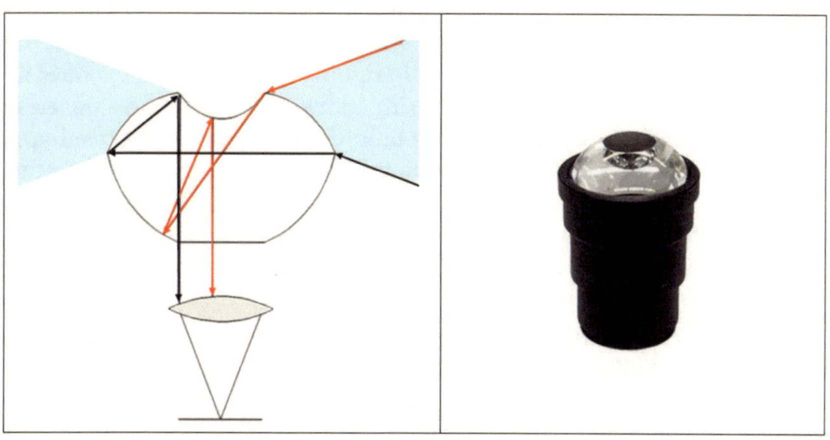

Fig. 5. Catadioptric optic with three surfaces. On the left the optic's schema, on the right a catadioptric lens.

The catadioptric optics projects the images with a transformation quite similar to the conformal projection:

$$r = 2 \cdot f \cdot tan\frac{\theta}{2} \tag{2}$$

where r is the distance on the sensor from the optical centre expressed in pixel, θ is the paraxial angle expressed in radiant and f is the focal length (expressed in pixels).
The peculiarity of the conformal projection is that both the angular resolutions (sagittal and tangential) are the same. Thus the image is not locally deformed. Furthermore the angular resolution increases with the distance from the optical centre.

Fig. 6. Comparison between the fisheye projection (on the left) and the catadioptric projection (on the right). In the catadioptric projection the local proportions are respected and the distortion at the centre of the image is lower than in the fisheye projection.

4. Video Content Analysis features

The Video Content Analysis is a technology that evaluates the contents of a video stream to extract specific information. The SuperVision system is a modular system that implements this kind of features according to the diagram in figure 7. Each module operates at different levels of abstraction. The first level deals with individual pixels (treated as individual entities). The output of these modules shows only the variation of the pixel appearing in different frames. The background updating module and the foreground detection module belong to this level. The purpose of these modules is to identify motion areas in the scene.
The second level does not consider pixel individually but as groups. At this level the clusterization of the foreground takes place, as well as the absorption of still groups in the background and clusters classification.
Finally the third level considers frame sequences and introduces temporal correlation among clusters. The tracking module belongs to this level.

4.1 Background updating

Moving object detection is a low level task necessary for the comprehension of high level events. There are different approaches (Elhabian et al., 2008). The SuperVision system

implements a statistical approach and considers each pixel independently basing its processing on the pixel temporal history.
First of all in a mobile temporal window the module calculates the average and the standard deviation of the pixel intensity. There is a state machine for each pixel that decides to update or not the tolerance and the reference. These four variables and the decision to update or not the background are stored in the "status of background" to be used in the next frame. Updating of background is based on the difference between the standard deviation and the tolerance. If the first is greater than the second the pixel is considered as belonging to a moving object and its reference and tolerance value are not updated.
A counter is initialized to measure the length of the lock, i.e. a measure of how long the background has been maintained unchanged. If the counter exceeds a predefined threshold a background update is forced (action performed by the "absorption of still clusters" module).

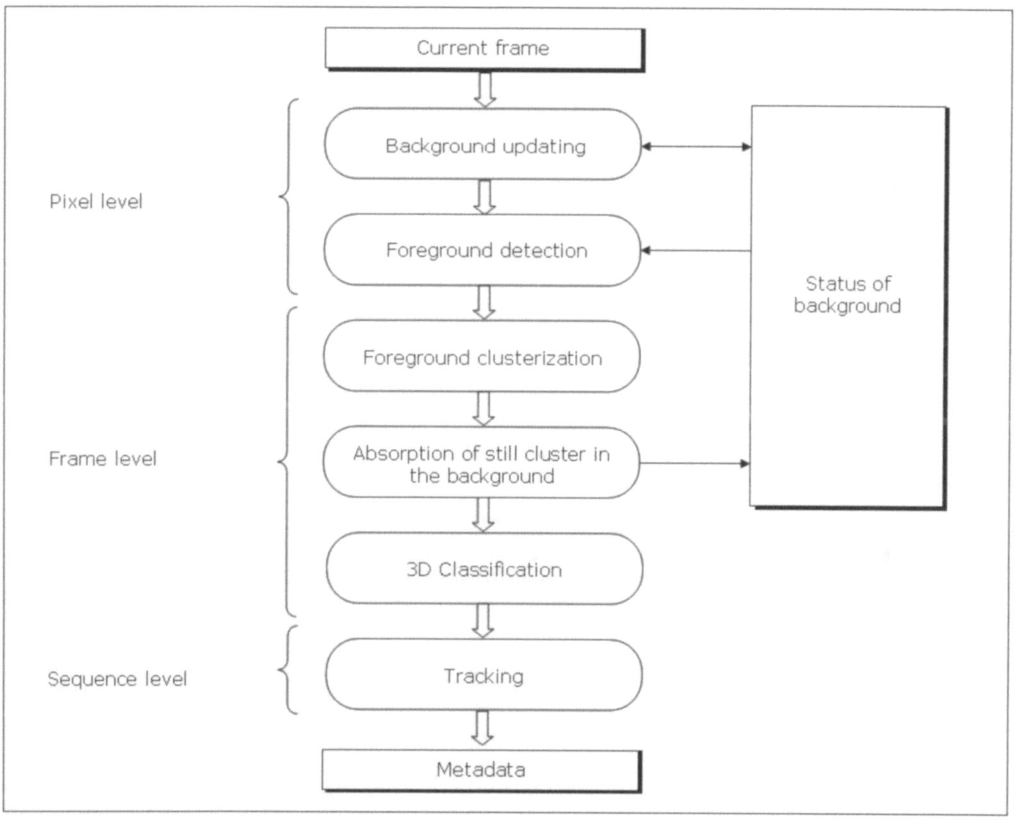

Fig. 7. SuperVision core algorithm flow diagram

4.2 Foreground detection

The foreground pixels are those with a considerable distance from the reference value of the background. The module decides if a pixel belongs to the foreground by comparing its intensity value with the reference and tolerance values. The module shows a noise tolerance as it is based on the signal standard deviation.

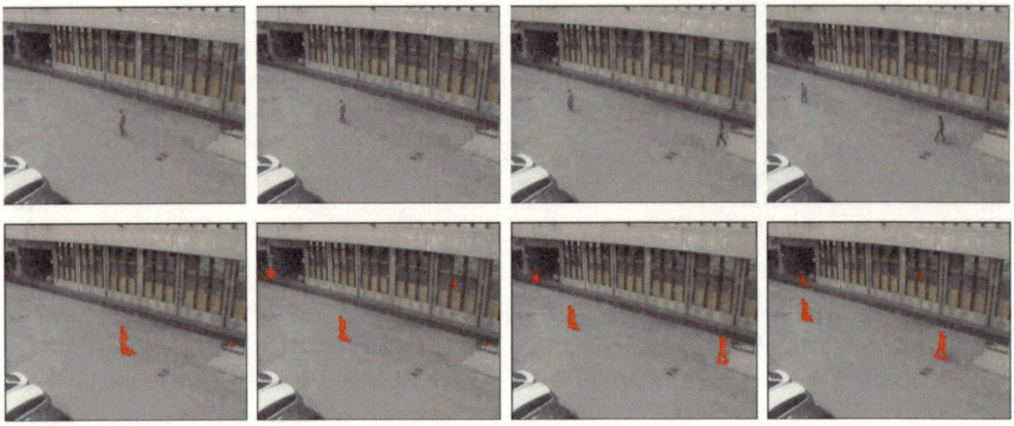

Fig. 8. Output of the foreground detection.

4.3 Foreground clusterization

The foreground clusterization module action is at frame level. It works aggregating neighbouring pixel. Pixels that are closer to each others have high probability of belonging to the same object. These clusters represent the area of interest for the next process steps.

4.4 Absorption of the cluster in the background

For each cluster of interest every pixel is under the control of the algorithm. When a considerable number of pixels are in a locked status, a background update is forced. All the information about the background and the foreground of the cluster are stored on a dedicated buffer. This way it is possible to control the absorption of stationary targets for a long time, by preserving their state in memory. Stationary targets do not interfere with moving objects and, if they start to move, they can be recognized thanks to the information saved in the status buffer.

This mechanism allows a multilayer management of the background.

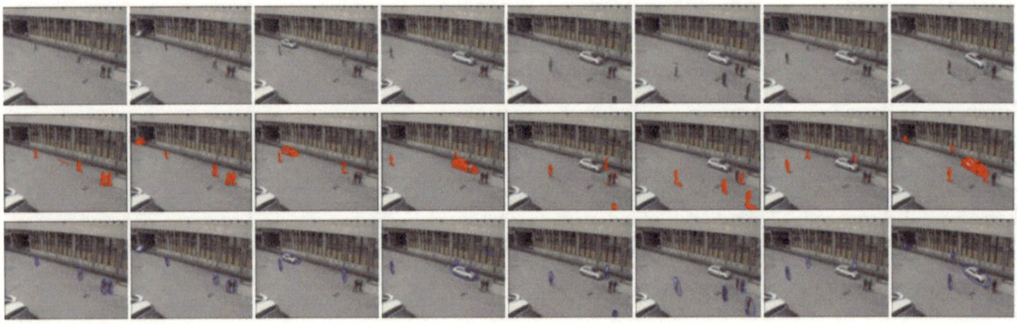

Fig. 9. Output of the foreground clusterization. In the first row some frame of the original sequence, in the middle the output of the foreground detection and in the bottom, circled in blue, the clusters. We can see how still cluster (like the two persons in the third frame and the car in the fifth frame) are reabsorbed into the background and they don’t interfere with the other moving targets.

4.5 3D classification

The 3D classification module works with real world coordinates. For each cluster of interest it projects, on the image, different 3D models of the target. For each 3D model the "silhouette" is calculated and is compared with the cluster. The model with the greatest likeness is chosen and its position and its orientation in world coordinate are calculated.
For the next step, the tracking module, the real position of the cluster and its radiometric information are also required. Finally this module can be used to segment clusters into different targets if they are too close. Alternatively the same module can fuse more clusters into a single target if they are fragmented. Camera calibration (to convert image coordinates into world coordinates) is needed to project the model on the image.

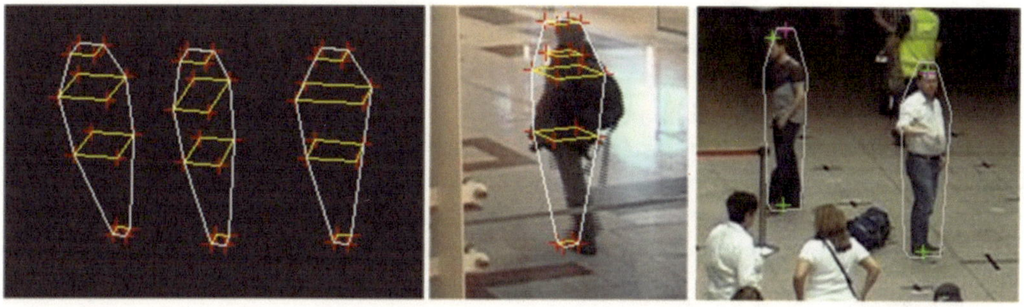

Fig. 10. On the left different 3D model of a person. In the middle and on the right the output of the 3D classification.

4.6 Tracking

The task of the tracking module is to estimate the trajectory of a moving object in the scene (Yilmaz et al. 2006). This module analyzes the target behavior in time, through the re-identification of the detected targets on a frame by frame basis.

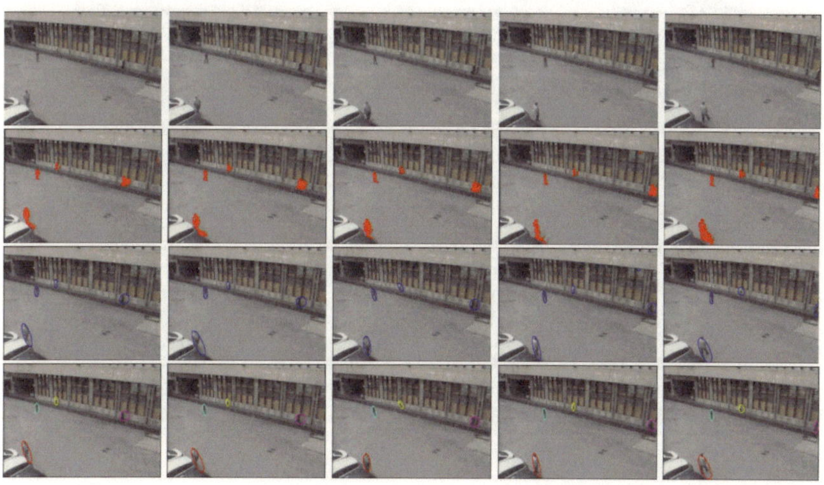

Fig. 11. Output of tracking module. In the first row the original sequence, in the second row the motion detection output, in the third one the foreground clusterization output and in the last row the tracking output. Each person is identified with a different colour, coherently with time.

The re-identification is based on the neighbourhood, the speed in world coordinates and the geometric and radiometric features of the target. It is then possible to associate a label coherent with time and thus it is possible to describe not only statically but also dynamically all the detected targets.
Each target is defined by its metadata: information about position, velocity (trajectory), dimension, radiometric features and classification (person, car, etc.)

5. Video Analytic applications

The effectiveness of the surveillance system operation can be considerably increased by Video Analytics. These are specialized applications that perform the task of real-time event detection as well as post-event analysis, saving manpower costs and providing an immediate alert upon detection of a relevant event. These applications are also called filters and they must be customized by parameterization. The parameterization is a procedure to customize the events to detect. Instead of general functions which produce output frame by frame, filters produce asynchronous events.
Typical filters are target tracking, tripwire, abnormal direction, speed, unattended object, loitering, graffiti and vandalism acts, falls, climbing, people counting and crowding detection. In the following readers can find a brief description of the most used filters.

1. ***Object detection.*** It's used to detect targets in one or more regions of the area under surveillance.
2. ***Tripwire detection.*** It's used to detect targets entering a restricted area. When a target passes on a tripwire, an alarm is raised.

Fig. 12. Example of tripwire detection. The detected target is circled in red.

3. ***Abnormal direction detection.*** The abnormal direction detection filter is used to detect objects moving in opposite direction with respect to the expected direction.
4. ***Detection of fast moving objects.*** This filter is used to detect moving targets travelling above a pre-defined speed.

5. ***Unattended/Removed object detection.*** Used to detect still targets in the scene. It can be used to detect unattended or removed objects.
6. ***Loitering detection.*** Unlike the speed detection filter, it is used to detect moving targets that remain in an area for longer than a predefined time.
7. ***Graffiti and vandalism acts detection.*** With this filter it is possible to detect relevant and permanent background changes. This event can be detected only with significant delay.
8. ***Detection of people laying (fall detection).*** It can be used to detect people laying, in particular to detect falling people.
9. ***Climbing detection.*** Similar to fall detection filter, climbing detection is used to detect people assuming abnormal position and pose. Generally is used to detect people that climb turnstiles or barriers.
10. ***People counting passing over a tripwire.*** This filter is used to define how many people pass across a tripwire and the direction of transit. The output of the filter is a series of event at the predefined frequency supplied with the following information: the tripwire label, the time and the number of people crossing the tripwire during the last interval of time. In this case the events are not random but at regular intervals.
11. ***People counting in a region of interest.*** Similar to counting people passing across a tripwire filter, it is used to evaluate how many people are in a predefined area. The output of the filter is a series of events at the predefined frequency with the following information: the area of interest, the time and the number of people in the area. As in the previous case the events are not random but at regular intervals.
12. ***Crowding detection.*** It can be used to detect the presence of excessive crowding in one or more predefined areas.

The parameters that can be customized are summarized in the following table:

	Area or Tripwire of interest (*)	Class of the object	Availability of a "SV controlled" PTZ	General parameters (i.e. inertia and radiometric sensitivity)	Motion or crossing direction	Minimum time of persistence in the detected status (**)	Dimensions of the object to detect	Threshold (***)	Counting frequency
Object detection	•	•	•			•			
Tripwire detection	•	•	•		•				
Abnormal direction detection	•	•	•		•	•			
Overspeed detection	•	•	•	•		•		•	
Unattended/ Removed object detection	•		•	•		•	•		

	Area or Tripwire of interest (*)	Class of the object	Availability of a "SV controlled" PTZ	General parameters (i.e. inertia and radiometric sensitivity)	Motion or crossing direction	Minimum time of persistence in the detected status (**)	Dimensions of the object to detect	Threshold (***)	Counting frequency
Loitering detection	•	•	•	•		•			
Graffiti and vandalism acts detection	•							•	
Detection of people laying (fall detection)	•		•	•		•		•	
Climbing detection	•		•	•		•		•	
People counting passing over a tripwire	•				•				•
People counting in a region of interest	•								•
Crowding detection	•		•	•		•		•	

Table 1. Customizable parameters

(*) The area or tripwire is defined by drawing a polygonal over the image or a ground projection of the area under surveillance.
(**) This parameter has different interpretation according to the filter. Its meaning is reported in the following table:

Filter	Minimum time of persistence in the detected status
Object detection	Minimum time the object must remain in the area to be detected
Abnormal direction detection	Minimum time the object must remain in the area to be detected
Overspeed detection	Minimum time of persistence of the object above the speed limit
Unattended/Removed object	Minimum time of persistence in the motionless

Filter	Minimum time of persistence in the detected status
detection	status
Loitering detection	Minimum time of persistence in the predefined area
Detection of people laying (fall detection)	Minimum time of persistence in the position
Climbing detection	Minimum time of persistence in the abnormal position
Crowding detection	Minimum time of persistence in the crowding status

Table 2. Meaning of the minimum time of persistence parameter

(***) This parameter has different interpretation according to the filter. Its meaning is reported in the following table:

Filter	Threshold
Overspeed detection	Speed limit
Graffiti and vandalism acts detection	Extension (in percentage) of the change to detect
Detection of people laying (fall detection)	Laying pose, expressed as percentage of the height of the object
Climbing detection	Abnormal pose, expressed as percentage of the height and the barycentre value
Crowding detection	Crowding (number of people)

Table 3. Meaning of the threshold parameter

6. Coordinate transformation support

A class of functions and tools that convert point's coordinates into different reference systems and to rectify images from omni-directional devices.
These operations are required to generate images that are more easily understood by surveillance operators and to generate ground projections of the images. The latter case is useful to define the tripwire and thus to generate alarms when these barriers are crossed. By coupling these features with the camera calibration, virtual PTZs can be implemented.

6.1 Coordinates conversion

As already stated, the SuperVision system works in real world coordinates, so it is necessary to convert the various coordinate reference systems.
The reference systems types are:

- Image coordinates, expressed in pixel, represent the point coordinates on the stored image buffer. They are indicated with the couple (U,V);
- Focal coordinates, expressed in pixel, represent the point coordinates on the focal plane. They are indicated with the vector $(Q_1, 0, Q_3)$;
- Local world coordinates, expressed in meters, represent the point coordinates on the local system of reference of the camera. They are indicated with the vector (P_1, P_2, P_3).

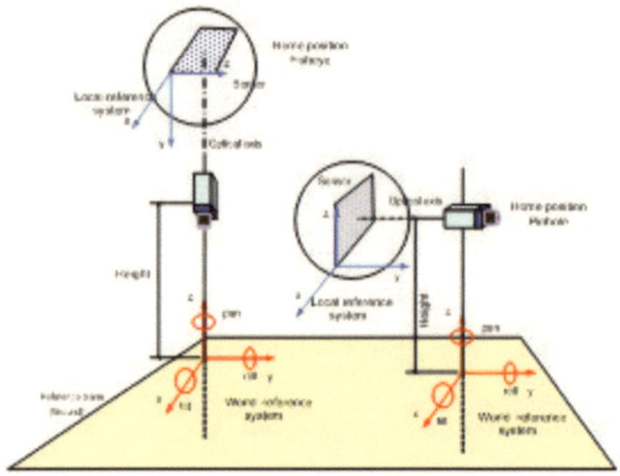

Fig. 13. Camera reference system for local world coordinates (ground projection of the camera position)

In the following sections the conversions between different systems of reference are described.

6.1.1 Image coordinates to focal coordinates

This conversion takes into account the optical centre position on the image (U_C, V_C), the anisotropy of the sensor (C_A) and the (possible) distortion. If the distortion is positive the warped image has distances from its centre greater than the original image (pin cushion distortion) and the focal coordinates are calculated as follows:

$$Q_1 = \frac{x}{y} \cdot \hat{Q}_1 \qquad Q_3 = \frac{x}{y} \cdot \hat{Q}_3 \tag{3}$$

where:

$$\hat{Q}_1 = U - U_C$$
$$\hat{Q}_3 = \frac{V}{C_A} - V_C$$
$$\hat{Q} = \sqrt{\hat{Q}_1^2 + \hat{Q}_3^2}$$
$$y = \frac{\hat{Q}}{R_{MAX}}$$

x is obtained inverting the polynomial $y = x + ax^3 + bx^5$, $a \geq 0$, $b \geq 0$.

a is the third order distortion coefficient, b is the fifth order distortion coefficient and R_{MAX} is the half diagonal of the image expressed in pixel.

If the distortion is negative ($a \leq 0$, $b \leq 0$) the warped image has distances from the centre less than the original (barrel distortion) and the focal coordinates are calculated as follows:

$$Q_1 = \hat{Q}_1 \cdot \left[1 - a \cdot \left(\frac{\hat{Q}}{R_{MAX}}\right)^2 - b \cdot \left(\frac{\hat{Q}}{R_{MAX}}\right)^4\right] \quad Q_3 = \hat{Q}_3 \cdot \left[1 - a \cdot \left(\frac{\hat{Q}}{R_{MAX}}\right)^2 - b \cdot \left(\frac{\hat{Q}}{R_{MAX}}\right)^4\right] \tag{4}$$

6.1.2 Focal coordinates to local world coordinates

This conversion varies with the camera type.

For a pin-hole camera the conversion from focal coordinates to world coordinates is obtained using the following formulas:

$$P_1 = Q_1 \qquad P_2 = F \qquad P_3 = Q_3 \tag{5}$$

where F is the focal of the camera.

For a fish-eye camera, instead, the conversion is obtained using the following formulas:

$$P_1 = Q_1 \qquad P_2 = E \qquad P_3 = Q_3 \tag{6}$$

where

$$E = \begin{cases} \dfrac{Q}{\tan\theta} & per \quad \theta \geq \dfrac{1}{500} \\ F & per \quad \theta < \dfrac{1}{500} \end{cases}$$

e

$$\theta = \frac{Q}{F}$$

6.2 Projections

The rotational symmetric lenses can be represented by a single general model. This model, in polar coordinates, is described by the equations:

$$\begin{cases} u = r(\theta)\cdot \cos\phi \\ v = r(\theta)\cdot \sin\phi \end{cases} \tag{7}$$

where

u,v are the coordinates of the point in the focal plane, θ is the paraxial angle of the field of view, *r* is a function of θ, and ϕ is the polar angle.

The local sagittal focal length is expressed by the formula:

$$F_S = \frac{\partial r}{\partial \theta} \tag{8}$$

while the local tangential focal length is the quantity:

$$F_T = \frac{r}{\sin\theta} \tag{9}$$

Different values of r(θ) produce different projections. The most common are:

- *Perspective projection or Gnomonic projection.* The pinhole camera is the simplest device to capture the geometry of perspective projection. The relationship between a point on the image plane and a point on the focal plane is:

$$r = F \cdot \tan\theta \tag{10}$$

with $\theta < \frac{\pi}{2}$.

Homogeneous coordinates handle the problem in a linear way. In this kind of projection the sagittal and the tangential focal length are different, that is the local object proportions in the projected image are not maintained, as can be inferred by the following formulas:

$$F_S = \frac{F}{\cos^2\theta} \tag{11}$$

$$F_T = \frac{F}{\cos\theta} \tag{12}$$

- *Conformal cylindrical projection.* It can be used to represent cylindrically a panoramic image. In this kind of projection the sagittal and the tangential resolution are equal, thus the local proportions of the object are maintained.

$$\begin{cases} U = F \cdot \phi \\ V = F \cdot \ln\left[\tan\frac{\theta}{2}\right] \end{cases} \tag{13}$$

$$F_S = F_T = \frac{F}{\sin\theta} \tag{14}$$

θ cannot reach the limit value 0 and π.

- *Stereographic projection.* It can be used for polar representation of a panoramic image (projection of a sphere onto a plane). Like the cylindrical projection it is a conformal transformation, that is it preserves angles and thus the local proportions of the objects. The r(θ) function for this projection is:

$$r = 2F \cdot \tan\frac{\theta}{2} \tag{15}$$

and the sagittal and the tangential focal length are:

$$F_S = F_T = F \cdot \cos^{-2}\frac{\theta}{2} \tag{16}$$

In the SuperVision system it is used for the virtual PTZ.

6.3 Virtual PTZ

The virtual PTZ function simulates the behaviour of a PTZ camera using as source the panoramic images. Coupling this feature with a high resolution sensor it's possible to produce detailed views of any part of an image, based on virtual parameters of pan, tilt and zoom. This allows the monitoring of areas that normally are not controlled by traditional camera and, thanks to the high resolution, to extract features of particular interest such as detail of the action occurring, plate numbers or faces. An example is shown in figure 15. The camera is mounted on a car. This allows to control what happens around it. The virtual PTZ can be activated in an automatic way, choosing on the rectified image the target of interest and requesting tracking, or manually when only the prospective projection of a portion of image is required.

Fig. 14. Example of a virtual PTZ. On the left a fisheye image. In the middle and on the right the prospective projections of the circled areas, based on the pan, tilt and zoom parameters.

Fig. 15. Example of a virtual PTZ. On the left an image from a catadioptric lens mounted over a car. In the middle the projection of the area circled in red and on the right the projection of the area circled in green.

7. Support features

Camera calibration and diagnostic functions are the support features of the SuperVision system. Camera calibration evaluates the real dimensions of the targets in the scene to track

their position and to classify them. It is also required to put in relation real points and the remote control parameters of the PTZ used to track objects.
The diagnostic functions, instead, allow the detection of tampering or faults in the system, such as the obscuring, shift of the camera, malfunctioning, etc.

7.1 Camera calibration

The target of the calibration is the evaluation of a set of parameters of the camera and the position of the camera in the world (camera coordinates and camera orientation) with respect to a reference plane (typically the ground plane). This process is necessary in those applications where metric information of the environment derives from images. In order to do the evaluation, the calibration process needs information about the image positions and world measures on a set of "calibration points".
The user specifies a set of segments anchored to the reference plane in two possible ways: either the segments lie on the plane (horizontal segments) or on a line normal to the plane with one end touching the horizontal plane (vertical segment). The only world information needed is the actual segment length.
Starting from the knowledge of some parameters such as the dimensions in pixel of the sensor, the position of the optical centre and, for a fisheye camera, the maximum radius of the image, it is possible to estimate the intrinsic parameters, that describe the internal geometry of the camera (focal expressed in pixel) and the extrinsic parameters, that define its position and its orientation (roll angle, tilt angle, height).
In this way the camera is calibrated on a reference system on the ground. The origin of this reference system corresponds to the on-ground camera projection, X and Y axes lay on the ground with Y direction parallel to the on-ground optical axis projection. In this reference system three camera extrinsic parameters (X, Y and pan angle) are always null.

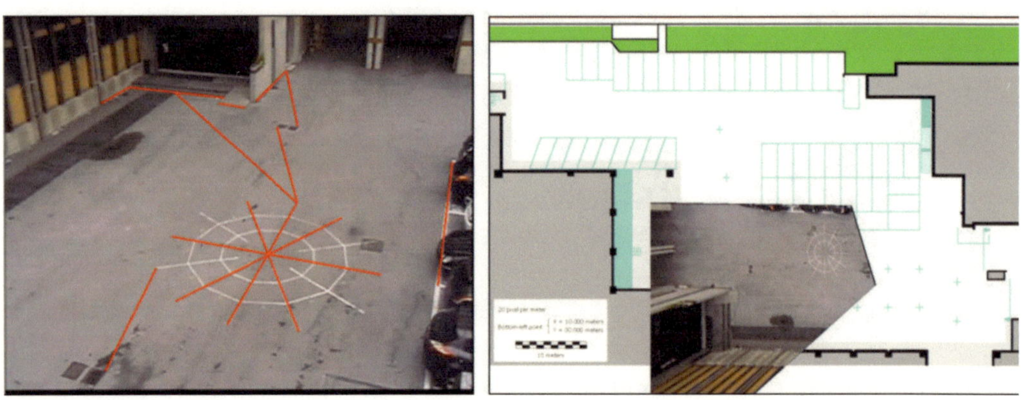

Fig. 16. On the left the image from the uncalibrated camera with the known length segments. On the right the ground projection of the image based on the calibration parameters (X=61.18 m, Y=18.52 m, Z=10.40 m, Pan=109.59°, Tilt=-30.75°, Roll=0.78°)

When two or more cameras have been calibrated, it is possible to link them to a common reference system. After selecting one of the cameras as the reference camera, the three null extrinsic parameters (X, Y and pan) of the other cameras are computed.

This process is called registration. For each camera the registration is equivalent to a rototranslation of the on-ground projection image. In order to evaluate the correct rototranslation, a set of corresponding points (on the ground) are selected on the two on-ground projection images, and a least-square method is applied. In this way it's possible to define not only the real dimensions of the objects in the scene, but also their position with respect to a reference system shared from all cameras (e.g. necessary for multicamera tracking). If a site map is available, it can be used as a substitute of the reference camera. Cameras position and orientation are anchored to any given reference system. After calibration and registration it is possible to generate a composite image using portions of the ground plane projection images.

Fig. 17. Map obtained with the multicamera calibration.

In the SuperVision system, the "controlled" PTZs are also calibrated. This is necessary in order to control these cameras based on the detected events referenced to world coordinates. The PTZ calibration is required to obtain correspondence between the PTZ camera and images from the traditional or omnidirectional camera. When the features of the camera (focal and dot pitch), the pan and the tilt angle and the target position in the image are known the system returns to the PTZ the relative angular shifts.

7.2 Diagnostic functions

The diagnostic functions provide alarms when the effectiveness of a camera is compromised. Lack of signal, voluntary or accidentally shift of the camera from its setup position, bad quality of the signal, due for example to the obscuring of the lens or to the loss of focus, are the detected events.

The operator is immediately alerted and solicited to take corrective actions.

Camera shift is detected comparing the background, which contains fixed elements of the scene, with the video stream. The background is periodically updated to take into account the environmental changes. The gradient of these images is calculated and then a binary threshold is applied. The Hausdorff's distance between the gradients is used to decide if a change in the background occurs or not. In the following picture the output of the comparison of the two gradients is reported. When a change in the scene occurs, the background superimposed on the new image tends to rapidly disappear (fig. 18 e) and the distance between the two images is high.

Fig. 18. Example of diagnostic function. The figure a) shows a "standard" scene, that contains its invariant elements (in this case the upper part of the image). The figure b) shows the gradient of the background after applying the binary threshold. Figures c) and d) show the scene before and after the shift of the camera and in figure e) the result of the comparison.

8. Automatic control of PTZ cameras

The PTZ camera is automatically controlled by the SuperVision system, based on the world coordinates received from the fixed system. This allows high resolution tracking of a specific target, extraction of interesting features and continuous pointing of the camera only to those areas where action is detected, avoiding the storage of video of limited interest.

When an event is detected, for instance the crossing of a tripwire, the PTZ camera sets itself on the target which has produced the event and it moves according to the target position upon the image plane. The quantity of shift is known thanks to the camera calibration. Once the tilt angle of the first position is known, the shifts are calculated whenever the target is too close to the image boundaries. In this way the object is always into the camera field of view.

Fig. 19. Examples of PTZ automatic control.

9. Conclusions and future works

The aim of all video surveillance automatic systems is to avoid tedious chores for the operators. In this paper we described Elsag Datamat approach to satisfy these requirements. The SuperVision system can analyze video streams from different types of camera, in particular omnidirectional, and to set alarms when preconfigured events are detected. The types of events detected are numerous, and can be composed according to the context and needs of applications. Future improvements will include new modules, such as face detection and recognition, for automatic check of people's identity.

10. References

Baker, S. & Nayar, S. K. (1999). A theory of single-viewpoint catadioptric image formation, *International Journal of Computer Vision (IJCV)*, Vol. 35, No. 2, pp. 175–196

Elhabian, S. Y., El-Sayed, K. M. & Ahmed, S. H. (2008). Moving object detection in spatial domain using background removal techniques - State-of-art, *Recent Patents on Computer Science*, Vol. 1, No. 1, January 2008, pp. 32-54, ISSN: 1874-4796

ISCAPS project (2006). www.iscaps.reading.ac.uk

McCahill, M. & Norris, C. (2003). CCTV systems in London: their structures and practices, In: *On the threshold to Urban Panopticon?: Analysing the Employment of CCTV in*

European Cities and Assessing its Social and Political Impacts, Technical University, Berlin.

SAMURAI project (FP7/2008-2011). www.samurai-eu.org

Smith, G.J.D. (2004). Behind the screens: examining constructions of deviance and informal practices among CCTV control room operators in the UK, *Surveillance & Society. CCTV Special,* Vol. 2 Issue 2/3, pp. 376–395.

SUBITO project (FP7/2009-2011). www.subito-project.eu

Yilmaz, A., Javed, O. & Shah, M. (2006). Object tracking: A survey. *ACM Computing Surveys,* Vol. 38, No. 4, December 2006, pp. 1-45, ISSN:0360-0300

9

Multi-Stage Video Analysis Framework

Andrzej Czyżewski, Grzegorz Szwoch, Piotr Dalka, Piotr Szczuko,
Andrzej Ciarkowski, Damian Ellwart, Tomasz Merta,
Kuba Łopatka, Łukasz Kulasek and Jędrzej Wolski
Gdansk University of Technology, Multimedia Systems Department,
Poland

1. Introduction

Video monitoring systems are a necessity in the modern times. Although some people object the idea of 'being watched', surveillance systems actually improve the level of public security, allowing the system operators to detect threats and the security forces to react in time. Surveillance systems evolved in the recent years from simple CCTV systems into complex structures, containing numerous cameras and advanced monitoring centers, equipped with sophisticated hardware and software. However, the future of surveillance systems belongs to automatic tools that assist the system operator and notice him on the detected security threats. This is important, because in complex systems consisting of tens or hundreds of cameras, the operator is not able to notice all the events.

In the last few years many publications regarding automatic video content analysis have been presented. However, these systems are usually focused on a single type of human or vehicle activity. No complex approach to the problem of automatic video surveillance system has been proposed so far. In order to address this problem, the authors designed a framework that analyses camera images on multiple levels, from basic detection of moving objects to advanced object recognition and automatic detection of important events. The proposed system has a flexible structure, with functional modules that may be selected so that the system suits the need of a particular application. These modules are based on algorithms proposed by various authors, adapted to the needs of the presented framework and enhanced by the authors in order to provide an efficient solution for automatic detection of important security threats in video monitoring systems.

The chapter is organized as follows. Section 2 presents the general structure of the proposed framework and a method of data exchange between system elements. Section 3 is describing the low-level analysis modules for detection and tracking of moving objects. In Section 4 we present the object classification module. Sections 5 and 6 describe specialized modules for detection and recognition of faces and license plates, respectively. In section 7 we discuss how video analysis results provided by other modules may be used for automatic detection of events related to possible security threats. The chapter ends with conclusions and discussion of future framework development.

2. Framework structure

The system for intelligent video analysis has a distributed architecture (Fig. 1), consisting of multiple node stations, one central station and operator stations. Node stations are placed in the monitored area, close to video acquisition sensors (i.e. cameras). They are responsible for camera management and for automatic analysis of images from all cameras in their vicinity. Each node station contains a small-factor PC running Linux operating system and equipped with video analysis software. The computer is enclosed in a weather-proof casing which makes possible to mount a node station outdoors. Results of video analysis are sent from node stations to the central station for storing, evaluating and notifying operators. Central station is also responsible for aggregation results coming from multiple node station in order to detect large-scale, global threats. Such configuration makes possible to use wide-band, short-distance cable connections between cameras and node stations to transfer high-quality video streams and wireless communication medium to send results of analysis to the central station. The system operator has access to the analysis results and camera images from the whole system through the operator station which consists of a monitor set, controllers and computers with the specialized software. Depending on the network throughput available, there is also a possibility to view live video streams from any camera in the system from an operator station.

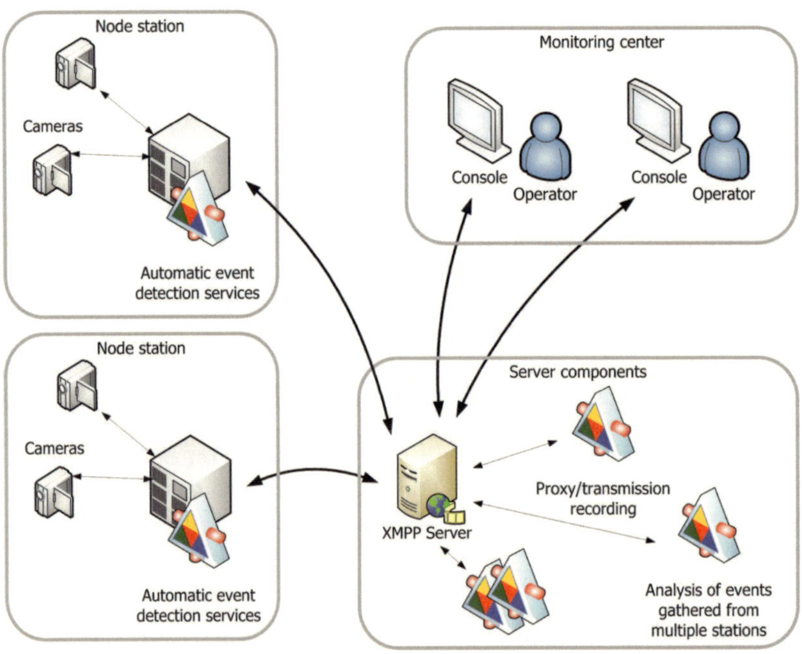

Fig. 1. Video analysis system architecture

An important aspect of the proposed system is the issue of data transmission. A layered approach was devised, based on TCP/IP protocols suite, which enables the sensitive data to be transferred by means of open Internet, regardless of the presence of Network Address Translators or firewalls which typically interfere with establishment of multimedia communication sessions. At the foundation of the developed solution lays the Extensible Messaging and Presence Protocol (XMPP), which is designed for building Instant Messaging systems, but thanks to its virtually-unlimited extensibility, it is an increasingly popular tool for general-purpose application servers and distributed applications. Its use provides an added value of security and message integrity layer (based on TLS standard), authorization, addressing scheme and a container for information structuring within self-describing, XML-based messages. Furthermore, XMPP grants access to a plethora of the protocol extensions developed by its mature community, which may be found surprisingly useful within the context of surveillance solution. Such particular extension, which is very important for the proposed system, is so-called Jingle protocol, which is a tool for establishing multimedia communication sessions. This forms the core of the system's audio and video streaming functionality. In fact Jingle is a session-control (signaling) protocol while the actual multimedia data transfer is performed out-of-band of XMPP connection due to performance reasons. For this purpose encrypted Realtime Transfer Protocol (RTP) sessions are utilized. As a consequence, the initiation of multimedia streaming may be problematic in the presence of NAT devices or firewall on the route between transmission endpoints. Therefore, an additional proxy service has been implemented within the system, which allows for the efficient multimedia transmission between any connected terminals regardless of their network conditions.

Two types of digital cameras are employed in the video monitoring system. Stationary (fixed), wide-angle cameras, especially megapixel ones, offer a wide field of view and are used for video content analysis and event detection. The other type - pan-tilt-zoom (PTZ) cameras - allow for adjusting their field of view as required and they are used for automatic tracking of objects, selected either manually by an operator or automatically by the event detection system. PTZ cameras provide an operator with a detailed view of the situation.

Video analysis performed in the node station is a multi-stage process (Fig. 2). It consists of low-level image processing modules and high-level event detection modules. First, all moving object present in a fixed camera field of view are detected in each video frame, independently. Then, all moving objects are tracked in the adjacent video frames, as long as they stay in the camera field of view, in order to obtain characteristics of their movements. Various static (e.g. shape, texture) and dynamic (e.g. location, speed, heading) object features are used to classify them into a few groups (e.g. humans, cars). Object features are used in the final, high-level analysis stage for automatic detection of important events. Event detection is supplemented by additional, specific modules, such as face detection and recognition, license plate recognition and others. The main functional modules of the framework will be presented in detail further in this chapter.

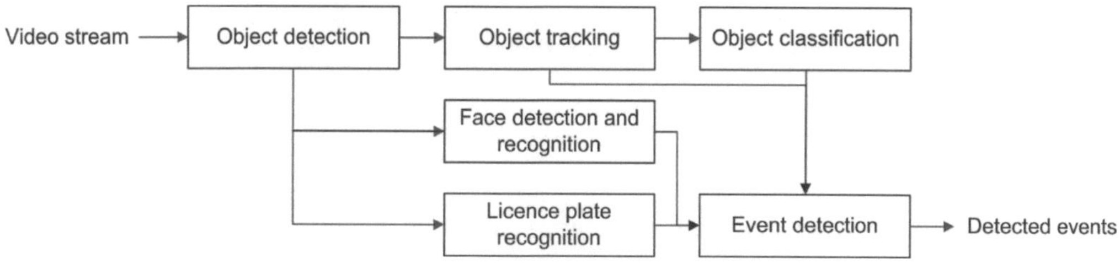

Fig. 2. Framework for video processing in the node station

3. Detection and tracking of moving objects

3.1 Object detection

Detection of moving objects is usually the first stage of video processing chain and its results are used by further processing modules. Most video segmentation algorithms usually employ spatial and/or temporal information in order to generate binary masks of objects (Li

& Ngan, 2007; Liu & Zheng, 2005; Konrad, 2007). However, simple time-averaging of video frames is insufficient for a surveillance system because of limited adapting capabilities. The solution implemented in the framework utilizes spatial segmentation for detection of moving objects in video sequences, using background subtraction algorithm (Yang et al., 2004). This approach is based on modeling pixels as mixtures of Gaussians and using an on-line approximation to update the model (Elgammal et al., 2000; Stauffer & Grimson, 2000). This method proved to be useful in many applications, as it is able to cope with illumination changes and to adapt to the background model accordingly to the changes in the scene, e.g. when motionless foreground objects eventually become a part of the background. Furthermore, the background model can be multi-modal, allowing regular changes in the pixel color. This makes it possible to model such events as trees swinging in the wind or traffic light sequences.

Background modeling is used to model current background of the scene and to differentiate foreground pixels of moving objects from the background (Dalka, 2006; Czyzewski & Dalka, 2007). Each pixel in the image is modeled with a mixture of K Gaussian distributions for this purpose. The probability that a pixel has the value x_t at the time t is given as:

$$p(x_t) = \sum_{i=1}^{K} w_t^i \eta\left(x_t, \mu_t^i, \Sigma_t^i\right) \tag{1}$$

where w_t^i denotes the weight and μ_t^i and Σ_t^i are the mean vector and the covariance matrix of i-th distribution at the time t, and η is the normal probability density function:

$$\eta(x_t, \mu, \Sigma) = \frac{1}{(2\pi)^{0.5 \cdot D} \sqrt{|\Sigma|}} e^{-0.5 \cdot (x_t - \mu)^T \Sigma^{-1} (x_t - \mu)} \tag{2}$$

where D is the number of elements describing pixel color; for the RGB color space D is equal to 3. It is assumed that each Gaussian distribution represents a different background color of a pixel. The longer a particular color is present in the video stream, the higher value of the weight parameter w of the corresponding distribution.

With every new video frame, the parameters w, μ and Σ of distributions for each pixel are updated according to the on-line K-means approximation algorithm. In the first step, distributions are ordered based on the value of the r coefficient given as:

$$r = \frac{w}{\sqrt{|\Sigma|}} \tag{3}$$

where $|\Sigma|$ is the determinant of the covariance matrix Σ. A particular color of the scene background is usually more often present in the observation data than any color of foreground objects and as such is characterized by the low variance. Thus a distribution with a higher r value represents the background color more accurately.

Every new pixel value x_t is checked against existing distributions, starting from the distribution with the highest value of the r coefficient, until the first match is found. The pixel matches the distribution if its color lies within 2.5 standard deviations of the distribution. If there is no match, a distribution with the lowest r value is replaced with the new one with the current pixel as its mean values, an initially low weight and high variances. The weight of the first matching distribution is increased, while the weights of other distributions are decreased based on the value of the learning rate parameter α (Dalka, 2006). The higher the α is the faster model adjusts to changes in the scene background (e.g. caused by gradual illumination changes), although moving objects, which remain still for a longer time (e.g. vehicles waiting at traffic lights), would quicker become a part of the background.

If there is a matching distribution, its mean and variance values are tuned according to the current value of the pixel; the speed of converging is determined by the learning rate α [7]. Only the first D distributions of pixel x in time t ordered by the decreasing r coefficient value are used as the background model where D is defined as:

$$D_x^t = \arg\min_d \left(\sum_{i=1}^{d} w_i^{\ t} > T \right) \tag{4}$$

If T is small, then the background model is usually unimodal. If T is higher, the background color distribution may be multimodal, which could result in more than one color being included in the background model. This make possible to model periodic changes in the background, properly. If the current pixel value does not match any of the first D distributions, it is considered as a part of a foreground object.

Object segmentation is supplemented with shadow detection and removal module. The shadow of a moving object moves together with the object and as such is detected as a part of the foreground object by a background removal algorithm. The shadow detection method is based on the idea that while the chromatic component of a shadowed background part is generally unchanged, its brightness is significantly lower (Horprasert et al., 1999; Dalka, 2006). Every new pixel recognized as a part of a foreground object during the background subtraction process is checked whether it belongs to a moving shadow. If the current pixel is darker than the distribution and its color lies within 2.5 standard deviations of the model for at least one of the first D distributions forming the background model, the current pixel is assumed to be a shadow and is considered as a part of the scene background.

In the result of background modeling, a binary mask denoting pixels recognized as belonging to foreground objects in the current frame is obtained. It needs to be refined by the means of morphological processing in order to allow object segmentation (Dougherty & Lotufo, 2003; Dalka, 2006). This process includes finding connected components, removing objects that are too small, morphological closing and filling holes in regions. Additionally, an algorithm for shadow removing from the mask using morphological reconstruction is implemented (Xiu et al., 2005). The morphological reconstruction procedure involves two binary images: a mask and a marker. In the mask image, all pixels belonging to either the moving object or the shadow have value of one, and all the background pixels have zero value. The marker is obtained by applying an aggressive shadow removal procedure to the object detection result, so that all the shadow pixels are removed, some pixels belonging to the moving object may also be removed in this process (the object mask is damaged). The marker is first 'cleaned' by removing isolated pixels, then it is dilated by a structural element which usually has a large size (typically, 9 x 9 structural element is used). The result of marker dilation is then combined with the mask using logical AND operation. As a result, shadows are removed and the moving object masks are properly reconstructed. Example results of moving object detection in a single video frame are presented in Fig. 3.

Fig. 3. Example results of moving object detection: original video frame (left) and binary mask denoting moving objects (right)

3.2 Object tracking

After the moving objects are found in each consecutive camera frame, movement of each object on the frame-by frame basis is needed. This is the task of an object tracking module. For each new detected moving object, a structure named a tracker is created. The position of the object in the current camera frame is found by comparing the results of object detection (the blobs extracted from the image) with the predicted position of each tracker. The prediction process estimates the state of each tracker from the analysis of the past tracker states. An approach based on Kalman filtering (Welch & Bishop, 2006) was used for prediction of trackers state in the presented framework.

The state of each tracked object is described by an 8-element vector, containing parameters related to object position in the camera image (x, y), the size of object's bounding box (width w, height h) and change of these parameters relative to the previous frame (Czyzewski & Dalka, 2008). Therefore, the state of the tracker in frame n is described by the vector X_n:

$$X_n = \left[x_n, y_n, w_n, h_n, dx_n, dy_n, dw_n, dh_n\right]. \tag{5}$$

The vector X is initialized in the first two frames in which the object was found. For each successive frame, the predicted state of the tracker is calculated by the Kalman filter. Next, the predicted state of the trackers is compared with the blobs found by object detection. A relation between a tracker and a blob is established if the bounding box of the tracker covers the bounding box of an object by at least one pixel. The tracker is then updated with the measurement - the position of the matching blob.

If there is an unambiguous one-to-one relation between one blob and one tracker, this tracker is updated by the state of the related blob. However, if there is more than one matching blob and/or tracker, a tracking conflict occurs. The authors proposed the following algorithm for conflict resolving. First, groups of matching trackers and blobs are formed. Each group contains all the blobs that match at least one tracker in the group and all the trackers that match at least one blob in the group. Next, all the groups are processed one by one. Within a single group, all the trackers are processed successively. If more than one blob is assigned to a single tracker, this tracker is updated with all blobs assigned to it, merged into a single blob. This is necessary in case of partially covered objects (e.g. a person behind a post) that causes the blob to be split into parts. In other cases. all the matching blobs are merged and the tracker is updated using its estimated position inside this blob group. This approach utilizes the ability of Kalman trackers to predict the state of the tracked object, provided that it does not rapidly change its direction and velocity of movement, so that the predicted state of the Kalman filter may be used for resolving short-term tracking conflicts. The estimated position is used for updating the tracker position, change of position is calculated using the predicted and the previous states. The predicted values of size and change in size are discarded and replaced by values from the previous filter state, in order to prevent disappearing or extensive growth of the tracker, if its size was unstable before entering the conflict situation. Therefore, it is assumed that the size of the object does not change during the conflict. The vector of parameters used for updating the Kalman tracker during the conflict may be written as:

$$X_n = \left[x_{pn}, y_{pn}, w_{n-1}, h_{n-1}, x_{pn} - x_{n-1}, y_{pn} - y_{n-1}, dw_{n-1}, dh_{n-1}\right] \quad (6)$$

where index p denotes the value predicted by the Kalman filter, n is the frame number.

A special case of tracking conflict is related to 'splitting objects', e.g. if a person leaves a luggage and walks away. In this situation, the tracker has to follow the person and a new tracker needs to be created for the luggage. This case is handled as follows (Szwoch et al, 2010). Within each group of matching trackers and blobs, subgroups of blobs separated by a distance larger than the threshold value are found. If there is more than one such subgroup it is necessary to 'split' the tracker: select one subgroup and assign the tracker to it, then create a new tracker for the remaining subgroup. In order to find the subgroup that matches the tracker, the image of the object stored in the tracker is compared with the image of each blob, using three measures: color similarity, texture similarity and coverage. The descriptors of the blob are calculated using the current image frame. The descriptors of the tracker are calculated during tracker creation and updated each time the tracker is assigned to only one blob (no conflict in tracking).

After the conflict resolving is done, the tracking procedure finishes with creating new trackers for unassigned blobs and removing trackers to which no blobs have been assigned for a defined number of frames. The process is repeated for each camera frame, allowing for tracking the movement of each object.

Fig. 4 presents an example of object tracking with conflict resolving, using the procedure described here. A person passes by a group of four persons walking together. During the conflict, positions of both objects are estimated using the Kalman filter prediction results. When these two objects become separated again, assignment of trackers to blobs is verified using the color, texture and coverage measures. As a result, both objects are tracked correctly before, during and after the conflict occurs.

The proposed algorithm for object tracking and conflict resolving provides correct results in case of short-term conflicts involving low to moderate number of objects. Performance of this procedure decreases in case of high number of objects conflicting with each other. It should be also noted that if the object detector passes incorrect data to the object tracker, e.g. masks of the objects are distorted because of improper lighting conditions, tracking errors are inevitable. Several directions of further work on the presented procedure are considered in order to improve the algorithm for long-term conflicts occurring with high frequency. For example, the parameters of Kalman filters related to estimation process may be selected adaptively, instead of being constant. This way, tracker may adapt to different tracking conditions. Moreover, a simplified estimation of tracker position, based solely on tracker estimation, may be enhanced by using an algorithm searching for the object in the image using characteristic features of the object. This way it will be possible to select the part of the blob that matches the tracked object, which will improve the tracking accuracy.

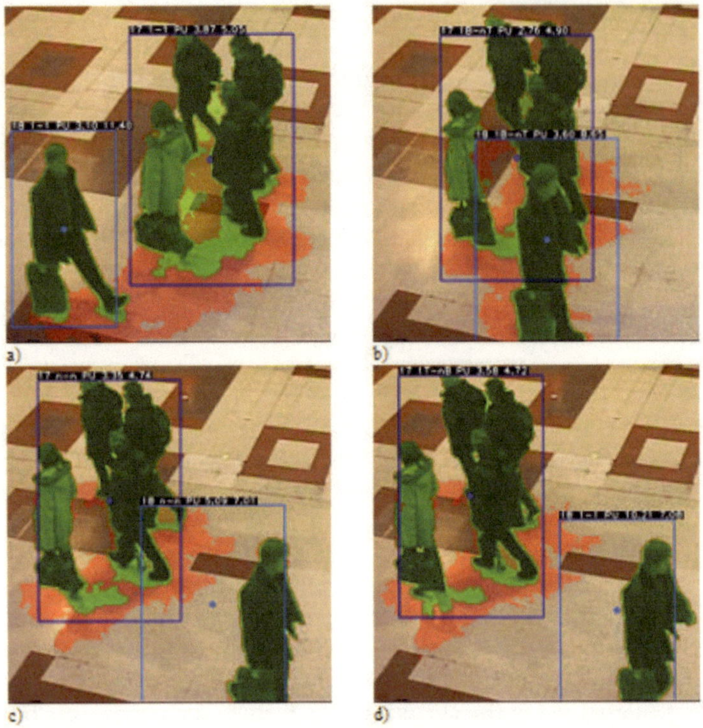

Fig. 4. Example of object tracking and conflict resolving results (images from the PETS 2006 database)

4. Object classification

4.1 Basic classification

Object classification is required for proper detection of various events involving specific types of moving objects (e.g. the presence of a person in the middle of a road is forbidden while vehicles are allowed). The video analysis framework provides a few modules devoted to object classification. The first module is responsible for dividing all objects into three groups: persons, vehicles and unanimated objects (e.g. luggage). Classification is based on object dimensions, therefore calibration of field of camera view is required. The calibration process involves selection of marked points in camera image and measuring their position in both image pixel space and in real world. For the purpose of presented system, a non-coplanar calibration mode should be used, meaning that calibration points with different height value should be used. Coordinates of calibration points are fed into the calibration procedure that calculates values for conversion between 2D image coordinates and 3D world coordinates (conversion from 2D to 3D requires that z coordinate, describing height, is provided). The authors used Tsai's calibration model to calculate 14 conversion parameters related to camera lens and camera orientation (Tsai, 1987). Using this conversion, the width and the height of the object is estimated (Szwoch et al., 2009). This estimation depends on the viewing angle, so time averaging has to be used to achieve good accuracy of size estimation. The objects are then assigned to classes using rules that test physical size and velocity of the objects (average and inter-frame change values are used).

If an object is 'removed' from the background (e.g. a luggage that was stationary for a prolonged time and was treated as a part of the background by the object detector, is taken by a person), it leaves a 'hole' in the background model, treated as a new object by the object tracker. The classification module has to decide whether a new tracker represents real object or part of the background. Otherwise, it would not be possible to detect e.g. abandoned luggage and taken (stolen) object, because these two situations would be treated in the same manner by the event detector. The proposed solution is based on observation that the contour of the detected object will contain edges only if it is not a part of background (Szwoch et al., 2010). Therefore, a grayscale image of the detected object (blob) and its mask (having non-zero values for pixels belonging to the blob and zero values otherwise) are processed by the Canny edge detector, resulting in E_B and E_M images. Next, E_M is morphologically dilated by a 7 x 7 structuring element *SE*, the result is combined with E_B and again dilated with the same element:

$$R_B = \left[\left(E_M \oplus SE \right) \cap E_B \right] \oplus SE \qquad (7)$$

A measure used for detection is calculated by dividing a number of non-zero pixels in R_B by a number of non-zero pixels in E_M dilated with *SE*. It was found during the experiments that if this measure is above 0.6, the blob represents the actual object, otherwise it is a part of the background.

4.2 Recognition of the object type

The second module is used to divide a general class of objects into specific subclasses (types). This module will be described using a vehicle type classifier (using types such as sedans, vans, trucks, etc.) as an example. Video-based object type classification utilizes results of moving object detection and tracking. Only images of objects classified as vehicles, without any occlusions with other objects, are analyzed in this example. Numerous vehicle image descriptors are used for vehicle type classification (Dalka & Czyzewski, 2010), they may be divided into two groups. The first group includes features based on vehicle mask only, such as: mask aspect ratio, eccentricity of the ellipse fitted to the mask, extent, defined as the proportion of the mask bounding box area to the mask area, solidity, defined as the proportion of the mask convex hull area to the mask area, proportion of the square of the mask perimeter to the mask area, 24 raw, central and normalized moments of the mask up to the third order (without trivial ones) and a set of seven Hu invariant moments of the mask (Flusser & Suk, 2006); the moments are invariant under translation, changes in scale and rotation. The second group of vehicle descriptors is based on image content. Because there is no correlation between vehicle type and its color, only luminance images are used. All image pixels outside of a vehicle mask are ignored. Two sets of vehicle image descriptors are computed; the first one is based on SURF (Speeded Up Robust Features) and the second one is derived from gradient images using Gabor filters.

Speed Up Robust Features (SURF) (Bay et al., 2006) is a scale- and rotation-invariant local image descriptor around a selected interest point. Its main advantages are repeatability, distinctiveness, and robustness as well as short computation time. Interest points (their location, orientation and size) may be chosen manually or automatically (e.g. using Fast-Hessian detector that is based on the determinant of the Hessian matrix. SURF descriptors ale calculated in the square regions centered around each interest point. The region is divided into 4×4 equal subregions. In each subregion, the Haar wavelet responses in horizontal d_x and vertical d_y directions (in relation to the interest point orientation) are calculated. Sums and absolute sums of wavelet responses form a four-element feature vector v for each subregion:

$$v = \left(\sum_{d_x<0} d_x, \sum_{d_x\geq 0} d_x, \sum_{d_x<0} |d_x|, \sum_{d_x\geq 0} |d_x|, \sum_{d_y<0} d_y \sum_{d_y\geq 0} d_y \sum_{d_y<0} |d_y| \sum_{d_y\geq 0} |d_y| \right) \quad (8)$$

This result in a SURF descriptor vector containing 128 elements for each interest point. The wavelet responses are invariant to illumination offset. Invariance to contrast is achieved by turning the descriptor into a unit vector.

SURF descriptor vectors are obtained for four interest points that are set manually in the centers of four rectangular, non-overlapping areas the vehicle image is divided into; the areas are located symmetrically around a center of gravity of the vehicle mask. The size of each interest point is equal to the height or width of the area, depending on which value is greater. Final vehicle feature vector based on SURF descriptors contains 128 × 4 = 512 elements.

The second set of vehicle image descriptors is based on filtering a gradient image with a bank of Gabor filters. Image gradients are calculated in vertical and horizontal directions independently using Sobel operator with an aperture size equal to 3. The final gradient image is obtained by adding squared vertical and horizontal gradients. Images are scaled to the fixed resolution 100×80 pixels. Gabor filter kernels are similar to the 2D receptive field profiles of the mammalian cortical simple cells. Therefore they reveal desirable characteristics of spatial locality and orientation selectivity (Daugman, 1988). In the spatial domain, a 2D Gabor filter is a Gaussian kernel function modulated by a sinusoidal plane wave (Grigorescu et al., 2002). A bank of eight Gabor filters based on two different wavelengths (2.5 and 4) and four different orientations (0°, 45°, 90° and 135°) is used. A scaled gradient image I is convolved with each Gabor filter g with two variants of phase offset φ, according to the equation:

$$I_G = \sqrt{\left(g_{\phi=0} * I\right)^2 + \left(g_{\phi=\pi/2} * I\right)^2} \quad (9)$$

This results in eight filtered vehicle images. For each image, seven Hu invariant moments are derived (Flusser & Suk, 2006). Final vehicle feature vector based on Gabor filters contains 7 × 8 = 56 elements.

A feed-forward Artificial Neural Network (ANN) with one hidden layer is used as a classifier for vehicle descriptors. The number of ANN inputs i_{ANN} corresponds with the number of vehicle features. The number of outputs o_{ANN} is equal to the number of vehicle types recognized. An expected output consists of a maximum value on one output and minimal values on other outputs. Therefore a vehicle type corresponding with the maximum output value is returned as the classification result. ANN is trained with a resilient backpropagation algorithm (RPROP). Sigmoid activation functions are used in all neurons. Vehicle descriptors are divided into training and validations sets randomly (Dalka & Czyzewski, 2010).

For the purpose of experiments, a 30-minute video recording from a traffic camera has been tested. All moving vehicle images have been automatically extracted using object detection and tracking algorithms, validated and hand-labeled with an appropriate vehicle class. Three vehicle subclasses were used: sedans, vans and trucks. Sample vehicle images are

presented in Fig 5. The database contained images of 525 different vehicles (367 sedans, 80 vans and 78 trucks). Each vehicle was represented by 40 images on average (Fig. 5). Therefore independent results of classifications of images of the same vehicle can be aggregated in order to increase total effectiveness. The final class assigned to a vehicle is equal to the most frequently labeled class for all images of the vehicle.
Vehicle type classification is a highly complex task because of large variety of vehicles belonging to each class and the fact, that vehicle physical dimensions and poses vary during their movement in a camera field of view. Nevertheless, up to 95% of vehicles can be classified correctly (Fig. 5). Experiments prove that feature vector consisting of vehicle mask statistical parameters and image features based on SURF and Gabor filters is sufficiently universal to characterize vehicles with different pose, size and resolution.

Vehicle type	No. of vehicles	% of correct classifications
sedan	315	97.4%
van	41	94.4%
truck	39	84.6%
all types	395	95.8%

Fig. 5. Sample vehicle images for each vehicle type: first row - sedans, second row - vans, third row - trucks; vehicle images are rescaled individually to the same vertical size (left) and results of vehicle type classification (right)

4.3 Shape analysis

Shape is one of the properties which could be analyzed to acquire more information describing an object. There are several task for which such data could be useful. After building a proper classifier, shape information could be applied for shape-based event detection or for object classification, providing additional information about the state of the object (e.g. person walking, sitting, running, etc.). Recognition of real objects in 2D images is a difficult task, but in comparison to methods which classify objects on the basis of their real dimensions and velocities, this method does not require any camera calibration techniques. Considering shape recognition for the purpose of object classification, a few things need to be denoted. Surveillance systems consist of multiple cameras placed and oriented variously. This causes the shape of an observed object to differ between cameras. Furthermore, objects may rotate around their own axis creating more various silhouette representations (Fig. 6).
The proposed shape-based object classification method assumes that the camera observation angle is known to the algorithm. With this condition fulfilled a set of binary images is prepared. These images correspond to objects representing various classes and types at a specified horizontal angle. In the simplified example presented here, three classes are considered: car, human and unknown.
Before training any classifier, all gathered shape images need to be parameterized (Fig. 7). This step is required to lower the amount of data being processed as well as to unify the shape representation. There are two general groups of methods used for shape parameterization (José, 2004). First group treats the shape as the whole region - i.e. Zernicke's Moments (Hae-Kwang, 2000). The other group operates on the shape contour - i.e. Chain Code, Pairwise

Geometric Histogram (Ashbrook, 1995). Independently from the group, each method can be characterized by its properties making it usefull for a certain purpose. In this paper a custom method is used. In the first step of this parameterization, the processed image is resized to a set dimensions (100x100 pix) preserving proportions. Next, pixels belonging to the shape are added in rows and columns. After this operation Hu moments are calculated and as the result of parameterization a final vector of 207 values is created for each image. Among all machine learning algorithms, Support Vector Machines classification method is chosen for the purpose of data clustering. SVM parameters are set during experiments for optimal performance and generalization (Chih-Wei 2003). Such approach analyzes objects independently in every video frame. In order to improve the algorithm performance, the final class assignment is done by averaging decisions from the last k frames equal to 0.5 s.

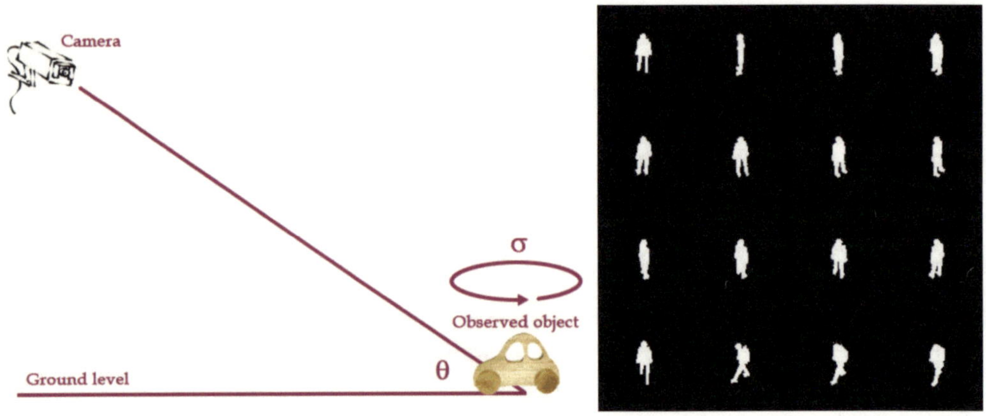

Fig. 6. 3D object recognition in 2D image problem (left) and sample 3D model projections at a set angle (right)

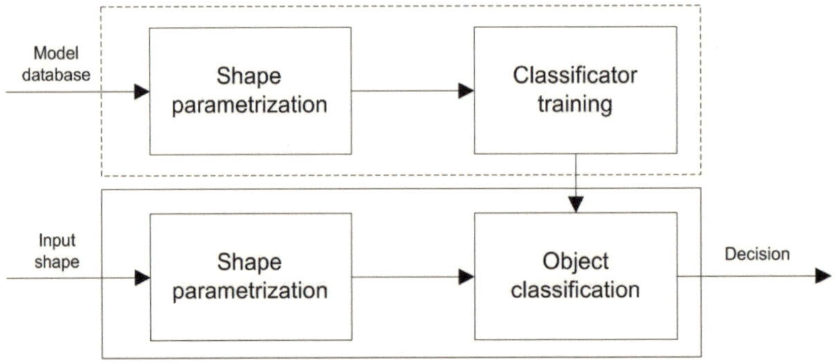

Fig. 7. Block diagram of data flow in the described method. Dotted border denotes the operation performed once per algorithm execution

The algorithm was tested using a set containing approximately 100 objects of each class. Classification results are presented in Fig. 8 and in Table 1, in the form of confusion matrix. In the tests, the proposed method worked as expected, achieving c.a. 90 percent accuracy. Experiments show that models for observation angle equal to 20, 40 and 60 are sufficient to cover the camera orientations from 10 to 70 degrees while sustaining similar performance. The described classifier distinguishes only three general classes but it is possible to recognize sub-classes within these by building a cascade classifier. As shown in this section, shape recognition can be successfully applied for object classification without the necessity of calibrating cameras but still providing the same or even better degree of accuracy.

Fig. 8. Examples of classification results obtained using the shape recogniser, with temporal probability denoted

	Car [%]	Human [%]	Unknown [%]
Car [%]	95.51	2.49	2.00
Human [%]	4.22	84.21	11.57
Unknown [%]	6.74	2.55	90.71

Table 1. Results of shape based object classification for camera angle approx. 40°

5. Face detection and recognition

The modules of the proposed framework described so far provide essential data for automatic event detection. However, in practical applications, more sophisticated modules may be needed, such as face detection and recognition algorithm described in this section. This optional module may be used e.g. for detection of presence of a particular person in the camera view or to check whether the detected person is in database of wanted people.

Two algorithms have to be implemented in this module. First, face detection is performed in order to select the image parts that contain faces. For this task we use an approach based on cascade of Haar classifiers (Viola & Jones, 2001). The classifier is trained with a set of face images scaled to the same size. During analysis, the classifier is applied to the image sections containing detected moving objects and classified as persons. If a face is detected, the classifier outputs a region of the image containing the face.

The second part of the module performs face recognition and is much more complex. The algorithm is expected to identify the detected person based on a series of face images. Face recognition techniques are under constant development since late 60s of 20th century, beginning with primitive local attempts trying to employ face geometry analysis. As this prototypic techniques failed due to intra-personal variability being greater than extra-personal one, some new approaches have arisen in late 80s, targeting at synthesis of effective face image representation, including so called holistic (global) approaches such as EigenFaces, based on principal component analysis (PCA)(Turk & Petland, 1991), FisherFaces (Fisher's Linear Discriminant, FLD)(Fisher, 1936) and neural network classifiers.

Moreover, hybrid methods emerged like *3D Morphable Models* (3DMM)(Vetter & Blanz, 1999). Next step in this area was possible thanks to advances in video surveillance and digital image processing systems which has occurred in the late 90s. Using a sequence of video frames instead of static face image allowed for employing probabilistic frameworks, able to exploit additional context contained in frame sequence. Contemporary attempts focus mostly on exploring probabilistic frameworks and excelling hybrid approaches like 3D modeling and active appearance modeling.

The main problem of implementing face recognition algorithms in real systems, such as the presented framework, is the insufficient number of image samples per person in the database. In most cases, the database contains a single photo of a wanted person, e.g. a passport photo. Using this sample image only, it is not possible to recognize a person if the pose is different from the sample. Our efforts focused on exploring possibilities of 3DMM method for creation of additional sample images. For this task, 3D face scanner based on phase shifting interferometry (PSI) method was constructed and programmed to acquire 3D face image data and build 3D image database. The collected 3D scans (29 women and 25 men faces) were used to create three models of face geometry (male, female and generic one, Fig. 9). In each scanned image, a set of 13 facial features was marked manually. In each group, faces were aligned using facial points and normalized. The algorithm for fitting a 2D image to the 3D face model works by finding a minimum of the function S:

$$S = \sum_{n=1}^{N} (\alpha_n - \beta_n)^2 \tag{10}$$

where N is a number of facial features (N = 13), α_n and β_n are coordinates of n-th facial point in 2D image and in 3D model, respectively. After the best match is found, texture of the image is transferred to the model and a new, textured 3D face model is constructed. This model may be then rotated in 3D space and compared with face images, e.g. the ones detected in the camera image.

The image matching algorithm using the created 3D models was tested using 200 sample images from FERET database. In most cases, reconstruction results were correct. However, the algorithm failed to match smaller regions such as eye-corners or the iris. The future work in this area will focus on automatic detection of facial points and implementing a geometry morphing algorithm in order to increase the reconstruction accuracy.

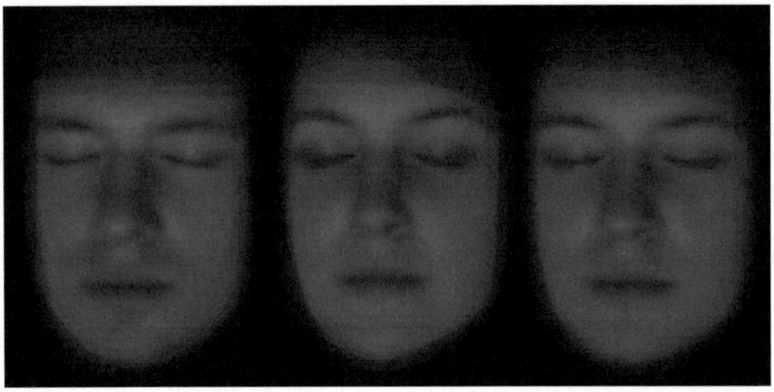

Fig. 9. The averaged 3D face models, from left: male, female and generic

For creation of facial features vector, needed for face matching, both Eigenface and Fisherface methods were implemented and compared using 2 training sets of 100 images each, from FERET database. The second set contained the same identities as the first one, but with some occlusions added and mimic expressions present. These images were rendered on the 3D averaged face model in order to simulate variations in exposition (pose and illumination) and then converted back to 2D in order to obtain virtual samples. This allowed using databases with varying number of samples per identity (from 1 sample to 40 samples). Simulations revealed that for substantial pose variation (around 40 degrees), Fisherfaces outperforms Eigenfaces approach, but its accuracy spans between 90% (for 10÷30 identities) and 10% (for sets of 50÷70 identities) which is locally less than Eigenfaces. With moderate pose variation (around 22 degrees), Eigenfaces approach substantially outperforms Fisherfaces approach as the latter yields very diverse accuracy in function of number of samples per identity and in function of trained identities number (Fig. 10). It also appeared that PCA-based approaches are highly sensitive to pose variation but they have nearly constant accuracy ratio along increasing sizes of training databases. Repeating simulations for the second set (the one with mimic variations and occlusions) confirmed the earlier observations, although overall accuracy decreased to 50% in best case.
Additionally, an optimal number of meaningful eigenvectors for both methods was investigated. It was observed that PCA-based algorithms perform with steadily increasing accuracy along with increasing number of meaningful eigenvectors. In case of FLD-based method, there is a threshold below which the accuracy is significantly below 50%. It was also observed that FLD accuracy drops rapidly if all eigenvectors are kept. For satisfactory scores in FLD it is necessary to remove c.a. 2% of the least meaningful eigenvectors.

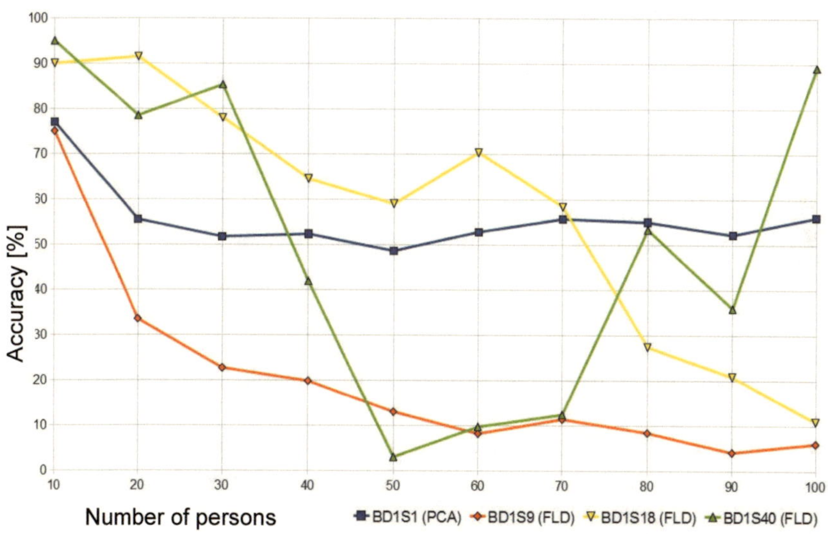

Fig. 10. Comparison of Fisherface (FLD) approach accuracy vs. Eigenface (PCA) method in function of number of identities in training set, for different numbers of samples per identity (PCA - 1, FLD - 10, 20, 40); only pose variation of 22 degrees applied

Although the results of the tests performed so far are promising, the algorithm is not ready yet for implementation in the proposed framework in real-world scenarios. Further research is needed in order to improve accuracy of the face matching algorithm and efficiency of the

3D face model construction. A larger database of faces will be constructed and used for testing face recognition algorithm against results of face detection performed in monitoring system camera images. It has be also noted that due to complexity of the algorithm and very high memory requirements, it seems reasonable to use a computer cluster for concurrent face recognition in a large number of cameras.

6. License plate detection and number recognition

A module for detection of license plate and recognition of license number is another example of a specialized algorithm that may be useful for automatic event detection in the proposed framework. For example, if a parked car is detected in the camera image, the module may read the license plate number and verify it in the database, in order to check e.g. if the vehicle is authorized to park in the particular place. In secured areas, the module may be used to register all vehicles entering and leaving the area. Moreover, if the system has access to an appropriate database, it is possible to detect stolen cars or traffic law violations. Performance of the algorithm depends on resolution of the image, placement of the camera and its view angle. Other factors such as speed of the passing cars, light and weather conditions may also require special approach.

Detection of a license number plate location is a problematic issue. Approaches to the detection problem are mainly based on combination of morphology and edge detection (Dong et al., 2006) which are fast, but detection errors occur when complex background is present. Methods using color features (Shi et al., 2005) are usually sensitive to light changes and night conditions. Algorithms that use Hough transform (Liu & Luo, 2010) usually need some restriction to image size or background.

The proposed algorithm is a solution which uses mainly color information about car back red light, edge detector and morphology. In this case, processed color does not change visibly according to light conditions. The algorithm was tested in real-world conditions in the Gdansk University of Technology campus, with a fixed camera pointed at an entrance gate, where the back of a car stopping at the gate is visible in the camera view. The size of the image was 704x576 pixels and the frame rate of the camera was 25 images per second. The expected size of the number plate in this image was 100x25 pixels.

The module operates on results of object detection and tracking, described earlier. Two processing stages are employed: license plate detection in the image of a moving object classified as a vehicle and license number recognition using optical character recognition (OCR). The plate detection part of the algorithm is responsible for finding coordinates of the number plate in a single video frame and for transmitting the results to the OCR module. For proper localization, the information about plate size and camera view angle is needed. Both parameters are constant in a given setup. It is also assumed that a car is visible for at least 1 second, which results in at least 25 images of the vehicle (the camera's fps rate is 25). The condition is met in the mentioned situation, when a car stops for a few seconds before passing through a gate.

The plate detection algorithm implements several image processing operations such as Sobel filtering, mathematical morphology or contours finding. The input image is extracted from the video frame. The output data is an integer vector of plate coordinates. A block diagram of the detection algorithm is shown in Fig. 11. The proposed approach is based on detecting red back lights and finding a location of the license plate in a space between them. First, the input image is rotated according to camera position. In order to reduce noise influence, the image is blurred using Gaussian smooth operator. Next, red areas are detected by finding pixels with dominant red channel value. For 8-bit per channel image, the threshold is set to 40. The selected red areas are saved as separate objects represented as contours. Car lights must be of appropriate size. Therefore, the area of every contour is checked in relation to the zoom of the camera and the expected size of the light. If a contour size is too small, it is not included in further processing. In the described setup the lights should be larger than 200 pixels. In case of finding a very large contour (in our case bigger than 5000 pixels), it is assumed that a red car is present. If at least two contours with correct sizes are found, the contour data is processed by the plate detection block.

In all valid contours, the alignment of every possible contour pair is checked. If the contours are in proper distance from each other and a horizontal line can be drawn between them, they are considered the contours of car back lights. For given conditions, the tolerance of horizontal placement is about 30 pixels. The distance between contours should be in the range of 2–4 plate lengths. If a large red contour is detected, it is assumed that it represents the whole car or a part of the car. In the latter case, the contour needs to be expanded to cover the whole vehicle. In both situations, the result of contour processing is a region that contains the license plate. In the next step, the original image is processed with Sobel operator and then dilated. As a result of this operation, an image containing vertical edges is obtained. The number plate is searched for in this image by moving a window vertically through the area containing the plate. The height of this window equals the expected height of a number plate. The result of this search is a rectangle with highest vertical edge concentration. Next, this area is swept horizontally with a window having width equal to the expected plate width. If hard edges, which represent the border of the number plate, are detected, the detection algorithm finishes its work and the rectangle covering the number plate is finally obtained. In example shown in Fig. 12, the result of number plate detection is presented. Red contours, including lights, are visible. The area where the number plated is searched for is marked by a blue rectangle and the final detected region is marked by a green rectangle.

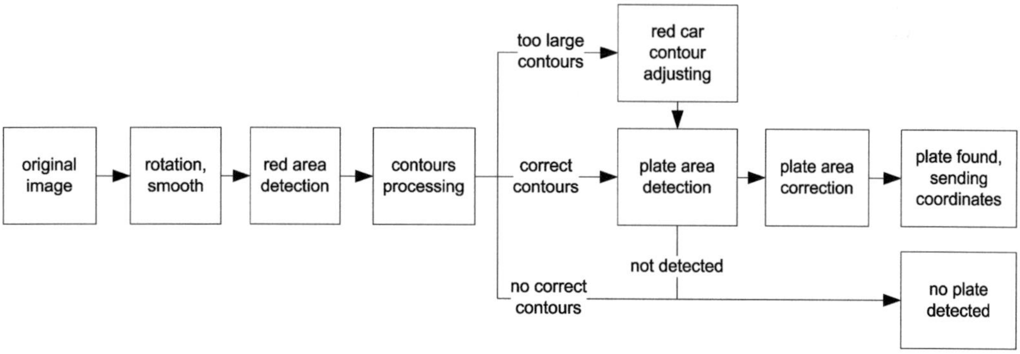

Fig. 11. Block diagram of the license plate detection algorithm

The area of the image containing the detected number plate is used by the OCR module to recognize the license number of a vehicle. The open source library GOCR was implemented in the presented module for recognizing characters. The GOCR algorithm can be divided into four parts. First, the image is converted to greyscale. Then, thresholding of the image is

Fig. 12. Example of the license plate detection: original frame from the camera (left) and the processed image (right)

performed. Next, the cluster detection algorithm detects areas in the image which may contain letters. In the final step, the detected clusters are compared with the patterns in the database. The performance depends on several configuration parameters of the GOCR engine, such as:

- *grey threshold* – the maximum luminance of a pixel (0 to 255), which is recognized as black (automatic setting of this parameter may be used);
- *dust size* – maximum size (in pixels) of a detected cluster which is not treated as a character; since the size of the number plate's area is at least 100x25 pixels and there are no lowercase characters, the characters are expected to occupy at least 100 pixels;
- *certainty* – each decision of recognizing a detected cluster as a letter depends on the certainty threshold (0-100) required to accept the decision; in the presented example, high certainty of recognized numbers is required, therefore the parameter is set to 95;
- *char filter* - list of characters that are expected to be found in the image; in this case the possible characters are capital Latin letters (A-Z) and numbers (0-9).

The use of the database has a large influence of the efficiency of the OCR engine. Prior to recognizing number plates, the engine needs to be trained with examples of number plates. Some images in the database are distorted with noise and blur and simulate different light conditions.

The recognition of characters usually comes with some errors, due to light conditions or insufficient resolution of the image. Therefore, some processing of the results is needed to increase the certainty of the final decision. In the first stage, the output of the GOCR engine is verified using certain rules concerning number plates. It is common that zeros, ones or blank spaces are inserted at the beginning of the registration number. Such characters need to be deleted, since number plates in Poland have to begin with a capital letter. The other aspect is the length of the detected character string. Polish registration numbers are always 7 characters long with a space after the second or third character. Therefore, if the string recognized by the OCR engine is longer, it needs to be cropped. For further improvement, a majority voting of the results is performed. OCR is performed independently for each frame in which a car is present in the view. The resulting char arrays are stored in a result buffer. After the buffer of 25 OCR results (one second of video stream) is filled, majority voting check is evaluated. The final number plate string is the most frequently appearing in the result buffer.

The results of the tests indicate that the proposed module provides satisfactory level of recognition accuracy. Most of the errors result from inaccuracy of the plate detection part of the algorithm. Therefore, future work will concentrate on improving the procedure for license plate detection, especially in difficult conditions (adverse lighting, dimmed car lights, etc.).

7. Event detection

An event detector is the final module in the proposed framework (Fig. 2). It utilizes results obtained during the earlier analysis stages in order to check whether defined rules that describe important events are fulfilled. In other words, this module interprets the data concerning all the objects visible by the camera and tests if a situation that may be a potential security threat has occurred. If this is the case, further actions are performed, e.g. notification is sent to the system operator (visual alert, logging or using a camera to view the area in which the event was observed).

The system for event detection is rule-driven. The rules may be selected by the operator from a predefined list of typical events or they may be constructed using a graphical user interface by combining elementary conditions and setting their parameters, so that the rules allow for detection of any desired situation. In the system developed by the authors, the event detection module uses only deterministic IF-THEN conditions. In future work, application of more advanced rule interpretation systems, e.g. based on fuzzy logic is planned. This will provide more flexible approach for determining whether a complex condition is fulfilled.

The rule interpretation system operates on data provided by the analysis modules situated lower in the framework hierarchy. This data may include positions of moving objects, their current state (size, velocity, etc.), type (class and subclass) and specific object information (recognized person name or license plate number). The event detector also analyses interactions between objects and the scene (e.g. whether the object is inside a defined area), as well as interactions between objects themselves (e.g. whether two objects are close to each other). Additionally, the event detector uses information about previously detected events (e.g. whether a particular event has occurred recently), so there is a feedback loop in this module. Therefore, it may be stated what while other modules analyze the camera image to provide information about what happened in the observed scene, the event detector interprets this data and informs the system operator what does this situation mean and whether it is a potential security threat.

In the presented framework, the authors divided the event detector into two parts. The low-level event detector operates on data provided by other modules and detects elementary events. The high-level detector analyses the detected low-level events, maintains history of the previous events and notifies the operator on detected security threats. For example, the low-level module will analyze the data provided by the object detector, tracker and classifier modules and it will detect the event described as 'a vehicle inside the defined area'. The high-level detector will check how long the vehicle remains inside the area, what type of area it is and whether the vehicle is permitted to park in the area. If the conditions are fulfilled, the operator will be notified with an alarm such as 'the car XX1234 is parking inside the Restricted Zone 1 for longer than 3 minutes without an authorization'.

There is a large number of potential security threats for which high-level detection rules may be created. Typical events that are commonly regarded as security threats include trespassing, loitering, burglary, theft, assault, vandalism (e.g. graffiti painting or destroying bus stops), etc. Detection of luggage that was left unattended in public spaces such as airports or railway stations is of particular interest, as it often results in closing the facility, evacuation of people and costly action of special forces. Therefore, there is a strong need to implement a detection of abandoned luggage in monitoring systems. A test version of detector for this type of events was developed and implemented by the authors (Szwoch et al, 2010). It will be presented here as an example of the working automatic event detector.

Detection of abandoned luggage using a high-level rule is possible if several low-level events have been detected before. The first condition is that a person has to leave a luggage. This is detected if an object of class 'person' (or 'person with luggage', if objects subclasses are used) is split into two objects: 'person' (now without luggage, but with the same tracker still assigned to it) and 'luggage' (which remains stationary and receives a new tracker). The second rule checks if the luggage remains within an area in which detection is performed. The third rule is fulfilled if distance between the person and the luggage exceeds the threshold. The fourth rule tests whether the person does not return to the left luggage for a defined period. The final, high-level rule examines all the low-level events detected in a number of last analyzed camera frames. If all four rules described above were fulfilled, the high-level event described as 'a person left unattended luggage in area A' is detected and notification is sent to the system operator. All the rules described here, written in natural language using IF…THEN clauses, are presented in Fig. 13.

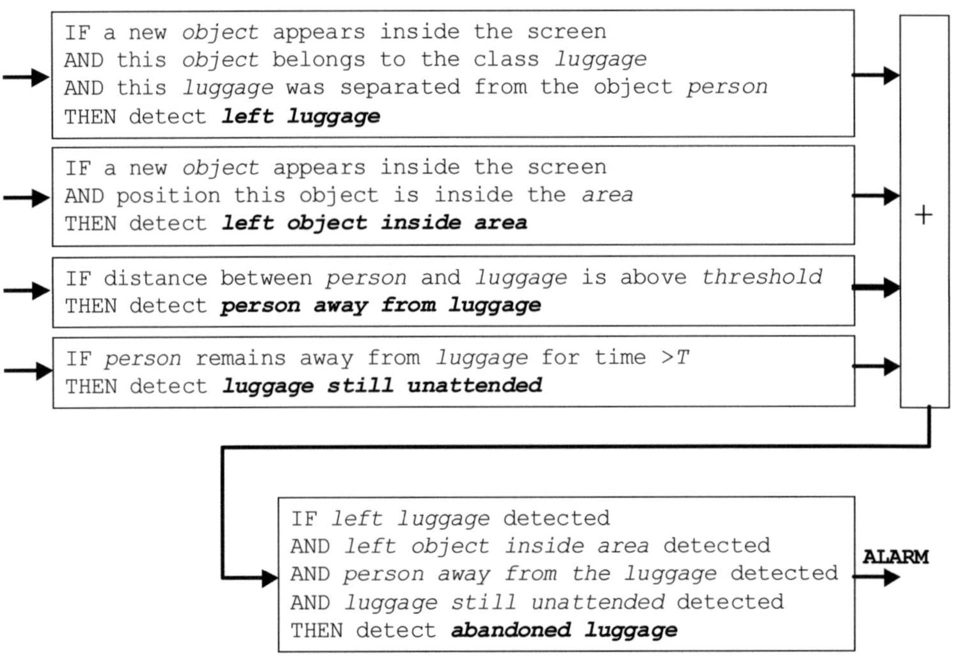

Fig. 13. Rules for detection of abandoned luggage

An example of abandoned luggage detection in real-life application, in the Poznan-Lawica airport in Poland, is presented in Fig. 14. It can be seen that all the necessary low-level events are detected, which results in detection of abandoned luggage using the high-level rule and visual alert on the screen. Results of tests performed at the airport proved that the proposed event detection module works correctly in simple situations, when the view on the person leaving luggage is not obstructed. However, performance of the event detector

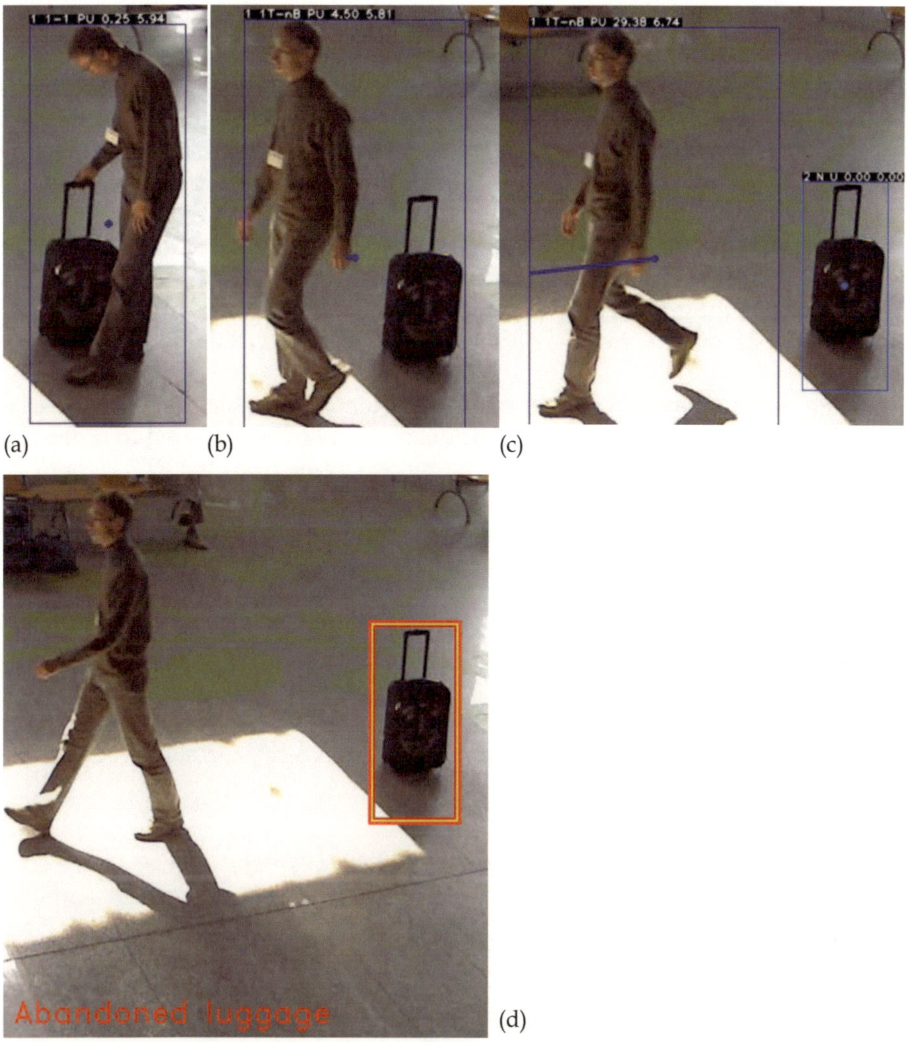

Fig. 14. An example of abandoned luggage detection: (a) initial state, (b) detected left luggage, (c) detected person away form luggage, (d) detected luggage still unattended, high-level event 'abandoned luggage' detected, visual alert

depends greatly on accuracy of the data provided by low-level modules, especially the object detector and the object tracker. In case of high number of conflicting objects (e.g. during rush hours at the airport) and adverse lighting conditions (e.g. reflections on the floor), a high number of errors in object detection and tracking significantly decreased the accuracy of event detection. Therefore, further work will be focused on improving object detection and tracking in difficult conditions.

Whenever a potentially dangerous event is detected by the video analysis framework, it is useful to provide a detailed view of the situation to an operator by aiming a PTZ camera at an object of interest and tracking it automatically as it moves. For example, if abandoned luggage is detected, the camera may track the person that left the luggage. This task requires finding pan p, tilt t and zoom z settings for a dome camera that will guarantee that an object of a known location will be present in a video stream from the camera (Szwoch & Dalka, 2010). Object position is obtained from object detection and tracking modules that analyze video streams from fixed cameras. The position must be expressed in real-world coordinates (e.g. meters), therefore the fixed camera has to be calibrated. Furthermore, the PTZ camera position and object location must be defined in a common, real-world, Cartesian 3D coordinate system. Alternatively, a conversion between both coordinate systems has to be available.

It is assumed that all objects move on the ground plane, therefore an object height coordinate is equal to zero. Object position is defined as $(x, y, 0)$ and current velocity of the object along both axes is denoted as v_x and v_y. A dome camera settings include its position (x_c, y_c), height above the ground h_c, and pan offset α_c, that is defined as an angle (in degrees) between the Y-axis of the world coordinate system and camera's zero pan position (clockwise).

There is a significant delay in a system caused by video processing, data transmission and executing PTZ command by the camera. This delay must be compensated in order to assure that a fast-moving object is always present in a video frame from the PTZ camera. System delay compensation is performed by setting the PTZ camera to the predicted position of the object. Prediction time should be equal to the total delay in the system. A linear predictor is used that estimates object position based on its current estimated speed and heading (direction of movement).

Predicted object position $(\hat{x}, \hat{y}, 0)$ is given with equations:

$$\hat{x} = x + d \cdot v \cdot \sin(\Theta) \qquad \hat{y} = y + d \cdot v \cdot \cos(\Theta) \tag{11}$$

where d is the system delay in seconds and v and Θ are object's current speed and heading calculated as follows:

$$v = \sqrt{v_x^2 + v_y^2} \qquad \Theta = \operatorname{atan2}(v_y, v_x) \tag{12}$$

The pan p and tilt t parameters for the camera are calculated with equations:

$$p = 90 - \operatorname{atan2}(\hat{y} - y_c, \hat{x} - x_c) - \alpha_c \qquad t = \begin{cases} -\arctan\left(\dfrac{h_c}{\sqrt{(\hat{x} - x_c)^2 + (\hat{y} - y_c)^2}}\right) & \hat{x} \neq x_c \vee \hat{y} \neq y_c \\ -90 & \text{otherwise} \end{cases} \tag{13}$$

The last camera parameter setting, the zoom, is set based on the object's distance from the PTZ camera. The closer the object is to the camera, the smaller is the zoom value. This approach assures that object dimensions in a video stream remain more or less constant.

8. Conclusions and future research

The multi-stage video analysis framework proposed by us and described in this chapter is a flexible and efficient solution for automatic analysis of camera images in the monitoring systems. The framework is intended mainly for automatic event detection in video. It was shown that successful event detection requires performing several stages of image processing. Some of the modules, such as object detection, tracking and classification, are necessary for event detection, because the rules describing potential security threats require data provided by these modules. Other modules, such as face recognition or license number recognition, are supplementary and they enhance the framework, providing additional data for event detection and allowing use of more complex detection rules, e.g. searching for a particular person or a vehicle. A flexible structure of the framework makes it possible to adapt the system to different needs, adding new modules in the future.

The functional modules described in this chapter were implemented in the current version of the framework that was used for preliminary testing. Most of these modules utilize algorithms found in the literature, enhanced and modified to suit the needs of the framework. The main contribution of the authors, apart from the design of the framework and method of data exchange between modules, is implementation of the object tracking algorithm with resolving of tracking conflicts, the algorithm for vehicle classification, the method for creating database of 3D face models and using them in face recognition, and a structure for interpretation of event detection rules.

It has to be noted that errors that occur at the lowest level of image processing significantly decrease the accuracy of event detection at the highest analysis level. This was observed in the test system for automatic detection of abandoned luggage at the Poznan airport in Poland (Szwoch et al, 2010). As long as the number of moving objects is small and the lighting is good, the event detection is successful. However, with a large number of moving persons and unfavorable light, errors in object detection and tracking are propagated throughout the framework, resulting in undetected events at the system output.

The future research will be aimed mainly at improving and enhancing the functional modules. The possible areas of improvement were indicated earlier for each algorithm presented in this chapter. Current work is focused mainly on reduction of number of errors in the object detection and tracking phases, by improving the background subtraction procedure (elimination of artifacts resulting from adverse lighting conditions) and by enhancing the procedure for resolving tracking conflicts (e.g. using feature matching algorithm for finding the object in the image region). We believe that with these enhancement, accuracy of the event detection will be improved significantly.

Apart from enhancing the existing modules, new modules will be developed and added to the framework. There is already an ongoing research on module for analysis and prediction of crowd behavior. It will allow for detection of advanced situations, such as a potential fight between groups of football fans, the riot on the street or a panic situation.

One possible enhancement of the framework that was not addressed so far is concurrent analysis of images from multiple cameras. Real video monitoring systems consist of a large number of cameras. Therefore, implementation of an algorithm for tracking movement of objects between cameras (capturing a known object as it enters a field of view of the camera) is planned for the next stage of research. Moreover, after enhancing the framework, tests will be performed that will provide quantitative assessment of its performance.

Video content analysis in large monitoring systems, e.g. in the modern football arena with several hundreds of cameras, imposes very high demand for the processing power, memory and data storage. Therefore, the framework was designed in such a way that it is possible to perform the video analysis using either a centralized 'supercomputer' cluster or a distributed network of typical personal computers ('node stations'), so that available processing resources may be utilized optimally.

The proposed framework, after enhancing its functional modules and the framework it self, will provide an useful solution for automatic detection of a wide range of events that may be potential security threats. It should noted here that the framework is not intended to be a fully automatic surveillance system that is able to detect every event occurring in the observed area. The system operator will still be the one that makes decisions and the framework will be only an automated 'assistant' that notifies the operator on the detected events. This system may also help in shifting the focus in modern monitoring systems from reviewing the recordings after an event occurred to a real-time identification of security threats, resulting in improved level of public security in the monitored areas.

9. Acknowledgements

Research funded within the project No. POIG.02.03.03-00-008/08, entitled "MAYDAY EURO 2012 - the supercomputer platform of context-depended analysis of multimedia data streams for identifying specified objects or safety threads". The project is subsidized by the European regional development fund and by the Polish State budget.

10. References

Ashbrook, A.P.; Thacker, N.A. & Rockett, P.I. Multiple shape recognition using pairwise geometric histogram based algorithms, *IEEE 5th International Conference on Image Processing and its Applications*, pp. 90-94, Edinburgh, July 1995

Bay, H.; Tuytelaars, T. & Van Gool, L. (2006). SURF: Speeded up robust features, *9th European Conference on Computer Vision*, Graz, May 2006

Czyzewski, A. & Dalka, P. (2007). Visual traffic noise monitoring in urban areas. *Int. Journal of Multimedia and Ubiquitous Engineering*, Vol. 2, No. 2, pp. 91–101

Czyzewski, A. & Dalka, P. (2008). Examining Kalman filters applied to tracking objects in motion, *9th International Workshop on Image Analysis for Multimedia Interactive Services*, pp. 175-178, Klagenfurt, May 2008

Dalka, P. (2006). Detection and segmentation of moving vehicles and trains using Gaussian mixtures, shadow detection and morphological processing. *Machine Graphics and Vision*, Vol. 15, No. 3/4, pp. 339–348

Dalka, P. & Czyzewski, A. (2010). Vehicle classification based on soft computing algorithms, *7th Conf. on Rough Sets and Current Trends in Computing*, Warsaw, June 2010

Daugman, J. G. (1988). Complete Discrete 2-D Gabor transforms by neural networks for image analysis and compression. *IEEE Trans. Acoustic, speech and signal processing*, Vol. 36, No. 7, pp. 1169-1179

Dong P., Yang J-h & Dong J-j. (2006). The application and development perspective of number plate automatic recognition technique, *Proc. 2nd Conference on Information and Communication Technologies ICTTA '06*, pp. 744-747, October 2006, Damascus

Dougherty, E. & Lotufo, R. (2003). *Hands-on morphological image processing*, SPIE Press

Elgammal, A.; Harwood, D. & Davis, L. (2000). Non parametric model for background subtraction. *Lecture Notes in Computer Science*, Vol. 1843, pp. 751-767

Fisher, R.A. (1936). The use of multiple measures in taxonomic problems. *Ann. Eugenics*, Vol. 7, pp. 179-188

Flusser, J. & Suk, T. (2006). Rotation moment invariants for recognition of symmetric objects. *IEEE Transactions on Image Processing*, Vol. 15, No. 2, pp. 3784–3790

Grigorescu, S.E.; Petkov, N. & Kruizinga, P. (2002). Comparison of texture features based on Gabor filters. *IEEE Trans. on Image Processing*, Vol. 11, No. 10, pp. 1160-1167

Horprasert, T.; Harwood, D. & Davis, L. (1999). A statistical approach for real-time robust back-ground subtraction and shadow detection, *Proc. of IEEE Frame Rate Workshop*, pp. 1–19, Kerkyra, Greece, September 1999

Hsu, C-W.; Chang, C-C. & Lin, C-J. (2003). A practical guide to support vector classification, Technical report. Dept. of Computer Science, National Taiwan University

Kim, H-K.; Kim, J-D.; Sim, D-G. & Oh, D-I (2000). A modified Zernike moment shape descriptor invariant to translation, rotation and scale for similarity-based image retrieval, *IEEE Int. Conference on Multimedia and Expo*, Vol. 1, pp. 307-310, New York, July 2000

Konrad, J. (2007). Videopsy: Dissecting visual data in space time. *IEEE Communication Magazine*, Vol. 45, No. 1, pp. 34-42

Li, H. & Ngan, K. (2007). Automatic video segmentation and tracking for content-based applications, *IEEE Communication Magazine*, Vol. 45, No. 1, pp. 27–33

Liu, Y. & Zheng, Y. (2005). Video object segmentation and tracking using y-learning classification, *IEEE Trans. Circuits and Syst. For Video Tech.*, Vol. 15, No. 7, pp. 885-899

Liu Ch-Ch. & Luo Z-Ch. (2010). An extraction algorithm of vehicle license number using pixel value projection and license plate calibration, *2010 International Symposium on Computer Communication Control and Automation (3CA)*, pp. 256-259, Tainan, May 2010

Martinez, J.M (2004). *MPEG-7 overview (version 10)*. MPEG Consortium, Palma de Mallorca

Shi X., Zhao W. & Shen Y (2005). Automatic license plate recognition system based on color image processing, In: *Computational Science and Its Applications*, Vol. 3483, Ed. O. Gervasi et al., Springer-Verlag, New York

Stauffer, C. & Grimson, W. (2000). Learning patterns of activity using real-time tracking. *IEEE Trans. on Pattern Analysis and Machine Intelligence*, Vol. 22, No. 8, pp. 747–757

Szwoch, G.; Dalka, P. & Czyzewski, A. (2009). Estimation of object size in the calibrated camera image. *Elektronika*, Vol. 50, No. 3, pp. 10-13.

Szwoch, G. & Dalka, P. (2010). Automatic detection of abandoned luggage employing a dual camera system, *3rd IEEE Int. Conf. on Multimedia Communications, Services & Security*, pp. 56-61, Krakow, May 2010

Szwoch, G.; Dalka, P. & Czyzewski, A. (2010). A framework for automatic detection of abandoned luggage in airport terminal, *3rd International Symposium on Intelligent and Interactive Multimedia: Systems and Services*, Baltimore, July 2010

Tsai, R. (1987). A versatile camera calibration technique for high accuracy 3D machine vision metrology using off-the-shelf TV cameras and lenses. *IEEE Journal of Robotics and Automation*, Vol. 3, No. 4. pp. 323-344

Turk, M. & Petland, A (1991). Eigenfaces for recognition. *Journal of Cognitive Neurosicence*, Vol. 3, No. 1, pp.71-86

Xiu, L.; Landabasso, J. & Pardas, M. (2005). Shadow removal with blob-based morphological reconstruction for error correction, *Proc. of IEEE International Conference on Acoustics, Speech, and Signal Processing*, pp. II–729–732, Philadelphia, March 2005

Vetter, T. & Blanz, V. (1999). A morphable model for the synthesis of 3D faces, *Computer Graphics Proceedings. Siggraph 1999*, pp. 187–194, Los Angeles, August 1999

Viola, P. & Jones, M (2001). Rapid object detection using boosted cascade of simple features, *IEEE Conference on Computer Vision and Pattern Recognition*, Vol. 1, pp. 511-518, Kauai, December 2001

Welch, G. & Bishop G. (2006). *An introduction to the Kalman filter*. Technical report, TR-95041, Department of Computer Science, Univ. of North Carolina, Chapel Hill

Yang, T.; Li, S.; Pan, Q. & Li, J. (2004). Real-time and accurate segmentation of moving objects in dynamic scene, *ACM 2nd International Workshop on Video Surveillance and Sensor Networks*, pp. 136-143, New York, October 2004

Part 3

Object Segmentation, Detection, and Tracking

10

Background Subtraction and Lane Occupancy Analysis

Erhan A. Ince, Nima S. Naraghi and Saameh G. Ebrahimi
Eastern Mediterranean University
North Cyprus

1. Introduction

In the last decade or so traffic monitoring has attracted considerable attention from intelligent transportation systems (ITS). ITSs are generally designed to collect traffic data such as vehicle count, vehicle speed, vehicle path, vehicle density, and vehicle classification. The information gathered may be used by traffic lights controllers, and toll collectors to regulate traffic flow, reduce congestion and improve safety. Traffic information can be obtained through physical devices like buried loop sensors, radars, and infrared detectors however these conventional systems have the disadvantage that they can only count but they cannot differentiate or classify. Nowadays, most ITSs essentially rely on wireless IP cameras which are either fixed or movable type. These systems employ state of the art machine vision technologies to automatically analyze traffic data collected by the camera system(s) and forward their findings to control devices or points. Video based surveillance systems (VBSS) can be categorized as indicated below:

1. Tripwire Systems,
2. Tracking Systems,
3. Spatial Analysis based systems.

In Tripwire systems the camera is used to simulate usage of a conventional detector by using small localized regions of the image as detector sites. Such a system can be used to detect the state of a traffic light (red, yellow, green) check if a reserved section has been violated, and detect wrong-way traffic etc.
Tracking systems detect and track individual vehicles moving through the camera scene. They provide a description of vehicle movements (east bound, west bound, etc.) which can also reveal new events such as sudden lane changes and help detect vehicles travelling in the wrong direction. Tracking systems can also compute trajectories and conclude on accidents when different trajectories cross each other and then motion stops.
Spatial analysis based systems on the other hand concentrate on analyzing the two-dimensional information that video images provided. Instead of considering traffic on a vehicle-to-vehicle basis, they attempt to measure how the visible road surface is being utilized.
Whichever approach is employed, the segmentation of mobile objects present in frames of a video sequence is a fundamental step for many video based applications. In the literature this step is referred to as the background subtraction. The process includes creation of a background model and then updating it with each newly arriving frame from a sequence. Newly arriving frame from a video sequence. The updating of the background model can be

done exploiting various predictive, non-predictive, recursive and non-recursive algorithms. Current frame pixels with considerable deviation from the background model are considered to belong to the moving objects (vehicles, people etc). Over the years many background estimation algorithms have been proposed. This is mainly because no single algorithm is able to cope with all the challenges in this area. While some of the proposed algorithms are best for indoor applications, others may be better for outdoors. The section that follows provides a general introduction on the classification of background subtraction algorithms and then gives a comparative study of five selected background subtraction algorithms.

2. Classification of background subtraction algorithms

In visual surveillance applications, a common approach for differentiating moving objects from the static part of the video frames is detection by background subtraction. According to (Christani, Bicego & Murino), a background modeling process has three phases:

1. Model representation,
2. Model initialization,
3. Model adaptation.

The first part describes the kind of model used to represent the background; the second part is about the initialization of the assumed model; and the third part is the mechanism used for adapting to illumination changes in the background. (Mittal & Paragios, 2004) state that existing state of the art methods for background adaptation may be classified as either predictive or non-predictive. Predictive algorithms are known to model the scene (background) as a time series and they would make use of a dynamic model to recover the current input based on past observations. The absolute error between the predicted and the actual observation can then be used as a measure of change. On the other hand non-predictive methods do not rely on the order of the input observations but rather try to build probabilistic representation for the observations at a particular pixel.

An alternative way for classifying background adaptation methods is to group them as either non-recursive or recursive. This was first proposed by (Cheung &Kamath, 2004). A non-recursive technique uses a sliding-window approach for background estimation. For non-recursive estimation the L previous video frames are first stored in a buffer and then a background image is constructed making use of the temporal variation of each pixel in the buffer. One disadvantage of non-recursive methods is that for slow moving objects a large storage may be required. Recursive techniques do not rely on a buffer for estimating the scene. Instead, they recursively update a single or multiple background model(s) based on each input frame (Elhabian, El-Sayed & Ahmed,2008). Even though recursive techniques have much lower memory requirements, any error in the background model can remain around for a longer time. To alleviate this problem exponential weighting and/or positive decision feedback can be used.

Non-recursive adaptation techniques include temporal differencing (frame differencing), average filter, Median filtering and Minimum-Maximum filtering. Recursive techniques on the other hand include Approximated Median filtering, Single Gaussian, Kalman Filtering, Mixture of Gaussians (MoG), Clustering based segmentation methods, and Hidden Markov Models.

2.1 Study of selected adaptation algorithms

Although many background subtraction methods are listed in the literature, foreground detection specially for outdoor scenes is still a very challenging problem. The performance of video based surveillance systems will vary based on several environmental changes like the ones listed below:

1. Variable lighting conditions, during sunset and sunrise,
2. Adverse weather conditions such as fog, rain, snow, etc,
3. Non-stationary backgrounds such as swaying grass, leaves and branches,
4. Presence of camera vibration due to wind and heavy vehicles.

Another important consideration while trying to choose an appropriate background estimation method is the time required for processing a frame. If a system has to run in real-time, its computational complexity should not be too high.

In this section we will first provide a summary for each of the five different adaptation algorithms that we have chosen to discuss and follow with the segmentation quality performance evaluations.

2.2 Temporal median filtering

(Nixon & Aguado, 2005) et al., state that finding the background given a sequence of frames is an example application of statistical operators. For conventional median filtering the median is the center of a rank-ordered list of values usually taken from a template centered on the point of interest. A temporal median filter (TMF) on the other hand is different from a conventinal median filter in that each point in the TMF produced image is the median of the points in a mask placed over the same positions in the N sample frames.

TMF computes the median intensity for each pixel from all the stored frames in a buffer. Considering the computation complexity and storage limitations it is not practical to store all the incoming video frames and make the decision accordingly. Hence the frames are stored in a limited size buffer. In some cases the number of stored frames is not large enough (buffer limitations), therefore the basic assumption will be violated and the median will estimate a false value which has nothing to do with the real background model. An example where temporal median filtering algorithm fails to extract a proper foreground mask is shown in Fig. 1.

In comparison to average or temporal average filters a background image that is obtained using TMF would have more detail and less blur.

2.3 Approximated median filtering

Shortly after the non-recursive median filtering became popular among the background subtraction algorithms, (McFarlane & Schofield, 1995) presented a simple recursive filter for estimating the median of each pixel over time. This filtering process which is named as the approximated median filtering (AMF) would simply increment the background model intensity by one, if the incoming intensity value (in the new input frame) is larger than the previous existing intensity in the background model. The reverse is also true, meaning that when the intensity of the new input is smaller than that of the background model the corresponding intensity will be decreased by one. Over time this process will converge to the median of the observed intensities.

Unlike TMF, this approach does not require storing any frames in a buffer and tries to update the estimated background model online. Hence it is extremely fast and suitable for real time applications. AMF used for estimating the background scene in a simulated indoor environment is shown in Fig. 2.

This method has also been adopted by some for background subtraction for urban traffic monitoring due to its considerable speed. A sample output showing the foreground background separation for an outdoor scene has been provided in Fig. 3.

(a) Original Frame

(b) Estimated Background (c) Mask of Extracted Foreground

Fig. 1. Foreground-Background detection using temporal median filtering

(a) Original Scene (b) Estimated Background

Fig. 2. Background detection using approximated median filtering for indoors

(a) Original Frame

(b) Estimated Background

(c) Mask of Extracted Foreground

Fig. 3. Foreground-Background separation using approximated median filtering

Note that even though the AMF produced background is more correct the technique still has some difficulty in handling shaking leaves and swaying branches.

2.4 K-Gaussian mixture model

The Mixture of Gaussians technique was first introduced by (Stauffer & Grimson, 1999). It sets out to represent each pixel of the scene by using a mixture of normal distributions so that the algorithm will be ready to handle multimodal background scenes. In the mixture model each pixel is modeled as a mixture of K Normal distributions. Typically values for K varies from 3 to 5. For $K < 3$, the mixture model is not so helpful since it cannot adapt to multimodal environments and if K is selected a value over 5, often the disadvantage of processing speed reduction (not able to be performed in real time) outweighs the improvement in quality of background model. At any time t, K Gaussian distributions are fitted to the intensities seen by each pixel up to the current time t:

$$P(X_{i,t}) = \sum_{i=1}^{K} w_{i,t} \cdot \eta(X_{i,t}, \mu_{i,t}, \Sigma_{i,t}) \tag{1}$$

In the adaptive K-MoG model $X_{i,t}$ is the current pixel value vector which consists of Red, Green and Blue components, $w_{i,t}$ is an estimate of the weight of the ith Gaussian in the mixture at time t, $\mu_{i,t}$ and $\Sigma_{i,t}$ are the mean value and the covariance matrix of the ith Gaussian in the mixture. $P(X_{i,t})$ denotes the probability of observing the current pixel value vector given the mixture of K Gaussian distributions and $\eta(X_{i,t}, \mu_{i,t}, \Sigma_{i,t})$ is a Gaussian probability density function.

$$X_{i,t} = (x^R_{i,t}, x^G_{i,t}, x^B_{i,t}) \tag{2}$$

$$\mu_{i,t} = (\mu^R_{i,t}, \mu^G_{i,t}, \mu^B_{i,t}) \tag{3}$$

$$\Sigma_{i,t} = \begin{pmatrix} \sigma^2_R & 0 & 0 \\ 0 & \sigma^2_G & 0 \\ 0 & 0 & \sigma^2_B \end{pmatrix} \tag{4}$$

$$\eta(X_{i,t}, \mu_{i,t}, \Sigma_{i,t}) = \frac{1}{(2\pi)^{n/2}|\Sigma|^{-1/2}} \exp^{1/2 \cdot (X_{i,t}-\mu_{i,t})^T \cdot \Sigma^{-1} \cdot (X_{i,t}-\mu_{i,t})} \tag{5}$$

Background/foreground separation consists of two independent steps: 1) estimating the parameters of Kdistributions; and 2) evaluating the likelihood of each distribution to represent the background.

2.4.1 Parameter updating

Since at the start of modelling all the Gaussians have an equal probability for representing the background the weights $w_{i,t}$, i ϵ (1...K), are all set to the value $\frac{1}{K}$ and the variances are set randomly to high values. Then every new pixel value vector $X_{i,t}$ is checked against the existing K Gaussian distributions until a match is found (a match is defined as a pixel value vector whose Euclidean distance is within 1.5 standard deviations of a distribution). The parameters of the matched component are then updated using the recursive equations below:

$$\mu_{i,t} = (1-\rho) \cdot \mu_{i,t-1} + \rho \cdot X_{i,t} \tag{6}$$

$$\Sigma_{i,t} = (1-\rho) \cdot \Sigma_{i,t-1} + \rho \cdot diag\{(X_{i,t} - \mu_{i,t})^T (X_{i,t} - \mu_{i,t})\} \tag{7}$$

$$\rho = \alpha \cdot (X_{i,t} | \mu_{i,t-1}, \Sigma_{i,t-1}) \tag{8}$$

Here α represents the user-defined learning rate and has a value in the range $0 < \alpha < 1$. ρ on the other hand is a learning rate for the parameters.

For the case when there are no matches the Gaussian distribution with the least weight is replaced by a new component with a mean equal to the current pixel vector. The variance for this new distribution is set high and the weight is set to a low prior value. Finally, the weight of all the K Gaussians at time t are updated and normalized using:

$$w_{i,t} = (1-\alpha) \cdot w_{i,t-1} + \alpha \cdot M_{i,t} \tag{9}$$

$$w_{i,t} = \frac{w_{i,t}}{\Sigma^K_{m=1} w_{m,t}}$$

When there is a match $M_{i,t}$ can be assumed as 1 and 0 otherwise.

2.4.2 Background estimation

Once the parameters for all the Gaussian distributions are updated the ones that are most likely produced by background processes are determined. First, the K Gaussians are sorted in descending order by the value of $\frac{w_{i,t}}{\Sigma_{i,t}}$ and then the first B distributions are chosen to be in the background model using the value of B as given by:

$$B = \arg\min_b \{\Sigma^b_{k=1} w_k > T\} \tag{10}$$

where, T can assume any value from the interval 0.5 - 1.
Generally the segmented foreground would contain some noise. It is possible to get rid of this noise by making use of standard morphological operations as suggested by (Gonzales, 2002). Figure 4 depicts some estimated backgrounds using the K-Gaussians mixture model. For all video sequences $K = 3$, $\alpha = 0.05$, $\beta = 1.5$, and $T = 0.85$ values were used in the adaptive K-MoG model.

(a) Frame from Highway-I sequence (b) Estimated Background

(c) Frame from Yeni Izmir Sequence (d) Estimated Background

Fig. 4. MoG based Background Generation

2.5 Progressive background estimation

This method was first introduced by (Chung et al., 2002). A progressive background image is generated by utilizing a histogram to record the changes in intensity for each pixel of the image, however, unlike its other histogram based background generator counterparts, progressive method does not directly use the input frames to create the histogram. The progressive method constructs the histograms from the preprocessed images also referred to as the partial backgrounds.
In order to generate the partial backgrounds, the progressive method follows the following steps. First, the current frame $I(t)$ at time t of an input video sequence $S(t)$ is captured into the system and this image is compared with the previous frame image, $I(t-1)$ to generate a current partial background $B(t)$. Each pixel at location i at time t of the corresponding partial background is called $b_i(t)$ and is computed using;

$$b_i(t) = \begin{cases} bg & , |p_i(t) - b_i(t-1)| < \epsilon \\ non-bg & , \text{otherwise.} \end{cases} \quad (11)$$

Here bg stands for pixels related to the background image whose intensity value difference from the previous partial background $b_i(t-1)$ does not exceed a small predefined threshold ϵ. If the incoming intensity varies from the partial background more than the selected threshold, the corresponding pixel will be classified as $non-bg$. There are several possible ways to assign value to bg pixels; one is to take the minimum intensity between the new $b_i(t)$ and $b_i(t-1)$, another way is to average these two values and yet another is by simply taking the new value as $b_i(t)$. This last approach requires less computational time and hence is more suitable for real-time processing. For $non-bg$ pixels a specific value should be assigned, so that it will be possible to distinguish them since we are not interested in them. To separate them from bg pixels, usually they are assigned 0 or -1. After all the pixels have been classified and the numbers are assigned to them, the whole partial background at time t can be created as;

$$B_i(t) = \bigcup b_i(t) \qquad , i \epsilon I(t) \tag{12}$$

By creating the partial background images, the moving objects are discarded due to their intensity differences from the background and only the pixels which are more likely to be a part of background will be kept. In some cases slow moving objects or similarity among foreground objects and background scene may cause some parts of moving objects to be misclassified as background related pixels. This problem can be avoided if color information is used as shown below:

$$b_i(t) = \begin{cases} bg & , \cap_c |p_i^c(t) - b_i^c(t-1)| < \epsilon^c \\ non-bg & ,\text{otherwise.} \end{cases} \tag{13}$$

Here, c is the different components of the RGB. In other words the classification is done separately for each color channel and then their intersection is obtained in order to set aside the pixels that vary in all channels in comparison to previous partial background.
The next step of the progressive background estimation method would be generating a histogram called $h_p(t)$ using the partial backgrounds obtained from the previous step. The index p indicates that there is a histogram for every pixel of the image and t stands for time. For each pixel at time t a certain number of generated partial background depending on the size of our buffer are processed and then the histograms are created per pixel location in time. This process is shown by Fig. 5.

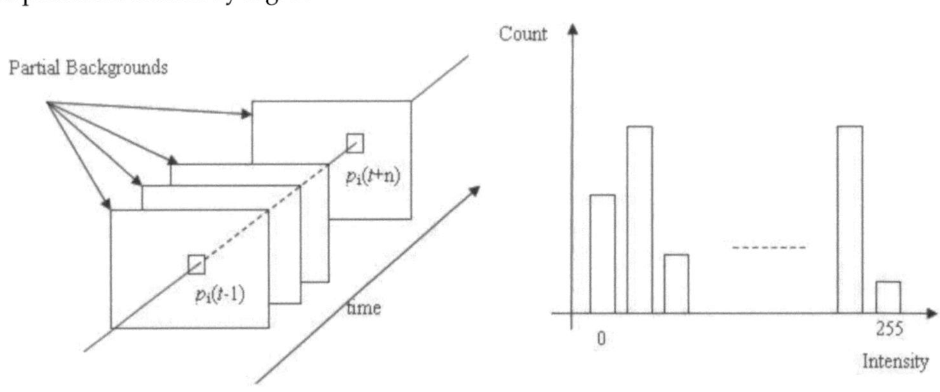

Fig. 5. Partial Background Images and Histogram

The histogram updating procedure is done simultaneously with the generation of histograms. For each pixel the incoming intensity from partial background is checked by the algorithm to discover whether the new intensity is within the local neighborhood of the previous background intensities or not. If the mentioned condition is satisfied (the intensity belongs to the neighborhood) then the frequency of that intensity is incremented by a constant factor. If the constraint is violated and the newly gained intensity is located outside the boundaries of our neighborhood domain, the recorded frequency for corresponding pixel in the histogram will be decreased by a factor less than mentioned incrementing factor. The preceding discussion can be summarized as in:

$$v = v + A\delta(b_i(t), a) - D \tag{14}$$

Here, v is the count (frequency) of the intensity index a, in the histogram. A represents the rising factor while on the contrary D is the descending factor. The δ function in equation 14 is defined as:

$$\delta(l, r) = \begin{cases} 1 \ , |l - r| < \lambda \\ 0 \ , \text{otherwise.} \end{cases} \tag{15}$$

After the histograms are generated and updated, the maximum frequency of each histogram along with its corresponding intensity for each pixel in the image are recorded in a table. The histogram table can be utilized as a reference for intensities which are responsible for background generation at any time. Whenever the background image is required, the recently updated intensity values in the table are used to generate the desired background.
At the beginning of the processing some cells of the table may not have a value and hence the background image contains leakages (undesired black dots). This problem occurs because the histograms are built over partial backgrounds which include black parts in the position of moving objects but as time passes, intensities related to the background image come to the pixel view more and more. Therefore this leakage effect will be gradually removed. A stable background image would be expected when the counts recorded in the histogram table are approximately 75-80 % of a predetermined upper limit.
Figure 6, depicts an example where leakage problem is resolved after 5 frames of the video sequence.

(a) Existence of leakage (b) Leakages removed after 5 frames

Fig. 6. Estimated background using progressive method

2.6 Group-based histogram estimation

Group Based Histogram (GBH) algorithm construct background models by using histogram of intensities for each pixel on the image. However, unlike the other histogram based methods, in group based histogram, each of the individual intensities is considered along with its neighboring intensity levels and forms an accumulative frequency. The frequency of coming intensity is summed up with its neighboring frequency to create a Gaussian shape histogram.

The accumulation can be done by using an average filter of width $2w + 1$ where w stands for half width of the window. The output $n^*_{u,v}(l)$ of the average filter at level l can be expressed as:

$$n^*_{u,v}(l) = \Sigma^{w}_{r=-w} n_{u,v}(l+r) \qquad ,0 \le (l+r) \le (L-1) \tag{16}$$

Here $n_{u,v}(l+r)$ is the count of the pixel having the intensity $(l+r)$ at the location (u,v), and L is the total number of possible intensity levels. The maximum probability density $p^*_{u,v}$ of a pixel can be computed through a simple division of the occurrence for a pixel by the total frequency N^*:

$$p^*_{u,v} = \frac{\max_{0\le l \le L-1}\{n^*_{u,v}(l)\}}{N*} \tag{17}$$

Since the filter smoothens the histogram curve, if the width of the averaging window is chosen to be less than a preset value, the location of the maximum will be closer to the center of the Gaussian model (which corresponds to background value). Therefore the mean intensity of the background model will be:

$$\mu_{u,v} = \arg\max_{l}\{n^*_{u,v}(l)\} \tag{18}$$

Choice of the window size is a critical task since a smaller window width can save the processing time, while a larger window will lead to smoother GBH and therefore more accurate estimation of the real value of the pixel related to the background model. The mean intensity can be computed by selecting the maximum frequency of the smoothened histogram. When a new intensity$l$ is captured, the algorithm does not process all the possible intensities, just the new one and its adjacent intensities which fall in the selected window.
If the current pixel intensity is represented by $I_{(u,v)}$ where (u,v) corresponds to the location of pixel on the image,then background objects are extracted by using:

$$BG(u,v) = \begin{cases} 1 & , if|I(u,v) - \mu(u,v)| < 3\sigma(u,v) \\ 0 & ,\text{otherwise.} \end{cases} \tag{19}$$

Figure 7, depicts an estimated background using GBH method for a video frame taken in Famagusta city.

(a) Original Frame (b) Estimated background (c) Extracted foreground mask

Fig. 7. Background / Foreground separation using group based histogram method

3. Segmentation performance

According to (Mezaris et al., 2003), comparison of algorithms trying to achieve the same task are possible either using standalone evaluations or by the application of relative evaluation methods. In this work the latter approach was used.

To have a precise comparison between BE/FS algorithms video sequences with ground truths are necessary. These are video sequences that are created by first recording a scene without any foreground objects and then superimposing animated moving objects on the recorded background manually. Therefore, the exact location of the pixels related to foreground items is known (in other words the ground-truths of these sequences are available). A second advantage of using a test sequence with ground truth is that the superimposed objects would not contain shadows and hence the focus will be on the BE/FS performance only.
The comparisons of the afore mentioned algorithms were based on a synthetically generated video sequence ,video7long.avi, which was developed for the *Background Competition of the 4th ACM International Workshop on Video Surveillance Sensor Networks* and a custom recorded video taken in the electrical and electronics engineering department of Eastern Mediterranean University. The custom video sequence contains an indoor scene showing students walk through the corridor, stop for a while, then continue walking again. To compare our achieved results with the ground truths two well known scales *recall* and *precision* were employed for each pixel. Recall is a measure of completeness and is defined as the number of correctly identified pixels (true positives) divided by the total number of pixels that actually belong to the foreground objects (pixels in ground truth). On the other hand precision is defined as the ratio of correctly detected pixels in the region of interest to the number of all pixels in relevant detection regions.

$$\begin{aligned} R &= \frac{TP}{TP+FN} \\ P &= \frac{TP}{TP+FP} \end{aligned} \tag{20}$$

where, TP, FN and FP stand for true positive, false negative and false positive respectivelt.
During evaluation of the five different algorithms introduced in section 2, all the frames belonging to video7long were used and average recall and precision percentages were computed for each technique separately. These results have been summarized in Table 1. To test which one of the algorithms generate the background model faster, we have also applied them to a video sequence which does not start with an empty frame and average processing times required to process a single frame have been recorded for each method. During the simulations also the number of frames required to generte an acceptable estimate of the foreground mask has been noted. These values are summarised in Table 2 .
A visula comparison showing how well each algorithm can cope with multi-modal background scenes (shaking leaves, swaying branches etc.) is depicted in Fig. 8. Similarly, Fig. 9 depicts how well each algorithm perform under indoor environment with transient stops.
A quick look at the results indicate that the MoG Model is not robust against transient stops but it suppresses the multi-modal backgrounds best. Also for indoor environments with transient stops the AMF technique surpasses the PG, MoG and GBH methods.

BG Est. Method	Recall (%)	Precision (%)
TMF	77.88	49.65
AMF	82.34	58.19
PG	72.30	60.92
MOG	85.38	77.96
GBH	86.18	74.42

Table 1. Average recall and precision results for five background estimation algorithms

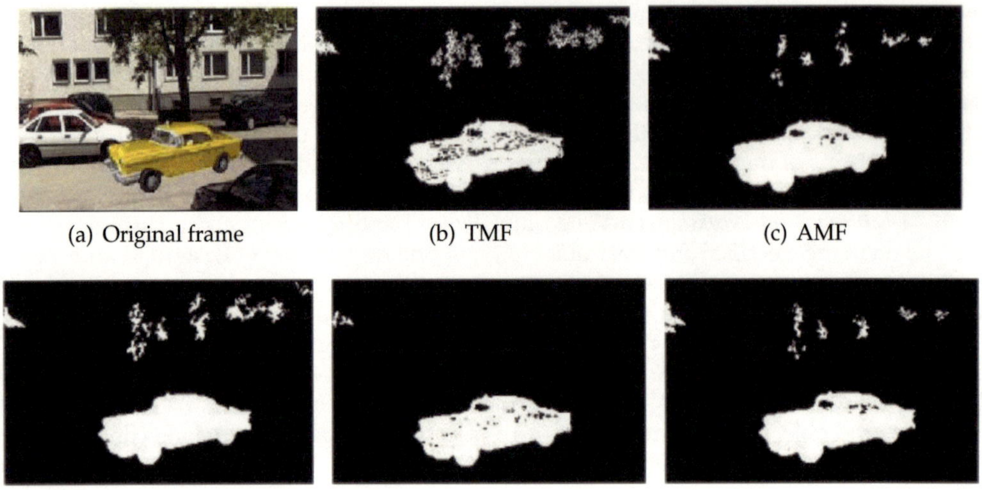

(a) Original frame (b) TMF (c) AMF (d) PG (e) MoG (f) GBH

Fig. 8. Visual comparison between algorithms in handling multi-modal background scenes

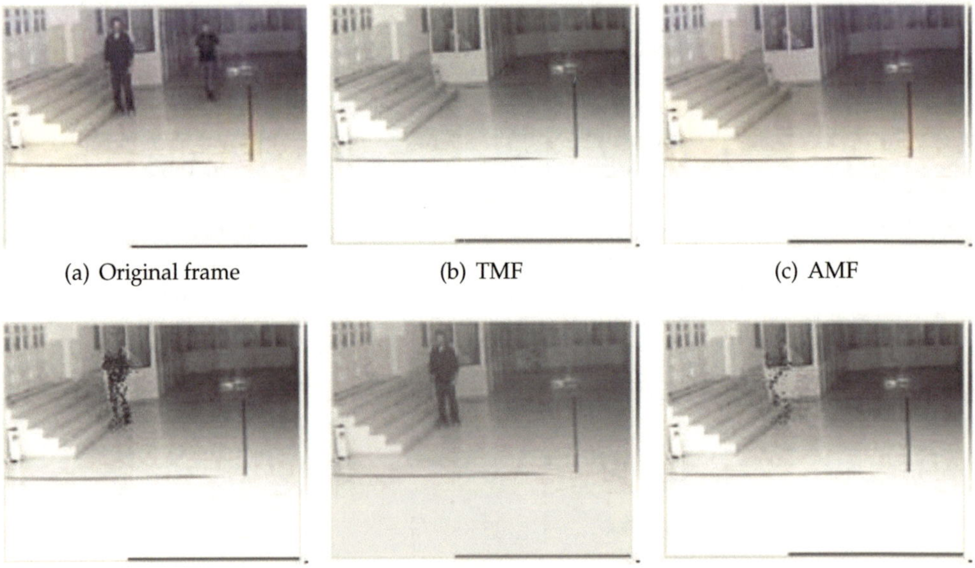

(a) Original frame (b) TMF (c) AMF (d) PG (e) MoG (f) GBH

Fig. 9. Visual comparison between algorithms in handling transient stops

Method	Average Processing Time Per Frame (sec)	Frames to Generate Acceptable FG
TMF	1.8570	12
AMF	0.0490	44
PG	2.7422	10
MOG	1.4152	9
GBH	4.0214	6

Table 2. Comparison of algorithm with respect to time

4. Cast shadow detection and removal

Cast shadows are generated due to occlusion of sun light by moving objects. The resultant shadows are the projected areas on the scene which move along side of the moving object. From a camera's point of view, cast shadows have many of the same characteristics as vehicles. They move in similar patterns and directions, and they are considerably different from the background. The cast shadows that are projected on the road surface can change in size based on how high or how low the illuminating light source might be. In cases when the cast shadows stretch, two or more independent objects can appear to be connected together and this makes classification a more difficult job. In fact, incorrect detection of moving cast shadows as part of the foreground scene will cause serious problems in all applications that deal with recognition, classification and traffic analysis.

4.1 Classification of shadow detection algorithms

As stated by (Prati et al., 2003), cast shadow detection algorithms can be classified using a two layer taxonomy. On the first layer are the *deterministic* and *statistical* methods. In the second layer, the statistical approaches can be subdivided into *parametric* and *non-parametric*. Similarly, deterministic methods can be sub-classified as *model-based* and *non-model based*.Choosing a model-based approach undoubtedly achieves the best results, but is, most of the time, too complex and time consuming compared to the nonmodel-based. In this chapter we will summarize the HSV color space and Shadow Confidence Score (SCS) based shadow removal algorithms and provide results based on custom and/or standard video sequences.

4.1.1 Shadow detection in the HSV space

The HSV system described by (Cucchiara et al., 2001) is an example of the deterministic nonmodel-based approaches. HSV color space corresponds closely to human perception of color and it has high accuracy in detecting shadow pixels. The shadow point mask defined by the HSV method is as follows:

$$SP_k(x,y) = \begin{cases} 1 \;, \left\{\alpha \leq \frac{I_k{}^V(x,y)}{B_k{}^V(x,y)} \leq \beta\right\} \cap \left\{(I_k{}^S(x,y) - B_k{}^S(x,y)) \leq \tau_S\right\} \cap \\ \left\{(I_k{}^H(x,y) - B_k{}^H(x,y)) \leq \tau_H\right\} \\ 0 \;, \text{otherwise.} \end{cases} \quad (21)$$

where $I_k{}^H(x,y)$, $I_k{}^S(x,y)$ and $I_k{}^V(x,y)$ are the HSV components of the input frame at time instant k and location (x,y) and $B_k{}^H(x,y)$,$B_k{}^S(x,y)$ and $B_k{}^V(x,y)$ are the HSV components of the background frame.

The lower bound α is used to define a minimum value for the darkening effect of shadows on the background and it is almost proportional to the light source intensity and the upper

bound β prevents the system from identifying noise which slightly changes the background in the shadow regions. It has been shown that the chrominance values for both the shadow and non-shadow pixels would vary only slightly. The choice of τ_H and τ_S is done according to this assumption. This choice is complicated and the threshold values have to be chosen by trial and error.
Figure 10 , shows the background subtraction and shadow removal processes applied to a frame from a custom video taken at the Yeni Izmir junction of Famagusta city.

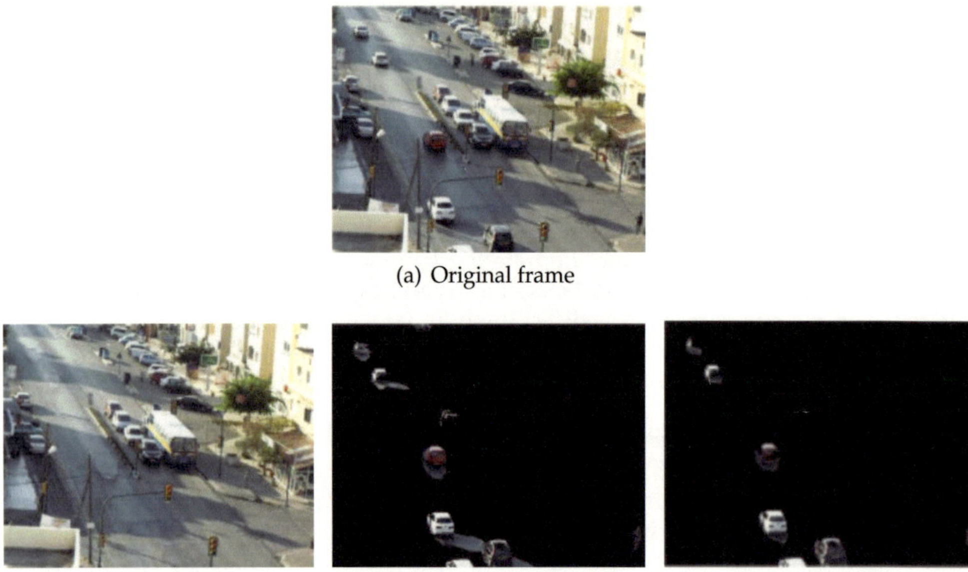

(a) Original frame

(b) BG estimate (c) FG with cast shadows (d) FG objects

Fig. 10. Shadow detection and removal using HSV method

4.1.2 Shadow confidence score based shadow removal

The shadow confidence score (SCS) based shadow removal was first proposed by (Andrew et al., 2002). This method requires that firstly, a background subtraction algorithm is used to generate the moving foreground mask (MFM) and then extracted blobs corresponding to binary mask locations in the color image are converted to YC_bC_r . For creating the SCSs one needs to combine the characteristics of the cast shadow in the luminance, chrominance and gradient density domains. The characteristics of the cast shadow in the luminance, chrominance and gradient density domain dictates that:

1. Luminance values of the cast shadow pixels are lower than those of the corresponding pixels in the background image,
2. The chrominance values of the cast shadow pixels are identical or only slightly different from those of the corresponding pixels in the background,
3. The difference in gradient density values of the cast shadow pixels and the corresponding background pixels is relatively low. The difference in gradient density values between the vehicle pixels and the corresponding background pixels is relatively high.

The three scores $S_{L,i}(x,y)$, $S_{C,i}(x,y)$ and $S_{G,i}(x,y)$ can be calculted using the equations below:

$$S_{L,i}(x,y) = \begin{cases} 1 & L_i \leq 0 \\ \frac{(T_L - L_i(x,y))}{T_L} & ,0<L_i(x,y)<T_L \\ 0 & L_i(x,y) \geq T_L \end{cases} \tag{22}$$

where, $L_i(x,y) = l_{I,i}(x,y) - l_{B,i}(x,y)$.

$$S_{C,i}(x,y) = \begin{cases} 1 & C_i \leq T_{C1} \\ \frac{(T_{C2} - C_i(x,y))}{T_{C2} - T_{C1}} & ,T_{C1}<C_i(x,y)<T_{C2} \\ 0 & C_i(x,y) \geq T_{C2} \end{cases} \tag{23}$$

where, $C_i(x,y) = |Cb_{I,i}(x,y) - Cb_{B,i}(x,y)| + |Cr_{I,i}(x,y) - Cr_{B,i}(x,y)|$.

$$S_{G,i}(x,y) = \begin{cases} 1 & GD_i(x,y) \leq T_{G1} \\ \frac{(T_{G2} - GD_i(x,y))}{T_{G2} - T_{G1}} & ,T_{G1}<GD_i(x,y)<T_{G2} \\ 0 & GD_i(x,y) \geq T_{G2} \end{cases} \tag{24}$$

where, $GD_i(x,y) = GD_{I,i}(x,y) - GD_{B,i}(x,y)$.

Figures 11 and 12, depict the shadow removal process applied to frames extracted from a custom and a standard video sequence. The threshold values used by the SCS calculator have been summarized in Table 3 for each video used.

Video Sequence	T_L	T_{C1}	T_{C2}	T_{G1}	T_{G2}
Yeni Izmir Junction	180	9.5	19	0.3	0.6
Highway I	200	7.5	15	0.5	1.0

Table 3. SCS Algorithm Parameters

It is possible that sometimes parts of the objects can be misclassified as shadows (incorrect decisions led to undesired erosion on the foreground mask). To fix this problem a convex hull can be fitted to the remaining shadow free foreground mask as described by (Ince et al., 2009). Generating a polygon that completely and closely surrounds a given set of points in 2D is called convex hull fitting. In the literature there are many algorithms for convex hull generation. Some well-known ones include incremental, gift wrapping, divide and conquer and quick hull algorithms. The one adopted here is the incremental algorithm. The processing starts with a single point and then using two more points a triangle is created. Next a new point is selected. If the new point is inside the hull there is nothing to do. Otherwise one must delete all the edges that the new point can see and add two new edges to connect the new point to the remainder of the old hull. This process is then repeated for all the remaining new points.

5. Analysis of lane occupancy

In a conventional traffic lights controller, the lights either change at constant cycle times or at times proportional to the length of each leg of the intersection. Such approaches clearly are not perfect for optimizing traffic flow. Waiting times proportional to lane length may work well for a single-lane road but when roads with multiple lanes are considered this solution would not be optimal. Assuming that in real life each leg of an intersection is being monitored simultaneously by fixed surveillance cameras, this section presents a framework as suggested by (Ince et al., 2009) to analyse the lane fullness for individual legs of an intersection. This way adaptive signalling based on the computed values would become possible. During simulations the segmentation of foreground objects from frames of the surveillance video

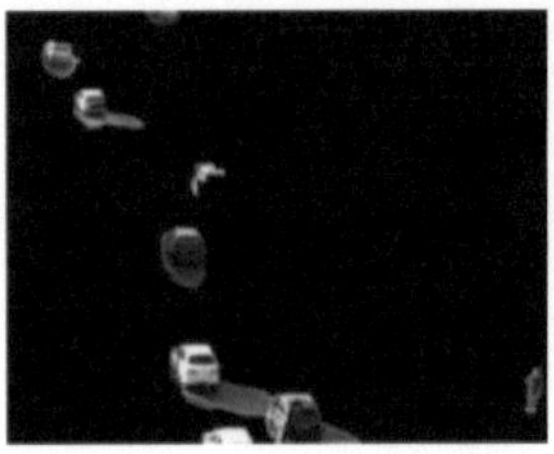

(a) FG with shadow

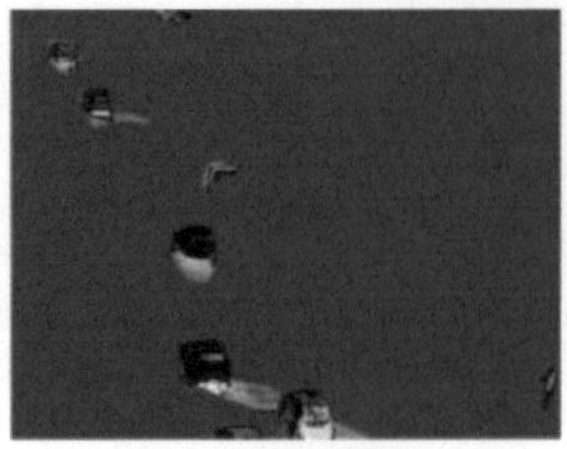

(b) total SCS

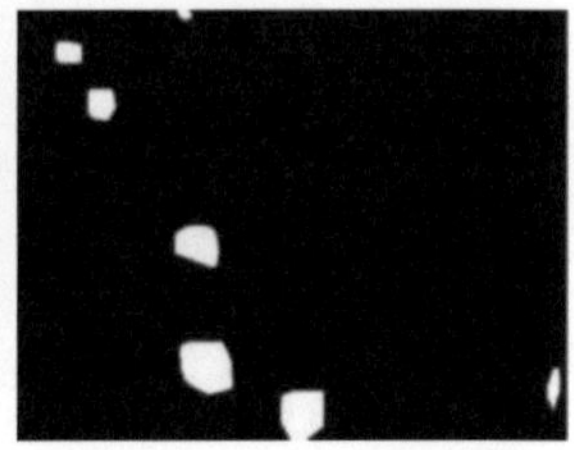

(c) shadow free foreground mask

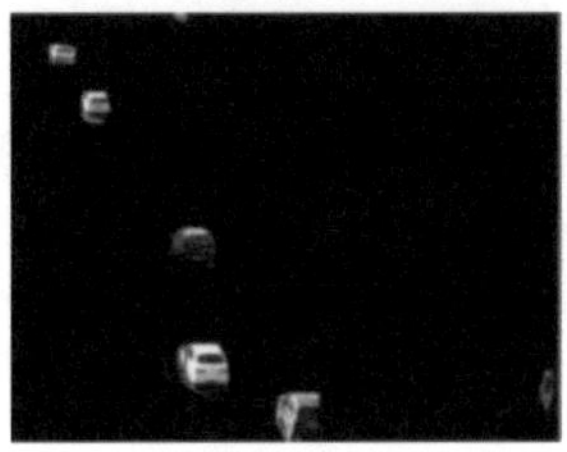

(d) FG objects

Fig. 11. Shadow detection and removal using SCS method

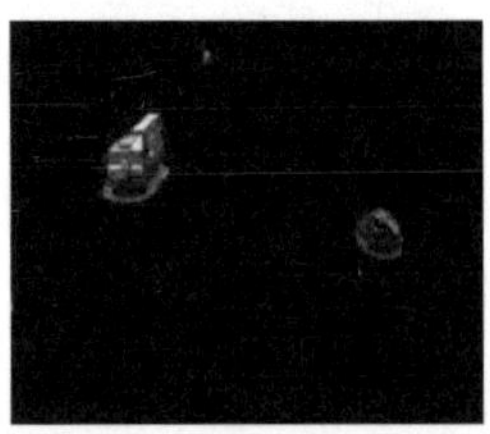

(a) FG with shadow

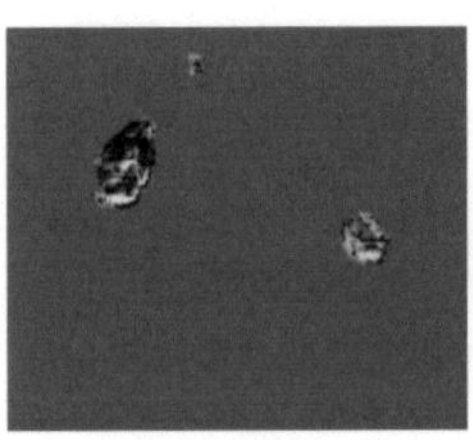

(b) total SCS

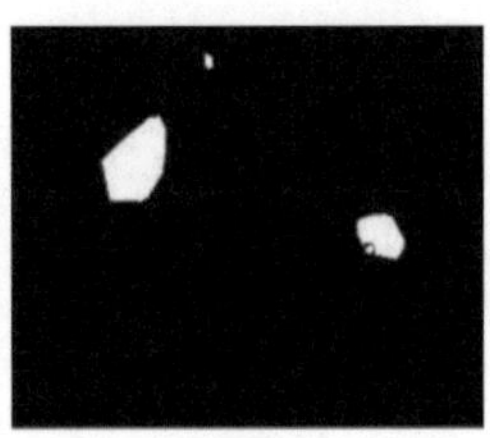

(c) shadow free foreground mask

(d) FG objects

Fig. 12. Shadow detection and removal using SCS and Highway I sequence.

are done using an adaptive K-Gaussian mixture model and cast shadows present in the segmented foregrounds are removed using the shadow confidence score earlier discussed.
In systems using fuzzy logic each leg houses two sensors behind traffic lights separated by a distance D. The sensor at distance D from the light counts the number cars coming to the intersection and the second counts the cars passing the traffic light. The amount of cars between the sensors is determined by the difference of the readings. However, this approach can not differentiate between a truck, a bus or a car. Hence determining what percent of the road is full based on size becomes fairly difficult.
A better approach that would not require any information on the type of cars present behind the traffic lights would be the use of the foreground mask(with shadows removed) together with two lane masks for determining how much each lane and the detected foreground overlap outside a designated region A. Afterwards we test to see if any of the foreground objects fall in this designated region. If region A contains no moving objects it is assumed 100% full. Otherwise the overlap between the extracted FG over region A and the ground truth mask of region A can be computed.
The application of the fullness analysis to the north leg of the intersection for frame #1890 of the video sequence shot at Yeni Izmir junction is depicted in Fig. 13.

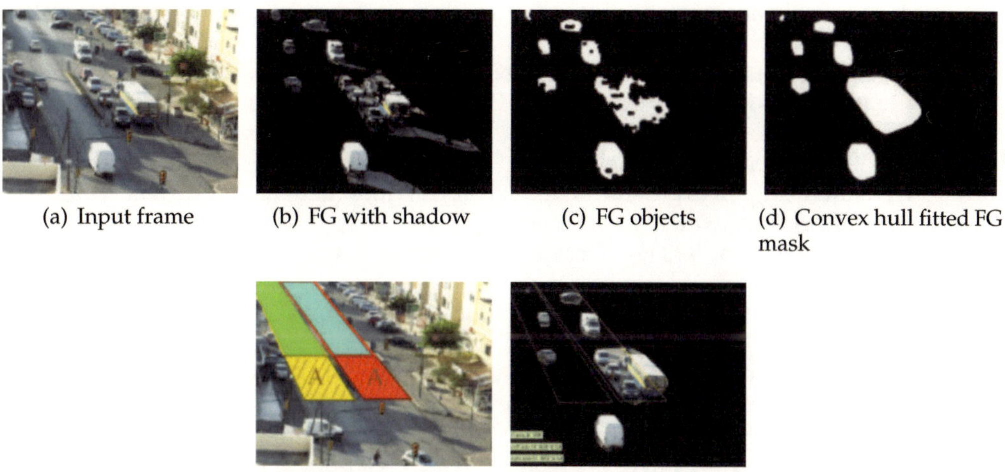

(a) Input frame (b) FG with shadow (c) FG objects (d) Convex hull fitted FG mask

(e) lane masks (f) degree of fullness

Fig. 13. Lane fullness analysis.

While computing percentage fullness of left and right lanes, the depth for the designated region A which is close to the traffic lights, can be adaptively changed after tracing every five minute of the video sequence and obtaining a speed for the traffic flow. This will allow estimates taken during different times of the day to be more realistic.

6. Summary

The simulation results indicate that critical tradeoffs are always present between the accuracy of estimated background model and the real time performance of the method. The choice of algorithm for background modeling should be made according to the desired application. For instance if it is desired to monitor an indoor scene environment, one of the most suitable choices would be the AMF, however, the same algorithm is not a proper choice when it comes to outdoor scenes due to the fact that it cannot deal with multi-modal background scenes or

cope with changes in weather condition. Among the five algorithms discusses in section 2, the MoG algorithm is best in handling the multi-modal backgrounds.
Both the HSV and the SCS based shadow removal algorithms need to use different thresholds and this constitudes a disadvantage since for each video sequence the set of thresholds have to be optimized empirically. On the other hand the HSV runs fast and accurately and if the selection of thresholds can be automized based on the content of each frame and its layers then it would constitude a good solution for real time systems.
For various examples it was observed that after shadow detection and removal step, applying a convex hull to the shadow free FG mask will help enhance the final FG mask by fixing errors like partial erosions and/or holes. This holds in general regardless of the shadow detection and removal method adopted.

7.References

Christani, M.; Bicego, M. & Murino, V. (2003). Multi level background initialization using Hidden Markov models, *In first ACM SIGMM Int. workshop on video surveillance*, pp. 11-20, 2003.

Mittal, A. & Paragios, N. (2004). Motion-based background subtraction using adaptive kernel density estimation, *In Proceedings of the Int. Conf. on Computer Vision and Pattern Recognition*, pp. 302-309, 2004.

Cheung, S-C. & Kamath, C. (2004). Robust techniques for background subtraction in urban traffic video, *In Proceedings of Electrical Imaging: Visual Communications Image Processing* , pp. 881-892, 2004.

Elhabian, S. Y.; El-Sayed, K. M. & Ahmed, S.H. (2008). Moving Object Detection in Spatial Domain using Background Removal Techniques-State-of-Art, *Recent Patents on Computer Science* , Vol. 1, pp. 32-54, 2008.

Nixon, M. & Aguado, A. (2005). *Feature Extraction and Image Processing*, Elsevier Inc., 0-7506-5078-8, UK.

McFarlane, N. & Schofield, C. (1995). Segmentation and tracking of piglets in images, *In Proc. of Machine Vision Applications*, 8(3), pp. 187-193, 1995.

Stauffer, C. & Grimson, W. (1999). Adaptive background mixture models for real-time tracking, *In Proceedings of the Int. Conf. on Computer Vision and Pattern Recognition*, pp. 246-252, 1999.

Gonzales, R.C. (2002). *Digital Image Processing*, Prentice Hall Inc.,0-20-118075-8, New Jersey USA.

Chung, Y., Wang, J. & Chen, S. (2002).Progressive Background Images Generation, *In Proc. of 15th IPPR Conf. on Computer Vision*, 2002.

Mezaris, V., Kompatsiaris, I. & Strintzis, M.G. (2003). Still Image Objective Segmentation Evaluation using Ground Truth, *In 5th COST 276 Workshop*, pp. 9-14, 2003.

Prati, A., Mikic, I., Trivedi, M.M.& Cucchiara, R. (2003). Detecting Moving Shadows: Algorithms and Evaluation, *In IEEE tracsactions on pattern analysis and machine intelligence* , Vol. 25, No. 7, pp. 918-923, 2003.

Cucchiara, R., Grana, C., Neri, G., Piccardi, M. & Prati, A. (2001). The Sakbot System for Moving Object Detection and Tracking, *In Video-Based Surveillance SystemsâĂŤComputer Vision and Distributed Processing* , pp. 1458-157, 2001.

George, S.K.F., Nelson, H.C.Y.,Grantham, K.H.P. & Andrew, H.S.L. (2002). Effective moving cast shadow detection for monocular colour traffic image sequences, *In Optical Engineering. 41(6)* , pp. 1425-1440, June 2002.

Seifnaraghi, N., Ebrahimi, S.G.& Ince, E.A. (2009). Novel traffic lights signalling technique based on lane occupancy rates, *In ISCIS 09* , pp. 592-596 , Sept 2009.

11

Block Matching-Based Background Generation and Non-Rigid Shape Tracking for Video Surveillance

Taekyung Kim and Joonki Paik
Graduate School of Advanced Imaging Science, Multimedia, and FilmChung-Ang University, Korea

1. Introduction

Video analysis and tracking is a fundamental problem of dynamically extracting two-dimensional (2D) information in most visual applications including; image processing, computer vision, video surveillance, image synthesis for contents creation, human-computer-interaction (HCI), video compression, and etc. Most existing video surveillance systems simply record and transmit video for crime investigation and traffic flow monitoring. Recent advances in video technology, however, realize intelligent features such as motion detection, tracking, classification, recognition, synthesis, and behaviour analysis.

A video tracking system consists of a series of computational modules, each of which performs location, recognition, and trace of an object. Since the tracking system utilizes spatio-temporally dynamic information, a moving object should first be differentiated from stationary background. The difference-based tracking algorithm, however, cannot detect an object that moves very slowly. Furthermore two or more objects are considered as a single object when occlusion occurs. Occlusion is another challenge, and adaptive background generation is necessary for robust tracking under unstable environment including illumination change, dynamic shading, and camera jitter [Mckenna et al. 1999]-[Javed et al. 2004].

The active shape model (ASM)-based tracking algorithm localizes non-rigid objects with a priori trained shape information [Mckenna et al. 1999], [Cootes et al. 1992], [Nascimento et al. 2004], [Calvagno et al. 2004], and [Koschan et al. 2003]. After modeling an object's shape, it iteratively performs model fitting with possible combination of motion information. The hierarchical extension of the ASM has been proposed by Lee et al. to accelerate the iterative model fitting process with higher matching accuracy [Lee et al. 2007]. Model fitting in the low-resolution image significantly reduces the amount of computation, and coarse-to-fine estimate of the shape together with Kalman filter provides more robust tracking results.

Both the original and the extended versions of ASM-based tracking are, however, highly dependent on prior knowledge such as the number of landmark points and the shape of models in the training sets. In most cases the number of landmark points is manually determined by examining the training data.

To reduce the computational load a feature-based shape tracking method, called non-prior training active feature model (NPT-AFM), has been proposed in [Shin et al. 2005]. This feature-based object modeling method can track objects by using the greatly reduced number of feature points rather than taking entire shapes in the existing shape-based methods. The on-the-fly update of the training set and the reduced number of feature points can make a real-time, robust tracking system possible. In spite of improved computational efficiency and occlusion handling performance, the NPT-AFM method still requires additional grouping and updating object's feature points. In addition it does not utilize background information, which contains the most part of information in the image.

Another successful tracking technique is block-matching algorithm to find a matching block from a frame to another one. A block-matching algorithm makes use of a matching criterion to determine whether a given block in a frame matches the search block in the reference frame [Zhang et al. 2004] The major advantages of the block-matching algorithms are twofold (i) its direct matching nature simplifies motion estimation procedures, and (ii) the block preserves object's features that cannot be easily parameterized. There are many variations of the block-matching algorithm that improves the estimation accuracy and computational efficiency [Zhang et al. 2000], [Stefano et al. 1999], [Hariharakrishnan et al. 2005].

On the other hand the drawbacks of the block-matching algorithm include poor performance with non-rigid shapes and the existence of similar patterns in the background. For example, irregular deformation of non-rigid objects decreases the matching accuracy of block-matching algorithms.

In this paper we present a combined shape and feature-based video analysis for non-rigid object tracking that tightly coupled with an adaptive background generation method to compensate the weakness of block matching. The proposed algorithm includes motion detection using background information, feature extraction, and block matching. The background information is acquired by checking the correlation of block located at the same location in the consecutive frames. The proposed method generates a set of features called shape control points (SCPs) by detecting edges in the neighbouring four directions. SCPs are evenly distributed on the contour of the object, and the block- matching-based tracking algorithm is performed on the block containing the corresponding SCP.

In order to further improve the accuracy of block matching together with background generation, we additionally adopt periodic evaluation of the centroid of SCPs in every few frames to preserve the overall shape. We then compare and update each SCP with the centroid during the tracking process, where stray SCPs are removed, and the tracking continue with only qualified SCPs. As a result, the proposed method efficiently removes potential failing factors caused by spatio-temporal similarity between object and background, object deformation, and occlusion.

This chapter is organized as follows. Section 2 presents the fundamentals of ASM. We briefly introduce the NPT-AFM method in section 3, and the definition of SCP and the associated block matching-based non-rigid object tracking algorithm is explained in section 4. We present experimental results in section 5 and finally conclude the chapter in section 6.

2. Active shape model (ASM)

Finding the shape and location of an object is a fundamental task for tracking an object in sequential video images. Within the class of deformable models, the boundary information of the object is used to represent the object. For tracking a non-rigid object with prior knowledge ASM is one of the best approaches in the sense of both accuracy and efficiency.

In order to track an object, ASM uses a priori information about the target object such as the shape. Thus it can match and extract the outline of the object in the noisy, or occluded image. The prior knowledge about the object forms a training set that includes variously posed target objects. The training set can be built either automatically or manually by selecting landmark points on the boundary of the object in the sample images. The landmark points should have the distinguishable features of the object such as corner point. ASM-based object detection algorithm consists of four steps; (i) assignment of landmark points, (ii) principal component analysis (PCA), (iii) local structure modeling, and (iv) model fitting.

2.1 Obtaining landmark points

Given an input image, landmark points can be obtained by selecting proper feature points on the object's boundary. The feature points in one frame should be correlated to those in the next frame. We can represent n landmark points as a $2n$ dimensional vector in a two-dimensional (2D) image as

$$X = [x_1, \ldots, x_n, y_1, \ldots, y_n]^T \tag{1}$$

We used 42 landmark points in the experiments. [Tanimoto et al. 1975] proposed an automatic landmark assignment method. The positions of landmark points are iteratively updated to minimize the differences with the real boundary of the target object.

2.2 Principal Component Analysis (PCA)

A set of n landmark points which is one member of the training set represents the shape of an object. Instead of using all landmark points in a member of the training set, PCA technique helps to model the shape of the object with less number of parameters. Let us assume that there are m members in the training set and x_i represents each member ($i = 1, \ldots, m$). The PCA algorithm is summarized in the following.

1. Find an average of m members.

$$\bar{x} = \frac{1}{m} \sum_{i=1}^{m} x_i \tag{2}$$

2. Find a covariance matrix from the training set.

$$S = \frac{1}{m} \sum_{i=1}^{m} (x_i - \bar{x})(x_i - \bar{x})^T \tag{3}$$

3. Obtain an eigenvector that has the q biggest eigenvalues from the covariance matrix S. q is defined to cover 98% of the variance of total data.

$$\Phi = [\varphi_1 \mid \varphi_2 \mid \varphi_3 \mid \cdots \mid \varphi_q] \tag{4}$$

4. Approximate the shape of the object from the obtained φ and $\overline{x}$ as

$$x_i \approx \bar{x} + \Phi b_i \tag{5}$$

and

$$b_i = \Phi^T (x_i - \bar{x}) \tag{6}$$

Vector b can be defined as a set of deformable model parameters and implies the shape of the object.

2.3 Local structure modeling

In order to analyze the shape of the target object we have to find the best set of landmark points that matches the object and the model. At each iteration the landmark points selected by PCA algorithm are relocated to the edge of the object along the line which is vertical to the boundary of the real object as shown in fig. 1.

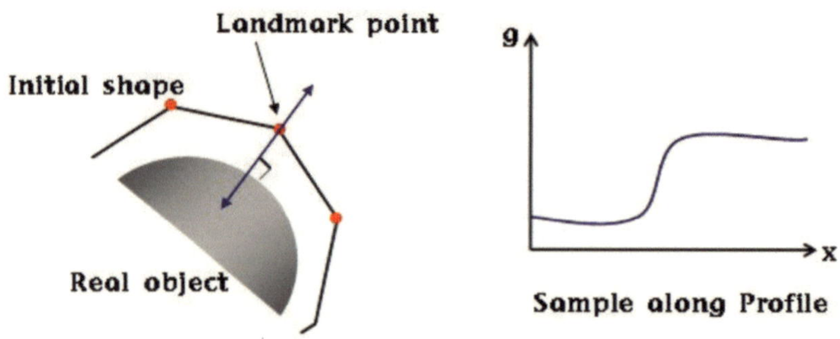

Fig. 1. Local structure modeling

2.4 Model fitting

The best parameters that represent the optimal location and shape of the object can be obtained by matching the shape of models in the training set to the real object in the image. The matching is performed by minimizing the error function as

$$E = (y - Mx)^T W (y - Mx) \tag{7}$$

where x represents the coordinates of the model, y the coordinate of the real object, W a diagonal matrix whose diagonal element is the weight to each landmark points, M a matrix for the geometrical transformation which consists of rotation θ, transition t, and scaling factor s. The weight decides the distance between previous and new landmark points.
The geometrical transformation matrix for a single point $(x_0, y_0)^T$ can be represented as

$$M\begin{bmatrix} x_0 \\ y_0 \end{bmatrix} = s\begin{bmatrix} \cos\theta & \sin\theta \\ -\sin\theta & \cos\theta \end{bmatrix}\begin{bmatrix} x_0 \\ y_0 \end{bmatrix} + \begin{bmatrix} t_x \\ t_y \end{bmatrix} \tag{8}$$

Once the set of geometrical parameters (θ, t, s) is determined, the projection of y to the frame of model parameters is given as

$$x_p = M^{-1} y \tag{9}$$

The new model parameter b is updated as

$$b = \Phi^T (x_p - \bar{x}) \quad (10)$$

With the model parameters from equation (10) a new shape that consists of new landmark points is obtained by equation (5). The new shape can be used in equation (7) and the model fitting process repeats until optimal landmark points are achieved. After some iteration of model fitting, we can achieve the final shape x .

3. Non prior training active feature model (NPT-AFM)

In this section we present a feature-based object tracking algorithm using optical flow under the non-prior training active feature model (NPT-AFM) framework which generates training shapes in real-time without pre-processing. The NPT-AFM algorithm extracts moving objects by using motion between frames, and determines feature points inside the object. Selected feature points in the next frame are predicted by a spatio-temporally adaptive algorithm. If a feature point is missing or tracking fails, correction process restores feasible feature points. The NPT-AFM can track deformable, partially occluded objects by using the greatly reduced number of feature points rather than taking entire shapes in the existing shape-based methods. Therefore, objects can be tracked without a priori information or constraint with respect to the camera position or object motion.
The flowchart of NPT-AFM algorithm is shown in fig. 2.

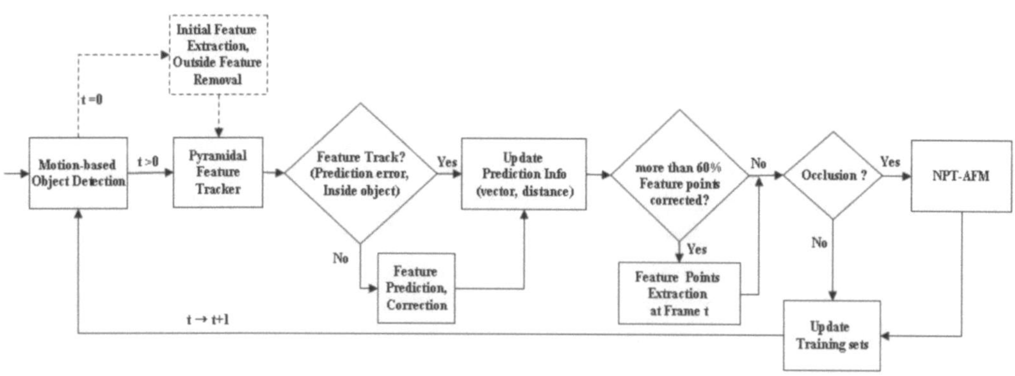

Fig. 2. Non-prior training active feature model (NPT-AFM) algorithm

In fig. 2, the upper, dotted box represents the algorithm of initial feature extraction. The remaining part of the flowchart relates two consecutive frames. In the motion-based object detection block, we extract motion by the simple Lucas-Kanade optical flow [Tekalp 1995] and classify object's movement into four directions such as left, right, up, and down. As a result, the region of moving objects can be extracted and the corresponding region is then labelled based on the direction of motion.
After detecting moving objects from background, we extract a set of feature points inside the object and predict the corresponding feature points in the next frame. We keep checking and restoring any missing feature points during the tracking process. If over 60% of feature points are restored, we decided the set of feature points are not proper for tracking, and

redefine new set of points. If occlusion occurs, the NPT-AFM process, which updates training sets at each frame to restore entire shapes from the occluded input, is performed to estimate the position of occluded feature points.
The advantages of the NPT-AFM algorithm can be summarized as: (i) it can track both rigid and deformable objects because a general feature-based tracking algorithm is applied, (ii) it is robust against object's sudden motion because motion direction and feature points are tracked at the same time, (iii) its tracking performance is not degraded even with complicated background because feature points are assigned inside an object rather than near boundary, and (iv) it contains the NPT-AFM procedure that can restore partial occlusion in real-time.

3.1 Feature point extraction

After detecting an object from background, we extract a set of feature points inside the object by using the Bouguet tracking algorithm [Isard et al. 1996][Bouguet 2000]. Due to the nature of motion estimation, motion-based object detection algorithms usually extract the object slightly larger than the real size of the object, which results in false extraction of feature points outside the object. Let the position of a feature point at frame t be v_i^t, where i represents the index of feature points and $v_i^t = [x_i^t, y_i^t]^T$. These outside feature points are removed by considering the distance between feature points given as

$$v_i^t = \begin{cases} v_i^t, & d_i \geq T \\ 0, & d_i < T \end{cases} \tag{11}$$

where $d_i = \sum_{t=0}^{K-1} \sqrt{\left(x_i^{t+1} - x_i^t\right)^2 + \left(y_i^{t+1} - y_i^t\right)^2}$, t represents the index of frames, and i the index of feature points. Here d_i represents the sum of distance between t-th and $t+1$-st frames with respect to the i-th feature point. In general, the moving distance of a feature point in the background (outside object) is much less than that of a feature point in the tracked object. Although the value of T is equal to 3.5 or 7 was used for all test sequences, users can control the value depending on the environmental factors such as illumination, noise, and the complexity of background. The results of outside feature point removal are shown in fig. 3. Three feature points outside the 'Tang' indicated by circle in fig. 3(a) are efficiently removed in fig. 3(b).

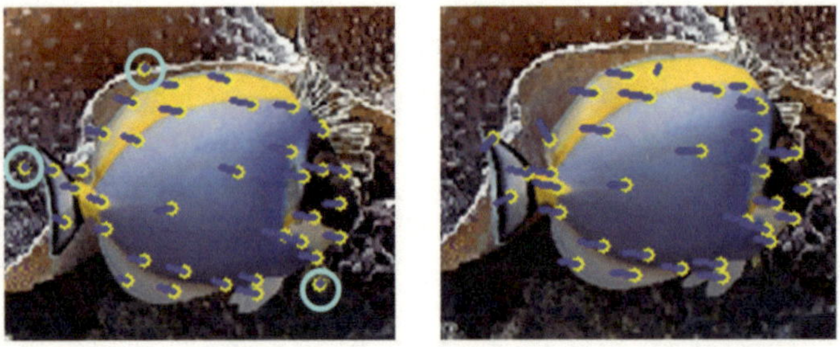

(a) (b)

Fig. 3. Results of outside feature point removal: (a) the 2nd frame with three outside feature points highlighted by circles and (b) the 7th frame without outside feature points.

3.2 Feature point prediction and correction

Sometimes, a tracking algorithm may fail in tracking a proper feature point in the next frame. We stop tracking a feature point when an error value within small window is larger than a pre-specified threshold. More specifically, a threshold value is determined by the distance between spatio-temporally predicted vectors. After the spatio-temporal prediction, re-investigation is performed. Then, both tracked and untracked feature points are updated in a list.

In many real-time, continuous video tracking applications, a feature-based tracking algorithm fails due to the following reasons: (i) self or partial occlusions of an object and (ii) feature points on or outside the boundary of the object, which are affected by dynamic background.

In order to deal with the tracking failure, we should correct the erroneously predicted feature points by using the location of the previous feature points and inter-pixel relationship between the predicted points. This algorithm is summarized in table 1.

Step 1	**Temporal Prediction:** If the i th feature point at the t th frame is lost in tracking, it is re-predicted as $$\hat{v}_i^{t+1} = v_i^t + \frac{1}{K}\sum_{k=0}^{K-1} m_i^{t-k} \quad (12)$$ where $m_i^t = v_i^t - v_i^{t-1}$, and K represents the number of frames for computing the average motion vector.
Step 2	**Spatial Prediction:** We can correct the erroneous prediction by replacing with the average motion vector of successfully predicted feature points. The temporal and spatial prediction results of Step 1 and Step 2 can be combined to estimate the position of feature points.
Step 3	**Re-Investigation of the Predicted Feature Point:** Assign the region including the predicted and corrected feature points in the spatio-temporal prediction step. If a feature point is extracted within a certain extent in the following frame, it is updated as a new feature point. While the re-predicted feature points are more than 60% of the entire feature points, feature points keeps being estimated.

Table 1. Spatio-temporal algorithm for correction of predicted feature points

A temporal prediction is suitable for deformable objects while a spatial prediction is good for non-deformable objects. Both temporal and spatial prediction results can also be combined with proper weights. Users can control the number of frames, K. The larger the value of K is, the better the performance of the algorithm is. Because of the trade-off between processing time and accuracy, the value around 7 was found to be reasonable for temporal prediction.

The existing ASM algorithm manually assigns landmark points on an object's boundary to make a training set. A good landmark point has balanced distance between adjacent landmark points and resides on either high-curvature or "T" junction position. A good feature point, however, has a different requirement from that of a good landmark point. In other words, a feature point is recommended to locate inside the object because a feature point on the boundary of the object easily fails in optical flow or block matching-based tracking due to the effect of dynamic, complicated background.

A set of feature points form an element shape in the training set. We update this training set at each frame of input video, and at the same time align the shape onto the image coordinate using Procrustes analysis [Goodall 1991]. In this work, the training set has 70 element shapes.

4. Combined shape and feature-based analysis for non-rigid object tracking

After motion detection, surveillance systems generally track moving objects from one frame to another in the image sequence. Tracking over time typically involves matching an object-of-interest in temporally consecutive frames using features such as a point, a line, or a blob.

The major contribution of the proposed algorithm is the high reliability resulting from the use of background and shape boundary in detecting and tracking a moving object. In the block matching process to extract object's region, there are many empty blocks with only background information. On the other hand the use of the shape boundary significantly alleviates this problem by selecting blocks containing the object and placing feature points on the boundary of the shapes. Also, the proposed method can efficiently remove the misplaced feature points within the given block area using measures explained in the following sections. From the selected feature points it is also possible to select the feature points called as shape control points (SCPs) which play a significant role in the tracking the object.

The proposed combined shape and feature-based object tracking system is depicted in fig. 4. Three modules of the proposed system respectively represent (i) background generation, (ii) motion detection and shape control point (SCP) extraction, and (iii) object shape tracking modules.

As mentioned in the previous section, simple difference-based methods without appropriately generated background often fail to track an object when adjacent frames have little difference. In order to overcome this problem we evaluate difference between the generated background and the input image to detect object region. The detected region is considered as a rough estimate the object's shape, and is tracked by the system using the block matching algorithm (BMA).

In the background generating process, we exclude blocks with moving objects that cause large matching errors. Additional median filtering is necessary to compensate blocking artifacts due to discarded blocks. Since the effect of moving object is blocked by the median filter, the proposed background generation block can detect moving regions and shape variation with higher accuracy.

After detecting the region of moving objects, we compute the object's boundary using morphological edge operations. The boundary information differentiates the object from the background by classifying SCPs and the candidate of shape control points (CSCPs). SCPs are used for tracking object's shape, while CSCPs are used for updating SCPs when deformation or occlusion occurs. The block matching method is used for tracking deformable objects as well as background generation. If occlusion occurs, the current SCPs are replaced by suitable CSCPs depending on the size of moving region and the number of SCPs.

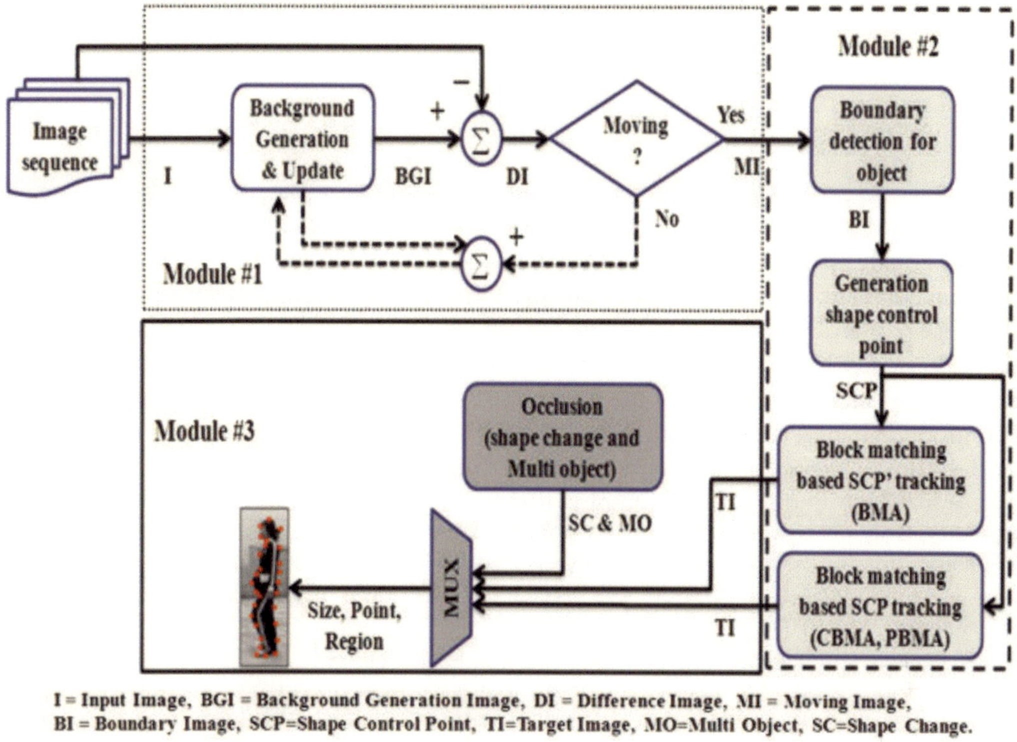

Fig. 4. The block diagram of proposed block matching-based object shape tracking

4.1 Background generation and updating

Once a stable background is generated, the object's moving region can easily be detected by comparing the generated background and the current input frame. The background is generated using only blocks with the matching error lower than a pre-specified threshold. Thus we can avoid the undesired effects caused by the internal motion and illumination change. Fig. 5 shows a typical process of BMA.

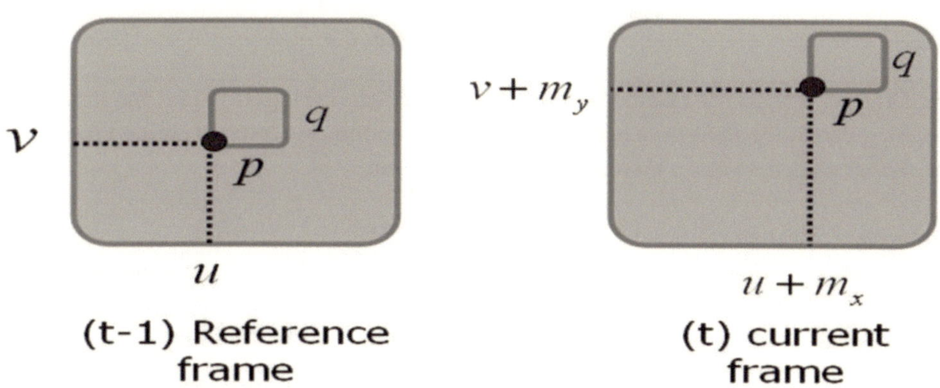

Fig. 5. Block matching algorithm between two temporally adjacent frames

The sum of absolute difference (SAD) is adopted as a measure of matching error as

$$SAD(u,v,t;m_x,m_y)=\sum_{i=0}^{p-1}\sum_{j=0}^{q-1}\begin{vmatrix}I(i+u,j+v,t-1)-\\ I(i+u+m_x,j+v+m_y,t)\end{vmatrix}, \tag{13}$$

where (u,v) represents the horizontal and vertical coordinates, (m_x,m_y) the motion vector, and (p,q) the horizontal and vertical sizes of the image block. If SAD is smaller than an experimentally chosen threshold, background is updated at the corresponding block region. In the experiment we have used 0.05 for the threshold value. For a block with high SAD value the background is generated by minimizing the SAD value, while the median filter is used for the rest blocks. Although the median filter is robust against noise and illumination change, it is still possible to lose the object due to dynamic environmental factors such as background change, internal reflection, and motion change, to name a few. For removing such dynamic factors, it is necessary to keep updating the background.

The desirable property of background is that it has a constant distribution. Based on this property, only change in video should not affect the constant distribution. For this reason W4 algorithm, for example, separates objects and background using temporal median filter, and as a result it can provide the constant distribution against illumination change [Haritaoglu et al. 2000]. W4 algorithm can also handle fast motion or abrupt change in the image because of the use of median filter.

Object motion can be detected if its amount is greater than the error of a block motion. So the background is generated such that the error is minimized. The background updating process can be expressed as

$$B(t)=(1-\sigma)I(t)+\sigma B(t-1), \tag{14}$$

where $B(t)$ represents the background at time t, $I(t)$ the input image at time t, and σ the mixing ratio in the range $[0,1]$. To differentiate object's moving region from the background, we use the following equation. The initial background $B(O)$ takes the first frame of the sequence.

$$D(t)=\begin{cases}1, & if\ \lVert B(t-1)-I(t)\rVert \geq T\\ 0, & otherwise\end{cases}, \tag{15}$$

where $D(t)$ represents the existence of difference between background and the input image frame. As given in (3), if $D(t)$ is equal to 1, the corresponding region is defined the moving region. Otherwise, the region is considered as background.

4.2 Detection of moving object

Incorporation of shape, feature, motion, and other possible information significantly increases the amount of computation in the video tracking system, which makes real-time tracking difficult. The proposed algorithm uses only SCPs from boundary information for detecting object's shape. The proposed method expresses object's moving region using binary data that is refined by morphological operations and edge detection. It is possible to estimate the object's boundary using the 2nd order derivative method.

The 2nd order derivative can be applied in both horizontal and vertical directions and object's boundary information can be calculated based on the results. Derivative information together with morphological operations enables simple, efficient edge extraction. The proposed method is similar to colour composition between background and objects to reduce errors generated by the background difference image. In the proposed algorithm we apply morphological operations on the binary image that is made from the difference image between the previous and the current images. We then finalize the boundary of the object by merging the result of morphological operations with the result of Laplacian. Fig. 6 shows the procedures of the proposed background generation and motion detection algorithm, and fig. 7 show the corresponding experimental results of each step.

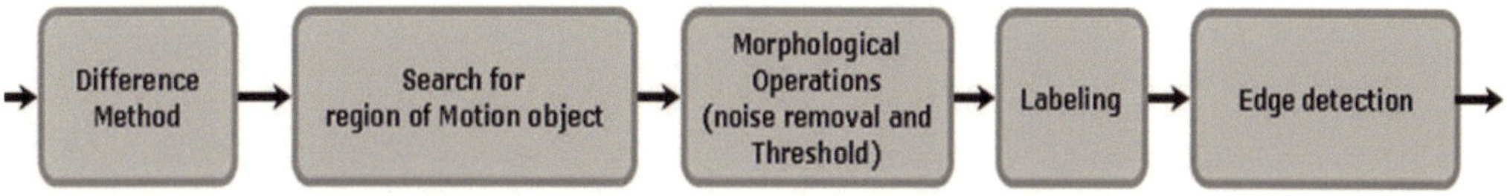

Fig. 6. Moving region detection algorithm based on background generation

(a) (b) (c) (d) (e)

Fig. 7. Experimental results of the proposed moving region detection algorithm: (a) input image, (b) difference image, (c) object's moving region, (d) result of morphological operation, and (e) result of edge detection

4.3 Shape control points (SCPs)

The object's boundary information, as shown in fig. 6(e), is used to define SCPs. Since the feature-based tracking methods often fail due to the misidentification of an object, it is necessary to group object's features by storing the boundary information. Fig. 8 shows the classification result of an image region into one of the background, the object, and the boundary.

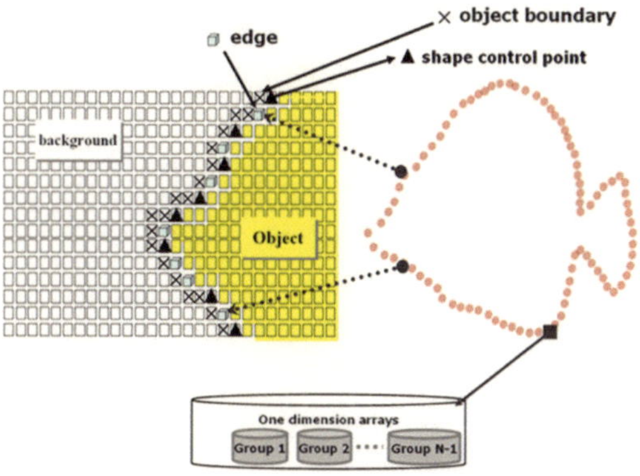

Fig. 8. Classification of meaningful regions for object detection

SCPs are obtained from the object's boundary that is produced by the moving region. Spurious edges are removed by using an empirically chosen threshold. Because matching the entire image is unrealistic in the sense of computational efficiency, the object containing region R is defined as

$$R(x,y) = \{(r,c) | x_1 \le r \le x_2 \text{ and } y_1 \le c \le y_2\}, \tag{16}$$

where (x_1, y_1) and (x_2, y_2) respectively represent the minimum and maximum coordinates of horizontal and vertical projections. Based on (16) R represents the minimum rectangular box enclosing the object, whose boundary is detected by Laplacian operator as

$$\nabla^2 R = \frac{\partial^2 R}{\partial x^2} + \frac{\partial^2 R}{\partial y^2}. \tag{17}$$

Only feasible boundary edge points are defined as SCPs, More specifically the $i-th$ SCP A_i represents the corresponding coordinate in the minimum rectangle $R(x,y)$ as

$$A_i = \{(x_i, y_i) | i = 1,2,\ldots,z\}, \tag{18}$$

where Z represents the total number of edge coordinates.

$$SCP_j = A_{jk} \text{ for } j = 1,2,\ldots,J,\ J = \lfloor I / k \rfloor. \tag{19}$$

where k represents the interval of skipping redundant SCPs. The selected set of SCPs is finally stored in a one-dimension (1D) array.

4.4 Combined shape and feature-based object tracking

Although the primary assumption on BMA is that the original and the compared blocks have significantly high correlation, it is not always true in real applications. In this paper we present a modified BMA-based tracking approach, which is robust to occlusion and illumination change, as shown in fig. 9.

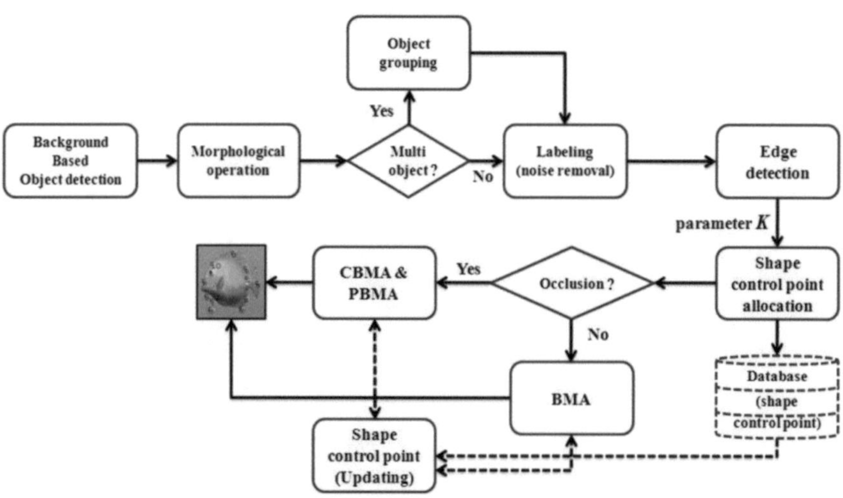

Fig. 9. Block diagram of combined shape and feature-based object tracking

Fig. 9 shows the tracking procedure given a detected object by using the generated background. The detected object is refined by the morphological operation. After labelling the object pixels, edges are detected for extracting SCPs. Extracted SCPs are saved in the database one hand and go through either BMA or CBMA/PBMA depending on whether occlusion occurs or not. By matching and updating the SCPs, a deformable, moving object can robustly be detected and tracked.
Fig. 10 shows an elaborated illustration for the SCP generation process, where an SCP is allocated at the center of the block. Each block consists of background, an object, CSCPs and SCPs at the center of the block. Location of a deformable object can be detected by using only the SCP.

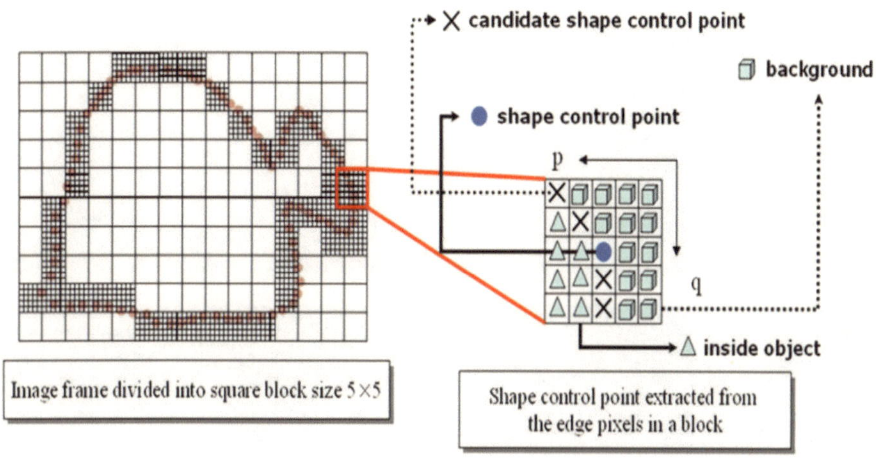

Fig. 10. Generation of an SCP

If an object deforms or occlusion occurs, SCPs cannot provide the correct location of the object. Thus CSCPs are used in this case.

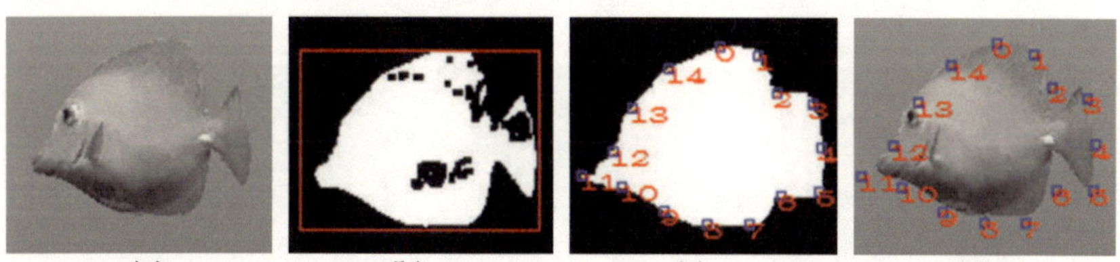

(a) (b) (c) (d)

Fig. 11. Model matching: (a) input image, (b) moving region of the object, (c) SCPs on the object's boundary, and (d) assigned SCPs on the input image.

Fig. 11 shows the step-by-step results of the SCP generation process. Fig. 11(b) shows the initially detected object's area, fig. 11(c) shows the SCP's detected on the object boundary, and fig. 11(d) shows the detected SCP's superimposed on the input image.
An object can be tracked by using BMA without background information. However, the result using BMA can easily be affected by similarity between object and background, object deformation, occlusion, illumination change, and etc. In order to minimize the tracking errors we propose two additional methods that combine background generation and block matching.

The first method, which is called the center-of-gravity-based block matching (CBMA) algorithm, preserves the relative location of each SCP by computing distances among SCPs. More specifically, SCPs are maintained inside the possible range of errors, while others are replaced by new SCPs.

The second approach extracts SCPs from the region without motion, which is called the periodic-update-based block matching (PBMA) algorithm. This method can update missing or oscillating SCPs by comparing the corresponding pair of SCPs between two consecutive input frames. SCPs outside the motion region are removed, and tracking is performed using only remaining SCPs. Fig. 12 compares results of the above mentioned three tracking methods, such as BMA, CBMA, and PBMA.

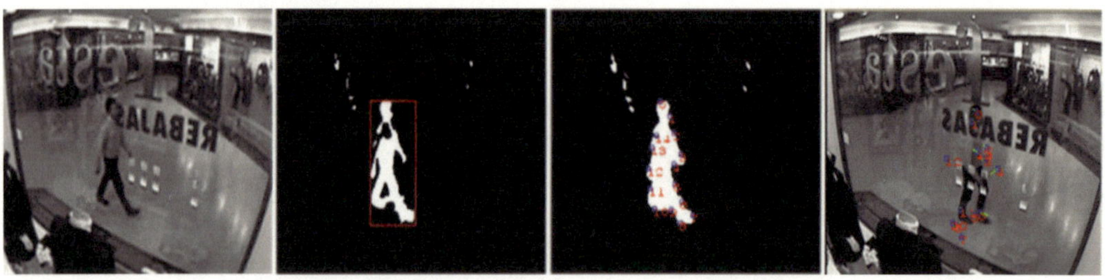

(a)

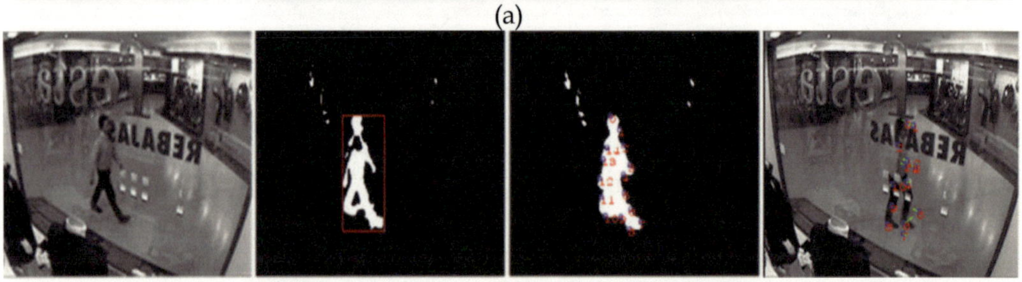

(b)

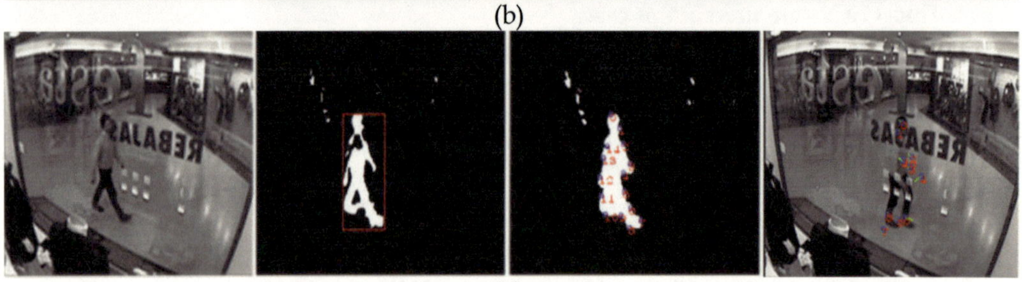

(c)

Fig. 12. Experimental results of three different block matching methods for object tracking: (a) BMA, (b) CBMA, and (c) PBMA.

5. Experimental results

The proposed object tracking algorithm was tested against shape deformation, occlusion, illumination change, and size change. The proposed algorithm is also quantitatively compared with the existing difference-based and active shape model-based algorithms.

Test sequences include (i) a computer-generated fish sequence, (ii) a PETS 2002 test sequence, (iii) in-house indoor and (iv) outdoor sequences. All test sequences have the same resolution of 320×240. To speed up the simulation we use only gray-scale images. For obtaining in-house test sequences, we sued a three-CCD colour video camera. The fish sequence has similar intensity distribution in both the object and background, while the shape of the fish keeps deforming. The PETS sequence has internal reflection on the glass window and scaled objects. The indoor sequence has external illumination and considerable amount of noise. The outdoor sequence has multiple objects with occlusion. Fig. 13 respectively summarize the experimental environment and test images.

(a) (b) (c) (d)

Fig. 13. The first image frames of four test sequences: (a) the fish, (b) the PETS 2002, (c) the indoor, and (d) the outdoor sequences

5.1 Combined shape and feature-based non-rigid object tracking

Fig. 12(a) has the worst case conditions for block matching, because texture of the object and background is similar and the object deforms. While existing block matching-based methods definitely fail in tracking the deformable fish in this sequence, the proposed algorithm provides reliable tracking results. Fig. 14 shows detection of object's moving region using background generation and the corresponding SCP extraction.

As shown in fig. 14(b) and (c), although there is no significant amount of noise in the input image, the initially detected object contains amplified noise during the subtraction process between the generated background and the input image. Such noise effect is removed by the proposed algorithm using a series of the morphological process, labelling, and SCP matching and updating.

Fig. 15 shows tracking results of the fish image using CBMA with 14 initial SCPs, $k = 30$, 5×5 blocks, and 65 frames. Most changes in the shape of fish occur especially at the tail part. In the dynamic tail part, we increase the number of SCPs, while keeping the same SCPs in the static region.

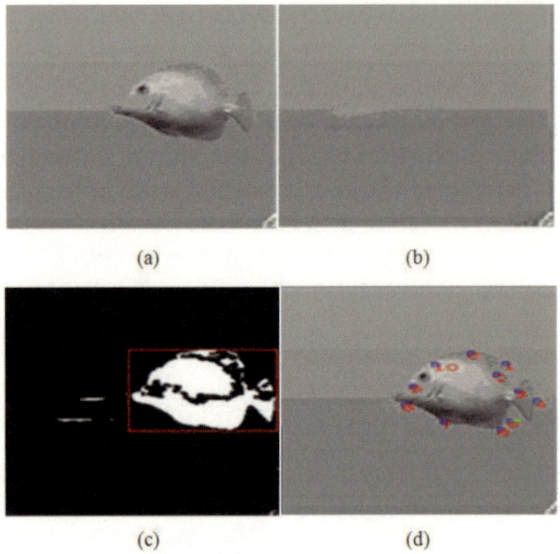

Fig. 14. Moving region detection and SCP extraction: (a) input image, (b) background generation, (c) region of object detection, and (d) SCPs superimposed on the input image

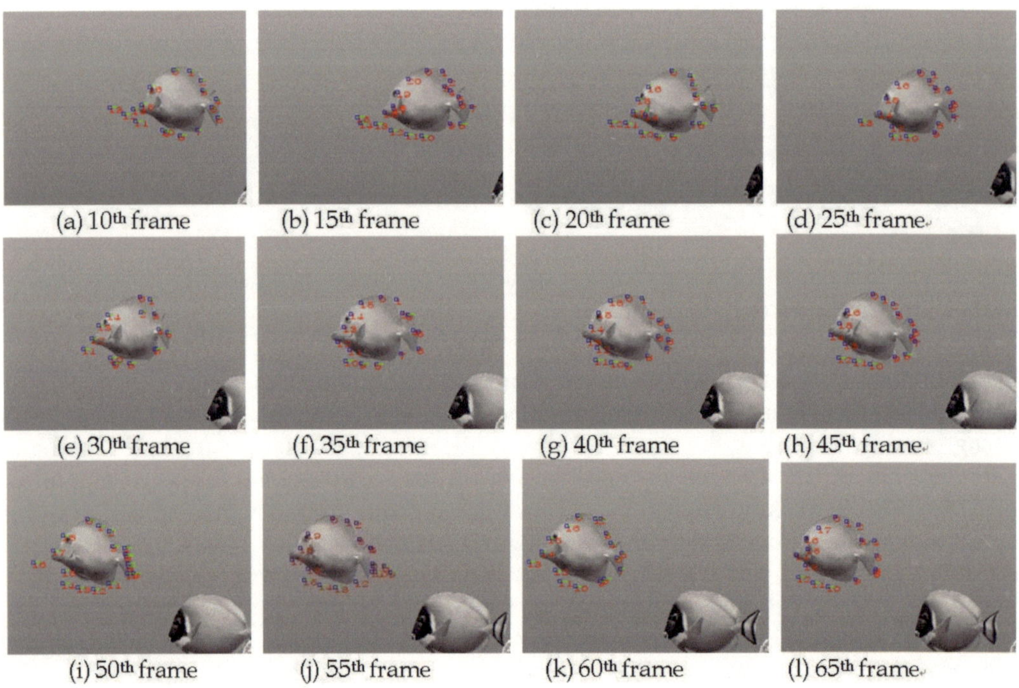

Fig. 15. Tracking results of the proposed shape and feature-based algorithm using CBMA

The block-matching method has weak from change of shape. But, because the proposed use to SCPs with some solved. Also Intensity trace in most of the block matching does not consider. Fig. 15 the result of the SCP in the background was of the location, object tracking, so that the gradient search is available in strengths. Since the block matching has its weakness we propose the use of SCP. In addition, to improve overall use of SCP we integrated additional information in the form of tracking and gradient search method which is illustrated in fig. 15.

Fig. 16 shows tracking results of the fish image using PBMA with 11 initial SCPs, $k=30$, 5×5 blocks, and 65 frames. We used 11 initial SCPs and $k=30$ for the BMA. PBMA updates SCPs at every 5 frames. CBMA shows recalculated SCPs, which represents replacement of SCPs.

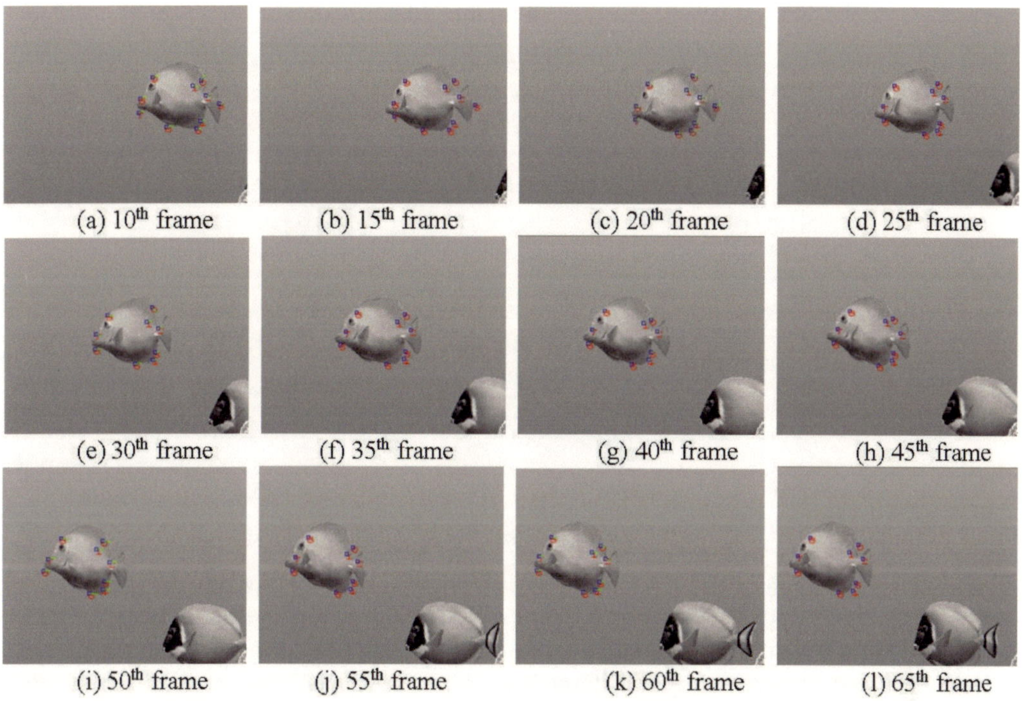

(a) 10th frame (b) 15th frame (c) 20th frame (d) 25th frame

(e) 30th frame (f) 35th frame (g) 40th frame (h) 45th frame

(i) 50th frame (j) 55th frame (k) 60th frame (l) 65th frame

Fig. 16. Tracking results of the proposed shape and feature-based algorithm using PBMA

5.2 Performance analysis

We compare the tracking performance of the proposed method with the frame difference-based method and the ASM-based method. The location of the reference object is represented by the centroid of all pixels inside the manually specified object boundary. The accuracy of tracking is measured by the Euclidean distance between two points (x,y) and $(\hat{x},\hat{y})$, called the similarity measure defined as

$$1/\rho = 1/\sqrt{(x-\hat{x})^2 + (y-\hat{y})^2}, \tag{20}$$

where

$$x = \frac{1}{N}\sum_{i=0}^{n-1} x_i,\ y = \frac{1}{N}\sum_{i=0}^{n-1} y_i,\ \hat{x} = \frac{1}{S}\sum_{j=0}^{s-1} \hat{x}_j,\ \hat{y} = \frac{1}{S}\sum_{j=0}^{s-1} \hat{y}_j. \tag{21}$$

where (x_i, y_i), $i = 0,1,\ldots,N-1$, represent pixels inside the manually specified object boundary, and $(\hat{x}_j, \hat{y}_j)$, $j = 0,1,\ldots,S-1$, the set of SCP's obtained by a tracking method to be compared. We can decide that a tracking algorithm is accurate if ρ is sufficiently small. Fig. 17 shows comparative results of the existing and the proposed tracking methods in the sense of the similarity measure.

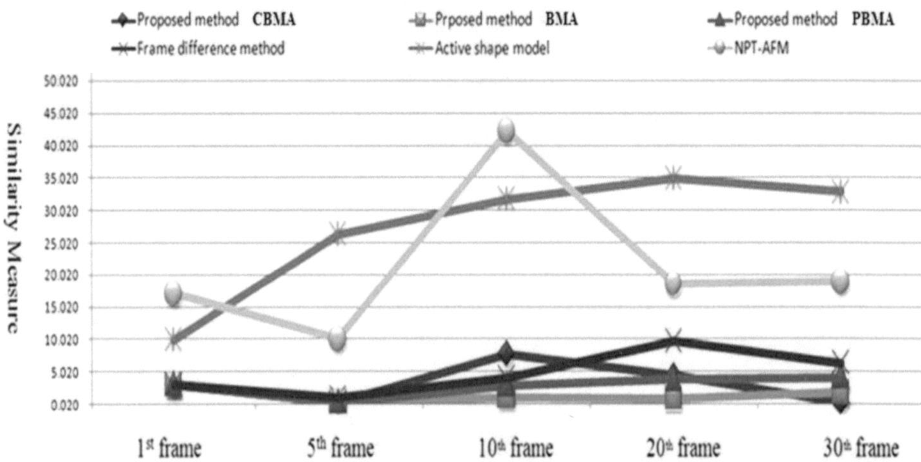

Fig. 17. Similarity curves: Comparison of various tracking methods using the fish sequence.

As shown in Fig. 17, all methods except the ASM-based method provide almost identical center points that coincides the reference center. As the number of frames increases, CBMA keeps increasing the similarity measure, while ASM and NPT-AFM methods become worse. It is to be noted that the simple difference-based method performs well in the starting frames, but the proposed method keeps increasing the similarity measure. We also note that ASM and NPT-AFM are both very sensitive to the initial training shape and boundary noise. Fig. 18 illustrates the comparison of tracking results between the proposed (CBMA and PBMA) with those of ASM and NPT-AFM. In case of ASM-based tracking lack of initialization in the starting frames led to poor convergence and increased error in the model fitting stages. This problem can be overcome using NPT-AFM-based method which yields higher feature detection and fitting accuracy. However the efficiency of NPT-AFM depends solely on the segmentation procedure which might lead to feature point's deviation from the object shape near the boundary. Both of the above mentioned drawbacks were overcome by using the proposed method because of the inclusion of SCP-based block matching and detection processes.

First column shows tracking results using ASM with 40 detected points in gray scale, Second column shows results of NPT-AFM algorithm in Y channel of YCrCb image format. Third column represents proposed CBMA and PBMA approach in gray scale.

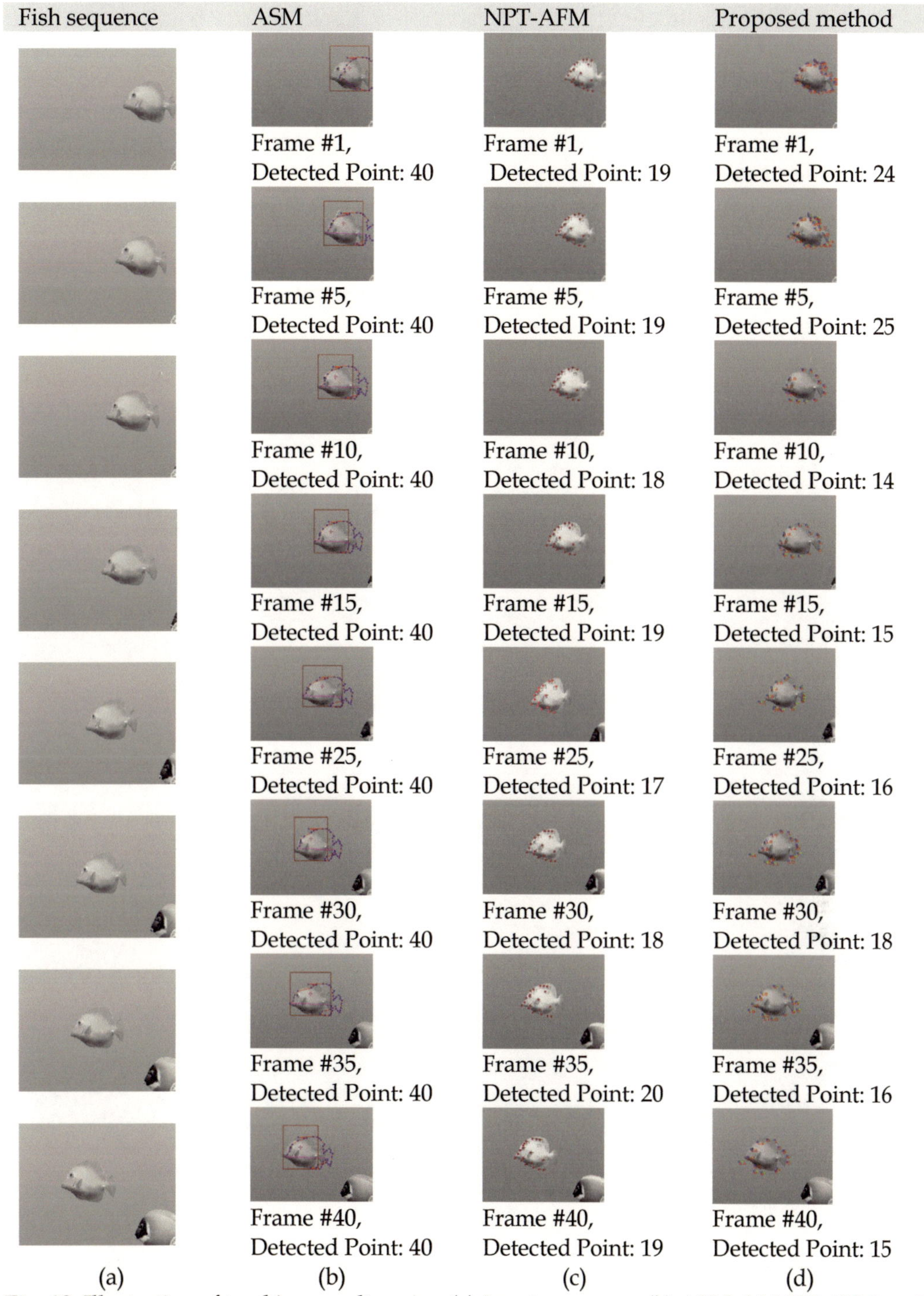

Fig. 18. Illustration of tracking results using (a) input sequence, (b) ASM, (c) NPT-AFM, and (d) the proposed method

As shown in fig. 18, although NPT-AFM accurately tracks control points in the head region, it fails to track in the tail region because of concave shape in the tail region does not satisfy NPT-AFM's assumption. On the other hand the proposed method keeps tracking all control points evenly. In conclusion, we can say that the proposed tracking methods outperform others in the sense of stability, robustness, and the least number of control points used.

Fig.19-21 shows the results of the proposed methods with different conditions of input images. Fig. 19 shows the result without reflection of illumination on change. On the other hand, fig. 20 and fig. 21 respectively show the results with reflection and illumination change. Based on the results shown in fig. 19-21, the proposed method is robust to various conditions such as reflection and illumination change.

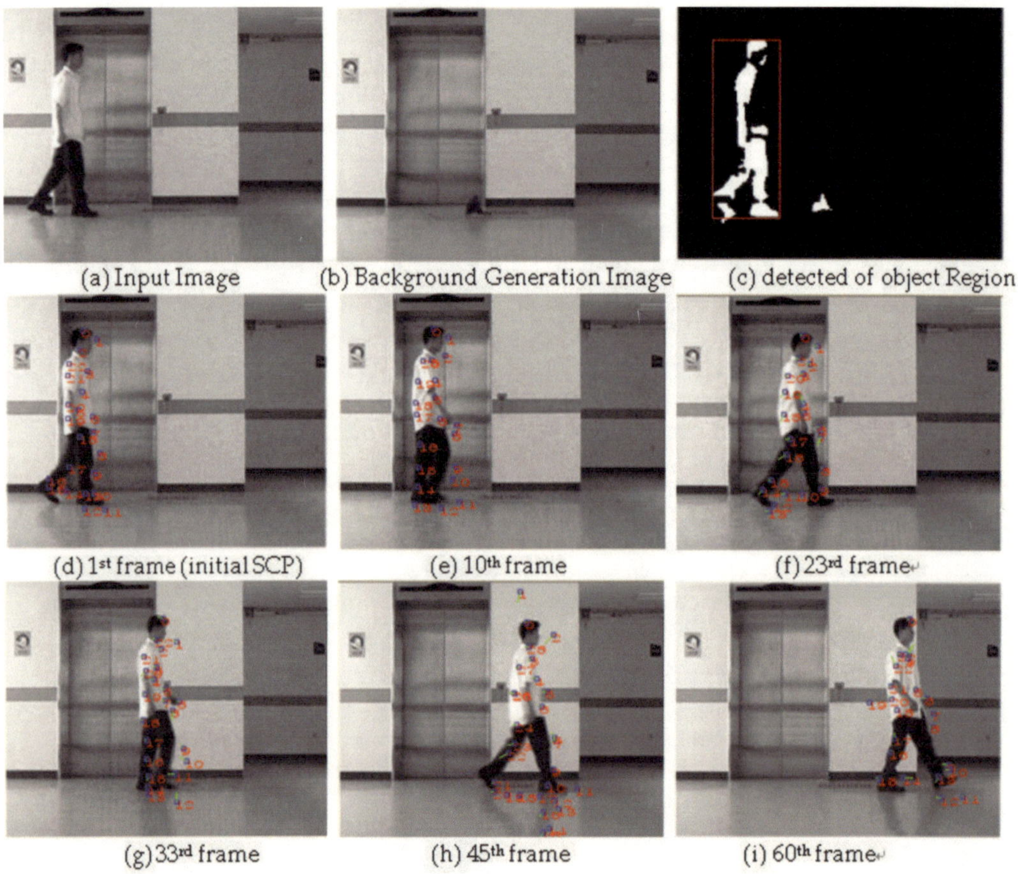

Fig. 19. Tracking results of the proposed method without any critical conditions. The initial background is generated using 50 frames. 5×5 blocks, 23 SCPs, and threshold of 25 are used.

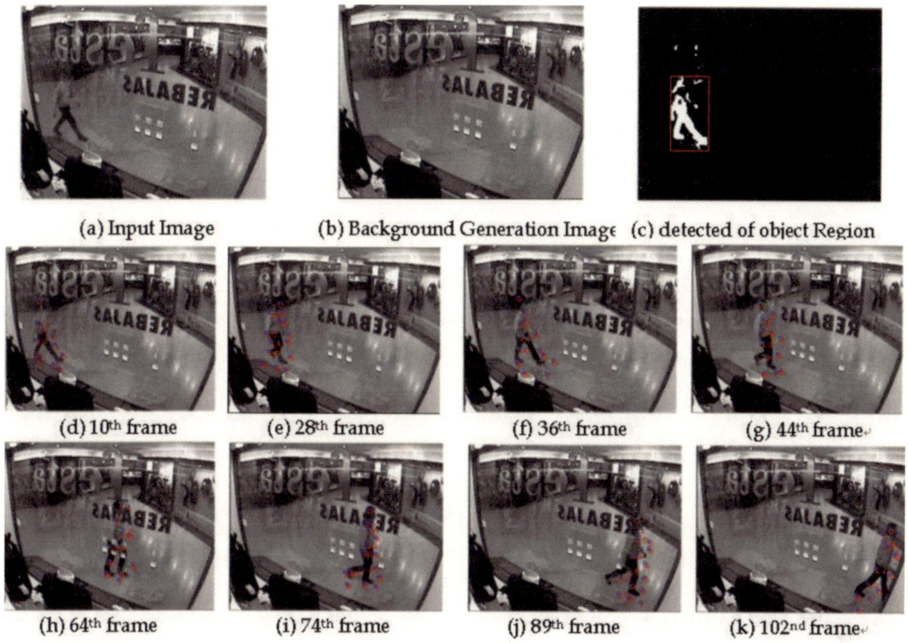

Fig. 20. Tracking results of the proposed method with strong reflections in the input image. The initial background is generated using 50 frames. 5×5 blocks, 12 SCPs, and threshold of 20 are used.

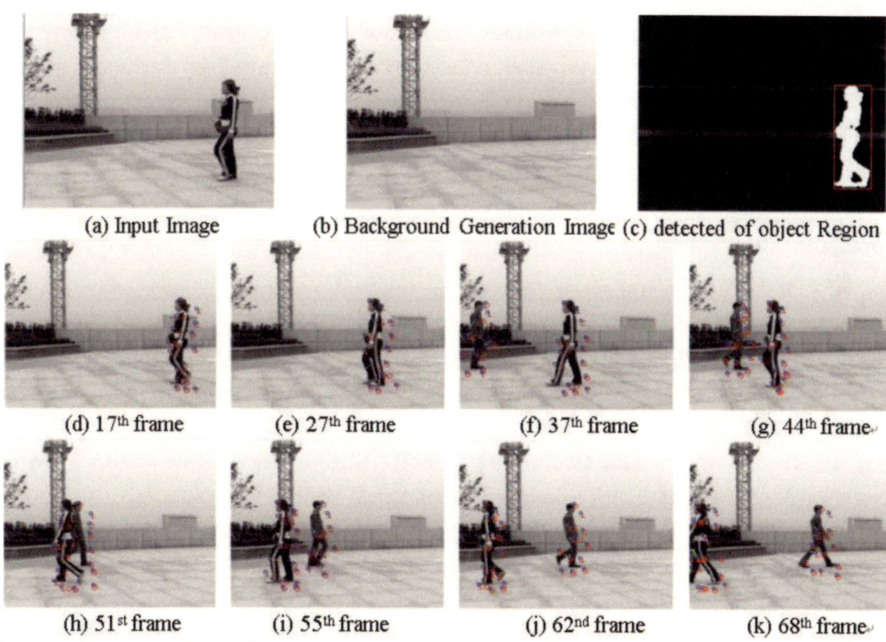

Fig. 21. Tracking results of the proposed method with illumination change in the input image. The initial background is generated using 50 frames. 5×5 blocks, 26 SCPs for group A, 12 SCPs for group B, and threshold of 25 are used.

The proposed method performs better than existing methods while maintaining the shape of an object is tracked. Therefore, the initial ASM generated shows good performance feature points to renew the NPT-AFM method does not use ASM initial feature points unstructured object to trace the missing feature points reconfiguration in test image(a) results were not good because it does not.

6. Conclusion

In this chapter we presented ASM, NPT-AFM, and combined shape and feature-based object tracking methods. The comined shape and feature-based method adaptively generates background, which serves as a fundamental building block for robust tracking by resolving inherent problems of existing BMA. After generating background the shape tracking module in the proposed algorithm determines object's moving region based on SCPs. Another contribution of this chapter is the CBMA method, which enables robust tracking with occlusion.

Extensive experiments have been performed using (i) computer generated fish sequence, (ii) PETS 2002 test sequence, (iii) in-house indoor sequence, and (iv) in-house outdoor sequence. Experimental results prove that the proposed method can provide robust tracking with complicated environment such as multiple objects, occlusion, and complicated background.

7. Acknowledgments

This research was supported by the Ministry of Knowledge Economy MKE of Korea, under the HNRC–ITRC support program supervised by the National IT Industry Promotion Agency (NIPA-2009-C1090-0902-0035) and by Basic Science Research Programs through National Research Foundation (NRF) of Korea funded by the Ministry of Education, Science and Technology (2009-0081059, 2009-0069382)

8. Reference

Mckenna, S, J ; Raja, Y. And Gong, S. (1999) Tracking colour objects using adaptive mixture models. *Image, vision Computing*, Vol. 17, pp. 225-231, March 1999.

Plankers, R. and Fuz, P. (2001) Tracking and modeling people in video sequences. Computer Vision, Image Understanding. *Computer Vision, Image Understanding*, Vol. 81, pp. 285-302, March 2001.

Cootes, T, F.; Taylor, C, T., and Graham, J. (1992) Training models of shape from sets of examples. *Proc. Int. Conf. Machine Vision*, pp. 9-18, 1992.

Lee, S, W., Kang, J., Shin, J., and Paik, J. (2007) Hierarchical active shape model with motion prediction for real-time tracking of non-rigid objects. *IET Computer Vision*, Vol. 1, pp. 17-24, March 2007.

Shin, J., Kim, S., Kang, S., Lee, S., and Paik, J. (2005) Optical flow-based real-time object tracking using non-prior training active feature model. *Real-Time Imaging*, Vol. 11, pp. 204-218, June 2005.

Zhang, X., and Minai, A. (2004) Temporally sequenced intelligent block-matching and motion-segmentation using locally coupled networks. *IEEE Trans. Neural Networks*, Vol. 15, pp. 1202-1214, September 2004.

Li, L., Huang, W., Gu, I., and Qi, T. (2002) Foreground object detection in changing background based on color co-occurrence statistics. *Proc. Int. Conf. Applications, Computer Vision*, pp. 269-274, 2002.

Chien, S., Ma, S., and Chen, L. (2002) Efficient moving object segmentation algorithm using background registration technique. *IEEE Trans. Circuits, Systems, Video Technology*, Vol. 12, pp. 577-586, July 2002.

Nascimento, J., and Marques, J. (2004) Robust shape tracking in the presence of cluttered background. *IEEE Trans. Multimedia*, Vol. 6, pp. 852-861, December 2004.

Javed, O., Shafique, K., and Shah, M. (2004) A hierarchical approach to robust background subtraction using color and gradient information. *Proc. Int. Conf. Motion, Video Computing*, pp. 22-27, December 2002.

Calvagno, G., Fantozzi, F., Rinaldo, R., and Viareggio, A. (2004) Model-based global and local motion estimation for videoconference sequences. *IEEE Trans. Circuits, Systems, Video Technology*, Vol. 14, pp. 1156-1161, September 2004.

Koschan, A., Kang, S., Paik, J., Abidi, B., and Abidi, M. (2003) Color active shape models for tracking non-rigid objects. *Pattern Recognition Letters*, Vol. 24, pp. 1751-1765, July 2003.

Zhang, D., and Lu, G. (2000) An edge and color oriented optical flow estimation using block matching. *Proc. Int. Conf. Signal Processing*, Vol. 2, pp. 1026-1032, August 2000.

Stefano, L., and Viarani, E. (1999) Vehicle detection and tracking using the block matching algorithm. *Proc. Int. Conf. Circuits, Systems, Communications, Compute*, Vol. 1, pp. 4491-4496, 1999.

Hariharakrishnan, K., and Schonfeld, D. (2005) Fast object tracking using adaptive block matching. *IEEE Trans. Multimedia*, Vol. 7, pp. 853-859, October 2005.

Tanimoto, S., and Pavlidis, T. (1975) A hierarchical data structure for picture processing. *Computer Graphics, Image Processing*, Vol. 4, pp. 104-119, June 1975.

Tekalp, A, M. (1995) Digital Video Processing. Prentice-Hall, 1995.

Isard, M., and Blake, A. (1996) Condensation-conditional density propagation for visual tracking. *Int. Jour. Computer Vision*, pp. 1-30, 1996.

Bouguet, J. (2000) Pyramidal implementation of the Lucas Kanade feature tracker description of the algorithms. *OpenCV Documentation, MicroProcessor Research Labs, Intel Corporation*, 2000.

Goodall, C. (1991) Procrustes methods in the statistical analysis of shape. *Jour. The Royal Statistical Society, Part B*, vol. 53, pp. 285-339, 1991.

Haritaoglu, I., Harwood, D., and Davis, L. (2000) W4: real-time surveillance of people and their activities. *IEEE Trans. Pattern Analysis, Machine Intelligence*, Vol. 22, pp. 809-830, August 2000.

Kim, T., Paik, D., and Paik, J. (2007) Block Matching-Based Background Generation and Non-Rigid Shape Tracking for Video Surveillance. *Proc. Int. Conf. ICWAPR*, vol. 1, PP. 415-420, November 2007.

12

Integrating Color and Gradient into Real-Time Curve Tracking and Feature Extraction for Video Surveillance

Huiqiong Chen and Qigang Gao
Faculty of Computer Science, Dalhousie University Nova Scotia, Canada

1. Introduction

Efficient curve detection and feature extraction is a very important step in many video-related applications, such as video content analysis and representation, surveillance systems, medical diagnoses, etc. For example, in video surveillance systems, curve tracking and feature extraction can be used in detecting moving targets from a video, allowing potential interesting events to be identified and analyzed for surveillance purposes. Curve detection usually includes edge detection and post processing procedures such as thinning, curve fitting or edge following, etc. Curve detection can significantly reduce less important data in a video frame while preserving structural information. Perceptual features can be extracted from curves for analysis or recognition purpose. However, Conventional edge detectors provide only an output of edge pixels. It is difficult to extract perceptual features directly from the edge detection results. Post-processing is then needed to remove noise, fill gaps, and fit edge pixels into curves. Unfortunately, most post-processing is too time-consuming for use in real-time applications (Fan et al., 2001).
Most edge detection techniques fall into two categories, gradient based methods and second order methods. Gradient-based methods detect edges based on the first derivative of the intensity. Examples include the Sobel, Prewitt, Roberts, and Canny operators, in which the Canny operator (Canny 1986) is the one of most commonly used edge detector. The second order methods find edges by searching for zero crossings in the second derivative of the intensity. Examples of the second order methods include the *Laplacian,* Marr-Hildreth *operators, etc.*
In color images, the color information also can be used to determine discontinuities in the color space (Cheng et al. 2001). Perez and Kock claimed in (Perez & Koch, 1994) that hue in HSI is more robust to certain types of highlights, shading, and shadows than the components in RGB, normalized RGB, or CIE color spaces. The edges with small hue change are removed from the Canny detector output in (Perez & Koch, 1994). A compass operator is proposed in (Ruzon & Tomasi, 1999), which considers distribution of pixel colors during edge detection. A 2D edge detection functional is used in (Qian & Huang, 1996), which is guided by the zero-crossing contours of the Laplacian-of-Gaussian (LOG) to find the edge locations.
In curve feature extraction, the Hough Transform is a well known technique for detecting curve features. It transforms the image space into the parameter space to find possible

features. Hough transform is tolerant to edge gaps, but its computational cost grows exponentially with the number of parameters used to represent the curves. Some efforts were made for modifying the Hough transform to reduce the dimensions of the parameter space (Yip et al. 1992). A constrained Hough transform is proposed in (Olson, 1999) for handling localization errors. Curve fitting divides a curve into segments and fits segment with lines, circular arcs or high order curves (Pei & Horng, 1995). Another way of finding curves is converting an edge image to a graph and search curves based on the criteria of the shortest path (Cheng et al. 2004). These methods use relatively complex mathematic models or search strategies; therefore they are computationally expensive.

Gao and Wong presented a curve detection technique called GET (Generic Edge Token) edge tracker in (Gao & Wong, 1993) based on gradient information. **The GET edge tracker** *can detect the edge traces and partition the traces in terms of Generic Edge tokens at the same time.* In this paper, we present an improved color-based GET tracker, which can produce more accurate GET map from image by using the integrated color and gradient information in tracking decision making. The new tracker can improve the accuracy and robustness of GTE detection while retains the real-time performance. Compared to other methods, the new tracker can provide perceptual curve features in video frames with low time expense, which makes it an effective solution for analysis and recognition tasks in video surveillance applications.

The rest of this paper is organized as follows. Section 2 presents the concepts of Generic Edge Token model. Sections 3 discusses the details of the new color-based GET tracker. In Section 4, experimental results and analysis are provided. Section 5 gives the conclusions.

2. Generic Edge Token model

Generic Edge Tokens (GETs) *are perceptually significant image primitives which represent classes of qualitatively equivalent shape features* (Gao & Wong, 1993). A complete set of GETs includes both Generic Segments (GSs) and curve partition points (CPPs). Each **GS** *is a perceptually distinguishable edge curve segment with linear or nonlinear feature* whereas each **CPP** is *some type of junction between GSs.*

The classification of GSs is ideally based on the best break-down curves in terms of the perceptual characteristics of GSs. Fig. 1 (a) shows curve partition examples with GSs and CPPs. This method partitions each curve based on the discontinuation of the monotonicity of descriptive characteristics including both direction information and geometry data. Each GS has its own unique descriptive characteristics and represents a general class of qualitatively equivalent curve segments. A generic segment gs is expressed by

$$\mathrm{gs} = \{x \mid p(x)\} \tag{1}$$

where x is an edge point, p indicates some perceptual property, and gs denotes a set of connected points sharing the property p (Zheng & Gao, 2003).

The property p is the monotonic characteristics of GS which can be qualitatively defined by a set of binary functions. Given a segment $y = f(x)$ and its inverse function $x = \varphi(y)$, their first derivatives are represented by $f'(x)$ and $\varphi'(y)$ respectively. The property p of a point x can be fully described by the function set:

$$p(x) = \{f(x), \varphi(y), f'(x), \varphi'(y)\} \tag{2}$$

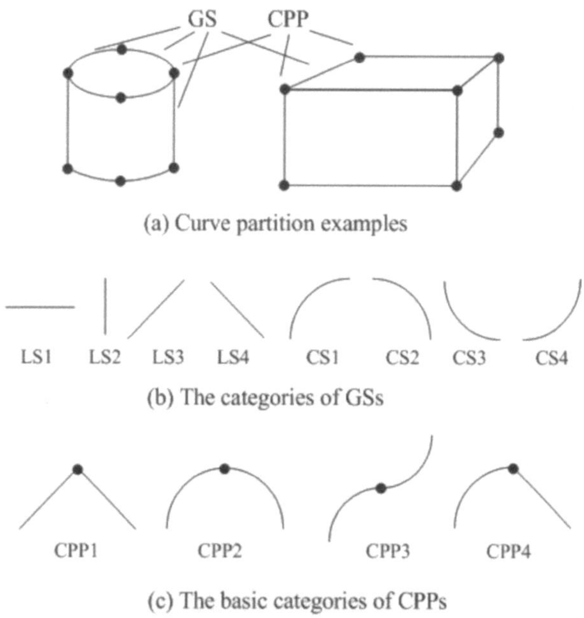

Fig. 1. Generic Edge Token model

GSs can be classified into 8 categories as Fig. 1(b) shows. Each type of GS shares one or more similar properties defined in Equation 2.

The points which break down curves into GSs are the positions on the curves at which the transitions of monotonicity take place. These perceptually significant breaking points, i.e., CPPs, are the general types of joints of GSs. A CPP can group two or more GSs into a perceptual structure. There are 4 basic categories of CPPs, as Fig. 1(c) shows. The CPPs are perceptually stable features and hence very useful for grouping curve structures.

The process of the GET tracker can be described as follows. A selective raster scan is first done to determine strong initial edge pixels, i.e. pixels with high significance, for edge tracking. The significance of a pixel $p(x, y)$, where (x, y) is the pixel location in an image, evaluates the difference between $p(x, y)$ and its neighbor pixels, therefore it can be used to measure the probability of the pixel $p(x, y)$ being an edge pixel.

Beginning from each strong edge pixel, the tracking processes search for the best neighbor edge pixel in order to form a trace. For any edge pixel $p(x, y)$, the next edge pixel on the trace will be picked up as follows. Let $p_n(x, y, d)$ be the neighbor of $p(x, y)$ in direction d, where d is the index of search direction as indicated in Fig. 2. There are eight search directions defined, where each direction is indexed by a number ranged in [0, 8), i.e. east (0), north-east (1), north (2), north-west (3), west (4), south-west (5), south (6), south-east (7). In the curving tracking process, the candidates of the next pixel following $p(x, y)$ on the trace can be expressed by a set of neighbors of $p(x, y)$ in specific tracking direction d:

$$S\left(p(x, y), d\right) = \left\{p_n(x, y, d), p_n\left(x, y, (d-1) mod8\right), p_n\left(x, y, (d+1) mod8\right)\right\} \quad (3)$$

The tracking direction d at $p(x, y)$ goes in the same direction as the tangent to the curve at the point (x, y):

$$d(p(x,y)) = \begin{cases} \lfloor (\arctan(\nabla p_y / \nabla p_x) + 90) / 45 \rfloor & \nabla p_x < 0 \\ 0 & \nabla p_x = 0, \nabla p_y > 0 \\ 0 & \nabla p_x = 0, \nabla p_y < 0 \\ \lfloor (\arctan(\nabla p_y / \nabla p_x) + 270) / 45 \rfloor & \nabla p_x > 0 \end{cases}$$

where $(\nabla p_x, \nabla p_y)$ is the significance of *p(x, y)* in horizontal and vertical directions respectively. The significance measurement will be discussed in section 3.2.

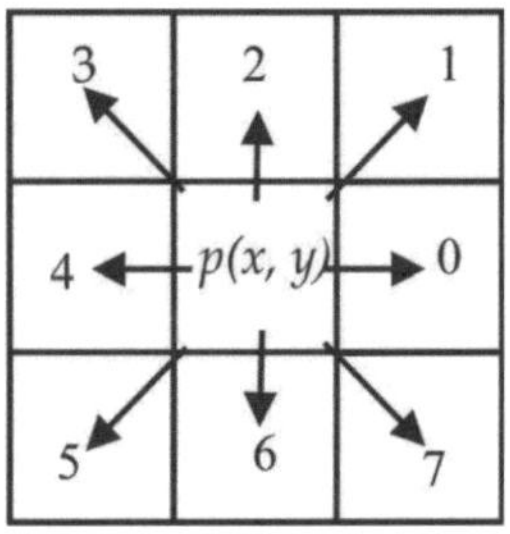

Fig. 2. 8-direction neighbors of a pixel *p(x, y)*. Each direction is labeled by an arrow and indexed by a number

The pixel *p(i, j)* in S (*p(x, y), d*) with the most significant is selected as the next edge pixel on the trace:

$$p(i,j) \in S(p(x,y),d) \mid (\forall (p(i',j') \in S(p(x,y),d),(i',j') \neq (i,j)):$$

$$\max(\nabla p_x(i,j), \nabla p_y(i,j)) > \max(\nabla p_x(i',j'), \nabla p_y(i',j'))) \quad (4)$$

The tracking continues upon reaching an endpoint where no more new edge pixels can be found. If the end point meets the initial point, a closed curve trace is formed; otherwise, this trace is an open trace and the endpoint is one end of the trace. The search of remaining trace pixels begins at the initial point again and proceeds in the opposite direction until the other endpoint of the trace is found. Once a curve has been found, it can be partitioned into GSs, and the type of partitioned GS is determined based on the GET model described in Fig. 1. The tracking processes repeats until all the selected initial edge pixels have been searched. CPPs can be dynamically detected in the edge tracking process.

3. Integrating color and gradient into curve tracking

A GET map provides a rich edge based description of image content including connected edge traces, GS and CPP features. However, in a gradient-based tracker, only gray level properties were applied for determining next best edge pixels in a GET map. The decision may not be sensitive to the situations where pixel candidates have weak gradient, but strong color difference. Since color is always an important factor for human perception of an image, a color-based GET tracker, which integrates color property into edge tracking for better performance of GET extraction, is proposed. Compared to the gradient-based tracker, the color-based tracker produces more accurate GET maps. Fig. 3 shows the processes of color-based edge tracking, which includes noise suppression, initial tracking point selection, and color-based curve tracking.

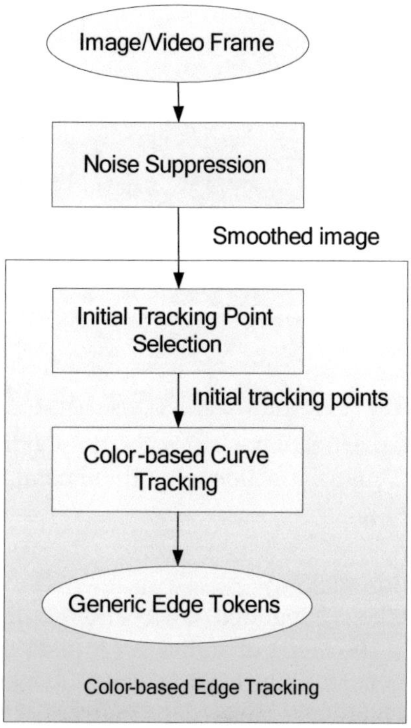

Fig. 3. The architecture of color-based edge tracking

3.1 Noise suppression

Noise suppression during GET tracking can help to reduce the effect of noise in an image during GET detection. Noise suppression is an important step for video surveillance applications. Compared to other images, image sequences in surveillance videos are likely to contain more noises due to the camera noise, light and other surveillance conditions. Before the tracking process starts, a bilateral filter is pre-applied to the image for noise removal to avoid possible jitter edges caused by noise.

Unlike tradition domain filters such as Gaussian filter, **bilateral filter** is a filter that *uses combined domain and range filtering for image smoothing*. It can smooth image noise while preserving most of edge information (Tomasi & Manduchi, 1998). Both domain and range filtering are combined in Bilateral filtering, that is, the spatial distribution of image intensities is considered in the filter. Each pixel value in an image is smoothed by an average of similar (domain) and nearby (range) pixel values, which can be expressed as a normalized weighted average of its neighbors:

$$k(p) = \int_{-\infty}^{\infty} \int_{-\infty}^{\infty} c(\xi, p) s(f(\xi), f(p)) d\xi \tag{5}$$

where $c(\xi, p)$ means the closeness between p and its neighborhood pixel ξ, and $s(f(\xi), f(p))$ measures the similarity between p and ξ.

Fig. 4 shows the comparison of GET map extraction on images with/without applying the bilateral filter. The bilateral filter efficiently preserves most of the useful edge information and partially removes noise edges.

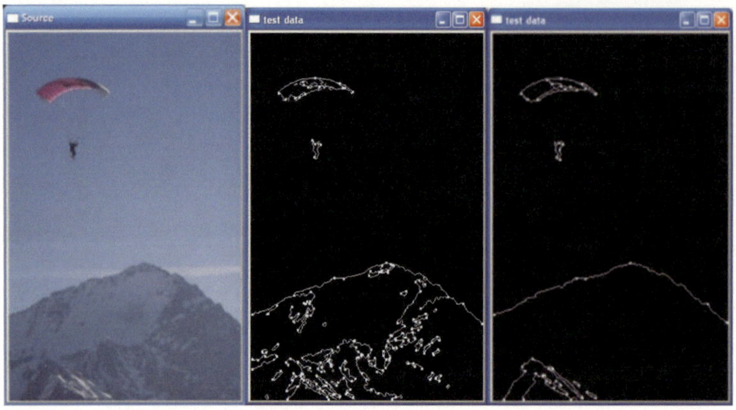

Fig. 4. Comparison of GET map extraction with/without applying bilateral filter. From left to right: A sample image; GET map extraction without bilateral filtering; GET map extraction with bilateral filtering.

3.2 Color based edge decision making

In the color-based GET tracker, integrated color and gradient information is used to determine the significance in the steps of initial edge pixel selection and edge tracking. Although RGB color space is commonly used in color image display, it is not generally appropriate for image representation because of the high correlation between the three color components and non-linearity with human perception. In other words, color differences perceived by human vision cannot be measured by their distance in RGB space. HSI space, which is more intuitive to human vision, is adapted for the color-based tracker. The HSI color space stands for Hue (H), Saturation (S), and Intensity (I), in which the color and intensity information are separated. The Hue value ranges from [0, 360) indicating color information. For example, red has a hue value of 0, green has a value of 120, and blue has a value of 240. The conversion between RGB and HSI can be found in many references (Cheng et al., 2001).

In the gradient-based tracker, the significance of an edge pixel $p(x, y)$ is measured by the gradient magnitude at (x, y) whereas in the color-based tracker, the significance $\nabla p(x,y)$ can be described by the normalized significance of $p(x, y)$ on both color and intensity in HSI color space.

$$\nabla p(x,y) = \left(\nabla p_x(x,y), \nabla p_y(x,y)\right) \tag{6}$$

$$\nabla p_x(x,y) = \| d_x h(x,y), d_x I(x,y) \|, \ \nabla p_y(x,y) = \| d_y h(x,y), d_y I(x,y) \|$$

where $(\nabla p_x(x,y), \nabla p_y(x,y))$ is the significance of $p(x, y)$ in horizontal and vertical directions, $h(x, y)$ and $I(x, y)$ indicate the hue and intensity components of $p(x, y)$ respectively, d_x/d_y is the normalized significance in x/y direction.

The significance of intensity can be calculated as

$$d_x I(x,y) = \frac{\partial I(x,y)}{\partial x}, \ d_y I(x,y) = \frac{\partial I(x,y)}{\partial y} \tag{7}$$

Since HSI space suffers from the hue value discontinuity, i.e. the colors close to hue value of 0 are similar to the colors close to hue value of 360, we define the normalized significance of color as:

$$d_x h(x,y) = \begin{cases} \nabla h_x(x,y) * 256/180 & \nabla h_x(x,y) <= 180 \\ (\nabla h_x(x,y) - 360) * 256/180 & \nabla h_x(x,y) > 180 \\ (\nabla h_x(x,y) + 360) * 256/180 & \nabla h_x(x,y) < -180 \end{cases}, \quad (8)$$

$$d_y h(x,y) = \begin{cases} \nabla h_y(x,y) * 256/180 & \nabla h_y(x,y) <= 180 \\ (\nabla h_y(x,y) - 360) * 256/180 & \nabla h_y(x,y) > 180 \\ (\nabla h_y(x,y) + 360) * 256/180 & \nabla h_y(x,y) < -180 \end{cases},$$

$$\nabla h_y(x,y) = \frac{\partial h(x,y)}{\partial y}, \quad \nabla h_x(x,y) = \frac{\partial h(x,y)}{\partial x}$$

Here *dh*(*x*, *y*) is normalized in consistency to *dI*(*x*, *y*), which is ranged in [-256, 256]. Specifically, in a gray level image, $d_x h(x,y) = d_y h(x,y) = 0$.

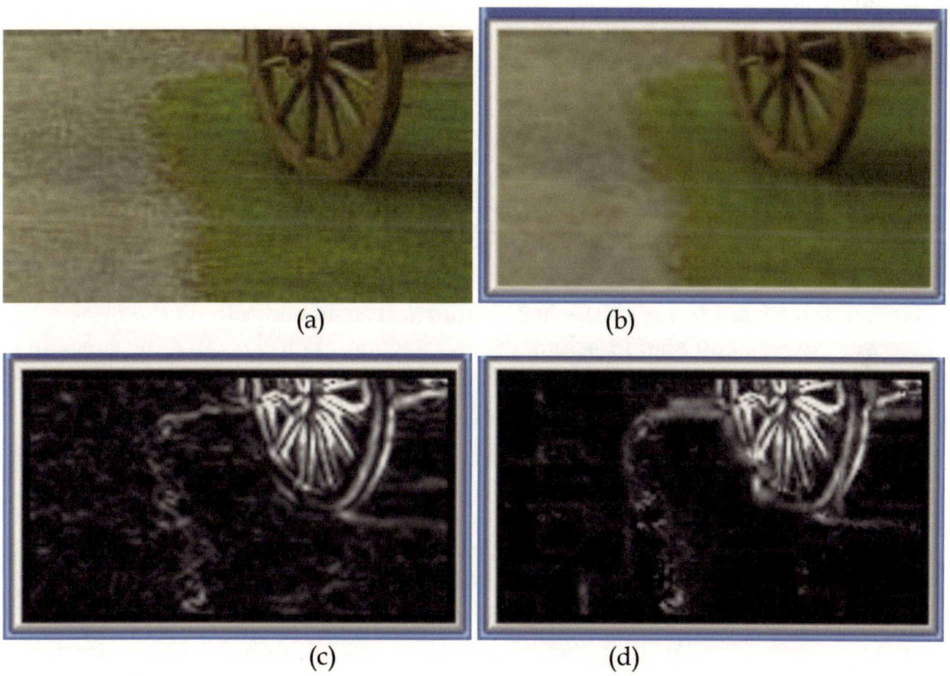

Fig. 5. Comparison of gradient-based and color-based significance map; a) an image; b) image after Bilateral filtering; c) gradient-based significance map ; d) color-based significance map

Fig. 5 shows a comparison between the gradient-based and color-based significance map of a sample within a green grass region. Each significance value is normalized to the range of

[0,255] for display purposes. The higher a pixel's intensity is in the gradient-based or color-based significance map, the greater its gradient-based significance or color-based significance value. The grass region still contains texture after bilateral filtering, as Fig. 5 (b) shows. The gradient-based significance map of the grass and gray ground regions contains many noise pixels due to texture in these areas. The gradient-based significance map in (c) has much more noise than the color-based significance map (d) in the texture areas; and the region boundary edges are more evident in the color-based significance map.

3.3 Color-based curve tracking

The curve tracking of the color-based tracker on an image I can be described as follows:

Step 1. Filtering; apply bilateral filtering to the image I.

Step 2. pick up initial pixels; image I is scanned both vertically and horizontally by pre-defined scan interval δ. Let t_{init} be the significance threshold for initial points, $S(p)$ be the set of initial pixels.

For any scanned pixel $p(x, y)$ do

if $\nabla p(x,y)$ satisfies $\nabla p_x(x,y) > t_{init} \vee \nabla p_y(x,y) > t_{init}$,

$S(p) = S(p) \cup p(x, y)$;

Step 3. Sort each pixel in $S(p)$ by significance descending.

Step 4. Edge tracking; From the first element in $S(p)$, for each initial pixel $p_{start} \in S(p)$ do

if p_{start} is not an edge pixel yet, perform the following curve tracking process:

1. Edge tracking starts from p in the initial direction $d_{init} = d(p_{start})$, where $d(p_{start})$ can be calculated using Equation 3.
2. In each step of tracking, if $p(x, y)$ is the current pixel on the trace, a pixel with highest normalized color significance $p(i, j)$ is selected as the possible next edge pixel from a set of candidates, i.e. $S(p(x, y), d(p(x,y))$, by using Equation 4.
3. Let t_s be the significance threshold for edge pixels:

if $max(\nabla p_x(i,j), \nabla p_y(i,j)) < t_s$,

one end of the trace has been reached; mark $p(i, j)$ as an endpoint of the trace; tracking goes back to p_{start} and starts tracking in the direction mod((d_{init}+4), 8) by repeating (2)-(3);

else if $p(i, j)$ is already marked as an edge pixel,

a closed trace is formed. A new tracking starts from a new initial point and repeats (1)-(3).

else

mark $p(i, j)$ as edge pixel, set $p(i, j)$ as current tracking point; go back to (2).

4. The curving tracking process of (1)-(3) repeats until no more initial points are left. GS partition and CPP detection can be dynamically found during the tracking process.

When the color-based tracker is applied to gray-scale images, only intensity information is considered during curve tracking. The tracker is efficient since the strategy of image sample scanning and edge tracking only needs to process a portion of relevant image pixels. Fig. 6 shows an example of edge tracking results by using gradient-based and color-based trackers. Compared to gradient-based tracker, the color-based tracker is able to pick up edges between regions with weak gradient but different colors (see the edge of green grass region). It gives a better edge map with more accurate edges.

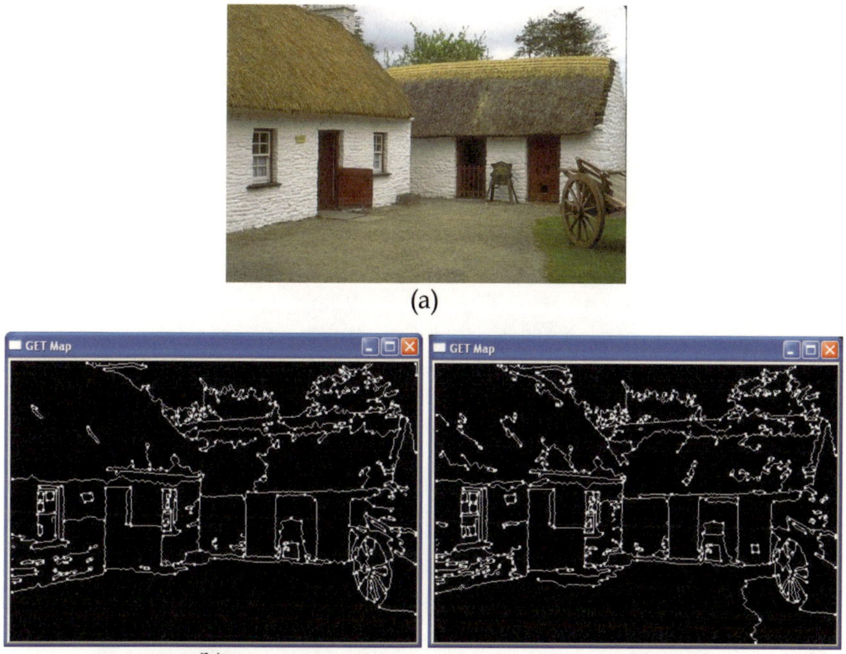

(a)

(b) (c)

Fig. 6. Edge tracking by using the gradient-based and color-based trackers; a) original image; b) result of edge tracking with gradient only; c) result of edge tracking with integrated color and gradient properties

4. Experiments and evaluation

In this section, the experimental results on both images and video sequencings are presented and analysis. The algorithm of the color-based GET tracker is implemented using C++.

Fig. 7 illustrates output of the color-based GET tracker on images. A comparison with alternative methods on the same set of test images is also provided in our testing. Since the Canny detector is one of the most efficient and commonly used edge detectors, we choose the Canny detector and a contour/curve detection method provided in (Grigorescu et al., 2004) for comparison. This contour/curve detection method is based on the Canny detector and it takes an additional surround suppression step which eliminates texture edges while leaves the contours of objects and region. A Gaussian filter is applied for noise suppression before Canny edge detection. The parameters in both methods are adjusted for each input image to obtain an optimal output edge map. The outputs of GET maps from the color-based GET tracker are also shown in Fig. 7. Bilateral filtering is applied to the GET tracker. Each CPP point is marked in the GET maps.

Fig. 7 shows that, compared to the other two methods, the color-based tracker performs qualitatively good in terms of 1) improving the accuracy of edge; the color-based tracker is able to apply both color and gradient evidence of an image for edge tracking in that the GETs are detected more accurately without increasing computation cost; 2) more robustness in suppressing noise and 3) providing perceptual structures that other methods cannot provide. The color-based tracker can extract GET structures at the same time as tracking, which are semantically sound curve features for image/video analysis.

Fig. 7. For each example: a) original image; b) edge map detected by Canny edge detector; C) curves detected by Canny-based curve detection (Grigorescu et al., 2004); d) GET map detected by the color-based GET tracker.

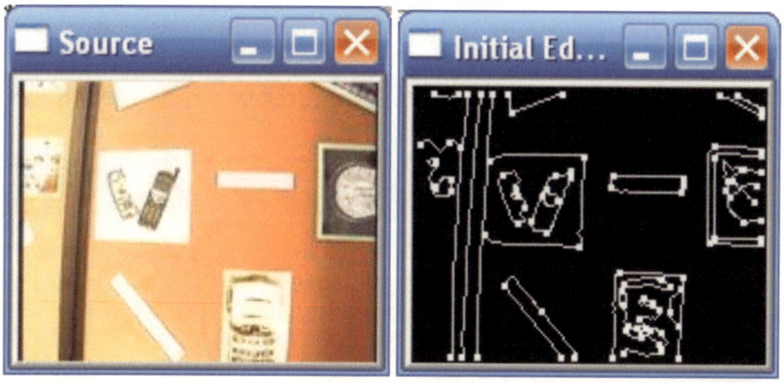

(a) Sample image from robot's left eye; (b) GET map;

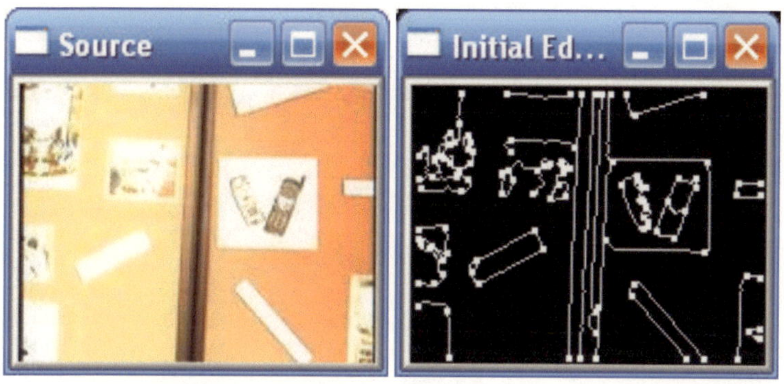

(c) Sample image from robot's right eye; (d) GET map;

Fig. 8. Robot vision system: edges maps and perceptual features detected by the color-based tracker.

The color-based tracker provides an ideal solution for video applications that requires content analysis and object recognition, such as video surveillance system, robot vision system, etc. The data used for performance testing on video applications come from IPAMI group, Dalhousie University (http://flame.cs.dal.ca/~IPAMI), KOGS/IAKS, Universität Karlsruhe (http://i21www.ira.uka.de/image_sequences/) and CAVIAR project (http://homepages.inf.ed.ac.uk/rbf/CAVIARDATA1/).

Fig. 8 gives an example of applying the color-based edge tracker to a robot vision system. Two video sequences are taken by robot eyes (two cameras). The size of each video frame is 160*120 pixels, and the frame rate reaches 9 fps. Fig. 8(a) shows an image taken by robot left eye and (c) shows the image with same scene taken by the right robot eye. The GET features detected from each frame will be used for motion analysis, object detection, 3D reconstruction in later stages. The average execution time of GET detection for each frame is 30 milliseconds when the color-based tracker runs under Intel 1.66GHZ CPU. It means that the color-based tracker can process each frame in the videos in real-time.

Fig. 9 shows GET maps of moving object detected from surveillance videos. For each frame pair in a video, the GET map is extracted from a frame by the GET tracker, and then moving GETs are used to group moving objects in the video sequence (Chen & Gao, 2008). Each moving object can be perceptually described by the GETs and CPPs extracted by the GET tracker. In our experiment, the size of each frame in the videos varies from 320 by 240 pixels to 640 by 480 pixels. For a video stream with the frame size of 320 by 240 pixels and the frame rate of 10 frames per second, the average processing time for GET extraction is 50 milliseconds under Intel 1.66GHZ CPU.

Fig. 9. Video surveillance system: GET maps and perceptual features of moving objects detected by the color-based tracker.

The tests above show that the computational cost of the color-based tracker is low enough for real-time applications. The execution time of curving detection and partitioning for an image depends on the number of edge pixels in the image. On average, the execution time for each image/video frame with 160*120 ~ 640*480 pixels is around 30-70 milliseconds when the color-based tracker runs, which gives the color-based tracker full capability of real-time processing for video applications, such as video content analysis, surveillance system, etc.

5. Conclusions

This paper presents an extended perceptual curve tracker using both color and gradient properties. The system can track edge traces and extract semantic curve features at same time. The enhanced GET tracker provides a more robust and effective solution for edge detection, curve feature extraction with real-time performance. The method has the following technique attributes. 1) It only needs to selectively process a subset of relevant pixels in an image. 2) It detects perceptual curve features without using parameter-based curve fitting, and the major computation involved is logic inference. 3) It integrates both color and gradient properties into edge decision making so that edges between two color regions with weak gradient can be accurately detected. 4) It improves the robustness in terms of noise handing. The tracker's real-time performance is achieved mainly because of the characteristics of 1) and 2). This edge tracking and curve detection method is very suitable for various real-time applications where edge-based features are needed (Chen et al., 2006) (Reilly & Chen, 2007) (Chen & Gao, 2008).

6. References

Canny, J. (1986) A Computational Approach to Edge Detection, *IEEE Trans. on Pattern Analysis and Machine Intelligence*, Vol. 8, No. 6, pp. 679-698

Chen, H.; Rivait D., & Gao Q. (2006) Real-Time License Plate Identification by Perceptual Shape Grouping and Tracking, *Proceedings of the 9th IEEE Conf. on Intelligent Transportation Systems*, pp. 1352-1357

Chen, H.; & Gao. Q. (2008) Intelligent Video Analysis for Vehicle Surveillance by Perceptual Edge Feature Grouping, *Computer Vision Research Progress*, Edited by F. Columbus, PA: Nova Science Inc., NY, USA, pp. 83-107

Cheng, H. D.; Jiang, X. H.; Sun, Y. & Wang, J. L. (2001) Color Image Segmentation: Advances and Prospects, *Pattern Recognition*, Vol. 34, No. 12, pp. 2259-2281

Cheng, Z.; Chen, M. & Liu, Y. (2004) A robust Algorithm for Image principal Curve Detection, *Pattern Recognition Letters*, Vol. 25, No. 11, pp. 1303-1313

Fan, J.; Yau, D. K. Y. & Aref, W. G. (2001) Automatic Image Segmentation by Integrating Color-Edge Extraction and Seeded Region Growing, *IEEE Trans. on Image Processing*, Vol. 10, No. 10, pp. 1454-1466

Gao, Q. & Wong, A. (1993) Curve Detection based on Perceptual Organization. *Pattern Recognition*, Vol. 26, No. 1, pp. 1039-1046

Grigorescu, C.; Petkov, N. & Westenberg, M. A. (2004) Contour and Boundary Detection improved by Surround Suppression of Texture Edges, *Image and Vision Computing*, Vol. 22, No. 8, pp. 609-622

Olson, C. F. (1999) Constrained Hough Transforms for Curve Detection, *Computer Vision and Image Understanding*, Vol. 73, No. 3, pp. 329-345

Pei, S. C. & Horng, J. H. (1995) Fitting Digital Curves using Circular Arcs, *Pattern Recognition*, Vol. 28, No. 1, pp. 107-116

Perez, F. & Koch, C. (1994) Toward Color Image Segmentation in Analog VLSI: Algorithm and Hardware, *International Journal of Computer Vision*, Vol. 12, No. 1, pp. 17-42

Qian, R. J. & Huang, T. S. (1996) Optimal Edge Detection in two-Dimensional Images, *IEEE Trans. Image Processing*, Vol. 5, pp. 1215–1220

Ruzon, M. A. & Tomasi, C. (1999) Color-Edge Detection with the Compass Operator, *Proceedings of the IEEE Conf. on Computer Vision and Pattern Recognition*, pp. 160–166

Reilly, D. & Chen, H. (2007) Toward fluid, mobile and ubiquitous interaction with paper using recursive 2D barcodes, *Proceedings of the 3rd International workshop on Pervasive Mobile Interaction Devices*, pp. 20-23

Tomasi, C. & Manduchi, R. (1998) Bilateral Filtering for Gray and Color Images, *Proceedings of the IEEE International Conf. on Computer Vision*, pp. 839-847

Yip, R.K.K.; Tam, P.K.S. & Leung, D.N.K. (1992) Modification of Hough Transform for Circles and Ellipses Detection using a 2-Dimension Array, *Pattern Recognition,* Vol. 25, No. 9, pp. 1007-1022

Zheng, X. & Gao, Q. (2003) Generic Edge Tokens, Representation, Segmentation and Grouping, *Proceedings of the 16th International Conf. on Vision Interface,* pp. 388-394

13

Targets Tracking in the Crowd

Cheng-Chang Lien
Department of Computer Science and Information Engineering,
Chung Hua University,
Taiwan

1. Introduction

Conventional video surveillance systems often have several shortcomings. First, target detection can't be accurate under the light variation environment or clustering backgrounds. Second, multiple targets tracking become difficult on a crowd scene because the split/merge and occlusions among the tracked targets occur frequently and irregularly. Third, it is difficult to the partition the tracked targets from a merged image blob and then the target tracking may be inaccurate. In this chapter, the methods for targets detection and tracking in the crowd are addressed. In general, the methods for targets tracking in the crowd can be categorized into the blob-based and point-based methods. The blob-based methods detect and track the targets based on the appearance models; while the point-based methods detect and track the moving targets with the reliable feature points.

2. Blob-based methods

In the conventional target detection systems, some typical methods are applied to extract the moving objects, e.g., background subtraction [1], and pixel-wise temporal difference analysis [2]. However, these methods are extremely sensitive to the variation of lighting or the dynamic background changing. Applying pixel-wise temporal differencing [4] may reduce the influence of the dynamic illumination change, but the regions of the moving objects are extracted incompletely when the background variation occurs. All the above mentioned methods do not utilize the motion information including the object and camera motions [3]. By applying the method of optical flow [2], the moving objects may be detected even in the presence of camera motion. However, the high computation complexity makes the real-time object detection difficult. In this study, we apply the pixel-wise temporal statistical model [5], voting rule for the Y, C_r, and C_b Bayesian classifiers, and foreground verification with the dynamic texture modeling to detect the targets on the crowd scene accurately.

In most target tracking systems, central point on the target is used as the reference location to predict the position at the next frame. However, central point can be influenced easily by the inaccurate foreground detection. Here, the methods of principle-axis detection [9] is applied to extract the ground point of each target to serve as the reference point in the target tracking algorithms, e.g., Kalman filter [6-7] and Particle filter [8]. Fig. 1 illustrates the block diagram of the proposed system.

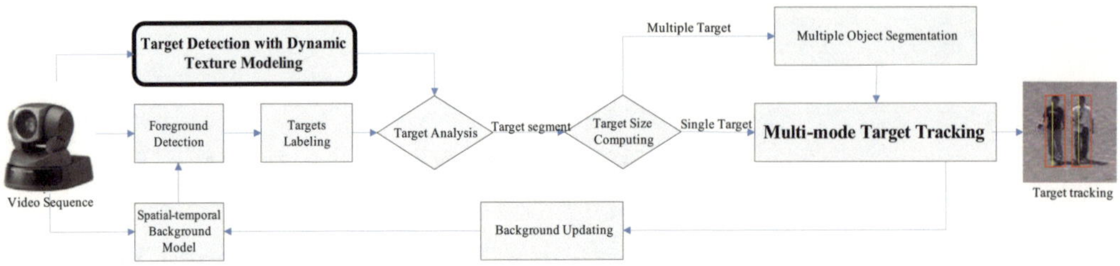

Fig. 1. The block diagram of the proposed system.

2.1 Temporal probability background model

In this section, the background model fusing with temporal and texture models is established to segment the foreground and background on a light variant or clustering background. In an image sequence, the intensity variation within a time period for each pixel can be modeled by the Gaussian distribution function [4]. The pixel-based MOG function is defined as:

$$p(I) = p(I \mid B)P(B) + \sum_{j=1}^{c-1} p(I \mid \omega_j)p(\omega_j), \tag{1}$$

where, I is the intensity value, B denotes the background, ω_j denotes the moving object and c denotes the number of Gaussians. The intensity distribution of the background pixel at a certain position x_b can be expressed as:

$$p(x_b \mid B) = \frac{1}{\sqrt{2\pi}\sigma} \exp\left(-\frac{(I - \bar{I}(x_b))^2}{2\sigma^2} \right), \tag{2}$$

where $\bar{I}(x_b)$ and σ are the mean and standard deviation of the pixel intensity at x_b. According to the Bayesian decision rule [9], whether the pixel belongs to the background or the foreground (the moving objects) can be determined by the following likelihood inequality.

$$\frac{p(I \mid B_{x_b})}{p(I \mid T_{x_b})} \geq \frac{P(T)}{P(B)} = \lambda, \tag{3}$$

where $P(T)$ and $P(B)$ are the prior probabilities for the background and moving objects respectively. By replacing $p(I \mid B_{xb})$ with Eq. (2), the likelihood ratio can be further simplified as:

$$\left| I - \bar{I}(x_b) \right| \leq k\sigma, \tag{4}$$

where $k = \sqrt{-2\ln(\sqrt{2\pi}\,\sigma\lambda/L)}$. If $| I - \bar{I}(x_b) | \leq k\sigma$, then the pixel is categorized as the background, otherwise, the pixel is categorized as the foreground.

2.2 Foreground detection rule

It can be very difficult to detect the moving objects when the intensity distribution is closed to the background model. The fusion of likelihood ratios of three color components (RGB or YC_rC_b) are then proposed to overcome this problem. In general, linear combination and voting rules are applied to detect the foreground, which are described in the following.

Linear combination rule:
If $w_y\ p_Y(u_y\,|\,B_x)+w_{cr}\ p_{Cr}(u_{Cr}\,|\,B_x)+w_{cb}\ p_{Cb}(u_{Cb}\ \,|\,B_x) > T$
pixel u is classified as background,
otherwise,
pixel u is classified as foreground,
where, w_y , w_{cr} , w_{cb} are weighting factors and sum of the weighting factors is equal to one.

Voting rule:
Given $p_Y(u_y\,|\,B_x)$, $p_{Cr}(u_{Cr}\,|\,B_x)$, $p_{Cb}(u_{Cb}\ \,|\,B_x\ )$, If a pixel is classified as background with more than two components' background models,
Pixel u is classified as background,
otherwise,
Pixel u is classified as foreground.

By comparing the above two fusion rules, we apply the voting rule to cope with the illumination variation problem. If a pixel is classified as background with more than two components' background models, then this pixel is classified as the background, otherwise, it is classified as the foreground. Fig. 2 illustrates the foreground detection using the voting rule. It is obvious that the foreground detection using voting rule outperform the one using the linear combination rule. Hence, we apply the voting rule to detect the objects on the outdoor crowd scene to cope with the illumination variation problem.

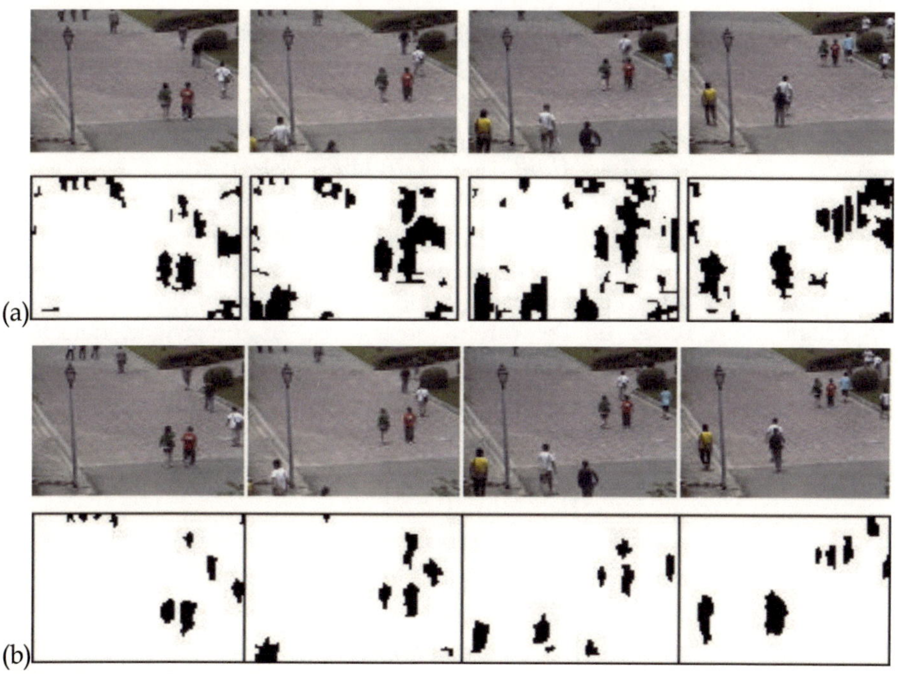

Fig. 2. (a) Foreground detection using the linear combination rule. (b) Foreground detection using the voting rule.

2.3 Foreground verification using texture modeling

Many environmental dynamic textures such as leaves, fire, smoke, and sea waves may reduce the accuracy of target detection. Here, the dynamic texture will be modeled by using the modified local binary pattern (LBP)[11] and then the target can be detected without the influence of dynamic textures in the crowd scene. Here, a local texture pattern T [11] centering the pixel g_c and having P neighboring pixels is defined as:

$$T \approx t(s(g_0 - g_c), s(g_1 - g_c), \ldots, s(g_{P-1} - g_c)), \tag{5}$$

where

$$s(x) = \begin{cases} 1, |x| \geq threshold \\ 0, |x| < threshold \end{cases}. \tag{6}$$

Then, we transform the modified LBP in (5) to an integer value with the formula in Eq. (7).

$$LBP_{PR} = \sum_{0}^{P-1} s(g_p - g_c) 2^P . \tag{7}$$

Finally, the modified LBP is utilized to model the dynamic texture background and remove the false foregrounds. In the LBP-based foreground detection, the bit difference η between the captured scene and LBP-based background model can be used to separate the foreground from the background. The LBP-based foreground detection rule is defined as:

$$P^{frame(t+1)}(\eta) = \begin{cases} foreground, & if \quad \eta \geq \eta\_th \\ background, & if \quad \eta < \eta\_th \end{cases}. \tag{8}$$

The bit difference η is calculated as:

$$\eta = \sum_{p=0}^{8} (LBP_p^{frame(t+1)} \ XOR \ LBP_p^{frame(t)}) \tag{9}$$

where, p is the index of the pixel on the circular chain. In this study, both the pixel-wise temporal probability model and LBP texture model are constructed to detect the foreground, but how to integrate both background models to reduce the false detection is a very important issue. Based on the careful observation of foreground detections, the foreground detection rule is then designed as:

If $R(O_c) \in$ **foreground**
  count $R(F_c^{LBP} | O_c)$,
  If $N(R(F_c^{LBP} | O_c)) > N_{th}$,
    $O_c \in$ **True foreground,**
    update $R(O_c)$,
  else
    $O_c \in$ **False foreground ,**
    clear $R(O_c)$,
Endif

where, $R(O_c)$ denotes the region of a detected object using the pixel-wise temporal probability model on the current frame c, $R(F^c_{LBP} | O_c)$ denotes the region of the foreground detected by pixel-wise LBP texture model on the current frame c around the region of O_c. In order to remove the false detections, we propose the update/clear method as follow:

$$\mathbf{R'(O_c)} = \begin{cases} R(O_c) \cup \mathbf{R(F_c^{LBP} | O_c)} \text{ , } \mathbf{if\ Update}_{foreground} \ \mathbf{is\ choosed.} \\ Null \qquad \text{ , } \mathbf{if\ Clear}_{foreground} \ \mathbf{is\ choosed.} \end{cases} \tag{10}$$

Consequently, we can not only detect the object regions precisely, but also can remove the false foregrounds.

2.4 Multi-mode target tracking

The targets tracking become complex on a crowd scene because the split and merging or occlusion conditions among the tracked targets occur frequently. In addition, the targets appear on the scene at the first time may be a single target or a merged multiple targets. In this study, the bottom-up tracking scheme is applied to develop the multi-modes tracking scheme. Each detected image blob is classified into single or multiple targets according to its area and then the tracked targets are examined whether they belong to the targets appeared on previous frames. Based on status classifications of target tracking on a crowd scene, there are six target tracking modes [13] shown in Fig. 3 are described as follows.

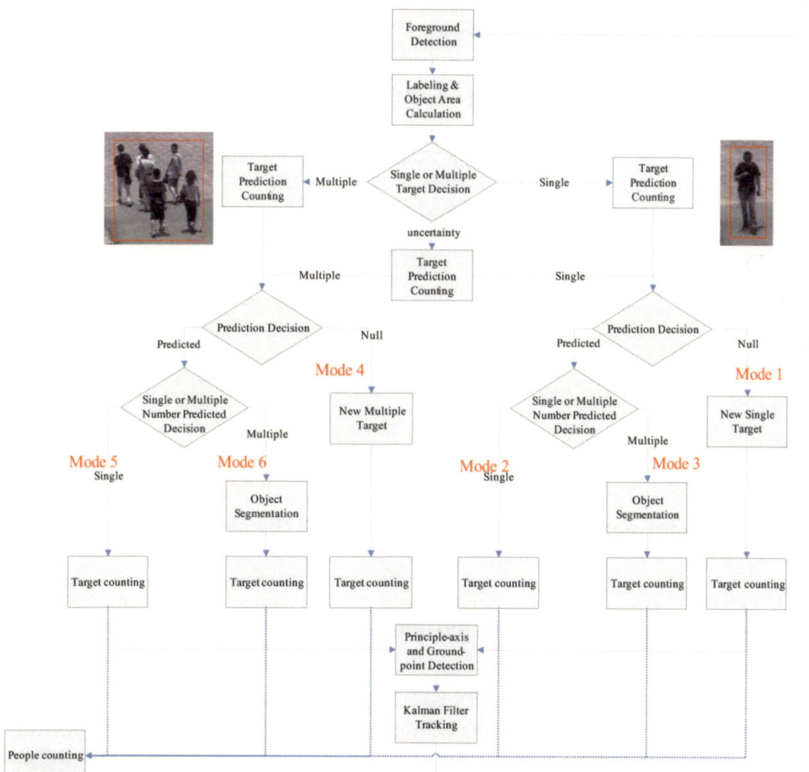

Fig. 3. Flowchart of the multi-mode multi targets tracking scheme.

Mode 1: An image blob is detected as a single target and its location is not predicted by other tracked targets from previous frames, i.e., the target is appeared on the scene at first time.
Mode 2: An image blob is detected as a single target and its location is predicted by one of the tracked targets from previous frames.
Mode 3: An image blob is detected as a single target and its location is predicted by a multiple target from previous frames, i.e., the object occlusion is occurred.
Mode 4: An image blob is detected as merged multiple targets and its location is not predicted by other tracked targets from previous frames, i.e., the merged multiple targets is appeared on the scene at first time.
Mode 5: An image blob is detected as a merged multiple targets and its location is predicted by one of the tracked merged multiple targets from previous frames.
Mode 6: An image blob is detected as a merged multiple targets and its location is predicted by a single target from previous frames, i.e., the objects' separation is occurred.
The detailed description of the multi-mode target tracking can be seen in [13].
When the tracked targets are slightly occluded it is possible to separate these targets. Then, the separated target can be tracked according to rules of modes 1 or 2. In general, color feature is effective to separate the merger targets. However, to develop robust target segmentation we apply the color-based difference projection to separate the targets from the merged targets. By observing the color difference projection histogram, we found the peak is not distinct for each color feature. To overcome this problem, the correlation for the color feature is used to find the segmentation line. In Fig. 4, the position of the prominent correlation peak is obtained to extract the segmentation line.

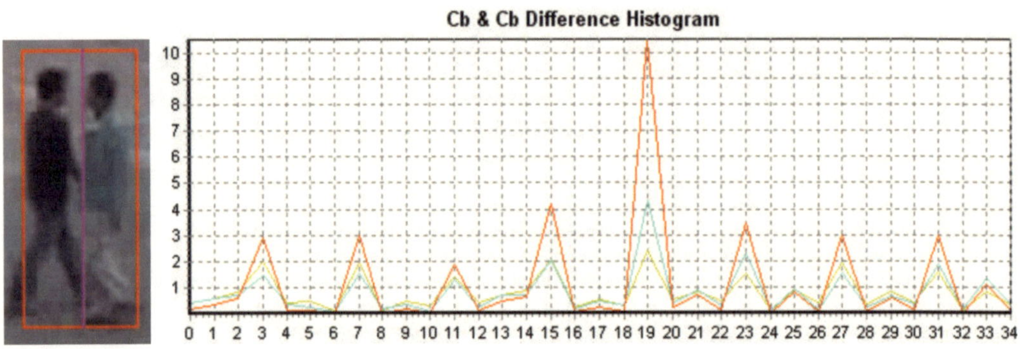

Fig. 4. The correlation for the color feature is used to find the segmentation line

2.5 Simulation results

2.5.1 Moving object filtering using the dynamic texture model

In Fig. 5-(a), it shows an outdoor scene. Fig. 5-(b) represents the foreground with the pixel-wise temporal probability model, and the dynamic texture detection model is described in Fig. 5-(c). By using the dynamic detection model, the targets will be separated into the truly foreground target and the constant texture object. If the object with too many constant textures, we will define the target as the noise, and it then will be removed, i.e. in Fig. 5-(d). Finally, we can improve the accuracy about the detected target.

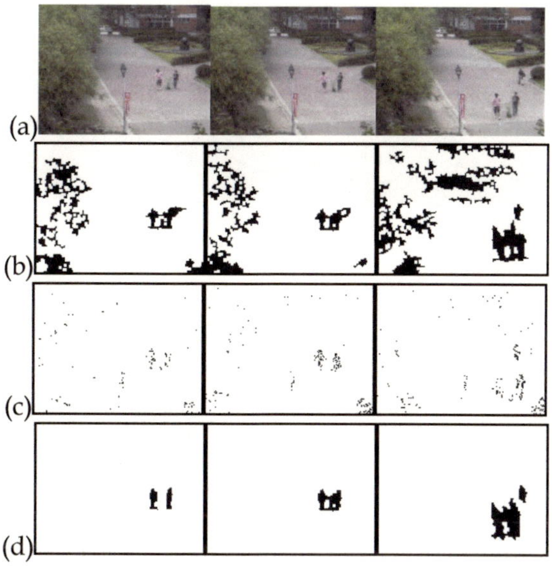

Fig. 5. (a) Outdoor scene. (b) The objects are detected by using pixel-wise temporal probability model. (c) Foreground detection using the dynamic texture model. (d) The extracted objects after the texture noise removing process.

2.5.2 Multi-mode target tacking scheme

In Fig. 6, the multi-mode target tracking on a crowd outdoor scene is illustrated. The split, merge, and occlusion among the targets occur repeatedly. The merged multiple-target is labeled "M". Meanwhile, some important features, e.g., color, weight, height, ground point position, are record as the tracking measurements for each target. The multi-mode multi targets detection on a crowd outdoor scene is shown in Fig. 7 and each target will be tracked with the mode according to the situation of target occlusion [13].

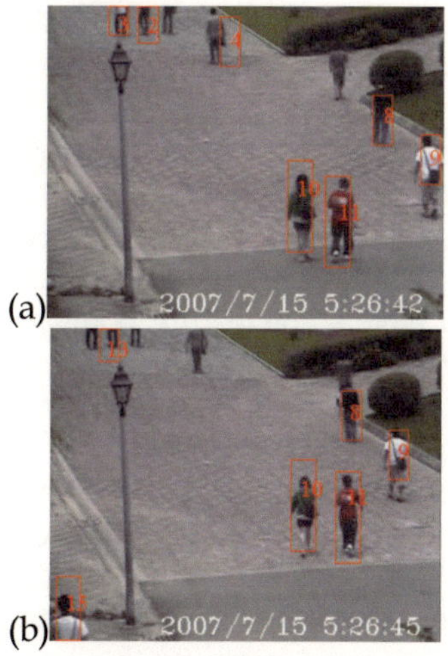

Fig. 6. Multi-mode tracking on an outdoor crowd scene.

Fig. 7. Multi-mode tracking on an outdoor crowd scene.

3. Point-based method

In the conventional blob-based object detection systems, some typical methods are applied to extract the moving objects, e.g., background subtraction [15], optical flow [16-18], frame difference analyses [19], and codebook model [20]. In [15], the regions of moving objects may be acquired precisely by using the method of background subtraction but it is extremely sensitive to the illumination variation and the dynamic background changing. In [16-18], the optical flow method is used to independently track each low-level object feature. Applying frame differencing method [19] may be adaptive to the illumination changes, but the moving objects are extracted incompletely when the objects move slowly. In [20], the codebook method can overcome the problems of changing backgrounds or illumination variations, but this method is difficult to detect and track the targets in the crowded scene.

In the novel video surveillance application, one of the most challenging problems is the target tracking in the crowded scene shown in Fig. 8. Generally, the serious occlusions make the conventional blob-based target detection/tracking methods failed. For example, to track a target in a crowded rail station or square, the tracked person can be partially occluded by other persons and only part of region can be served as a clue to track. Hence, to track the individual target in the dense crowds may face two major problems: 1) the target size can be small when we are monitoring a large space where the crowds move; 2) frequent partial occlusions make the target segmentation very difficult. Therefore, the point-based features are considered to be applied to tackle the problems of tracking in the crowd. Even in the crowded scenes, there may still have some feature points on the partial target regions that are not occluded. In Fig. 9-(b), the example of object extraction using the blob-based method is illustrated. It is obvious that the foreground region formed by merging several targets is difficult to segment each target. On the contrary, Fig. 9-(c) shows the feasibility for applying the point-based method to detect and track each individual target in the crowded scene.

With the same concept of feature point tracking, Brostow and Cipolla [21] proposed a Bayesian clustering algorithm that can segment each individual entity within the crowd with the space-time proximity and trajectory coherence. However, the efficiency is unsatisfied. In this study, we propose a novel method to detect and track the individual target in the crowd.

Fig. 8. (a) Crowded scene in tunnel. (b) Crowded scene in Chu-Hua University. (c) Occlusion occurs in the scene.

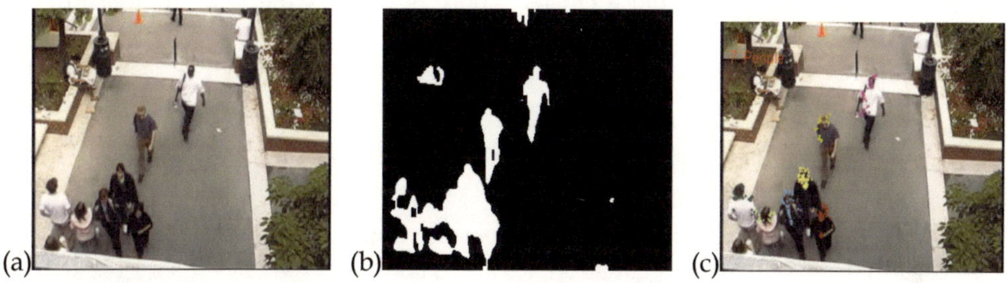

Fig. 9. (a) Original image. (b) The foreground detection with the method of blob-based background subtraction. (c) Target detection and tracking using the point-based feature and each color represents each individual target.

3.1 Point-based target tracking

In general, the conventional object detection in the crowd may have several problems in the individual segmentation process. First, it's difficult to find accurate boundaries by using background subtraction methods [23] in the crowded scenes. Second, the supervised learning or any subject-specific model [20] needs more computation cost to train. Third, the moving subjects may have different moving directions but merge together. In order to tackle these problems, we propose a coarse-to-fine approach based on the corner points extraction and tracking processes, in which the C-means algorithm is used to extract the coarse clusters and the spatial-temporal shortest spanning tree is proposed to segment each individual subject.

In the proposed system framework, we firstly detect the low-level feature points with the Shi-Tomasi-Kanade detector [16]. In the Kanade's algorithm, once the corner points are extracted, each feature point can be tracked by the Kanade-Lucas-Tomasi(KLT) optical flow [22] between two successive frames. Each trace of the tracked corner point can be represented as:

$$\{\{(x_t^i, y_t^i), t = T_{init}^i, \ldots, T_{final}^i\}, i = 1, \ldots, N\} ,$$

where (x_t^i, y_t^i) denotes the image coordinate of the corner point i at frame t, N denotes the total number of feature point tracks, and T denotes the frame number. By the careful observation, the corner points on each individual object can have high spatial-temporal correlation. The spatial correlation measures the geometrical relationship among the corner points that belong to an object; while the temporal correlation measures the trajectory consistency for the corner points that belong to an object. Here, the C-means algorithm is used to roughly cluster the dynamic feature points based on the spatial correlation measure.

3.1.1 Individual segmentation with spatial-temporal shortest spanning tree

Based on the rough segmentations from the C-means clustering, the corner points located on a subject should be close on both the geometrical distribution and moving trajectory. To this end, the cluster refining process implemented with spatial shortest spanning tree is applied to the rough segmented clusters to partition the individual objects. The algorithm of individual segmentation with the spatial shortest spanning tree [25] is described as follows.

1. Construct a spatial shortest spanning tree in each cluster. Let set $C^i = \{p^1, p^2..., p^N\}$ represent the point set within a cluster where N denotes the total number of cluster members.
2. Calculate the weighted distance according to the following formula.

$$d_{ij} = \left\{ \sqrt{\beta_x \left(p_x^i - p_x^j\right)^2 + \beta_y \left(p_y^i - p_y^j\right)^2} \ , i = 1,2,\ldots,N \ , j = 1,2,\ldots,N \right\},$$

where β_x, β_y are weights on x and y directions separately.

1. According to the distance calculation in step 2, construct the spatial shortest spanning tree sequentially for each cluster.
2. Retain the weighting table and the linking order in the spatial shortest spanning tree for constructing the spatial-temporal shortest spanning tree.

In the following, we will modify this algorithm by combining the trajectory correlation to segment the individual more precisely.

Given two tracks T_u and T_v generated from two feature points, if the track variance defined in Eq. (11) for the two tracks is small, then the two feature points are likely to belong to same target.

$$Correlation(T_u, T_v) = \frac{1}{1 + Variance(T_u, T_v)}, \tag{11}$$

where $Variance(T_u, T_v) = Variance(DistanceEucl(T_u, T_v))$ within N frames. Finally, we can establish a spatial-temporal conformance measure as:

$$Conformance = \frac{\sqrt{\beta_x \left(p_x^i - p_x^j\right)^2 + \beta_y \left(p_y^i - p_y^j\right)^2}}{Correlation\left(T_i \ , \ T_j\right)}, i = 1,2,\ldots,N-1 \ , j = i+1, \tag{12}$$

If the conformance value is larger than a predefined threshold, then it means that the two points don't belong to the same subject. But sometimes we may face a situation that a feature point belong to subject A may be mis-located on subject B when two subject are crossing. Fig. 10 illustrates that a lot points are possible to be mis-located when two person are crossing each other. To overcome the above-mentioned problem, we propose the voting method with temporal information to ensure the trajectory conformance of tracked feature points in a cluster. The voting rule for trajectory conformance is described as follows.

Fig. 10. A lot points are mis-located when two person are crossing each other.

1. The vector $\boldsymbol{d}_{(x,y)}(F_t, F_{t-10})$ acquired from successive 10 frames is defined to record the moving direction for each feature point.
2. Based on the x and y components of $\boldsymbol{d}_{(x,y)} = (d_x , d_y)$, there are four possible sign pairs to denote the rough moving direction shown in Fig. 11. They are defined as (+ , +), (+ , -), (- , +), and (- , -) separately. We record the direction of all dynamic points that belong to each subject.
3. By observing the recorded direction list, there may have a direction with the highest votes. We assume that it is the dominant moving direction in this cluster, and then delete other dynamic points with different directions.
4. Repeat steps 1~3 until all cluster are processed.
5. Once the cluster's direction list is modified, the cluster center must be recalculated.

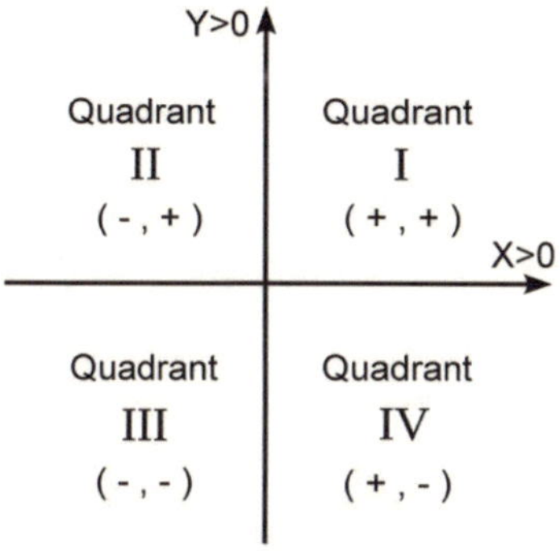

Fig. 11. The possible moving direction for each feature point.

3.1.2 Object tracking

In order to accurately track all targets, to develop a stable and reliable point-based object tracking method is necessary. According to the mechanism of feature tracking, we know the corner feature would be tracked efficiently between two successive frames. Therefore, the characteristic of KLT tracking algorithm are adopted for tracking the existed dynamic feature points with the inheritance of the points' attributes in last frame. On the other hand, the new points can appear while the existed points' tracking fail or vanish. Hence, it's important to link the tracking relation between old and new points.

Point-Based Target Tracking Algorithm

1. If the corner points are tracked successfully and continuously, they will inherit the attribute of the segmented individual cluster. Otherwise, if the corner points are newly generated in the area of ROI, we will classify the feature points into the set $P_{NEW} = \{p^1, p^2 \ldots p^N\}$. Furthermore, the distance between the new points and existed cluster centers C_j are calculated as:

$$Distance = \left\{ \left\{ \sqrt{\alpha_x \left(p_x^i - C_x^j\right)^2 + \alpha_y \left(p_y^i - C_x^j\right)^2} \; , i = 1,2,\ldots(5),N \right\} , j = 1,2,\ldots,N \right\}, \tag{13}$$

where a_x and a_y are weights on x-axis and y-axis that are similar to the C-means clustering process. Then, we add the new points into the closest cluster.

2. After adding the new points to the nearest cluster, the cluster centers may change. In addition, the situation that multiple objects moving together may occur and then the individual segmentation are required to perform again. The individual segment mechanism is based on normal width of human body. First we calculate the width of the cluster as:

$$ClusterWidth = \mathbf{RightBoundary_y} - \mathbf{LeftBoundary_y}.$$

If the width of the cluster is larger than the predefined threshold TWIDTH (evaluated by the normal width of human body), then the cluster is required to be segmented. The new segmented cluster will be given a new ID. Fig. 12 illustrates the situation that needs to be re-segmented.

3. If some new points are not classified into any existed clusters, then theses point are classified into the new set $P'_{NEW} = \{p'^1, p'^2 \ldots p'^N\}$ and regarded as new moving objects. Fig. 13 illustrates existed cluster (existed objects) and the new clusters (new objects). For this reason, we use C-means algorithm to classify them but without comparing to the existed clusters.
4. Integrate the new and old clusters' information.
5. Check the consistence of all points in each cluster and execute the process of individual segmentation with the spatial-temporal shortest spanning tree for each cluster. Fig. 14 shows the final results.

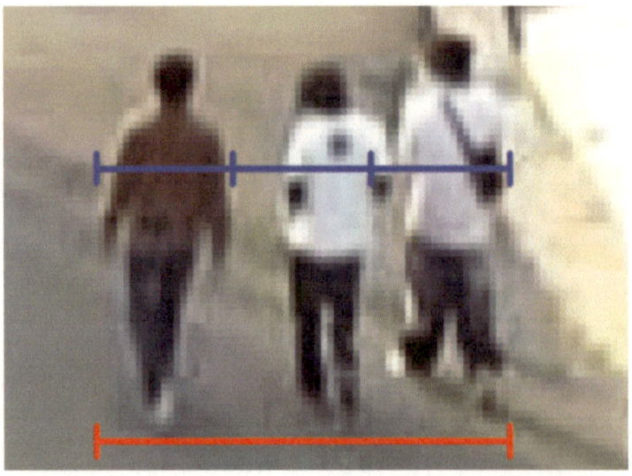

Fig. 12. The red line denotes the cluster width. The blue line denotes the normal width of human body.

Fig. 13. Grouping of new points. (a) Green points are the new generated points that are distant from other existed red clusters. (b) The result of clustering.

Fig. 14. Final result of segmenting the tracked objects

3.2 Simulation results

Two test videos: "Commons01" and "Tunnel-A125" are used to evaluate the performance of individual segmentation and object tracking. The video "Commons01" is obtained from the web site in [24]. Another test video "Tunnel-A125" is provided from professor Brostow [21], which is captured from a tunnel where the people are walking side by side. The object tracking is based on the concept of feature points' inheritance. The proposed point-based object tracking algorithm can make the target tracking more accurate and efficient. Fig. 15 illustrates the experimental results for the point-based object tracking. In Fig. 15, there are 3 people walking closely and the occlusion problem is serious. The proposed method can segment each individual person even the occlusion problem exists.

In order to evaluate the accuracy of the proposed system, we compare the proposed method to other methods proposed in recent years. Table 1 shows the accuracy analysis among the methods in [21, 26] and ours. It can be seen that the performance in detection rate and miss detection rate outperforms the other methods and the false detection rate is close to the other methods. In the accuracy analysis, we select 400 successive frames from the video "tunnel-A125". The efficiency of our system can approach 8 fps and it can be further improved with the adjustment of the amount of feature points. The method of Bayesian detection [21] selected the test video frames from "tunnel-A125" randomly. In order to calculate the likelihoods between many image features, the computational complexity of the method in [21] is higher. They take about 5 seconds to perform the spatial clustering process for each frame. In our experiment, we analyze and count the detection rate in the area between the blue lines. Some results of individual segmentation are shown in Fig. 16.

frame #247 frame #307 frame #637

Fig. 15. Segmentation and tracking for the targets in the crowd.

frame #2762 frame #2981

Fig. 16. Analysis of the detection rate in the area between the two blue lines.

	Brostow & Cipolla	Zhao & Nevatia	Ours
distinct detections	144	8466	1319
correctly detected	136	7881	1254
missed detections	8	585	65
false detections	33	291	56
detection rate	94%	93.09%	95.07%
miss detection rate	22.9%	6.91%	4.92%
false detection rate	5.6%	3.43%	4.25%

Table 1. The accuracy analyses for the methods of Brostow & Cipolla, Zhao & Nevatia, and ours.

4. Conclusions

In this chapter, the methods for targets detection and tracking in the crowd are addressed. In general, the methods for targets tracking in the crowd can be categorized into the blob-based and point-based methods. The blob-based methods detect and track the targets based on the appearance models; while the point-based method detect and track the moving targets with the reliable feature points. For the blob-based method, the spatial-temporal probability background model, multi-mode tracking scheme, color-based difference projection, and ground point detection are proposed to improve the conventional target tracking systems. Experimental results show that the targets in the crowd scene may be tracked with the correct tracking modes and with rate above 15fps. For the point-based method, a novel system for tracking in the crowd is proposed. The spatial-temporal shortest spanning tree and target tracking with point inheritance are proposed to improve the problems for the object tracking in the crowd. The experimental results show that the accuracy of individual segmentation in the crowd can be higher than 90%, and the efficiency of our system can approach 8 fps. The future works in the subsystem of tracking in crowd is focus on refining the accuracy of targets' segmentation and tracking.

5. Reference

[1] A. Elgammal, D. Harwood, and L. Davis, "Non-parametric model for background subtraction," in *Proceedings of the 6th European Conference on Computer Vision, 2000,* pp. 751-767.

[2] X. Dai, and S. Khorram, "Performance of optical flow techniques," *Int J Compute Vision 12(1),* pp. 42-77, 1994.

[3] R. Jain, W. Martin and J. Aggarwal, "Segmentation through the detection of changes due to motion," *Compute Graph Image Process 11, 1979,* pp. 13–34.

[4] Y. Ren, C. S. Chua and Y. K. Ho, "Motion detection with nonstationary background," *Machine Vision and Application, Mar. 2003,* Vol. 13, No. 5-6, pp. 332–343.

[5] C. C. Lien and S. C. Hsu, "The target tracking using the spatial-temporal probability model," *IEEE Nonlinear Signal and Image Processing, NSIP 2005, May 2005,* pp. 34-39.

[6] C. Wren, A. Azarbayejani, T. Darrell, and A. Pentland, "Pfinder: real-time tracking of the human body," *IEEE Transactions on Pattern Analysis and Machine Intelligence, July 1997,* Vol. 19, No. 7, pp. 780-785.

[7] M. Xu, J. Orwell, L. Lowey and D. Thirde, "Architecture and algorithms for tracking football players with multiple cameras" *Image and Signal Processing, IEE Proceedings, 8 April 2005,* Vol. 152, Issue 2, pp. 232-241

[8] K. Nummiaro, E. K. Meier, L. J. V. Gool, "An adaptive color-based particle filter" *Journal: Image Vision Computing,* Vol. 21, Issue. 1, pp. 99-110.

[9] W. Hu, M. Hu, X. Zhou, Tieniu Tan, "Principal axis-based correspondence between multiple cameras for people tracking" *IEEE Transactions on Pattern Analysis and Machine Intelligence, APRIL 2006,* Vol. 28, No. 4, pp. 663-671.

[10] D. Salmond, "Target tracking: introduction and Kalman tracking filters," *IEEE Target Tracking: Algorithms and Applications, 2001,* Vol. 2, pp. 1/1-1/16.

[11] E. Alpaydin, Introduction to Machine Learning, *MIT Press, Cambridge 2004.*

[12] Y. Yang and M. Levine, "The background primal sketch: an approach for tracking moving objects," *Machine Vision and Applications, 1992,* Vol. 5, pp. 17-34.

[13] C. C. Lien, J. C. Wang and Y. M. Jiang, "Multi-mode target tracing on s crowd scene," *IEEE International Conference on Intelligent Information Hiding and Multimedia Signal Processing 2007 (IIH-MSP 2007),* Nov. 26-28, Kaohsiung, Taiwan.

[14] G. J. Brostow and R. Cipolla, "Unsupervised Bayesian detection of independent motion in crowds," in Proc. of IEEE Conference on Computer Vision and Pattern Recognition, 2006, vol. 1, pp. 594-601.

[15] C. R. Jung, "Efficient Background Subtraction and Shadow Removal for Monochromatic Video Sequences," *IEEE Transactions on Multimedia*, Vol. 11, No. 3, April 2009, pp. 571-577.

[16] J. Shi and C. Tomasi, "Good Features to Track," *Proceedings of the IEEE Conference Computer Vision and Pattern Recognition*, June 1994, pp. 593-600.

[17] D. G. Lowe, "Distinctive Image Features from Scale-Invariant Keypoints," *International Journal of Computer Vision*, Vol. 60, No. 2, Jan. 2004, pp. 91-110.

[18] H. Bay, A. Ess, T. Tuytelaars, and L. V. Gool, "Speeded-Up Robust Features (SURF)," *Proceedings of the 9th European Conference on Computer Vision*, Vol. 3951, May 2006, pp. 404-417.

[19] S. Wang, X. Wang, and H. Chen, "A Stereo Video Segmentation Algorithm Combining Disparity Map and Frame Difference," *International Conference on Intelligent System and Knowledge Engineering*, Vol. 1, Nov. 2008, pp. 1121-1124.

[20] K. Kim, T. H. Chalidabhongse, D. Harwood, and L. Davis, "Real-Time Foreground–Background Segmentation Using Codebook Model," *Real-Time Imaging*, Vol. 11, No. 3, June 2005, pp. 172-185.

[21] G. Brostow and R. Cipolla, "Unsupervised Bayesian Detection of Independent Motion in Crowds," *Proceedings of the IEEE Conference Computer Vision and Pattern Recognition*, Vol. 1, June 2006, pp. 594-601.

[22] C. Tomasi and T. Kanade, "Detection and Tracking of Point Features," *Carnegie Mellon University Technical Report CMU-CS-91-132*, April 1991.

[23] J. Rosen, "A Cautionary Tale for A New Age of Surveillance," *The New York Times Magazine*, Oct. 2001.

[24] A. M. Cheriyadat and R. J. Radke, "Detecting Dominant Motions in Dense Crowds," *IEEE Journal of Selected Topics in Signal Processing*, Vol. 2, No. 4, Aug. 2008, pp. 568-581.

[25] O. J. Morris, M. J. Lee, and A. G. Constantinides, "Graph theory for image analysis: an approach based on the shortest spanning tree," *IEE Proceedings F. Communications, Radar and Signal Processing*, Vol. 133, No. 2, April 1986, pp. 146-152.

[26] T. Zhao and R. Nevatia, "Tracking Multiple Humans in Complex Situations," *IEEE Transactions on Pattern Analysis and Machine Intelligence*, Vol. 26, No. 9, Sep. 2004, pp. 1208-1221.

14

Measurement of Pedestrian Traffic Using Feature-based Regression in the Spatiotemporal Domain

Gwang-Gook Lee and Whoi-Yul Kim
Hanyang University,
Republic of Korea

1. Introduction

Measurement of pedestrian traffic in public areas (e.g., stations, airports, shopping malls or complex buildings) provides valuable information. For safety management, congestions can be detected to prevent accidents in their early stage by monitoring the pedestrian traffic continuously. Knowing the number of people working in a large building may help to when designing evacuation plans. For marketing purposes, value assessments of shopping areas can be achieved based on traffic data because higher pedestrian traffic is directly linked to more sales. In building management, pedestrian traffic data can be utilized to optimize the number and working hours of staff. Power savings can be achieved by adjusting air-conditioning and heating based on pedestrian traffic.

Over the last decade, various computer vision methods have been studied to automatically measure the pedestrian traffic. One popular approach to pedestrian traffic measurement is the use of top-view cameras. In this approach, a camera is mounted vertically at the top of a gate or over a region of interest. Because of the superior viewpoint of the camera, pedestrians do not obscure each other in video frames. Hence the problem of pedestrian traffic measurement may be solved easily by detecting moving objects using foreground segmentation and tracking the detected blobs (Sexton et al., 1995; Kim et al., 2003). However, these methods fail when a number of people move close or slightly touch each other creating a single blob. Chen et al. resolved this problem by comparing the area of detected moving object with the area of one person to estimate the number of people in the blob (2006). Velipasalar *et al.* employed two-level hierarchical tracking to deal with pedestrians of complex movements interacting with each other (2006).

Pedestrian traffic also can be studied by detecting humans using standard surveillance cameras that do not require a specific viewpoint. Similar to top-view camera based methods, some of these methods perform foreground segmentation to distinguish moving objects. However, for oblique camera angles, multiple pedestrians easily appear as merged blobs in a video frame. The detected foreground blobs are segmented into individuals by modeling humans as ellipsoids (Zhao et al, 2004, 2008) or rectangles (Liu et al, 2005; Beleznai et al., 2006) cooperating with the known camera geometry. Based on based on their shapes and apperances, humans can also be detected directly from image frames without separating out foreground blobs. Viola *et al.* detected humans using appearance and motion information together in a boosting sceheme (2003). Dalal and Triggs used histograms of oriented gradients as features to describe human shapes (2005). Detection of whole human bodies often suffer due to occlusions in dense crowds. To resolve miss-detection due to occlusions, only upper body shapes (Sidla et al., 2006) or contours around heads (Yuk et al., 2006) may be used in detection. Part-based detection methods have been studied extensively (Wu and Nevatia, 2005; Lin et al., 2007) to improve detection performance in dense crowds. Once pedestrians are detected, they are then tracked to analyze their movement and to collect traffic data. Bayesian inference (Zhao et al., 2004 & 2008), Kalman filter (Sidla, 2006) or other trackers (Yuk et al, 2006) have been used to track individual pedestrians.

Even though various efforts have been made, existing methods are not suitable for measuring pedestrian traffic in large public areas. The top-view camera based method shows good performance with relatively low computational burden. However the top-view camera based methods cannot be applied to exisitng CCTV systems because they require a dedicated camera system of specific angles. Currently, most of large buildings have their own video surveillance system but they have oblique views to enable wide coverage of cameras and to deliver better scene understanding to human operators. Installation of additional video camera system only for pedestrian traffic measurement would be a great burden. Unlike the top-view camera based methods, the detection-based methods can be applied to ordinary CCTV cameras with an oblique view. However, the computational complexity of detection-based methods is relatively high in general. This complexity is a restriction to real systems where the computational power is low and the number of cameras is large. Moreover, the computation time tends to increase as the scene gets more complex with large crowds because more pedestrians should be detected and tracked.

A pedestrian traffic measurement method should satisfy the following requirements to be useful in a practical system that covers a large public area:

- Low computational complexity: The computational complexity of the algorithm should be as low as possible. Real-time execution on a PC is not sufficient for large systems because tens or hundreds of cameras are often used in a complex building. When such a large number of cameras is involved, the algorithm should be able to process a number of CCTV inputs on a single computer or the method should be executable on an embedded system with a computational power that is much lower than that of a standard PC.
- Compatibility with existing system: Most large buildings have their own video surveillance systems. The pedestrian traffic measurement method should make use of existing surveillance systems. To achieve this compatibility, traffic measurement algorithms solely rely on video camera input, and not require other kinds of input such as range data. This also implies that the algorithms should not be constrained by camera angle.
- Stability under high traffic: In public places, such as railway stations or shopping malls, the number of people can be large. Hence the method should be able to measure pedestrian traffic successfully not only for small numbers of people, but also for large crowds. Moreover, the computation time of the method should not increase for larger numbers of people.

An alternative method for measuring pedestrian traffic is introduced in this chapter. The method is a statistical approach which uses feature-based regression. The feature-based regression is widely used for crowd size estimation. In crowd size estimation, the number of people or the level of crowdedness in an image frame is measured by examining image features. As image features, foreground pixels (Velastin *et al.*, 1994; Celik *et al.*, 2006), edges (Cho *et al.*, 1999), textures (Manara *et al.*, 1999) or combinations of various features (Kong *et al.*, 2006; Chan *et al.*, 2008) are employed. Based on the extracted image features, the count of people or the level of crowdedness is measured by linear relation (Velastin *et al.*, 1994), a neural network (Cho *et al.*, 1999; Kong *et al.*, 2006), a SVM classifier (Xiohua *et al.*, 2006) or a Gaussian process regression (Chan *et al.*, 2008).

In a similar manner to the crowd size estimation, the size of pedestrian traffic is estimated from the amount of image features. That is, the traffic is measured by setting a relation between image features and the number of pedestrians. To count passing people rather than static humans, the analysis is performed in a spatiotemporal domain rather than an image domain. Because it is a statistical method which is applied in the spatiotemporal domain, it requires very low computation, its performance remains stable under high traffic and it is also less sensitive to camera viewpoints.

2. Overview

The basic concept underlying the pedestrian traffic measurement method can be easily understood from Fig. 1. In the video frame, a measurement line, called a *virtual gate*, is set up as in Fig. 1 (a). Here s connects a pixel location (x, y) to the corresponding pixel on the virtual gate. Fig. 1 (b) is an example of a spatiotemporal image.

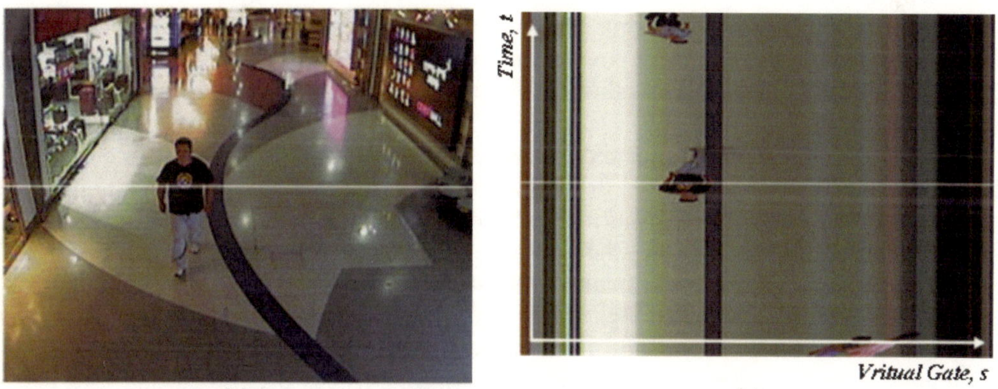

(a) (b)

Fig. 1. (a) A virtual gate to measure pedestrian traffic size, (b) a spatiotemporal image created using the virtual gate

Observing the image pixels on the virtual gate over time can be interpreted as examining a spatiotemporal image whose two coordinates correspond to time t and the linear coordinate along the virtual gate s, respectively. When a person passes the virtual gate, his body shape is produced in the spatiotemporal image as in Fig. 1 (b). The spatiotemporal image, which is obtained over a certain period of time, contains the images of people who passed the gate during that period. Hence the pedestrian traffic or the number of people passing the virtual gate, can be acquired by counting the number of people in this spatiotemporal image.

When counting pedestrians in spatiotemporal images, we cannot use conventional detection or segmentation techniques because human shapes suffer severe distortions in the spatiotamporal images. Fig. 2 shows some examples of these distortions. In Fig. 2 (a) the shape of objects are slanted because they changed direction while passing the virtual gate. Fig. 2 (b) gives an example of size variations of people in the spatiotemporal image. Because the two people on the left side moved very slowly, their shapes are elnogated resulting in a larger image size that of the people on the right side. Also, in Fig 2. (c), part of some people are occluded by others and their whole body shapes cannot be seen.

(a) (b) (c)

Fig. 2. Distortions occur in the spatiotemporal image. (a) Slanted shape occurred due to a pedestrian passing to the left. (b) Elongated shape caused by very slow pedestrian movement. (c) Occlusions due to dense crowd.

Because of these problems, counting pedestrians as individuals in spatiotemporal images using conventional detection or segmentation method is not feasible. Rather than trying to detect individuals, a statistical method is adopted to count pedestrians as a whole from image features.

Fig. 3 shows the block diagram of the traffic flow measurement method. As shown in the figure, image features are extracted first followed by feature integration process to measure pedestrian traffic. Foreground pixels and motion vectors are extracted as image features. In the traffic flow measurement step, the foreground pixels are accumulated along the virtual gate over continuous frames to calculate pedestrian traffic. In the feature accumulation, a feature normalization process is employed to account for size variation of the human images caused by perspective projection. Also, different moving speeds of individuals are considered to adapt different motions of pedestrians. Because occlusions due to a dense crowd yields under-estimation of pedestrian traffic size, the accumulated feature size is compensated to deliver an accurate estimate of pedestrian traffic.

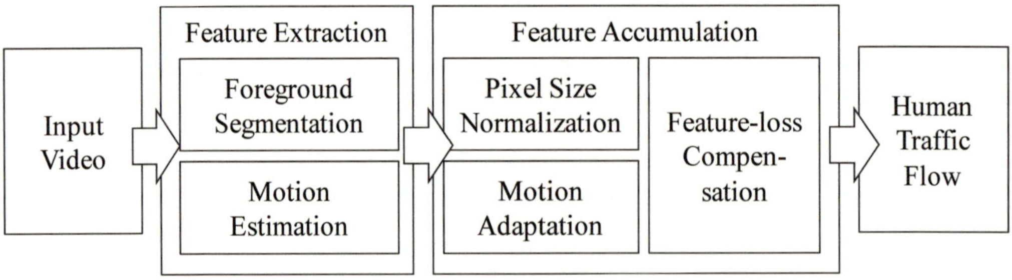

Fig. 3. Block diagram of the traffic flow measurement method

3. Feature extraction

3.1 Foreground segmentation

As the image feature for human traffic estimation, regions of moving objects are first isolated. We avoided using other features such as edges or textures because of their sensitivity to noise level or lighting changes. Foreground segmentation is achieved by comparing an input frame with a reference background. In creating and updating the reference background, a background modeling method proposed by Stauffer and Grimson (1999) is employed with a light modification.

In the Stauffer and Grimson's method, each pixel in a video frame is modeld by mixture of Gaussian distributions. An update of the background model is performed incrementally by the online K-means algorithm given by (1):

$$\Theta_{k,t}(x) = (1-\alpha)\cdot\Theta_{k,t-1}(x) + \alpha\cdot\Lambda\left(I_t(x), \Theta_{k,t-1}(x)\right). \tag{1}$$

In (1), $\Theta_{k,t}$ and I_t are model k and an observation at time t for a pixel x. Each model updates its parameter based upon a local estimate $\Lambda(I_t(x), \Theta_{k,t-1}(x))$. The learning rate a is a small constant which determines the learning speed of the background model. Because the model parameters are updated incrementally using online K-means, the background model is adaptable to scene changes such as lighting variation or new background objects.

The incremental update of the model parameter in (1) can be thought as a pixel observation process that uses a temporal window of length $L = 1/a$. The underlying assumption of the model update is that the background pixel occurs most frequently in this temporal window. Hence the model update process tries to find the dominant mode by estimating its density using online clustering. However, such assumption is often violated when high traffic of pedestrians occurs constantly in a scene. For example, if pedestrians pass the observation area continuously leaving only a small time window for backgroud pixels, foreground pixels may occupy the majority of the pixel statistics resulting in a defective background models as shown in Fig. 4.

Because the traffic flow measurement method introduced in this chapter is designed for use in public areas with high traffic rates, the background modeling method must be able to cope with the defective backgrounds with high traffic. To resolve this problem, another assumption is made which is that background pixels are not only the most frequent but also are static. Hence, to avoid creating an erroneous background model, the learning rate of each pixel is adjusted by examining its static level. If a pixel is not static at a time, a lower learning rate is applied because the pixel might belong to a foreground object.

(a) (b) (c)

Fig. 4. (a) a scene with continuous pedestrian movements, (b) method clear background model under low human traffic, (c) a defected background model due to continuous movements of humans.

To identify static pixels, we first define its activity of a pixel as (2). In (2), $A(x, t)$ represents the activity of a pixel x at time t and $I_d(x, t)$ is interframe difference which is defined as $|I(x, t) - I(x, t\text{-}1)|$. Hence, the activity is decided as the maximum value between the interframe difference and the activity of previous frame decreased by a constant ratio β.

$$A(x,t-1) = \max\left(I_d(x,t), \beta \cdot A(x,t-1)\right) \tag{2}$$

By comparing its activity to a given threshold level T_{act}, each pixel is classified as static or non-static. Fig. 5 shows an example of a static pixel classification where (a) is the input frame and (b) is the classification result. In Fig. 5 (b), static pixels and non-static pixels are represented in black and white, respectively. Pixels around moving objects show large activity values and are labelled as non-static pixels. We used 0.2 for β and 40 for T_{act}.

Even though pixels around moving objects show large activity values, pixels inside a large object or nearly static objects might be labeled as static pixels as shown in Fig. 5 (b). Hence the labeled result is expanded using a morphological operation. The size of the window used for the morphological operation is determined as the expected size of a human at each pixel location, which will be explained in Section 5.1. Fig. 5 (b) shows the result of the morphological operation in which gray pixels indicate non-static pixels reclassified from static pixels.

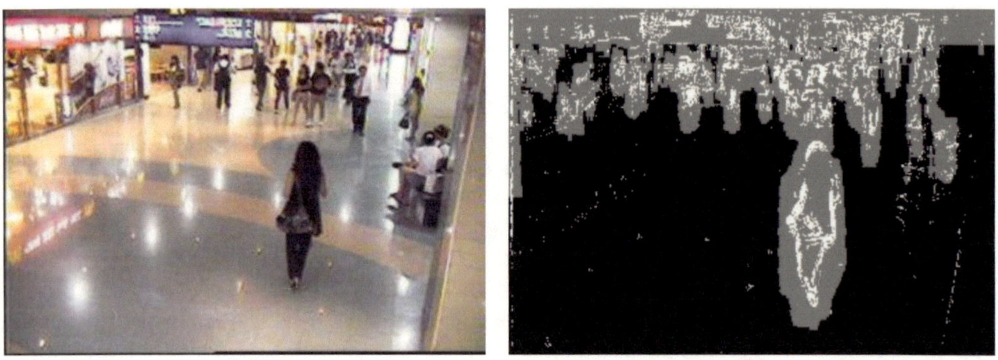

(a) (b)

Fig. 5. Distinguishing static and non-static pixels: (a) input video frame; (b) black pixels and white pixels correspond to static and non-static pixels, respectively. Gray pixels are expanded from white pixels by morphological operations.

Once static and non-static pixels are distinguished, a low learning rate is used for the model to update to the non-static pixels. The lower learning rate α_l is set to be 10 times lower than the regular learning rate. Controlling the learning rate according to the activity of the pixel can be thought as changing background model update according to the history of the pixel. When a pixel shows static characteristic, its background model is updated by a general Gaussian mixture model. If a pixel is determined to be non-static, its update rate is significantly reduced making the background model similar to a static reference.

To reduce computational complexity, the background model is generated and maintained only for the pixels at the virtual gate. The activity value is computed only for regions around the virtual gate to control the learning rate of the background models. Because computation of activity value is quite simple compared to the maintenance of background models, the overall computational load is significantly reduced.

3.2 Motion estimation

To measure pedestrian traffic separately in different directions, the moving directions must be observed. Motion information is also required to obtain the exact traffic size because the size of an object in the spatiotemporal image varies according to the time taken the object to pass the virtual gate. For these reasons, a motion vector is chosen as a feature to examine moving directions and speeds of pedestrians. Hence, motion vectors are employes as image features too.

Motion vectors are obtained by a coarse-to-fine estimation of optical flow using pyramids (Bouguet, 1999). Because the estimation of optical flow includes a differential equation, which is solved iteratively, it introduces computational complexity. Hence, to reduce computation, motion vectors are computed for every two pixels on the line of the virtual gate and then interpolated.

Fig. 6 illustrates an example of motion vector computation. The computed motion vectors are displayed in different colors. The green lines indicate motion vectors that pass the virtual gate in the upward direction and the red lines represents motion vectors in the downward direciton. The lengths of the lines coincide with the maginitudes of the motion vectors.

Fig. 6. An example of extracted motion vectors

4. Feature accumulation

4.1 Estimating human traffic flow from image features

As a result of the feature extraction described in the previous section, a foreground map $fg(t, s)$ and a motion vector map $v(t, s)$ for the spatiotemporal image are created. In the foreground map, $fg(t, s)$ is equal to one when a pixel s on the virtual gate belongs to the foreground at time t, otherwise it is zero. Similarly, the motion vector map $v(t, s)$ contains the motion vector for a pixel s on the virtual gate at time t. Fig. 7 gives an example of the foreground map and the motion vector map. Fig. 7 shows an example of feature extraction.

For convenience, the traffic away from the camera is refered to as the upward direction and the opposite as the downward direction. To determine the traffic flow size of humans for upward and downward directions separately, the direction of traffic flow $k \in \{+1, -1\}$ is introduced. The direction of traffic flow is defined as +1 when the inner product of the motion vector and the normal vector of the virtual gate line is equal to or greater than zero and vice versa.

(a) (b) (c)

Fig. 7. Feature extraction results: (a) spatiotemporal image, (b) foreground map, (c) motion vector map

Based on the assumption that the number of people in the image is proportional to the amount of image features, the traffic flow size for a direction k during the time from t_i to t_j is obtained by integrating the extracted image features by using the following formula.

$$F_k(t_1,t_2)=\sum_{t=t_1}^{t_2}\sum_{s=1}^{N}\alpha\cdot\rho(s)\cdot fg(t,s)\cdot\delta\left(k,d(t,s)\right). \tag{3}$$

In (3), N is the number of pixels on the virtual gate and $d(t, s)$ is the direction of the traffic flow for a pixel s at time t. A delta function $\delta(i, j)$ (which equal one if $i = j$, but otherwise is zero) is used to integrate the image features from one direction only. Hence, the summation of $fg()$ multiplied by $\delta()$ gives us the amount of foreground pixels that have the same direction and occur between time t_1 and t_2.

The amount of image features (i.e., foreground pixels) is converted into the number of pedestrians by introducing two scaling factors a and $\rho(s)$ in (3). To determine $\rho(s)$, humans are modeled as rectangles with sizes that vary linearly with vertical image coordinates as shown in Fig. 8. The rectangle size for each pixel position can be easily calculated by annotating the human size manually at several locations and interpolating. Then, for a pixel s, $\rho(s)$ is set to $1/W(s)\cdot H(s)$ where $W(s)$ and $H(s)$ are the width and height of a rectangle. Because the area covered by a human is generally smaller than its bounding box, another scaling factor a is employed to fill this gap. The scaling factor a can be determined using a short video sequence with a known number of pedestrians.

Fig. 8. Pixel size normalization

4.2 Adaptation to motions of pedestrians

As mentioned in Section 2.1, different moving speeds and directions of people influences to feature observation in the spatiotemporal domain. For example, a person who moves slowly produces larger traffic estimate by taking a longer time to pass through the virtual gate. To deal with the different moving speeds and direction of pedestrians, the feature accumulation in (3) is modified to (4).

$$F_k(t_1,t_2)=\sum_{t=t_1}^{t_2}\sum_{s=1}^{N}\alpha\cdot\rho(s)\cdot\|\mathbf{v}(t,s)\|\cdot|\cos\theta_{\mathrm{v}}|\cdot fg(t,s)\cdot\delta(k,d(t,s)). \tag{4}$$

In this equation, the motion magnitude is multiplied to include the moving speeds of people in the traffic flow. Also, to consider only the motion components that contribute to passing by the virtual gate, the motion vector is projected onto the normal vector of the virtual gate where θ_v is the angle between the motion vector $v(t, s)$ and the normal vector of the line of the virtual gate.

Fig. 9 shows some examples of this pixel counting process. Fig. 9 (a), (b) and (c) are examples of the test sequence in which one person passes the gate. Fig. 9(d), (e) and (f) are the results of pixel counting obtained by integrating $F()$. Therefore, the feature integration results approached one because the pixel count was normalized by the average area of one person using a and $\rho(s)$. Note that the moving speeds of (a) and (b) are different (21 frames vs. 16 frames, respectively). Also, the viewpoints are different in (a) and (c). However, the traffic flow obtained by (4) approach to one in all three sequences proving its robustness to changes in camera angle and different speeds of pedestrians.

(a) (b) (c)

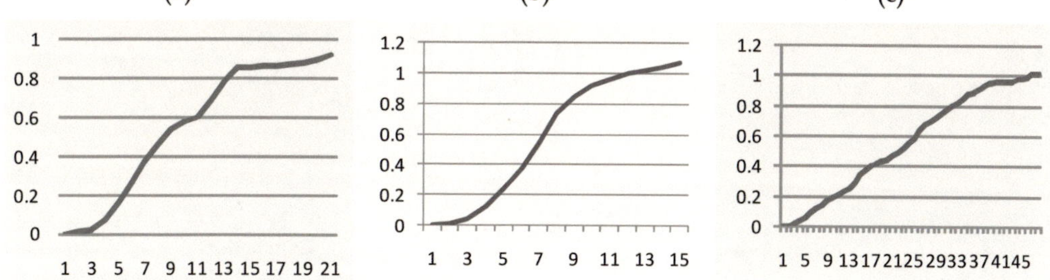

(d) (e) (f)

Fig. 9. Examples of traffic flow estimation for one person

4.3 Compensating feature loss due to a dense crowd

Although different pedestrian speeds and directions can be handled using motion vectors, the pedestrian traffic given by (4) cannot handle the problems caused by a dense crowd. When a scene is crowded, occlusions take place between individuals that make foreground pixels less observable. Hence, the traffic estimates obtained from (4) tend to underestimate the actual traffic value when the scene becomes crowded.

To compensate for the loss of feature observation due to occlusion, the traffic flow computed by (4) is compensated using nonlinear regression,

$$F_k^{'}(t_1,t_2) = a \cdot F_k(t_1,t_2)^b. \tag{5}$$

where a and b are the regression parameters that are learned during initial training. Because the loss of feature observation increases as the crowd level in the scene grows, a function of the power form is chosen for the regression. The measurement duration t_2-t_1 must be fixed because the feature integration result of (4) is used as input to the nonlinear regression. It was set to 60 seconds in our experiments. For parameter learning, the gradient descent method is employed as the optimization algorithm.

Fig. 10 shows an example of nonlinear regression used to compensate for the under-estimation in a dense crowd. In the graphs, 40 sample data are displayed. The points were obtained by estimating the sizes of the pedestrian traffic in one minute video segments. The x-axis represents the actual number of people passing in a video segment and the y-axis indicates the estimated human traffic size for the same video segment. Sample data were obtained from the two different video sequences containing low and high pedestrian traffic, which are represented as "o" and "+" in the graphs. Samples from each video were fitted linearly, as illustrated by solid and dotted lines for better comparison. The estimated flow size (obtained by (4)) versus ground truth is given in Fig. 10 (a). As shown in the figure, the slope of the fitted line for the video containing high pedestrian traffic is lower than that of the video for low pedestrian traffic. This indicates that the pedestrian traffic was underestimated for the high traffic segments. On the other hand, we can see that the lines nearly coincide in Fig. 10 (b) where the flow estimation results were adjusted by nonlinear regression as in (5).

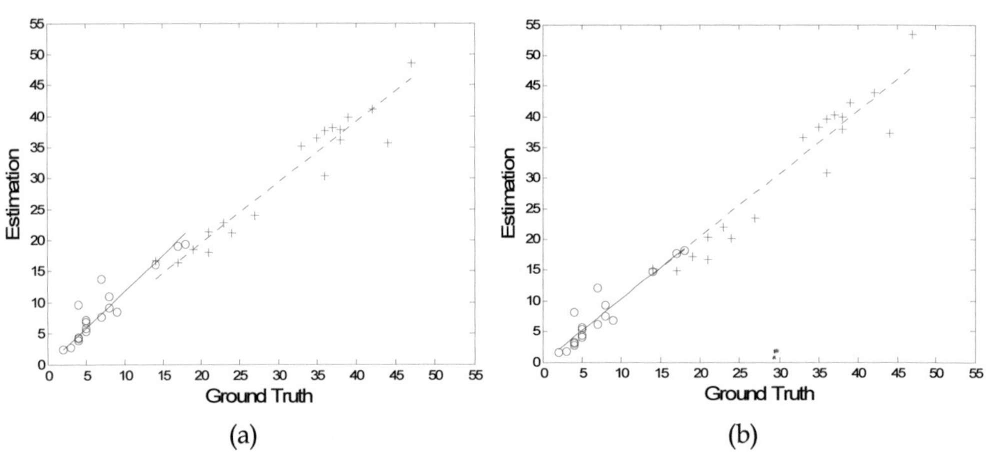

Fig. 10. Result of the nonlinear regression to compensate for feature loss. Graphs of ground truth vs. estimates (a) without and (b) with feature loss compensation as in (5).

5. Experiments

For the evaluation, an experimental dataset of 4 hours of video sequences was used. The video data were acquired at two different locations of the most crowded shopping mall in Korea. Fig. 11 shows an example of the test video of two different locations ((a) Video 1 and (b) Video 2). Because the characteristics of traffic flow in the shopping mall differ early and late in the day, we recorded video sequences at two different times (10:00 - 11:00 AM and 7:00 - 8:00 PM).

(a) (b)

Fig. 11. Test sequences for the evaluation: (a) Video 1 and (b) Video 2.

As the ground truth for evaluation, the number of people passing the virtual gate was counted manually each minute. The initial 20 minutes of each sequence were employed as a training set to calculate parameters (i.e., *a*, a and *b* in (4) and (5)) and the remaining 40 minutes of the video sequences were used for evaluation. The same coefficients were maintained across experiments for video sequences obtained from the same camera.

Table 1 summarizes the evaluation results. The relative accuracy of the proposed method was 95% to 100% and 97.20% on average. The processing speed of the proposed method reached 70 frames/second on an Intel Pentium IV 2.67 GHz PC. Figs. 12 and 13 provide evaluation results for Video 1 and Video 2 in a graphical representation. It should be noted that the accuracy remained stable in spite of the significant differences of traffic levels between video sequences of different times (200 at minimum and 1,200 at maximum in for 40 minutes).

		Upward			Downward		
		Ground Truth	Estimation	Accuracy	Ground Truth	Estimation	Accuracy
Video 1	10 AM	268	257	95.98	522	522	100
	7 PM	910	901	98.98	1025	1054	97.12
Video 2	10 AM	813	785	96.58	211	201	95.22
	7 PM	1194	1238	96.32	1215	1284	97.44

Table 1. Evaluation results

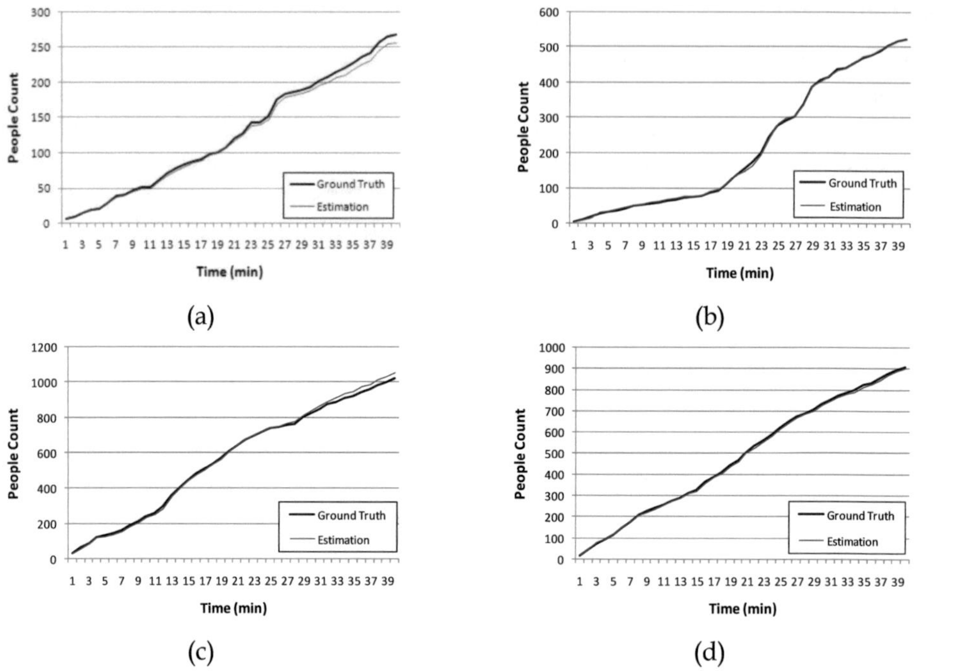

Fig. 12. Evaluation results for Video 1: (a) 10 AM and upward, (b) 10 AM and downward, (c) 7 PM and upward, (d) 7 PM and downward

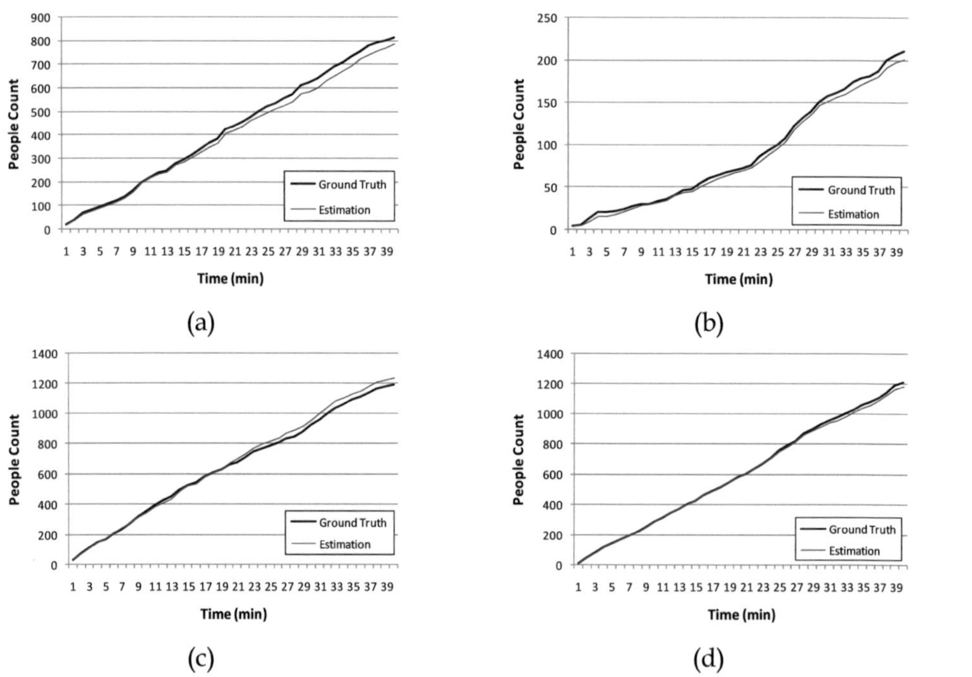

Fig. 13. Evaluation results for Video 2: (a) 10 AM and upward, (b) 10 AM and downward, (c) 7 PM and upward, (d) 7 PM and downward

6. Discussions

The method introduced in this chapter is a statistical approach that estimates the size of human traffic flow from the amount of image features. This basic concept, estimating traffic size from image features, is discovered from (3), which integrates foreground pixels of the same directions. This process in (3) is similar to that used for crowd size estimation, but the proposed method performs an online update. Instead of gathering image features from a whole frame, the proposed method extracts image features only from the virtual gate line and accumulates them over sequential frames. This incremental accumulation makes the traffic measurement process the same as image analysis in the spatiotemporal domain.

The use of statistical analysis in the spatiotemporal domain yields some advantages in the pedestrian traffic measurement method. First, the computational burden of the method is greatly reduced. Human traffic is measured by extracting image features and accumulating them, not by detection or tracking. Instead of analyzing an entire video frame, only pixels on the line of the virtual gate are reqruied to be processed, requiring much less computation. Hence the proposed method incurs much lower computational complexity than previous methods. Second, the performance of the method remains stable in high traffic areas in terms of both accuracy and computation time. Because previous methods are based on the identification of objects, as the number of people in a scene is increased, the accuracy of previous methods decreases while the computation time increases. In the proposed method, the measurement process is not related to individual objects; hence the same execution time can be maintained regardless of the number of people in the scene. Because of the statistical method relies on training, it shows good performance even for scenes with high traffic.

When comparing to previous methods, the human traffic measurement method introduced in this chapter provides similar or even a higher accuracy with much less computation. It has been reported that the top-view camera method proposed by Chen et al. (2006) showed an accuracy of 100% with simple movements of a few people. However, the accuracy was reduced to 85% for pedestrians with complex moving patterns. The frame rate of their method varied from 10 Hz to 30 Hz depending on the number of people in the scene. The detection-based by Sidla *et al.* (2006), which used a head-shoulder shape for human detection, counted passing people with 98% accuracy with a 15 Hz frame rate. However, they applied a linear regression to the result of human detection because the automatic count was overestimated. Without the aid of linear regression, the accuracy fell to 85%-90%. Since all of their test sequences contain only one hour of video, it is not guaranteed that the same linear regression could be applied to other video showing a different level of pedestrian traffic. Zhao *et al.* (2008) employed elliptical human models to detect pedestrians from foreground area and to track located humans. Because Zhao et al. evaluated the accuracy of tracking rather than pedestrian count, their accuracy was relatively low as 62%. Their method also could process about 2 frames per second on a 2.8GHz Pentium IV PC.

Besides the accuracies, it is also be noted that the statistical method is tested for video sequences of highly different traffic levels. Previous methods rarely tested for videos of different crowd levels. Hence the stability in varying level of pedestrian traffic, which is important for practical use, is not guranteed for the previous methods. On the contrary, the statistical method have been verified using two video sequences of mild and heavy traffic. Even though the test sequences showed huge differences in the level of crowdedness (six times at most), both the computation time and accuracy of the statistical method remained stable.

The main drawback of the statistical method is that it is based on training. The problems of training based methods are twofold. First they require human intervention during initial training process. This could be an obstacle applying the same method to multiple different locations. Another problem is that the performance could be dependent to the amount of training data and might not be guaranteed to a new input which is far from training data. Celik *et al.* (2006) proposed a pixel counting method for crowd size estimation that does not include training phase. It is expected that a similar concept could be applied to the statistical method to relieve its shortcomings.

7. Conclusions

In this chapter, a statistical method for measuring human traffic flow was introduced. Unlike previous methods that tried to count individuals by detection and tracking, the statistical method count pedestrians based on image features. Because it is a statistical method which does not include time consuming detection and tracking, it requires much smaller computation compared to previous methods. Through experiments on video data from real environments, it is shown that the proposed method gives similar or higher accuracy compared to previous methods even with the low computational cost. Because it does not rely on a specific camera viewpoint unlike blob-based methods, the method can be applied to existing CCTVs with oblique views. The low complexity, high accuracy and flexibility in viewpoints make the proposed method highly applicable to real systems.

8. References

Beleznai, C.; Fruhstuck, B. & Bishof, H. (2006). Human tracking by fast mean shift mode seeking. Journal of Multimedia 1(1): 1.

Bouguet, J. (1999). Pyramidal implementation of the Lucas Kanade feature tracker description of the algorithm. Technical Report, Intel Corporation, Microprocessor Research Labs.

Celik, H.; Hanjalic, A. & Hendriks, E. (2006). Towards a robust solution to people counting, *Proceedings of International Conference on Image Processing*, pp. 2401-2404

Chan, A.; Liang, Z. & Vasconcelos, N. (2008). Privacy preserving crowd monitoring: Counting people without people models or tracking. *Proceedings of IEEE Conference on Computer Vision and Pattern Recognition*, Anchorage. 30: 40-50.

Cho, S.; Chow, T. & Leung, C. (1999). A neural-based crowd estimation by hybrid global learning algorithm, *IEEE Transactions on Systems, Man, and Cybernetics--Part B: Cybernetics*, 29(4): 535.

Dalal, N.; Triggs, B., Rhone-Alps, I. & Montbonnot, F. (2005). Histograms of oriented gradients for human detection, *Proceedings of IEEE Conference on Computer Vision and Pattern Recognition*, vol. 1, pp. 8860893.

Kim, J.-W.; Choi, K.-S., Choi, B.-D., Lee, J.-Y. & Ko, S.-J. (2003). Real-Time System for Counting the Number of Passing People Using a Single Camera. *Pattern Recognition*, Springer Berlin / Heidelberg. 2781: 466-473.

Kong, D.; Gray, D & H. Tao. (2006). A viewpoint invariant approach for crowd counting, Proceedings of International Conference on Pattern Recognition, pp. 1187-1190.

Lin, Z.; Davis, L., Doermann, D. & DeMenthon D. (2007). Hierarchical part-template matching for human detection and segmentation,*Proceedings of International Conference on Computer Vision*, pp. 1-8.

Liu, X.; Tu, P., Rittscher, J., Perera, A., & Krahnstoever, N. (2005). "Detecting and counting people in surveillance applications." *Proceedings of Advanced Video and Signal Based Surveillance*, pp. 306-311.

Marana, A.; Costa, L. & Velastin, S. (1999). Estimating crowd density with Minkowski fractal dimension, *Proceedings of IEEE International Conference on Acoustics, Speech, and Signal Processing*, vol. 6, pp. 3521-3524.

Sexton, G.; Zhang, X., Redpath, G. & Greaves, G. (1995). Advances in automated pedestrian counting, Proceedings of European Convention and Security and Detection, pp. 106-110.

Sidla, O.; Lypetskyy, Y. Brandle, N. & Seer, S. (2006). Pedestrian detection and tracking for counting applications in crowded situations, *Proceedings of International Conference on Video and Signal Based Surveillance*, pp. 70-70.

Stauffer, C. & Grimson, W. (1999). Adaptive background mixture models for real-time tracking, Proceedings of IEEE Conference on Computer Vision and Pattern Recognition, pp. 246-252.

Thou-Ho, C.; Tsong-Yi, C. & Chen, Z.-X. (2006). An Intelligent People-Flow Counting Method for Passing Through a Gate, *Proceedings of International Conference on Robotics, Automation and Mechatronics*, pp. 1-6.

Velastin, S.; Yin, J., Davies, A., Vicencio-Silva, M., Allsop, R. & Penn. A. (1994). Automated measurement of crowd density and motion using image processing, Proceedings of International Conference on Road Traffic Monitoring and Control, pp. 127-132.

Velipasalar, S.; Ying-Li, T. & Hampapur, A.(2006). Automatic Counting of Interacting People by using a Single Uncalibrated Camera, Proceedings of International Conference on Multimedia and Extp, pp. 1265-1268.

Viola, P.; M. Jones & D. Snow. (2005). Detecting pedestrians using patterns of motion and appearance, *Proceedings of International Journal of Computer Vision* pp. 153-161.

Wu, B. & Nevatia, R. Detection of multiple, partially occluded humans in a single image by bayesian combination of edgelet part detectors,Proceedings of International Conference on Computer Vision, pp. 90-97.

Xiaohua, L.; Lansun, S. & Huanqin, L. (2006). Estimation of crowd density based on wavelet and support vector machine, *Transactions of the Institute of Measurement & Control*, Vol. 28, pp. 299.

Yuk, J.; Wong, K, Chung, F & Chow, K. (2006). Real-time multiple head shape detection and tracking system with decentralized trackers, *Proceedings of Intelligent Systems Design and Applications*, pp. 382-389.

Zhao, T. & R. Nevatia (2004). Tracking multiple humans in crowded environment, *Proceedings of IEEE Conference on Computer Vision and Pattern Recognition*, pp. II-406 – II-415.

Zhao, T. & Nevatia, R. and Wu, B. (2008). Segmentation and tracking of multiple humans in crowded environments, *IEEE Transactions on Pattern Analysis and Machine Intelligence*, Vol. 30, pp. 1198-1211.

15

The Management of a Multicamera Tracking System for Videosurveillance by Using an Agent Based Approach

Bethel Atohoun and Cina Motamed
Laboratoire LISIC, Université du Littoral Côte d'Opale, France

1. Introduction

The development of vision systems for monitoring or surveillance of wide area sites is an interesting field of investigation. In order to maximize the capabilities and performance of such system, it is often necessary to use a variety of sensor devices that complement each other. The standard configuration consists in completely covering a scene with a set of cameras with adjacent Fields Of View (FOV). Many people from the computer vision community have worked on the geometrical aspect of this configuration. By using several overlapping calibrated cameras, the system generates a global virtual view of the scene. The use of multiple views of the same scene in the tracking process provides the ability to resolve a part of occlusion situations. A second and less explored configuration is based on a network of non-overlapping cameras. This second configuration is economically attractive because it permits to efficiently decrease the number of sensors. However, the incomplete coverage makes the tracking problem more difficult. The main difficulty is the establishment of correspondence between the objects captured by multiple sensors (cross-camera data association).

In this work we present a high level sensor management strategy in a context of video-surveillance including both of the two configurations: overlapping and distant cameras. The global objective of the system is the development of the object tracking task.

The general problems of multi-sensor management are related to decisions about what sensors to use and for which purposes, as well as when, where and how to use them. This last side of high level management is closely linked with the concept of active perception strategy (Bajcsy, 1998). This strategy is particularly adapted where real-time performance is needed such as tracking, robot navigation, surveillance, visual inspection. The active perception has been widely developed for designing the perception for mobile robotic. In fact real-time perception systems have theirs limitation in the computation of massive amount of input data with processing procedures in a reduced and fixed amount of time. The active strategy has the capacity to filter data and to focus the attention of the perception to relevant information and also can choose the best alternative by using the contextual information. Such approaches are closely linked with the design of cognitive system which permits to combine knowledge and reasoning in order to develop smart and robust perception system.

An important objective of an intelligent multi-sensor system is to exploit the complementarity and the redundancy of sensors. For homogenous sensors the complementarity permits to enlarge the field of perception and the redundancy permit to improve the accuracy of measurements. For a given configuration some area of the scene can be covered by a unique sensor, or by several sensors or none of them. In the case of heterogeneous sensor it permits to increase the number of the perception modalities, in order to cope, for example, with several perception conditions (night/day).
In order to perform the high level management, it is essential to characterize each sensor with respect to its utility for the task. Generally the main characterization of the sensor is given by the measurement uncertainty. Many sensors have a variable uncertainty with respect to their functioning condition. And generally it is difficult to model the uncertainty globally. Another sensor characterization feature concerns its field of coverage.
Tracking is an important task of computer vision with many applications in surveillance, scene monitoring, navigation, sport scene analysis and video database management. One of the most critical parts of a multi-object-tracking algorithm is the data association step. It has to deal with new objects, short or long term disappearing objects and occlusions. Related works linked with the tracking of humans and vehicles with multiple visual sensors are numerous (Snidaro et al., 2004) (Nakazawa et al., 1998) (Utsumi et al., 1998) (Foresti et al, 1995).
Statistical approaches as the kalman filtering approach with its extensions are widely used in tracking and control (Bar-Shalom & Forthmann, 1988). They are particularly adapted for tracking targets in clutter. Qualitative approaches are an alternative for motion correspondence (Veenman et al, 2001)(Sethi & Jain, 1990)(Rangarajan & Shah, 1991). These approaches are less normative than conventional statistical methods used in tracking. The main advantage is their flexibility, because they permit an easy integration of several forms of a priori information and contextual information for constraining complex problem. Our approach belongs globally to the last category.
The section 2 presents the local tracking module. The section 3 details the global strategy of our distributed tracking system. The section 4 represents the management strategy in the presence of overlapping camera FOVs. The section 5 is focused on the problem of tracking based on distant camera without common FOV. Finally, the section 6 shows some experimental results over a real world application.

2. Local tracking module

The goal of this unit is to detect and track object locally in the field of view of each Local Vision System (LVS). The first step concerns the motion detection step. For a fixed sensor, the standard motion detection approach consists in modelling the stationary background which has to be updated in order to tolerate low illumination variation. We have used the Stauffer and Grimson algorithm based on the Mixture Gaussians in order to model the background with multiple possible states (Stauffer & Grimson, 2000). The figure 1 shows an illustration of the moving objects detection.
The local tracking of objects under the FOV of a camera uses a region-based approach. It uses cinematic and visual constraints for establishing correspondence. In our problem of object tracking for a visual-surveillance application, observations representing the detected regions are complex, and are not corrupted by random noise only. They are also affected by detection errors, merging and splitting artefacts, which are difficult to model globally or statistically. In addition, the dynamic model of human activity may present significant

Fig. 1. Moving object segmentation, test images from the dataset PETS'2006, camera C3

variability according to the working context. For all these reasons, we have chosen a qualitative approach, which mainly focuses on the data association quality rather than the precision of the object motion estimation. Assumptions underlying our approach concern several points: objects move smoothly from a frame to another one, objects do not change quickly their appearance colour and objects can interact with other objects or groups of objects. The tracking algorithm uses the Nearest Neighbour (NN) strategy. However, in the presence of merging or splitting situations, two specific procedures are launched in order to solve the association ambiguity.

When a merging situation is detected, a notion of a temporary group of objects is defined in order to track the global region containing visually merged objects. In addition to the temporary group tracking, the algorithm attempts to maintain the track of each individual object inside the global group region. The estimation of position of the individual objects during the merging situation is based on their appearance model by using the Mean Shift algorithm (Comaniciu, 2000) (Cheng, 1995). When the system detects a splitting situation associated with a known group, a specific procedure focuses its attention toward the identity of objects. A visual comparison between objects before merging and after splitting permits to affect the best object identity for each region by using the colour histogram. After splitting, the group updates its individual object. When the group is reduced to a known sole object, the group entity is destroyed [Motamed, 2006].

A planar homography transformation H^s is performed in order to bring each local track estimation from sensor 's' into the same reference plan R_0. The position in image concerns the position of object on the ground plane obtained by the lower segment of the object bounding box. At each image sequence, the output of the local tracker is composed by the position of the tracked object and two complementary information.

3. Global organisation of the distributed multi-camera tracking system

Under a surveillance objective, the system has to react in real time and to manage efficiently its distributed sensors' resources. In particular, in a multi-camera organisation, raw image sequences cannot be easily sent over the network and in addition to this, the central unit has generally not enough capacity to compute alone all information in parallel. The distributed organisation is adapted to reduced network bandwidth constraint. In fact, all low level information can be processed locally and only high-level information is transmitted over the network.

It is important to explicitly manage the uncertainty of the object's identity. In other words, the system has to notify situations where the risk of object confusion becomes important. This capacity of self-evaluation is essential for a safety device and is known as the "positive security".

The proposed system integrates a hybrid strategy including a distributed and central organisation. It is composed of a network of distributed local vision systems (LVS). The system contains a supervisor level, whose role is to collect LVS decisions and performs the global task of high level tracking for surveillance.

In order to manage efficiently the information flow coming from LVSs at the supervisor level, we propose a specific logical organisation at the supervisor level. It is based on a multi-agent society framework, which is considered as an interesting approach when the distributed problem can be represented and solved with a group of cooperative intelligent entities (Matsuyama, 2001). The notion of agent is associated with each tracked object and is defined for each LVS. This organisation permits to join together agents in a specific "society" in order to solve specific tracking task.

As we have mentioned in the introduction the system has to deal with two general categories of multi-camera configuration (Fig. 2). The first is based on overlapping FOV of cameras and the second concerns distant cameras with separate FOVs. In order to efficiently operate with these different configurations, three independent management strategies are jointly implemented:

- The basic strategy is in the case of an object under the FOV of only one sensor. In this situation, the supervisor takes into account directly the result of the local tracker.
- For overlapping configuration, a logical society based on agents from these sensors is created. The society allows the fusion of object position estimations obtained by multiple views.
- For a configuration containing sensors with separate FOVs, another specific logical society is created in order to perform the cross camera object association. The society contains agents that are linked with each neighbouring sensors likely to perceive the object.

The instantaneous result of the local tracking system, encapsulated in the concept of an logical agent, is sent to the supervisor level. The agent contains the current position, indicators and status of the tracked object. Firstly, the identity indicator $Id^t(O_i)$ of each object O_i represents a degree of belief with respect to the identity of the object during the local tracking. The status of the object is associated with the notion of group of objects defined in the local tracking level. If the object belongs to a group, a third indicator delivers the degree of visibility of the object from the sensors. The last important information concerns the fact of entering and exiting the FOV of the local sensor. At each entry or exit the local sensor send to the supervisor a set of information resuming the appearance of object (color histograms, dimension). This last information linked with the entry and exit will be explicitly exploited by the cross camera tracking strategy.

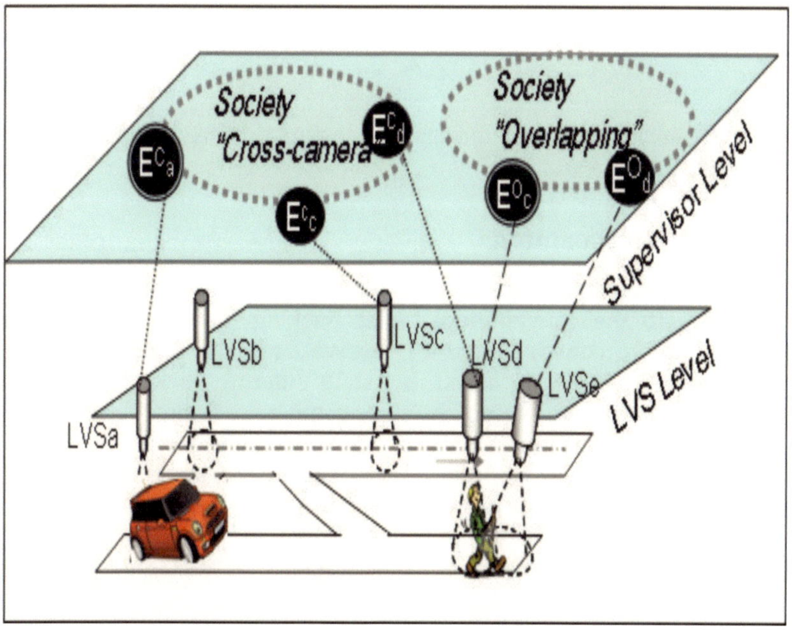

Fig. 2. Organisation of societies for distant cameras configuration (Cross camera) and for overlapping sensor FOVs configuration

4. Tracking with overlapping camera FOVs

In the presence of overlapping FOV, the system has to deal with the limitation of each sensor with respect to the occlusion problem. In the proposed approach, when a tracked object is detected inside an overlapping FOV area a society of agents is automatically created at the supervisor level society for each object. The society contains agents associated with each local tracker. The society operates as a centralized filter by combining agents results (local tracking).

The notion of group and the visibility indicator obtained from the local tracker allows the estimation of the dynamic suitability of a sensor in an overlapping situation with respect to the tracked object. The sensor suitability permits to guide the tracking process by a context driven strategy. The main objective is to favor the best views with respect to dynamic occlusion of each tracked object. This indicator clearly favor un-occluded tracked object with respect to the camera views.

For each object with respect to each sensor 's', the suitability indicator (λ_s) is set to its maximum=1 if the tracked object is known as sole object from the local sensor. When the object goes out of the field of the sensor the indicator takes the zeros value. In presence of occlusion, highlighted by the notion of group managed by the local sensor 's', the indicator takes the degree of visibility estimated during the merging procedure of the local tracker. The visibility degree is obtained directly from the Meanshift estimation in the case of the object occlusions.

For each society, the supervisor level performs a combination of positions estimation from local sensor weighted by their suitability indicators in order to generate a fused position P_{global}.

$$P_{global} = \frac{1}{\sum_{s} \lambda_s} . \sum_{s} H^S(P_s^*).\lambda_s \quad (1)$$

The homography transformation H^S brings each estimation from each sensor 's' into the same reference plan R_0.

5. Tracking with distant cameras

The tracking with distant camera, also known as the cross-camera tracking, can be considered as close to the conventional target tracking (radar or vision), because the trajectories of objects are constructed from observations. The main difference is that in conventional tracking algorithms based on state filtering, observations are obtained synchronously in a continuous space. In cross-camera tracking, objects move between discrete locations and can disappear for a long time (blind zones).

In addition to detection errors, or occlusions at the sensor level, the cross-camera data association over wide scene induces three levels of difficulties:

- There are numerous cases where objects look similar.
- Objects' behaviours between two sensors are unpredictable or coarsely defined.
- Variation of outdoor illumination, sensor response and object orientation, induces changes in the visual appearance of objects.

In order to make the re-identification feasible, in addition to the objects' visual signature, the system has to constrain the object motion in blind zones. It permits to focus the attention on interesting candidates in front of a set of sensors.

(Huang & Russell, 1997) and (Kettnaker & Zabih, 1999) have addressed the problem of data association in cross-camera tracking in the context of the Artificial Intelligence and Computer Vision communities, respectively. Huang's algorithm has been tested in freeway environments, and Kettnaker's algorithm has been designed for human re-identification inside an office. Both algorithms use the Bayesian formalism and attempt to track all possible detected objects over a network of cameras. The data association stage is transformed to a weighted assignment problem solving.

Previous algorithms do not contain an explicit temporal reasoning scheme. However Kettnaker proposes an online extension of their approach by selecting a set of active candidates. The main applications of previous re-identification systems are the link travel time between locations and origin-destination counting, except the kettnaker's system, which is designed for human activity monitoring. Our work is also inspired by the Bayesian approach. It permits to perform the data-association in a distributed manner by integrating prior information about visual and behavioural model of objects.

Once a new object is detected by an LVS, a first level society (Cross camera society) is generated at the supervisor level in order to wait for the future re-appearance of the object over the network. The society contains agents that are linked with each neighbouring LVSs likely to perceive the awaited object. The constitution of the society is performed offline by a human analyst by using contextual knowledge of the scene (topology of the scene and traffic behaviour) and depends on the configuration of the perception system. For example, if an object is detected by the LVS_a, the society, which is in charge of its tracking, will be by default, composed by the agents linked to LVS_a, LVS_c and LVS_d (Fig. 3).

The manager of the society is the agent associated with the LVS that has detected the object. The waiting procedure is activated during a time delay controlled by the temporal constraints. Under this organisation, the association is performed under a strategy of prediction-verification. This network organisation can be seen as an information routing layer from LVS information level to supervisor level. In other terms, each agent focuses on the messages from its associated LVS and waits for its awaited object. The manager sends, to each agent of its society, a message containing visual and temporal constraints associated with the appearance of the awaited object. These messages permit the creation of temporary tracks between the manager and each agent. When an agent E_i re-identifies the awaited object, it sends a message to the manager of the society and confirms the current track of the object. At each re-identification, the manager validates the decision of the association. The existing society is then destroyed, and recursively, the supervisor creates a new one in order to follow the object over the network.

Figure 3 illustrates these main steps during the crossing of a vehicle in front of a distributed network of LVS. At instant T1 the track of the object is initialized and a first society is launched. At instant T2, one of the agents of the current society re-identifies the awaited object and returns this decision to its manager for validation. The first society is then destroyed. The figure at instant T3 shows the second society which has been created to maintain the track of the object.

Temporal constraints are represented in our system by a fuzzy temporal interval called (DOP: Domain Occurrence Possibility) represented by a possibility distribution. The $DOP(O_i,E_m,E_n)$ is the prediction generated by the agent E_m, explaining the temporal appearance possibility of an awaited object O_i in the field of a specific agent E_n. Each society manager has to generate these coarse temporal constraints for each agent of its society. The DOP between two nodes is estimated by the kinematic equation:

$$d = v_0.t + \frac{A.t^2}{2}$$

$$=> \; t = \frac{-v_0 + \sqrt{{v_0}^2 + 2.A.d}}{A} \qquad (2)$$

$$or \;\; t = \frac{d}{v_0}, \qquad (if\, A=0)$$

with

V_0 : the measured local speed of the object

A : the model of object acceleration between the two nodes

d : the distance d between the two nodes

The computation of the prediction 't' has to integrate the acceleration variability and also the measurement errors. For this, all variables are approximated by a normal distribution with respect to their mean and variance values. The distribution of the variable $t(m_t,\sigma_t)$ is computed by using specific arithmetic operators for the normal distributions (Courtney & Thacker, 2001). This procedure allows the propagation of the theoretical errors over the expression of t. The DOP is then built by using the normal distribution of the variable t. A standard transformation from a normal distribution to a trapezoidal possibilistic distribution is applied. The trapezoidal model is centred at the instant m_t with a core and a base of 2. σ_t and 3. σ_t respectively. A human analyst coarsely initialises generic acceleration models A_i by using the contextual knowledge for each class of object Ci (human, car etc…). They represent essentially physical limitations of the class behaviour between two nodes.

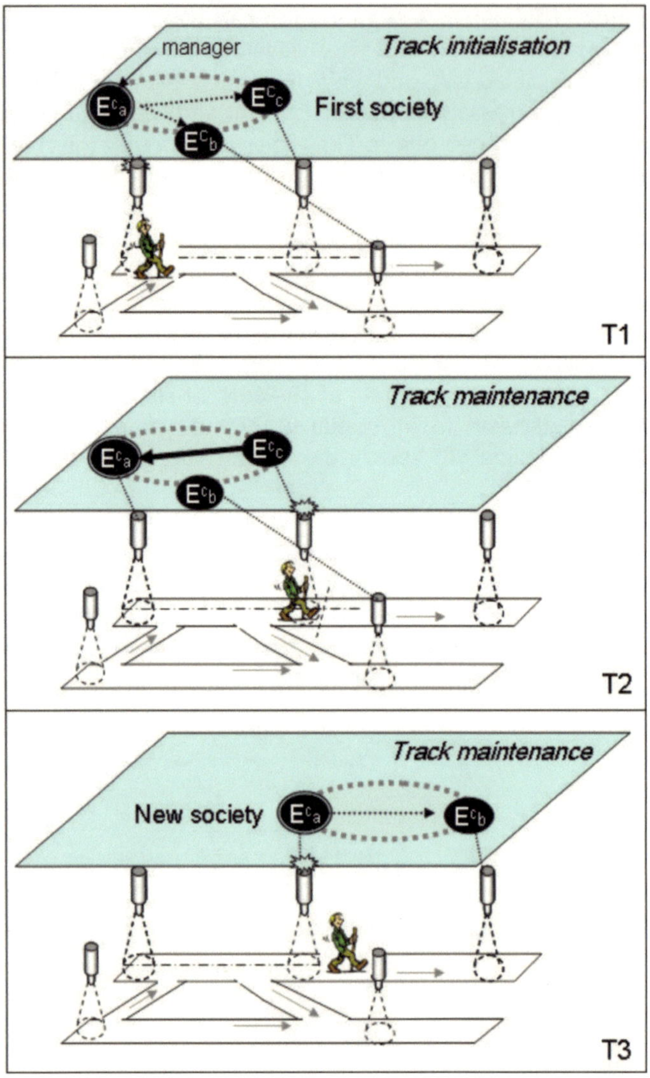

Fig. 3. Illustration of the creation of the first level "cross camera" society

In a complex multi-sensor network, there is no effective one to one correspondence between awaited objects and observed objects. A standard instantaneous approach has some limitations with asynchronous observations. In fact, in some ambiguous situations, the system may have not received all interesting information. An efficient approach is the "temporal fusion" strategy. This last strategy tries to improve dynamically the quality of decisions with more observations. In fact, for a distributed multi-sensor architecture with no common field of view, the system has to exploit the complementarities of observations over time and over the fields of sensors. The global compatibility between two objects is obtained by the product of their visual compatibility with their temporal compatibility. The temporal compatibility value represents the value of the DOP at the instant of the object detection. The proposed distributed tracking approach uses as in conventional tracking systems three main steps linked to track initialisation, maintenance, and termination.

The strategy of creation of new objects is chosen close to the Open-world assumption existing in the Demspter Shafer Theory of Evidence. In other terms, when the observation is not compatible with any of the awaited objects, the occurrence of the new object is favoured. The track termination of an object is decided when an awaited object is not detected by its current society during its lifespan controlled by its DOPs.

When several objects are tracked simultaneously, multiple societies have to work together. For each observation, within a LVS, measures of compatibility with all awaited objects represent a local distribution of preference. The validation of an association H_i by an agent is performed by computing the possibility $P(H_i)$ and the necessity $N(H_i)$ of the association. The possibility distribution is then built by normalizing the distribution of preference inside the segment [0,1]. The necessity of a hypothesis translates the notion of uniqueness of the hypothesis with respect to other alternatives. If the necessity is high, it means that no ambiguity is present. In this situation, the agent can validate the association solely. When the necessity of the association is low, a notion of ambiguity is declared.

$$N(H_i) = 1 - P(\bar{H}_i)$$

With

$$\bar{H}_i = \Phi - \{H_i\} \qquad (3)$$

$$P(\bar{H}_i) = \max_{H_j \in \bar{H}_i} P(H_j)$$

We present in figure 4, the two situations of ambiguity appearing during the association of two visually compatible objects. Dop1 and Dop2 represent predictions of object O1 and object O2, respectively, on the downstream sensor. Obs1 and Obs2 are the observations of O1 and O2 detected by the downstream sensor. In the first scenario (Type 1), the first observation, with respect to the predictions cannot be associated to a unique object. The second observation can remove the ambiguity by using a temporal fusion strategy. In the second scenario (Type 2), the two observations are detected within the intersection of the two predictions. The system decides that it cannot make the association. However, the system reacts quickly, once it has detected the two observations, without waiting for the end of awaited objects lifespan.

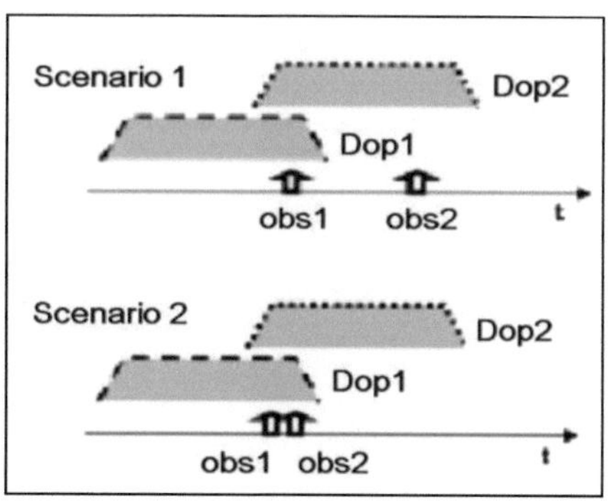

Fig. 4. Scenarios of ambiguity Type 1 and Type 2 with two similar objects

When a first level agent detects an ambiguity containing two or more objects, a second level society is generated by integrating all concerned first level societies containing ambiguous objects. The objective of the second level society is to develop a Temporal Fusion procedure. In

order to compare efficiently all hypotheses, the temporal fusion uses a MHT tree (Multiple Hypotheses Testing) (Reid, 1979). When a second level society is activated, the attached first level societies stop their own decisions and wait for the decisions of the temporal fusion.
The MHT tree describes all possible hypotheses resulting from observations obtained by the set of LVS concerned by the second level society. A MHT hypothesis integrates a set of associations with their global degree of compatibility. For each MHT hypothesis, a possibility and a necessity measurement is estimated. The possibility measurement of a MHT hypothesis is built by the product of the compatibility of its associations. At each observation, the tree is updated. A pruning procedure removes a MHT hypothesis when its possibility is low (< 0.1). The data association decision is then deferred as long as the confidence level of one of MHT hypothesis is not significant enough compared to the other ones. This decision is controlled by the necessity of the hypotheses. The MHT tree is stopped when the relative necessity measurement of a MHT hypothesis is sufficient (> 0.3).
Figure 5 illustrates a basic example where the temporal fusion strategy efficiency resolves an ambiguity associated to a scenario of type 1 in a configuration with four LVS. The ambiguity concerns two visually similar vehicles (Object_1, Object_2) appearing at instants T1 et T2.

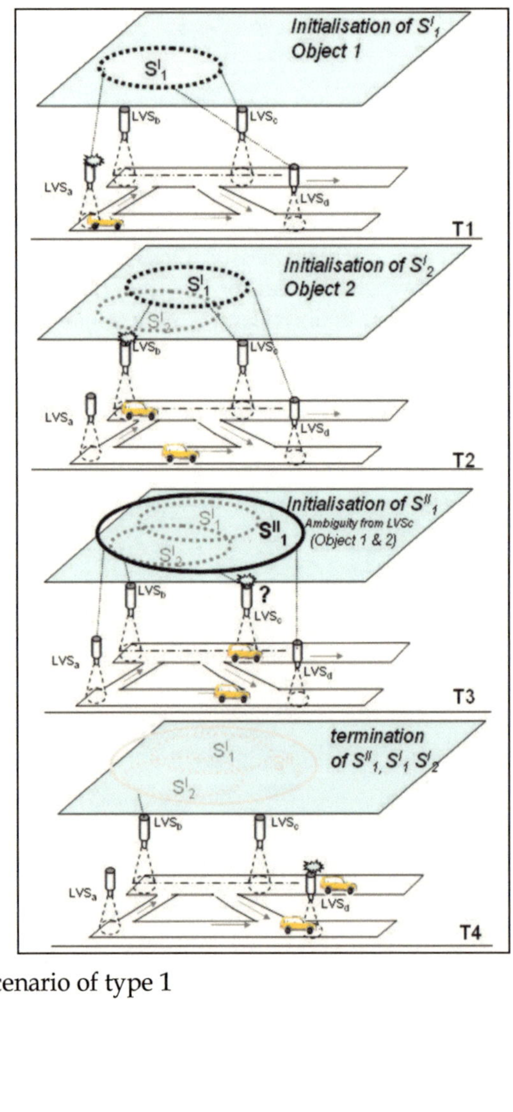

Fig. 5. Resolution of scenario of type 1

The detection of the Object_1 at the instant T1 from LVS_a, induces the creation of a first level society S^I_1 to perform the tracking of the object. At instant T2, another society S^I_2 is created for the Object_2. The observation of the an object Obs(T3) (at instant T3) on the LVS_c generates an ambiguity for experts of S^I_1 and S^I_2, linked with LVS_c. In fact, two awaited objects are visually similar and temporally compatible with the observation. So a second level society S^{II}_1 is created at instant T3, in order to perform a temporal fusion strategy. The figure 6 shows the predictions (DOPs) used by experts linked to LVS_c and LVS_d.

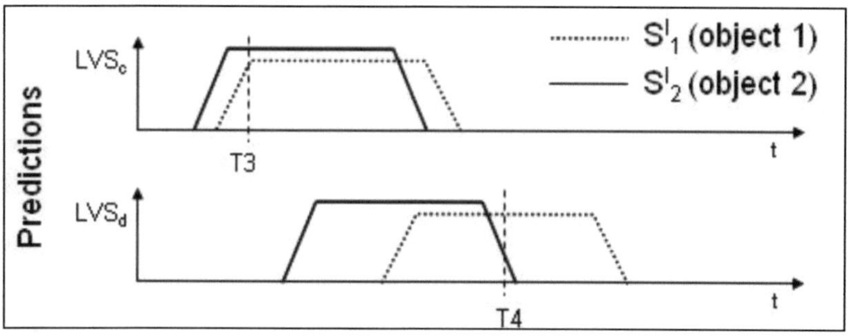

Fig. 6. Temporal prediction for the example

In our example, a second observation Obs(T4) from LVS_d permits the elimination of the ambiguity (table 1). The first observation generates two hypotheses 1.1 and 1.2 indicating a low necessity. Hypothesis 1.1 represents the association of the Obs(T3) to objet_1. Hypothesis 1.2 represents the association of the obs(T3) to object_2. After the second observation Obs(T4), Hypothesis 2.1 with a necessity value of (0.73) is accepted and finally the Obs(T3) is associated to Object_1 and the Obs(T4) to Object_2.

MHT Hyp. N°	Obs(T3) From LVSc (compatibility degree)	Obs(T4) From LVSd (compatibility degree)	Possibility of the MHT hyp.	Necessity of the MHT hyp.
1.1	(1.0) /Object_1		**1.00**	**0.10**
1.2	(0.9) /Object_2		**0.90**	**0.00**
2.1	(1.0) /Object _1	(1.0) /Object_2	**1.00**	**0.73**
2.2	(0.9) /Object_2	(0.3) /Object_1	**0.27**	**0.00**

Table 1. a MHT tree with the degree of possibility and necessity of the hypotheses

Unfortunately, there are three distinct cases where the Temporal Fusion decides that it cannot resolve the ambiguity:

- The first case is when all observations are detected and the MHT tree is performed without success. It means that the system has detected a scenario of ambiguity of type 2 (fig.4). This situation is detected by the MHT tree, when the necessity of each hypothesis remains low. The temporal fusion is then stopped after the last awaited observation.
- The second case is when a part of awaited objects is not detected at the end of predicted DOPs. The temporal fusion is stopped at the end of their DOPs. These problems may occur when objects do not verify their prediction, and also when objects are not correctly detected by the LVSs.

- The third case is when the number of awaited objects, interacting within the MHT tree, becomes too important (object count > 5). The temporal fusion prematurely stops in order to avoid the explosion of the MHT tree.

Decisions of success or non-decision obtained by the temporal fusion are sent to managers of each primary society. Then, in their turn, they forward their final decisions to the supervisor. In a surveillance context, as we have mentioned in the section 3, this notion of a controlled non-decision is more acceptable than standard errors.

6. Experiments

In this section we present a first experiment based on the proposed global management approach. Real sequences are obtained by recording synchronised image sequences from four cameras observing a campus. The figure 7 illustrates the multi-camera configuration of the scene.

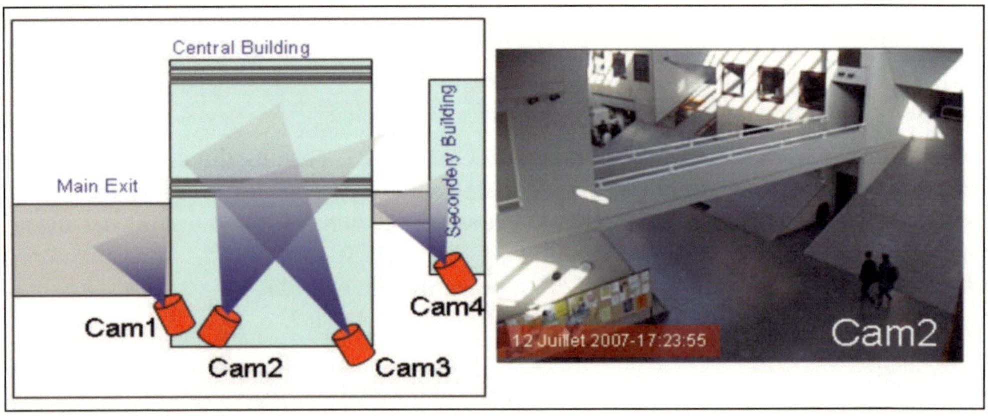

Fig. 7. The multi-camera configuration of the observed campus and an image from the second camera.

The table 2 summarizes the results of the data association decisions with a comparison with straightforward (basic) techniques. In fact, for cross camera tracking the basic NN algorithm decides the association of the observation with the best instantaneous candidate, and in the case of overlapping configuration, the track maintenance is performed only by the local tracker who has primary detected the object. The evaluation of performance of our system with respect to the above basic techniques is obtained by using ground truth data delivered by a human analyst.

The third line represents the notion of ambiguity rate (non decision rate) of our system which is essentially due to the resemblance of a part of tracked objects from the distant cameras societies. In the context of security such non-decision score is more acceptable than standard errors. In this experiment the global tracking results are satisfactory and the sum of the errors and non decision rate of the proposed approach is lower than the global tracking errors of the basic algorithm.

When the count of simultaneous compatible objects (temporally and visually) is low, the cross camera association based on the TF algorithm reacts efficiently with an acceptable non-decision rate. Otherwise the performance of the TF algorithm decreases significantly. In fact, an excessive augmentation of object, firstly favours scenarios of ambiguity of type 2 (fig. 4) which are detected but are not solved by the temporal fusion and secondly, it induces an excessive number of awaited objects interacting in the MHT trees. In this last situation, the temporal fusion prematurely stops in order to avoid the explosion of the MHT trees size.

Results	Proposed management strategy	Basic approach : NN algorithm (in distant configuration) & without track fusion (in overlapping situation)
Global count of objects (ground truth)	122	122
Correct global track (in term of identity)	90	69
non decision (distant camera)	23	X
Global Track errors	9	53

Table 2. Illustration of performance and comparison with basic algorithms

7. Conclusion

We have proposed an agent-based architecture in context of a distributed vision based tracking system. The objective of the system is the tracking of objects over a wide area scene by using a high level multi-sensor management strategy.

The main originality of this work with previous works concerns the capacity of management of multi-camera systems for surveillance including both overlapping cameras FOV and distant cameras configuration. The proposed system has been successfully tested in a real indoor environment.

Our strategy of sensor management naturally copes explicitly with known modelled tracking ambiguities. At the local level the tracking takes into account the regions merging, splitting, and target missing. In the presence of muti-view configuration of the scene, it can solve efficiently a good part of occlusions situation. And finally, in the presence of distant cameras, the strategy of temporal fusion allows to control temporally the tracking system decisions over the time.

Future works concern the improvement of the survivability of such distributed tracking system with respect to the loss of LVSs by performing an automatic reconfiguration of the sensor network. It will permit to generate active societies based only on operational LVSs. This reconfiguration may be controlled as in conventional computer network by using a kind of "keep-alive" messages between LVS and the supervisor.

8. References

Bajcsy, R. (1998). Active Perception, *Proceedings of the IEEE*, 76 (8) (1998) 996-1005.

Bar-Shalom, Y. & Forthmann, T.E. (1988). *Tracking and data association*. Academic Press.

Cheng, Y. (1995). Mean Shift, Mode Seeking, and Clustering. *IEEE Trans. Pattern Analysis and Machine Intelligence*, Vol 17(8), 1995, pp.790-799.

Comaniciu, D.; Ramesh, V. & Meer P. (2000). Real-TimeTracking of Non-Rigid Objects using Mean Shift. *IEEE Computer Vision and Pattern Recognition*, Vol II, 2000, pp.142-149.

Courtney, P.; Thacker, N.A. (2001). Performance characterization in computer vision: The role of statistics in testing and design. *In Imaging and Vision Systems : Theory, Assessment and Applications, Jacques Blanc-Talon and Dan Popescu (Eds), 2001,* NOVA Science Book.

Foresti G.L.; Murino, V.; Regazzoni, C. & Vernazza, G. (1995). A multilevel fusion approach to object identification in outdoor road scenes. *International Journal of Pattern Recognition and Artificial Intelligence,* 1995, 9(1):23–65.

Huang, T. & Russell, S. (1997). Object identification in a Bayesian context. *In International Joint Conference on Artificial Intelligence* (1997), 1276-1282.

Kettnaker, V. & Zabih, R. (1999). Bayesian multi-camera surveillance. *In IEEE Conference on Computer Vision and Pattern Recognition (*1999) 253-259.

Matsuyama, T. (2001) Cooperative distributed vision: dynamic integration of visual perception, camera action, and network communication. *4th international Workshop on Cooperative Distributed Vision* (2001), Kyoto Japan.

Motamed, C. (2006). Motion detection and tracking using belief indicators for an automatic visual-surveillance system. *Image and Vision Computing,* Volume 24, Issue 11, 1, Pages 1192-1201, 2006.

Nakazawa, A.; Kato, H. & Inokuchi, S. (1998). Human tracking using distributed vision systems. *In Proceedings of the 14th ICPR,* pages 593–596.

Rangarajan, K. & Shah, M. (1991). Establishing Motion Correspondence. CVGIP: Image Understanding, 54 (1), (1991) pp. 56-73.

Reid, B. (1979). An algorithm for tracking multiple targets. *IEEE Transactions on Automatic Control,* AC-24(6) (1979) 843-854.

Sethi, I.K. & Jain, R. (1990). Finding trajectories of feature points in a monocular image sequence. *IEEE Transaction on Pattern Analysis and Machine Intelligence,* 9 (1), 56-73.

Snidaro, L.; Luca Foresti, G.; Niu, R. & Varshney, P. K. (2004). Sensor fusion for video surveillance, International Conference on Information Fusion (2004),pp. 739-746, Sweden.

Stauffer, C. & Grimson, W. (2000). Learning patterns of activity using real-time tracking. *IEEE Trans. Pattern Analysis and Machine Intelligence,* 22(8) (2000) 747–757.

Utsumi, A.; Mori, H.; Ohya, J. & Yachida, M. (1998). Multiple view-based tracking of multiple humans. *In Proceedings of the 14th ICPR,* pages 597–601.

Veenman, C.J.; Reinders, M.J.T.; & Backer, E. (2001). Resolving Motion Correspondence for Densely Moving Points. *IEEE Transactions on PAMI* vol23, pp. 54-72.

Part 4

Content Analysis and Event Detection for Video Surveillance

16

A Survey on Behaviour Analysis in Video Surveillance Applications

Teddy Ko
Raytheon Company,
USA

1. Introduction

There is an increasing desire and need in video surveillance applications for a proposed solution to be able to analyze human behaviors and identify subjects for standoff threat analysis and determination. The main purpose of this survey is to look at current developments and capabilities of visual surveillance systems and assess the feasibility and challenges of using a visual surveillance system to automatically detect abnormal behavior, detect hostile intent, and identify human subject.

Visual (or video) surveillance devices have long been in use to gather information and to monitor people, events and activities. Visual surveillance technologies, CCD cameras, thermal cameras and night vision devices, are the three most widely used devices in the visual surveillance market. Visual surveillance in dynamic scenes, especially for humans, is currently one of the most active research topics in computer vision and artificial intelligence. It has a wide spectrum of promising public safety and security applications, including access control, crowd flux statistics and congestion analysis, human behavior detection and analysis, etc.

Visual surveillance in dynamic scene with multiple cameras, attempts to detect, recognize and track certain objects from image sequences, and more importantly to understand and describe object behaviors. The main goal of visual surveillance is to develop intelligent visual surveillance to replace the traditional passive video surveillance that is proving ineffective as the number of cameras exceed the capability of human operators to monitor them. The goal of visual surveillance is not only to put cameras in the place of human eyes, but also to accomplish the entire surveillance task as automatically as possible. The capability of being able to analyze human movements and their activities from image sequences is crucial for visual surveillance.

In general, the processing framework of an automated visual surveillance system includes the following stages: Motion/object detection, object classification, object tracking, behavior and activity analysis and understanding, person identification, and camera handoff and data fusion.

Almost every visual surveillance system starts with motion and object detection. Motion detection aims at segmenting regions corresponding to moving objects from the rest of an image. Subsequent processes such as object tracking and behavior analysis and recognition are greatly dependent on it. The process of motion/object detection usually involves background/environment modeling and motion segmentation, which intersect each other during the processing. Motion segmentation in image sequences aims at detecting regions corresponding to moving objects such as humans or vehicles. Detecting moving regions provides a focus of attention for later processes such as tracking and behavior analysis as only these regions need be considered and further investigated.

After motion and object detection, surveillance systems generally track moving objects from one frame to another in an image sequence. The tracking algorithms usually have considerable intersection with motion detection during processing. Tracking over time typically involves matching objects in consecutive frames using features such as points, lines or blobs.

Behavior understanding involves analysis and recognition of motion patterns, and the production of high-level description of actions and interactions between or among objects. In some circumstances, it is necessary to analyze the behaviors of people and determine whether their behaviors are normal or abnormal.

The problem of who enters the area and/or engages in an abnormal or suspicious act under surveillance is of increasing importance for visual surveillance. Human face and gait are now regarded as the main biometric features that can be used for personal identification in visual surveillance systems.

Motion detection, tracking, behavior understanding, and personal identification at a distance can be realized by single camera-based visual surveillance systems. Multiple camera-based visual surveillance systems can be extremely helpful because the surveillance area is expanded and multiple view information can overcome occlusion. Tracking with a single camera easily generates ambiguity due to occlusion or depth. This ambiguity may be eliminated from another view. However, visual surveillance using multiple cameras also brings problems such as camera installation (how to cover the entire scene with the minimum number of cameras), camera calibration, object matching, automated camera switching, and data fusion.

The video process of surveillance systems has inherited same difficult challenges while approaching a computer vision application, i.e., illumination variation, viewpoint variation, scale (view distance) variation, and orientation variation. Existing surveillance solutions to object detection, tracking, and identification from video problems tend to be highly domain specific. An indication of the difficulty of creating a single general purpose surveillance system comes from the video surveillance and monitoring (VSAM) project at CMU (Collins et al., 2000) and other institutions (Borg et al., 2005; PETS, 2007). VSAM at CMU is one of the most ambitious surveillance projects yet undertaken, and has advanced the state of the art in many areas of surveillance research. This project was intended as a general purpose system for automated surveillance of people and vehicles in cluttered environments, using a range of sensors including color CCD cameras, thermal cameras, and night vision cameras. However, due to the difficulty of developing general surveillance algorithms, a visual surveillance system usually has had to be designed as a collection of separate algorithms, which are selected on a case by case basis.

The flow and organization of this review paper has followed four very thorough, excellent surveys conducted by (Ko, 2008; Wang et al., 2003; Hu et al., 2004; Kumar et al., 2008) when discussing the general framework of automated visual surveillance systems as shown in Fig. 1, enriching with the general architecture of a video understanding system (Bremond et al., 2006) in behavior analysis and with expandable network system architecture as illustrated in (Cohen et al., 2008). The main intent of this paper is to give engineers, scientists, and/or managers alike, a high-level, general understanding of both the theoretical and practical perspectives involved with a visual surveillance system and its potential challenges while considering implementing or integrating a visual surveillance system.

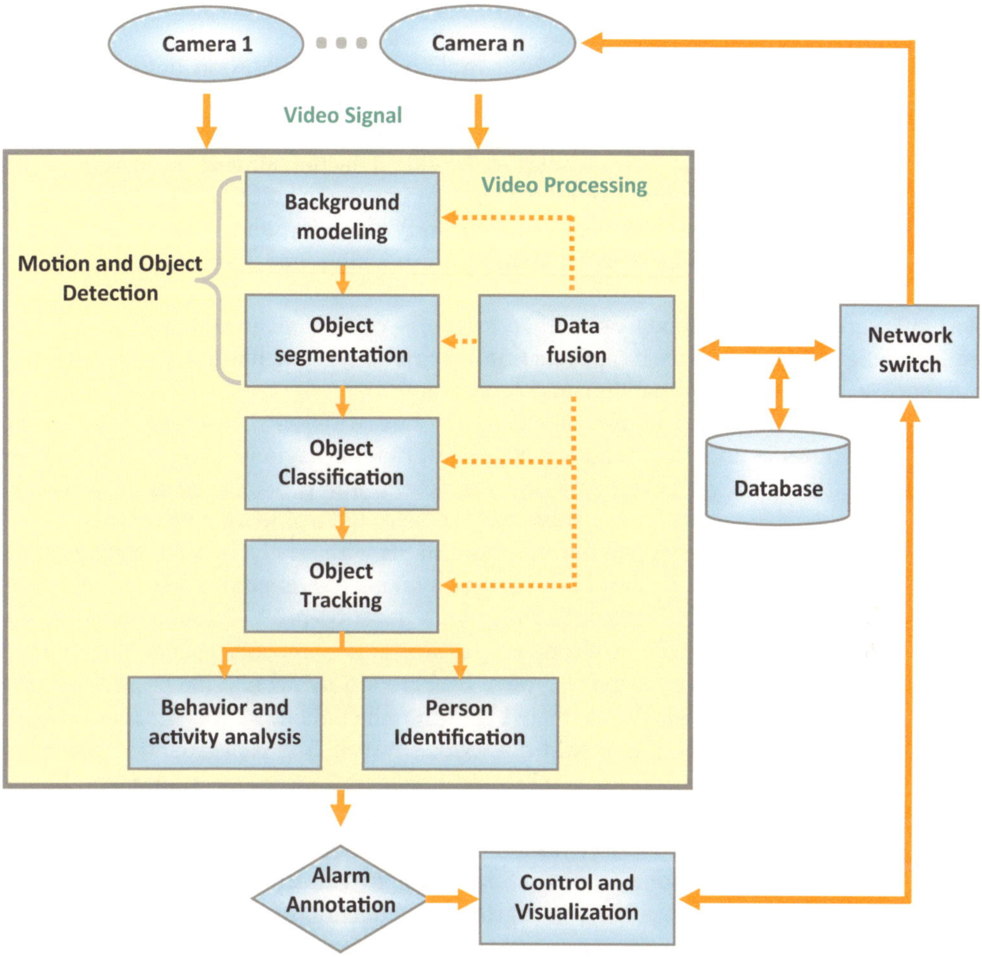

Fig. 1. A general framework of an automated visual surveillance system

This paper reviews and exploits developments and general strategies of stages involved in video surveillance, and analyzes the challenges and feasibility for combining object tracking, motion analysis, behavior analysis, and biometrics for stand-off human subject identification and behavior understanding. Behavior analysis using visual surveillance involves the most advanced and complex researches in image processing, computer vision, and artificial intelligence. There were many diverse methods (Saligrama et al., 2010) have been used while approaching this challenge; and they varied and depended on the required speed, the scope of application, and resource availability, etc. The motivation of writing and presenting a survey paper on this topic instead of a how-to paper for a domain specific application is to review and gain insight in visual surveillance systems from a big picture first. Reviewing/surveying existing available works to enable us to understand and answer the following questions better: Developments and strategies of stages involved in a general visual surveillance system; how to detect and analyze behavior and intent; and how to approach the challenge, if we have opportunities.

2. Motion and object detection

Most visual surveillance systems start with motion detection. Motion detection methods attempt to locate connected regions of pixels that represent the moving objects within the scene; different approaches include frame-to-frame difference, background subtraction and motion analysis using optical flow techniques. Motion detection aims at segmenting regions corresponding to moving objects from the rest of an image. The motion and object detection process usually involves environment (background) modeling and motion segmentation. Subsequent processes such as object classification, tracking, and behavior recognition are greatly dependent on it.

Most of segmentation methods use either temporal or spatial information in the image sequence. Several widely used approaches for motion segmentation include temporal differencing, background subtraction, and optical flow.

Temporal differencing makes use of the pixel-wise difference between two to three consecutive frames in an image sequence to extract moving regions. Temporal differencing is very fast and adaptive to dynamic environments, but generally does a poor job of extracting all the relevant pixels, e.g., there may be holes left inside moving entities.

Background subtraction is very popular for applications with relatively static backgrounds as it attempts to detect moving regions in an image by taking the difference between the current image and the reference background image in a pixel-by-pixel fashion. However, it is extremely sensitive to changes of environment lighting and extraneous events. The numerous approaches to this problem differ in the type of background model and the procedure used to update the background model. The estimated background could be simply modeled using just the previous frame; however, this would not work too well. The background model at each pixel location could be based on the pixel's recent history. Background subtraction methods store an estimate of the static scene, accumulated over a period of observation; this background model is used to find foreground (i.e., moving objects) regions that do not match the static scene. Recently, some statistical methods to extract change regions from the background are inspired by the basic background subtraction methods as described above. The statistical approaches use the characteristics of individual pixels or groups of pixels to construct more advanced background models, and the statistics of the backgrounds can be updated dynamically during processing. Each pixel in the current image can be classified into foreground or background by comparing the statistics of the current background model. This approach is becoming increasingly popular due to its robustness to noise, shadow, changing of lighting conditions, etc. (Stauffer & Grimson, 1999).

Optical flow is the velocity field, which warps one image into another (usually very similar) image, and is generally used to describe motion of point or feature between images (Watson & Ahumada, 1985). Optical flow methods are very common for assessing motion from a set of images. However, most optical flow methods are computationally complex, sensitive to noise, and would require specialized hardware for real-time applications.

3. Object classification

Different moving regions may correspond to different moving objects in natural scenes. To further track objects and analyze their behaviors, it is essential to correctly classify moving objects. For instance, the moving objects are humans, vehicles, or objects of interest of an investigated application. Object classification can be considered as a standard pattern recognition task. There are two main categories of approaches for classifying moving objects: shape-based classification and motion-based classification

Different descriptions of shape information of motion regions such as points, boxes, silhouettes and blobs are available for classifying moving objects. In general, human motion exhibits a periodic property, so this has been used as a strong cue for classification of moving objects also.

4. Object tracking

The task of tracking objects as they move in substantial clutter, and to do it at, or close to, video frame-rate is challenging. The challenge occurs if elements in the background mimic parts of features of the foreground objects. In the most severe case, the background may consist of objects similar to the foreground object(s), e.g., when a person is moving past a person, a group of people, or a crowd (Cavallaro et al., 2005).

The object tracking module is responsible for the detection and tracking of moving objects from individual cameras; object locations are subsequently transformed into 3D world coordinates. The camera handoff and data fusion module (or algorithm) then determines single world measurements from the multiple observations. Object tracking can be described as a correspondence problem and involves finding which object in a video frame related to which object in next frame (Javed & Shah, 2002). Normally, the time interval between two successive frames is small, thus the inter-frame changes are limited, allowing the use of temporal constraints and/or object features to simplify the correspondence problem. Tacking methods can be roughly divided into four major categories, and algorithms from different categories can be integrated together (Cavallaro et al., 2005, Javed & Shah, 2002).

a. Region-based Tracking

Region-based tracking algorithms track objects according to variation of the image regions corresponding to the moving objects. For these algorithms, the motion regions are usually detected by subtracting the background from the current images.

b. Contour-based Tracking

In contour-based methods instead of tracking the whole set of pixels comprising an object, the algorithms track only the contour of the object (Isard & Blake, 1996).

c. Feature-based Tracking

Feature-based methods use features of a video subject to track parts of the object. Feature-based tracking algorithms perform recognition and tracking of objects by extracting elements, clustering them into higher level features and then matching the feature between images.

d. Model-based Tracking

Model-based tracking algorithms track objects by matching projected object model. The models are usually constructed off-line with manual measurement, CAD tools or computer vision techniques. Generally, model-based human body tracking involves three main tasks: 1) construction of human body models; 2) representation of a priori knowledge of motion models and motion constraints; and 3) prediction and search strategies. Construction of human body models is the base of model-based human tracking. In general, the more complex a human body model, the more accurate the tracking results, but the more expensive the computation. Traditionally, the geometry structure of a human body can be represented in four styles: Stick figure, 2-D contour, volumetric model, and hierarchical model.

e. Hybrid Tracking

Hybrid approaches are designed as a hybrid between region-based and feature-based techniques. They exploit the advantages of two by considering first the object as an entity and then by tracking its parts.

5. Extraction and motion information

Before discussing the details of the extraction of motion information, Fig. 3 shows how a surveillance system may extract and learn motion patterns, e.g., a walk cycle, using an example of 4-level decomposition of the human dynamics as illustrated in (Bregler, 1997). Each level represents a set of random variables and probability distributions over hypotheses. The lowest level is a sequence of input images. For each pixel, we represent the spatio-temporal image gradient and optionally the color value as a random variable. The second level shows the blob hypotheses. Each blob is represented with a probability distribution over coherent motion (rotation and translation or full affine motion), color (HSV values), and spatial "support-regions". In the third level, temporal sequences of blob tracks are grouped to linear stochastic dynamical models. At the fourth and highest level, each dynamic model corresponds to the emission probability of the state of a Hidden Markov Model (HMM).

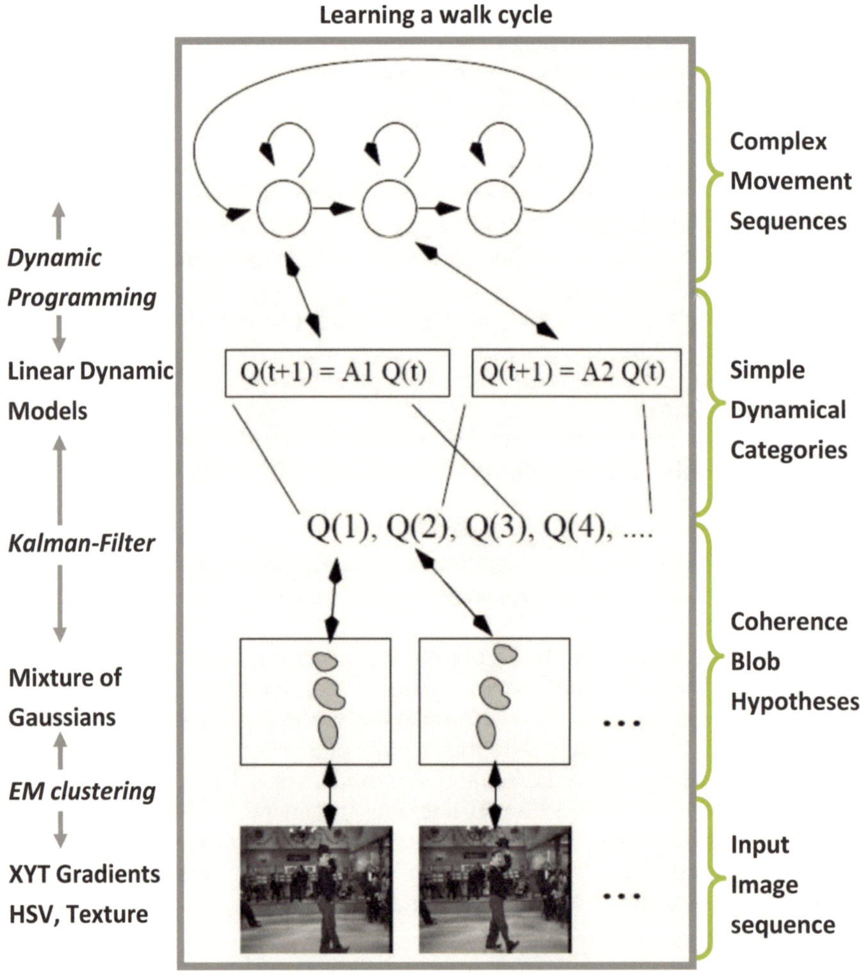

Fig. 2. Learning and recognizing human dynamics in video sequences (Bregler, 1997)

For example, the movement of one leg during a walk cycle can be decomposed into one coherent motion blob for the upper leg, and one coherent motion blob for the lower leg; one dynamic system for all the time frames while the leg has ground support, and one dynamic system in case the leg is swinging above ground, and a "cycle" HMM with multiple states. The state space of the dynamic systems is the translation and angular velocities of the blob hypothesis. The HMM stays in the first state for as many frames as the first dynamical system is valid, transitions to the second state once the second dynamic system is valid, and then cycles back to the first state for the next walk cycle.

The first important step in motion-based recognition is the extraction of motion information from a sequence of images. Motion perception and interpretation plays a very important role in a visual surveillance system. There are generally three methods for extracting motion information from a sequence of images: Optical flow, trajectory-based features, and region-based features.

a. Optical Flow Features

Optical flow methods are very common for assessing motion from a set of images. Optical flow is an approximation of the two-dimensional flow field from image intensities. Optical flow is the velocity field, which warps one image into another (usually very similar) image. Several methods have been developed, however, accurate and dense measurements are difficult to achieve (Cedras & Shah, 1995).

b. Trajectory-based Features

Trajectories, derived from the locations of particular points on an object in time, are very popular because they are relatively simple to extract and their interpretation is obvious (Morris & Trivedi, 2008). The generation of motion trajectories from a sequence of images typically involves the detection of tokens in each frame and the correspondence of such tokens from one frame to another. The tokens need to be distinctive enough for easy detection and stable through time so that they can be tracked. Tokens include edges, corners, interest points, regions, and limbs. Several proposed solutions (Cavallaro et al., 2005; Koller-meier & Van Gool, 2001; Makris & Ellis, 2005; Bobick & Wilson, 1997) for human actions modeling and recognition using the trajectory-based features approach. In the first step, an arbitrary changing number of objects are tracked. From the history of the tracked object states, temporal trajectories are formed which describe the motion paths of these objects. Secondly, characteristic motion patterns are learned by e.g. clustering these trajectories into prototype curves. In the final step, motion recognition is then tackled by tracking the position within these prototype curves based on the same method used for the object tracking.

c. Region- or Image-based Features

For certain types of objects or motions, the extraction of precise motion information for each single point is neither desirable nor necessary. Instead, the ability to have a more general idea about the content of a frame might be sufficient. Features generated from the use of information over a relatively large region or over the whole image are referenced here as region-based features. This approach has been used in several studies (Jan, 2004).

6. Behaviour analysis and understanding

One of most difficult challenges in the domain of computer vision and artificial intelligence is semantic behavior learning and understanding from observing activities in video (visual) surveillance. The research in this area concentrates mainly on the development of methods for analysis of visual data in order to extract and process information about the behavior of physical objects (e.g., humans) in a scene.

In automated visual surveillance systems, reliable detection of suspicious or endangering human behavior is of great practical importance (Regazzoni et al., 2010; Lao et al., 2010). An automated visual surveillance system generally requires a reliable combination of image processing and artificial intelligence techniques. Image processing techniques are used to provide low level image features. Artificial intelligence techniques are used to provide expert decisions. Extensive research has been reported on low level image processing techniques such as object detection, recognition, and tracking; however, relatively few researches has been reported on reliable classification and understanding of human activities from the video image sequences.

Detection of suspicious human behavior involves modeling and classification of human activities with certain rules. Modeling and classification of human activities are not trivial due to the randomness and complex nature of human movement. The idea is to partition the observed human movements into some discrete states and then classify them appropriately. Apparently, partitioning of the observed movements is very application-specific and overall hard to predict what will constitute suspicious or endangering behavior (Cohen et al., 2008; Jan, 2004; Saligrama et al., 2010).

Most approaches in the field of video understanding incorporated methods for detection of domain-specific events (Bremond et al., 2006). Examples of such systems use dynamic time warping for gesture recognition (Bobick & Wilson, 1997) or self-organizing networks for trajectory classification (Ivanov & Bobick, 2000; Bobick & Davis, 2001). The main drawback of these approaches is the usage of techniques that are specific only for a certain application domain which causes difficulties when applying these techniques to other areas (Bremond et al., 2006). Therefore, some researchers (Bremond et al., 2006; Ivanon & Bobick, 2000) have proposed and adopted a two-step approach to the problem of video understanding:

- A lower-level image processing visual module is used to extract visual cues and primitive events
- This collected information is used in a higher-level artificial intelligence module for the detection of more complex and abstract behavior patterns

By dividing the problem into two or three sub-problems, researchers can use simpler and more domain-independent techniques in each stage. The first stage usually involves and uses image processing and stochastic techniques for data analysis while the second stage conducts structural analysis of the symbolic data gathered at the previous step.

In the general visual surveillance process framework as shown in Fig. 1, the motion detection/segmentation and object classification are usually grouped as lower-level vision tasks. Human behavior recognition is based on successfully tracking the human subject through image sequences, and is considered a high-level vision task. The tracking process as discussed in (Wang et al., 2003) can be considered an intermediate-level vision task, or it can be split into lower and higher two stages as proposed in (Bremond et al., 2006) and shown in Fig. 3.

As shown in Fig. 3, at the first level of a general video surveillance system, geometric features, like areas of motions, are extracted. Based on those extractions, objects are recognized and tracked. At the second level, events in which the detected objects participate are recognized. For performing this task, a selected representation of events is used that defines concepts and relations in the domain of human activity monitoring.

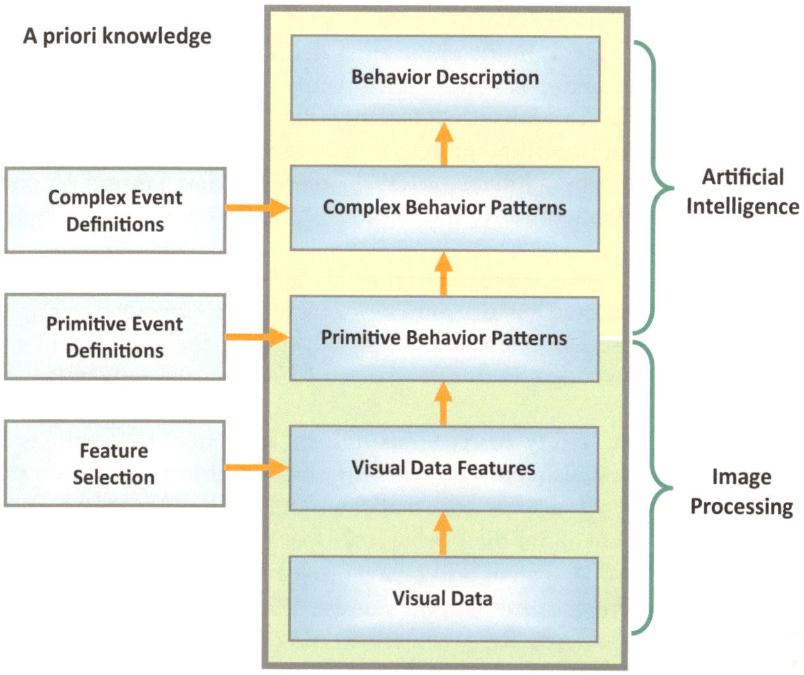

Fig. 3. A general architecture of a video understanding system.

For the computer vision community, a natural approach to recognize scenarios consists of using a probabilistic or neural network. The nodes of this network correspond usually to scenarios that are recognized at a given instance with a computed likelihood.

For the artificial intelligence community, a natural way to recognize a scenario is to use a symbolic network where nodes correspond usually to the Boolean recognition of scenarios. The common characteristic of these approaches is that all totally recognized behaviors are stored.

Another development that has captured the attention of researchers, is the unsupervised behavior learning and recognition, consisting of the capability of a vision interpretation system of learning and detecting the frequent scenarios of a scene without requiring the prior definitions of behaviors by the user.

Any scene object involved in a behavior/action should also include other individuals, groups of people, crowds, or static objects (e.g., equipments). Activities involve a regularly repeating sequence of motion events. The automatic video understanding and interpretation needs to know how to represent and recognize behaviors corresponding to different types of concepts, which include (Bremond et al., 2006; Medioni et al., 2001; Levchuk et al., 2010):

- **Basic Properties**: A basic property is a characteristic of an object such as its trajectory or speed.
- **States**: A state describes a situation characterizing one or several objects (actors) defined at given time (e.g., a subject is agitated) or a stable situation defined over a time interval. For the state: "an individual stays close to the ticket vending machine," two subjects (actors) are involved: an individual and a piece of equipment.
- **Events**: An event is a change of state at two consecutive times (e.g., a subject enters an area of interest).

- **Scenarios**: A scenario is a combination of states, events or sub-scenarios. Behaviors are specific scenarios, dependent on the application defined by the users. For example, to monitor metro stations, end-users could have defined targeted behaviors: "Loitering", "Unattended Luggage", "Vandalism", "Overcrowding", "Fighting", etc.

The ability to extract semantic information from human biologic motion has been known for some time. In his seminal work, Johansson (1973) revealed that presenting coordinated human joint motion was sufficient for rendering the impression of a human being walking or running through space.

With respect to detecting hostile intent (Cohen et al., 2008), each point in the point-light walker (PLW) might have its own gesture motion - which when examined in relation to the links in the object, can be used to determine the overall state of the system. Unusual events such as vandalism or overcrowded areas can be detected by unusual movements as well as unlikely object positions.

People have had the innate ability to recognize others' emotional dispositions based on intuition; this innateness must also manifest itself physically. For instance, when someone is experiencing emotion, what visual cues exist that communicate this? Facial expression, is an immediate indicator, but what about their behavior? Does posture, gesture, or specific body parts communicate this also? A system will be able to learn the visual cues found to be of some significance in identifying an emotion (Johansson, 1973) by identifying specific regions of the body that identify emotions,. Researchers will discover that motions of certain body parts may identify an emotion more than others (Cohen et al., 2008; Johansson, 1973; Montepare et al., 1987). For instance, researchers may discover that in anger the torso is most evocative of that emotion.

The review of available and state of the art techniques show the large diversity of video understanding techniques in automatic behavior recognition. The challenge is to efficiently combine these techniques to address the large diversity of the real world. Behavior pattern learning and understanding may be thought of as the classification of time varying feature data, i.e., matching an unknown test sequence with a group of labeled reference sequences representing typical or learned behaviors (Bobick & Davis, 2001). The fundamental problem of behavior understanding is to learn the reference behavior sequences from training samples, and to devise both training and matching methods for coping effectively with small variations of the feature data within each class of motion pattern. The major existing methods for behavior understanding include the following:

a. Hidden Markov Models (HMMs): A HMM is a statistical tool used for modeling generative sequences characterized by a set of observable sequences (Brand & Kettnaker, 2000).
b. Dynamic Time Warping (DTM): DTW is a technique that computes the non-linear warping function that optimally aligns two variable length time sequences (Bobick & Wilson, 1997). The warping function can be used to compute the similarity between two time series or to find corresponding regions between the two time series.
c. Finite-State Machine (FSM): FSM or finite-state automaton or simply a state machine, is a model of behavior composed of a finite number of states, transitions between those states, and actions. A finite state machine is an abstract model of a machine with a primitive internal memory.
d. Nondeterministic-Finite-State Automaton (NFA): A NFA or nondeterministic finite state machine is a finite state machine where for each pair of state and input symbols,

there may be several possible next states. This distinguishes it from the deterministic finite automaton (DFA), where the next possible state is uniquely determined. Although the DFA and NFA have distinct definitions, it may be shown in the formal theory that they are equivalent, in that, for any given NFA, one may construct an equivalent DFA, and vice-versa.

e. Time-Delay Neural Network (TDNN): TDNN is an approach to analyzing time-varying data. In TDNN, the delay units are added to a general static network, and some of the preceding values in a time-varying sequence are used to predict the next value. As larger data sets become available, more emphasis is being placed on neural networks for representing temporal information. TDNN methods have been successfully applied to applications, such as hand gesture recognition and lip reading.
f. Syntactic/Grammatical Techniques: The basic idea in this approach is to divide the recognition problem into two levels. The lower level is performed using standard independent probabilistic temporal behavior detectors, such as HMMs, to output possible low-level temporal features. These outputs provide the input stream for a stochastic context-free grammar parser. The grammar and parser provide longer range temporal constraints, disambiguate uncertain low-level detection, and allow the inclusion of a priori knowledge about the structure of temporal behavior (Ivanov & Bobick, 2000).
g. Self-Organizing Neural Network: The methods discussed in (a) - (f) all involve supervised learning. They are applicable for known scenes where the types of object motions are already known. The self-organizing neural networks are suited to behavior understanding when the object motions are unrestricted.
h. Agent-Based Techniques: Instead of learning large amounts of behavior patterns using a centralized approach, agent-based methods decompose the learning into interactions of agents with much simpler behaviors and rules (Bryll et al., 2005).
i. Artificial Immune Systems: Several researchers have exploited the feasibility of learning behavior patterns and hostile intents in the optical flow level using artificial immune system approaches (Sarafijanovic & Leboudec, 2004).

7. Person identification

In most of video surveillance system literatures, the person identification is achieved by motion analysis and matching, such as gait, gesture, posture analysis and comparison (Hu et al., 2004). In model-based methods, parameters for gait, gesture, and/or posture, such as joint trajectories, limb lengths, and angular speeds are measured. Statistical recognition techniques usually characterize the statistical description of motion image sets and have been well developed in automatic gait recognition. Physical-parameter-based methods make use of geometric structural properties of a human body to characterize a person's gait pattern. The parameters used included height, weight, stride cadence, length, etc. For motion recognition based on spatio-temporal analysis, the action or motion is characterized via the entire 3-D spatio-temporal data volume spanned by the moving person in the image sequence.

Human gait and face are now regarded as the main biometric features that can be used for personal identification in visual surveillance systems. The fusion of gait and face information with other standoff biometrics to further increase recognition robustness and reliability has been exploited by new surveillance systems. The problem of who is (are) now in the area, is (are) engaging in an abnormal/suspicious act under surveillance is of increasing important for visual surveillance.

8. Camera handoff and data fusion

To expand the surveillance area and provide multiple view information to overcome, most of visual (or video) surveillance systems are multiple camera-based. In a multi-camera surveillance system, with overlapping fields of view to track objects and recognize their activities predefined by a set of activities or scenarios, or even learns new behavior patterns or new knowledge. Each camera agent performs per frame detection and tracking of scene objects, and the output data is transmitted to a centralized server where data associated and fused object tracking is performed. This tracking result is fed to a video event recognition module where spatial and temporal events relating to the objects are detected and analyzed. Tracking with a single camera easily generates ambiguity due to occlusion or depth. This ambiguity may be eliminated from another view. However, visual surveillance using multiple cameras also brings problems such as camera installation (how to cover the entire scene with the minimum number of cameras), camera calibration, object matching, automated camera switching, and data fusion (Collins et al., 2000).

Most of proposed systems use cameras as the sensor since the camera can provide resolution needed for accurate classification and position measurement. The disadvantage of image-only detection systems is the high computational cost associated with classifying a large number of candidate image regions. Accordingly, it has been a trend for several years to use a hierarchical detection structure combining different sensors. In the first step low computational cost sensors identify a small number of candidate regions of interest (ROI). LIDAR (**Li**ght **D**etection **a**nd **R**anging) is an optical remote sensing technology that measures properties of scattered light to find range and/or other information of a distant target. The prevalent method to determine distance to an object or surface is to use laser pulses. Like the similar RADAR technology, which uses radio waves instead of light, the range to an object is determined by measuring the time delay between transmission of a pulse and detection of the reflected signal. As shown in (Szarvas et al., 2006; Premebida et al., 2007), the region of interest (ROI) detector in their proposed systems receives the signal from the LIDAR sensor and outputs a list of boxes in 3 dimensional (3D) world-coordinates. The 3D ROI-boxes are obtained by clustering the LIDAR measurements. Each 3D box is projected to the image plane using the intrinsic and extrinsic camera parameters.

9. Performance evaluation

The methods of evaluating the performance of object detection, object tracking, object classification, and behavior and intent detection and identification in a visual surveillance system are more complex than some of the well-established biometrics identification applications, such as fingerprint or face, due to unconstrained environments and the complexity of challenge itself. Performance Evaluation for Tracking and Surveillance (PETS) is a good starting place when looking into performance evaluation (PETS, 2007). As shown in Fig. 4, PETS has several good data sets for both indoor and outdoor tracking evaluation and event/behavior detection.

Fig. 4. Surveillance scenario dataset shows sample images captured from multiple cameras.

PETS datasets, starting from 2000 to 2007, include:

- Outdoor people and vehicle tracking using single or multiple cameras,
- Indoor people tracking (and counting) and hand posture classification,
- Annotation of a smart meeting, including facial expression, gaze and gesture/action,
- Multiple sensor (camera) sequences for unattended luggage,
- Multiple sensor (camera) sequences for attended luggage removal (theft), and
- Multiple sensor (camera) sequences for loitering.

In addition to surveillance datasets, there are efforts, like TRECVid Evaluation (Smeaton et al., 2009), with the goal to support the development of technologies to detect visual events through standard test datasets and evaluation protocols.

10. Conclusions

Visual (or video) surveillance systems have been around for a couple of decades. Most current automated video surveillance systems can process video sequence and perform almost all key low-level functions, such as motion detection and segmentation, object tracking, and object classification with good accuracy. Recently, technical interest in video surveillance has moved from such low-level functions to more complex scene analysis to detect human and/or other object behaviors, i.e., patterns of activities or events, for standoff threat detection and prevention.

Existing behavior/event analysis systems focus on the predefined events/behaviors, e.g., to combine the results of an automated video surveillance system with spatiotemporal reasoning about each object relative to the key background regions and other objects in the scene. Advanced behavior/event analysis systems have begun to exploit the capability to automatically capture and define (learn) new behaviors/events by pattern discovery, and

further present the behavior/events to the specialists for confirmation. The increasing need for sophisticated video surveillance systems and the move to digital video surveillance infrastructure, has transformed automated video surveillance into a large scale data analysis and management challenge (Brown et al., 2006).
This paper reviews and exploits developments and general strategies of stages involved in video surveillance and analyzes the challenges and feasibility for combining object tracking, motion analysis, behavior analysis, and biometrics for stand-off human subject identification and behavior understanding. Behavior analysis using visual surveillance involves the most advanced and complex researches in image processing, computer vision, and artificial intelligence. There were many diverse methods have been used while approaching this challenge; and they varied and depended on the required speed, the scope of application, and resource availability, etc. The motivation of writing and presenting a survey paper on this topic instead of a how-to paper for a domain specific application is to review and gain insight in visual surveillance systems from a big picture first. Reviewing/surveying existing available works to enable us to understand and answer the following questions better: Developments and strategies of stages involved in a general visual surveillance system; how to detect and analyze behavior and intent; and how to approach the challenge, if we have opportunities.

11. References

Bobick, A. & Wilson, A. (1997). "A State-Based Approach to the Representation and Recognition of Gesture," *IEEE Transactions on Pattern Analysis and Machine Intelligence*, Vol. 19, No. 12, pp. 1325-1337.

Bobick, A. & Davis, J. (2001). "The Recognition of Human Movement Using Temporal Templates," *IEEE Transactions on Pattern Analysis and Machine Intelligence*, Vol. 23, No. 3, pp. 257-267.

Borg, M., Thirde, D., Ferryman, J., Fusier, F., Valentin, V., Bremond, F. & Thonnat, M. (2005). "Video Surveillance for Aircraft Activity Monitoring," IEEE Conference on Advanced Video and Signal Based Surveillance, pp. 16-21.

Brand, M. & Kettnaker, V. (2000). "Discovery and Segmentation of Activities in Video," *IEEE Transactions on Pattern Analysis and Machine Intelligence*, Vol. 22, No. 8, pp. 844-851.

Bregler, C. (1997). "Learning and Recognizing Human Dynamics in Video Sequences," *Proceedings of IEEE Conference on Computer Vision and Pattern Recognition*, San Juan, Puerto Rico, pp. 568-574.

Brown, L., Hampapur, A., Connell, J., Lu, M., Senior, A., Shu, C. & Tian, Y. (2005). "IBM Smart Surveillance System (S3): An open and extensible architecture for smart video surveillance."

Bremond, F., Thonnat, M. & Zuniga, M. (2006). "Video-understanding framework for automatic behavior recognition," *Behavior Research Methods*, Vol. 30, No. 3, pp. 416-426.

Bryll, R., Rose, R. & Quek, F. (2005). "Agent-Based Gesture Tracking," *IEEE Transactions on Systems, Man and Cybernetics*, Part A, Vol. 35, No. 6, pp. 795-810.

Cavallaro, A., Steiger, O. & Ebrahimi, T. (2005). "Tracking video objects in cluttered background," *IEEE Transactions on Circuits and Systems for Video Technology*, Vol. 15, No. 4, pp. 575-584.

Cedras, C. & Shah, M. (1995). "Motion-Based Recognition: A Survey," *Image and Vision Computing*, Vol. 13, No. 2, pp. 129-155.

Cohen, C., Morelli, F. & Scott, K. (2008). "A Surveillance System for Recognition of Intent within Individuals and Crowds," *IEEE Conference on Technologies for Homeland Security*, Waltham, MA, pp. 559-565.

Collins, R., Lipton, A., Kanade, T., Fujiyoshi, H., Duggins, D., Yin, Y., Tolliver, D., Enomoto, N. & Hasegawa, O. (2000). "A System for Video Surveillance and Monitoring," Technical Report CMU-RI-TR-00-12, Carnegie Mellon University.

Dick, A. & Brooks, M. (2003). "Issues in Automated Visual Surveillance," in *Proceedings of International Conference on Digital Image Computing: Techniques and Application*, pp. 195-204.

Hu, W., Tan, T., Wang, L. & Maybank, S. (2004). "A Survey on Visual Surveillance of Object Motion and Behaviors," *IEEE Transactions on Systems, Man, and Cybernetics*, Part C: Application and Review, Vol. 34, No. 3, pp. 334-352.

Isard, M. & Blake, A. (1996). "Contour tracking by stochastic propagation of conditional density," in *Proceedings of European Conference on Computer Vision*, Cambridge, UK, pp. 343-356.

Ivanov, Y. & Bobick, A. (2000). "Recognition of Visual Activities and Interactions by Stochastic Parsing," *IEEE Transactions on Pattern Analysis and Machine Intelligence*, Vol. 22, No. 8, pp. 852-872.

Jan, T. (2004). "Neural Network Based Threat Assessment for Automated Visual Surveillance," in *Proceedings of IEEE International Joint Conference on Neural Networks*, Vol. 2, pp. 1309-1312.

Javed, O. & Shah, M. (2002). "Tracking and Object Classification for Automated Surveillance," *Proceedings of the 7th European Conference on Computer Vision*, Part-IV, pp. 343-357.

Johansson, G. (1973). "Visual perception of biological motion and a model for its analysis," *Perception and Psychophysics*, Vol. 14, No. 2, pp. 201-211.

Ko, T. (2008). "A Survey on behavior analysis in video surveillance for homeland security application," *AIPR*, pp. 1-8, 37th IEEE Applied Imagery Pattern Recognition Workshop.

Koller-meier, E. & Van Gool, L. (2001). "Modeling and recognition of human actions using a stochastic approach," in *Proceedings of 2nd European Workshop on Advanced Video-Based Surveillance Systems*, London, UK, pp. 17-28.

Kosmopoulos, D. & Chatzis, S. (2010). "Robust Visual Behavior Recognition: A framework based on holistic representations and multicamera information fusion," *IEEE Signal Processing Magazine*, Vol. 27, No. 5, pp. 34-45.

Kumar, P., Mittal, A. & Kumar, P. (2008). "Study of Robust and Intelligent Surveillance in Visible and Multi-modal Framework," *Informatica* 32, pp. 63-77.

Lao, W., Han, J. & With, P. (2010). "Flexible Human Behavior Analysis Framework for Video Surveillance Application," *International Journal of Digital Multimedia Broadcasting*, Vol. 2010, Article ID 920121, 9 pages.

Levchuk, G., Bobick, A. & Jones, E. (2010). "Activity and function recognition for moving and static objects in urban environments from wide-area persistent surveillance inputs," *Proc. SPIE 7704*, p. 77040P.

Makris, D. & Ellis, T. (2005). "Learning Semantic Scene Models From Observing Activity in Visual Surveillance," *IEEE Transactions on Systems, Man, and Cybernetics – Part B: Cybernetics*, Vol. 35, No. 3, pp. 397- 408.

Medioni, G.. Cohen, I, Bremond, F., Hongeng, S. & Nevatia, R. (2001). "Event Detection and Analysis from Video Streams," *IEEE Transactions on Pattern Analysis and Machine Intelligence*, Vol. 23, No. 8, pp. 873-889.

Montepare, J., Goldstein, S. & Clausen, A. (1987). "The Identification of Emotions from Gait Information," *Journal of Nonverbal Behavior*, 11(1), pp. 33-42.

Morris, B. & Trivedi, M. (2008). "A Survey of Vision-Based Trajectory Learning and Analysis for Surveillance," *IEEE Trans. on Circuits and Systems for Video Technology*, Vol. 18, No. 8, pp. 1114-1127.

PETS. (2007). Performance Evaluation and Tracking and Surveillance (PETS) 2007; Web site: http://pets2007.net/

Premebida, C., Monteiro, C., Nunes, U. & Peixoto, P. (2007). "A Lidar and Vision-based Approach for Pedestrian and Vehicle Detection and Tracking," *IEEE Intelligent Transportation Systems Conference*, pp. 1044-1049.

Regazzoni, C., Cavallaro, A., Wu, Y., Konrad, J. & Hampapur, A. (2010). "Video Analytics for Surveillance: Theory and Practice," *IEEE Signal Processing Magazine*, Vol. 27, No. 5, pp. 16-17.

Saligrama, V., Konrad, J. & Jodoin, P.-M. (2010). "Video Anomaly Identification: A Statistical Approach," *IEEE Signal Processing Magazine*, Vol. 27, No. 5, pp. 18-33.

Sarafijanovic, S. & Leboudec, J.-Y. (2004). "An Artificial Immune System for Misbehavior Detection in Mobile Ad-Hoc Networks with Virtual Thymus, Clustering, Danger Signal and Memory Detectors," in *Proceedings of ICARIS-2004* (Third International Conference on Artificial Immune Systems), Catania, Italy, pp. 342-356.

Smeaton, A., Over, P. & Kraaij, W. (2009). "High-Level Feature Detection from Video in TRECVid: a 5-Year Retrospective of Achievements," in *Multimedia Content Analysis, Theory and Applicaitons*, Editor, Divakaran, A., pp. 151-174, Springer Verlag, ISBN: 978-0-387-76567-9, Berlin.

Stauffer, C. & Grimson, W. (1999). "Adaptive Background Mixture Models for Real-Time Tracking," *Proceedings of the IEEE Conference on Computer Vision and Pattern Recognition*, Vol. 2, pp. 246-252.

Szarvas, M., Sakai, U. & Ogata, J. (2006). "Real-time Pedestrian Detection Using LIDAR and Convolutional Neural Networks," *IEEE Intelligent Vehicles Symposium*, pp. 213-218.

Wang, L, Hu, W. & Tan, T. (2003). "Recent developments in human motion analysis," *Pattern Recognition* Vol. 36, No. 3, pp. 585-601.

Watson, A. & Ahumada, A. Jr. (1985). "Model of Human Visual-Motion sensing," *J. Opt. Soc. Am.*, A 2, pp. 322-342.

17

Automatic Detection of Unexpected Events in Dense Areas for Videosurveillance Applications

Bertrand Luvison[1,2], Thierry Chateau[1], Jean-Thierry Lapreste[1],
Patrick Sayd[2] and Quoc Cuong Pham[2]
[1] *LASMEA, Blaise Pascal University*
[2] *CEA, LIST, LVIC*
France

1. Introduction

Intelligent videosurveillance is largely developping due to both the increasing population, especially in cities, and the exploding number of videosurveillance cameras deployed. When interesting to dense areas, mainly two kinds of scenes come to mind : crowd scenes and traffic ones. A usual treatment on these videos, usually done by security officers, is to monitore several video streams looking for anomalities. A survey of Dee & Velastin (2008) report a camera to screen ratio between 1:4 in best cases and 1:78 in worst ones. As a consequence, the chances to react quickly to an event are very low. This is the reason why this task need to be assisted. Nevertheless automatically detecting anomalies in these kinds of video is particularly difficult because of the large amount of information to be processed simultaneously and the complexity of the scenes.
Most of computer vision methods perform well in visual surveillance applications where the number of objects is low. Individuals can be successfully detected and tracked in scenarios where they appear in images with a sufficient resolution, and in the case of very limited and/or temporary occlusions. However, in crowded scenes, such as in public areas (for example, airports, stations, shopping malls), the video analysis task becomes much more complex. Abnormal behaviour definition is very scene and context dependent. Objects of interest may be small with respect of the global view, and only partially visible thus very difficult to model. Moreover, permanent interaction between individuals in a crowd even complicates the analysis.

1.1 State of the art

Crowd analysis methods can be divided in two main categories Zhan et al. (2008).
Local (or microscopic) approaches which try to segment individuals and track them. Tracking people can be performed in the monocamera case (Zhao & Nevatia (2004), Bardet et al. (2009) and Yu & Medioni (2009)), with stereo sensor (Tyagi et al. (2007)), or in the multicamera setup (Wang et al. (2010)). Learning paths enables the detection of abnormal trajectories (Junejo & Foroosh (2007), Hu et al. (2006), Saleemi et al. (2008)), or infering people interaction (Blunsden et al. (2007), Oliver et al. (2000)). The analysis of trajectories is also used in intrusion detection applications where crossing a virtual line raises an alarm or increase a counter

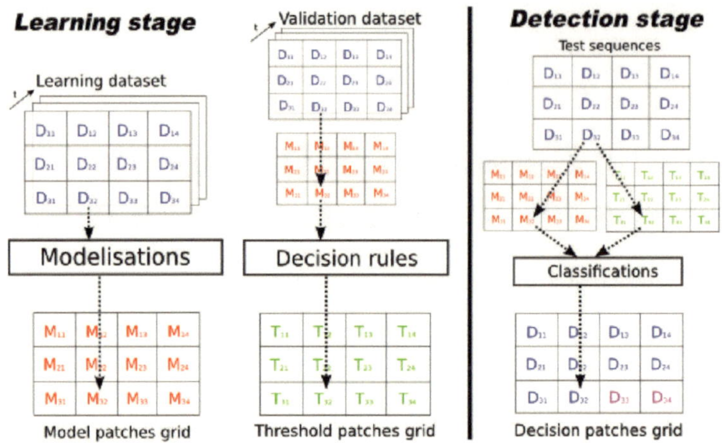

Fig. 1. System outline.

(Rabaud & Belongie (2006) or Sidla & Lypetskyy (2006)). Local approaches also tackles the problem of posture recognition in crowded area (Zhao & Nevatia (2004), Pham et al. (2007)).
Global (or macroscopic) approaches that treat crowd as a single object without segmenting persons. Most of global methods are based on motion analysis. Depending on the context, abnormal motion may be absence of movement, or unexpected movement direction in monocamera (Kratz & Nishino (2009) and Zhong et al. (2007)) or with multiple camera (Adam et al. (2008)). The problem of event detection in a crowd can consist in characterizing small perturbations, such as a person lying down (Andrade & Blunsden (2006)), in a global view of the scene, like in aerial images (Saad & Shah (2007)) or with a scene saliency measure (Mahadevan et al. (2010)). In Mehran et al. (2009) and Wu et al. (2010) the authors propose a way to detect bursting crowd. Varadarajan & Odobez (2009) and others (Wang et al. (2009)) detects pedestrians crossing streets in forbidden areas, cars stopping in unauthorized zones, wrong way displacements, etc. In Breitenstein et al. (2009), a method is proposed to detect all scenes that differ from a learned corpus of observed situations. Küttel et al. (2010) implement a framework for correlating vehicle and pedestrian typical trajectories. The recognition of a person particular movement in a crowd is also an addressed issue in crowd analysis (Shechtman & Irani (2005)) or tracking a particular person in very crowded scenes (Kratz & Nishimo (2010)).

1.1.1 Crowd features

1.1.1.1 Microscopic approches

The basic idea here is to segment individuals in order to recover their trajectory by tracking them. Methods differ in both the human appearance models (descriptors) used for segmenting people and the way datas are associated.
In Zhao & Nevatia (2004), Sidla & Lypetskyy (2006) and Pham et al. (2007), individuals are segmented using several ellipses or rectangles to represent body parts or the omega shape to model both the head and the shoulders. Yu & Medioni (2009) reinforce people tracking with occlusion by adding information on the appearance of the persons before they are occluded and an assumption on the speed continuity of tracked blobs. Kratz & Nishimo (2010) distinguish people inside a crowd using both color histogram and global mouvement model.

In tracking, the assumption is that the shape of persons does not vary much at the scale of and individual in a crowd, and that physical points lying on a person move in the same way (same trajectory and same speed) (Brostow & Cipolla (2006), Rabaud & Belongie (2006), Sidla & Lypetskyy (2006) and Hu et al. (2006)). Tracking algorithms are widely used to recover people trajectories. Kalman filtering (Stauffer & Grimson (2000), Oliver et al. (2000) and Zhao & Nevatia (2004)) and particle filtering (Bardet et al. (2009) and Yu & Medioni (2009)) are the most popular tracking algorithms. These filters can also integrate classification data and a priori information on objects.

The main drawback of tracking methods is the complexity which grows linearly with the number of targets which becomes untractable in the case of dense crowd. The second drawback is the occlusion handling, difficult to take into account in a crowd.

1.1.1.2 Macroscopics approaches

Global approaches require less assumption than local methods. They are based on global information on the crowd which can be more or less locally studied. As pedestrians are not precisely segmented, the detection of unusual motion provides unclassified information, i.e. the detection does not necessarily originate from a human, but for instance from objects in the background such as trees or shadows.
Motion is the most direct feature that can be analysed in a crowd. Motion is generally measured by computing the optical flow in the image. The Lucas-Kanade algorithm is employed in Adam et al. (2008) where the result is filtered using a block median filter (Varadarajan & Odobez (2009), Wang et al. (2009)). In Andrade & Blunsden (2006), the robust piecewise affine method of Black and Anandan is used. Saad & Shah (2007) or Wu et al. (2010) analyze the motion of a huge crowd by building an analogy with fluid dynamics. Spatiotemporal structures ar used in Shechtman & Irani (2005), in Kratz & Nishino (2009) and (2010). Zhong et al. (2007) model a movement energy and search for abnormal discontinuities of this function.
In contrast to the previous methods, some approaches are based on the modelling of the interaction forces between people inside the crowd (Mehran et al. (2009)). Dynamic textures proposed by Chan & Vasconcelos (2008) in crowd analysis context (Mahadevan et al. (2010)), it enables the detection of non pedestrian entities (bikers, skaters, etc.) in walkways or usual motion patterns. Beyond the scope of crowd analysis, Breitenstein et al. (2009) present an approach to store in an efficient way all past scenes and detect new ones. One of the applications of the method is the detection of non moving vehicles in a dense area.

1.1.2 Learning methods

Two different techniques are commonly employed to classify detected events in a crowd. The first one is based on ad-hoc rules that are defined thanks to prior depending on the context, or the application (Junejo & Foroosh (2007)). The second relies on a learning process. The assumption in the learning approach is that "normal" observations are the most frequently observed ones, whereas "abnormal" situations come from rare or unseen observations. Classification methods based on learning focus on specific features or descriptors extracted from the crowd analysis.
Data clustering approaches aim at subdividing datas in homogenous groups. One can mention K-means used in Hu et al. (2006) for finding blob centroid or Wu et al. (2010) to gather similar trajectories with a special method automatically finding the number of cluster.

In the Bayesian framework, the learning approach is expressed as the estimation of the maximum posterior density function. Several algorithms are proposed, the most commonly used are the expectation-maximization algorithm (EM) (Mahadevan et al. (2010)) and the Kernel Density Estimation (KDE) (Saleemi et al. (2008)). Markov Chain Monte Carlo Methods are also proposed in several approaches (Pham et al. (2007), Saleemi et al. (2008), Yu & Medioni (2009)). Breitenstein et al. (2009) propose an ad-hoc method for updating the maximum posterior density function once a day.
Zhao & Nevatia (2004), Andrade & Blunsden (2006) and Kratz & Nishino (2009) exploit the temporal consistency by computing spatiotemporal patterns using Hidden Markov Models (HMM). Moreover, Kratz & Nishino (2009) introduce a spatial consistency between local movement patterns by modelling them with coupled HMM, also used in Oliver et al. (2000) for trajectories interaction analysis. Küttel et al. (2010) combine HMM with natural language processing approaches for creating behaviour dependency networks.
Approaches inspired by natural language processing try to analyse the relationship between documents and the words they contain, by building topics. Varadarajan & Odobez (2009) use a probabilistic Latent Semantic Analysis (pLSA) to learn position, size and motion features. Mehran et al. (2009) use the Latent Dirichlet Allocation (LDA) algorithm with words based on the social forces computation whereas Wang et al. (2010) use motion-drawn words. Küttel et al. (2010) rely on Hierarchical Dirichlet Process (HDP) which automatically find the number of topics as opposed to LDA. Wang et al. (2009) compare an extension of HDP, the dual-HDP with LDA, showing outperforming results.

1.2 Our approach

In order to anwser to the problem of automatic crowded area analysis, several choices has been done:

- A system without calibration step to avoid complex deployement process.
- A global approch, using motion, to be independent of the number of targets in the scene and to be more persistant. Indeed, motion is estimated with few frames whereas a trajectory is issued from a long term process and can be hardly recovered if failed. The motion has the advantage to work on intensity gradient, so these kind of features are very robust various weather and illumination condition changes.
- A learning approach to be as generic as possible, working at the same time on traffic or crowd scenes.
- A supervised approach because no labeled dataset can be made when dealing with anomalies which are by definition infrequent.

Giving an video stream from a fixed camera, the proposed system is able to generate, in an offline process, a statistical model of frequently observed (considered as normal) motion. The scene is divided into blocs from a regular grid. The motion is characterized by a new spatio-temporal descriptor computed on each blocks. The detection stage consists in searching motion patterns that deviate from the model and considered as unexpected events. The decision rule is given thanks to a confidence criteria. An overview of the system is given on figure 1. This method has the asset to be completely automatic: no camera calibration is needed, no labelling task has to be done on the learning database. Moreover, the approach is independent of the number of targets and runs in real-time.
This paper is organized as follows. Section 2 introduces a new characterisation of the mouvement using a spatio-temporal structure as a feature. Section 3 presents the classification

framework. It relies on a new density estimation method competing with classical algorithm such as KDE or EM. Final section 4, compares improvements obtained using our motion features compared to classical optical flow movement estimation with our classification framework and both quantitative and qualitative results concerning unexpected event detections.

2. Movement characterisation

2.1 Opical Flow

Global movement on a scene is generally determined using optical flow estimation algorithms. These algorithms rely on the gradient constraint which suppose a constant illumination of object between two frames. This poor assumption combined with spatial constraint still manages to estimate on each pixel a displacement from one frame to another. Different optical flow techniques have been tested, such as Lucas & Kanade (1981) and its variants, Horn & Schunck (1981) or "Block matching method" (Barron et al. (1992)). From all the different techniques, the Black & Anandan (1996) has been chosen for its robustness and the cleanliness of its result compared to others methods, but also for its relative fast computation. This method is based on a piecewise affine motion assumption which is generally satisfied for our type of scene. Moreover, its computation time remains sustainable for real-time analysis.

When using displacement flow as a descriptor for our system, some special cares need to be taken. The movement magnitude for example, is not as meaningful as the orientation because of the gradient constraint. As a consequence, only the movement direction is studied. To compare two directions an angular distance can be used :

$$d_\theta(\theta_1,\theta_2) = min(\ |\theta_2 - \theta_1|, |\theta_2 - (\theta_1 + 2\pi)|\ )\ with\ \theta_1 < \theta_2 \tag{1}$$

2.2 Spatio-temporal descriptors

The more the movement characterisation is continuous over time, the better it is. Indeed, optical flow usually estimates the movement between two frames and can sometimes be biased by ponctual perturbations. Spatio-temporal structures are convinient to filter such phenomenons. Kratz & Nishino (2009) use this kind of structure in a crowd analysis context, modeling gradients along x,y and t computed on a greyscale cuboid extracted from a sub area of the video through several frames, with a 3D gaussian. To compare two cuboids, Kratz & Nishino (2009) use the symmetric Kullback-Leibler divergence.

Shechtman & Irani (2005) work also tackles the problem of spatio-temporal movement characterisation. We will describe the theory of this method because the new descriptor proposed in this paper relies on the same theory. When considering a uniform mouvement inside a cuboid, constant grey level pixels are all aligned following the same direction through the cuboid. This direction $[u\ v\ w]^T$ is perpendicular to the space-time gradients $\mathbf{\nabla I_i} = [I_{i,x} I_{i,y} I_{i,t}]^T = [\frac{\partial I(i)}{\partial x} \frac{\partial I(i)}{\partial y} \frac{\partial I(i)}{\partial t}]^T$. Figure 2 represents this linear relationship. Let G be the matrix gathering $\mathbf{\nabla I_i}$ gradients of all the N pixel of the cuboid, $G = [\mathbf{\nabla I_1} \dots \mathbf{\nabla I_N}]^T$. We obtain $G[u\ v\ w]^T = [0\ 0\ 0]^T$ which can be reformulated using the Gram matrix :

$$G^T G \begin{bmatrix} u \\ v \\ w \end{bmatrix} = \begin{bmatrix} 0 \\ 0 \\ 0 \end{bmatrix} \tag{2}$$

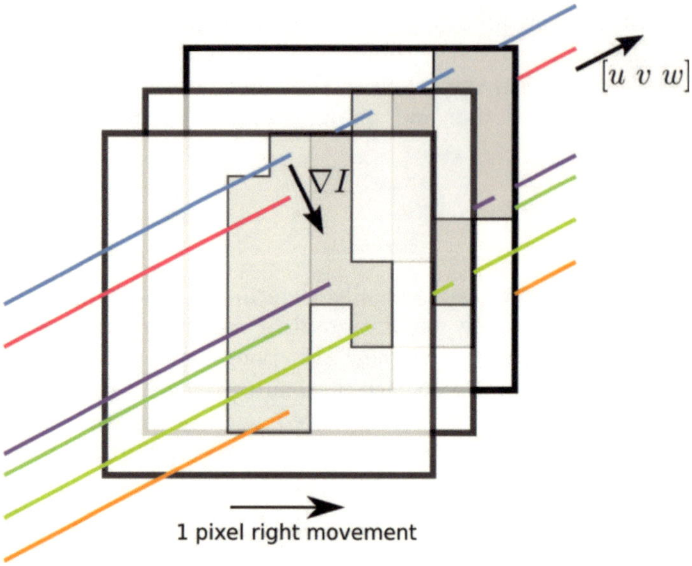

Fig. 2. Spatio-temporal structures in a translation movement case. The constant greyscale lines are all parrallel.

Let M be the Gram matrix $G^T G$ associated :

$$M = G^T G = \begin{bmatrix} \sum_i I_{i,x}^2 & \sum_i I_{i,x} I_{i,y} & \sum_i I_{i,x} I_{i,t} \\ \sum_i I_{i,y} I_{i,x} & \sum_i I_{i,y}^2 & \sum_i I_{i,y} I_{i,t} \\ \sum_i I_{i,t} I_{i,x} & \sum_i I_{i,t} I_{i,y} & \sum_i I_{i,t}^2 \end{bmatrix} \tag{3}$$

M can be considered as a extension of the Harris matrix (Harris & Stephens (1988)), whose definition is :

$$M^\diamond = \begin{bmatrix} \sum_i I_{i,x}^2 & \sum_i I_{i,x} I_{i,y} \\ \sum_i I_{i,y} I_{i,x} & \sum_i I_{i,y}^2 \end{bmatrix} \tag{4}$$

Matrix M contains all information needed for spatio-temporal corner detection.
Note that equation (2) has a solution only if matrix M is rank-deficient ($rg(G) = rg(M) \neq 3$). Otherwise, the movement inside the cuboid is not uniform, it is a spatio-temporal corner considering intensity lines. As a consequence, no increase in rank between the upper left minor $M^\diamond$ of M define on equation (4) and matrix M notices a uniform motion in the cuboid.
Two cuboids are motion consistent if appending the two cuboids along the temporal dimension still verifies the rank criteria cited above. However, this criteria provides a binary answer. As a consequence, Shechtman & Irani (2005) define a continous rank-increase measure to take into account the natural image noise and to give a graduated answer. This measure is defined by :

$$\Delta \hat{r} = \frac{\det(M)}{\det(M^\diamond).\|M\|_F} \tag{5}$$

where $\|M\|_F$ is the Frobenius norm of matrix M. Note that $\Delta\hat{r_{ii}} = \Delta\hat{r_1}$ is not necessarily equal to zero. Shechtman & Irani (2005) define another measure, m_{ij}, to ensure that m_{ii} is minimal. m_{ij} which captures the degree of local inconsistency between two cuboids, is equal to :

$$m_{12} = \frac{\Delta\hat{r}_{12}}{min(\Delta\hat{r}_1, \Delta\hat{r}_2) + \epsilon} \quad (6)$$

These spatio-temporal structures can model smoother movements or even more complex movements. In order to have the best classification results possible, we proposed a new spatio-temporal descriptor that rely on the same assumption than Shechtman & Irani (2005) descriptor.

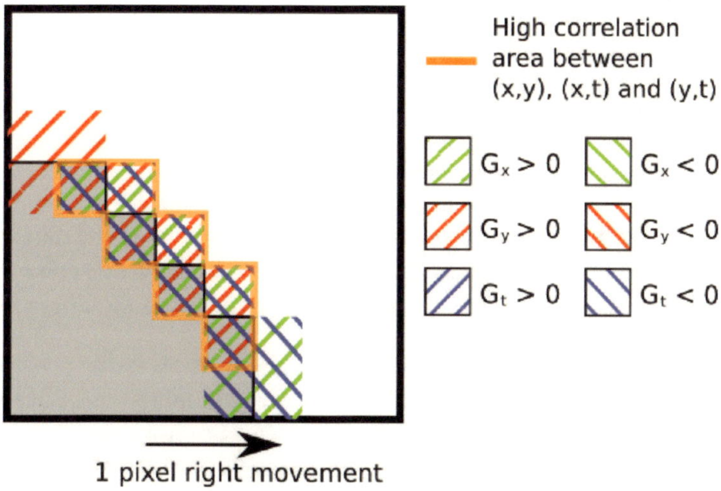

(a)

Fig. 3. Shape influence on linear relationship estimation for translation movement.

2.3 Our descriptor

Shechtman & Irani (2005) based their descriptor on studying the linear dependency between spatial gradients and the temporal gradient. Instead of using the rank of the matrix M, we propose to look for a possible linear dependency using a correlation measure. The correlation between two random variables $X = (x_1, ..., y_n)$ and $Y = (y_1, ..., y_n)$ is given by the Pearson formula :

$$\rho_{XY} = \frac{\sum_{i=1}^{N}(x_i - \bar{x})(y_i - \bar{y})}{\sqrt{\sum_{i=1}^{N}(x_i - \bar{x})^2}\sqrt{\sum_{i=1}^{N}(y_i - \bar{y})^2}} \quad (7)$$

with $E(.)$ the expected value. Other measures of dependence exist, such as mutual information but according to the application context, the Pearson correlation is the right mesure for searching linear relationship.

According to equation (7), standard deviations of each random variable need to be different to zero. In our case, the natural noise in the image is usually enough to ensure this property. Singular remaining cases represent either a perfect gradient color or a uniform image area. Both cases which are not interesting situations, can be filtered by thresholding the gradient magnitude.

The proposed descriptor is thus constructed looking on the linear correlation between both x and t and y and t. We obtain the movement characterisation $\mathbf{C} = [\rho_{xt}\ \rho_{yt}]^T$. The distance between two descriptors is defined by equation (8). Values are taken in $[0, 2]$.

$$d_{corr}(\mathbf{C_1}, \mathbf{C_2}) = 1 - \frac{\mathbf{C_1}.\mathbf{C_2}}{||\mathbf{C_1}||||\mathbf{C_2}||} \tag{8}$$

This feature is not an estimation of the movement since no movement magnitude is defined. Only a confidence measure on linear dependency existence is expressed with this feature. Since magnitude gradients are not taken into account, separation between diagonal mouvement in the same quartile is theorically impossible. For example, considering two translation movements $(2, 1)$ and $(1, 2)$, in both cases the correlation vector should be $\mathbf{C} = [1\ 1]^T$. In practice, correlations on real image gradients are never perfect. The more a movement is well defined in a direction, the more the correlation is high. This is the reason why two different diagonal movements from the same quartile will give different features **C**. Nevertheless, vector **C** magnitude gives a confidence criteria on the characterisation. If **C** magnitude is too low, one can consider that no main movement exists in the cuboid. This piece of information is analog to the consistency criteria defined by Shechtman & Irani (2005). Moreover, normalizing data through correlation computation makes the descriptor invariant to affine illumination changes of type $\widehat{I} = aI + b$ where I is the greyscale cuboid. Indeed, such a change, modify gradients such as $\widehat{G} = aG$ but does not change the linear relationship, so $C_{\widehat{G}} = C_G$.

However, the descriptor suffers, like optical flow estimation from the aperture problem. This problem appears along straight edge where only the normal component of the movement can be estimated. Here, the problem is similar, since gradients are computed in a given base (the image orthonormal basis x,y), a movement can be fully defined if part of edges are aligned along both axis in the cuboid. A gradient aligned along an axis can only give information on this axis component of the movement. Diagonal edges gives diagonal spatial gradients which may bias the movement characterisation. The positive correlation relationship is theorically not transitive except under some conditions. This transitivity relationship is discussed by Langford et al. (2001) who show that for three random variables A, B et C such as $\rho_{AB} > 0$ et $\rho_{BC} > 0$, the correlation between A et C is bounded by :

$$\rho_{AB}\rho_{BC} - \sqrt{(1-\rho_{AB}^2)(1-\rho_{BC}^2)} \le \rho_{AC} \le \rho_{AB}\rho_{BC} + \sqrt{(1-\rho_{AB}^2)(1-\rho_{BC}^2)} \tag{9}$$

For diagonal edges, components x and y are correlated. When the correlation is strong and if component x for example is correlated to component t, then component y will be correlated to. As a consequence, if a cuboid contains mainly a diagonal edge, the caracterisation will tend to be $\mathbf{C} = [\alpha\ \beta]$ with $|\alpha| \approx |\beta|$ whatever the true movement is, as shown with the orange area on figure 3.

To avoid such problem, only the thrustful information contained in the cuboid can be kept for linear relationship estimations. This subset is made from gradients aligned along x and y axis. Let S_x et S_{xt} be respectively gradient sets $I_{i,x}$ and $I_{i,t}$ for points with spatial gradient aligned along x axis. Such a filtering makes movement characterisation more precise and thus more discriminative but considering only subset of gradients can lead to singular cases. These cases occur when not enough gradients are aligned along one of the two axis. To avoid such a phenomenon, the alignement constraint is relaxed to accept gradients in an angular interval of $\frac{\pi}{4}$ around axis. In the same way,S_y and S_{yt} are defined with gradient aligned around axis y. Subset S_x, S_{xt}, S_y and S_{yt} are defined such as :

$$S_x = \{I_{i,x}| -\frac{\pi}{8} \leq \theta \leq \frac{\pi}{8}\} \text{ and } S_{xt} = \{I_{i,t}| -\frac{\pi}{8} \leq \theta \leq \frac{\pi}{8}\}$$
$$S_y = \{I_{i,y}| -\frac{3\pi}{8} \leq \theta \leq \frac{5\pi}{8}\} \text{ and } S_{yt} = \{I_{i,t}| -\frac{3\pi}{8} \leq \theta \leq \frac{5\pi}{8}\} \quad (10)$$

where $\theta = \arg(I_{i,x}, I_{i,y})\ [\pi]$. Finally, vector $\mathbf{C}$ is equal to $\mathbf{C} = [\rho_{S_x S_{xt}}$ $corrS_y S_{yt}]^T$. For the remaining singular cases where there are still not enough gradients along axis, typically very low frequencies image areas, instead of giving a wrong movement characterisation, an invalidate state for the feature is set.
In the rest of this paper this new descriptor is named "Separated Selected Correlation"(SSC).

2.4 Experimental results

2.4.1 Movement separation

In order to validate the proposed descriptor, movement class separation of descriptor SSC has been compared to the initial version our the proposed descriptor without filtering on spatial gradient orientation, but also compared to Shechtman & Irani (2005) and Kratz & Nishino (2009) descriptors. Cuboids have been generated and compared for movement in 16 different directions (cf. figure 4(a)). Descriptors have been computed on $T = 3$ frames. The movement generated are exact translations, thus parameter T does not have a lot of influence. On the contrary, for real uniform movement, parameter T smoothes and reinforces the movement characterisation. Spatio-temporal gradients have been computed with Canny method with gaussian standard deviation equal to 1 and filter size of 5 pixels.

(a) Movement indexes. (b) Interest regions for descriptor comparison.

Fig. 4. Synthetic movement generation.

Results are represented as a distance matrix $\mathcal{M}$ of size $(16, 16)$ for a given descriptor and the associated distance. This matrix is assumed to be symetric, with minimal diagonal and a sub-diagonal corresponding to the distance between a mouvement and the opposed one. Cuboids have been generated from real images in differents regions of interest $r_i \in R$ represented in red on figure 4(b) in translation along the 16 directions of figure 4(a). The blue boxes on figure 4(b) correspond to area possibly seen through the displacement. Movement characterisation has to be independant to the shape contained in the cuboid, as a consequence, distances between two direction i et j are computed for all the couples of regions of interest and then averaged.

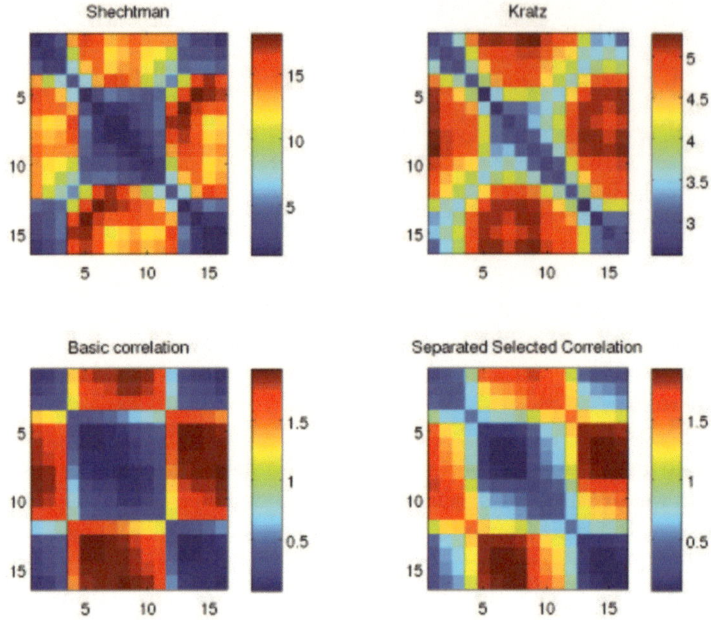

Fig. 5. Distance matrices for real images translation movement using different spatio-temporal descriptors.

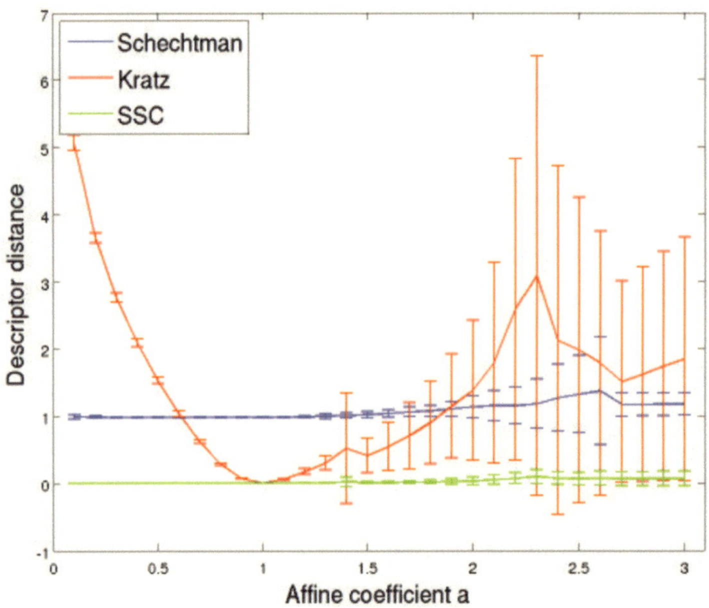

Fig. 6. Evolution of distance mean and standard deviation between descriptors with affine illumination change.

Movement separation results are shown on figure 5. All the three descriptors with their own distance roughly distinguish movements. However the SSC descriptor is more constant and precise. In order to measure distance matrix quality, the mean of the maximum relative position is computed. For a movement in direction i, the maximum distance is expected for opposed movement, that is to say movement with index $i + 8$ [16]. Table 1 shows that SSC descriptor is the nearest to the theoritical index 8 than other methods. Moreover, standard deviations on these maximum positions show that the separation is more stable whatever the shape contained in the cuboid is.

	Shechtman	Kratz	Simple correlation	SSC
i_{max}	6	8.5	7.625	7.875
$\sigma_{\overline{i_{max}}}$	2.7809	2.3094	0.8851	0.6191

Table 1. Average shift and standard deviation between two movement extremum.

One may note that concerning the simple correlation method, movement is distinguished in roughly two classes illustrating the shape influence phenomenon. The spatial correlation biases **C** computation to make it constant for a mouvement class whatever the true movement. SSC version of the algorithm decreases this effect in a significant manner.

2.4.2 Affine illumination change invariance

To validate this property, the distance between a cuboid without illumination change and one with it has been computed for a given direction on all regions of interest $r_i \in R$ represented in red on figure 4(b). The different curves on figure 6 represent distance mean and standard deviation on all region of interest of R function of coefficient a. Descriptors are characterizing the same direction, so distance between them should be minimal (0 for Kratz & Nishino (2009) and SSC descriptor and 1 for Shechtman & Irani (2005)). Except for Kratz & Nishino (2009) descriptor, other ones have a very low distance mean and standard deviation whatever the value of a until reasonable values. Indeed, a for very high value of a, pixels saturate to white which leads to a false descriptor characterization. On the contrary, Kratz & Nishino (2009) descriptor for low value of a does not return low distance as excepted. An affine illumination change modifies the 3D gaussian from $\mathcal{N}(\mu, \Sigma)$ to $\mathcal{N}(a\mu, a^2\Sigma)$ which are two different distributions according to Kullback-Leibler divergence. This deficiency is quite important when dealing with outdoor videos.

2.4.3 Computation efficiency

Because of the real-time constraint, motion characterisation computation time is important. We compared spatio-temporal SSC and Shechtman & Irani (2005) descriptors computation time with Black & Anandan (1996) optical flow method. The implementation was done in C++ with optimised code. Spatio-temporal cuboid have 16x16x5 size. Note that spatio-temporal descriptors gives blocks information whereas optical flow returns a dense information. Thus, performances are not really comparable, times are given for information.
Most of spatio-temporal computation time is caused by the gradients estimation as seen on table 2. Concerning correlation computation for the SSC descriptor, it can be optimised to calculate the correlation in one pass instead of two, dividing computation time by two as shown on figure 2. To do so, the following formula is used for the correlation computation :

$$\rho_{XY} = \frac{N\sum_{i=1}^{N}(x_i y_i) - \sum_{i=1}^{N} x_i \sum_{i=1}^{N} y_i}{\sqrt{N\sum_{i=1}^{N} x_i^2 - (\sum_{i=1}^{N} x_i)^2}\sqrt{N\sum_{i=1}^{N} y_i^2 - (\sum_{i=1}^{N} y_i)^2}} \tag{11}$$

Image size	Gradients	unoptimised SSC	optimised SSC	Shechtman	Black & Anandan
320x240	67.92	45.28	19.81	25.47	152.82
640x480	297.15	155.65	76.41	104.71	761.27

Table 2. Number of average clock cycle (million of cycles).

This formulation has to be taken with care because it is not numerically stable. Safegards need to be taken to avoid these cases, such as thresholding gradient magnitudes to consider only significant variations.
Table 2 show that SSC and Shechtman & Irani (2005) descriptors have the same complexity. Moreover, computation time is linear with image size as shown with times fourfold between image resolution 320x240 and 640x480.

3. Classification frameworks

Our application framework imposes us the use of unsupervised learning machines (no labelled databases with abnormal behaviours can be made). The main problem is to drawn a decision function from a set of features representing the "normal" behaviour. We will focus on probabilist approaches which aim at estimating a likelihood function and thresholding it to decide new sample class.
Likelihood functions are widely used into computed vision algorithms like recognition, detection or tracking. However, estimating such fonction from observations is still a challenging task because: 1) in the general case, no prior on the shape of the likelihood can be used to define a simple parametric function and 2) methods have to deal with high dimensionnal features and huge training sets.
For approximating the unknown likelihood distribution of the model, given observations (the learning features) drawn from this model, non parametric or parametric approaches can be used. For the non parametric one, Kernel Density Estimation (named KDE or Parzen windows model Duda et al. (2001)) relies on the choice of a kernel function. This method converges to the true distribution with the number of learning features but with a heavy computational cost which is generally not acceptable as we will see later. K-Nearest Neighbour estimation (KNN) is also a non parametric method that does not assume a window with a given size like KDE. Contrarily, this method defines a cell volume as a function of the training data Duda et al. (2001).
Other methods for approximating unknown distribution are parametric and generally assume that this distribution is a gaussian mixture (GMM). In Dempster et al. (1977) the authors propose an algorithm to estimate the parameters of a mixture of gaussians, using a prior on the number of gaussians. This well known algorithm called Expectation Maximisation has been improved. In Figueiredo & Jain (2002) the constraint on the number of gaussians which is usually unknown in practice, has been removed. Recently, Han et al. (2008) proposed a sequential approach, named SKDA, to approximate a given distribution with GMMs, adding gaussian one by one and mixing it in the previous gaussian mixture if needed. The main drawback of these parametric methods is to suppose a model which may not always fit to the real model. For example, EM or SKDA algorithms use intrinsic Mahalanobis distance to compare features. This may be complete out of sense for use of spatio-temporal features seen in section 2 which have their own comparison distance.
As a consequence, a parametric estimation using adhoc features distance like KDE or KNN, without computational cost constraint is proposed. The decision function needs for

classification context associated with this proposed estimation can be very simple with a fix threshold or more subtle. We choose to use a confidence criteria that will be presented with the proposed estimation method.

3.1 An hybride method

We propose to approximate the KDE with a sparse model composed by a weighted sum of kernel functions in order to withdraw the computational burden associated to the KDE while keeping its precision. Our method will be called SKDE for Sparse Kernel Density Estimation. It aims at selecting the most important features and weighted the kernel functions associated to it, as shown on figure 7. The weight of a feature defines its amplitude and thus its range.

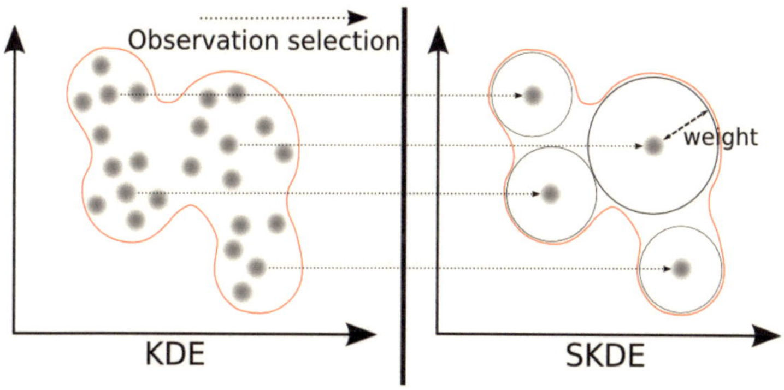

Fig. 7. Feature selection process for KDE approximation.

3.1.1 Likelihood Non-Parametric Approximation

Let $\mathbf{Z} \doteq (z_1, z_2, ..., z_K)^T$ denotes the features belonging to a given model. We choose to represent the likelihood $P(z)$ with a non-parametric model using KDE:

$$P_{\text{KDE}}(z) \approx K^{-1} \sum_{k'=1}^{K} \phi_{k'}(z) \tag{12}$$

where $\phi_{k'}(.)$ is a kernel function (not necessarily gaussian). With such an approach, no assumption needs to be done over the shape of the distribution. However, one of the drawbacks of this approach is that the estimation of the probability is proportional to the number of samples used. We propose a solution wherein a sparse model is obtained by approximating equation (12) by a weighted sum of basis functions.

3.1.2 A Sparse Kernel Density Estimation

Equation 12 can also be expressed as:

$$P_{\text{KDE}}(z) \approx \mathbf{w}^T (\phi(z)) \tag{13}$$

with $\mathbf{w}^T = (1, ...1)^T / K$ is a vector of size K and ϕ is a vector function defined by $\phi(z) = (\phi_1(z), \phi_2(z), ..., \phi_K(z))$.

We propose a sparse model formulation of equation (13) by fixing most of the coefficients of $\mathbf{w}$ to zero as it is classically done. This new vector will be called $\check{\mathbf{w}}$ and the reduced one, that is to say the vector of non zero coefficient, $\tilde{\mathbf{w}}$. As a consequence the new estimator expression is:

$$\widehat{P_{\mathrm{KDE}}}(z) \approx \tilde{\mathbf{w}}^T \tilde{\phi}(z) \tag{14}$$

with $\tilde{\phi}$ a vector function extracted from ϕ with the kernel function associated to non-zero weight kept in $\tilde{\mathbf{w}}$. To obtain equation (14), we solve the following least square problem:

$$\widetilde{\mathbf{w}_{\mathbf{LS}}} = \arg\min_{\tilde{\mathbf{w}}} \left(\sum_{k=1}^{K} (\mathbf{w}^T \phi(z_k)) - \tilde{\mathbf{w}}^T \tilde{\phi}(z_k))^2 \right) \tag{15}$$

The remaining question to solve problem (15) is how to choose $\tilde{\phi}$. Let Φ denote, a matrix of size $K \times K$ and built such as the element of the line i and column j is given by $\Phi_{i,j} = \phi_i(z_j)$. Φ is a square and symetric matrix, from which, an estimator of the likelihood associated to the sample z_k of the training set is given by the sum of elements of the line or the column k of Φ, that is to say:

$$P_{\mathrm{KDE}}(z_k) = K^{-1} \sum_{k'=1}^{K} \Phi_{k,k'} \tag{16}$$

A likelihood vector φ related to the training set is built:

$$\varphi = \Phi \times (\mathbf{1}_K)/K = (P_{\mathrm{KDE}}(z_1), ..., P_{\mathrm{KDE}}(z_K))^T \tag{17}$$

with $(\mathbf{1}_K)$ is a vector of one of size K. With these new notations, problem (15) can be rewritten:

$$\widetilde{\mathbf{w}_{\mathbf{LS}}} = \arg\min_{\tilde{\mathbf{w}}} (\|\Phi_v \, \tilde{\mathbf{w}} - \varphi\|) \tag{18}$$

with Φ_v the reduced matrix where only columns with index in set v are taken from Φ. To find this set v, we choose to keep iteratively, indexes of vectors with the maximum residual likelihood. Algorithm 1 is fully described by a two step recursive process:

Algorithm 1 Non parametric estimator approximation algorithm

Require: matrix Φ, stopping criterium Q_l
Likelihood vector computation: $\varphi_1 = K^{-1}\Phi \times \mathbf{1}_K$
Initialisation: $m = 0$
repeat
Maximum likelihood index extraction: $v(m) = \underset{i}{argmax}\, \varphi_{m,i}$
Computation of weight vector $\tilde{\mathbf{w}}_m$ solution of problem 18
Likelihood vector update $\varphi_{m+1} = \varphi_m - \Phi_v \, \tilde{\mathbf{w}}_m$
$m = m + 1$
until $\max \varphi_{m+1,i} > h(Q_l)$
return Weight vector $\tilde{\mathbf{w}}_M$ and the selected feature indexes: $\mathbf{v} = (v(1), v(2), ..., v(M))$

Steps one and two are repeated until $\max \varphi_{m+1,i} > h(Q_l)$. The parameter Q_l represents the precision of the likelihood approximation and h is the confidence criterium for the KDE distribution described in section 3.1.3. For a coarse approximation Q_l can be decreased. In this case the number of used vectors decreases. Illustrations of the effect of this parameter are given in section 3.2. This approach enables to give a good approximation of the likelihood with few vectors. Initially, the non parametric model set $\mathbf{Z}$ contained K elements whereas the sparse vector machine model $\widetilde{\mathbf{Z}} = \mathbf{Z}_v$ contains only M elements with $M \ll K$. Let note :

$$\widetilde{\mathbf{Z}} \doteq (\widetilde{\mathbf{z_1}}, \widetilde{\mathbf{z_2}}, ..., \widetilde{\mathbf{z_M}})^T \tag{19}$$

This reduction in size is mandatory since it makes the real-time classification possible.
In practice, the problem solved on equation (15) can be simplified in our case. Instead of solving the least square problem on all observations z_k, we use the same problem only at control points, that is to say on the selected features, $z_{v(k)}$. In this condition equation (15) can be rewritten:

$$\widetilde{\mathbf{w_{LS}}} = \arg\min_{\tilde{\mathbf{w}}} \left(\sum_{k=1}^{M} (\mathbf{w}^T \phi(z_{v(k)})) - \tilde{\mathbf{w}}^T \tilde{\phi}(z_{v(k)})) \right) \tag{20}$$

And with our notation :

$$\widetilde{\mathbf{w_{LS}}} = \arg\min_{\tilde{\mathbf{w}}} (\|\Phi_{v,v}\, \tilde{\mathbf{w}} - \varphi_v\|) \tag{21}$$

with $\Phi_{v,v}$ the reduced matrix where only rows columns with index in set v are taken from Φ. It amounts to solve a square linear system of reduced dimensionality.

3.1.3 Confidence criteria

Intuitively when approximating a likelihood distribution, regions with high probability are expected to be well approximated whereas regions with almost zero probability can be neglected. The problem is to define the threshold from which probabilities can be neglected (cf. figure 8). This problem is easy to solve for simple distribution such as gaussian density. But for more intricate density such as GMM, the problem could not have exact solution anymore. Nevertheless, approximated methods can be used. One solution is to use a confidence criteria (Paalanen et al. (2006)).

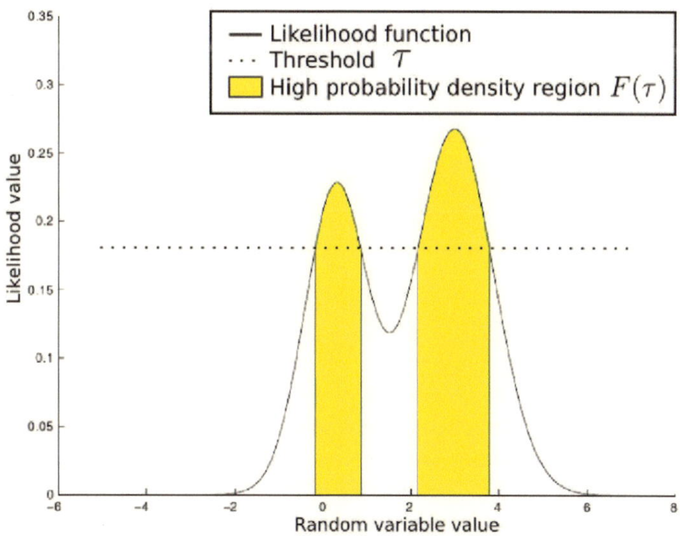

Fig. 8. How threshold τ should be chosen to keep only $F(\tau)\%$ of the highest probability of a given distribution (represented in yellow) ?

Let $F(\tau)$ be the density quantile for a given probability density value τ,

$$F(\tau) = \int_{p(\mathbf{x})\geq\tau} p(\mathbf{x})d\mathbf{x} \tag{22}$$

This density quantile corresponds to the highest density region for density value above τ. A reverse mapping $h(F) = \tau$ can be chosen such as $F \in [0, 1]$ is the density quantile needed (0.9 for 90% of the probability density for example).
The approximating method to solve this problem rely on a Monte Carlo algorithm. Let $X = (\mathbf{x}_1, \mathbf{x}_2, ..., \mathbf{x}_N)$ be N points randomly chosen following distribution p and $p_i = p(\mathbf{x}_i)\ \forall i \in [1, N]$. p_i are then sorted in an ascending order $\mathbf{Y} = (y_1, y_2, ..., y_N)$. This set is used to estimate $F(\tau)$ and $h(F)$ using linear interpolation. Let $i = \underset{i}{argmax}\{y_i | y_i \leq \tau\}$, we get :

$$F(\tau) \approx \begin{cases} 1 - \frac{l(0,\tau)}{N} & if\ \tau < y_1 \\ 0 & if\ \tau \geq y_N \\ 1 - \frac{i+l(i,\tau)}{N} & otherwise \end{cases} \tag{23}$$

with

$$l(i, \tau) = \begin{cases} \frac{\tau}{y_1} & if\ i = 0 \\ 0.5 & if\ y_{i+1} - y_i = 0 \\ \frac{\tau - y_i}{y_{i+1} - y_i} & otherwise \end{cases} \tag{24}$$

The inverse transform $h(F)$ can be deduced by:

$$\tau = h(F) \approx \begin{cases} y_N & if\ i = N \\ (N(1-F))y_1 & if\ i = 0 \\ y_i + (N(1-F) - i)(y_{i+1} - y_i) & otherwise \end{cases} \tag{25}$$

with $i = \lfloor N \times (1 - F) \rfloor$.
This confidence criteria is used as a stopping criteria during the iterative approximation algorithm presented on algorithm 1 but it can also be used to determine the decision function for classification purpose thanks to equation (25). Indeed, in classification context once likelihood density is estimated thanks to SKDE, new observations $\mathbf{Z}$ can be considered as random points drawn from the estimated model, that is to say set X. Quantil parameter F will make detections more or less strict, considering F% of observation belonging to the estimated model.

3.2 Experiments

In this section, we present result of our algorithm with other classical method. Several density estimation approximation algorithm have been tested: the KDE, the SKDA and Figueiredo-Jain EM algorithm. The tests have been done on both synthetic and real datas. For synthetic ones, given a known gaussian mixture, a learning set Z of points are randomly drawn from the known distribution. On the way back, we compare the gaussian mixture retrieved from this learning set Z with the different methods. As a consequence, the kernel chosen for the KDE and all more reason for our method, will be gaussian one.

3.2.1 SKDE parameters influence

First of all, some results concerning simplified approximation of SKDE method expressed with equation (21) and parameters influence, realized on monodimensional synthetic data, can be seen on figures 9. The KDE distribution which is the ground truth of our method has been represented by the black dashed curve. The sparse probability $\widetilde{\mathbf{Z}}$ has been drawn for the original problem approximation of equation (15) and for the simplified one of equation (20). With equal Q_l, the original problem tends to converge oscillating around the true distribution whereas the simplified one, converges toward the KDE distribution without overestimating it. The convergence speed is also shown on figure 10 which represents the Mean Integrated Square Error (MISE) between each approximation and the KDE. We can see on this semilog curves that both methods roughly converge at the same speed. For the rest of the tests the simplified version of the approximation will be used.

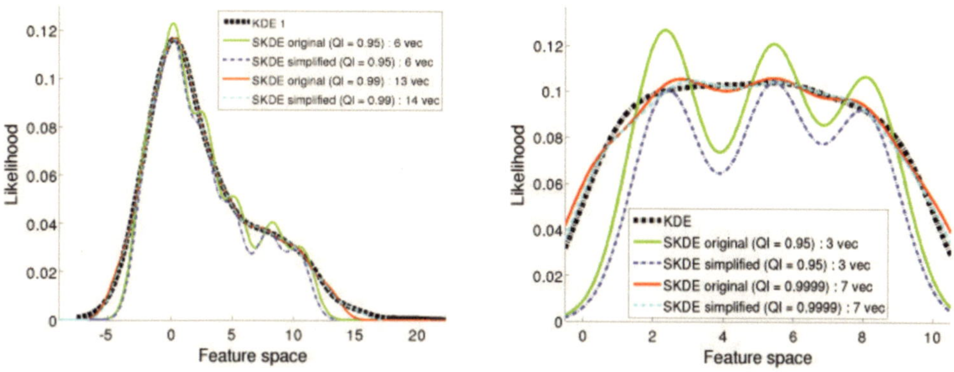

(a) Two gaussians distribution (b) Uniform distribution

Fig. 9. Approximation of the kernel based non parametric density estimation with the original SKDE and simplified one.

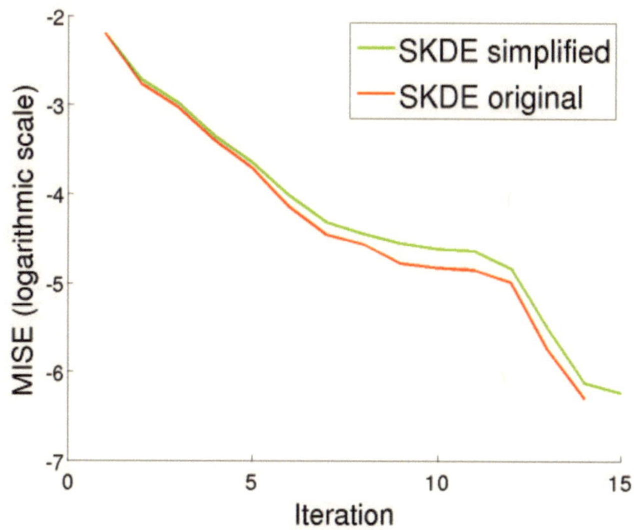

Fig. 10. MISE evolution through iteration process for original SKDE and simplified one.

Concerning the Q_l parameter influence, we can see figures 9 that with low Q_l values the approximation underestimates the distribution for some features (blue curves) whereas cyan curves obtained with a high Q_l fairly well approximate KDE distribution.

3.2.2 Estimation comparative results

We compare the four algorithms in term of precision, sparseness and computation time. The precision is computed thanks to MISE between the true distribution if known (TD) or the KDE distribution. The error is computed only at learning sample locations. Different databases have been used for the comparison, from the monodimensional ones used before to real databases:

- B_1 is drawn from a two gaussian mixtures ($N(0, 2^2, 0.6)$ and $N(7, 4^2, 0.4)$). It contains 3000 monodimensional features.
- B_2 is drawn from a uniform distribution between 1 and 10, it also contains 3000 monodimensional features.
- B_{ripley} containing 2 different classes with 125 2D learning features for each class. Result criteria have been computed on each class separately and averaged.

In order to conveniently compare the different methods, we assume that observations follow a gaussian mixture distribution. As a consequence, the kernel chosen for the KDE and SKDE, will be gaussian one. The comparison results are summed up in table 3. The parameter set for each method are the same than those used in figure 11 for databases B_1 and B_2. They have been chosen in order to have the closest results to the true distribution. For B_{ripley}, the parameter of each method have been chosen in order to have the best classification result as shown in section 3.2.3. Compared to other method, SKDE gives similar results in term of precision. As expected, we are very close to KDE distribution since it is the refered distribution. Concerning the number of support vectors kept, we largely reduced the KDE model, but we generally keep more vectors than SKDA or EM method. The reason is the kernel fixed bandwidth, that may need several gaussians for approximating a unique one with larger bandwith whereas SKDA or EM method will just adapt the bandwidth. On more difficult distribution such as uniform one which are not easily approximated by gaussian mixture, we see that our method fits quite well to the true distribution. For the learning computation time, the time given in number of cycles, should be taken with care. All the algorithm have been run under Matlab, the times presented are given for information only since algorithms coding are not necessarily optimized and EM algorithm complexity is unknown. The SKDA has a linear time complexity and it is clearly the fastest method but also the less accurate which is the exact opposite of EM algorithm. SKDE method is balanced between the two. Most of SKDE computation time is due to the Φ computation which is $O(K^2)$. Concerning B_{ripley} database, no true distribution is known. As a consequence, the comparison is done with KDE distribution. The very large MISE of EM algorithm are not due to wrong gaussian means but to overestimation. Moreover, our method with a coarse approximation (only 2 vectors kept) still gives comparable results with other methods.

A graphical representation is given on figure 11. The true distribution, that is to say the original gaussian mixture from which the learning observation have been drawn, is represented with the black dashed curve. Note that, the KDE distribution does not necessarily fit perfectly the true distribution. Theoretically the KDE converges to the true distribution for an infinite number of observations, whatever kernel bandwidth. Here the learning set is 3000 features long. As a consequence, the bandwidth selection is very important. For the moment this bandwidth is experimentally chosen. It should be large enough to avoid the KDE

Databases	Method s	MISE / TD	MISE / KDE	Support vectors	Computation time
B_1	KDE	$7.02e^{-5}$		3000	
	SKDE	$6.93e^{-5}$	$\mathbf{6.71e^{-7}}$	14	4.23
	SKDA	$4.31e^{-4}$	$2.76e^{-4}$	**2**	**0.13**
	EM	$\mathbf{8.13e^{-6}}$	$3.1e^{-5}$	**2**	163.06
B_2	KDE	$2.64e^{-4}$		3000	
	SKDE	$2.8e^{-4}$	$\mathbf{6.6e^{-6}}$	7	4.3
	SKDA	$1.76e^{-3}$	$1.22e^{-3}$	1	**0.13**
	EM	$\mathbf{1.8e^{-4}}$	$3.65e^{-4}$	7	180.12
B_{ripley}	KDE			150	
	SKDE		$\mathbf{2.2e^{-3}}$	2	**0.005**
	SKDA		$3.8e^{-3}$	**1**	**0.0005**
	EM		1.75	3	0.237

Table 3. Learning results. Each methods is evaluated on different criteria: MISE compared to true distribution, MISE compared to KDE, number of support vectors and learning computation time expressed in billion of clock cycle.

distribution to look like a Dirac comb, each pseudo Dirac being the gaussian of a learning feature, but also not too large in order not to melt different modes in one. We can see on the two mode distribution that except for SKDA, the other methods are quite similar and have roughly found the two modes. The second one is just slightly underestimated. On the uniform distribution, EM gives an oscillating approximation whereas SKDA approximate the square by a very large gaussian which is not acceptable. Our method fit quite well to KDE as expected.

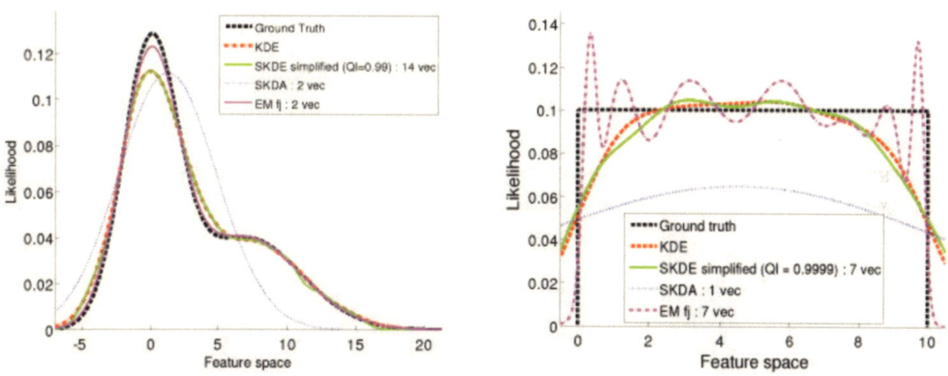

(a) Two gaussians distribution (b) Uniform distribution

Fig. 11. Density estimation algorithm comparison.

3.2.3 Classification comparative results

This section propose to test our likelihood approximation in a learning machine context. The classification decision rule for all the method is the same, deduce from confidence criteria presented in section 3.1.3 to take into account likelihood distribution kurtosis. B_{ripley} database has been used for this comparison. The learning has been done on each class separately and tested on a thousand features, half from one class and half from the other one. The ROC

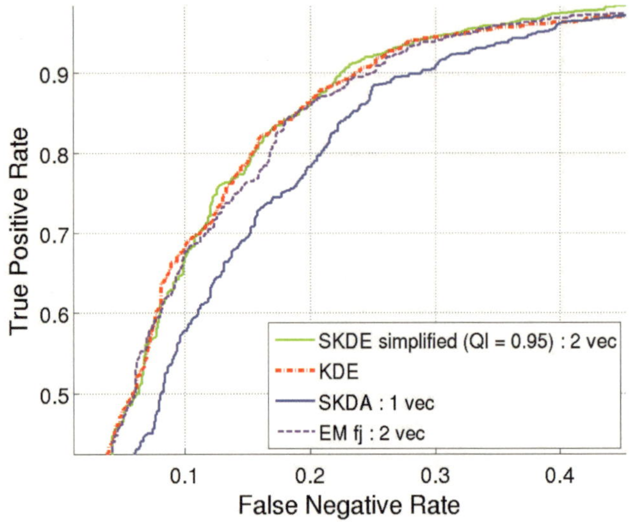

Fig. 12. ROC curves comparison.

curves on figure 12 show that the proposed method gives the best classification results with a reasonable number of control points (2 points).

4. Global experiments

4.1 Quantitative results

Giving quatified performances for such a kind of system is a difficult task. If a wrong way movement is clearly an anomality, other deviating movements can be harder to classify. Anyway, in order to give quantitative results we define permissive ground truth. We say permissive because defining exactly which blocks to consider as abnormal for every frames is impossible. Is shadow part of the anomaly ? What about neighbouring blocks ? etc. (cf. figure 13(a)). As a consequence the defined ground truth is spatially blurred on purpose (cf. firefighter truck going wrong way on figure 13(b)) but also temporally because first, defining the exact frame an event begins or ends is impossible.

(a) How to define groung truth ? (b) Ground truth example. (c) Augmented reality example.

Fig. 13. Evaluation database creation and definition.

With such a ground truth, we choose to make a frame counting for good detection and false alarms. ROC curves will be used for comparing descriptors and decision functions. A true positve is raised when at least one block in the ground truth is considered as abnormal at time t and one false positive when the block is outside the ground truth. Note that with the temporal blurring on ground truth definition, the true positive rate is decreased. **The ROC curves are not really well-shaped but since ground truth is the same for all the appoaches, comparing ROC curves is still valid.**

Roc curves have been drawn on a synthetic database with artifical events. Real sequences of a complex crossroad have been used for inserting a textured object following a user-defined trajectories (cf. figure 13(c)). The inserted object respect the scene perspective but is not photo-realistic since no 3D model of the scene was available. 15 abnormal trajectories with 9 different textures have been used, for creating a total of 135 video containing abnormal behaviours, that is to say about half an hour. Videos are 320x240 size at 12 fps. Trainings have been done on 33 real videos of 30 seconds each, with various illumination and weather conditions. Decision functions have been computed on another 24 real videos representing normal situations.

First of all, the influence of the decision function, the confidence threshold is compared with a fix threshold for all the blocks. The same descriptor (SSC) is used with SKDE as a machine learning. We can see on figure 14 that confidence threshold (red plain curve) improve classification results compared to a static threshold (blue dashed curve). Adapting detection threshold depending on the distribution shape is usefull to lower detection sensibility on area where movement is not well-defined (every direction may be seen) and to raise it in the opposite case. The improvement in classification context for the proposed descriptor is also shown on figure 15. SSC descriptor (red plain curve) has been compared with traditional optical flow features (blue dashed curve). The main orientation per block for optical flow feature is obtained with SKDE process ensuring to keep only the first found control point ($\tilde{K} = 1$). Once again, the proposed descriptor improves the classification task, decreasing ponctual false alarms and smoothing the detections. Only SSC descriptor will be used in the rest of these tests.

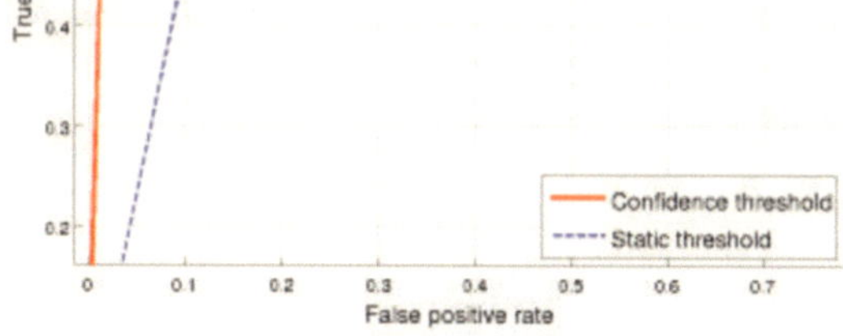

Fig. 14. ROC curves comparison between confidence threshold and static theshold decision function.

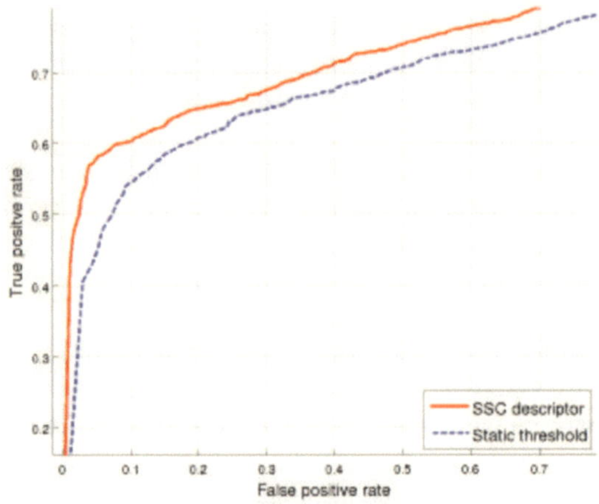

Fig. 15. ROC curves comparison between descriptors.

In order to evaluate the proposed algorithm in a more realistic context, we defined an event alarm when at least one bloc per frame is classified as abnormal on K consecutive frames, in the same neighbourhood. This filtering remove the remaining ponctual false alarms and give a more robust answer since an event usually lasts several seconds and propagates from one bloc to the adjacent ones. A diturbance rate is also defined as the coresponding false alarm rate with such a filtering.
For example, with $K = 8$ the proposed system is able to detect up to 70% of right event detection from a total of 145 events among the 135 videos analysed. With such a detection rate, the disturbance rate is less than $0,2\%$, representing less than 2 wrong alarms per hour on average. Such performances fit well with a video assistance system requirements, that is to say beeing able to detect most of the main problems while ensuring a low false alarm rate which can be very annoying for operators.

4.2 Qualitative results

To describe what kind of event can be detected thanks to the proposed application framework, different examples of detections in various illimination (indoor/outdoor sequence) and weather conditions are presented on figure 16. We can see that various events can be detected such as jaywalkers, wrong way movement, argument between people, etc. Conditions can be very different in terms of illumination with night detections in particularly hard conditions but also in term of population or traffic density with wrong way pedestrian detections in marathon crowd for example.

5. Conclusion

Crowded scenes are particularly difficult to analyse because of the large amount of information to be processed simultaneously and the complexity of the scenes. Tracking based systems cannot handle numerous targets at the same time. In this paper we consider the crowd as a whole. We propose a new framework that cut the problem in two, the movement characterisation and the learning and classifying procedure. Two main contributions can be pointed out.

Fig. 16. Example of detection such as jaywalkers, wrong way movement, car pulling out or chaotic movement due to people argument, etc. All the arrows respect the color legend given in the first on the top left image. Ground truth for each scene is represented with large arrows.

The first one is a new method of movement characterisation. We study the global scene movement thanks to a new descriptor based on a spatio-temporal structure. This descriptor outperforms other spatio-temporal descriptors studied in terms of movement separation. Moreover, it is invariant to affine illumination changes which is particularly usefull when treating outdoor sequences.

The second main contribution of this paper is a new framework for modelling motion pattern of any scene with structured motion. The proposed framework relies on a new density estimation method which is a sparse representation of the KDE distribution, adapted to real-time evaluations. This method gives results of same quality as other classical algorithms aiming at retrieving gaussian mixture parameters, but with a better compromise between precision, sparseness of the model and time computation.

Moreover, our approach requires neither camera calibration nor any 3D scene model, the learning phase is unsupervised and thus the framework applies to a large number of scenes such as outdoor or indoor areas, traffic or crowd monitoring, etc. It works under various illumination and weather conditions but also with various population or traffic density. It can reveal subtle perturbations in the global motion, such as wrong ways or movement deviations, jaywalkers dangerous behaviours or chaotic movements due to abnormal interactions between people of a crowd when they are arguing for example.

Currently, we are investigating temporal and spatial consistency in movement propagation through more sophisticated modelisation. We are also studying block size adaptation with a multiscale approach in order to adapt automatically to both scale change due to strong perspective projections or large movements that should need a lower resolution to be perceived conveniently.

6. References

Adam, A., Rivlin, E., Shimshoni, I. & Reinitz, D. (2008). Robust real-time unusual event detection using multiple fixed-location monitors, IEEE *Transactions on Pattern Analysis and Machine Intelligence* **30**(3): 555–560.

Andrade, E. & Blunsden, S.and Fisher, R. (2006). Hidden markov models for optical flow analysis in crowds, *Proceedings of the International Conference on Pattern Recognition*, Vol. 1, pp. 460–463.

Bardet, F., Chateau, T. & Ramasasan, D. (2009). Illumination aware mcmc particle filter for long-term outdoor multi-object simultaneous tracking and classification, *Proceedings of the International Conference on Computer Vision.*

Barron, J., Fleet, D., Beauchemin, S. & Burkitt, T. (1992). Performance of optical flow techniques, *Proceedings of the International Conference on Computer Vision and Pattern Recognition*, Vol. 92, pp. 236–242.

Black, M. & Anandan, P. (1996). The robust estimation of multiple motions: Parametric and piecewise-smooth flow fields, *Computer Vision and Image Understanding* **63**(1): 75–104.

Blunsden, S., Andrade, E. & Fisher, R. (2007). Non parametric classification of human interaction, *Pattern Recognition and Image Analysis*, pp. 347–354.

Breitenstein, M., Grabner, H. & Van Gool, L. (2009). Hunting nessie: Real time abnormality detection from webcams, *Proceedings of the International Conference on Computer Vision - Workshop on Visual Surveillance.*

Brostow, G. & Cipolla, R. (2006). Unsupervised bayesian detection of independant motion in crowds, *Proceedings of the International Conference on Computer Vision and Pattern Recognition.*

Chan, A. & Vasconcelos, N. (2008). Modeling, clustering, and segmenting video with mixtures of dynamic textures, IEEE *Transactions on Pattern Analysis and Machine Intelligence* **30**: 909–926.

Dee, H. & Velastin, S. (2008). How close are we to solving the problem of automated visual surveillance ? : A review of real-world surveillance, scientific progress and evaluative mechanisms, *Machine Vision Applications* **19**(5-6): 329–343.

Dempster, A., Laird, N. & Rubin, D. (1977). Maximum likelihood from incomplete data via the em algorithm (with discussion), *Royal Statistical Society* **B 39**: 1–38.

Duda, R., Hart, P. & Stork, D. (2001). *Pattern Classification*, John Wiley & Sons Inc.

Figueiredo, M. & Jain, A. (2002). Unsupervised learning of finite mixture models, IEEE *Transactions on Pattern Analysis and Machine Intelligence* **24**: 381–396.

Han, B., Comaniciu, D., Zhu, Y. & Davis, L. (2008). Sequential kernel density approximation and its application to real-time visual tracking, IEEE *Transactions on Pattern Analysis and Machine Intelligence* **30**: 1186–1197.

Harris, C. & Stephens, M. (1988). A combined corner and edge detector, *Proceedings of the Alvey Vision Conference*, pp. 147–151.

Horn, B. & Schunck, B. (1981). Determining optical flow, *Artificial Intelligence* **17**: 185–203.

Hu, W., Xiao, X., Fu, Z., Xie, D., Tan, T. & Maybank, S. (2006). A system for learning statistical motion patterns, IEEE *Transactions on Pattern Analysis and Machine Intelligence* **28**: 1450–1464.

Junejo, I. & Foroosh, H. (2007). Trajectory rectification and path modeling for video surveillance, *Proceedings of the International Conference on Computer Vision.*

Kratz, L. & Nishimo, K. (2010). Tracking with local spatio-temporal motion patterns in extremely crowded scenes, *Proceedings of the International Conference on Computer Vision and Pattern Recognition.*

Kratz, L. & Nishino, K. (2009). Anomaly detection in extremely crowded scenes using spatio-temporal motion pattern models, *Proceedings of the International Conference on Computer Vision and Pattern Recognition*, pp. 1446–1453.

Küttel, D., Breitenstein, M., Van Gool, L. & Ferrari, V. (2010). What's going on ? discovering spatio-temporal dependencies in dynamic scenes, *Proceedings of the International Conference on Computer Vision and Pattern Recognition.*

Langford, E., Schwertman, N. & Owens, M. (2001). Is the property of being positively correlated transitive ?, *The American Statistician* **55(4)**: 322–325.

Lucas, B. & Kanade, T. (1981). An iterative image registration technique with an application to stereo vision, *Proceedings of the International Joint Conference on Artificial Intelligence*, pp. 674–679.

Mahadevan, V., Li, W., Bhalodia, V. & Vasconcelos, N. (2010). Anomaly detection in crowded scenes, *Proceedings of the International Conference on Computer Vision and Pattern Recognition.*

Mehran, R., Oyama, A. & Shah, M. (2009). Abnormal crowd behavior detection using social force model, *Proceedings of the International Conference on Computer Vision and Pattern Recognition*, Vol. 0, pp. 935–942.

Oliver, N., Rosario, B. & Pentland, A. (2000). A bayesian computer vision system for modeling human interactions, IEEE *Transactions on Pattern Analysis and Machine Intelligence* **22**: 831–843.

Paalanen, P., Kamarainen, J., Ilonen, J. & Kälviäinen, H. (2006). Feature representation and discrimination based on gaussian mixture model probability densities : Practices and algorithms, *Pattern Recognition* **39**: 1346–1358.

Pham, Q., Gond, L., Begard, J., Allezard, N. & Sayd, P. (2007). Real time posture analysis in a crowd using thermal imaging, *Proceedings of the International Conference on Computer Vision and Pattern Recognition.*

Rabaud, V. & Belongie, S. (2006). Counting crowded moving objects, *Proceedings of the International Conference on Computer Vision and Pattern Recognition.*

Saad, A. & Shah, M. (2007). A lagrangian particle dynamics approach for crowd flow segmentation and stability analysis, *Proceedings of the International Conference on Computer Vision and Pattern Recognition.*

Saleemi, I., Shafique, K. & Shah, M. (2008). Probabilistic modeling of scene dynamics for applications in visual surveillance, IEEE *Transactions on Pattern Analysis and Machine Intelligence* **PP, Issue 99**: 1–1.

Shechtman, E. & Irani, M. (2005). Space-time behaviour based correlation, *Proceedings of the International Conference on Computer Vision and Pattern Recognition.*

Sidla, O. & Lypetskyy, Y. (2006). Pedestrian detection and tracking for counting applications in crowded situations, *Proceedings of the International Conference on Advanced Video and Signal Based Surveillance.*

Stauffer, C. & Grimson, W. (2000). Learning patterns of activity using real-time tracking, IEEE *Transactions on Pattern Analysis and Machine Intelligence* **22**: 747–757.

Tyagi, A., Keck, M., Davis, J. & Potamianos, G. (2007). Kernel-based 3d tracking, *Proceedings of the International Conference on Computer Vision and Pattern Recognition*.

Varadarajan, J. & Odobez, J. (2009). Topic models for scene analysis and abnormality detection, *Proceedings of the International Conference on Computer Vision - Workshop on Visual Surveillance*, Kyoto.

Wang, X., Ma, X. & Grimson, W. (2009). Unsupervised activity perception in crowded and complicated scenes using hierarchical bayesian models, IEEE *Transactions on Pattern Analysis and Machine Intelligence* **31**(1): 539–555.

Wang, X., Tieu, K. & Grimson, W. (2010). Correspondence-free activity analysis and scene modeling in multiple camera views, IEEE *Transactions on Pattern Analysis and Machine Intelligence* **32**(1): 56–71.

Wu, S., Moore, B. & Shah, M. (2010). Chaotic invariants of lagrangian particle trajectories for anomaly detection in crowded scenes, *Proceedings of the International Conference on Computer Vision and Pattern Recognition*.

Yu, Q. & Medioni, G. (2009). Multiple-target tracking by spatiotemporal monte carlo markov chain data association, IEEE *Transactions on Pattern Analysis and Machine Intelligence* **31**(12): 2196–2210.

Zhan, B., Monekosso, D., Remagnino, P., Velastin, S. & Xu, L. (2008). Crowd analysis: A survey, *Machine Vision Applications* **19**: 345–357.

Zhao, T. & Nevatia, R. (2004). Tracking multiple humans in complex situations, IEEE *Transactions on Pattern Analysis and Machine Intelligence* **26**: 1208–1221.

Zhong, Z., Yang, M. & Wang, S. (2007). Energy methods for crowd surveillance, *Proceedings of the International Conference on Information Acquisition*, pp. 504–510.

18

Automatic Scenario Recognition for Visual-Surveillance by Combining Probabilistic Graphical Approaches

Ahmed Ziani and Cina Motamed
Laboratoire LISIC, Université du Littoral Côte d'Opale, France

1. Introduction

The online recognition and indexing of video-surveillance sequence is firstly helpful for video-surveillance operator for an on-line alarm generation by highlighting abnormal situation. The second utility concerns the off-line retrieval of specific behavior from a stored image sequence in order to discover causes of an alarm. This capability becomes naturally more powerful when the monitoring concerns a network of IP-camera over a wide area or the Internet.

The scenario recognition also known as activity recognition is an old and still active topic in computer science and several complementary approaches have been proposed by the Computer vision and the Artificial Intelligence communities. A scenario is composed on a set of elementary events linked with temporal constraints. The difficulty of human activity lies in their complexity, their spatial and temporal variability and also the uncertainty existing over the whole interpretation task. The computer vision approaches are generally focused on numerical approach by using probabilistic (Bui et al., 2004) (Hongeng et al., 2000) (Rabiner, 1989) or neural network (Howell & Buxton, 2002) approach in order to deal with uncertainty of the low level vision tasks. On the other hand, the Artificial Intelligence community has proposed more flexible symbolic approaches permitting a high level recognition capability (Tessier, 2003) (Vu et al., 2003) (Dousson & Maigat, 2007). Our main contribution in this work concerns the integration of these two complementary approaches (probabilistic and symbolic) in the global scenario recognition system.

HHMs (Hidden Markov Model) are the most popular probabilistic approach in representing dynamic systems. They have been initially used in speech recognition (Rabiner, 1989) and successfully applied over gesture or activity recognition (Starner & Pentland, 1995). An interesting feature of HMM is its time scale invariance enabling activity with various speeds. Other extensions to the basic HMM have also been used such as the Coupled Hidden Markov Models (CHMMs) for modelling human interactions (Oliver et al., 2000), and variable length Markov models (VLMMs) to locally optimize the size of behavior models (Galata et al., 2001).

However Bayesian networks have also been widely used in the computer vision community for object, event or scenario recognition. One important advantage of the Bayesian network is its ability to encode both qualitative and quantitative contextual knowledge, and their dependence.

The time aspect in probabilistic domain has led to several approaches. The first category is known as "time-slice" approach. The main technique is the Dynamic Bayesian networks (Dean & Kanazawa, 1999). DBN which can be considered as an extension of Bayesian networks, is a generalization of both Hidden Markov Models (HMM) and technique based on linear dynamical system such as Kalman filters. It assumes a Markov property by considering that a single snapshot in the past is sufficient for predicting the future.
A second category, represents the "event-based approach" also known as the "interval based approach", which allows the integration of specific nodes associated to temporal information like in (Figueroa, 1999) by the Temporal Nodes Bayesian Networks (TNBN), or Net of Irreversible Events in Discrete Time (NIEDT) (Galan & Diez, 2000). In these networks, nodes represent events that can take place at a certain time interval. A state of the node is defined as being the event outcome and the time interval at which the event is occurred.
In our context of video based scenario recognition, generally many scenarios have to be recognized, and it is important to control efficiently the system resources by using an active perception strategy (Bajcsy, 1998). In other term, the system has to focus its attention only on a set of "active scenario" with respect to the current scene behaviors.
In our opinion, in the context of scenarios based on asynchronous events, the event-based approach seems to be more appropriate and intuitive with respect to the time slice approaches. In fact, the event-based approach permits naturally to develop an active perception strategy by controlling the recognition tasks when it is necessary and in particular when a change over a node is perceived. The event based approach is also particularly relevant when the system has to manage the notion of time at several temporal granularities. In fact, the time-sliced approach adds unnecessary complexity to the network because the networks are repeated for each time slice. In the context of scenario recognition, one other main limitation of time slice approaches as DBN or standard HMM, is that there is no way to naturally represent interval-based concept: as an event e1 appears with an event e2 and finish before the end of e2. However, several extensions of HHM have been developed in order to add explicitly such time constraints. First extension concerns the hierarchical temporal structure of the HMM. In such organization, long-term layers are designed for modeling higher-level activities evolving at slower timescales. The second extension is the semi-Markov model including explicit duration HMMs. In these models, a state remains unchanged for some duration before its transition to a new state.
The proposed recognition system integrates three main layers and uses an agent based approach. This first layer in based on agents focused on basic events (Section 3). The second layer contains agents which integrate the temporal reasoning capability by using an interval based approach (section 4). The third layer combines the results of agents of the previous layers.

2. Proposed recognition algorithm

The standard approach in automatic visual surveillance is to model normal scenarios and then the system has to recognize if the current activity is normal (dangerous or safe) or unknown.
A scenario is defined by a set of events and contains in particular its start event. Each event recognition process is considered as an autonomous logical agent. A set of start event detectors are permanently in action and permits to the system to activate specific agents of the awaited scenarios. The start events are for example, "*a door is opening*", "*a car entering*", "*a pedestrian starts a specific trajectory*" etc...

Each specific scenario controls the execution of its useful event detectors and verifies their responses. However some detectors have the possibility to be in common with other scenarios and may be previously activated.
The partial recognition strategy based on the notion of start event brings an efficient predictive capability for the high level scenario agents in order to prepare the activation of its future awaited events.

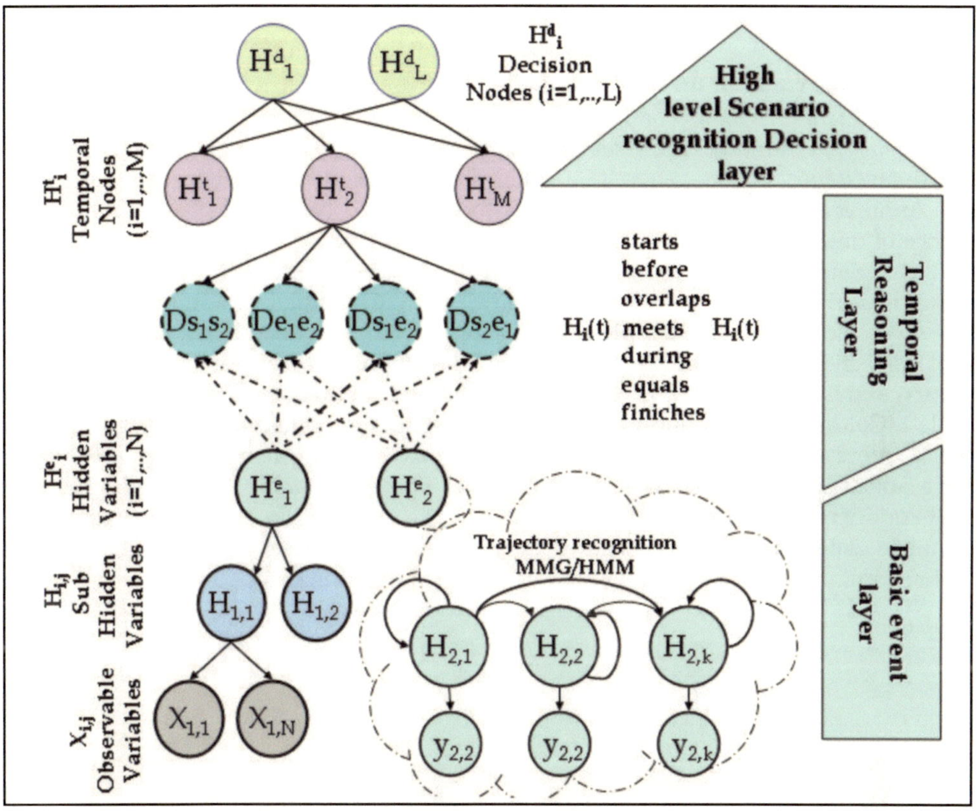

Fig. 1. Global architecture of the scenario model

The proposed approach uses probabilistic network and combines event based and HHM techniques. The system mainly takes the advantage of an event based approaches as a flexible temporal reasoning capability and it uses conventional time slice approaches for the trajectory recognition task. The global structure of the proposed network is based on the concept of the Hierarchical Bayesian Networks (fig. 1)

3. The basic events layer

3.1 Basic events with Bayesian network

The first layer the system has to recognize events as "running", "inside zone Z_i ", to detect interaction between objects as "object O_i meets objet O_j " or to recognize the trajectory of the object. Generally basic events are represented by a Bayesian network. However the trajectories recognition event is built over an hmm approach. The qualitative structure of the basic events based on Bayesian networks is defined by hand and the conditional

probabilities are adjusted easily by a learning procedure with a training data set in a supervised manner.
Generally, it is possible to learn the network parameters, from the experimental data, and in particular, the conditional probabilities parameters.

$$P\left(X_i = x_k \middle| parent(X_i) = c_j\right) = \theta_{i,j,k} = \frac{n_{i,j,k}}{\sum_k n_{i,j,k}} \quad (1)$$

Where $n_{i,j,k}$ is the count of the events in the learning database for which variable X_i is in the state x_k and its parents are in configuration c_j.
Unfortunately, in the context of visual-surveillance, it is not realistic to perform the standard learning procedure. In fact, generally it is not possible to have enough occurrences for each event. Another difficulty is that the learning process has to deal with uncertain inputs. In the presence of missing values or hidden variables, parameters for a known network structure from incomplete data can be estimated by the Expectation-Maximization (EM) algorithm.
We use the EM algorithm to learn the first layer network parameters. In order to illustrate this process, we present an example of a sub-network from an abandoned baggage scenario model used in our experiments (fig. 2). This sub-network is based on a 'naïve' Bayesian Network, and is composed by three nodes. The data collection used for learning is presented in table 1. Column "Count" shows the occurrence of a set of nodes values configuration. The value '?' represents the notion of incomplete or missing data. It highlights the situations when a node can not estimate its value. Such information is obtained by introducing a kind of self-confidence factor for the specific low-level detectors. By taking into account the incomplete data with the EM algorithm, the system naturally integrates some of the detectors limitations without reducing the quantity of learning data.

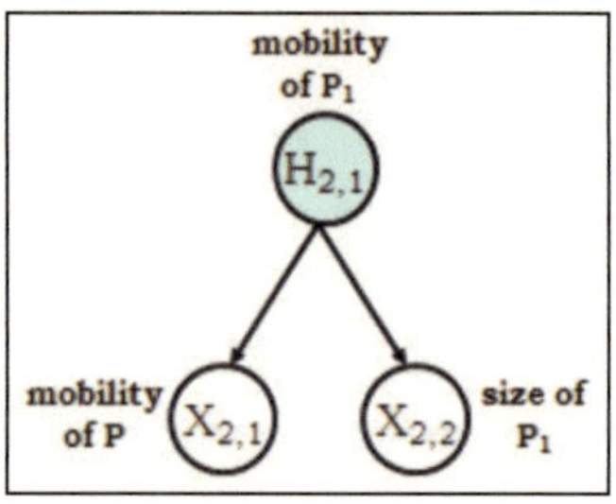

Fig. 2. An example of a naive Bayesian network

X2,1	X2,2	H2,1	Count
1	1	1	18
1	1	0	1
0	1	0	3
1	0	0	2
?	1	1	1
1	?	1	2
0	0	0	14
0	?	0	3

Table 1. A table of occurrence for the learning process

The EM algorithm is initialized with $P^{(0)}(H_{2,1}=1)=0.5$ and $P^{(0)}(H_{2,1}=0)=0.5$. Table 2 shows the evolution of the joint probabilities for the 1st and 2nd iteration. The convergence is obtained after the 13th iteration: $P^{(13)}(X_{2,1}=1 \mid H_{2,1}=1)=0.857$ and $P^{(13)}(X_{2,2}=1 \mid H_{2,1}=0)=0.985$. Figure 3 shows the evolution of these probabilities during the learning process.

Iterations		$X_{2,1}=0$	$X_{2,1}=1$	$X_{2,2}=0$	$X_{2,2}=1$
1	$H_{2,1}=0$	0.50	0.49	0.39	0.60
1	$H_{2,1}=1$	0.45	0.54	0.44	0.56
2	$H_{2,1}=0$	0.48	0.51	0.41	0.58
2	$H_{2,1}=1$	0.47	0.52	0.43	0.57

Table 2. Iterations of EM

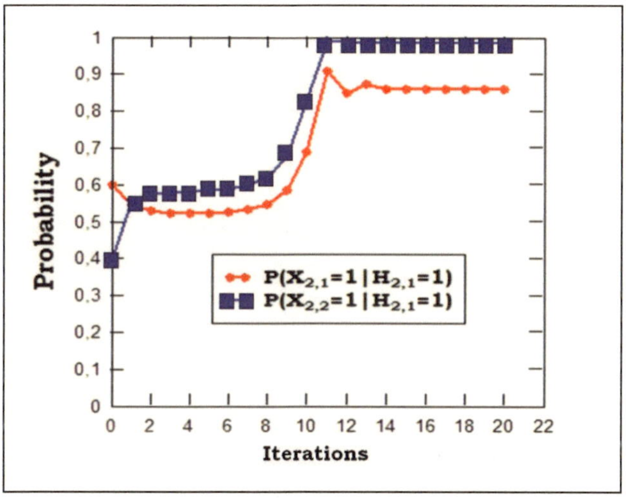

Fig. 3. Evolution of the estimated probabilities

3.2 The trajectory recognition

The trajectory recognition task represents an important feature of our scenario recognition system. It integrates a Hidden Markov Models (HMM) approach which is well adapted for sequential data recognition. The core of the proposed algorithm uses the approach of (Porikli, 2004) for modeling the trajectories and their temporal evolution. The feature vector representing a trajectory T_j is the vector containing the N successive values of object position $W=(x,y)$: $O_N = (W_1,..., W_N)$. Then a more compact representation of trajectory based on a vector quantization is built. It is based on a standard K-Means algorithm and it classifies trajectories into K clusters such that some metric relative to the centers of the clusters is minimized. The main drawback of the standard k-means concerns the number of cluster that should be known a priori. We have used an automatic estimation of this number for each trajectory model. The algorithm computes the mean length for each of trajectory collection in the image coordinate space. For a specific and controlled environment, the length estimation can be also obtained in the real coordinate by using a standard homography transformation. Then the number k of cluster is defined proportionally with

this length. This strategy permits a specific vector quantization by taking account the complexity of each trajectory model.
We have developed a predictive trajectory recognition algorithm in adequacy with the active strategy of the global scenario recognition. It permits to focus the recognition on the relevant trajectories and in the same manner to help the system to remove non plausible scenarios. The recognition is based on a recursive partial recognition of trajectory from their starts (sub-trajectory).
The HMM based recognition takes into account a set of learning data for each trajectory collection. At each instant the system uses partially these data with respect to the set of cluster that the object has crossed for each trajectory collection.
The conditional observation distribution model is based on a mixture of Gaussian (GMM). The Expectation-Maximization algorithm is used for computing the parameters of a parametric mixture model distribution GMM.
The main characteristic of our algorithm is the use a distance between current sub-trajectory and the sub-trajectories used for learning of each model of trajectory (trajectory collection). In order to compare two Hmm models of sub-trajectories λ_1 and λ_2, the similarity measure proposed by (Starner & Pentland, 1995) is used:

$$D_s(\lambda_1,\lambda_2)=\frac{1}{2}[D(\lambda_1,\lambda_2)+D(\lambda_2,\lambda_1)] \tag{2}$$

With

$$D(\lambda_1,\lambda_2)=\frac{1}{n_2}\left[\log P(S_{o_2}\mid\lambda_1)+\log P(S_{o_2}\mid\lambda_2)\right] \tag{3}$$

Where $S_{oj}=W1,W2,\ldots,W_{nj}$ and $P(S_{oj}\mid\lambda_j)$ represents the probability of observation of S_{oj} by the model λ_i. n_j is the length of the trajectory λ_j (number of states).
For each $collection_i$ of trajectories (length $\{l\}$), $T_{i,k,l}(k=1,\ldots,N)$, represents the set of HMM models linked with sub-trajectory used for learning. The algorithm estimates a distance: DM obtained by the mean of distances between current trajectory T_c and all the sub-trajectory $T_{i,k,l}$ of the $collection_i$.

$$DM(T_c,collection_i)=\frac{\sum_k D_s(T_c,T_{i,k,l})}{card(collection_i)} \tag{4}$$

The collection of trajectories which obtains the lowest distance DM with the trajectory T_c is chosen as the most likely predictive trajectory model. The figure 4 shows an illustration of trajectory prediction situation (Pets'2004 dataset). The prediction rate of the trajectory with the length $\{l\}$ is defined with the respect of the total number (n_f) of states in each collection:

$$P_{prediction}(T_c)=\frac{1}{n_f}P(S(o)|\lambda_l) \tag{5}$$

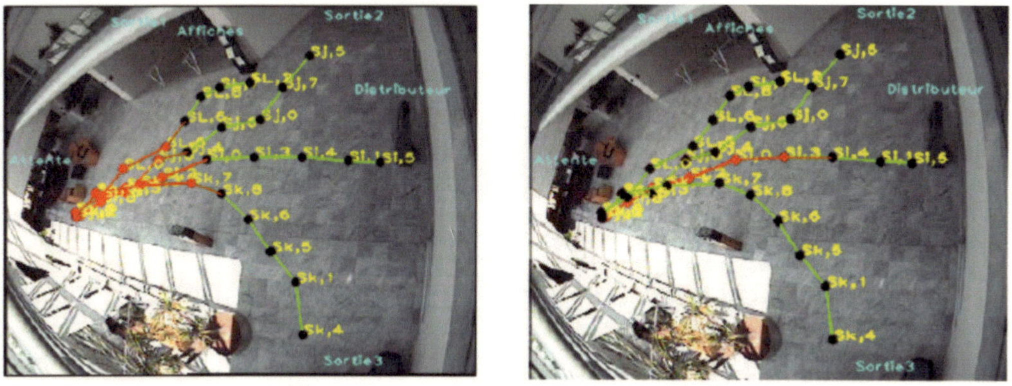

(t) (t+2)

Fig. 4. An illustration of predictive trajectory recognition at instants t and t+2

4. Temporal reasoning layer

The temporal reasoning layer uses explicitly the event-based approach. The objective of the proposed temporal layer is to evaluate temporal constraints for each event and also to estimate relations between coexisting events. The temporal constraints represent the duration of existence (relative or absolute) of an event. Relations between events reveal their mutual temporal dependency (before, after, during etc..).

The proposed temporal reasoning layer is based on a set of Bayesian networks and lies explicitly on the event-based approach. This approach is inspired by the work of (Burns & Morrison, 2003) in the context of Artificial Intelligence. It permits to incorporate temporal reasoning in a Bayesian blackboard system called *AIID*: Architecture for the Interpretation of Intelligence Data.

The temporal layer operates on the "start" and "end" time of each event (H_i from the first layer). For this, the network contains specific leaf nodes exploiting the lifespan of the events (duration of existence) estimated by the first layer. The tracking of the degree of belief of a hypothesis permits to detect its "Start" and "End" time. These time points are obtained by specific detectors operating on the temporal signal of the value of belief $H_i(t)$. In order to avoid false detection, the original signal has been filtered by a smoothing operator (fig. 5). Each start or end time is represented by a normal distribution approximated by its mean and variance values. It permits to propagate the uncertainty of these time estimations over the temporal layer. The start date (respectively the end time) is obtained once the probability of the hypothesis is higher (lower, respectively) than 80%. The variance of the time estimator is fixed off-line for each category of event and is obtained by a supervised learning procedure. It exploits N events for each category and compares ground-true duration with the results of the detector (N>10, in our experiments).

Then temporal relationships between the lifespan of events H_1 and H_2 are estimated by using a generic network structure called Temporal Relation Network TRN. This network has to check the temporal relation $H^t_{1,2}$ between two events H_1 and H_2. Its general structure is defined in figure 6. For each relation, a TRN needs four specific nodes Ds_1s_2, De_1e_2, Ds_1e_2 and Ds_2e_1 which verify the temporal positions of the two events based and their start (s_i) and end times (e_i). The signification of these nodes is detailed in the table 3 for each temporal relation. A signed distance D(A,B) between two time points A and B is computed. It uses

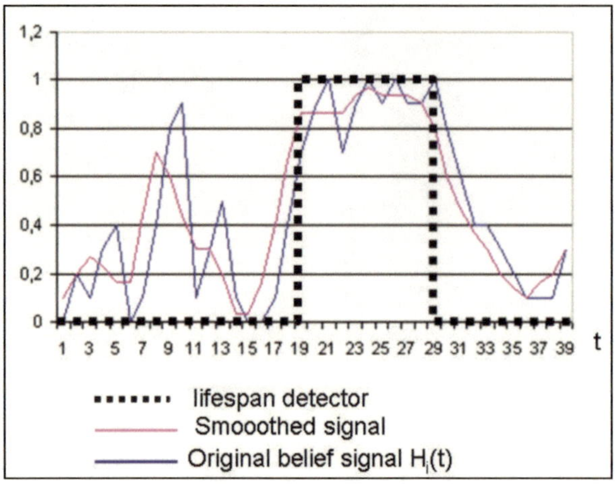

Fig. 5. Illustration of the lifespan detector based on the event belief signal

firstly the Mahalanobis distance for the normal distributions, and then the sign is obtained directly by estimating the difference between the means of the normal distributions. This signed distance permits to rank two time points by taking into account their temporal uncertainty.

In the case of the TRN "H1 equals H2" (table 3), the node Ds_1s_2 verifies the notion of start times equality of the events H_1 and H_2, ($s_i = s_2$) and the node De_1e_2 verifies the end times equality of the events. In this example, the node Ds_1s_2 is true when the signed distance $D(s_1,s_2)=0$.

The inference over the TRN uses explicitly an event-based approach and is activated only when one of its tracked event changes its state. The dotted lines, used in the temporal layer, represent specific links to the tracked node for the lifespan estimation.

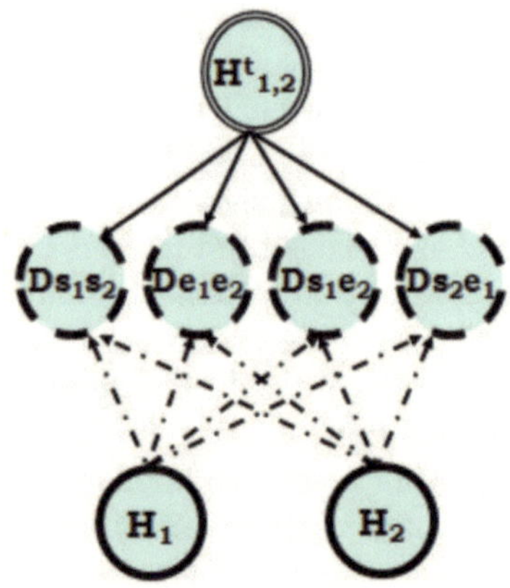

Fig. 6. The temporal relations network

The integration of the temporal constraints associated with an event, such as duration, can also be performed with the TRN presented above. It is easily obtained by linking the duration of the observed events with the constraints. Such constraint is also represented as a node and is actively controlled by the system. Generally, the constraints are defined by a relative time base with respect to other events.

Temporal Relation Network	Graphical Representation of the Relation	$D_{s_1 s_2}$ true if	$D_{e_1 e_2}$ true if	$D_{s_1 e_2}$ true if	$D_{s_2 e_1}$ true if
H_2 starts with H_1	H_1 : •—• H_2 : •——•	$D(s_1, s_2) = 0$	$D(e_1, e_2) < 0$	$D(s_1, e_2) < 0$	$D(s_2, e_1) < 0$
H_1 finishes H_2	H_1 : •—• H_2 : •——•	$D(s_1, s_2) > 0$	$D(e_1, e_2) = 0$	$D(s_1, e_2) < 0$	$D(s_2, e_1) < 0$
H_1 during H_2	H_1 : •—• H_2 : •———•	$D(s_1, s_2) > 0$	$D(e_1, e_2) < 0$	$D(s_1, e_2) < 0$	$D(s_2, e_1) < 0$
H_1 equals H_2	H_1 : •——• H_2 : •——•	$D(s_1, s_2) = 0$	$D(e_1, e_2) = 0$	$D(s_1, e_2) < 0$	$D(s_2, e_1) < 0$
H_1 meets H_2	H_1 : •—• H_2 : •—•	$D(s_1, s_2) < 0$	$D(e_1, e_2) < 0$	$D(s_1, e_2) < 0$	$D(s_2, e_1) = 0$
H_1 overlaps H_2	H_1 : •——• H_2 : •——•	$D(s_1, s_2) < 0$	$D(e_1, e_2) < 0$	$D(s_1, e_2) < 0$	$D(s_2, e_1) < 0$
H_1 before H_2	H_1 : •—• H_2 : •—•	$D(s_1, s_2) < 0$	$D(e_1, e_2) < 0$	$D(s_1, e_2) < 0$	$D(s_2, e_1) > 0$

Table 3. Temporal relationships and TRN nodes

5. Experiments

We present some results of our scenarios recognition system over two applications. The first one concerns a system for abandoned baggage scenario recognition. The second experiment is linked with an application of car park surveillance. The preliminary steps of these systems concern the motion detection, tracking of objects and their classification. The detection algorithm uses the Mixture of Gaussians in order to model the background with multiple possible states.

Our tracking algorithm basically uses a region-based approach. It uses cinematic and visual constraints for establishing correspondence. The tracking algorithm uses the Nearest Neighbor (NN) strategy. However, in the presence of merging or splitting situations, two specific procedures are launched in order to solve the association ambiguities (Motamed, 2006). The classification of object (pedestrian/car) is obtained directly by the estimation of their detection surface area in the image.

5.1 Experiment 1

The first experiment operates on the dataset delivered by the workshop PETS'2006 (PETS, 2006) (Fig. 7). It contains several challenging sequences dedicated for the performance evaluation of abandoned baggage recognition systems in the context of public transportation. The dataset is composed of multi-sensors sequences (4 overlapping cameras C1-C4) with variable complexity. All sequences are provided with information representing the calibration of camera, geometric information of the scene, and ground truth of the observed scenarios (baggage location, time of alarms). For our experiment, we have used the camera C3 which brings an interesting view of the global scene and contains less shadows artifacts. In order to compare our result with the ground truth data, a homographic transformation from the image to the ground plane is performed. The parameters of this transformation is estimated by a linear least square method by linking pairs of points from the images and their corresponding in the ground-plane.

In the figure 8, we present the model of an abandoned baggage scenario by using the proposed approach. H^t_{12} represents a temporal node verifying the relation between events

Fig. 7. Images from the dataset PETS'2006, camera C3

H_1 (detection of an object separation) and H_2 (checking an effective distant separation) The node H^t_3 in the temporal layer permits to verify a temporal duration of the node H_3 (verifying the fact that the Pedestrian P_1 goes away from the object 0_2) with a constraint node representing a duration (Δt). The lifespan of this constraint node is started after the validation of the H^t_{12} which detects the initial separation of P_1 and 0_2, this link is also drawn with dotted line.

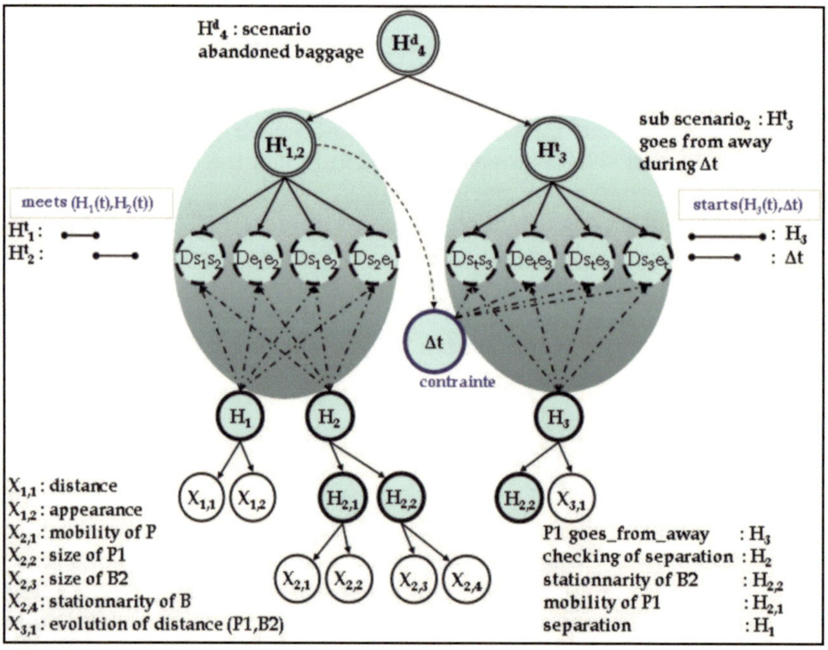

Fig. 8. Abandoned baggage model

The table 4 shows the result of our algorithm on seven sequences S1-S7. It represents the error position of the abandoned baggage, the temporal error of the alarms activation and the tracking statistics. The proposed algorithm has correctly detected the majority of the high level scenarios (6 of 7). Over the dataset S7, we can mention some image analysis errors inducing some false interpretations. This sequence contains many interacting objects involving merging situations in images. The object tracker makes few false associations and miss-classifications (2 errors on identity associations and 1 error for human/baggage classification).

Sequence	S1	S2	S3	S4	S5	S6	S7
Alarm time errors / GT(in s)	0.3	0.2	--	0,3	0.1	0.2	--
Baggage location errors / GT (in cm)	24	26	30	18	32	40	31
# True Positive alarm/ GT	1/1	1/1	0/0	1/1	1/1	1/1	0/1
# False positive alarm	0	0	0	1	0	0	1
# of tracked persons/ GT	1/1	2/2	1/1	1/1	1/1	2/2	7/6
Subjective difficulty	*	***	*	****	**	***	******

Table 4. Result of our algorithm on the PETS'2006 datasets S1-S7, camera 3

5.2 Experiment 2

The second experiment is based on two sub-scenarios linked with the entering of a pedestrian inside a car park area. Scenarios contain a set of temporal constraints and specific trajectories. The first sub-scenario verifies if the pedestrian takes a car in area P and exits the scene with the car. The second sub-scenario represents a pedestrian visiting a car with an exit from the scene without taking the car.

The figure 9 shows the global model of the car park surveillance. It contains trajectory recognition agents and temporal agents.

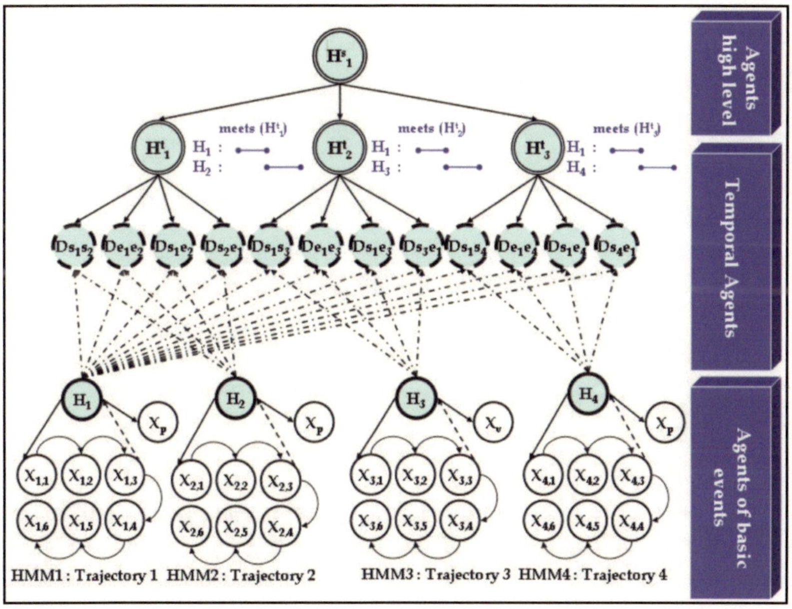

Fig. 9. Parking surveillance model

At the beginning, during the first scenario, the trajectories T_i, T_j, T_k (fig. 10:b) are partially recognized then only the trajectory T_k is confirmed (fig. 10:c). With the respect of the pedestrian paths, when the pedestrian is near the first car, the algorithm activates the second scenario. Then the second scenario as well as the first one is abandoned, because the tracked object deviates from its normal trajectories T_L or T_m (fig. 10:d). In such situation, the recognition system decides the occurrence of an atypical scenario. Fig. 11 illustrates the prediction rate of each trajectory recognition (Fig11: a, b, c, d) and its associated state evolution indicator (fig 11: e, f, g, h).

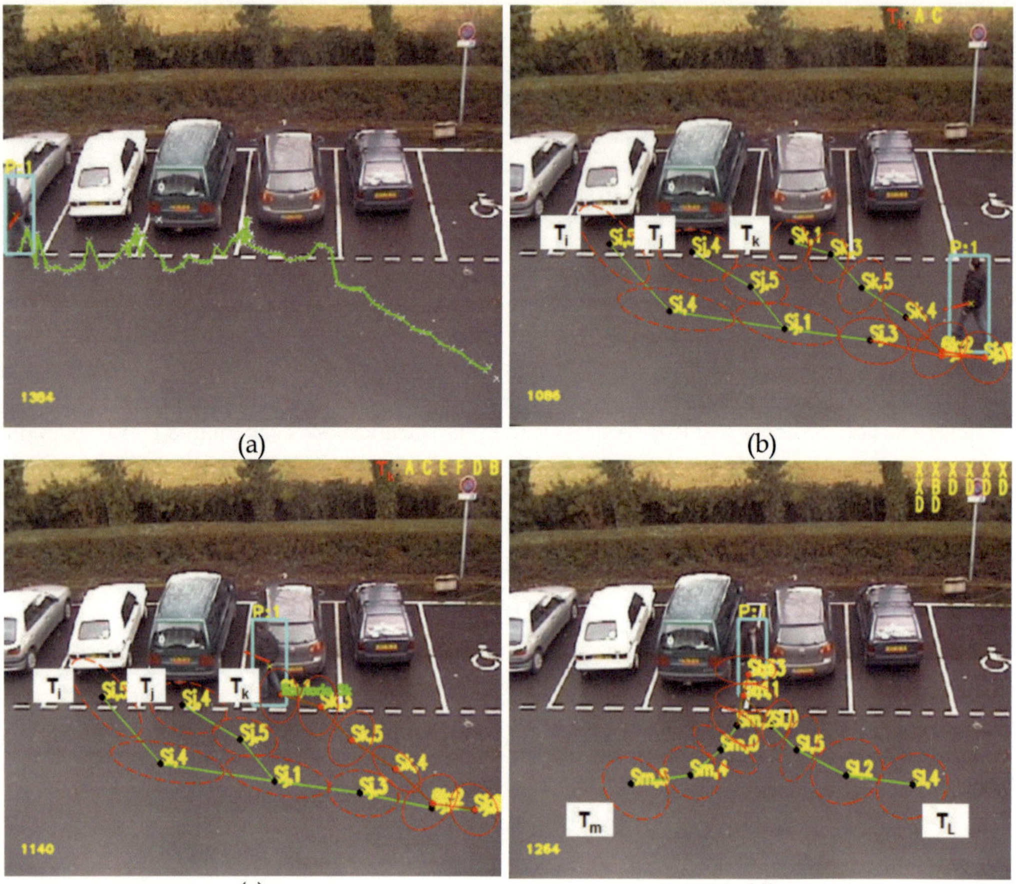

(a) (b) (c) (d)

Fig. 10. (a) a global trajectory example; (b,c): recognition of trajectories T_i, T_j, T_k linked with the 1st sub-scenario; (d) : recognition of trajectories T_L, Tm linked with the 2nd sub-scenario

6. Conclusion

The global proposed model combines in a flexible manner, graphical probabilistic techniques in order to manage efficiently decisions uncertainty. The recognition system takes the advantage of an active perception strategy by focusing on the awaited scenarios with respect to the scene behavior. The partial recognition strategy brings efficient predictive capabilities for the high level scenario agent in order prepare the activation of its future awaited events. The first layer of the recognition permits to highlight basic events from the observed visual features. At this level, the trajectory recognition task represents an important event. We have also proposed a predictive trajectory recognition approach based on GMM-HMM model.

In a second layer, the use of nodes integrating temporal information in a specific Bayesian Networks, allows the temporal reasoning capabilities over the recognition task by managing various types of time constraint (qualitative, quantitative, relative and absolute). The global recognition algorithm is validated over two real world applications.

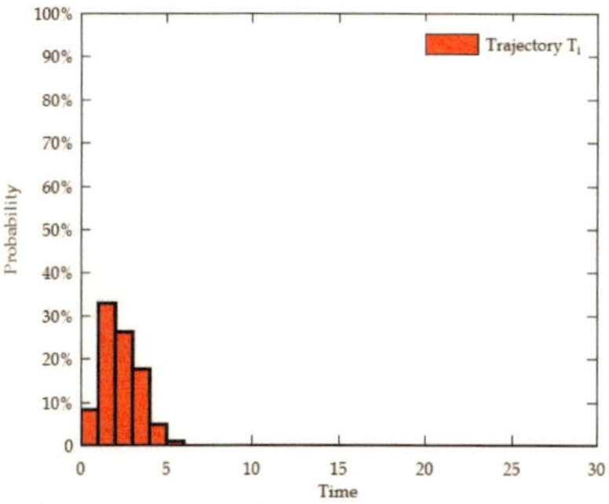

(a) Prediction rate of the trajectory Ti

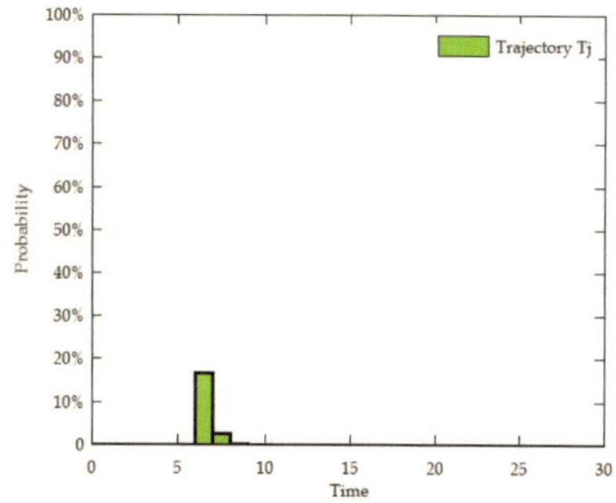

(b) Prediction rate of the trajectory T_j

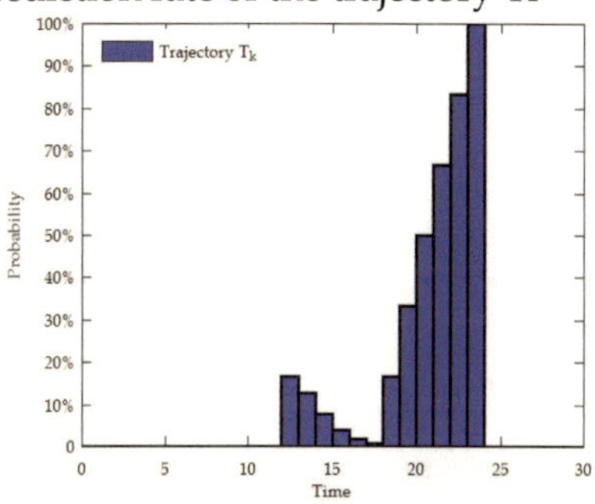

(c) Prediction rate of the trajectory T_k

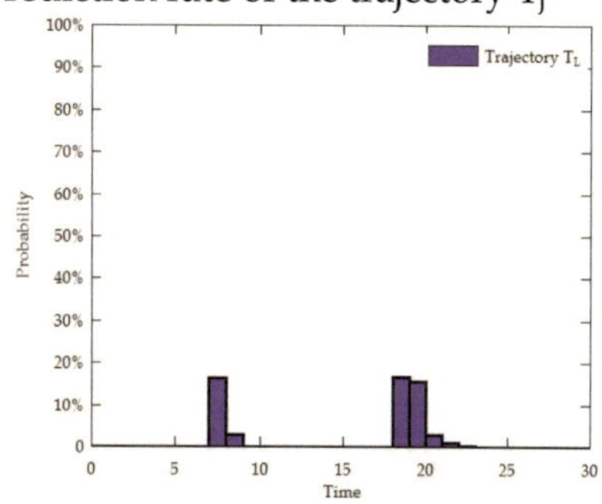

(d) Prediction rate of the trajectory T_L

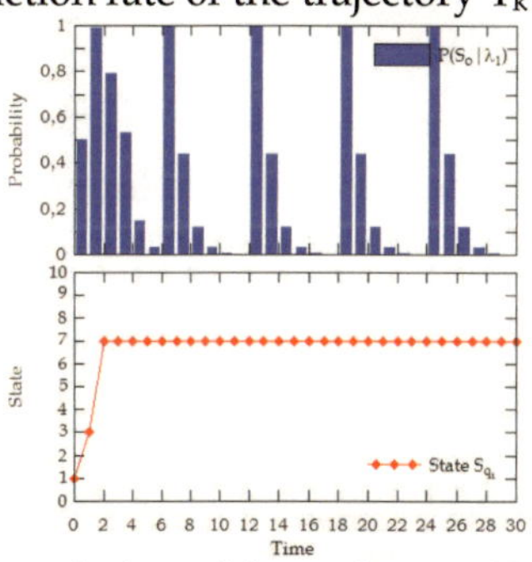

(e) State evolution of the trajectory T_i

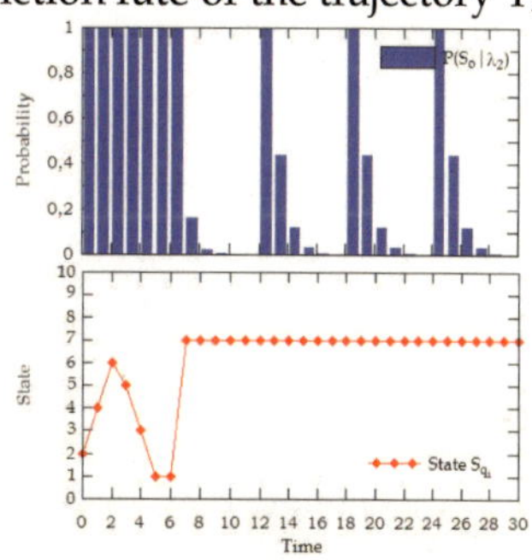

(f) State evolution of the trajectory T_j

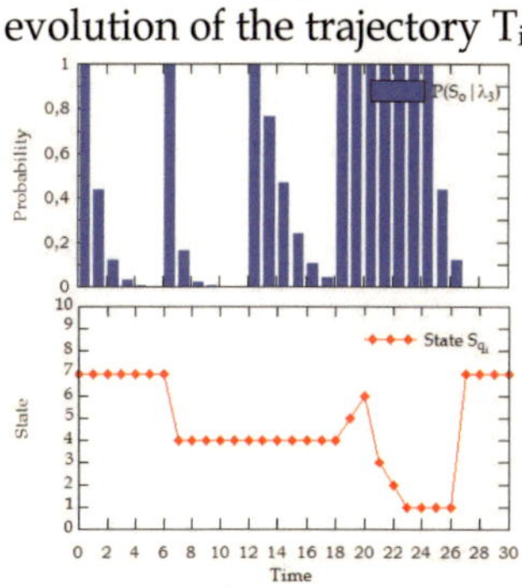

(g) State evolution of the trajectory T_k

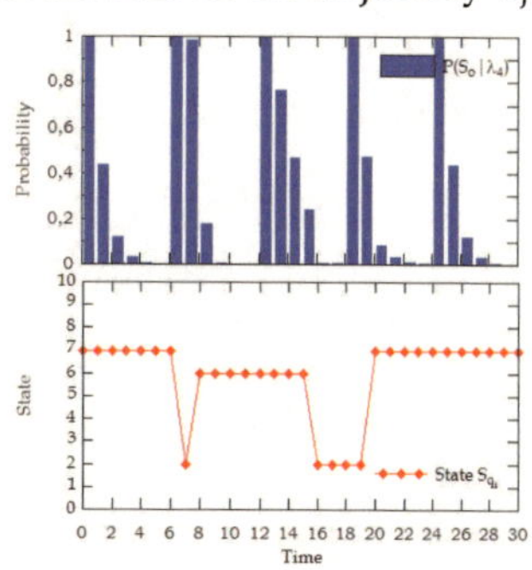

(h) State evolution of the trajectory T_L

Fig. 11. Prediction of trajectories Ti, Tj, Tk, TL,: (a,b,c,d) and respectively their states evolution: (e,f,g,h)

7. References

Arroyo-Figueroa, G. (1999). A Temporal Bayesian Network for Diagnosis and Prediction. Uncertainty in artificial intelligence. Proc15th Conf Uncertainty Artificial Intelligence pp: 13-20., 1999.

Bajcsy, R. (1998). Active Perception. Proceedings of the IEEE, 76(8):996-1005, 1998.

Bui, H.H.; Phung, Q. and Venkatesh. S. (2004). Hierarchical Hidden Markov Models with General State Hierarchy. In Proceedings of the Nineteenth National Conference on Artificial Intelligence, 2004, pp: 324–329, San Jose, California,

Burns, B. & Morrison, C.T. (2003). Temporal Abstraction in Bayesian Networks. In Working Notes of AAAI Spring Symposium Workshop: Foundation and Applications of Spatio-Temporal Reasoning, 2003, pp:41-48.

Dean, T. & Kanazawa, K. (1999). A model for reasoning about persistence and causation. Computational Intelligence, 5(3), pp:142-150., 1999.

Dousson, C. & Le Maigat, P. (2007). Chronicle Recognition Improvement Using Temporal Focusing and Hierarchization. IJCAI 2007, pp: 324-329.

Galan, S.F. & Diez, F.J. (2000). Modeling dynamic causal interactions with bayesian networks: temporal noisy gates. CaNew', the 2nd InternationalWorkshop on Causal Networks held in conjunction with ECAI, pp: 1-5., 2000, Berlin, Germany.

Galata, A.; Johnson, N. & Hogg. D. (2001). Learning variable length Markov models of behaviour. Int. Journal of Comp. Vision and Image Understanding, 81(3), 2001, pp: 398–413.

Hongeng, S.; Bremond, F. & Nevatia, R. (2000). Bayesian Framework for Video Surveillance Application, ICPR00, pp: 164-170, Barcelona, Spain.

Howell, A.J. & Buxton, H. (2002). RBF Network Methods for Face Detection and Attentional Frames, Neural Processing Letters (15)(2002), pp.197-211.

Motamed, C. (2006). Motion detection and tracking using belief indicators for an automatic visual-surveillance system. Image and Vision Computing, Volume 24, Issue 11, 1, Pages 1192-1201, 2006.

Oliver, M.; Rosario, B. & Pentland. A. (2000). A Bayesian computer vision system for modeling human interactions. IEEE Transactions on Pattern Analysis and Machine Intelligence, 2000, 22(8):831–843.

PETS'2006 http://www.cvg.rdg.ac.uk/PETS2006/data.html

Porikli, F. (2004) Trajectory distance metric using hidden Markov model based representation. In PETS 2004 Workshop, Prague.

Rabiner. L. R. (1989). A tutorial on Hidden Markov models and selected applications in speech recognition. In Proceedings of the IEEE, volume 77, February 1989, pp 257–286.

Starner, T. & Pentland (1995) A. Real-time American Sign Language Recognition from Video Using Hidden Markov Models," Proceedings of International Symposium on Computer Vision, 1995, pp. 265-270. Miami Beach.

Tessier. C. (2003). Towards a commonsense estimator for activity tracking. In AAAI Spring Symposium, 2003, pp: 111-119, Palo Alto, CA.

Vu, T.; Bremond, F. & Thonnat, M. (2003). Automatic Video Interpretation: A Novel Algorithm for Temporal Scenario Recognition. The Eighteenth International Joint Conference on Artificial Intelligence (IJCAI'03), August 2003, pp: 9-15, Acapulco, Mexico.

19

A Parallel Non-Linear Surveillance Video Synopsis System with Operator Eye-Gaze Input

Ulas Vural and Yusuf Sinan Akgul
GIT Vision Lab, Department of Computer Engineering,
Gebze Institute of Technology
Turkey

1. Introduction

Most living areas such as parks, streets, metro stations, shopping centers, schools and houses are monitored by technologically varied surveillance camera systems. While the first generation primitive systems are still largely used to view and record visual data, the semi-autonomous second generation systems started to emerge to help human operators by processing video data to alert them for abnormal situations (Ahmad et al., 2007). These systems generally include an advanced component for motion detection, object recognition, tracking, behavior understanding, video indexing, or video retrieval (Hampapur et al., 2007). Although these systems intend to handle the events automatically (Hu et al., 2004), fully automated surveillance systems are still inadequate (Keval & Sasse, 2006) and therefore human operators are still indispensable (Siebel & Maybank, 2004).

The number of cameras in surveillance systems is getting larger with the increased demand for security in public spaces (Koskela, 2000). While the number of cameras increases, the amount of data and the amount of visual stimuli for an operator become extremely large. Human operators sometimes have to monitor many video feeds at the same time but the visual limitations of human being give permission to handle only a small subset (Preece et al., 1994). These limitations cause operators to overlook some important actions, requiring more operators to maintain a reliable surveillance system. However, the increased number of operators makes the system more reliable but less efficient. The cost of manpower becomes the dominating factor in the total operational cost and it is generally much larger than the costs of software and storage medium (Dick & Brooks, 2003).

Indispensability of human power in surveillance systems increases the human workload. Performance of human operators become a key point on the total performance of surveillance systems. Attention levels of operators, their monitoring strategies, characters and moods effect the system's success. It is claimed that the performances of human operators are not stable and even expert operators loses their attention after twenty minutes(Green, 1999). While surveillance systems are so common and the operators are the most important part of these systems, many micro-social studies have been conducted for better understanding of security rooms(Keval & Sasse, 2006; Norris & Armstrong, 1999; D., 2004). All these studies, which show that human attention levels have to be monitored regularly.

The field of Human Computer Interaction (HCI) became very interested in analyzing and designing systems for the interaction between the human operators and the surveillance systems. A large amount of work has been conducted on surveillance systems (Ahmad et al., 2007) to achieve higher efficiency and reliability, which can be separated into two groups. The first group generally works at real-time rates while human operators are monitoring the scene. These systems support operators by placing the views of detected threats in conspicuous places (Steiger et al., 2005). Although these systems are generally limited with a fixed number of objects or actions, they successfully decrease the amount of workload where properties of monitored objects or actions are known. An automated surveillance system consists of a number of complex mechanisms according to its objectives (Hu et al., 2004) like tracking pedestrians, making crowd analysis (Siebel & Maybank, 2004), extracting motion patterns (Gryn et al., 2009) and object recognition (López et al., 2006). Some surveillance systems use advanced user interface designs to make themselves convenient and manageable. The efficiency of operators can be increased by utilizing hand gestures for selecting cameras, zooming, tilting and focusing instead of using traditional mouse and keyboard units (Iannizzotto et al., 2005). Although advanced user interfaces and automatic detection of suspicious threats make the operators more efficient on the monitoring process, the operators might still overlook some important actions.

Retrieving a previously overlooked threat is in the scope of the second group. Since the amount of surveillance-video data is very large, manual reexamination of all the recorded data is time consuming even in accelerated modes. The solution is the searching of actions or objects by using image and video understanding methods. Indexing video data and collecting them in databases increase the speed of subsequent searches (Dick & Brooks, 2003). Content-based video retrieval methods can retrieve objects by considering their shape, color or texture properties but cannot successfully determine specified behaviors (Hu et al., 2004). Tracking of actions and spatial positions of objects are also used for detecting anomalies in surveillance videos (Buono & Simeone, 2010). These systems need the knowledge of event locations and can only work after the event occurs. There are also systems that perform semantic analysis of actions in videos for video indexing (Snoek & Worring, 2005). These methods are more advanced than content-based methods but they have to find low-level visual features and handle semantic video indexing.

These two groups largely cover almost all the approaches of interactive surveillance systems but there is still a gap between the two groups. Methods in the first group aim to decrease the rate of overlooking but they cannot do anything when operator overlooks suspicious actions. They do not know if the operator perceives the action or not. Methods in the second group support indexing and retrieving of actions. While these methods can be used off-line, they cannot preclude damages of suspicious actions. In addition, actions and their features have to be precisely described to the system. We propose a new eye-gaze based user interface system that can help close this gap. The system neither processes video for the known threats nor indexes actions but it catches the overlooked actions and prepares a summarized video of these actions for later viewing. Our user interface increases the reliability of the surveillance system by giving a second chance to the operator. The system increases the efficiency of operators and decreases the workload by re-showing only a summary of overlooked actions. The system can also be used to summarize video sections where the operator pays most attention. Such a video can be used to review the surveillance video by other operators in a much shorter amount of time.

Our system employs eye-gaze positions to decide operator's Region Of Interest (ROI) on the videos. Eye-gaze based ROIs are used on images for personalized image retrieval and indexing (Jaimes et al., 2001; Jing & Lansun, 2008) but they are not popular on videos. Eye-gaze information is used as a semantic information on images and they cooperate with other content-based methods. While images contain only objects, there are both objects and actions on videos, so finding semantic rules for videos is harder. We do not try to form semantic rules for actions, we only focus on how people watch videos and track motion (Jacob, 1991). Psychological studies show that humans can track only 5 to 8 moving objects at a time (Franconeri et al., 2007; Pylyshyn & Storm, 1988; Sears & Pylyshyn, 2000) by focusing at the center of moving objects instead of making saccades between them (Fehd & Seiffert, 2008). Although expert human operators can track slightly more actions than untrained operators (R. et al., 2004), they may still overlook some important actions at rush times. We propose to estimate video sections that correspond to these overlooked actions by finding video regions with actions away from the center of focus. These estimated video sections are used to produce the final summary video. Similarly, as mentioned before, our system allows video summaries that include only the video sections where the surveillance operator pays attention, which could be used for fast peer reviewing of already monitored videos.

There are many video summarization methods available in the literature (Komlodi & Marchionini, 1998; Li et al., 2009; Truong & Venkatesh, 2007). A classification of linear video summarization methods is given by Li et al. (2001). The most popular video summarization methods are based on discarding frames with least activity (Kim & Hwang, 2000; Li et al., 2000), but this simple method cannot compress a video shorter than number of possible key frames. These methods need a threshold and it is not generally possible to determine this threshold perfectly, lower thresholds increase size of the summarized video and higher thresholds discard the frames with activities.

Another important problem with the methods that discard whole-frames is that the summarized videos might contain both overlooked and focused actions if they are in the same frame. We need a summary method that lets objects move on the time axis independently to compress the activity from different time intervals into a very small time volume. One such method is the non-linear video summarization approach by Acha et al. (2006) who represented the video summary as an energy minimization over the whole video volume. The chronology of a single pixel value is allowed to change, meaning that events of different time steps for the same region of the video image can be collated in any order. In the final summarized video, a single frame is most likely composed of activity from different frames of the original video. For example, for an input video where two persons walk in different frames (Fig 1. (a)), they are seen walking together in its non-linear summary (Fig. 1. (b)). While this method may seem like a good solution for a compact video for later viewing, the overall energy minimization is very complex and it is not suitable for our real-time purposes.

Non-linear video summarization methods are getting popular on surveillance domain (Choudhary & Tiwari, 2008;Slot et al., 2009;Pritch et al., 2009;Chen & Sen, 2008). An extension of 2D seam carving (Avidan & Shamir, 2007) is applied for achieving a content-aware synopsis video for stationary cameras (Slot et al., 2009). A more complex non-linear method using min-cut optimization technique on 3D video volume is proposed by (Chen & Sen, 2008). This method better preserves the actions in a very compact synopsis, it requires large memory space. Another original approach for non-linear synopsis is the grouping of actions(Pritch et al., 2009). Pritch et al. propose an unsupervised system that clusters similar actions. A more

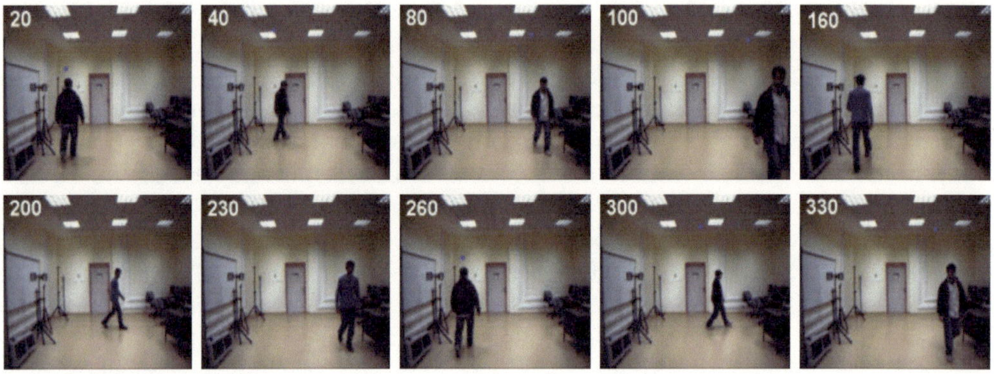

(a) Sample frames from an input video sequence of 366 frames. Small blue circles are eye gaze points of operator.

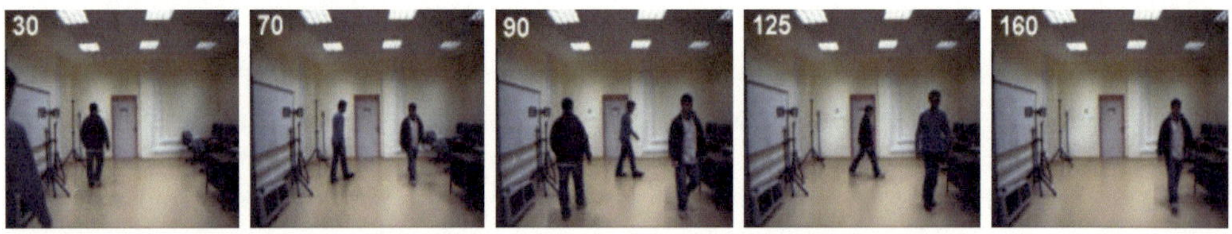

(b) Sample frames from full synopsis video sequence of 185 frames.

(c) Sample frames from the synopsis of monitored parts. The result video contains 147 frames.

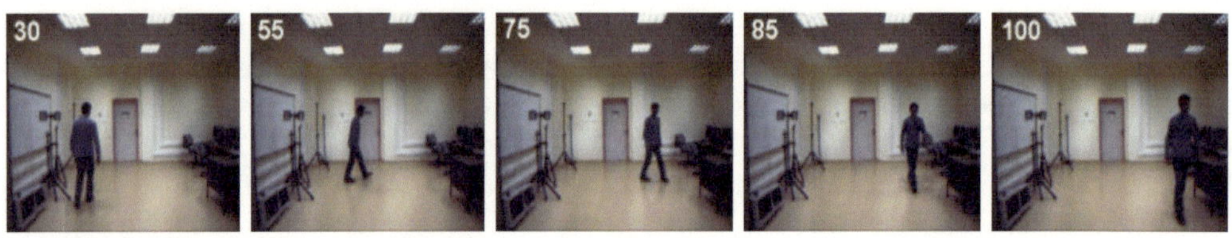

(d) Sample frames from the synopsis of where operator overlooks. It contains 130 frames.

Fig. 1. Sample frames from the first input video and its corresponding summaries.

compact video synopsis can be achieved after the clustering and overlapping actions but the learning stage takes very long time.

A fast approximation of non-linear video summarization method is proposed by Yildiz et al. (2008). The method works on 2D projections of the video volume instead of working on 3D volume itself. This projection reduces the complexity of the problem. Therefore, an efficient dynamic programming algorithm can be employed to optimize the video energy. The video energy is represented by an energy image after the projection. Every pixel of the energy image corresponds to a column of a video frame and a pixel has a higher energy value if there is an action on the corresponding column. A path with the minimum energy can be found and discarded on this image to decrease the video length. After removing these columns from the original video, the non-linearly summarized video is obtained.

The main contribution of the proposed system is the novel integration of the eye-gaze focus points with the improved real-time non-linear video summarization method of (Yildiz et al., 2008). We use a new efficient background subtraction algorithm that provides information about the number of frames to be discarded without limiting the summarization capacity. The overall system can be used with practical surveillance systems without complicating the task of the operator (Fig. 1). The system runs at real-time speeds on average hardware, which means that while the operator is working, the summary video of the overlooked (Fig. 1. (d)) or the attentively monitored (Fig. 1. (c)) video sections are already available at the end of the monitoring process. We also describe some improvements over our previous work (Vural & Akgul, 2009). Today's surveillance cameras generally produce low resolution videos that could not be useful for human identification (Keval & Sasse, 2006). So, the recorded videos are not accepted as an evidence in court(Sasse, 2010). Technological foresights on digital surveillance video systems indicate that most of the surveillance video cameras are going to be replaced with higher resolution ones. Our method reaches the real-time rates on high resolution videos by using parallelism and a better optimization method.

2. Background information

Video summarization methods are useful in video surveillance systems for decreasing the operational costs. They decrease the demand of manpower on video searching tasks as well as cutting down the storage costs. We use video summarization in surveillance somehow differently from the previous methods. We utilize the operator eye-gaze positions in summarizing the interesting sections of the surveillance videos, where interesting sections might include the overlooked or most attentively monitored sections. We employ a non-linear video summarization method for its efficiency and nonlinear treatment of its time dimension. The method depends on an observation of motion in real life activities. It assumes that almost all dynamic objects in surveillance scenes move horizontally on the ground and cameras are placed such that x axis of the camera reference frame is parallel to the ground. If we project the video volume onto the plane orthogonal to its y axis, the resulting projection reduces the size of the problem in exchange for losing the information of motion on the y axis (Fig. 2 Step-1). The projection keeps horizontal motion information on a 2D projection matrix, P. Despite the 3D nature of the video summarization problem, the method works on 2D projection matrix. The projection matrix P contains W x H elements for a video sequence of T frames each of which is W x T. Each element of matrix P represents a column of input video V, and their values are equal to the sum of the gray level pixels in the corresponding columns.

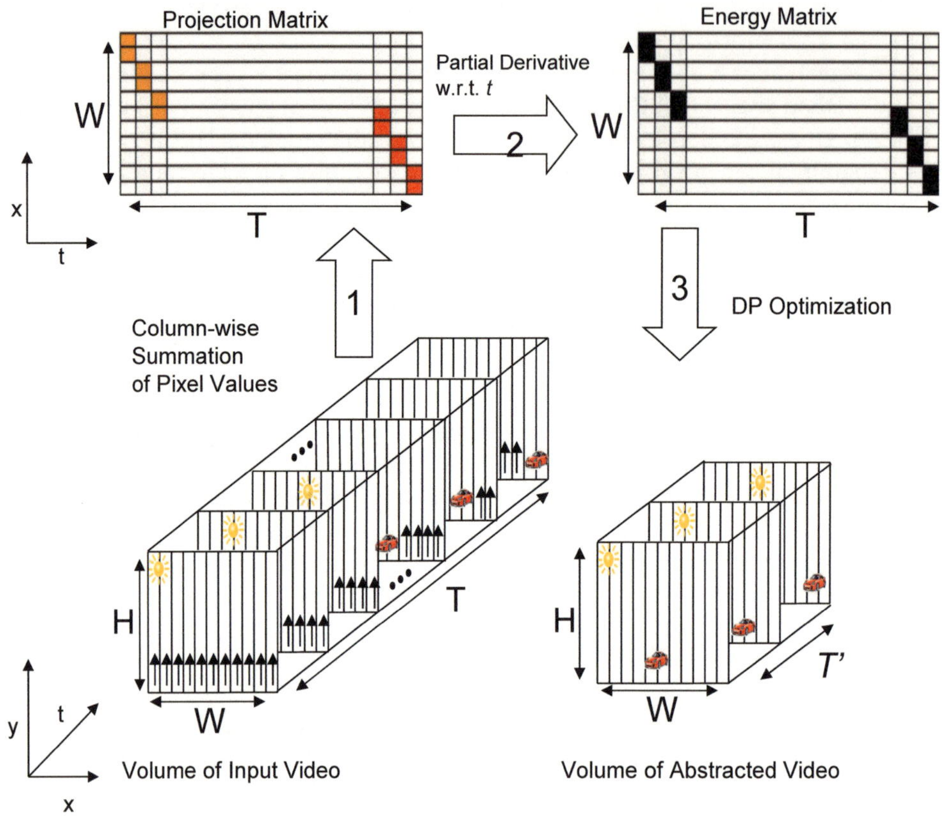

Fig. 2. Non-linear video summarization of an input video sequence with T frames. All frames of input video have width of W and height of H. A summarized video with T number of frames is obtained after 3 steps: 1- Projection of the columns, 2- Computation of Energy Matrix, 3- Optimization using dynamic programming.

$$P(w,t) = \sum_{h=1}^{H} V(w,h,t), \forall\, w,\ t,\ c,\ s.t.\ w \in [1,W],\ t \in [1,T]. \tag{1}$$

Although the projection operation reduces the problem size, the values in P are the summations of the pixel intensities and cannot be used alone in the optimizations. The second step of the summarization method constructs an energy matrix E with the same size of P(Fig. 2 Step-2). The elements of E are computed as a partial derivative of P with respect to time (Eq. 2) so the motion information is obtained from the brightness changes of the video columns.

$$E(w,t) = \left|\frac{\partial P(w,t)}{\partial t}\right|, \forall\, w,\ t,\ s.t.\ w \in [1,\ W],\ t \in [2,\ T]. \tag{2}$$

We briefly explain the dynamic programming based optimization here and leave the details to the next subsection (Fig. 2 Step-3). The method discards the video columns by running dynamic programming on the energy matrix E. While higher energy values in E mean there can be an action, lower energy values most probably represent background columns. The method uses dynamic programming to find a path with the minimum energy on E and removes the corresponding pixels from the original video. These removed pixels make a surface in the 3D video volume which means that removing this surface makes the video shorter. Since the removed surface contains only the low energy pixels, background columns in the video are discarded. Matrix E is partially changed after the removal of the columns. New surfaces can be discarded by applying dynamic programming after computing the changed parts of matrix E. Applying these steps several times makes the video shorter and the video summary is obtained. Although the above method is similar to the non-linear image resizing method of Avidan & Shamir (2007), our employment of this method is original because we use it not for the image resizing but for video summarization. The energy matrix E_{img} of an image can be defined as the gradient magnitude of the original image I. Edges and textured regions in the image are most likely preserved.

Our video summarization method is based on the non-linear image resizing method of Avidan & Shamir (2007). In non-linear image resizing, an energy matrix of the original image is used for optimization. The energy matrix is specially formed from the original image such that matrix elements have higher energy values if they correspond to pixels with higher conceptual information. Dynamic programming runs on the energy matrix and finds a minimum energy path on the image. The pixels along the path are removed for shrinking the image. For horizontal shrinking, non-linear image resizing finds a vertical minimum energy path on the energy image and removes the pixels belonging to that path. Similarly, a horizontal minimum energy path is searched and its pixels are removed for vertical shrinking. Size of the new image is inversely proportional with the number of dynamic programming paths so for getting original image smaller more minimum energy paths must be found.

$$E_{img} = \sqrt{\left(\frac{\partial I}{\partial x}\right)^2 + \left(\frac{\partial I}{\partial y}\right)^2} \tag{3}$$

A vertical path on E_{img} should be found for horizontal shrinking and the path should have only one element for each row of the image. This rule enforces all rows to have the same number of pixels after every path removal. On a WxH image, a vertical path is defined as

$$S^v = \{col(h), h)\}, \text{ s.t. } \forall h, h \in [1, H], \ |col(h) - col(h-1)| \leq 1, \tag{4}$$

where $col(h)$ is the column position of path element on row h. A vertical path S^v is composed of h points and the neighboring points of the path can have at most 1 displacement in the horizontal direction. Similarly, a horizontal path S^h is defined as

$$S^h = \{(w, row(w))\}, \text{ s.t. } \forall w, w \in [1, W], \ |row(w) - row(w-1)| \leq 1. \tag{5}$$

Finding the vertical or the horizontal minimum energy paths on E_{img} and removing the corresponding pixels will shrink the image in the desired dimension. The minimum energy path is found using dynamic programming. Dynamic programming first fills a table M with the cumulative cost values of the paths then back traces on this table to find the actual path elements. The values of M are computed using the following recursion

$$M(w,h) = E_{img}(w,h) + min\{M(w-1,h-1), M(w,h-1), M(w+1,h-1)\}. \tag{6}$$

When M is fully constructed, the minimum costs for the paths are placed at the last row of M. The minimum cost value of the last row equals to the total cost of the minimum energy vertical path and the position of the minimum cost value gives the last element of the path.

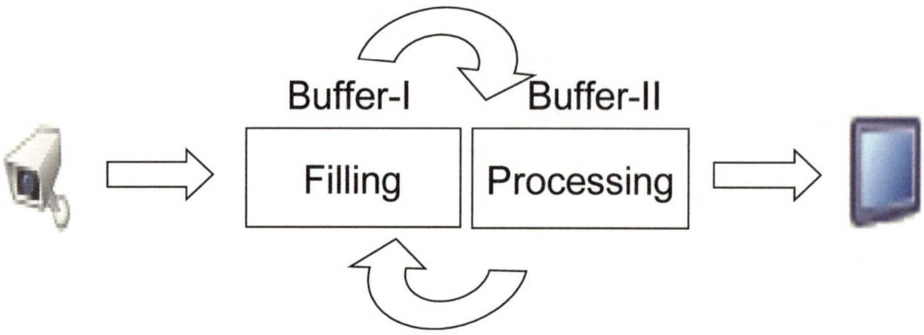

Fig. 3. Our method works on two buffers for handling real-time video summarization.

Dynamic programming finds all path elements by back tracing from that position. At the end of this process we have the minimum path across the energy image. All pixels belonging to this path are discarded to shrink the image by one column.
This method can be used in 3D space-time video volume as well as 2D images. A non-linear video summarization from the space-time video volume can be achieved by shrinking the time dimension. A naive approach would search a 3D surface of pixels with least motion information instead of a 2D path. The video summary can then be produced by discarding a surface with the minimum energy but finding such a surface with dynamic programming would take exponential time. This problem is solved by projecting the video volume onto a plane orthogonal to its x or y axes (Yildiz et al., 2008).

3. The method

Our method employs the projection technique used in (Yildiz et al., 2008) to obtain a projection matrix. We then use a novel frequency based background subtraction method on the projection matrix. The video sections with motion information in the background matrix B are then filtered according to the eye-gaze positions obtained from the operator. The filtering can be performed to produce overlooked sections or the sections that have the operator focus. At the last step, we run the dynamic programming algorithm for producing the video summary.
We use two buffers for the real-time processing of the video. Each buffer is processed by a separate process. One of the processes fills its buffer with video frames and computes the corresponding row of projection matrix P just after grabbing the frame. Since computing projection of a frame does not depend on other frames, one process can handle grabbing and projection together. Once the first process fills its buffer, it hands the current buffer over to the second process and it starts filling the other. The second process begins processing the full buffer by computing energy matrix from the present projection matrix and continuously finds the minimum energy paths for summarizing the video.
The following subsections include novel contributions of our method for the background subtraction and the employment of eye-gaze positions.

3.1 Frequency based background subtraction

Although the video abstraction method of (Yildiz et al., 2008) is fast, direct employment of this method in our application has several problems. First, computed values on E are the absolute differences of total intensity values between two consecutive columns (Eq. 2). The value

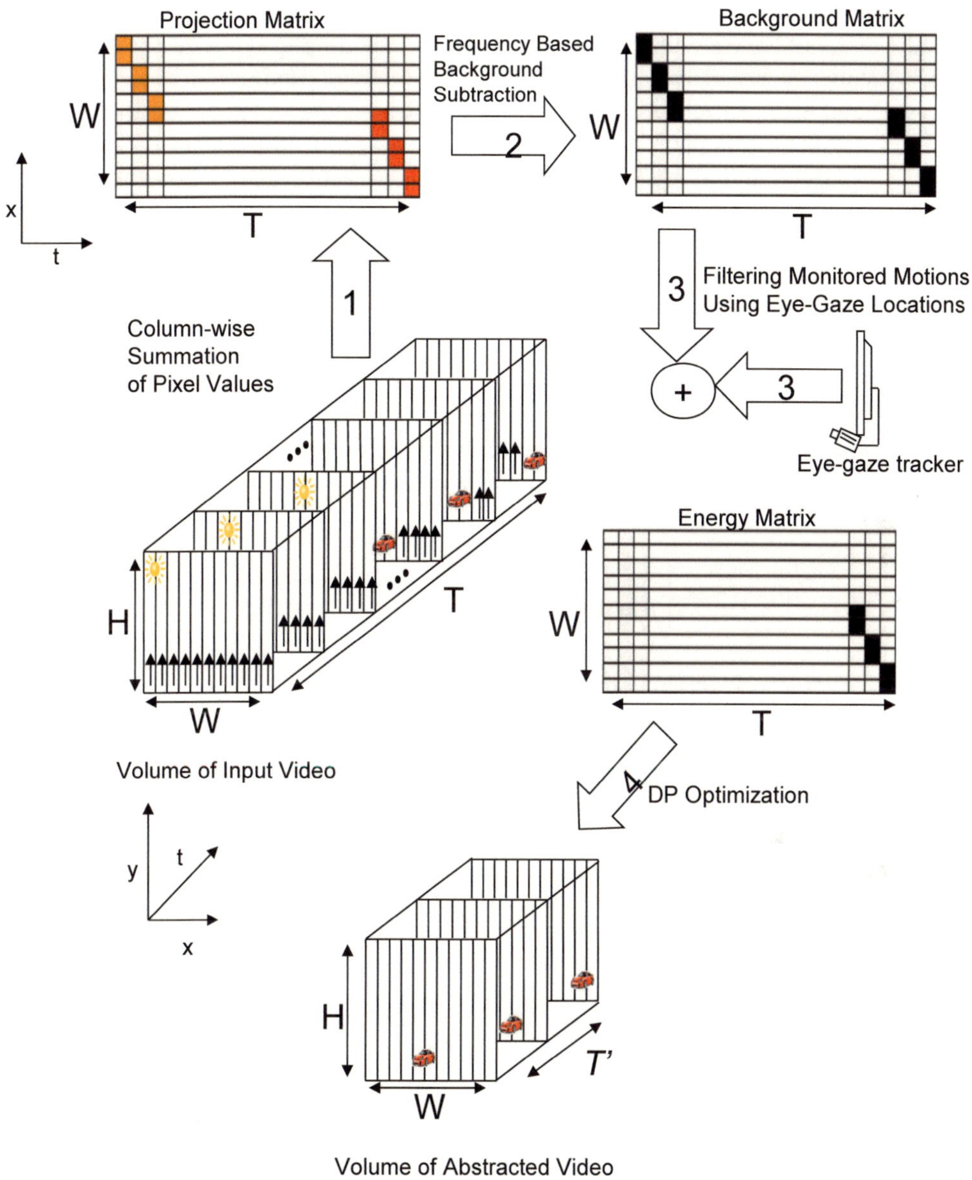

Fig. 4. Non-linear video summarization of the interesting sections contains 4 steps: 1- Projection of the video columns, 2- Background subtraction, 3- Computing Energy Matrix E_{gaze} considering eye-gaze positions, 4- Optimization using dynamic programming.

gets larger while the intensity dissimilarity between the moving object and the background increases. Second, the system produces positive costs for the video columns with no motion information, if there are lighting variations. Third, the system cannot determine how many frames have to be discarded because it does not know what values represent an action. Finally, the system does not have any mechanisms of filtering according to eye-gaze positions.
Our new frequency based background subtraction method produces a binary map B of background and actions. Values of the projection matrix elements are scaled to the interval of $[0, S]$ for a scaling parameter S. This scaling operation limits the maximum value with a relatively small number and lets us use a histogram based fast frequency transform.
Our method counts the number of scaled intensity values for the rows of matrix P using an histogram array A with a size of S. The values of histogram array for a row $w \in [1, W]$ are computed as follows:

$$A_w[P(w,t)] = A_w[P(w,t)] + 1 \;\; \forall t \; s.t., \; 1 \leq t \leq T. \tag{7}$$

The last step of computing frequency based background matrix is extracting the background and actions. We use a technique similar to one described by Zhang & Nayar (2006), for extracting background from the video frames. Since the histogram values for the action pixels of matrix P is expected to be less than the pixels of the background, a simple thresholding method can be used to form the background matrix B.

$$B(w,k) = \begin{cases} ACTION & if \; A_w(k) \leq threshold_1, \\ BACKGROUND & otherwise. \end{cases} \tag{8}$$

3.2 Tracking eye-gaze positions of human operator

The proposed system requires both background matrix B and eye-gaze positions of the operator for computing energy matrix of interesting video sections (Fig. 4 Step-3). Although we use the eye-gaze tracker of LCTechnologies(LCTechnologies (1997)), any eye-gaze tracker (Hutchinson et al., 1989; Morimoto & Mimica, 2005) that does not disturb operators would work with our system. The tracker communicates with our application and returns the x and y positions of the operator's eye-gaze position for each video frame. First, we label each frame as 'monitored' or 'not monitored' by checking if the eye-gaze position of the operator is within the display area.

$$L(t) = \begin{cases} monitored & if (G_x(t) \in [0, W] \wedge G_y(t) \in [0, H], \\ not \; monitored & otherwise, \end{cases} \tag{9}$$

where $L(t)$ is the label of the frame, $G_x(t)$ and $G_y(t)$ are x and y positions of eye-gaze position at time t. We preprocess $G_x(t)$ and $G_y(t)$ before they are used in Eq. 9 for suppressing the effect of eye blinking. Our system uses an outlier detection approach for determining the frames with eye blinking. For such blinking frames the last valid eye-gaze position is applied as G_x and G_y.
The above formulations are sufficient to find if the operator misses the whole frame. For such cases, our dynamic programming based abstraction method includes the action sections of the frame in the video summary because it is known that none of the actions are monitored by the operator.

If the eye-gaze positions of the operator is on the display area, we need a mechanism of what sections of the video the operator is focused on. Although sensing and tracking actions generally can be done fast, operators cannot focus to see all the actions on a monitor if there are several independently moving objects (Sears & Pylyshyn, 2000). Detecting such a situation is also important to understand if the action is seen by operator or not. Human visual system has a good and efficient mechanism for tracking moving objects. The eye focuses near the moving object if there is only one object (Fig. 8. (a)). It focuses at the center of moving objects if there are more than one related object (Fehd & Seiffert, 2008) (Fig. 8. (b)). We also observe this behavior in our experiments, which led us to use a circular attention window for covering action sections. A circular area around the eye gaze position is assumed as the visual field where a human can catch actions. The radius of the circle is determined experimentally in our work and we set it as quarter of the screen dimensions.

Our summarization method uses a weight array ω for ignoring or accepting the video sections according to eye-gaze positions of the operator. The weight array with values larger than 1 increases the acceptance chance (ω^+) of the section and the values smaller than 1 decreases the chance (ω^-). These arrays are filled with constant numbers, however our formulations do not prevent any employment of varying numbers that increases the weights of the center pixels. Since our system cannot discard a video column partially due to the projection of the 3D video volume to a 2D projection image, vertical weighting is unnecessary. Therefore, using a simple weight array is sufficient. The ω contains $2r + 1$ elements where r is the radius of attention circle. The system can have either one of two different special abstracts using one of the weight arrays above. The abstract video can show either 'attentively monitored' or 'overlooked' parts depending on which weight array is used.

We construct our eye-gaze based energy matrix E_{gaze} from background matrix B using a weight array ω.

$$E_{gaze}(w,t) = \begin{cases} B(w,t)\ \omega[G_x(t) - w] & if\ |G_x(t) - w| \leq r, \\ B(w,t) & otherwise. \end{cases} \tag{10}$$

The new energy matrix E_{gaze} is the matrix that will be used to run the dynamic programming based video summary method.

3.3 A more efficient and parallelizable method

It is expected that most of the surveillance cameras are going to be replaced with higher resolution cameras(Sasse, 2010). New generation cameras produce high quality videos which are more useful for accurate recognition of objects and actions but processing these videos will require more CPU power. Some of the existing surveillance video synopsis methods work in delayed real-time with today's surveillance cameras but further improvements are required for handling higher resolution videos. Analysis of our existing synopsis method shows that the method is highly parallelizable and dynamic programming based optimization can be replaced with an efficient binary optimization method. In order to speed up the synopsis system, we use binary energy images more effectively both for finding minimum energy paths and for the regeneration of synopsis video.

The slowest part of the existing method is the regeneration of synopsis video after removing the minimum energy paths. Video columns that do not correspond to the minimum energy path elements are moved on time axis to reconstruct synopsis video. Moving the input video columns to their new locations in the synopsis video volume is a time consuming

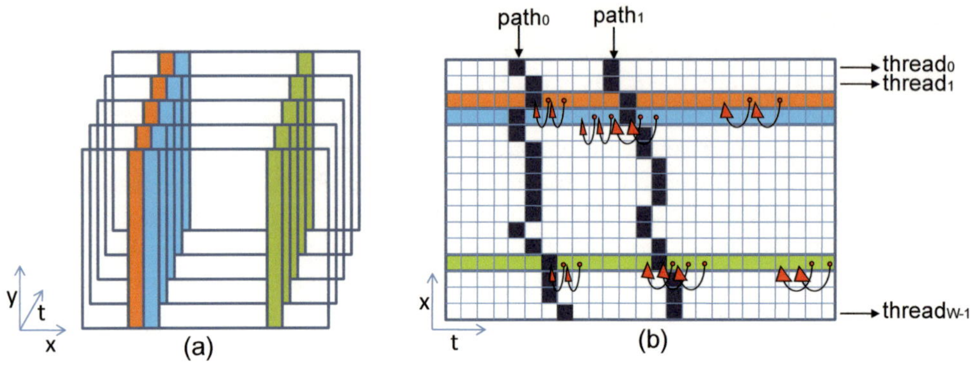

Fig. 5. (a) An input video volume. Each different color shows columns with different column indexes. (b) Energy matrix E of (a). Two sample paths are found so the video will be two frames shorter. One of these paths is used for constituting the background frame $F_{background}$. Each column index is represented with a different color on the rows of the energy matrix E. One thread is assigned for each row of E. Sample movements of video columns are also shown.

task. Existing non-linear synopsis methods spend most of their computation times on the reconstruction phase. In experiments, it is shown that total processing time decreases when the number of extracted minimum energy paths increases. The methods get faster when the number of moving columns is smaller. While the reconstruction of synopsis video is the most time consuming phase, it is important to improve this phase for speeding up the whole synopsis system. We propose two improvements for this phase: first improvement is to prevent to movement of redundant columns and the second improvement is using parallel programming techniques for the reconstruction of synopsis video.

Although the system ensures that a path element represents a background column, the video columns to be moved do not only contain actions but also background columns which do not include any minimum energy path(Fig. 7). Fast non-linear synopsis method of Yildiz et al. uses a real valued energy matrix E_r and this map does not know anything about if a map element represents an action or background (Yildiz et al., 2008). Thus, this method has to move all columns for the reconstruction. A large number of video columns can be skipped in the moving process by using the binary energy matrix E_b effectively. First, a background image is obtained using one of the minimum energy paths (Fig. 5(b)). Video columns that correspond to a zero energy path constitute a background frame $F_{background}$ by using Eq. 11.

$$F_{background}(i,j) = V(i,j,path[i].t), \forall\, i,\ j,\ s.t.\ i \in [1,W],\ j \in [1,H] \tag{11}$$

where path[i].t is the frame number of the ith element of the minimum energy path stack.

We first create a synopsis video volume whose frames are $F_{background}$ and then only move the action columns to their new locations in the synopsis video volume. The moving operation is similar to the moving operation of (Vural & Akgul, 2009).

The second improvement on the synopsis video volume reconstruction is using parallelism. An input video column can only be moved to a synopsis video column on the same column index (Fig. 5(a)). In other words, a column can only be moved on the time axis. This operation is independent from other columns with different w indexes. We assign one thread for each

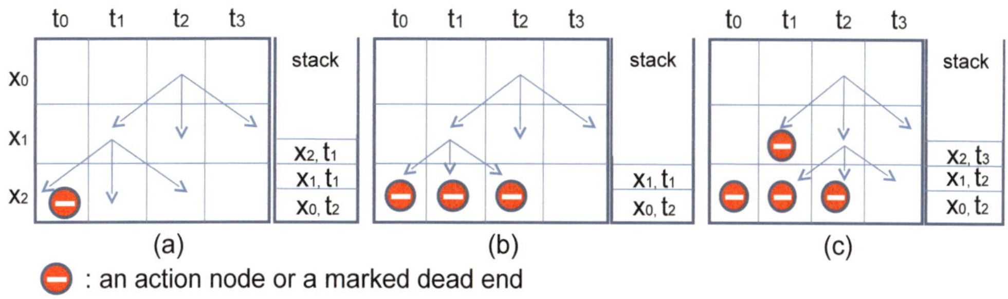

Fig. 6. (a) A path starting from (x_0,t_2) finishes on (x_2,t_1). A stack holds the path elements. (b) Dead-end: (x_1,t_1) is chosen as a next path element from the node (x_0,t_2) but there are no available path elements in the neighborhood of (x_1,t_1). (c) (x_1,t_1) is removed from the stack and marked as an unavailable node. (x_1,t_2) is chosen instead of (x_1,t_1). A complete path is found after this choice.

row of the energy matrix E(Fig. 5(b)). Each thread handles the movement of all columns in a row of binary energy matrix E.

Another time consuming part of the existing non-linear synopsis methods is the DP optimization. In DP optimization it is required to find total costs of all minimum energy paths. When a path is found and removed from the energy matrix E, neighborhood of video columns is changed and recalculations of total path energies are needed for a partial region of E. DP finds all the paths and then it requires a back-tracing for the one with the minimum energy to find path elements. A more efficient method that uses binary energy matrix E can be applied instead of DP. Total energy of a permitted path on a binary energy map must be zero. While we know the total energy, computation of path's total energy is redundant. A path can only contain elements which represent the background columns with zero energy values. The proposed method tries to find paths for all background elements of the first row of the binary energy matrix E. A stack data structure is used for storing path elements. The first element of the stack is chosen from the first row of the binary energy matrix E. The method seeks a path for each background element of the first row. The stack is initialized for each path and the next background element from the first row of E is added to the stack. The top element of the stack is the active node. From the active node, next element of the path can be one of the three neighbors on the next row. A background element from the active node's neighborhood is added to the stack. A path is completed when the stack includes an element from the last row of the energy image E (Fig. 6(a)). In some cases, there can be no available background nodes in the neighborhood of an active node as seen in Fig. 6(b). If there is not any path from an active node, the method marks that node as a dead-end node. A dead-end node is removed from the stack and a new path is tried from the previous active node (Fig. 6(c)). A marked dead-end node loses its availability and further paths never traverse it again.

Although there are some other parallelism mechanisms could be found for the computation of the projection matrix P and the energy matrix E, their effect will be marginal on the total processing time. A pipeline mechanism could also be used while computing the projection matrix P. Each row of the projection matrix P is only depended on one input video frame, so a row of P could be computed just after the frame is graped. We tested the proposed

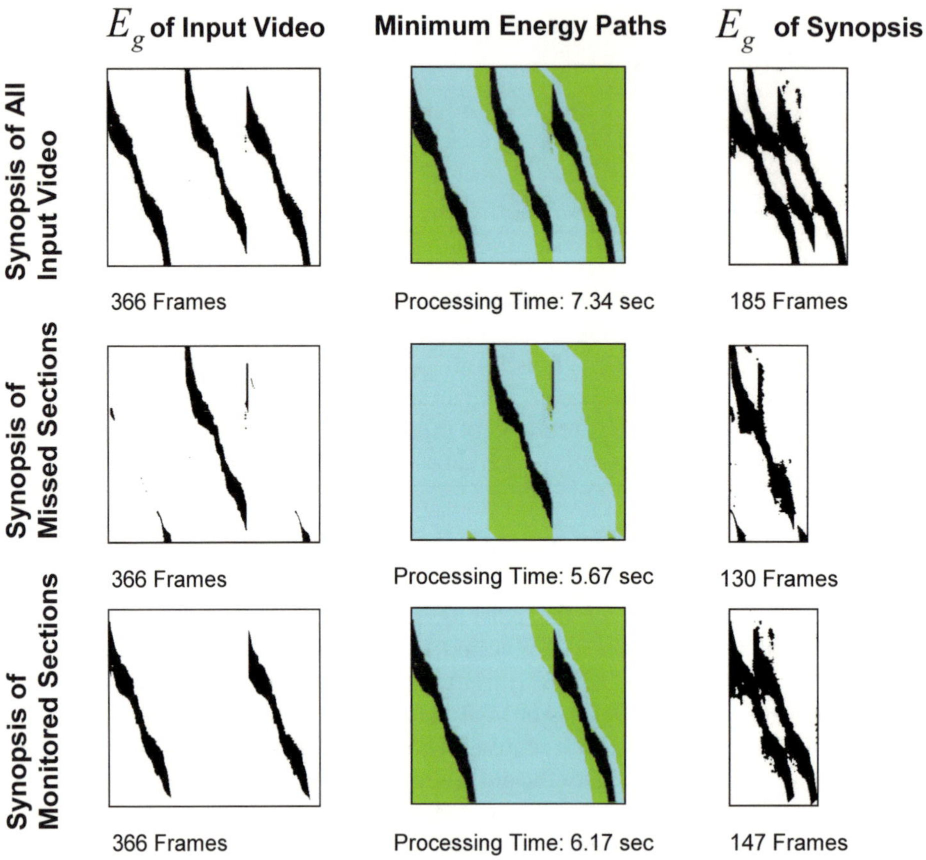

Fig. 7. E_{gaze} images and the minimum energy paths of the first input video. Black regions show action trajectories and the cyan colored regions represent minimum energy paths. Green regions are also representing background columns like cyan regions but the difference is that there is not any minimum energy path passing from green elements. One improvement on synopsis video reconstruction phase skips over working on these columns. Processing times are for single threaded method running on 3.2Ghz CPU.

improvements on different computers with varied sized sample videos. The results show that our method reaches the real-time rates for high resolution images by using above improvements.

4. Experiments

We group our experiments into two parts. The videos of these experiments can be viewed at http://vision. gyte. edu. tr/projects. php?id=5.In the first group we analyze how humans track and sense moving objects. This analysis is important to understand the relationship between eye movements and observed actions. We prepared six synthetic movies with different number of moving objects and motion characteristics to test on a group of people. The experiments show us how an eye-gaze position gets its initial position when an action

	Intel P4 3.2Ghz with hyper-threading		Intel QuadCore 2.5Ghz	
	Single Threaded	Multi Threaded	Single Threaded	Multi Threaded
320x240	7.349	2.532	4.578	0.859
640x480	23.51	10.17	16.06	2.844
1024x768	104.3	39.98	48.30	10.81
1920x1080	182.1	87.76	126.4	30.07

Table 1. Running times (sec) of single thread method of (Vural & Akgul, 2009) and improved multi-threaded method on different resolutions. Experiments are done on two different computer setups.

appears and how the tracking is continued. The eye moves totteringly when it first recognizes a moving object and nearly after two seconds all the subjects' eyes find a stable trajectory for tracking. Tracking is more complex for multiple moving objects on different sections of the monitor. Although most of the subjects prefer to track as many objects as possible, eyes move towards crowded sections of the monitor (Fig. 8. (c)). This initial latency and tottering can cause overlooking some actions. We also observed that our experiments support the thesis about multiple moving objects in (Fehd & Seiffert, 2008). Human eyes are rather focused around moving objects instead of focusing directly on the objects conference (Fig. 8. (a,b)). Therefore using an attention area to represent this adjacency is required and we represent this area in a circular form.

In the second group of experiments, we tested our method on two different scenarios of surveillance videos with varied resolutions. We show the results of our video summarizations and compare them with each other according to their frame numbers and processing times. The videos are recorded in our laboratory and we instruct our operators to monitor some actions and overlook others. Our videos are at 15fps and the resolutions are 320 x 240, 640x480, 1024x768 and 1920x1080.We select the scaling parameter S as 255 and $threshold_1$ of Eq. 8 as 5 for all our experiments. We tested our methods on two different computer setups. First computer is a hyper-threaded Intel Pentium-4 3.2GHz PC with 1GB of memory and the second one has 2GB memory and an Intel QuadCore 2.5Ghz CPU.

In the first video a person walks and another person traces nearly the same route after the first person leaves the field of view of the camera. The first person then again walks in the room. We instructed our operator to direct his eye-gaze out of the display area when the second person appears on the screen. Sample frames from this scenario are shown in Fig. 1. We also show images of the minimum energy paths and the E_{gaze} matrices of both input and result videos (Fig. 7). First input video is 24 second long and our single threaded method summarizes the overlooked sections of it in 5.67 seconds with the DP optimization. The processing time of attentively monitored sections is a little longer than the overlooked parts and it takes 6.17 seconds. The processing time of the video decreases when the number of minimum energy paths increases for the single threaded method of (Vural & Akgul, 2009). This shows that the most time consuming part of the system is reconstruction of the video volume for summarization. Time requirement of this step increases with the number of frames in the video.

We compare the running time of single-threaded synopsis method of Vural et. al (2009) with the proposed multi-threaded method. In Table. 1 we tested several different resolutions of first input video on two different computers. We run each method ten times and the values

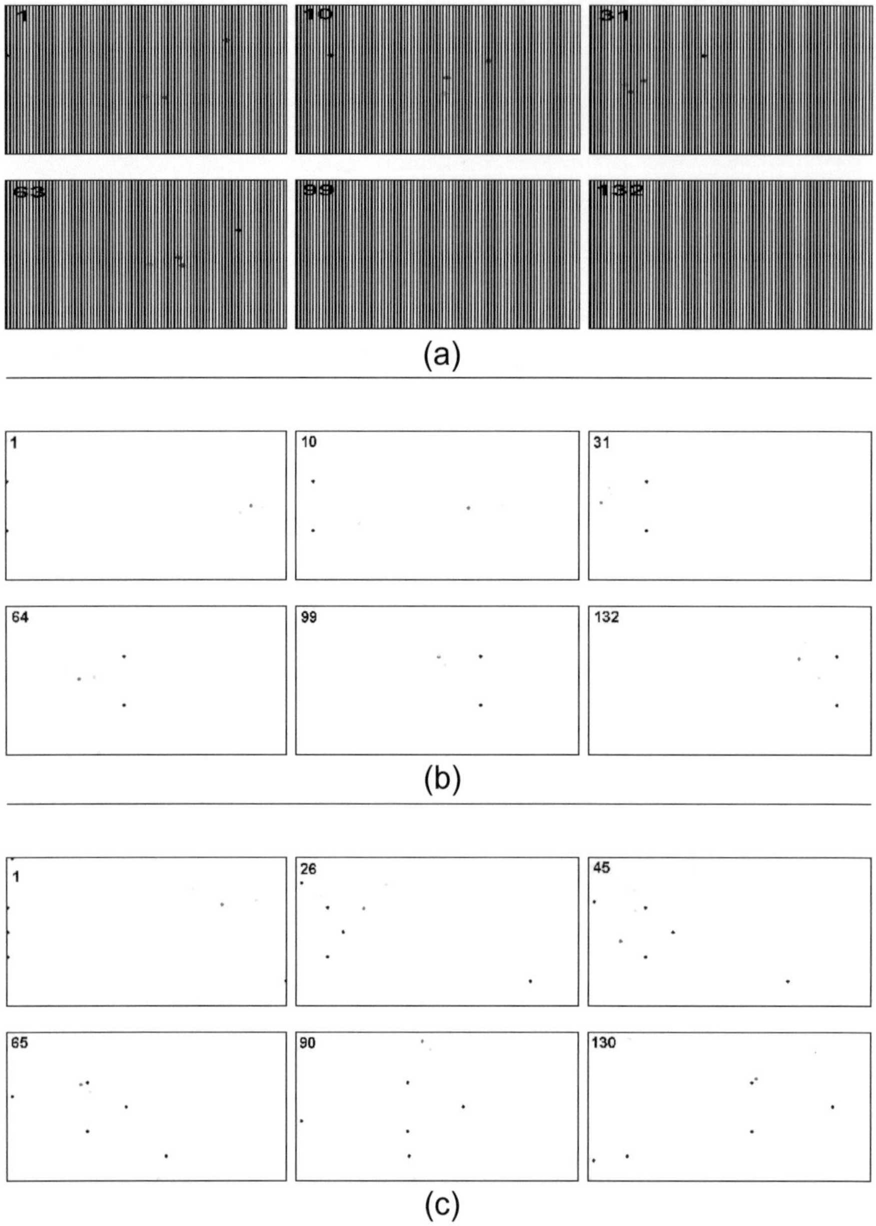

Fig. 8. How an eye tracks moving objects: Black circles are moving objects and the circles with other colors represent the eye gaze points of different subjects. (a) Tracking one moving object, (b) Tracking two objects moving same direction. (c) Tracking five objects moving different directions.

	A	B	C	D
Full synopsis (1920x1080)	126.4	101.0 (125%)	52.59 (240%)	30.07 (420%)
Full synopsis (1024x768)	48.30	39.94 (121%)	22.38 (216%)	10.81 (447%)
Full synopsis (320x240)	4.578	2.375 (193%)	1.094 (418%)	0.859 (533%)
Overlooked (320x240)	3.962	1.782 (222%)	1.031 (384%)	0.750 (528%)
Monitored (320x240)	4.047	2.031 (199%)	1.203 (336%)	0.843 (480%)

Table 2. Speeding up effects of the improvements on the first input video. Column A: Single-threaded synopsis method, Column B: Single-threaded method without DP optimization, Column C: Multi-threaded method without DP optimization, Column D: Multi-threaded method without DP optimization and with skipping redundant video columns from moving. Running times are (sec) achieved on Intel QuadCore 2.5 CPU with 2GB memory. Percentages represent the speeding up ratio of that column from the Column A.

in the table are averages. The experiments show that the multi-threaded synopsis method is at least the number of CPU cores times faster than the single threaded method. While the limited memory sizes limit the speeding up, the improvement is nearly two times more on lower resolution videos.

We also show how each improvement effects on the running times. In Table. 2. running times of single threaded synopsis method and the effects of different combination of improvements are shown. In higher resolution videos dynamic programming based optimization takes less percentage of time on total running time. So, the removing DP can only effect up to 240% over single-threaded method. Multi-threading decreases running time between 50% to 75%. The last column of the table shows multi-threaded synopsis method without DP and skipping background columns from moving. The improvement is up to 533% and this improvement is proportional with the number of background nodes which are not marked as minimum energy path elements. All of our running times on the last column except for 1920*1080 resolution are shorter then the original input video length. Our multi-threaded method runs on delayed real-time for other resolutions of video on 15 fps. The method reaches only 11 fps on 1920x1080 resolution but this speed is also acceptable on today's high resolution surveillance cameras. High resolution surveillance cameras works at 25 fps for 1024x768 (768.) resolution and at 10fps for 1920x1080 (1080p). In the last table (Table. 3 we show the running time results of second input video.

Our last experiment is for analyzing the behavior of our system when an operator overlooks an action while watching another action on the same monitor (Fig. 9.) In this scenario a bag is stolen but our operator watches the other side of the monitor. We then show the rubbery again to the operator by processing the 24 second long input video in only 4.39 seconds. There are some artifacts in summarized videos. These artifacts occur because of the constant radius of visual attention circle. If the attention circle covers only some part of the action, the other parts can be discarded. One solution to this problem could be a simple motion segmentation module that prevents segments from partial omission. We prefer not to use such a mechanism due to the real-time requirements of our system.

	A	B	C	D
Full synopsis (320x240)	3.782	2.406 (157%)	1.297 (292%)	0.797 (475%)
Overlooked (320x240)	3.632	1.516 (240%)	0.969 (375%)	0.698 (520%)
Monitored (320x240)	3.657	2.324 (157%)	1.188 (308%)	0.765 (478%)

Table 3. Speeding up effects of the improvements on the second input video. Column A: Single-threaded synopsis method, Column B: Single-threaded method without DP optimization, Column C: Multi-threaded method without DP optimization, Column D: Multi-threaded method without DP optimization and with skipping redundant video columns from moving. Running times are (sec) achieved on Intel QuadCore 2.5 CPU with 2GB memory. Percentages represent the speeding up ratio of that column from the Column A.

5. Conclusions

We introduced a novel system for the real-time summarization of the high resolution surveillance videos under the supervision of an surveillance operator. The system employs an eye-gaze tracker that returns the focus points of the surveillance operator. The resulting video summary is an integration of the actions observed in the surveillance video and the video sections where the operator pays most attention or overlooks. The unique combination of the eye-gaze positions with the non-linear video summaries results in a number of important advantages: First, it is possible to review what actions happened in the surveillance video in a very short amount of time. If there are many operators monitoring different cameras, the supervisor of the surveillance system can check what the operators observed without going through all the videos. Second, it is possible to review the overlooked actions of the surveillance videos efficiently. Finally, as a side benefit of the second advantage, it is possible to evaluate the performance of the surveillance operators by analyzing the overlooked sections of the videos. This advantage makes it possible to adjust the number of operators, their work durations and the work environment conditions.

The proposed system requires the tracking of the operators gaze for the gaze positions, which might seem like a disturbance for the operator. However, eye-gaze tracking is becoming very popular and seamless systems started to appear in the market for very low costs. We expect that the advantages of the proposed system far exceed the disadvantage of the added eye-gaze tracker.

Another limitation of the system might be the employment of the 3D video projection to the 2D images that loses some of the action information. However, our experiments with the real surveillance scenes indicated that this is not a serious problem because in surveillance videos most of the action happens on a horizontal plane and vertical actions are always coupled with horizontal actions. The experiments we performed on real and synthetic videos indicated that our system is actually works in the real world and can easily be employed in practice.

Although the system is formulated and the experiments are performed under the assumption that only the video sections with movements are interesting, the system can be easily modified to change what is interesting. There are systems that classify the video sequences as interesting or not interesting, which could be easily integrated with our system for other types of video summaries.

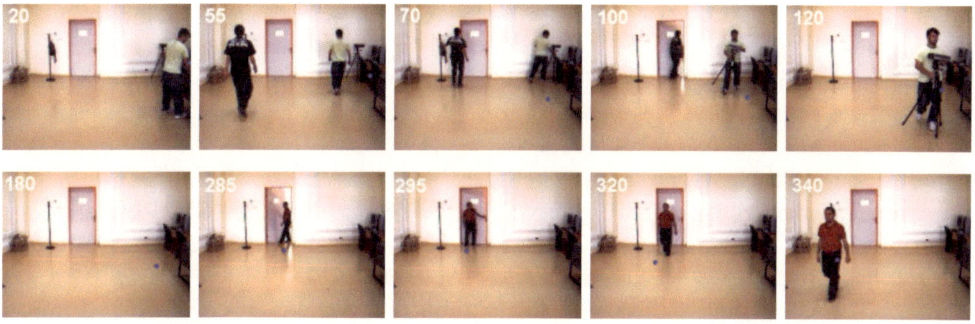

(a) Sample frames from an input video sequence of 359 frames. Small blue circles are eye gaze points of operator.

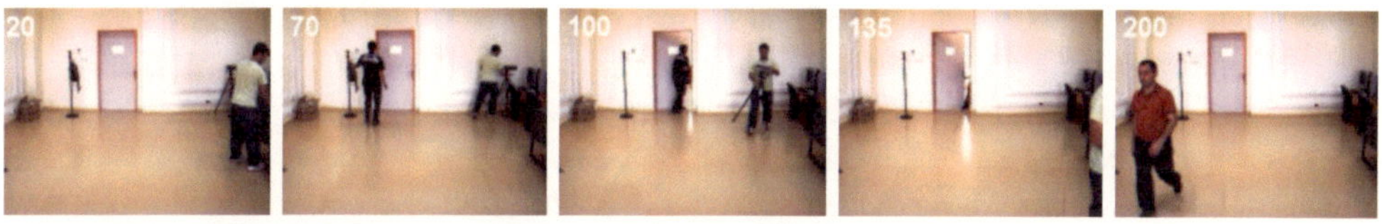

(b) Sample frames from full synopsis video sequence of 209 frames. Processing time is 7.78 seconds.

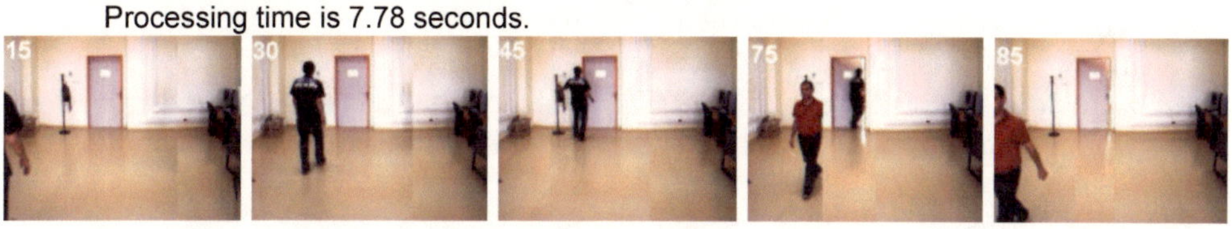

(c) Sample frames from the synopsis of where operator overlooks. It contains 95 frames. The summary is extracted in 4.39 seconds.

(d) Sample frames from synopsis of monitored parts. The result video contains 137 frames and is processed in 5.47 seconds.

Fig. 9. Sample frames from the second input video and its corresponding abstracted videos. Processing times are for single threaded method on 3.2Ghz CPU.

6. Acknowledgements

This work is supported by TUBITAK Project 110E033.

7.References

Acha, A. R., Pritch, Y. & Peleg, S. (2006). Making a long video short: Dynamic video synopsis, *IEEE Computer Vision and Pattern Recognition or CVPR*, pp. I: 435–441.

Ahmad, I., He, Z., Liao, M., Pereira, F. & Sun, M. (2007). Special issue on video surveillance, *Circuits and Systems for Video Technology, IEEE Transactions on* 17(9): 1271–1271.

Avidan, S. & Shamir, A. (2007). Seam carving for content-aware image resizing, *ACM Trans. Graph.* 26(3): 10.

Buono, P. & Simeone, A. L. (2010). Video abstraction and detection of anomalies by tracking movements, *AVI '10: Proceedings of the International Conference on Advanced Visual Interfaces*, ACM, New York, NY, USA, pp. 249–252.

Chen, B. & Sen, P. (2008). Video carving, *In Short Papers Proceedings of Eurographics*.

Choudhary, V. & Tiwari, A. K. (2008). Surveillance video synopsis, *ICVGIP '08: Proceedings of the 2008 Sixth Indian Conference on Computer Vision, Graphics & Image Processing*, IEEE Computer Society, Washington, DC, USA, pp. 207–212.

D., S. G. J. (2004). Behind the screens: Examining constructions of deviance and informal practices among cctv control room operators in the uk., *Surveillance and Society*, Vol. 2(2/3), pp. 376–395.

Dick, A. R. & Brooks, M. J. (2003). Issues in automated visual surveillance, *In International Conference on Digital Image Computing: Techniques and Applications*, pp. 195–204.

Fehd, H. M. & Seiffert, A. E. (2008). Eye movements during multiple object tracking: Where do participants look, *Cognition* 108(1): 201–209.

Franconeri, S. L., Alvarez, G. A. & Enns, J. T. (2007). How many locations can be selected at once?, *J Exp Psychol Hum Percept Perform* 33(5): 1003–1012.

Green, M. (1999). The appropriate and effective use of security technologies in us schools. a guide for schools and law enforcement, *Technical report*.

Gryn, J. M., Wildes, R. P. & Tsotsos, J. K. (2009). Detecting motion patterns via direction maps with application to surveillance, *Computer Vision and Image Understanding* 113(2): 291 – 307.

Hampapur, A., Brown, L., Feris, R., Senior, A., Shu, C., Tian, Y., Zhai, Y. & Lu, M. (2007). Searching surveillance video, *AVSBS07*, pp. 75–80.

Hu, W., Tan, T., Wang, L. & Maybank, S. (2004). A survey on visual surveillance of object motion and behaviors, *IEEE Trans. Syst., Man, Cybern* pp. 334–352.

Hutchinson, T. E., White, K. P., Martin, W. N., Reichert, K. C. & Frey, L. A. (1989). Human-computer interaction using eye-gaze input, *Systems, Man and Cybernetics, IEEE Transactions on* 19(6): 1527–1534.

Iannizzotto, G., Costanzo, C., Rosa, F. L. & Lanzafame, P. (2005). A multimodal perceptual user interface for video-surveillance environments, *ICMI*, pp. 45–52.

Jacob, R. (1991). The use of eye movements in human-computer interaction techniques: What you look at is what you get, *ACM Transactions on Information Systems* 9(3): 152–169.

Jaimes, R., Pelz, J., Grabowski, T., Babcock, J. & fu Chang, S. (2001). Using human observers' eye movements in automatic image classifiers, *Proceedings of SPIE Human Vision and Electronic Imaging VI*.

Jing, Z. & Lansun, S. (2008). A personalized image retrieval based on visual perception, *Journal of Electronics (China)*, Vol. 25.

Keval, H. & Sasse, M. A. (2006). Man or gorilla? performance issues with cctv technology in security control rooms, *16th World Congress on Ergonomics Conference, International Ergonomics Association* .

Kim, C. & Hwang, J.-N. (2000). An integrated scheme for object-based video abstraction, *MULTIMEDIA '00: Proceedings of the eighth ACM international conference on Multimedia*, ACM, New York, NY, USA, pp. 303–311.

Komlodi, A. & Marchionini, G. (1998). Key frame preview techniques for video browsing, *DL '98: Proceedings of the third ACM conference on Digital libraries*, ACM, New York, NY, USA, pp. 118–125.

Koskela, H. (2000). The gaze without eyes: Video-surveillance and the nature of urban space, *Progress in Human Geography* 24(2): 243–265.

LCTechnologies (1997). The eyegaze communication system.
URL: *http://www.eyegaze.com*

Li, F. C., Gupta, A., Sanocki, E., wei He, L. & Rui, Y. (2000). Browsing digital video, *CHI '00: Proceedings of the SIGCHI conference on Human factors in computing systems*, ACM, New York, NY, USA, pp. 169–176.

Li, T., Mei, T., Kweon, I.-S. & Hua, X.-S. (2009). Multi-video synopsis for video representation, *Signal Process.* 89(12): 2354–2366.

Li, Y., Li, Y., Zhang, T., Zhang, T., Tretter, D. & Tretter, D. (2001). An overview of video abstraction techniques, *Technical report*, Imaging Systems Laboratory, HP Laboraties, Palo Alto.

López, M. T., Fernández-Caballero, A., Fernández, M. A., Mira, J. & Delgado, A. E. (2006). Visual surveillance by dynamic visual attention method, *Pattern Recogn.* 39(11): 2194–2211.

Morimoto, C. H. & Mimica, M. R. M. (2005). Eye gaze tracking techniques for interactive applications, *Comput. Vis. Image Underst.* 98(1): 4–24.

Norris, C. & Armstrong, G. (1999). Cctv and the social structuring of surveillance, *Surveillance of Public Space: CCTV, Street Lighting and Crime Prevention.*, Monsey: Criminal Justice Press.

Preece, J., Rogers, Y., Sharp, H., Benyon, D., Holland, S. & Carey, T. (1994). *Human-Computer Interaction*, Addison-Wesley Longman Ltd., Essex, UK, UK.

Pritch, Y., Ratovitch, S., Hendel, A. & Peleg, S. (2009). Clustered synopsis of surveillance video, *AVSS '09: Proceedings of the 2009 Sixth IEEE International Conference on Advanced Video and Signal Based Surveillance*, IEEE Computer Society, Washington, DC, USA, pp. 195–200.

Pylyshyn, Z. W. & Storm, R. W. (1988). Tracking multiple independent targets: evidence for a parallel tracking mechanism., *Spatial vision* 3(3): 179–197.

R., A., P., M., D., P. & B., M. A. (2004). Attention and expertise in multiple target tracking, *Applied Cognitive Psychology* 18: 337–347.

Sasse, M. A. (2010). Not seeing the crime for the cameras?, *Commun. ACM* 53(2): 22–25.

Sears, C. R. & Pylyshyn, Z. W. (2000). Multiple object tracking and attentional processing, *Canadian Journal of Experimental Psychology* 54(1): 1–14.

Siebel, N. T. & Maybank, S. J. (2004). The advisor visual surveillance system, *in* M. Clabian, V. Smutny & G. Stanke (eds), *Proceedings of the ECCV 2004 workshop "Applications of Computer Vision" (ACV'04), Prague, Czech Republic*, pp. 103–111.

Slot, K., Truelsen, R. & Sporring, J. (2009). Content-aware video editing in the temporal domain, *SCIA '09: Proceedings of the 16th Scandinavian Conference on Image Analysis*, Springer-Verlag, Berlin, Heidelberg, pp. 490–499.

Snoek, C. G. M. & Worring, M. (2005). Multimodal video indexing: A review of the state-of-the-art, *Multimedia Tools Appl.* 25(1): 5–35.

Steiger, O., Cavallaro, A. & Ebrahimi, T. (2005). Real-Time Generation of Annotated Video for Surveillance, *Proceedings of IEEE Workshop on Image Analysis for Multimedia Interactive Services, WIAMIS 2005*, ISCAS, SPIE.

Truong, B. T. & Venkatesh, S. (2007). Video abstraction: A systematic review and classification, *ACM Trans. Multimedia Comput. Commun. Appl.* 3(1): 3.

Vural, U. & Akgul, Y. S. (2009). Eye-gaze based real-time surveillance video synopsis, *Pattern Recogn. Lett.* 30(12): 1151–1159.

Yildiz, A., Ozgur, A. & Akgul, Y. (2008). Fast non-linear video synopsis, *23rd of the International Symposium on Computer and Information Sciences, Istanbul, Turkey* .
URL: *http://vision.gyte.edu.tr/projects.php?id=5*

Zhang, L. & Nayar, S. (2006). Projection defocus analysis for scene capture and image display, *ACM Trans. Graph.* 25(3): 907–915.

20

Video Surveillance for Fall Detection

Caroline Rougier[1], Alain St-Arnaud[2], Jacqueline Rousseau[3] and Jean Meunier[4]
[1,4] *Department of Computer Science and Operations Research, University of Montreal*
[2,3] *Research Center of the Geriatric Institute, University of Montreal*
Canada

1. Introduction

1.1 Context

Developed countries have to face the growing population of seniors. In Canada for example, while one Canadian out of eight was older than 65 years old in 2001, this proportion will be one out of five in 2026 (PHAC, 2002), due in particular to the "baby boomers" post-world war II and the increase of life expectancy. Several studies (Chappell et al., 2004; Senate, 2009) have shown that helping elderly people staying at home is interesting from a human perspective, but also from a financial perspective. Hence the interest to develop new healthcare systems to ensure the safety of elderly people at home.

Falls are one of the major risk for seniors living alone at home, often causing severe injuries. The risk is amplified if the person cannot call for help. Usually, wearable fall devices are used to detect falls. For example, an elderly person can call for help using a push button (DirectAlert, 2010), but it is useless if the person is immobilized or unconscious after the fall. Automatic wearable devices are more interesting as no human intervention is required. Some are based on accelerometers (Kangas et al., 2008; Karantonis et al., 2006) which detect the magnitude and the direction of the acceleration. Others are based on gyroscopes (Bourke & Lyons, 2008) which measure the body orientation. A combination of an accelerometer and a gyroscope was used by (Nyan et al., 2008) to detect falls at an earlier stage. The major drawback of these technologies is that these sensors are often embarrassing to wear, and require batteries which need to be replaced or recharged regularly for adequate functioning. Floor vibration-based fall detector (Alwan et al., 2006) can also be used to detect falls but depends on the floor dynamics. This idea has been successfully improved by (Zigel et al., 2009) by adding a sound sensor. They obtained high detection rates, but they admitted that low-impact real human falls may not be detected. Video surveillance offers a new and promising solution for fall detection, as no body-worn devices are needed. For this purpose, a (possibly miniaturized) camera network is placed in the elderly apartment to automatically detect a fall to prevent an emergency center or the family.

1.2 Fall detection problem

1.2.1 General fall detection problem

The main fall detection problem is to recognize a fall among all the daily life activities, especially sitting down and crouching down activities which have similar characteristics to falls (especially a large vertical velocity). A fall event can be decomposed in four phases (Noury et al., 2008) as shown in Fig. 1:

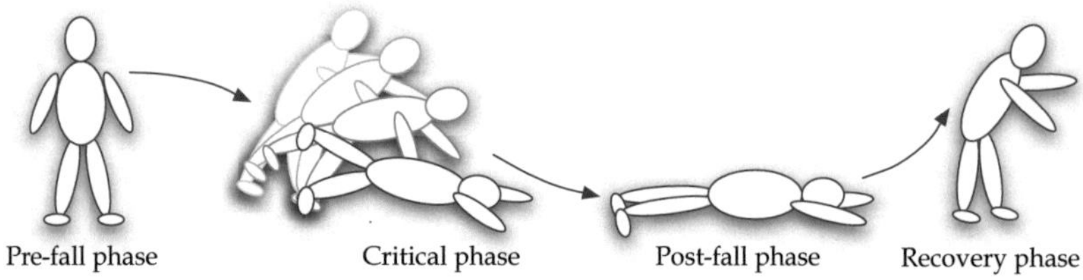

Fig. 1. The different phases of a fall event.

The pre-fall phase corresponds to daily life motions, with occasionally sudden movements directed towards the ground like sitting down or crouching down. These activities should not generate alarm with a fall detection system.

The critical phase, corresponding to the fall, is extremely short. This phase can be detected by the movement of the body toward the ground or by the impact shock with the floor.

The post-fall phase is generally characterized by a person motionless on the ground just after the fall. It can be detected by a lying position or by an absence of significative motion.

A recovery phase can eventually occur if the person is able to stand up alone or with the help of another person.

1.2.2 Specific video surveillance problems

Video surveillance systems need to be robust to image processing difficulties. One of them comes from the camera choice. With inexpensive cameras, the video sequences will contain a *high video compression* (MPEG4 for example) which can generate artifacts in the image. Sometimes, a *variable illumination* can be observed, which must be taken into account during the background updating process. The lighting can also be a source of problems with the appearance of *reflections* in the scene (colors brighter than usual) or *shadows* from the moving person (colors darker than usual). The problem with *reflections* and *shadows* is their detection erroneous as moving objects with a basic segmentation method. *Occlusions* are also a well-known source of errors, mainly due to furniture (chairs, sofa, etc) or entry/exit from the field of view. *Carried objects,* like bags or clothes, can also generate occlusions. Moving objects of no interest (e.g. chair moved) can cause "phantoms" in the image and must be finally integrated in the background image somehow. The silhouette of the person can also be disturbed by the action of *putting on/taking off a coat*. *Clothes with different textures and colors* need to be tested to evaluate their influence on the algorithms, as well as realistic *cluttered and textured backgrounds*.

Robust fall detection systems using video surveillance should not generate alarms because of image processing problems. Some precautions can be taken to limit these sources of problems. Beyond the choice of the camera, the placement of the cameras is important. They need to be placed highly in the room to limit occluding objects and to have a larger field of view. The use of infrared lights can also be considered for lighting problems or for use at night. For our experiments, we have acquired in our laboratory a realistic video data set (Auvinet et al., 2010) of simulated falls and normal daily activities with a multi-camera system. It is composed of inexpensive cameras with a wide angle to cover all the room. This video data set contains all types of problems described previously, and has been made publicly available for the scientific community to test their fall detection algorithms.

1.3 User perception and receptivity of video surveillance systems

We have conducted a research project (Londei et al., 2009), funded by the Social Sciences and Humanities Research Council of Canada, to explore the perception and the receptivity of the potential users of the Intelligent Videomonitoring System. The study specifically focuses on two objectives:

- to explore their receptivity towards the system (cameras, computer at home) and
- to explore their perception related to the data transmitted (eg. images) and the transmission modes (eg. cell phone).

The study uses a mixed-methods design (Creswell & Clark, 2007). Participants (potential users) include: professionals from the health care and social system (n=31) (nurses, occupational therapists, physiotherapists, social workers and managers), elderly living at home who have fallen during the last year (n=30) and caregivers (n=18). Focus group technique (Krueger, 1994) and structured interviews (Mayer & Ouellet, 1991) were used for data collection. Data analyses were performed with (SPSS, 2007) and (QSR, 2002) softwares. The results of the three main questions are presented here:

1. *What do you think about the Intelligent Videomonitoring System?*

   Fifteen caregivers (83,3%) are in favor of this system as well as 26 seniors (86,7%). Advantages of the system are:

   a) security and quickness of intervention for the seniors,

   b) a relief from stress, for caregivers, related to their fear that the elder falls and stays a long time without assistance while hurt, and

   c) for the professionals, images videotaped a few seconds before the fall occurrence would be a valuable source of information to document fall events in a way to improve security and interventions.

2. *Would you actually use a system such as the Intelligent Videomonitoring System?*

   a) Most of the caregivers (n=15, 83,3%) would like to use the system.

   b) For the elderly, results show that a little less than fifty percent would use the system. The explanation of these results is that elders mention that they don't want it because they don't need it at this time. When they will be "old enough", they would certainly agree to have one in order to stay at home as long as they could.

   c) For the professionals and the managers, this system allows new opportunities for home care: 1) to improve security for elderly living at home focusing on the quickness of the emergency intervention and 2) to document the fall events in a way to better understand the origins of falls and to improve interventions.

3. *What is your choice of images to be transmitted?*

   Figure 2 shows the images presented to the participants. The original image (a) is preferred by all participants: 25 elders (92,6%), 14 caregivers (82,4%) and 5 groups of professionals. In accordance with the professionals, the silhouette images (g-h-i) seem to be more appropriate for videotaping in the bathroom but the original image (a) remains the first choice for elders and caregivers.

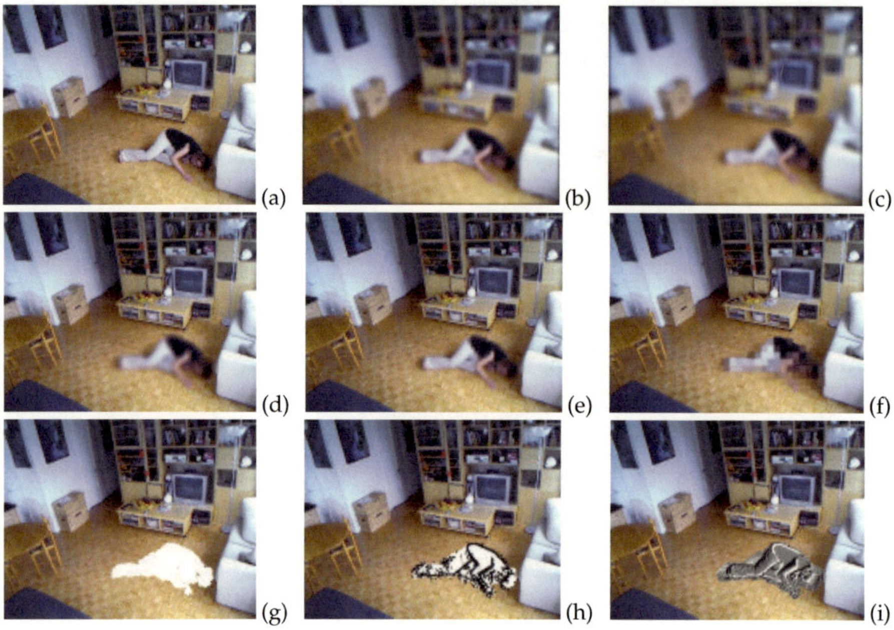

Fig. 2. Images presented to the participants: original image (a) and eight processed images (images (b)-(i) with blurring, pixelization or silhouette extraction)

To summarize: the results show receptivity from the potential users (for example: safety and quick intervention) but some concerns about safety of the transmission system (eg. Images). Intelligent Videomonitoring System is a very promising technology to support the elderly living at home respecting their privacy.

2. Related works on fall detection using video surveillance

The reader can find a good study on fall detection techniques using wearable devices or video surveillance in a recent article by (Noury et al., 2007). In this section, an overview of fall detection methods using video surveillance is proposed.

2.1 Using monocular systems

A commonly used method to detect falls consists of analyzing the person bounding box in the image (Anderson et al., 2006; Tao et al., 2005; Töreyin et al., 2005). This simple method works well with a camera placed sideways, but can fail because of occluding objects. In a more realistic way, other researchers (Lee & Mihailidis, 2005; Nait-Charif & McKenna, 2004) have placed the camera higher in the room for a larger field of view and to avoid occluding objects. The person silhouette and the 2D image velocity were analyzed by (Lee & Mihailidis, 2005) to detect falls with special thresholds for usual inactivity zones like the bed or the sofa (manually initialized). An ellipse representing the person was tracked with a particle filter by (Nait-Charif & McKenna, 2004) to obtain the trajectory used to detect abnormal inactivities outside usual inactivity zones (automatically learned). The vertical velocity is an interesting way to detect falls, either with the 2D vertical image velocity (Sixsmith & Johnson, 2004) or the 3D vertical velocity (Wu, 2000). In this chapter, some new monocular methods will be shown based on human shape change (see Sections 4 and 5) or on 3D head trajectory (see Section 6).

2.2 Using multi-camera systems

A calibrated multi-camera system is useful to reconstruct a three-dimensional representation of the human shape as done by (Anderson et al., 2009) in the voxel space from foreground silhouettes. Their fall detection step was performed by analyzing the states of the voxelized person with a fuzzy hierarchy. For different heights relative to the ground, the homographic transformations of the foreground silhouettes were fused by (Auvinet et al., 2008) in a plane parallel to the ground to reconstruct the 3D human blob. An analysis of the volume distribution along the vertical axis is performed to detect abnormal events like a person lying on the ground after a fall. An alarm is triggered when the major part of this distribution is concentrated near the floor during a predefined period of time. Without reconstructing the 3D human blob, a Layered Hidden Markov Model (LHMM) was used by (Thome et al., 2008) to distinguish falls from walking activities. Their method was based on motion characteristics extracted from a metric image rectification in each view. With two uncalibrated cameras, a Principal Component Analysis (PCA) was performed by (Hazelhoff et al., 2008) on the human silhouette to obtain the direction of the principal component and the variance ratio used for fall detection. A head tracking module was used to improve their recognition results.

3. Our fall detection system

Concretely, a camera network would be placed in the apartment of the person in order to automatically detect a fall. Figure 3 shows an overview of our fall detection system. The images acquired from the video cameras are processed by the local workstation to automatically detect a fall. When a fall is detected, a message could be sent to an emergency center or to the family through a secure Internet connection.

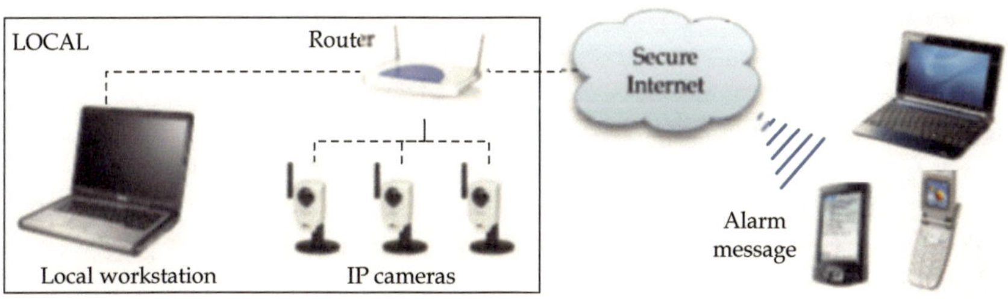

Fig. 3. Our fall detection system.

To limit the cost of our system, inexpensive cameras (IP cameras or webcams) are used and their number is limited to only one per room for cost effectiveness and for simplicity. Indeed, a multi-camera system is more difficult to implement than a monocular one, as reliable 3D information can only be computed if the system is well synchronized and calibrated.
The next sections will describe some of our solutions for fall detection using monocular systems. First, 2D information for fall detection can be used by detecting a fall as a large motion along with changes in the human shape (described in Section 4) or by analyzing the deformation of the human silhouette during and after the fall (described in Section 5). However, some 3D information can be very useful for fall detection as it becomes possible to recover the localization of the person relative to the ground. Usually a multi-camera system is required to have 3D information, but we will show in Section 6 that it is possible to compute the 3D head trajectory of the person from a monocular system. Then, a fall can be detected when the 3D vertical head velocity is too high or when the head is too close to the ground.

Notice that all our algorithms are implemented in C++ using the OpenCV library (Bradski & Kaehler, 2008) and can run in quasi-real-time.

4. 2D information for fall detection: human shape and Motion history image

A fall is characterized by a *large motion* combined with a *change in the human shape*. The idea in this work was to detect and analyze these two characteristics (Rougier et al., 2007).

4.1 Human shape change

The moving person is first extracted from the image with a background subtraction method (Kim et al., 2005) taking into account the problem of shadows, highlights and high image compression. Using moments (Jain, 1989; Pratt, 2001), the person is then approximated by an ellipse defined by its center $(\bar{x}, \bar{y})$, its orientation θ and the length a and b of its major and minor semi-axes. The approximated ellipse gives us information about the shape and orientation of the person in the image. Some examples of background subtraction results and ellipse approximation are shown in Fig. 5 and 6.
Two features are computed for a $1s$ duration to analyze the human shape change:

The orientation standard deviation σ_θ of the ellipse If a person falls perpendicularly to the camera optical axis, then the orientation will change significantly and σ_θ will be high. If the person just walks, σ_θ will be low.

The a/b ratio standard deviation $\sigma_{a/b}$ of the ellipse If a person falls parallelly to the camera optical axis, then the ratio will change and $\sigma_{a/b}$ will be high. If the person just walks, $\sigma_{a/b}$ will be low.

4.2 Motion history image

A serious fall generally occurs with a large movement which can also be quantified with the Motion History Image (Bobick & Davis, 2001). The Motion History Image (MHI) is an image representing the recent motion in the scene, and is based on a binary sequence of motion regions $D(x,y,t)$ from the original image sequence $I(x,y,t)$ using an image-differencing method. Then, each pixel of the Motion History Image H_τ is a function of the temporal history of motion at that point, occurring during a fixed duration τ (with $1 \leq \tau \leq N$ for a sequence of length N frames):

$$H_\tau(x,y,t) = \begin{cases} \tau & if\ D(x,y,t) = 1 \\ \max(0, H_\tau(x,y,t-1) - 1) & otherwise. \end{cases} \tag{1}$$

The more recent moving pixels are seen brighter in the MHI image. Then, to quantify the motion of the person, we compute a coefficient C_{motion} based on the motion history (accumulation of motion during $500ms$) within the blob representing the person using:

$$C_{motion} = \frac{\sum_{Pixel(x,y)\in blob} H_\tau(x,y,t)}{\#\ pixels \in blob} \quad \text{with} \begin{cases} blob \text{ the person silhouette pixels} \\ H_\tau \text{ the Motion History Image} \end{cases} \tag{2}$$

Only the largest blob is considered here. This coefficient is then scaled to a percentage of motion between 0% (no motion) and 100% (full motion). Some examples of MHI images and corresponding coefficients C_{motion} are shown in Fig. 5 and 6.

4.3 Fall detection

Our complete fall detection algorithm, shown in Fig. 4, is composed of three steps:

1. **Motion quantification**
   A large suspicious motion is detected when the coefficient C_{motion} is higher than 65%. However, a walking person moving perpendicularly to the camera optical axis can also generate a large movement in the MHI image. Thus, we need to analyze further this abnormal motion to discriminate a fall from a normal movement.
2. **Human shape analysis**
   A large motion is considered as a possible fall if σ_θ is higher than 15 *degrees* or if $\sigma_{a/b}$ is higher than 0.9 (sufficient to be insensitive to little ellipse variations due to image segmentation problems or variation in human gait).
3. **Lack of motion after a fall**
   The last step is used to check if the person is immobile on the ground just a few seconds after the fall (during 5 seconds). An unmoving ellipse must respect all these criteria:
   • $C_{motion} < 5\%$
   • $\sigma_{\bar{x}} < 2$ pixels and $\sigma_{\bar{y}} < 2$ pixels, with $\sigma_{\bar{x}}$ and $\sigma_{\bar{y}}$ the standard deviations of the centroid position.
   • $\sigma_a < 2$ pixels, $\sigma_b < 2$ pixels and $\sigma_\theta < 15$ degrees, with σ_a, σ_b and σ_θ the standard deviations of the ellipse parameters.

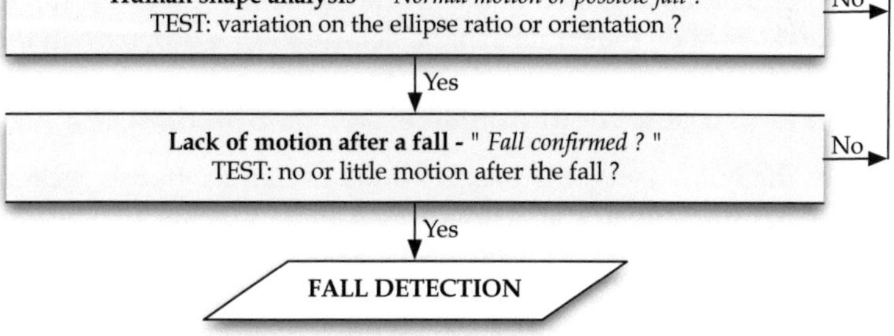

Fig. 4. Our fall detection algorithm based on the Motion History Image and human shape.

4.4 Experimental results

For a low-cost system, our video sequences were acquired using a USB webcam with a wide angle of more than 70 degrees to cover all the room (model Live! Ultra from Creative Technology Ltd). Our system works with a single uncalibrated camera (image size 320x240 pixels) and runs in real-time (computational time of less than 80 *ms* which is adequate for our application as 10 fps is sufficient to detect a fall).

Some examples of falls are shown in Fig. 5 and normal activities in Fig. 6. The human silhouette, extracted from the background, is approximated by an ellipse shown in red. This figure shows also the MHI image obtained and the coefficient values used for fall detection. When a fall occurs, a large motion appears (high C_{motion}) with a significant change in orientation and/or scale (high σ_θ and/or $\sigma_{a/b}$).

(a) Fall with direction perpendicular to the camera axis, which is detected as C_{motion} and σ_θ are high.

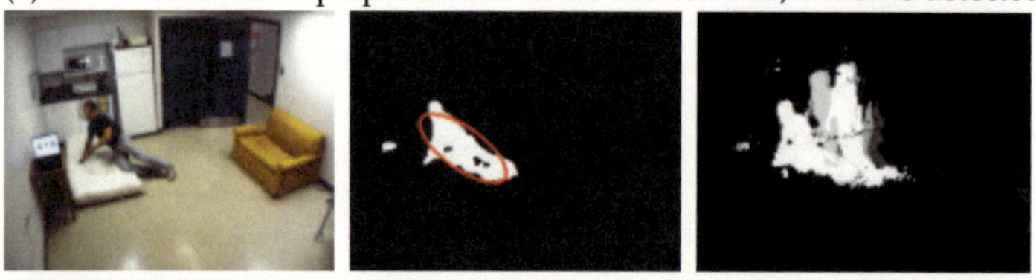

$C_{motion} = \mathbf{93.3\%}$
$\sigma_\theta = \mathbf{15.98}$
$\sigma_{a/b} = 0.74$

(b) Fall with direction parallel to the camera axis. C_{motion} and $\sigma_{a/b}$ are sufficiently high to detect the fall.

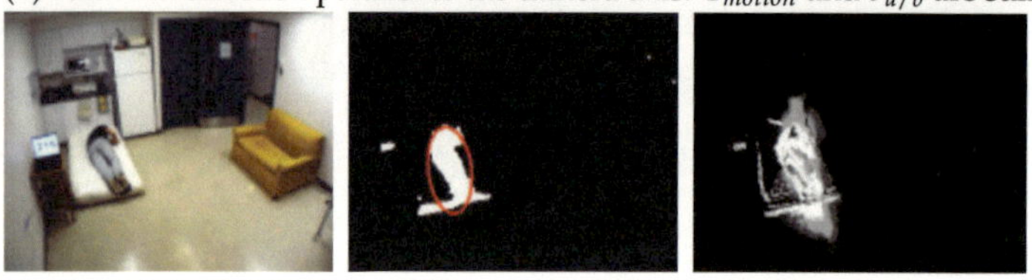

$C_{motion} = \mathbf{74.3\%}$
$\sigma_\theta = 3.26$
$\sigma_{a/b} = \mathbf{0.97}$

For our experiments, our data set was composed of realistic video sequences representing 24 daily normal activities (walking, sitting down, standing up, crouching down) and 17 simulated falls (forward falls, backward falls, falls when inappropriately sitting down, loss of balance). We obtained a good fall detection rate with a sensitivity of 88% and an acceptable false detection rate with a specificity of 87.5%, in spite of the bad video quality and the fluctuant frame rate of the webcam. We have demonstrated that the combination of motion and change in the human shape gives crucial information on human activities. Some thresholds were experimentally defined in this work, but could be learned from training data. An automatic method based on the human shape deformation is proposed in the next section.

5. 2D information for fall detection: human shape deformation

As seen previously, the human shape is useful for fall detection. In this section, we describe our method to quantify the human shape *deformation* and automatically detect falls (Rougier et al., 2008; 2010b). The idea is that the human shape changes drastically and rapidly during a fall, while during usual activities, this deformation is more progressive and (relatively) slow. In this section, the human shape deformation is quantified to discriminate real falls from normal activities. First, some edge points are extracted from the human silhouette by combining a foreground segmentation with a Canny edge detection in the image. Then, two consecutive silhouettes can be matched using Shape Context to quantify the human shape deformation. Finally, a GMM classifier based on shape analysis is used to detect falls.

5.1 Silhouette edge point matching using shape context

The shape descriptor "Shape Context" (Belongie et al., 2002) is used to match two consecutive sets of edge points. As Shape Context is sensitive to background edges, we improve the method by only considering moving silhouette edge points. They are extracted by combining

(c) The person walks with direction parallel to the camera axis, all coefficients are low.

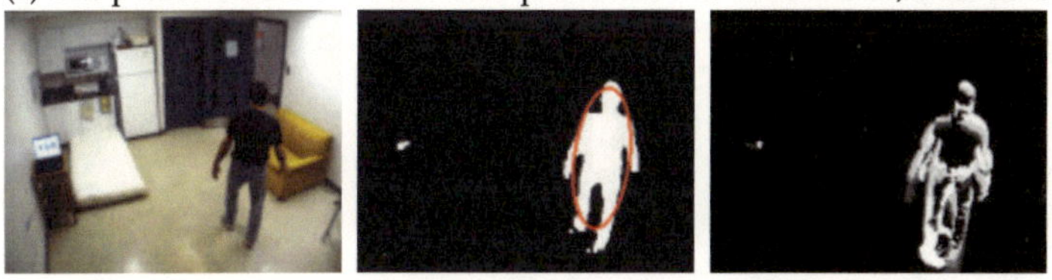

$C_{motion} = 39.6\%$
$\sigma_\theta = 1.64$
$\sigma_{a/b} = 0.26$

(d) The person walks with direction perpendicular to the camera axis, which generates a large C_{motion}. However, as σ_θ and $\sigma_{a/b}$ are low, no fall is detected.

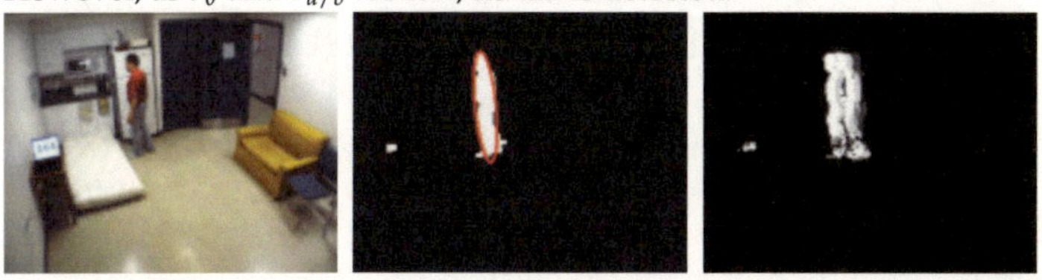

$C_{motion} = \mathbf{74.6\%}$
$\sigma_\theta = 0.69$
$\sigma_{a/b} = 0.32$

(e) A sitting person generates a moderate coefficient C_{motion} which can be sufficient for a suspicious fall. However, as σ_θ and $\sigma_{a/b}$ are low, no fall is detected.

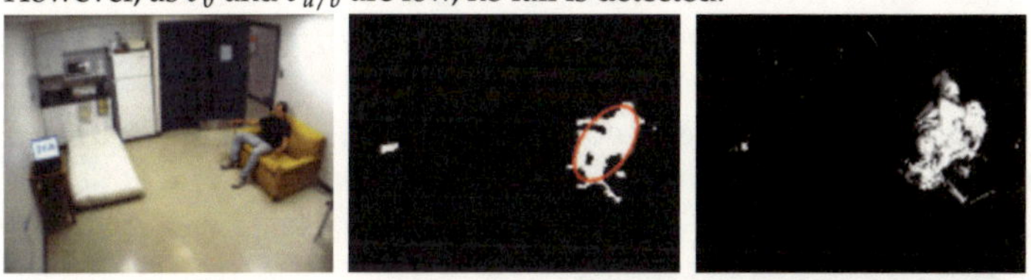

$C_{motion} = \mathbf{72.3\%}$
$\sigma_\theta = 10.4$
$\sigma_{a/b} = 0.8$

(f) The person, doing housekeeping, only moves the arm which do not increase the different coefficients.

$C_{motion} = 9.3\%$
$\sigma_\theta = 4.02$
$\sigma_{a/b} = 0.02$

Fig. 6. Examples of normal activities.

the foreground silhouette, obtained from a background subtraction method (Kim et al., 2005), with an edge image of the scene, obtained from a Canny edge detector (Canny, 1986), to provide additional shape information. For real-time purpose, N landmarks, regularly-spaced, are selected for each silhouette ($N = 250$ for our experiment).

For each point p_i of the first shape, the best corresponding point q_j of the second shape needs to be find. A log-polar histogram h_i is used to encode local information about each point relative to its neighbours. h_i is centered on each point p_i and contains the relative coordinates of the remaining $n-1$ points:

$$h_i(k) = \#\{q \neq p_i : (q - p_i) \in bin(k)\}, \qquad h_i \text{ contains 5 bins for } \log r \text{ and 12 bins for } \theta \quad (3)$$

Similar points on the two shapes can be found using the matching cost computed with the χ^2 statistic. This matching cost C_{ij} is computed for each pair of points (p_i, q_j):

$$C_{ij} = C(p_i, q_j) = \frac{1}{2} \sum_{k=1}^{K} \frac{\left[h_i(k) - h_j(k)\right]^2}{h_i(k) + h_j(k)} \tag{4}$$

where $h_i(k)$ and $h_j(k)$ denote the K-bin histograms respectively for p_i and q_j.
Using the resulting cost matrix, the best corresponding points are obtained by minimizing the total matching cost $H(\pi) = \sum_i C(p_i, q_{\pi(i)})$ given a permutation $\pi(i)$. The Hungarian algorithm (Kuhn, 1955) for bipartite matching is used by the authors of (Belongie et al., 2002) to find corresponding points, but this algorithm is time consuming and some bad matching points can appear in spite of the inclusion of dummy points. As we want to keep only reliable points for the shape deformation quantification, we find those that have their cost minimal for the row and the column of the matrix ($\min_i C_{ij} = \min_j C_{ij}$). To discard some bad landmarks which may still remain, the set of matching points is also cleaned based on the motion of the person, by computing the mean motion vector $\bar{v}$ and the standard deviation σ_v from the set of matching points. Only the vectors within 1.28 standard deviation from the mean, which corresponds to 80% of the motion vectors, are kept. The *mean matching cost* $\bar{C}$ is then obtained by averaging all the best matching points costs. An example of Shape Context matching is shown in Fig. 7. While the foreground silhouette is not clean enough to be used for shape analysis, due to segmentation problems, the moving edge points are perfect to match the two consecutive silhouettes.

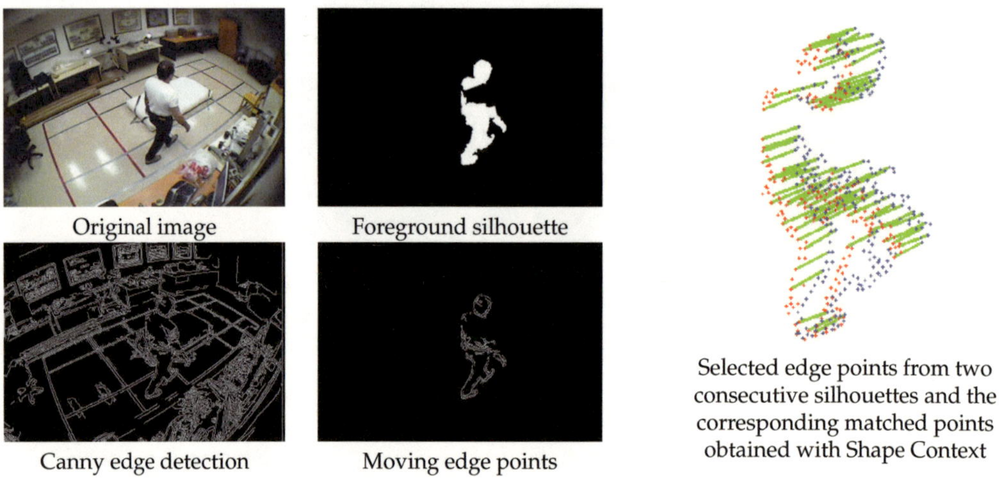

Fig. 7. Example of silhouette matching with Shape Context

5.2 Shape analysis

When a fall occurs, the human shape will drastically change during the fall ($\bar{C}_1$ or D_1) and finally will remain motionless just after ($\bar{C}_2$ or D_2) as shown in Fig. 8. These features are analyzed in two ways:

With the mean matching cost i.e. features $(\bar{C}_1, \bar{C}_2)$
$\bar{C}_1$ should be high during the fall as the human shape change drastically in a short period of time, while just after, $\bar{C}_2$ should be low as the person remains unmoving on the ground.

With the full Procrustes distance i.e. features (D_1, D_2)

The Procrustes shape analysis (Dryden & Mardia, 1998) is used to quantify the shape deformation, which consists in comparing the shapes once translational, rotational and scaling components are removed to normalize them. The full Procrustes distance should increase in case of a fall (feature D_1), and should be low just after the fall (feature D_2).

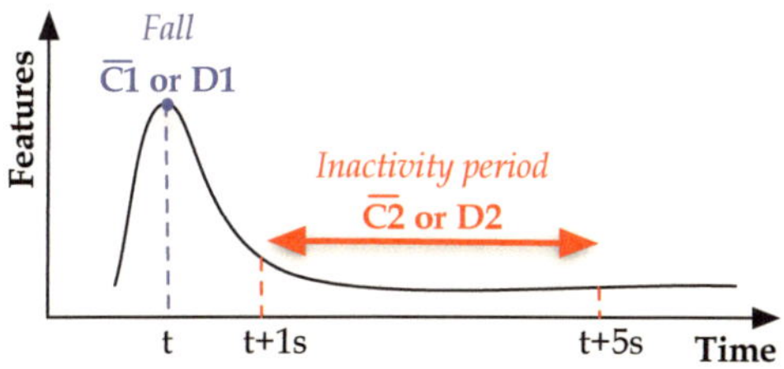

Feature $\bar{C}_1$ or D_1 represents the fall at time t.

Feature $\bar{C}_2$ or D_2 represents the lack of movement after the fall. This feature was computed between $t + 1s$ and $t + 5s$, this time interval was determined experimentally.

Fig. 8. The features $(\bar{C}_1, \bar{C}_2)$ and (D_1, D_2).

5.3 Fall detection using GMM

The fall detection problem consists in detecting an abnormal event from a training data set of normal activities, which is known as novelty detection methods (Hodge & Austin, 2004). For our experiment, our normal activities are modeled by a GMM (Gaussian Mixture Model) which is defined by a weighted sum of Gaussian distributions (Nabney, 2001). The GMM parameters are determined using the EM (Expectation-Maximisation) algorithm by maximizing the data likelihood.

Specifically in our case, the parameters of the GMM are estimated from a training data set of daily normal activities (walking, sitting down, crouching down, housekeeping, etc) with the GMM features $(\bar{C}_1 \text{ } or \text{ } D_1, \bar{C}_2 \text{ } or \text{ } D_2)$ described previously. For training and testing, a leave-one-out cross-validation is used. The data set is divided into N video sequences which contain some falls and/or normal activities (including lures). For testing, one sequence is removed from the data set, and the training is done using the $N - 1$ remaining sequences (where falls are deleted because the training is only done with normal activities). The removed sequence is then classified with the resulting GMM. This test is repeated N times by removing each sequence in turn. The sensitivity and the specificity of the system give an idea of the classifier performance. Considering the number of falls correctly detected (*True Positives, TP*) and not detected (*False Negatives, FN*), and the number of normal activities (including lures) detected as a fall (*False Positives, FP*) and not detected (*True Negatives, TN*), the sensitivity is equal to $Se = TP/(TP + FN)$ and the specificity $Sp = TN/(TN + FP)$. An efficient fall detection system will have a high sensitivity (a majority of falls are detected) and a high specificity (normal activities and lures are not detected as falls).

5.4 Experimental results

Our method was tested on our video data set of simulated falls and normal daily activities (Auvinet et al., 2010) taken from 4 different camera points of view. The acquisition frame rate was 30 fps and the image size was 720x480 pixels. The shape matching is implemented in C++ using the OpenCV library (Bradski & Kaehler, 2008) and the fall detection step is done with Matlab using the Netlab toolbox (Nabney, 2001) to perform the GMM classification. The computational time of the shape matching step is about 200*ms* on an Intel Core 2 Duo processor (2.4 GHz), which is adequate for our application as a frame rate of 5 fps is sufficient to detect a fall. A 3-component GMM was used in our experiment as we have shown (Rougier et al., 2010b) that it was the best compromise between a low classification error rate, a good repeatability of the results and a reasonable computation time. Figure 9 shows a log-likelihood example obtained with a 3-component GMM for the full Procrustes distance features, and a fall event in light blue superimposed on the graphic. The input features are normalized to unit standard deviations and zero means.

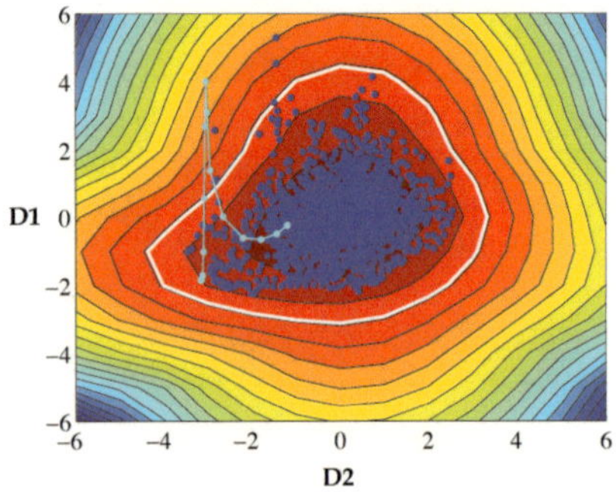

The dark blue points represent the normalized training data set (normal activities).

The white boundary represents the boundary for the chosen log-likelihood threshold.

The light blue points corresponds to a sequence where a fall occurs. The fall is detected when the points are outside the boundary.

Fig. 9. Example of log-likelihood obtained with a 3-component GMM and a fall event.

A ROC analysis was performed for each camera independently and for a majority vote (fall detected if at least 3 of 4 cameras returned a fall detection event). Figure 10 shows the curves obtained for the full Procrustes distance (a) and mean matching cost features (b).

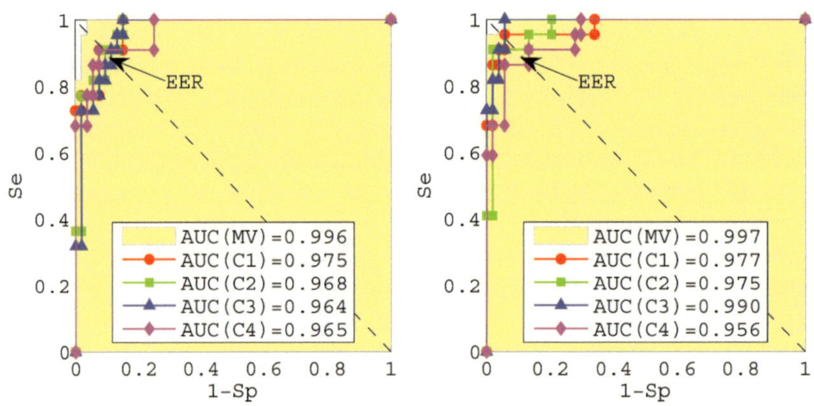

(a) For the full Procrustes distance (b) For the mean matching cost

Fig. 10. ROC curves (log-likelihood threshold ranging from -50 to -1) obtained for each camera independently (C1, C2,C3, C4) and for a majority vote (MV, at least 3 of 4 cameras).

Table 1 shows our recognition results for the *full Procrustes distance* and the *mean matching cost* regarding several evaluation tests:

1. *Using the best matching points*
   Our results are quite good for each camera independently and increase with a majority vote. The similar ROC curves prove that our method is view-independent for the two features. The *full Procrustes distance* and the *mean matching cost* gave similar results with, respectively, an Equal Error Rate of 3.8% and 4.6% with a majority vote.

2. *Using the Hungarian matching*
   The results obtained with the Hungarian matching are not statistically different from those obtained with our methodology. However, Hungarian matching is more time consuming, requires to choose the percentage of dummy points (a parameter that affect considerably the quality of the results) and can leave bad matching points.
3. *Using normal inactivity zones*
   A solution to increase the recognition results could be to define normal inactivity zones (Lee & Mihailidis, 2005) like the bed or the sofa, where the detection thresholds should be less sensitive. Normal inactivity zones were defined manually in our video sequences, and when the person centroid was localized inside one of these zones, the detection threshold was fixed at 1.5 times the normal threshold. As shown in Table 1, the use of normal inactivity zones can really increase the recognition results. These inactivity zones could be automatically learned before installing the system.

Camera	Features	Best matching* points	Hungarian† matching	Inactivity‡ zones
Camera 1	(D_1, D_2)	9.1% (0.978)	13.2% (0.963)	5.7% (0.983)
Camera 2		9.4% (0.968)	9.4% (0.965)	9.1% (0.979)
Camera 3		11.3% (0.964)	7.6% (0.988)	7.6% (0.971)
Camera 4		9.1% (0.966)	13.6% (0.930)	9.1% (0.983)
Majority vote		3.8% (0.996)	9.1% (0.907)	0% (1)
Camera 1	$(\bar{C}_1, \bar{C}_2)$	5.7% (0.977)	11.3% (0.953)	4.6% (0.984)
Camera 2		9.1% (0.975)	9.1% (0.979)	0% (1)
Camera 3		5.7% (0.990)	9.4% (0.979)	5.7% (0.988)
Camera 4		13.2% (0.956)	13.6% (0.935)	9.4% (0.972)
Majority vote		4.6% (0.997)	0% (1)	1.9% (0.999)

* *Our matching method considering only the best matching points.*
† *The Hungarian algorithm (Kuhn, 1955) for bipartite matching with 20% of dummy points.*
‡ *Results obtained when normal inactivity zones are added for classification (best matching points).*

Table 1. EER and AUC values obtained for the full Procrustes distance (D_1, D_2) and the mean matching $(\bar{C}_1, \bar{C}_2)$ features.

In conclusion, the human shape deformation is a useful tool for fall detection, as the full Procrustes distance and the mean matching cost are really discriminant features for classification. By using only reliable landmarks, our silhouette matching using Shape Context is robust to occlusions and other segmentation difficulties (the full Procrustes distance or the mean matching can be sensitive to bad matching points). Our GMM classification results are quite good with only one uncalibrated camera, and the performance can increase using a majority vote with a multi-camera system. Detection errors generally occur when the person sits down too brutally which generates a high shape deformation detected as a fall, or with a slow fall which do not generate a sufficiently high shape deformation to be detected. With such cases, it becomes difficult to chose the best detection threshold. A solution is the use of known inactivity zones which increases the results as shown in this work.

6. 3D information for fall detection

The head trajectory can be very useful for activity recognition and video surveillance applications. A new method is shown here to compute the 3D head trajectory of a person in a room with only one calibrated camera (Rougier et al., 2006; 2010a). The head, represented by a 3D ellipsoid, is tracked with a hierarchical particle filter based on color histograms and shape information. The resulting 3D trajectory is then used to detect falls.

6.1 Related works in 3D head tracking

The head has been widely used to track a person as it is usually visible in the scene and its elliptical shape is simple. The head can be track by a 2D ellipse in the image plane, for example, using gradient and/or color information with a local search (Birchfield, 1998) or with a particle filter (Charif & McKenna, 2006; K. Nummiaro & Gool, 2003). However, a 3D head trajectory gives more information about the localization and the movement of a person in a room. The easy way to recover some 3D information is to use several cameras. For example, the 3D head trajectory has been extracted using stereo cameras (Kawanaka et al., 2006; Mori & Malik, 2002) or multi-camera systems (Kobayashi et al., 2006; Usabiaga et al., 2007; Wu & Aghajan, 2008). However, tracking the head to recover a 3D trajectory in real-time with only one camera is a real challenge. One attempt by (Hild, 2004) was to compute the top head 3D trajectory of a walking person. However, his assumptions are that the person is standing and that the camera optical axis is parallel to the (horizontal) ground plane, which is not practical in video surveillance applications. Indeed, the camera must be placed higher in the room for a larger field of view and to avoid occluding objects, and the person is not always standing or facing the camera. In our previous work (Rougier et al., 2006) with a single calibrated camera, the head was tracked with a 2D ellipse which was used to compute the 3D head localization by knowing the 3D model of the head. The resulting 3D trajectory for a standing person was well estimated, but some errors occurred with a falling person (need to deal with oriented head). An improvement is shown here using an oriented 3D ellipsoid to represent the head which is tracked with a particle filter through the video sequence.

6.2 Head model projection

The head, represented by a 3D ellipsoid, is projected in the image plane as an ellipse (Stenger et al., 2001). The 3D head model will be tracked in the world coordinate system attached to the XY ground plane as shown in Fig. 11. The projection of the 3D head model in the image plane is possible by knowing the camera characteristics (intrinsic parameters) and the pose of the XY ground plane relative to the camera (extrinsic parameters).

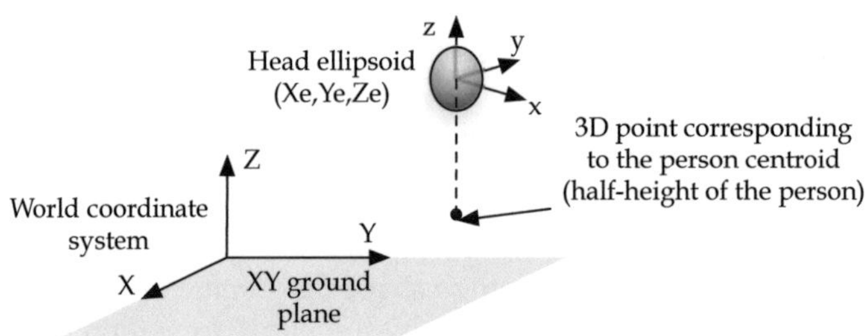

Fig. 11. The 3D head ellipsoid model.

- **Camera parameters**

  The intrinsic parameters were computed using a chessboard calibration pattern and the camera calibration toolbox for Matlab (Bouguet, 2008). The focal length (f_x, f_y) and the optical center (u_0, v_0) in pixels define the camera's intrinsic matrix K. Notice that image distortion coefficients (radial and tangential distortions) are also computed to correct the images for distortion before processing. From a set of ground points in the real world and the corresponding image points, the plane-image homography is computed to obtain the extrinsic parameters (Zhang, 2000). The extrinsic matrix M_{ext} is defined by R and T which are respectively a 3D rotation matrix and a 3D translation vector.

$$K = \begin{pmatrix} f_x & 0 & u_0 & 0 \\ 0 & f_y & v_0 & 0 \\ 0 & 0 & 1 & 0 \end{pmatrix} \qquad M_{ext} = \begin{pmatrix} R & T \\ 000 & 1 \end{pmatrix} \tag{5}$$

- **Ellipsoid projection**

  An ellipsoid is described by a positive definite matrix Q_C in the camera coordinate system, such that $[x, y, z, 1]^T Q_C [x, y, z, 1] = 0$, with (x, y, z) a point belonging to the ellipsoid. The ellipsoid Q_C is then projected in the image plane, using the projection matrix P, as a conic C (Hartley & Zisserman, 2004; Stenger et al., 2001):

$$C = Q_{C_{44}} Q_{C_{1:3,1:3}} - Q_{C_{1:3,4}} Q_{C_{1:3,4}}^T \tag{6}$$

  From the conic, the ellipse is described by $[u, v, 1]^T C [u, v, 1] = 0$ for a point (u, v) in the image plane.

- **From the head coordinate system to the ellipse in the image plane**

  Our 3D head ellipsoid model expressed in the head coordinate system, has the form:

$$Q_H = \begin{pmatrix} \frac{1}{B^2} & 0 & 0 & 0 \\ 0 & \frac{1}{B^2} & 0 & 0 \\ 0 & 0 & \frac{1}{A^2} & 0 \\ 0 & 0 & 0 & -1 \end{pmatrix} \quad \text{with the semi-major } A \text{ and the semi-minor } B \text{ ellipsoid head axes} \tag{7}$$

  The projection matrix $P = K M_{ext} M_{Head/World}$, which represents the transformation from the head ellipsoid coordinate system to the image plane, is used to project the head ellipsoid in the camera coordinate system such that $Q_C = P^{-1T} Q_H P^{-1}$. The translation and rotation of the head in the world coordinate system, which corresponds to the matrix $M_{Head/World}$, will be defined by the head tracking (see Section 6.3). Finally, the parameters of the ellipse representing the head in the image plane are obtained from the conic defined in eq. 6.

6.3 3D head tracking with particle filter

Tracking with particle filters has been widely used, for example, to track the head with an ellipse (K. Nummiaro & Gool, 2003; Rougier et al., 2006) or a parametric spline curve (Isard & Blake, 1998) using color information or edge contours. Their particularity is that they allow abrupt trajectory variations and can deal with small occlusions.

Particle filters are used to estimate the probability distribution $p(S_t|Z_t)$ of the state vector S_t of the tracked object given Z_t, representing all the observations. This probability can be approximated from a set $S_t = \{s_t^n, n = 1, \ldots, N\}$ of N weighted samples (also called particles) at time t. A particle filter is composed of three steps:

1. **Selection**

   N new samples are selected from the previous sample set by favoring the best particles to create a new sample set S'_t.

2. **Prediction**

   A stochastic dynamical model is used to propagate the new samples $s_t^n = A_l s_t'^n + B_l w_t^n$, where w_t^n is a vector of standard normal random variables, and A_l and B_l are, respectively, the deterministic and stochastic components of the dynamical model.

3. **Measurement**

   The new weights $\pi_t^n = p(z_t|s_t^n)$ are computed and normalized so that $\sum_n \pi^n = 1$.

The final step corresponds to the mean state estimation of the system at time t using the N final weighted samples i.e. $E[S_t] = \sum_{n=1}^{N} \pi_t^n s_t^n$
Our implementation of the particle filter is similar to the annealed particle filter (Deutscher et al., 2000) in a hierarchical scheme with several layers. Each layer is composed of the three main particle filter steps, and at the end of the layer, the stochastic component is reduced for the next layer: $B_{l+1} = B_l/2$ (see Section 6.5). Our ellipsoid particles are represented by the state vector:

$$s_t^n = [X_e, Y_e, Z_e, \theta_{Xe}, \theta_{Ye}]_t^n \tag{8}$$

where (X_e, Y_e, Z_e) is the 3D head ellipsoid centroid expressed in the world coordinate system (translation component of the matrix $M_{Head/World}$), and $(\theta_{X_e}, \theta_{Y_e})$ are respectively the rotation around the X and the Y axes (rotation component of the matrix $M_{Head/World}$) [1]. No motion is added in our dynamical model as the previous velocity between two successive centroids is already added to the particles to predict the next 3D ellipsoid localization before propagating the particles (i.e. A_l is an identity matrix).

6.4 Particles weights

The particle weights are based on foreground, color and body coefficients:

- **Foreground coefficient** C_F

  Role The 3D pose precision is obtained with the foreground coefficient when the ellipsoid is well matched to the head contour

  Definition The foreground silhouette of the person is extracted with a background subtraction method which consists in comparing the current image with an updated background image (Kim et al., 2005). The foreground coefficient is computed by searching for silhouette contour points along N_e line segments normal to the ellipse, distributed uniformly along the ellipse and centered on its contour. An example of foreground coefficient is shown in Fig. 12.

$$C_F = \frac{1}{N_e} \sum_{n=1}^{N_e} \frac{D_e(n) - d_e(n)}{D_e(n)}, \quad C_F \in [0 \ldots 1] \tag{9}$$

  where d_e is the distance from the ellipse point to the detected silhouette point and D_e, the half length of the normal segment, is used to normalize the distances.

[1] Notice that two angles (instead of three) are sufficient to define the position and orientation of the ellipsoid since its minor axes have both the same length in our model.

For an ellipse defined by the semi-axis parameters a and b, each segment begins from the inner ellipse (axes $a/2$ and $b/2$) to the outer ellipse (axes $a + a/2$ and $b + b/2$).

Fig. 12. Foreground segmentation and foreground coefficient computation examples.

- **Color coefficient** C_C

  Role The color coefficient is used to prevent the ellipsoid from hanging on something else inside the silhouette when large movement occurs.

  Definition The color coefficient is based on a normalized 3D color histogram of the head (K. Nummiaro & Gool, 2003). The histogram H is computed in the RGB color space inside a rectangular zone included in the head ellipse and composed of $N_b = 8 \times 8 \times 8$ bins. The updated color head model and the target model are compared by calculating the normalized histogram intersection:

$$C_C = \sum_{i=1}^{N_b} \min\left(H(i), H_{ref}(i)\right), \quad C_C \in [0 \ldots 1] \tag{10}$$

- **Body coefficient** C_B

  Role The body coefficient is used to link the head to the body through the body center, to avoid unrealistic 3D ellipsoid rotation.

  Definition The distance between the projection of the 3D point corresponding to the centroid of the person (see Fig. 11) and the 2D silhouette centroid (distance d_b compared to the half-major axis of the bounding box D_b) should be small. This coefficient is only used when the bounding box is valid (and thus not used in case of occlusion for example).

$$C_B = \frac{D_b - d_b}{D_b}, \quad C_B \in [0 \ldots 1] \tag{11}$$

The final ellipsoid coefficient is an amplified combination of these three coefficients to give larger weights to the best particles ($\sigma = 0.15$):

$$C_{final} = \frac{1}{\sqrt{2\pi}\sigma} \exp^{(C_F C_C C_B)/2\sigma^2} \tag{12}$$

As the mean state of the particle filter is a weighted combination of all particles, the weights amplification is important to obtain a more precise 3D localization.

6.5 Initialization and tracking

The ellipsoid size is calibrated from a manually initialized 2D ellipse representing the head. With this ellipse and by knowing the body height and the ellipse aspect ratio (The ratio of a human head ellipse is fixed at 1.2 (Birchfield, 1998)), the ellipsoid proportion can be computed.

Our system is automatically initialized with a head detection module which consists in testing several 2D ellipses from the top head point of the foreground silhouette. The one which has the biggest foreground coefficient C_F is kept, and if $C_F > 0.7$, the ellipse is supposed sufficiently reliable to begin the tracking with the particle filter.
An initial 3D head centroid localization can be computed from this 2D detected ellipse, by knowing the ellipsoid proportion and the camera calibration parameters using the iterative algorithm POSIT (Dementhon & Davis, 1995). This algorithm returns the relative position of the head in the camera coordinate system $P_{Head/Cam}$, which can be transformed in the world coordinate system attached to the XY ground plane using $P_{Head/World} = M^{-1}_{World/Cam} P_{Head/Cam}$ with the matrix $M_{World/Cam}$ representing the known position of the world coordinate system in the camera coordinate system. The head localization $P_{Head/World}$ is used to initialize the tracking and is then refined with the particle filter.
For a reliable 3D head localization, the head projection in the image need to be well adjusted to the head contour. With a conventional particle filter, a lot of particles are needed for precision which severely affects the computational performance and is incompatible with real-time operation. With several layers, a better precision can be reached in a shortest time, a good compromise between performance and computational time can be obtained with 250 particles and 4 layers. The stochastic component $B_l = \left[B_{X_e}, B_{Y_e}, B_{Z_e}, B_{\theta_{X_e}}, B_{\theta_{Y_e}}\right]$ for the model propagation is different for each layer, sufficiently large for the first layer and decreasing for the next layers, such as $B_{l+1} = B_l/2$ with l the current layer and $l+1$ the next layer. As the person is supposed to be standing up at the beginning, Z_e is approximately known and, θ_{X_e} and θ_{Y_e} are close to zero. Thus, our initial values are fixed to $B_l = [0.5\ 0.5\ 0.3\ 0\ 0]$ which corresponds to a large diffusion for the X and Y components ($\pm 50cm$) on the horizontal plane and a moderate one ($\pm 30cm$) for the Z component. For the next images, the current velocity is used to reinitialize B_l such that the particles spread towards the 3D trajectory direction (minimum of $0.1m$ or $0.1rad$ for B_l). Recall that A_l is an identity matrix (see Section 6.3). Figure 13 shows the usefulness of the hierarchical particle filter for a large motion. By considering only the first layer, the ellipsoid is badly estimated, while with the four layers, the ellipsoid is finally well adjusted.

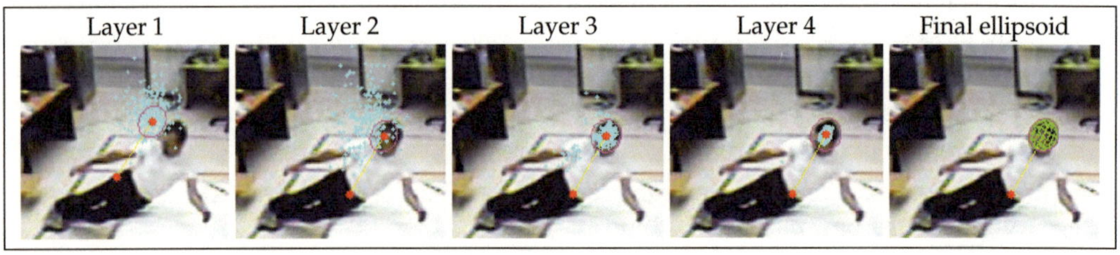

Fig. 13. Example of a large motion during a fall. The images show the particles and the mean state ellipsoid for each layer, and the resulting ellipsoid.

6.6 Experimental results

Our 3D head tracker is implemented in C++ using the OpenCV library (Bradski & Kaehler, 2008) and can run in quasi-real time (130ms/frame on an Intel Core 2 Duo processor (2.4 GHz), non optimized code and image size of 640x480).

6.6.1 3D localization precision using HumanEva data set

The 3D localization precision is evaluated with the HumanEva-I data set (Sigal & Black, 2006) which contains synchronized multi-view video sequences and corresponding MoCap data (ground truth 3D localizations). The results were obtained for each camera independently (color cameras C_1, C_2 and C_3) using the video sequences of 3 subjects (S1, S2 and S3). The motion sequences "walking" and "jogging" were used to evaluate our 3D trajectories at 30Hz, 20Hz and 10Hz. The resulting 3D head trajectories (top head point) obtained from different view points are similar to the MoCap trajectory as shown in Fig. 14. The small location error for the Z axis and the cyclical movement of the walking person visible on the curve prove that the head height is quite well estimated. The depth error (X and Y location) is a little higher due to the ellipsoid detection (noisy foreground images, artifacts on the silhouette) and depending on the orientation of the person relative to the camera (for simplicity, the frontal/back and lateral views of the head are considered identical in our 3D ellipsoid model).

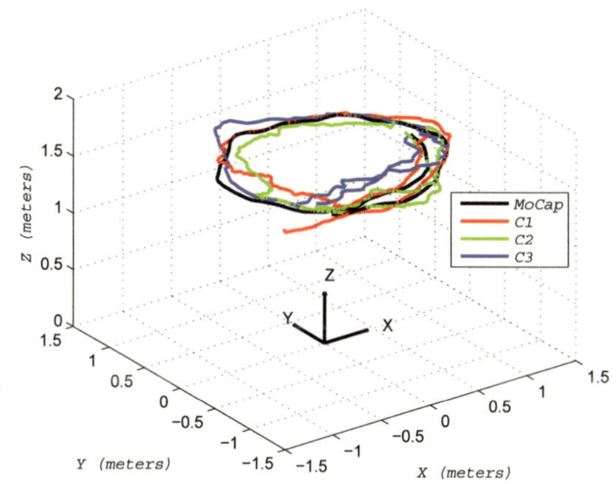

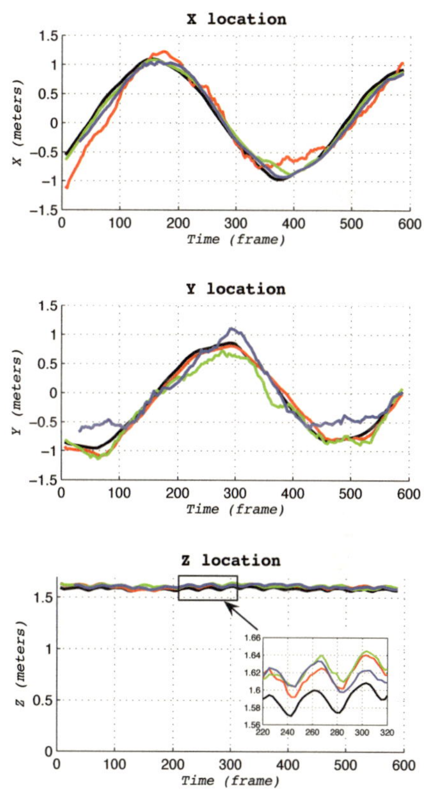

3D errors	C1	C2	C3
X error	17.7 ± 12.6	7.1 ± 4.8	8.3 ± 4.8
Y error	7.2 ± 4.4	11.9 ± 9.8	15.6 ± 12.3
Z error	2.3 ± 1.1	2.7 ± 0.9	2.4 ± 1

Fig. 14. 3D head trajectories for a walking sequence of subject S1 (20Hz). The table shows the mean 3D errors (in cm) for X, Y and Z location.

The 3D mean errors obtained for each subject and each camera are shown in Table 2. The mean error was about 5% at a 4 to 6 meters distance. As expected, the error tended to be slightly higher when the movement was larger, but the head still continues to be well tracked with the 3D ellipsoid.

Camera, Frame rate	Walking sequences S1	S2	S3	Jogging sequences S1	S2	S3
C1, 30Hz	20.6 ± 13.6	20.5 ± 7.3	21.3 ± 12.9	19.2 ± 9.5	24.1 ± 16.3	25.9 ± 15.3
C2, 30Hz	17.1 ± 13	21.3 ± 7.8	23.6 ± 10.7	20.6 ± 12.4	24.5 ± 10.6	17.4 ± 9.7
C3, 30Hz	17.3 ± 11.6	21.4 ± 8.4	25.9 ± 17	21.5 ± 13.6	23.7 ± 11.6	28.8 ± 17.2
C1, 20Hz	20 ± 12.4	21.2 ± 7.4	19.7 ± 11.5	16.6 ± 10.3	25.4 ± 17.4	25.5 ± 16.7
C2, 20Hz	15.1 ± 9.6	22.8 ± 8.5	22.8 ± 11.1	22.8 ± 10.1	26.3 ± 12	16.9 ± 10.3
C3, 20Hz	19 ± 11.5	20.6 ± 8.4	28.8 ± 19.4	15.3 ± 9.8	23 ± 11.5	30 ± 19
C1, 10Hz	24 ± 12.8	22.8 ± 8.2	21 ± 13	21 ± 11.4	25.9 ± 16.2	23.2 ± 16.1
C2, 10Hz	18.3 ± 12.6	22.5 ± 9.9	18.3 ± 14	22.1 ± 13.8	29.2 ± 13.7	22.8 ± 16.8
C3, 10Hz	22.6 ± 14	19.5 ± 8.5	28.8 ± 17.7	22 ± 10.5	24.1 ± 14.2	33.7 ± 20.7

Table 2. Mean 3D errors (in cm) obtained from walking and jogging sequences for different subjects (S1, S2, S3), several view points (C1, C2, C3) and several frame rates.

6.6.2 3D head trajectory for fall detection

A biomechanical study with wearable markers (Wu, 2000) showed that falls can be distinguished from normal activities using 3D velocities. In Fig. 13, we have shown that our 3D head tracker was efficient with an oriented person and large motion. We propose here to use the 3D head trajectory, obtained without markers, for fall detection. Two fall detection methods are explored:

The vertical velocity V_v of the head centroid is computed as a height difference for a 500 *ms* duration [2]: $V_v = Z_e(t) - Z_e(t - 500\ ms)$

The head height Z_e, corresponding to the centroid head height relative to the ground, should be small at the end of the fall as the person is supposed to be near the ground.

For our experiment, ten falls (forward falls, backward falls, loss of balance) from our video data set (Auvinet et al., 2010) were used with two cameras. The falls were done in different directions with respect to the two camera points of view, which were separated by 9 meters (deep field of view), placed at the entrance of the space and on the opposite wall. The acquisition frame rate was 30 fps, but 10 fps was sufficient to detect a fall. The image size was 720x480 pixels. Due to the wide angle, the images needed to be corrected for distortion before processing as shown in Fig. 15.

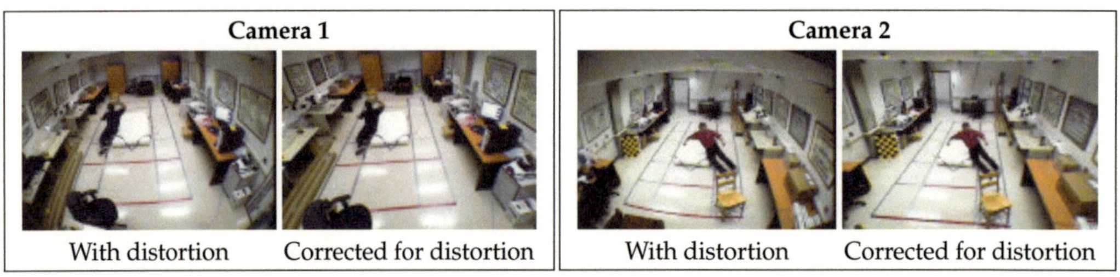

Fig. 15. Examples of images from the two viewpoints before and after distortion correction.

Figure 16 shows the vertical velocity V_v and the head height Z_e obtained for a video sequence of a fall viewed from the two points of view. The 3D head tracking was performed in spite of the deep field of view, and even if the person was not entirely in the image (camera 1 near the entry). Our tracker was automatically initialized when the head was correctly detected. As seen previously with the HumanEva-I data set, the head height was rather precise giving

[2] Duration of the fall critical phase (Noury et al., 2008)

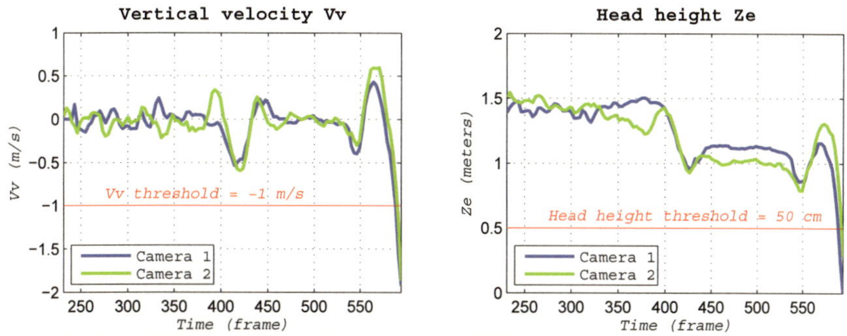

Walking (Frame 300)
The walking person until frame 400 generates a vertical velocity around 0m/s and a head height around 1.5m from the ground.

Sitting down (Frame 420)
When the person sits down, the head height decreases to 1m with a small vertical velocity.

Falling (Frame 588)
Finally, the person stands up again and falls with a high vertical velocity (V_v less than $-1m/s$) and the head height Z_e is below 50cm at the end of the fall.

Camera 1 **Camera 2**

Fig. 16. Vertical velocity and head height obtained for a video sequence of a fall.

similar head heights from the two views although 9 meters separates the two cameras. In spite of the low image quality, the 10 falls from the two views were successfully detected with the vertical velocity V_v (with a threshold at $-1m/s$). A person sitting down abruptly is also shown in Fig. 16 producing a vertical velocity equal to $-0.53m/s$ which was not sufficient to be detected as a fall. A head localization near the ground can be considered as a suspicious event for an old person. Thus, a fall can be detected when the head height Z_e is below 50cm. In this case, only one fall was not detected because of a tracking failure due to a noisy silhouette. However, this fall was detected with vertical velocity ($V_v = -1.17m/s$). Notice in Fig. 16 that the head height was about 1m when the person was seated.
To summarize, a 3D head trajectory can be extracted with only one calibrated camera. Our tracker was able to give similar results for different viewpoints, different frame rates and different subjects as shown with the HumanEva-I data set. These tests showed that the 3D locations were estimated with a mean error of around 25cm (5% at 5 meters) which

is sufficient for most activity recognition based on trajectories. One important point is that our 3D head tracker is automatically initialized with a well-detected 2D head ellipse. The hierarchical particle filters with 4 layers is useful for the head tracking precision in a reasonable computational time. Our method can deal with body occlusions (for example with chairs or occlusion due to entry into the scene), however the head need to be appropriately visible to have a reliable 3D pose, as the 3D localization is inferred from the head foreground detection. For example, our 3D head tracker sometimes fails at the end of a fall towards the camera. Indeed, the head tends to be merged with the body of the person which can give some 3D errors. However, even if the 3D pose is not well estimated, a high vertical velocity generally occurs at the beginning of a fall. Thus, the vertical velocity is a better criterion for fall detection than the location of the head because head height can lead to failure because of occlusion or tracking problem when the head is near the ground.

7. Conclusion and future work

An overview of fall detection techniques using video surveillance has been proposed in this chapter. Several fall detection methods using a single camera have been shown and have shown that monocular video surveillance systems are a good solution for fall detection with high detection rates. A robust method for fall detection is the analysis of the human shape motion and deformation. Even with realistic and difficult video data sets, such system are able to discriminate falls from normal daily activities automatically (Sections 4 and 5). The 3D localization of the person is also a useful tool for fall detection, and we have demonstrated that it is feasible with only one calibrated camera. All these methods are view-independent, automatically initialized and can run in real-time, considering that 5 to 10 fps is sufficient for fall detection.

When developping such systems, we must ensure the privacy of the person, which can be satisfied here, as our systems are entirely automated and access to the images could be forbidden except in case of emergency. For instance, the system will send an alarm signal toward an outside resource (e.g. via a cell phone or Internet) if and only if an abnormal event is detected (e.g. falling). Moreover, recall that this technology do not hamper the movement of the person as no devices are required and no button needs to be pushed.

How to improve the robustness

To reduce the risk of false alarms, a hybrid method combining 2D and 3D information could be considered. Considering only the human shape deformation, slow falls are sometimes more difficult to discriminate from a person sitting down brutally. By using the 3D head velocities or the 3D head localization, these two events can be discriminated. Inversely, when the 3D tracking is not sufficiently reliable (for example when the head is occluded), the human shape deformation could help to detect falls.

Multi-camera systems could also be used to improve the recognition results by combining information from several cameras to take a decision. However, these systems are more expensive and difficult to implement requiring an accurate calibration and synchronization. Some stereo systems entirely calibrated and directly usable e.g. (PointGrey, 2010) could be used to provide a more reliable depth information than a monocular system. Although these systems are still expensive, with the renewed interest in 3D technologies, some 3D digital cameras and webcams are now proposed for general public (Fujifilm, 2010; Minoru, 2010) suggesting that stereo systems will become more affordable in the future. **Next challenges for**

healthcare video surveillance systems
Beyond fall detection, gait analysis could help to identify persons at risk with unstable gait patterns requiring reeducation to reduce the risk of falling. Moreover, a video surveillance system can provide a large amount of information about the person, but also his/her interaction with the environment. A computer vision system could be used to check other daily activities like medication intake (Valin et al., 2006), or meal/sleep time and duration. Information about his/her environment could also be analyzed for fire detection, forgotten oven or running faucet and other home hazards.
Healthcare video surveillance systems are a new and promising solution to improve the quality of life and care for elderly, by preserving their autonomy and generating the safety and comfort needed in their daily lives. This corresponds to the hopes of the elderly themselves, their families, the caregivers and the governments. The positive receptivity for video surveillance systems suggests that this technology has a bright future for healthcare and will advantageously complement other approaches (e.g. fixed or wearable sensors, safer home modifications, etc) by overcoming many of their limitations.

8. Acknowledgements

This work was supported by the Natural Sciences and Engineering Research Council of Canada (NSERC).

9. References

Alwan, M., Rajendran, P., Kell, S., Mack, D., Dalal, S., Wolfe, M. & Felder, R. (2006). A smart and passive floor-vibration based fall detector for elderly, *2nd Information and Communication Technologies*, Vol. 1, pp. 1003–1007.

Anderson, D., Keller, J., Skubic, M., Chen, X. & He, Z. (2006). Recognizing falls from silhouettes, *International Conference of the IEEE Engineering in Medicine and Biology Society*, pp. 6388–6391.

Anderson, D., Luke, R. H., Keller, J. M., Skubic, M., Rantz, M. & Aud, M. (2009). Linguistic summarization of video for fall detection using voxel person and fuzzy logic, *Computer Vision and Image Understanding* 113(1): 80–89.

Auvinet, E., Reveret, L., St-Arnaud, A., Rousseau, J. & Meunier, J. (2008). Fall detection using multiple cameras, *30th Annual International Conference of the IEEE Engineering in Medicine and Biology Society*, pp. 2554–2557.

Auvinet, E., Rougier, C., Meunier, J., St-Arnaud, A. & Rousseau, J. (2010). Multiple cameras fall data set, *Technical Report 1350*, University of Montreal, Canada.
URL: *http://vision3d.iro.umontreal.ca/fall-dataset*

Belongie, S., Malik, J. & Puzicha, J. (2002). Shape matching and object recognition using shape context, *IEEE Transactions on Pattern Analysis and Machine Intelligence* 24(4): 509–522.

Birchfield, S. (1998). Elliptical head tracking using intensity gradients and color histograms, *Proc. IEEE Computer Vision and Pattern Recognition (CVPR)*, pp. 232–237.

Bobick, A. & Davis, J. (2001). The recognition of human movement using temporal templates, *IEEE Transactions on Pattern Analysis and Machine Intelligence* 23(3): 257–267.

Bouguet, J.-Y. (2008). Camera calibration toolbox for matlab.
URL: *http://www.vision.caltech.edu/bouguetj/calib_doc*

Bourke, A. & Lyons, G. (2008). A threshold-based fall-detection algorithm using a bi-axial gyroscope sensor, *Medical Engineering & Physics* 30(1): 84–90.

Bradski, G. & Kaehler, A. (2008). *Learning OpenCV: Computer Vision with the OpenCV Library*, O'Reilly.
URL: *http://opencv.willowgarage.com/wiki*

Canny, J. (1986). A computational approach to edge detection, *IEEE Transactions on Pattern Analysis and Machine Intelligence* 8(6): 679–698.

Chappell, N. L., Dlitt, B. H., Hollander, M. J., Miller, J. A. & McWilliam, C. (2004). Comparative costs of home care and residential care, *The Gerontologist* 44: 389–400.

Charif, H. N. & McKenna, S. J. (2006). Tracking the activity of participants in a meeting, *Machine Vision and Applications* 17(2): 83–93.

Creswell, J. & Clark, V. P. (2007). *Designing and Conducting Mixed Methods Research*, Thousands Oaks, CA: SAGE.

Dementhon, D. & Davis, L. (1995). Model-based object pose in 25 lines of code, *International Journal of Computer Vision* 15(1-2): 123–141.

Deutscher, J., Blake, A. & Reid, I. (2000). Articulated body motion capture by annealed particle filtering, *Proc. IEEE Computer Vision and Pattern Recognition*, Vol. 2, pp. 126–133.

DirectAlert (2010). Wireless emergency response system.
URL: *http://www.directalert.ca/emergency/help-button.php*

Dryden, I. & Mardia, K. (1998). *Statistical Shape Analysis*, John Wiley and Sons, Chichester.

Fujifilm (2010). 3d digital camera finepix real 3d w3.
URL: *http://www.fujifilm.com*

Hartley, R. I. & Zisserman, A. (2004). *Multiple view geometry in computer vision*, 2nd edn, Cambridge University Press.

Hazelhoff, L., Han, J. & de With, P. H. N. (2008). Video-based fall detection in the home using principal component analysis, *Advanced Concepts for Intelligent Vision Systems*, Vol. 1, pp. 298–309.

Hild, M. (2004). Estimation of 3d motion trajectory and velocity from monocular image sequences in the context of human gait recognition, *International Conference on Pattern Recognition (ICPR)*, Vol. 4, pp. 231–235.

Hodge, V. J. & Austin, J. (2004). A survey of outlier detection methodologies, *Artificial Intelligence Review* 22: 85–126.

Isard, M. & Blake, A. (1998). Condensation – conditional density propagation for visual tracking, *International Journal of Computer Vision* 29(1): 5–28.

Jain, A. (1989). *Fundamentals of digital image processing*, 2nd edn, Prentice Hall, Englewood Cliffs, New Jersey.

K. Nummiaro, E. K.-M. & Gool, L. V. (2003). An adaptive color-based particle filter, *Image and Vision Computing* 21(1): 99–110.

Kangas, M., Konttila, A., Lindgren, P., Winblad, I. & Jämsä, T. (2008). Comparison of low-complexity fall detection algorithms for body attached accelerometers, *Gait & Posture* 28(2): 285–291.

Karantonis, D., Narayanan, M., Mathie, M., Lovell, N. & Celler, B. (2006). Implementation of a real-time human movement classifier using a triaxial accelerometer for ambulatory monitoring, *IEEE Transactions on Information Technology in Biomedicine* 10(1): 156–167.

Kawanaka, H., Fujiyoshi, H. & Iwahori, Y. (2006). Human head tracking in three dimensional voxel space, *International Conference on Pattern Recognition (ICPR)*, Vol. 3, pp. 826–829.

Kim, K., Chalidabhongse, T., Harwood, D. & Davis, L. (2005). Real-time foreground-background segmentation using codebook model, *Real-Time Imaging* 11(3): 172–185.

Kobayashi, Y., Sugimura, D., Hirasawa, K., Suzuki, N., Kage, H., Sato, Y. & Sugimoto, A. (2006). 3d head tracking using the particle filter with cascaded classifiers, *Proc. of British Machine Vision Conference (BMVC)*, pp. 37–46.

Krueger, R. (1994). *Focus group: a practical guide for applied research*, 2nd edn, Thousands Oaks, CA: SAGE.

Kuhn, H. W. (1955). The hungarian method for the assignment problem, *Naval Research Logistic Quarterly* 2: 83–97.

Lee, T. & Mihailidis, A. (2005). An intelligent emergency response system: preliminary development and testing of automated fall detection, *Journal of telemedicine and telecare* 11(4): 194–198.

Londei, S. T., Rousseau, J., Ducharme, F., St-Arnaud, A., Meunier, J., Saint-Arnaud, J. & Giroux, F. (2009). An intelligent videomonitoring system for fall detection at home: perceptions of elderly people, *Journal of Telemedicine and Telecare* 15(8): 383–390.

Mayer, R. & Ouellet, F. (1991). *Méthodologie de recherche pour les intervenants sociaux*, Boucherville: Gaëtan Morin.

Minoru (2010). Webcam minoru 3d.
URL: *http://www.minoru3d.com*

Mori, G. & Malik, J. (2002). Estimating human body configurations using shape context matching, *European Conference on Computer Vision LNCS 2352*, Vol. 3, pp. 666–680.

Nabney, I. T. (2001). *NETLAB - Algorithms for Pattern Recognition*, Springer.

Nait-Charif, H. & McKenna, S. (2004). Activity summarisation and fall detection in a supportive home environment, *Proceedings of the 17th International Conference on Pattern Recognition (ICPR)*, Vol. 4, pp. 323–326.

Noury, N., Fleury, A., Rumeau, P., Bourke, A., Laighin, G., Rialle, V. & Lundy, J. (2007). Fall detection - principles and methods, *29th Annual International Conference of the IEEE Engineering in Medicine and Biology Society (EMBS 2007)*, pp. 1663–1666.

Noury, N., Rumeau, P., Bourke, A., ÓLaighin, G. & Lundy, J. (2008). A proposal for the classification and evaluation of fall detectors, *IRBM* 29(6): 340–349.

Nyan, M., Tay, F. E. & Murugasu, E. (2008). A wearable system for pre-impact fall detection, *Journal of Biomechanics* 41(16): 3475–3481.

PHAC (2002). Canada's aging population, Public Health Agency of Canada, Division of Aging and Seniors.

PointGrey (2010). Stereo vision camera system - bumblebee2.
URL: *http://www.ptgrey.com*

Pratt, W. (2001). *Digital Image Processing*, 3rd edn, John Wiley & Sons, New York.

QSR (2002). QSR international pty. QSR N'Vivo (2nd version for IBM). Melbourne, Australia.

Rougier, C., Meunier, J., St-Arnaud, A. & Rousseau, J. (2006). Monocular 3d head tracking to detect falls of elderly people, *International Conference of the IEEE Engineering in Medicine and Biology Society*, pp. 6384–6387.

Rougier, C., Meunier, J., St-Arnaud, A. & Rousseau, J. (2007). Fall detection from human shape and motion history using video surveillance, *IEEE 21st International Conference on Advanced Information Networking and Applications Workshops*, Vol. 2, pp. 875–880.

Rougier, C., Meunier, J., St-Arnaud, A. & Rousseau, J. (2008). Procrustes shape analysis for fall detection, *ECCV 8th International Workshop on Visual Surveillance (VS 2008)*.

Rougier, C., Meunier, J., St-Arnaud, A. & Rousseau, J. (2010a). 3d head tracking using a single calibrated camera, *Image and Vision Computing (Submitted)* .

Rougier, C., Meunier, J., St-Arnaud, A. & Rousseau, J. (2010b). Robust video surveillance for fall detection based on human shape deformation, *IEEE Transactions on Circuits and Systems for Video Technology (Accepted)* .

Senate (2009). Canada's aging population: Seizing the opportunity, *Technical report*, Special Senate Committee on Aging, Senate Canada.

Sigal, L. & Black, M. J. (2006). Humaneva: Synchronized video and motion capture dataset for evaluation of articulated human motion, *Technical Report CS-06-08*, Brown University, Department of Computer Science, Providence, RI.

Sixsmith, A. & Johnson, N. (2004). A smart sensor to detect the falls of the elderly, *IEEE Pervasive Computing* 3(2): 42–47.

SPSS (2007). SPSS 15.0. Statistical Package for the Social Sciences Inc. Chicago.

Stenger, B., Mendonça, P. & Cipolla, R. (2001). Model-based hand tracking using an unscented kalman filter, *Proc. BMVC*, Vol. 1, pp. 63–72.

Tao, J., Turjo, M., Wong, M.-F., Wang, M. & Tan, Y.-P. (2005). Fall incidents detection for intelligent video surveillance, *Fifth International Conference on Information, Communications and Signal Processing*, pp. 1590–1594.

Thome, N., Miguet, S. & Ambellouis, S. (2008). A real-time, multiview fall detection system: A lhmm-based approach, *IEEE Transactions on Circuits and Systems for Video Technology* 18(11): 1522–1532.

Töreyin, B., Dedeoglu, Y. & Çetin, A. (2005). Hmm based falling person detection using both audio and video, *Proc. IEEE International Workshop on Human-Computer Interaction*, pp. 211–220.

Usabiaga, J., Bebis, G., Erol, A., Nicolescu, M. & Nicolescu, M. (2007). Recognizing simple human actions using 3d head movement, *Computational Intelligence* 23(4): 484–496.

Valin, M., Meunier, J., St-Arnaud, A. & Rousseau, J. (2006). Video surveillance of medication intake, *International Conference of the IEEE Engineering in Medicine and Biology Society*, pp. 6396–6399.

Wu, C. & Aghajan, H. (2008). Head pose and trajectory recovery in uncalibrated camera networks - region of interest tracking in smart home applications, *ACM/IEEE International Conference on Distributed Smart Cameras*, pp. 1–7.

Wu, G. (2000). Distinguishing fall activities from normal activities by velocity characteristics, *Journal of Biomechanics* 33(11): 1497–1500.

Zhang, Z. (2000). A flexible new technique for camera calibration, *IEEE Transactions on Pattern Analysis and Machine Intelligence* 22(11): 1330–1334.

Zigel, Y., Litvak, D. & Gannot, I. (2009). A method for automatic fall detection of elderly people using floor vibrations and sound - proof of concept on human mimicking doll falls, *IEEE Transactions on Biomedical Engineering* 56(12): 2858–2867.

21

Uncertainty Control for Reliable Video Understanding on Complex Environments

Marcos Zúñiga[1], François Brémond[2] and Monique Thonnat[3]
[1]*Electronics Department, Universidad Técnica Federico Santa María, Av. España 1680, Valparaíso*
[2,3]*Project-Team PULSAR, INRIA, 2004 route des Lucioles, Sophia Antipolis*
[1]*Chile*
[2,3]*France*

1. Introduction

The most popular applications for video understanding are those related to video-surveillance (e.g. alarms, abnormal behaviours, expected events, access control). Video understanding has several other applications of high impact to the society as medical supervision, traffic control, violent acts detection, crowd behaviour analysis, among many others. This interest can be clearly observed through the significant number of research projects approved in this domain: GERHOME [1], CARETAKER [2], ETISEO [3], BEWARE [4], SAMURAI [5], among many others.
We propose a new generic video understanding approach able to extract and learn valuable information from noisy video scenes for real-time applications. This approach is able to estimate the reliability of the information associated to the objects tracked in the scene, in order to properly control the uncertainty of data due to noisy videos and many other difficulties present in video applications. **This approach comprises motion segmentation, object classification, tracking and event learning phases.**
A fundamental objective of this new approach is to treat the video understanding problem in a generic way. This implies implementing a platform able to classify and track diverse objects (e.g. persons, cars, air-planes, animals), and to dynamically adapt to different scene and video configurations. This generality will allow to adapt the approach to different applications with minimal effort. Achieving a completely general video understanding approach is an extremely ambitious goal, due to the complexity of the problem and the infinite possibilities of situations occurring in real-time. That is why it must be considered as a long term goal, considering many building blocks in the process. **This work is focused on building the first fundamental blocks allowing a proper management of uncertainty of data in every phase of the video understanding process.**

---

[1] GERHOME Project 2005, `http://gerhome.cstb.fr`
[2] CARETAKER Project 2006, `http://cordis.europa.eu/ist/kct/caretaker_synopsis.htm`
[3] ETISEO Project 2006, `http://www-sop.inria.fr/orion/ETISEO/`
[4] BEWARE Project 2008, `http://www.eecs.qmul.ac.uk/~sgg/BEWARE/`
[5] SAMURAI Project 2008, `http://www.samurai-eu.org/`

To date, several video understanding platforms have been proposed in the literature (Hu et al., 2004; Lavee et al., 2009). These platforms are normally designed for specific contexts or for treating specific issues. Normally, they are tested over well-known videos or in extremely controlled environments in order to be validated. Moreover, reality is not controlled and it is hardly well-known. **The main novelty of this research is to treat the video understanding problem in a general way**, by modelling different types of uncertainty introduced when analysing a video sequence. Modelling uncertainty allows to understand when something will go wrong in the analysis and then to prepare the system to take the necessary actions for preventing this situation.

The main contributions of the proposed approach are: (i) a new algorithm for tracking multiple objects in noisy environments, (ii) the utilisation of reliability measures for modelling uncertainty in data and for proper selection of valuable information extracted from noisy data, (iii) the improved capability of tracking to manage multiple visual evidence-target associations, (iv) the combination of 2D image data with 3D information in a dynamics model governed by reliability measures for proper control of uncertainty in data, and (v) a new approach for event recognition through incremental event learning, driven by reliability measures for selecting the most stable and relevant data.

This chapter is organised as follows. First, Section 2 describes the state-of-the-art focused on justifying the decisions taken for each phase of the approach. Next, Section 3 describes the proposed approach and the involved phases. Then, Section 4 presents results for different benchmark videos and applications.

2. Related work

As properly stated in (Hu et al., 2004), general structure in video understanding is comprised by four main phases: motion segmentation, object classification, tracking, and behaviour analysis (event recognition and learning). In general, two phases can be identified as critical for the correct achievement of any further event analysis in video: image segmentation and object tracking. Image segmentation (McIvor, 2000) consists in extracting motion from a currently analysed image frame, based on information extracted from previously acquired information (e.g. background image or model). Multi-target tracking (MTT) problem (Yilmaz et al., 2006) consists in estimating the trajectory of multiple objects as they move in a video scene. In other words, tracking consists in assigning consistent labels to the tracked objects in different frames of a video.

One of the first approaches focusing on MTT problem is the Multiple Hypothesis Tracking (MHT) algorithm (Reid, 1979), which maintains several correspondence hypotheses for each object at each frame. Over more than 30 years, MHT approaches have evolved mostly on controlling the exponential growth of hypotheses (Bar-Shalom et al., 2007; Blackman et al., 2001). For controlling this combinatorial explosion of hypotheses all the unlikely hypotheses have to be eliminated at each frame (for details refer to (Pattipati et al., 2000)). MHT methods have been extensively used in radar (Rakdham et al., 2007) and sonar tracking systems (Moran et al., 1997). In (Blackman, 2004) a good summary of MHT applications is presented. However, most of these systems have been validated with simple situations (e.g. non-noisy data).

The dynamics models for tracked object attributes and for hypothesis probability calculation utilised by the MHT approaches are sufficient for point representation, but are not suitable for this work because of their simplicity. The common feature in the dynamics model of these algorithms is the utilisation of Kalman filtering (Kalman, 1960) for estimation and prediction of object attributes.

An alternative to MHT methods is the class of Monte Carlo methods. The most popular of these algorithms are CONDENSATION (CONDitional DENSity PropagATION) (Isard & Blake, 1998) and particle filtering (Hue et al., 2002). They represent the state vector by a set of weighted hypotheses, or particles. Monte Carlo methods have the disadvantage that the required number of samples grows exponentially with the size of the state space. In these techniques, uncertainty is modelled as a single probability measure, whereas uncertainty can arise from many different sources (e.g. object model, geometry of scene, segmentation quality, temporal coherence, appearance, occlusion).

When objects to track are represented as regions or multiple points other issues must be addressed to properly perform tracking. Some approaches have been found pointing in this direction (e.g. in (Brémond & Thonnat, 1998), the authors propose a method for tracking multiple non-rigid objects; in (Zhao & Nevatia, 2004), the authors use a set of ellipsoids to approximate the 3D shape of a human).

For a complete video understanding approach, the problem of obtaining reliable information from video concerns the proper treatment of the information in every phase of the video understanding process. For solving this problem, each phase has to measure the quality of the concerning information, in order to be able of evaluating the overall reliability of a framework. Reliability measures have been used in the literature for focusing on the relevant information, allowing more robust processing (e.g. (Heisele, 2000; Nordlund & Eklundh, 1999; Treetasanatavorn et al., July 2005)). Nevertheless, these measures have been only used for specific tasks of the video understanding process.

The object representation is a critical choice in tracking, as it determines the features which will be available to determine the correspondences between objects and acquired visual evidence. Simple 2D shape models (e.g. rectangles (Cucchiara et al., 2005), ellipses (Comaniciu et al., 2003)) can be quickly calculated, but they lack in precision and their features are unreliable, as they are dependant on the object orientation and position relative to camera. In the other extreme, specific object models (e.g. articulated models (Boulay et al., 2006)) are very precise, but expensive to be calculated and lack of flexibility to represent objects in general. In the middle, 3D shape models (e.g. cylinders (Scotti et al., 2005), parallelepipeds (Yoneyama et al., 2005)) present a more balanced solution, as they can still be quickly calculated and they can represent various objects, with a reasonable feature precision and stability. As an alternative, appearance models utilise visual features as colour, texture template, or local descriptors to characterise an object (Quack et al., 2007). They can be very useful for separating objects in presence of dynamic occlusion, but they are ineffective in presence of noisy videos, low contrast, or objects too far in the scene, as the utilised features become less discriminative.

In the context of video event learning, most of these approaches are supervised using general techniques as Hidden Markov Models (HMM) and Dynamic Bayesian Network (DBN) (Ghahramani, 1998), requesting annotated videos representative of the events to be learnt. Few approaches can learn events in an unsupervised way using clustering techniques. For example, in (Xiang & Gong, 2008) the authors propose a method for unusual event detection, which first clusters a set of seven blob features using a Gaussian Mixture Model, and then represents behaviours as an HMM, using the cluster set as the states of the HMM.

Some other techniques can learn on-line the event model by taking advantage of specific event distributions. For example, in (Piciarelli et al., 2005), the authors propose a method for incremental trajectory clustering by mapping the trajectories into the ground plane decomposed in a zone partition. Their approach performs learning only on spatial information, it cannot take into account time information, and do not handle noisy data.

Briefing, among the main issues present in video analysis applications are their lack of generality and adaptability to new scenarios. This lack of generality can be observed in several aspects: (a) applications focused on few object attributes and not suited to process new ones, (b) processes not capable of interpreting uncertainty in input, processed data, and algorithms, (c) tracking approaches not properly prepared to treat several observations (visual evidences) associated to the same target (or object) (e.g. detected object parts), (d) learning approaches incorporating data that can be really noisy or even false, (e) applications focused in scenarios with very restricted environmental (e.g. illumination), structural (e.g. cluttered scene) and geometric conditions (e.g. camera view angle).
Next section details a new video understanding approach, facing several of the main issues previously discussed.

3. Video analysis approach with reliability measures for uncertainty control

All the issues involved with the different stages of the video understanding process introduce different types of uncertainty. For instance, different zones of an image frame can be affected by different issues (e.g. illumination changes, reflections, shadows), or object attributes at different distances with respect to the camera present different estimation errors, and so on. In order to properly control this uncertainty, reliability measures can be utilised. Different types of uncertainty can be modelled by different reliability measures, and these measures can be scaled and combined to represent the uncertainty of different processes (e.g. motion segmentation, object tracking, event learning).
This new video understanding approach is composed of four tasks, as depicted in Figure 1.

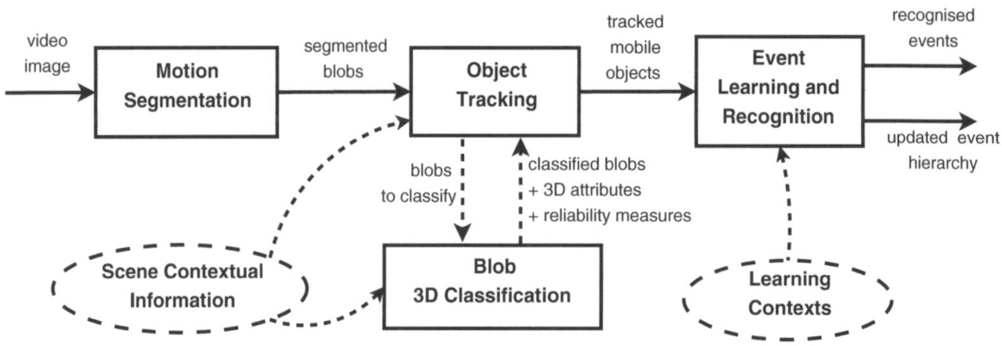

Fig. 1. Proposed video understanding approach.

First, at each video frame, a segmentation task detects the moving regions, represented by bounding boxes enclosing them. We first apply an image segmentation method to obtain a set of moving regions enclosed by a bounding box (*blobs* from now on). More specifically, we apply a background subtraction method for segmentation, but any other segmentation method giving as output a set of blobs can be used. The proper selection of a segmentation algorithm is crucial for obtaining quality overall system results. For the context of this work, we have considered a basic thresholding algorithm (McIvor, 2000) for segmentation in order to validate the robustness of the tracking approach on noisy input data. Anyway, keeping the segmentation phase simple allows the system to perform in real-time.
Second, and using the output blobs from segmentation as input, a new tracking approach is performed to generate the hypotheses of tracked objects in the scene. The tracking phase

uses the blobs information of the current frame to create or update hypotheses of the mobiles present in the scene. These hypotheses are validated or rejected according to estimates of the temporal coherence of visual evidence. The hypotheses can also be merged or split according to the separability of observed blobs, allowing to divide the tracking problem into groups of hypotheses, each group representing a tracking sub-problem. The tracking process uses a 2D merge task to combine neighbouring blobs, in order to generate hypotheses of new objects entering the scene, and to group visual evidence associated to a mobile being tracked. This blob merge task simply combines 2D information. A new 3D classification approach is also utilised in order to obtain 3D information about the tracked objects, which provides new means of validating or rejecting hypotheses according to a priori information about the expected objects in the scene.

This new 3D classifier associates an object class label (e.g. person, vehicle) to a moving region. This class label represents the object model which better fits with the 2D information extracted from the moving region. The objects are modelled as a 3D parallelepiped described by its width, height, length, position, orientation, and visual reliability measures of these attributes. The proposed parallelepiped model representation allows to quickly determine the type of object associated to a moving region and to obtain a good approximation of the real 3D dimensions and position of an object in the scene. This representation tries to cope with the majority of the limitations imposed by 2D models, but being general enough to be capable of modelling a large variety of objects and still preserving high efficiency for real world applications. Due to its 3D nature, this representation is independent from the camera view and object orientation. Its simplicity allows users to easily define new expected mobile objects. For modelling uncertainty associated to visibility of parallelepiped 3D dimensions, reliability measures have been proposed, also accounting for occlusion situations.

Finally, we propose a new general event learning approach called **MILES** (**M**ethod for **I**ncremental **L**earning of **E**vents and **S**tates). This method aggregates on-line the **attributes** and **reliability information** of tracked objects (e.g. people) to **learn** a hierarchy of concepts corresponding to **events**. Reliability measures are used to focus the learning process on the most valuable information. Simultaneously, MILES **recognises** new occurrences of events previously learnt. The only hypothesis of MILES is the availability of tracked object attributes, which are the needed input for the approach, which is fulfilled by the new proposed tracking approach. MILES is an incremental approach, which allows on-line learning, as no extensive reprocessing is needed upon the arrival of new information. The incremental aspect is important as the available examples of the training phase can be insufficient for describing all the possible scenarios in a video scene. This approach proposes an automatic bridge between the low-level image data and higher level conceptual information, where the learnt events can serve as building blocks for higher level behavioural analysis. The main novelties of the approach are the capability of learning events in general and on-line, the utilisation of a explicit quality measure for the built event hierarchy, and the consideration of measures to focus learning in reliable data.

The 3D classification method utilised in this work is discussed in the next section 3.1. Then, in section 3.2 the proposed tracking algorithm is described. Next, in section 3.3, MILES algorithm for event learning is described.

3.1 Reliable classification using 3D generic models

The proposed tracking approach interacts with a 3D classification method which uses a generic parallelepiped 3D model of the expected objects in the scene. The parallelepiped model is described by its 3D dimensions (width w, length l, and height h), and orientation α with respect to the ground plane of the 3D referential of the scene, as depicted in Figure 2(a). The utilised representation tries to cope with several limitations imposed by 2D representations, but keeping its capability of being a general model able to describe different objects, and a performance adequate for real world applications.

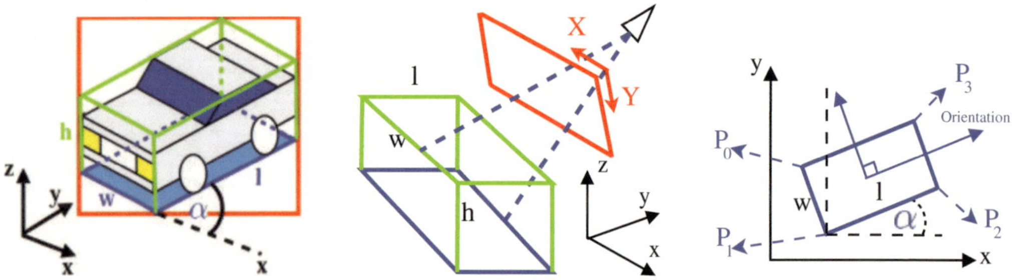

Fig. 2. 3D parallelepiped model for detected objects. (a) Vehicle enclosed by a 2D bounding box (coloured in red) and by the parallelepiped representation (blue base and green projections). (b) 3D view of the scene. (c) Top view of the scene.

A large variety of objects can be modelled (or, at least, enclosed) by a parallelepiped. The proposed model is defined as a parallelepiped perpendicular to the ground plane of the analysed scene. Starting from the basis that a moving object will be detected as a 2D blob b with 2D limits $(X_{left}, Y_{bottom}, X_{right}, Y_{top})$, 3D dimensions can be estimated based on the information given by pre-defined 3D parallelepiped models of the expected objects in the scene. These pre-defined parallelepipeds, which represent an object class, are modelled with three dimensions w, l, and h described by a Gaussian distribution (representing the probability of different 3D dimension sizes for a given object), together with a minimal and maximal value for each dimension.

Formally, a pre-defined 3D parallelepiped model $Q_{\mathbf{C}}$ for an object class **C** can be defined as:

$$Q_{\mathbf{C}} = \{(\mathcal{N}(\mu_q, \sigma_q), q_{min}, q_{max}) | q \in \{w, l, h\}\}, \tag{1}$$

The objective of the classification approach is to obtain the class C for an object **O** detected in the scene, which better fits with an expected object class model $Q_{\mathbf{C}}$.

A 3D parallelepiped instance $S_{\mathbf{O}}$ for an object O (see Figure 2) is described by:

$$S_{\mathbf{O}} = (\alpha, (w, R_w), (l, R_l), (h, R_h)), \tag{2}$$

Note that the orientation α corresponds to the angle between the length dimension l of the parallelepiped and the x axis of the 3D referential of the scene. where α represents the parallelepiped orientation angle (Figure 2(c)), defined as the angle between the direction of length 3D dimension and x axis of the world referential of the scene. The orientation of an object is usually defined as its main motion direction. Therefore, the real orientation of the object can only be computed after the tracking task. Dimensions w, l and h represent the 3D values for width, length and height of the parallelepiped, respectively. l is defined as the 3D dimension which direction is parallel to the orientation of the object. w is the 3D dimension which direction is perpendicular to the orientation. h is the 3D dimension parallel to the z axis

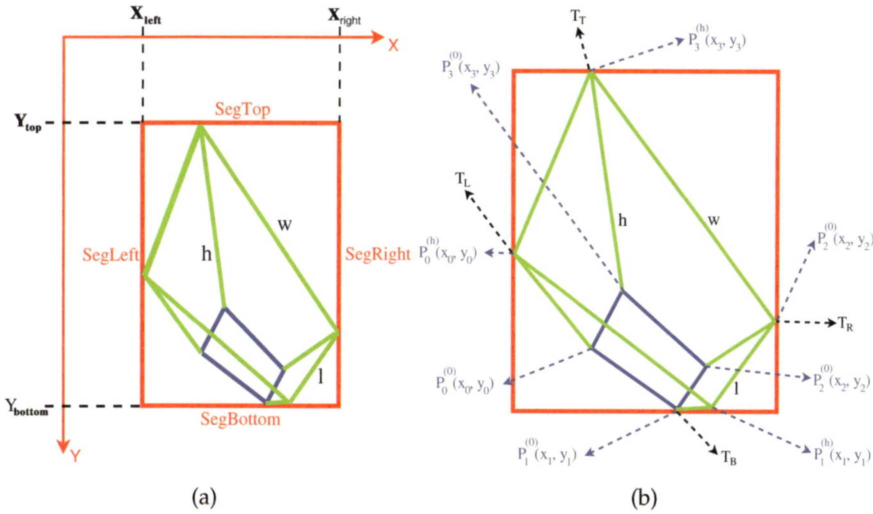

Fig. 3. Camera view of 3D parallelepiped model for detected objects. (a) Image 2D referential variables. (b) World 3D referential variables.

of the world referential of the scene. R_w, R_l and R_h are 3D visual reliability measures for each dimension. These measures represent the confidence on the visibility of each dimension of the parallelepiped and are described in Section 3.1.2.

The dimensions of the 3D model are calculated based on the 3D position of the vertexes of the parallelepiped in the world referential of the scene. Eight points $P_i^z(x_i, y_i) = (x_i, y_i, z)$ are defined, with $i \in \{0,1,2,3\}$ and $z \in \{0,h\}$, as the 3D points that define the parallelepiped vertexes, with $P_i^{(0)}$ corresponding to the i-th base point and $P_i^{(h)}$ corresponding to the i-th vertex on height h, as shown in Figure 3(b). Also, P_i are defined (and respectively E_i), with $i \in \{0,1,2,3\}$, as the 3D points (x_i, y_i) on the ground plane xy representing each vertical edge E_i of the parallelepiped, as depicted in Figure 2(b). The parallelepiped position (x_p, y_p) is defined as the central point of the rectangular base of the parallelepiped, and can be inferred from points P_i.

The idea of this classification approach is to find a parallelepiped bounded by the limits of the 2D blob b corresponding to a group of moving pixels. For completely determining the parallelepiped instance S_O, it is necessary to determine the values for the orientation α in 3D scene ground, the 3D parallelepiped dimensions w, l, and h and the four pairs of 3D coordinates from $P_i = (x_i, y_i)$, with $i \in \{0,1,2,3\}$, defining the base of the parallelepiped. Therefore, a total of 12 variables have to be determined.

To find these values, a system of equations has to be solved. A first group of four equations arise from the constraints imposed by the vertexes of the parallelepiped which are bounded by the 2D limits of the blob. Other six equations can be derived from the fact that the parallelepiped base points P_i, with $i \in \{0,1,2,3\}$, form a rectangle. Then, considering the parallelepiped orientation α, these equations are written in terms of the parallelepiped base points $P_i = (x_i, y_i)$, as shown in Equation (3).

$$\begin{array}{ll} x_2 - x_1 = l \times cos(\alpha) & ; \; y_2 - y_1 = l \times sin(\alpha) \; ; \\ x_3 - x_2 = -w \times sin(\alpha) & ; \; y_3 - y_2 = w \times cos(\alpha) \; ; \\ x_0 - x_3 = -l \times cos(\alpha) & ; \; y_0 - y_3 = -l \times sin(\alpha) \end{array} \tag{3}$$

These six[6] equations define the rectangular base of the parallelepiped, considering an orientation α and base dimensions w and l. As there are 12 variables and 10 equations (considering the first four from blob bounds), there are two degrees of freedom for this problem. In fact, posed this way, the problem defines a complex non-linear system, as sinusoidal functions are involved, and the indexes $j \in \{L, B, R, T\}$ for the set of bounded vertexes T are determined by the orientation α. Then, the wisest decision is to consider α as a known parameter. This way, the system becomes linear. But, there is still one degree of freedom. The best next choice must be a variable with known expected values, in order to be able to fix its value with a coherent quantity. Variables w, l and h comply with this requirement, as a pre-defined Gaussian model for each of these variables is available. The parallelepiped height h has been arbitrarily chosen for this purpose.
Therefore, the resolution of the system results in a set of linear relations in terms of h of the form presented in Equation (4). Just three expressions for w, l, and x_3 were derived from the resolution of the system, as the other variables can be determined from the four relations arising from the vertexes of the parallelepiped which are bounded by the 2D limits of the blob and the relations presented in Equation (3).

$$\begin{aligned} w &= M_w(\alpha; M, b) \times h + N_w(\alpha; M, b) \\ l &= M_l(\alpha; M, b) \times h + N_l(\alpha; M, b) \\ x_3 &= M_{x_3}(\alpha; M, b) \times h + N_{x_3}(\alpha; M, b) \end{aligned} \tag{4}$$

Therefore, considering perspective matrix M and 2D blob $b = (X_{left}, Y_{bottom}, X_{right}, Y_{top})$, a parallelepiped instance $S_{\mathbf{O}}$ for a detected object $\mathbf{O}$ can be completely defined as a function f:

$$S_{\mathbf{O}} = f(\alpha, h, M, b) \tag{5}$$

Equation (5) states that a parallelepiped model O can be determined with a function depending on parallelepiped height h, and orientation α, 2D blob b limits, and the calibration matrix M. The visual reliability measures remain to be determined and are described below.
The obtained solution states that the parallelepiped orientation α and height h must be known in order to calculate the parallelepiped. Taking these factors into consideration h and α are found for the optimal fit for each pre-defined parallelepiped class model, based on the probability measure PM defined in Equation (6)).

$$PM(S_{\mathbf{O}}, C) = \prod_{q \in \{w,l,h\}} Pr_{qC}(q_{\mathbf{O}} | \mu_{qC}, \sigma_{qC}) \tag{6}$$

After finding the optimal model for each class based on PM, the class of the model with the highest PM value is considered as the class associated to the analysed 2D blob. This operation is performed for each blob on the current video frame.

3.1.1 Solving ambiguity of solutions

As the determination of a parallelepiped has been considered as an optimisation problem of only geometric features, this can lead to solutions far from the visual reality. A typical example is the one presented in Figure 4, where two solutions are very likely geometrically given the model, but the most likely from the expected model has the wrong orientation.

[6] In fact there are eight equations of this type. The two missing equations correspond to the relations between the variable pairs $(x_0; x_1)$ and $(y_0; y_1)$, but these equations are not independent. Hence, they have been suppressed.

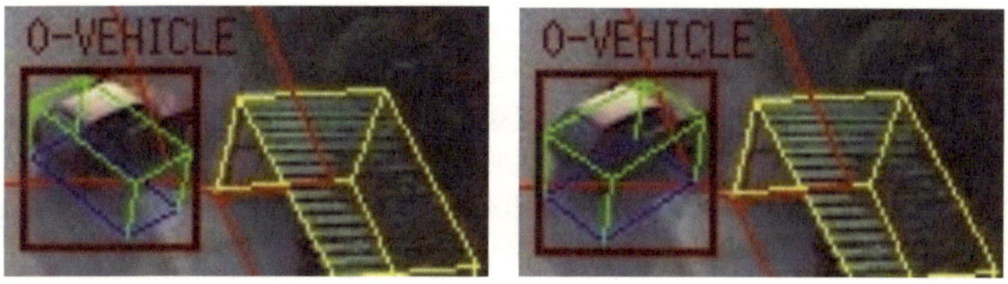

(a) (b)

Fig. 4. Geometrically ambiguous solutions for the problem of associating a parallelepiped to a blob. Figure (a), shows an ambiguity between vehicle model instances, where the one with incorrect orientation has been chosen. In Figure (b), the correct solution to the problem.

A good way for discriminating between ambiguous situations is to return to pixel level. A simple solution is to store the most likely found parallelepipeds and to select the instance which better fits with the pixels inside the blob. This way, a moving pixel analysis is associated to the most likely parallelepiped instances by sampling the pixels enclosed by the blob and analysing if they fit the parallelepiped model instance. The sampling process is performed at a low pixel rate, adjusting this pixel rate to a pre-defined interval of sampled pixels number. True positives (TP), and true negatives (TN) are counted. A TP is considered as a moving pixel which is inside the 2D image projection of the parallelepiped, and TN as a background pixel outside the parallelepiped projection. Then, the chosen parallelepiped will be the one with higher $TP + TN$ value.

3.1.2 Dimensional reliability measures

A reliability measure R_q has been defined for each dimension $q \in \{w, l, h\}$ in the parallelepiped. This measure quantifies the visual evidence for the estimated dimension, by analysing how much of the dimension can be seen from the camera view. The measure gives a minimal value 0 when attribute is not visible, and a maximal value 1 when the attribute is totally visible. It is also influenced by static occlusion (image borders, static objects). The chosen function for modelling this reliability is $R_q \to [0,1]$ (Equation (7)).

$$R_q = \min\left(\frac{dY_q \cdot Y_{occ}}{H} + \frac{dX_q \cdot X_{occ}}{W}, 1\right), \quad with\ q \in \{l, w, h\} \tag{7}$$

dX_q and dY_q represent the length in pixels of the projection of the dimension q on the X and Y reference axes of the image plane, respectively. H and W are the 2D height and width of the currently analysed 2D blob. Y_{occ} and X_{occ} are occlusion flags, which value is 0 if occlusion exists with respect to the Y or X reference axes of the image plane, respectively. These measures represent visual reliability as the sum of contributions of each 3D dimension projection onto the image axes, in proportion with the magnitude of each 2D blob limiting segment. Thus, the maximal value 1 is achieved if the the sum of the partial contributions for each 2D axis is higher than 1. The occlusion flags are used to eliminate the contribution to the reliability for a 2D axis projection in case of occlusion possibility in this axis direction.

3.2 Reliability multi hypothesis tracking

In this section, the new tracking algorithm, Reliability Multi-Hypothesis Tracking (RMHT), is described in detail. In general terms, this method presents similar ideas in the structure for creating, generating, and eliminating mobile object hypotheses compared to the MHT methods presented in Section 2. The main differences from these methods are induced by the object representation utilised for tracking (section 3.1), and the dynamics model enriched by uncertainty control (section 3.2.1). The utilisation of region-based representations implies that several visual evidences could be associated to a mobile object (object parts). This consideration implies adapting the methods for creation and updating of object hypotheses. For further details on these adaptations, refer to (Zuniga, 2008).

3.2.1 Dynamics model

The dynamics model is the process for computing and updating the attributes of the mobile objects. Each mobile object in a hypothesis is represented as a set of statistics inferred from visual evidences of their presence in the scene. These visual evidences are stored in a short-term history buffer of blobs representing these evidences, called **blob buffer**. The attributes considered for the calculation of the mobile statistics belong to the set $A = \{X, Y, W, H, x_p, y_p, w, l, h, \alpha\}$. (X, Y) is the centroid position of the blob, W and H are the 2D blob width and height in image plane coordinates, respectively. (xp, yp) is the centroid position of the calculated 3D parallelepiped base. w, l, and h correspond to the 3D width, length, and height of the calculated parallelepiped in 3D scene coordinates. At the same time, an attribute V_a for each attribute $a \in A$ is calculated, representing the instant speed based on values estimated from visual evidence at different frames.

3.2.1.1 Modelling Uncertainty with reliability measures

Uncertainty on data can arise from many different sources. For instance, these sources can be the object model, the geometry of the scene, segmentation quality, temporal coherence, appearance, occlusion, among others. Following this idea, the proposed dynamics model integrates several reliability measures, representing different uncertainty sources.
Let RV_{a_k} be the **visual reliability** of the attribute a, extracted from the visual evidence observed at frame k. The visual reliability of an attribute RV_{a_k} changes according to the attribute. In the case of 3D dimensional attributes w, l, and h, these measures are obtained with the Equation (7). For 3D attributes x_p, y_p, and α, their visual reliability is calculated as the mean between the visual reliability of w and l, because the calculation of these three attributes is related to the base of the parallelepiped 3D representation. For 2D attributes W, H, X and Y a visual reliability measure inversely proportional to the distance to the camera is calculated, accounting for the fact that the segmentation error increases when objects are farther from the camera.
To account for the coherence of values obtained for attribute a throughout time, the **coherence reliability** measure $RC_a(t_c)$, updated to current time t_c, is defined:

$$RC_a(t_c) = 1.0 - min\left(1.0, \frac{\sigma_a(t_c)}{a_{max} - a_{min}}\right), \tag{8}$$

where values a_{max} and a_{min} in (8) correspond to pre-defined minimal and maximal values for a, respectively. The standard deviation $\sigma_a(t_c)$ of the attribute a at time t_c (incremental form) is defined as:

$$\sigma_a(t_c) = \sqrt{\hat{RV}(a) \cdot \left(\sigma_a(t_p)^2 + \frac{RV_{a_c} \cdot (a_c - \bar{a}(t_p))^2}{RVacc_a(t_c)}\right)}, \tag{9}$$

where a_c is the value of attribute a extracted from visual evidence at frame c, and $\bar{a}(t_p)$ (as later defined in Equation (14)) is the mean value of a, considering information until previous frame p.

$$RVacc_a(t_c) = RV_{a_c} + e^{-\lambda \cdot (t_c - t_p)} \cdot RVacc_a(t_p), \tag{10}$$

is the **accumulated visual reliability**, adding current reliability RV_{a_c} to previously accumulated values $RVacc_a(t_p)$ weighted by a cooling function, and

$$\hat{RV}(a) = \frac{e^{-\lambda \cdot (t_c - t_p)} \cdot RVacc_a(t_p)}{RVacc_a(t_c)} \tag{11}$$

is defined as the ratio between current and previous accumulated visual reliability, weighted by a cooling function.

The value $e^{-\lambda \cdot (t_c - t_p)}$, present in Equations (10) and (11), and later in Equation (16), corresponds to the cooling function of the previously observed attribute values. It can be interpreted as a *forgetting factor* for reinforcing the information obtained from newer visual evidence. The parameter $\lambda \geq 0$ is used to control the strength of the forgetting factor. A value of $\lambda = 0$ represents a perfect memory, as forgetting factor value is always 1, regardless the time difference between frames, and it is used for attributes w, l, and h when the mobile is classified with a rigid model (i.e. a model of an object with only one posture (e.g. a car)).

Then, the **mean visual reliability measure** $\overline{RV}_a(t_k)$ represents the mean of visual reliability measures RV_a until frame k, and is defined using the accumulated visual reliability (Equation (10)) as

$$\overline{RV}_a(t_c) = \frac{RVacc_a(t_c)}{sumCooling(t_c)}, \tag{12}$$

with

$$sumCooling(t_c) = sumCooling(t_p) + e^{-\lambda \cdot (t_c - t_p)}, \tag{13}$$

where $sumCooling(t_c)$ is the accumulated sum of cooling function values.

In the same way, reliability measures can be calculated for the speed V_a of attribute a. Let V_{a_k} correspond to current instant velocity, extracted from the values of attribute a observed at video frames k and j, where j corresponds to the nearest valid previous frame index in time to k. Then, $RV_{V_{a_k}}$ corresponds to the visual reliability of the current instant velocity and is calculated as the mean between the visual reliabilities RV_{a_k} and RD_{a_j}.

3.2.1.2 Mathematical formulation of dynamics

The statistics associated to an attribute $a \in A$, similarly to the presented reliability measures, are calculated incrementally in order to have a better processing time performance, conforming a **new dynamics model** for tracked object attributes. This dynamics model proposes a new way of utilising reliability measures to weight the contribution of the new information provided by the visual evidence at the current image frame. The model also incorporates a cooling function utilised as a forgetting factor for reinforcing the information obtained from newer visual evidence.

Considering t_c as the time-stamp of the current frame c and t_p the time-stamp of the previous frame p, the obtained statistics for each mobile are now described. The **mean value** $\bar{a}$ for attribute a is defined as:

$$\bar{a}(t_c) = \frac{a_{exp}(t_c) \cdot R_{a_{exp}}(t_c) + a_{est}(t_c) \cdot R_{a_{est}}(t_c)}{R_{a_{exp}}(t_c) + R_{a_{est}}(t_c)}, \tag{14}$$

where the expected value a_{exp} corresponds to the expected value for attribute a at current time t_c, based on previous information, and a_{est} represents the value of a estimated from the observed visual evidence associated to the mobile until current time t_c. These two values are intentionally related to respective **prediction** and **filtering** estimates of Kalman filters (Kalman, 1960). Their computation radically differs from these estimates by incorporating reliability measures and cooling functions to control pertinence of attribute data. $R_{a_{exp}}(t_c)$ and $R_{a_{est}}(t_c)$ correspond to reliability measures weighting the contributions of each of these elements.

The **expected value** a_{exp} of a corresponds to the value of a predictively obtained from the dynamics model. Given the **mean value** $\bar{a}(t_p)$ for a at the previous frame time t_p, and the estimated speed $V_a(t_p)$ of a at previous frame p, it is defined as

$$a_{exp}(t_c) = \bar{a}(t_p) + V_a(t_p) \cdot (t_c - t_p). \tag{15}$$

$V_a(t_c)$ corresponds to the estimated velocity of a (equation (17)) at current frame c.

The reliability measure $R_{a_{exp}}$ represents the reliability of the estimated value a_est of attribute a. It is determined as the mean of the **global reliabilities** R_a and R_{V_a} of a and V_a, respectively, at the previous time t_p. This way, the uncertainty of elements used for the calculation of a_{exp} as $\bar{a}(t_p)$ and $V_a(t_p)$, is utilised for modelling the uncertainty of a_{exp}. A **global reliability** measure $R_x(t_k)$ for an attribute x can be calculated as the mean between $R_{a_{exp}}$ and $R_{a_{est}}$ at t_k.

The **estimated value** a_{est} represents the value of a extracted from the observed visual evidence associated to the mobile, and is defined in Equation (16). This way, $a_{est}(t_c)$ value is updated by adding the value of the attribute for the current visual evidence, weighted by the visual reliability value for this attribute value, while previously obtained estimation is weighted by the forgetting factor.

$$a_{est}(t_c) = \frac{a_c \cdot RV_{a_c} + e^{-\lambda \cdot (t_c - t_p)} \cdot a_{est}(t_p) \cdot RVacc_a(t_p)}{RVacc_a(t_c)}, \tag{16}$$

where a_k is the value and RV_{a_k} is the visual reliability of the attribute a, extracted from the visual evidence observed at frame k. $RVacc_a(t_k)$ is the accumulated visual reliability until frame k, as described in Equation 10). $e^{-\lambda \cdot (t_c - t_p)}$ is the cooling function.

The reliability measure $R_{a_{est}}$ represents the reliability of the estimated value a_est of attribute a. It is calculated as the mean between the visual reliability $RV_a(t_c)$ (Equation (12)) and coherence reliability $RC_a(t_c)$ (Equation (8)) values at current frame c, weighted by the reliability measure R_{valid}. The R_{valid} reliability measure corresponds to the number of *valid* blobs in the blob buffer of the mobile over the size of the buffer. For a 2D attribute, a *valid* blob corresponds to a blob not corresponding to a lost object (no visual evidence correspondence), while for a 3D attribute, a *valid* blob corresponds to a blob which has been classified and has then valid 3D information. Not classified blobs correspond to blobs where the 3D classification method was not able to find a coherent 3D solution with respect to the current mobile attributes 3D information.

The statistics considered for velocity V_a follow the same idea of the previously defined equations for attribute a, with the difference that no expected value for the velocity of a is calculated, obtaining the value of the statistics of V_a directly from the visual evidence data. The velocity V_a of a is then defined as

$$V_a(t_c) = \frac{V_{a_c} \cdot RV_{V_{a_c}} + e^{-\lambda \cdot (t_c - t_p)} \cdot V_a(t_p) \cdot RVacc_{V_a}(t_p)}{RVacc_{V_a}(t_c)}, \tag{17}$$

where V_{a_k} corresponds to current instant velocity, extracted from the a attribute values observed at video frames k and j, where j corresponds to the nearest previous valid frame index previous to k. $RV_{V_{a_k}}$ corresponds to the visual reliability of the current instant velocity as defined in previous Section 3.2.1.1. Then, visual and coherence reliability measures for attribute V_a can be calculated in the same way as for any other attribute, as described in Section 3.2.1.1.

Finally, the **likelihood measure p_m for a mobile** m can be defined in many ways by combining the present attribute statistics. The chosen likelihood measure for p_m is a weighted mean of the probability measures for different group of attributes (group $\{w, l, h\}$ as D_{3D}, $\{x, y\}$ as V_{3D}, $\{W, L\}$ as D_{2D}, and $\{X, Y\}$ as V_{2D}), weighted by a joint reliability measure for each group, throughout the video sequence, as presented in Equation (18).

$$p_m = \frac{\sum\limits_{k \in K} R_k C_k}{\sum\limits_{k \in K} R_k} \tag{18}$$

with $K = \{D_{3D}, V_{3D}, D_{2D}, V_{2D}\}$ and

$$C_{D_{3D}} = \frac{\sum\limits_{d \in \{w,l,h\}} (RC_d + P_d)\overline{RV}_d}{2 \sum\limits_{d \in \{w,l,h\}} RD_d} \tag{19}$$

$$C_{V_{3D}} = \frac{MP_V + P_V + RC_V}{3.0}, \tag{20}$$

$$C_{D_{2D}} = R_{valid_{2D}} \cdot \frac{RC_W + RC_H}{2}, \tag{21}$$

$$C_{V_{2D}} = R_{valid_{2D}} \cdot \frac{RC_{V_X} + RC_{V_Y}}{2.0}, \tag{22}$$

where $R_{valid_{2D}}$ is the R_{valid} measure for 2D information, corresponding to the number of not *lost* blobs in the blob buffer, over the current blob buffer size. From equation (18), $R_{D_{2D}}$ is the mean between mean visual reliabilities $\overline{RV}_W(t_c)$ and $\overline{RV}_H(t_c)$, multiplied by $R_{valid_{2D}}$ measure. $R_{V_{2D}}$ is the mean between $\overline{RV}_X(t_c)$ and $\overline{RV}_Y(t_c)$, also multiplied by $R_{valid_{2D}}$ measure. $R_{D_{3D}}$ is the mean between $\overline{RV}_w(t_c)$, $\overline{RV}_l(t_c)$, and $\overline{RV}_h(t_c)$ for 3D dimensions w, l, and h, respectively, and multiplied by $R_{valid_{3D}}$ measure. $R_{valid_{3D}}$ is the R_{valid} measure for 3D information, corresponding to the number of not *classi ed* blobs in the blob buffer, over the current blob buffer size. $R_{V_{3D}}$ is the mean between $\overline{RV}_x(t_c)$ and $\overline{RV}_y(t_c)$ for 3D coordinates x and y, also multiplied by $R_{valid_{3D}}$ measure. Measures $C_{D_{2D}}$, $C_{D_{3D}}$, $C_{V_{2D}}$, and $C_{V_{3D}}$ are considered as measures of temporal coherence (i.e. discrepancy between estimated and measured values) of the dimensional attributes (D_{2D} and D_{3D}) and the position velocities (V_{2D} and V_{3D}). The measures $R_{D_{3D}}$, $R_{V_{3D}}$, $R_{D_{2D}}$, and $R_{V_{2D}}$ are the accumulation of visibility measures in time (with decreasing factor).

P_w, P_l, and P_h in Equation (19) correspond to the mean probability of the dimensional attributes according to the a priori models of objects expected in the scene, considering the cooling function as in Equation (16). Note that parameter t_c has been removed for simplicity. MP_V, P_V, and RC_V values present in Equation (20) are inferred from attribute speeds V_x and V_y. MP_V represents the probability of the current velocity magnitude $V = \sqrt{V_x^2 + V_y^2}$

with respect to a pre-defined velocity model for the classified object, added to the expected object model, defined in the same way as described in Section 3.1. P_V corresponds to the mean probability for the position probabilities P_{V_x} and P_{V_y}, calculated with the values of P_w and P_l, as the 3D position is inferred from the base dimensions of the parallelepiped. RC_V corresponds to the mean between RC_{V_x} and RC_{V_y}.
This way, the value p_m for a mobile object m will mostly consider the probability values for attribute groups with higher reliability, using the values that can be trusted the most. At the same time, different aspects of uncertainty have been considered in order to better represent and identify several issues present in video analysis.

3.2.2 Hypothesis representation

In the context of tracking, a hypothesis corresponds to a set of mobile objects representing a possible configuration, given previously estimated object attributes (e.g. width, length, velocity) and new incoming visual evidence (blobs at current frame).
The representation of the tracking information corresponds to a *hypothesis set list* as seen in figure 5. Each *related hypothesis set* in the *hypothesis set list* represents a set of hypotheses exclusive between them, representing different alternatives for mobiles configurations temporally or visually related. Each hypothesis set can be treated as a different tracking sub-problem, as one of the ways of controlling the combinatorial explosion of mobile hypotheses. Each hypothesis has associated a likelihood measure, as seen in equation (23).

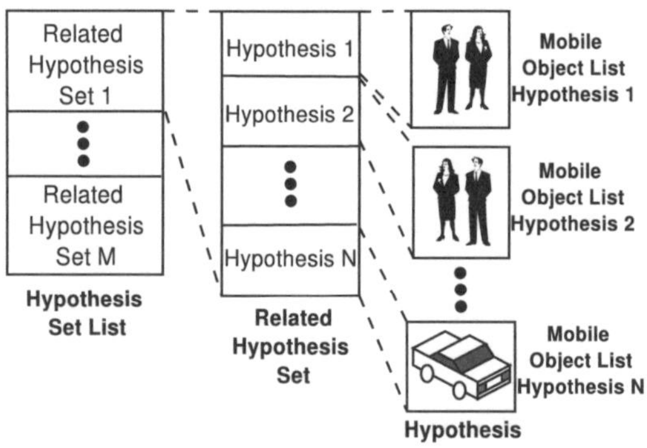

Fig. 5. Representation scheme utilised by our new tracking approach. The representation consists in a list of hypothesis sets. Each hypothesis set consists of hypotheses temporally or visually related. Each hypothesis corresponds to a set of mobile objects representing a possible objects configuration in the scene.

$$P_H = \sum_{i \in \Omega(H)} p_i \cdot T_i, \tag{23}$$

where $\Omega(H)$ corresponds to the set of mobiles represented in hypothesis H, p_i to the likelihood measure for a mobile i (as previously obtained from the dynamics model in Equation (18)), and T_i to a temporal reliability measure for a mobile i relative to hypothesis H, based on the life-time of the object in the scene.
Then, the likelihood measure P_H for an hypothesis H corresponds to the summation of the likelihood measures for each mobile object, weighted by a temporal reliability measure for each mobile, accounting for the life-time of each mobile. This reliability measure allows to

give higher likelihood to hypotheses containing objects validated for more time in the scene, and is defined in equation (24).

$$T_i = \frac{F_i}{\sum_{j \in \Omega(H)} F_j}. \tag{24}$$

This reliability measure intends to grant the survival of hypotheses containing objects of proved existence.

3.3 MILES: A new approach for incremental event learning and recognition

MILES is based on *incremental concept formation models* (Gennari et al., 1990). Conceptual clustering consists in describing classes by first generating their conceptual descriptions and then classifying the entities according to these descriptions. *Incremental concept formation models* is a conceptual clustering approach which incrementally creates a new concept without extensive reprocessing of the previously encountered instances. The knowledge is represented by a hierarchy of concepts partially ordered by generality. A *category utility* function is used to evaluate the quality of the obtained concept hierarchies (McKusick & Thompson, 1990).

MILES is an extension of incremental concept formation models for learning video events. The approach uses as input a set of attributes from the tracked objects in the scene. Hence, the only hypothesis of MILES is the availability of tracked object attributes (e.g. position, posture, class, speed). MILES constructs a **hierarchy of state and event concepts h**, based on the **state and event instances** extracted from the tracked object attributes.

A **state concept** is the model of a spatio-temporal property valid at a given instant or stable on a time interval. A **state concept** $S^{(c)}$, in a hierarchy **h**, is modelled as a **set of attribute models** $\{n_i\}$, with $i \in \{1,..,T\}$, where n_i is modelled as a random variable N_i which follows a Gaussian distribution $N_i \sim \mathcal{N}(\mu_{n_i};\sigma_{n_i})$. T is the number of attributes of interest. The state concept $S^{(c)}$ is also described by its **number of occurrences** $N(S^{(c)})$, its **probability of occurrence** $\mathcal{P}(S^{(c)}) = N(S^{(c)})/N(S^{(p)})$ ($S^{(p)}$ is the root state concept of **h**), and the **number of event occurrences** $N_E(S^{(c)})$ (number of times that state $S^{(c)}$ passed to another state, generating an event).

A **state instance** is an instantiation of a state concept, associated to a tracked object **o**. The state instance $S^{(o)}$ is represented as the set attribute-value-measure triplets $\mathbf{T_o} = \{(v_i; V_i; R_i)\}$, with $i \in \{1,\ldots,T\}$, where R_i is the reliability measure associated to the obtained value V_i for the attribute v_i. The measure $R_i \in [0,1]$ is 1 if associated data is totally reliable, and 0 if totally unreliable.

An **event concept** $E^{(c)}$ is defined as the change from a starting state concept $S_a^{(c)}$ to the arriving state concept $S_b^{(c)}$ in a hierarchy **h**. An **event concept** $E^{(c)}$ is described by its **number of occurrences** $N(E^{(c)})$, and its **probability of occurrence** $\mathcal{P}(E^{(c)}) = N(E^{(c)})/N_E(S_a^{(c)})$ (with $S_a^{(c)}$ its starting state concept).

The state concepts are hierarchically organised by generality, with the children of each state representing specifications of their parent. A unidirectional link between two state concepts corresponds to an event concept. An example of a hierarchy of states and events is presented in Figure 6. In the example, the state S_1 is a more general state concept than states $S_{1.1}$ and $S_{1.2}$, and so on. Each pair of state concepts ($S_{1.1}$; $S_{1.2}$) and ($S_{3.2}$; $S_{3.3}$), is linked by two events concepts, representing the occurrence of events in both directions.

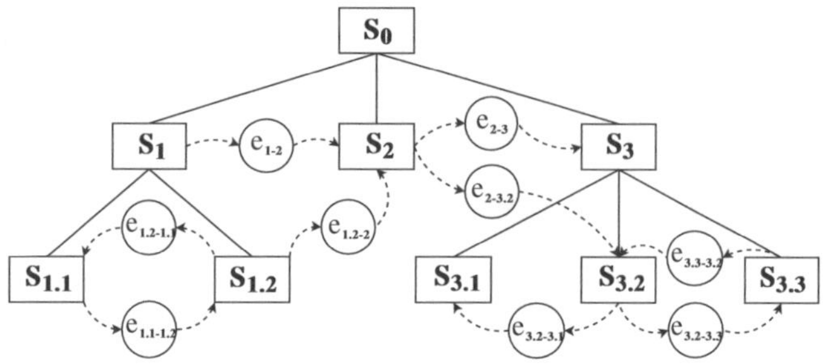

Fig. 6. Example of a hierarchical event structure resulting from the proposed event learning approach. Rectangles represent states, while circles represent events.

3.3.1 MILES learning process

The input of MILES corresponds to a list of tracked object attributes. MILES needs that the objects are tracked in order to detect the occurrence of *events*. There is no constraint on the number of attributes, as MILES has been conceived for learning state and event concepts in general. For each attribute, MILES needs a normalisation value to be defined prior to its computation. This value corresponds to the concept of *acuity*.

The **acuity** (Gennari et al., 1990) is a system parameter that specifies the minimal value for numerical attributes standard deviation σ in a state concept. In psycho-physics, the *acuity* corresponds to the notion of a *just noticeable difference*, the lower limit on the human perception ability. This concept is used for the same purpose in MILES, but the main difference with its utilisation in previous work (Gennari et al., 1990) is that the *acuity* was used as a single parameter, while in MILES each numerical attribute n_i has associated an acuity value A_{n_i}. This improvement allows to represent different normalisation scales and units associated to different attributes (e.g. kilo, meter, centimetre) and to represent the interest of users for different applications (more or less coarse precision). The acuity parameter needs to be set-up manually to enable the user to regulate the granularity of the earned states.

Initially, before the first execution of MILES, the hierarchy **h** is initialised as an empty tree. If MILES has been previously executed, the incremental nature of MILES learning process allows that the resulting hierarchy **h** can be utilised as the initial hierarchy of a new execution. At each video frame, MILES utilises the list of all tracked objects **O** for updating the hierarchy **h**. For each object **o** in **O**, MILES first gets the set of triplets $\mathbf{T_o}$, which serves as input for the state concept updating process of **h**. This updating process is described in Section 3.3.2. The updating process returns a list $\mathbf{L_o}$ of the current state concepts recognised for the object **o** at each level of **h**.

Then, the event concepts $E^{(c)}$ of the hierarchy **h** are updated comparing the new state concept list L_o with the list of state concepts recognised for the object **o** at the previous frame.

Finally, MILES gives as output for each video frame, the updated hierarchy **h** and the list of the currently recognised state and event concepts for each object **o** in **O**.

3.3.2 States updating algorithm

The hierarchy updating algorithm incorporates the new information at each level of the tree, starting from the root state.

The algorithm starts by accessing the analysed state **C** from the current hierarchy **h**. If the tree is empty, the initialisation of the hierarchy is performed by creating a state with the triplets $\mathbf{T_o}$, for the first processed object.

Then, for the case that $\mathbf{C}$ corresponds to a terminal state (the state has no children), a *cutoff* test is performed. The **cutoff** is a criteria utilised for stopping the creation (i.e. specialisation) of children states. It can be defined as:

$$\text{cutoff} = \begin{cases} \text{true} & \text{if} \quad \{ \quad \mu_{n_i} - V_{n_i} \leq A_{n_i} \\ & \qquad\qquad \mid \; \forall \, i \in \{1,..,T\} \quad \} \, , \\ \text{false} & \text{else} \end{cases} \tag{25}$$

where V_{n_i} is the value of the i-th triplet of $\mathbf{T_o}$. This equation means that the learning process will stop at the concept state $S_k^{(c)}$ if no meaningful difference exists between each attribute value of $\mathbf{T_o}$ and the mean value μ_{n_i} of the attribute n_i for the state concept $S_k^{(c)}$ (based on the attribute *acuity* A_{n_i}).
If the *cutoff* test is passed, two children are generated for $\mathbf{C}$, one initialised with $\mathbf{T_o}$ and the other as a copy of $\mathbf{C}$. Then, passing or not passing the *cutoff* test, $\mathbf{T_o}$ is incorporated to the state $\mathbf{C}$ (state incorporation is described in Section 3.3.3). In this terminal state case, the updating process then stops.
If $\mathbf{C}$ has children, first $\mathbf{T_o}$ is immediately incorporated to $\mathbf{C}$. Next, different new hierarchy configurations have to be evaluated among all the children of $\mathbf{C}$. In order to determine in which state concept the triplets list $\mathbf{T_o}$ is next incorporated (i.e. the state concept is recognised), a quality measure for state concepts called **category utility** is utilised, which measures how well the instances are represented by a given category (i.e. state concept).
The category utility CU for a class partition of K state concepts (corresponding to a possible configuration of the children for the currently analysed state $\mathbf{C}$) is defined as:

$$CU = \frac{\displaystyle\sum_{k=1}^{K} \frac{\mathcal{P}(S_k^{(c)}) \displaystyle\sum_{i=1}^{T} \left(\frac{A_{n_i}}{\sigma_{n_i}^{(k)}} - \frac{A_{n_i}}{\sigma_{n_i}^{(p)}} \right)}{2 \cdot T \cdot \sqrt{\pi}}}{K}, \tag{26}$$

where $\sigma_{n_i}^{(k)}$ (respectively for $\sigma_{n_i}^{(p)}$) is the standard deviation for the attribute n_i of $\mathbf{T_o}$, with $i \in \{1, 2, .., T\}$, in the state concept $S_k^{(c)}$ (respectively for the root state $S_p^{(c)}$).
It is worthy to note that the category utility CU serves as the major criteria to decide how to balance the states given the learning data. CU is an efficient criteria because it compares the relative frequency of the candidate states together with the relative Gaussian distribution of their attributes, weighted by their significant precision (predefined acuity).
Then, the different alternatives for the incorporation of $\mathbf{T_o}$ are:
(a) The incorporation of $\mathbf{T_o}$ to a existing state $\mathbf{P}$ gives the best CU score. In this case, the hierarchy updating algorithm is recursively called, considering $\mathbf{P}$ as root.
(b) The generation of a new state concept $\mathbf{Q}$ from instance $\mathbf{T_o}$ gives the best CU score $\mathbf{x}$. In this case, the new state $\mathbf{Q}$ is inserted as child of $\mathbf{C}$, and the updating process stops.
(c) Consider the state $\mathbf{M}$ as the resulting state from merging the best state $\mathbf{P}$ and the second best state $\mathbf{R}$. Also, consider $\mathbf{y}$ as the CU score of replacing states $\mathbf{P}$ and $\mathbf{R}$ with $\mathbf{M}$. If the best CU score is $\mathbf{y}$, the hierarchy is modified by the **merge operator**. Then, the hierarchy updating algorithm is recursively called, using the sub-tree from state $\mathbf{M}$ as the tree to be analysed. The **merge operator** consists in merging two state concepts S_p and S_q into one state S_M, while S_p and S_q become the children of S_M, and the parent of S_p and S_q becomes the parent of S_M,

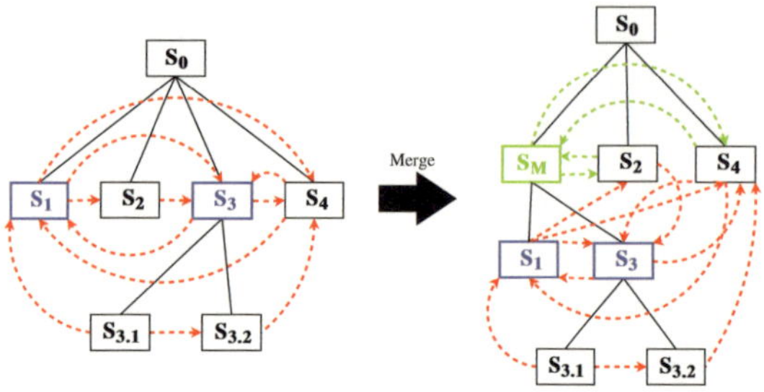

Fig. 7. Result of a merging operation. Blue boxes represent the states to be merged. The green box represents the resulting merged state. Red dashed lines represent the existing events, while the green dashed lines are the new events from the merging process.

as depicted in Figure 7. The merge operator also generates new events for state S_M which generalise the transitions incoming and leaving states S_p and S_q.
(d) Consider **z** as the CU score of replacing state **P** with its children. If the best CU score is **z**, the hierarchy is modified by the **split operator**. Then, the hierarchy updating algorithm is recursively called, using the sub-tree from the current state **C** again. The **split operator** consists in replacing a state S with its children, as depicted in Figure 8. This process implies to suppress the state concept S together with all the events in which the state is involved. Then, the children of the state S must be included as children of the parent state of S.

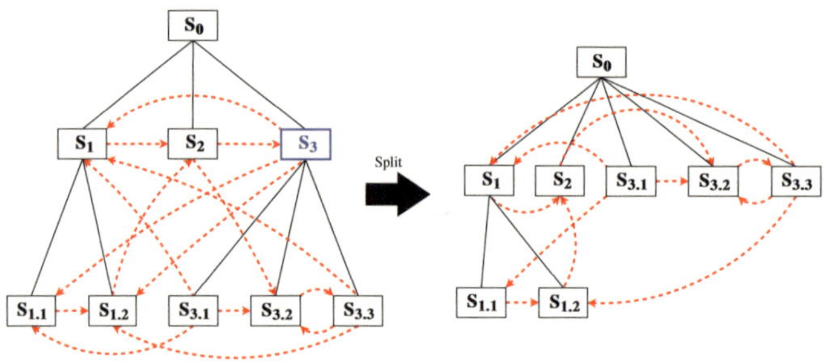

Fig. 8. Split operator in MILES approach. The blue box represents the state to be split. Red dashed lines represent events.

At the end of the hierarchy updating algorithm, each current state **C** for the different levels of the hierarchy is stored in the list **L** of current state concepts for object **o**.

3.3.3 Incorporation of new object attribute values

The incorporation process consists in updating a state concept with the triplets $\mathbf{T_o}$ for an object **o**. The proposed updating functions are incremental in order to improve the processing time performance of the approach. The incremental updating function for the mean value μ_n of an attribute n is presented in Equation (27).

$$\mu_n(t) = \frac{V_n \cdot R_n + \mu_n(t-1) \cdot Sum_n(t-1)}{Sum_n(t)}, \tag{27}$$

with

$$Sum_n(t) = R_n + Sum_n(t-1), \tag{28}$$

where V_n is the attribute value and R_n is the reliability. Sum_n is the accumulation of reliability values R_n.

The incremental updating function for the standard deviation σ_n for attribute n is presented in Equation (29).

$$\sigma_n(t) = \sqrt{\frac{Sum_n(t-1)}{Sum_n(t)} \cdot \left(\sigma_n(t-1)^2 + \frac{R_n \cdot \Delta_n}{Sum_n(t)}\right)}.$$
$$with \tag{29}$$
$$\Delta_n = (V_n - \mu_n(t-1))^2$$

For a new state concept, the initial values taken for Equations (27), (28), and (29) with $t = 0$ correspond to $\mu_n(0) = V_n$, $Sum_n(0) = R_n$, and $\sigma_n(0) = A_n$, where A_n is the *acuity* for the attribute n.

In case that, after updating the standard deviation Equation (29), the value of $\sigma_n(i)$ is lower than the *acuity* A_n, $\sigma_n(i)$ is reassigned to A_n. This way, the acuity value establishes a lower bound for the standard deviation of an attribute.

4. Evaluation and results

4.1 Evaluating tracking

For evaluating the tracking approach, four benchmark videos publicly accessible have been evaluated. These videos are part of the evaluation framework proposed in ETISEO project (Nghiem et al., 2007). The obtained results have been compared with other algorithms which have participated in the ETISEO project. These four chosen videos are:

- **AP-11-C4:** Airport video of an apron (AP) with one person and four vehicles moving in the scene over 804 frames.
- **AP-11-C7:** Airport video of an apron (AP) with five vehicles moving in the scene over 804 frames.
- **RD-6-C7:** Video of a road (RD) with approximately 10 persons and 15 vehicles moving in the scene over 1200 frames.
- **BE-19-C1:** Video of a building entrance (BE) with three persons and one vehicle over 1025 frames.

The tests were performed with a computer with processor Intel Xeon CPU 3.00 GHz, with 2 Giga Bytes of memory. For obtaining the 3D model information, two parallelepiped models have been pre-defined for person and vehicle classes. The precision on 3D parallelepiped height values to search the classification solutions has been fixed in $0.08[m]$, while the precision on orientation angle has been fixed in $\pi/40[rad]$.

4.1.1 Results

The **Tracking Time** metric utilised in ETISEO project for evaluating object tracking has been used ($T_{Tracked}$ from now on). This metric measures the ratio of time that an object present in the reference data has been observed and tracked with a consistent ID over tracking period. The results using this metric are summarised in Figure 9.

The results are very competitive with respect to the other tracking approaches. Over 15 tracking results, the proposed approach has the second best result on the apron videos, and the third best result for the road video. The worst result for the proposed tracking approach has been obtained for the building entrance video, with a fifth position. For understanding these

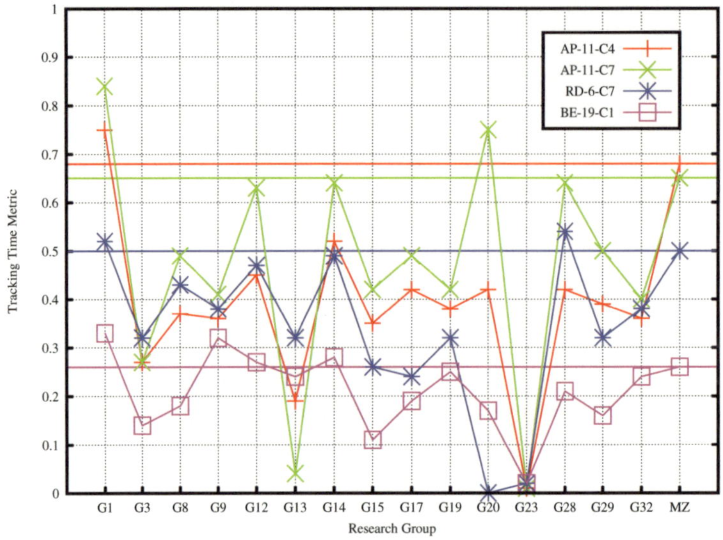

Fig. 9. Summary of results for the Tracking Time metric $T_{Tracked}$ for the four analysed videos. The labels at the horizontal axis represent the identifiers for anonymous research groups participating to the evaluation, except for the **MZ** label, which represents the proposed tracking approach. Horizontal lines at the level of the obtained results for the proposed approach have been added to help in the comparison of results with other research groups.

results it is worthy to analyse the videos separately. In further figures, the green bounding box enclosing an object represents the currently associated blob. The white bounding box enclosing a mobile corresponds to its 2D representation, while yellow lines correspond to its 3D parallelepiped representation. Red lines following the mobiles correspond to the 3D central points of the parallelepiped base found during the tracking process for the object. In the same way, blue lines following the mobiles correspond to the 2D representation centroids found. Images of these results are shown in Figure 10.

The processing time performance of the proposed tracking approach has been also analysed in this experiment. Unfortunately, ETISEO project has not incorporated the processing time performance as one of its evaluation metrics, thus it is not possible to compare the obtained results with the other tracking approaches. Table 1 summarises the obtained results for time metrics: mean processing time per frame $\overline{T_p}$, mean frame rate $\overline{F_p}$, standard deviation of the processing time per frame σ_{T_p}, and maximal processing time utilised in a frame $T_p^{(max)}$. The

Video	Length	$\overline{F_p}[frames/s]$	$\overline{T_p}[s]$	$\sigma_{T_p}[s]$	$T_p^{(max)}[s]$
AP-11-C4	804	76.4	0.013	0.013	0.17
AP-11-C7	804	85.5	0.012	0.027	0.29
RD-6-C7	1200	42.7	0.023	0.045	0.56
BE-19-C1	1025	86.1	0.012	0.014	0.15
Mean		**70.4**	**0.014**		

Table 1. Evaluation of results obtained for both analysed video clips in terms of processing time performance.

(a) AP-11-C7

(b) AP-11-C4

(c) RD-6-C7

(d) BE-19-C1

Fig. 10. Results for tracking experiment.

results show a high processing time performance, even for the road video **RD-6-C7** ($\overline{F_p} = 42.7[frames/sec]$), which concentrated several objects simultaneously moving in the scene. The fastest processing times for videos **AP-11-C7** ($\overline{F_p} = 85.5[frames/sec]$) and **BE-19-C1** ($\overline{F_p} = 86.1[frames/sec]$) are explained from the fact that there was a part of the video where no object was present in the scene, and because of the reduced number of objects. The high performance for the video **AP-11-C4** ($\overline{F_p} = 76.4[frames/sec]$) is because of the reduced number of objects. The maximal processing time for a frame $T_p^{(max)}$ is never greater than one second, and the $\overline{T_p}$ and σ_{T_p} metrics show that this maximal value can correspond to isolated cases.

The comparative analysis of the tracking approach has shown that the proposed algorithm can achieve a high performance in terms of quality of solutions for video scenes of moderated complexity. The results obtained by the algorithm are encouraging as they were always over the 69% of the total of research groups. It is important to consider that no system parameters reconfiguration has been made made between different tested videos, as one of the advantages on utilising a generic object model.

In terms of processing time performance, with a mean frame rate of $70.4[frames/s]$ and a frame rate of $42.7[frames/s]$ for the hardest video in terms of processing, it can be concluded that the proposed object tracking approach can have a real-time performance for video scenes of moderated complexity.

The road and building entrance videos show the need of new efforts on the resolution of harder static and dynamic occlusion problems. The interaction between the proposed parallelepiped model with appearance models can be an interesting first approach to analyse in the future for these cases. Nevertheless, appearance models are not useful in case of noisy data, bad contrast, or objects too far in the scene, but the general object model utilised in the proposed approach, together with a proper management of possible hypotheses, allows to better respond to these situations.

4.2 Evaluation of MILES

The capability of MILES for automatically learning and recognising real world situations has been evaluated, using two videos for elderly care at home. The video scene corresponds to an apartment with a table, a sofa, and a kitchen, as shown in Figure 11. The videos correspond to an elderly man (Figure 11(a)) and an elderly woman (Figure 11(b)), both performing tasks of everyday life as cooking, resting, and having lunch. The lengths of the sequences are 40000 frames (approximately 67 minutes) and 28000 frames (approximately 46 minutes).
The input information is obtained from a tracking method which computes reliability measures to object attributes, which is not included due to space constraints. The attributes

(a) (b)

Fig. 11. Video sequences for elderly care at home application. Figures (a) and (b) respectively show the observed elderly man and woman.

of interest for the evaluation are 3D position (x, y), an attribute for standing or crouching posture, and interaction attributes $SymD_{table}$, $SymD_{sofa}$, and $SymD_{kitchen}$ between the person and three objects present in the scene (table, sofa, and kitchen table). For simplicity, The interaction attributes are represented with three flags: $FAR : distance \geq 100[cm]$, $NEAR : 50[cm] < distance < 100[cm]$, and $VERY\_NEAR : distance \leq 50[cm]$. The contextual objects in the video scene (sofa, table, and kitchen) have been modelled in 3D.
All the attributes are automatically computed by a tracking method, which is able to compute the reliability measures of the attributes. These reliability measures account the quality and coherence of the acquired data.
The learning process applied over the 68000 frames have resulted in a hierarchy of 670 state concepts and 28884 event concepts. From the 670 states, 338 state concepts correspond to terminal states (50.4%). From the 28884 events, 1554 event concepts correspond to events occurring between terminal states (5.4%). This number of state and event concepts can be reduced considering a state stability parameter, defining the minimal duration for considering a state as stable.
This evaluation consists in comparing the recognised events with the ground-truth of a sequence. Different 750 frames from the elderly woman video are used for comparison,

corresponding to a duration of 1.33 minutes. The recognition process has obtained as result the events summarised in Figure 12.

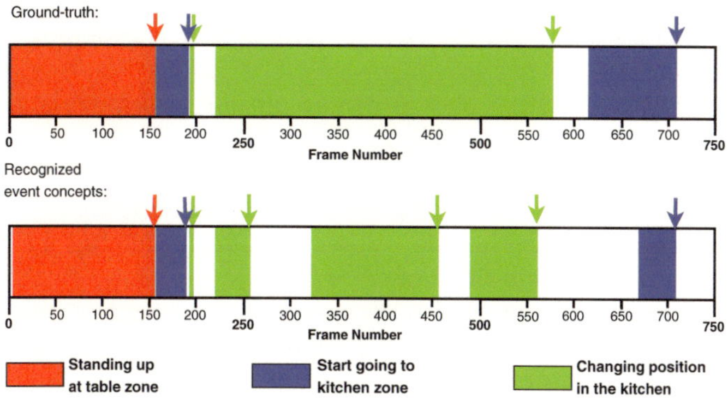

Fig. 12. Sequence of recognised events and ground-truth for the elderly woman video. The coloured arrows represent the events, while coloured zones represent the duration of a state before the occurrence of an event.

The evaluation has obtained 5 true positives (TP) and 2 false positives (FP) on event recognition. This results in a precision (TP/(TP+FP)) of 71%. MILES has been able to recognise all the events from the ground-truth, but also has recognised two nonexistent events, and has made a mean error on the starting state duration of 4 seconds. These errors are mostly due to bad segmentation near the kitchen zone, which had strong illumination changes, and to the similarity between the colours of the elderly woman legs and the floor. The results are encouraging considering the fact that the description of the sequence generated by a human has found a very close representation in the hierarchy.

The results show that the system is able to learn and recognise meaningful events occurring in the scene. The computer time performance of MILES is $1300[frames/second]$ for a video with one tracked object and six attributes, showing the real-time capability of the learning approach. However, the learnt events are frequent and stable, but are not always meaningful for the user. Despite the calculation of the category utility, which formally measures the information density, an automatic process for measuring the usefulness of the learnt events for the user is still needed.

5. Conclusion

Addressing real world applications implies that a video analysis approach must be able to properly handle the information extracted from noisy videos. This requirement has been considered by proposing a generic mechanism to measure in a consistent way the reliability of the information in the whole video analysis process.

The proposed tracking method presents similar ideas in the structure of MHT methods. The main difference from these methods lies in the dynamics model, where features from different models (2D and 3D) are combined according to their reliability. This new dynamics model keeps redundant tracking of 2D and 3D object information, in order to increase robustness. This dynamics model integrates a reliability measure for each tracked object feature, which accounts for quality and coherence of utilised information. The calculation of this features considers a forgetting function (or cooling function) to reinforce the latest acquired information.

The reliability measures have been utilised to control the uncertainty in the obtained information, learning more robust object attributes and knowing which is the quality of the obtained information. These reliability measures have been also utilised in the event learning task of the video understanding framework to determine the most valuable information to be learnt.
The proposed tracking method has shown that is capable of achieving a high processing time performance for sequences of moderated complexity. But nothing can still be said for more complex situations. The results on object tracking have shown to be really competitive compared with other tracking approaches in benchmark videos, with a minimal reconfiguration effort. However, there is still work to do in refining the capability of the approach on coping with occlusion situations.
MILES algorithm allows to learn a model of the states and events occurring in the scene, when no a priori model is available. It has been conceived for learning state and event concepts in a general way. Depending on the availability of tracked object features, the possible combinations are large. MILES has shown its capability for recognising events, processing noisy image-level data with a minimal configuration effort. The proposed method computes the probability of transition between two states, similarly as HMM. The contribution MILES is to learn the global structure of the states and the events and to structure them in a hierarchy.
This work can be extended in several ways. Even if the proposed object representation serves for describing a large variety of objects, the result from the classification algorithm is a coarse description of the object. More detailed and class-specific object models could be utilised when needed, as articulated models, object contour, or appearance models. The proposed tracking approach is able to cope with dynamic occlusion situations where the occluding objects keep the coherence in the observed behaviour previous to the occlusion situation. Future work can point to the utilisation of appearance models utilised pertinently in these situations in order to identify which part of the visual evidence belongs to each object. The tracking approach could also be used in a feedback process with the motion segmentation phase in order to focus on zones where movement can occur, based on reliable mobile objects.
For the event learning approach, more evaluation is still needed for other type of scenes, for other attribute sets, and for different number and type of tracked objects. The anomaly detection capability of the approach on a large application must also be evaluated. Future work will be also focused in the incorporation of attributes related to interactions between tracked objects (e.g. meeting someone). The automatic association between the learnt events and semantic concepts and user defined events will be also studied.

6. References

Bar-Shalom, Y., Blackman, S. & Fitzgerald, R. J. (2007). The dimensionless score function for measurement to track association, *IEEE Transactions on Aerospace and Electronic Systems* 41(1): 392–400.

Blackman, S. (2004). Multiple hypothesis tracking for multiple target tracking, *IEEE Transactions on Aerospace and Electronic Systems* 19(1): 5–18.

Blackman, S., Dempster., R. & Reed, R. (2001). Demonstration of multiple hypothesis tracking (mht) practical real-time implementation feasibility, *in* . E. Drummond (ed.), *Signal and Data Processing of Small Targets*, Vol. 4473, SPIE Proceedings, pp. 470–475.

Boulay, B., Bremond, F. & Thonnat, M. (2006). Applying 3d human model in a posture recognition system, *Pattern Recognition Letter, Special Issue on vision for Crime Detection and Prevention* 27(15): 1788–1796.

Brémond, F. & Thonnat, M. (1998). Tracking multiple non-rigid objects in video sequences, *IEEE Transaction on Circuits and Systems for Video Technology Journal* 8(5).

Comaniciu, D., Ramesh, V. & Andmeer, P. (2003). Kernel-based object tracking, *IEEE Transactions on Pattern Analysis and Machine Intelligence* 25: 564–575.

Cucchiara, R., Prati, A. & Vezzani, R. (2005). Posture classification in a multi-camera indoor environment, *Proceedings of IEEE International Conference on Image Processing (ICIP)*, Vol. 1, Genova, Italy, pp. 725–728.

Gennari, J., Langley, P. & Fisher, D. (1990). Models of incremental concept formation, *in* J. Carbonell (ed.), *Machine Learning: Paradigms and Methods*, MIT Press, Cambridge, MA, pp. 11 – 61.

Ghahramani, Z. (1998). Learning dynamic bayesian networks, *Adaptive Processing of Sequences and Data Structures, International Summer School on Neural Networks*, Springer-Verlag, London, UK, pp. 168–197.

Heisele, B. (2000). Motion-based object detection and tracking in color image sequences, *Proceedings of the Fourth Asian Conference on Computer Vision (ACCV2000)*, Taipei, Taiwan, pp. 1028–1033.

Hu, W., Tan, T., Wang, L. & Maybank, S. (2004). A survey on visual surveillance of object motion and behaviors, *IEEE Transactions on Systems, Man, and Cybernetics - Part C: Applications and Reviews* 34(3): 334–352.

Hue, C., Cadre, J.-P. L. & Perez, P. (2002). Sequential monte carlo methods for multiple target tracking and data fusion, *IEEE Transactions on Signal Processing* 50(2): 309–325.

Isard, M. & Blake, A. (1998). Condensation - conditional density propagation for visual tracking, *International Journal of Computer Vision* 29(1): 5–28.

Kalman, R. (1960). A new approach to linear filtering and prediction problems, *Journal of Basic Engineering* 82(1): 35–45.

Lavee, G., Rivlin, E. & Rudzsky, M. (2009). Understanding video events: A survey of methods for automatic interpretation of semantic occurrences in video, *SMC-C* 39(5): 489–504.

McIvor, A. (2000). Background subtraction techniques, *Proceedings of the Conference on Image and Vision Computing (IVCNZ 2000)*, Hamilton, New Zealand, pp. 147–153.

McKusick, K. & Thompson, K. (1990). Cobweb/3: A portable implementation, *Technical report*, Technical Report Number FIA-90-6-18-2, NASA Ames Research Center, Moffett Field, CA.

Moran, B. A., Leonard, J. J. & Chryssostomidis, C. (1997). Curved shape reconstruction using multiple hypothesis tracking, *IEEE Journal of Oceanic Engineering* 22(4): 625–638.

Nghiem, A.-T., Brémond, F., Thonnat, M. & Valentin, V. (2007). Etiseo, performance evaluation for video surveillance systems, *Proceedings of IEEE International Conference on Advanced Video and Signal based Surveillance (AVSS 2007)*, London (United Kingdom), pp. 476–481.

Nordlund, P. & Eklundh, J.-O. (1999). Real-time maintenance of figure-ground segmentation, *Proceedings of the First International Conference on Computer Vision Systems (ICVS'99)*, Vol. 1542 of *Lecture Notes in Computer Science*, Las Palmas, Gran Canaria, Spain, pp. 115–134.

Pattipati, K. R., Popp, R. L. & Kirubarajan, T. (2000). Survey of assignment techniques for multitarget tracking, *in* Y. Bar-Shalom & W. D. Blair (eds), *Multitarget-Multisensor Tracking: Advanced Applications, chapter 2*, Vol. 3, Artech House, Norwood, MA, pp. 77–159.

Piciarelli, C., Foresti, G. & Snidaro, L. (2005). Trajectory clustering and its applications for video surveillance, *Proceedings of the IEEE International Conference on Advanced Video and Signal-Based Surveillance (AVSS 2005)*, IEEE Computer Society Press, Los Alamitos, CA, pp. 40–45.

Quack, T., Ferrari, V., Leibe, B. & Van Gool, L. (2007). Efficient mining of frequent and distinctive feature configurations, *International Conference on Computer Vision (ICCV 2007)*, Rio de Janeiro, Brasil, pp. 1–8.

Rakdham, B., Tummala, M., Pace, P. E., Michael, J. B. & Pace, Z. P. (2007). Boost phase ballistic missile defense using multiple hypothesis tracking, *Proceedings of the IEEE International Conference on System of Systems Engineering (SoSE'07)*, San Antonio, TX, pp. 1–6.

Reid, D. B. (1979). An algorithm for tracking multiple targets, *IEEE Transactions on Automatic Control* 24(6): 843–854.

Scotti, G., Cuocolo, A., Coelho, C. & Marchesotti, L. (2005). A novel pedestrian classification algorithm for a high definition dual camera 360 degrees surveillance system, *Proceedings of the International Conference on Image Processing (ICIP 2005)*, Vol. 3, Genova, Italy, pp. 880–883.

Treetasanatavorn, S., Rauschenbach, U., Heuer, J. & Kaup, A. (July 2005). Model based segmentation of motion fields in compressed video sequences using partition projection and relaxation, *Proceedings of SPIE Visual Communications and Image Processing (VCIP)*, Vol. 5960, Beijing, China, pp. 111–120.

Xiang, T. & Gong, S. (2008). Video behavior profiling for anomaly detection, *IEEE Transactions on Pattern Analysis and Machine Intelligence* 30(5): 893–908.

Yilmaz, A., Javed, O. & Shah, M. (2006). Object tracking: A survey, *ACM Computer Surveillance* 38(4). Article 13, 45 pages.

Yoneyama, A., Yeh, C. & Kuo, C.-C. (2005). Robust vehicle and traffic information extraction for highway surveillance, *EURASIP Journal on Applied Signal Processing* 2005(1): 2305–2321.

Zhao, T. & Nevatia, R. (2004). Tracking multiple humans in crowded environment, *Proceedings of the IEEE Computer Society Conference on Computer Vision and Pattern Recognition (CVPR04)*, Vol. 2, IEEE Computer Society, Washington, DC, USA, pp. 406–413.

Zuniga, M. (2008). *Incremental Learning of Events in Video using Reliable Information*, PhD thesis, Université de Nice Sophia Antipolis, École Doctorale STIC.

Part 5

Advanced Topics

22

Animal Eyes and Video Imagery

Tomasz P. Jannson and Ranjit Pradhan
Physical Optics Corporation,
USA

1.Introduction

1.1 "Natural engineering", human engineering, and "artificial abstraction"

Nature created a multitude of forms of animal eyes as a manifestation of "natural engineering." *Human engineering* (HE) came much later, creating its own forms of artificial vision or video imagery, some of them as repetitions of *natural engineering* (NE) and some of them as supposed-to-be NE-repetitions (i.e., possibly wrong guesses); these latter we call "*artificial abstractions*" (AAs), being an interesting product of human imagination. This paper is about relationships among these various forms of engineering in respect to animal eyes.

Although the earth has existed for several billion years, the vast majority of animal forms having eyes similar to those in existence today appeared during the so-called *Cambrian explosion*, about 530 million years ago, probably related to development of a new NE-based *concept of operation* (CONOPS): *visually-guided-predation*, which, in turn, created new NE-constructions: larger (macroscopic) animals with hardened tissue. This hardened tissue was necessary to create pigment-based *vignetting effect*, a precursor of animal vision (Fig. 1).

Through the movement of such a primitive eye (through all-body movement), various photoreceptors would receive different optical signals, thus, creating a kind of *spatial* vision. Further NE developments have bifurcated into two basic directions: *apposition* eyes (such as bug eyes) and *imaging* eyes, the latter to be found in almost all vertebrates.

In Section 2, we will discuss one of the first attempts to study the animal eye, Maxwell's "fish-eye," and *aquatic* eyes based on *Graded-Index* (GRIN) optics, including an *Artificial Abstraction* (AA): "fish-eye" *catadioptric* systems.

In Section 3 the recently discovered concept of the lobster eye is reviewed in detail, while in Section 4 both natural vision and artificial color vision are studied.

In Section 5, optical imaging resolution/sensitivity, in the context of animal eyes, are studied, while in Section 6, animal mirrors, vignetting, anti-reflection (AR) structures, total internal reflection, camouflage, and the other natural optical elements are discussed.

In Section 7, a new concept of spectral imaging as a manifestation of HE-based apposition eyes, is introduced.

In Section 8, the neurophysiology of the retina and visual cortex, in the context of video imagery, is analyzed, and, finally, a summary and overall discussion of AA examples, are presented in Section 9.

Abbreviations are reduced to a minimum, although some of them, such as HE, NE, and AA, are used throughout the text for the sake of space. Some others, such as TIR, GRIN, CONOPS are commonly used in engineering literature. Others, containing a great many words, are used only locally for the sake of space.

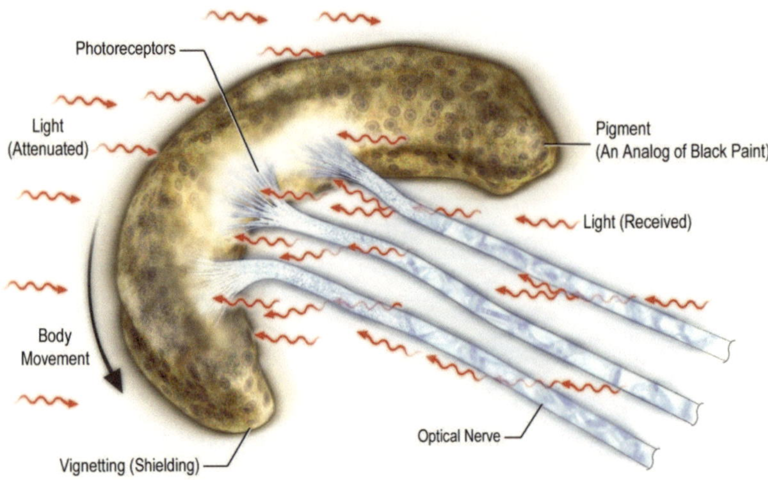

Fig. 1. Illustration of a lensless vision system based on the vignetting effect, a precursor of the animal eye. We see that optical nerves are blocking the view, an unwanted effect to be discussed later, in the context of the human eye

2. Maxwell's "Fish-eye," GRIN lenses, and Aquatic eyes

Starting with apposition eyes (Land & Nilsson, 2002) investigated by Robert Hook in 1665, Maxwell's "fish-eye" in 1854 (Born & Wolf, 1999; Maxwell, 1854), and the Luneburg lens (Luneburg, 1964), in the 1950s, animal eye systems, including *fish-eyes, bug eyes, lobster eyes*, and others, have been adopted for artificial vision. In particular, it has been proven that the lobster eye can be considered an advanced bug eye in biologic evolution. Attractive military and Homeland Security HE applications have been developed, including an IR/visible lobster-eye system as a hemispheric awareness sensor (Grubsky et al., 2006), and an X-ray lobster eye as the first X-ray lens for improvised explosive device (IED) detection and "see through" applications (Gertsenshteyn et al., 2005; Jannson et al., 2006b; Jannson et al., 2007a, and Gertsenshteyn at al., 2007).

The primary concern in mimicking animal eyes, within the scope of geometrical and physical optics, has been connected with so-called *absolute imaging* instruments, which provide precise point-to-point imaging (i.e., without aberrations). Unfortunately, such systems, including the Maxwell fish-eye and Luneburg lens, require 3D Graded-Index distribution, which complicates fabrication. The practical response to these problems has been *catadioptric* systems, which combine the imaging properties of refractive and reflective optics (Baker & Nayar, 1999). While these systems do not preserve absolute imaging properties, they have an almost hemispheric (or, rather, omni-directional) view, sometimes also using the "fish-eye" name.

2.1 Maxwell's "Fish-eye" and the Luneburg Lens

Consider a Graded-Index (GRIN) 3D medium, with spherical symmetry:

$$n(r) = \frac{1}{1+(r/a)^2} n_o \qquad (1)$$

where, a, and n_o are constants, as shown in Fig. 2, where:

$$r = \left(x^2 + y^2 + z^2\right)^{1/2} \quad . \tag{2}$$

We discuss the ray equation in spherical-coordinates (r,θ), with a solution for: r = a, and $\theta = \alpha$, or $\theta = \pi +$ d. We obtain the one-parameter (α) family of rays,

$$\frac{r^2 - a^2}{r\,sin(\theta - \alpha)} = \frac{r_o^{\,2} - a_o^{\,2}}{r_o\,sin(\theta_o - \alpha)} \tag{3}$$

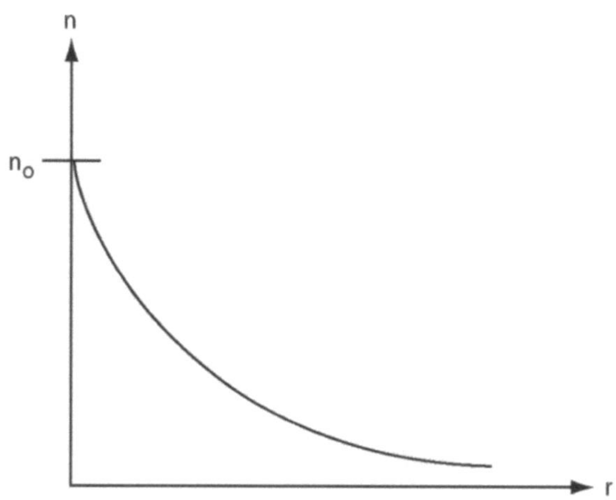

Fig. 2. Illustration of Eq. (1)

This family of rays has two fixed points: P_o (r_o, θ_o), and $P_1(r_1, \theta_1)$, where

$$r_1 = \frac{a^2}{r_o}, \quad \theta_1 = \pi + \theta_o \tag{4ab}$$

independently on α. Therefore, all the rays pass those two points; thus, the fish-eye is an absolute instrument; this is further discussed in Born & Wolf, 1999, and Jagger, 1992.
The disadvantage of the Maxwell fish-eye is that all media must be GRIN (Graded Index). To avoid this disadvantage, Luneburg designed his lens, also with spherical symmetry, in the form:

$$n(r) = \begin{cases} n(r) = \sqrt{2 - r^2}; & 0 \le r \le 1 \\ 1, \ for\ r > 1 \end{cases} \tag{5}$$

The Luneburg lens's GRIN medium is limited to $r \le 1$. For any collimated beam passing through this medium, we obtain the focusing into point P_o lying on the medium boundary, shown in Fig. 3. We see that the Luneburg lens has a continuum of optical axes passing through the center. It is still difficult to realize in optics (except planar optics as in Jannson & Sochacki, 1980a), with practical applications in microwave antennas.

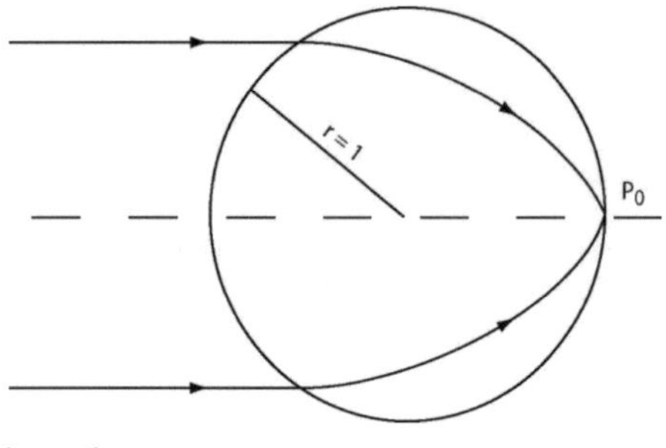

Fig. 3. Illustration of Luneburg lens

2.2 Catadioptric systems

The catadioptric systems are based both on mirrors (catoptric) and lenses (dioptric). They were designed to continue the idea of absolute instruments, such as the Maxwell fish-eye, yet without introducing a GRIN medium. Although they are not absolute instruments, they have an omni-directional view, as shown in Fig. 4, where a parabolic cylindrical mirror is shown. The rays at the bottom are directed to a (refractive) projection lens, where they are imaged at the CCD array. At Physical Optics Corporation (POC), they are applied for periscopic views and video surveillance, where *electronic zoom* is introduced, in particular, and electronic pan, tilt, zoom (PTZ), in general, with a high-resolution cylindrical view, without the necessity of mechanical camera motion.

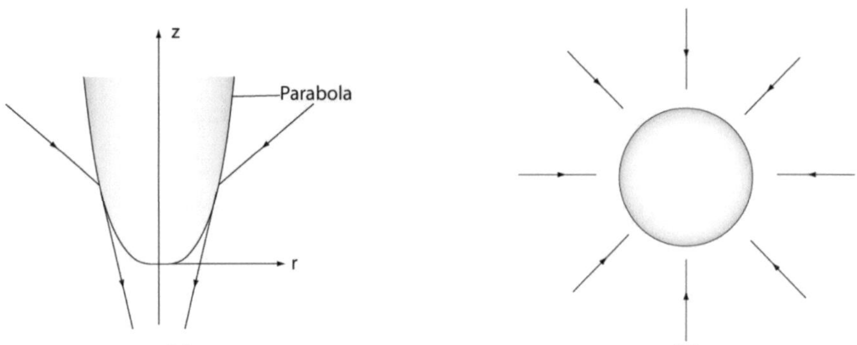

(a) (b)

Fig. 4. Illustration of catadioptric system including: (a) Parabolic cylindrical mirror; (b) Omnidirectional cylindrical top view

Catadioptric systems have panoramic (360°) view; thus, they are similar to Maxwell's "fish-eye." However, they are not GRIN structures. Therefore, calling them "fish-eye" systems (as they sometimes are called in video surveillance applications for panoramic dioptric systems) is a rather unfortunate example of *Artificial Abstraction* (AA), as defined in Section 1.

2.3 Aquatic eyes

In contrast to terrestrial eyes (such as the human eye), when the 1st interface (cornea) has some focusing power due to the difference in refractive indices between air (n_1) and a medium (n_2), the aquatic lenses have zero focusing power for the 1st interface. Therefore, in general, lens focusing is a problem in an aquatic (water) medium. To show this, consider the lens geometry in Fig. 5.

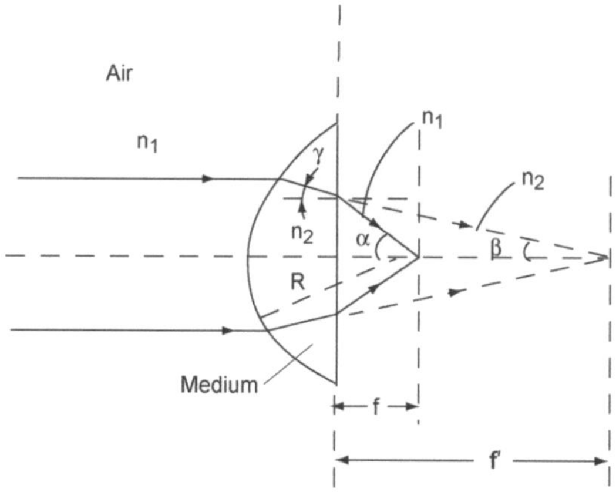

Fig. 5. Lens geometry, illustrating the difference between focusing powers of an aquatic lens (1/f') and a terrestrial lens (1/f) (here the front interface is the back interface and vice versa). The broken-line ray illustrates an aquatic lens, while the continuous line ray illustrates a terrestrial lens; $\beta = \gamma$

According to Fig. 5, the focusing power of a plano-convex lens (for illustration), 1/f, is (f is focal length),

$$\frac{1}{f} = \left(\frac{n_2}{n_1} - 1\right)\left(\frac{1}{R}\right) = \left(\frac{n_2 - n_1}{n_1}\right)\left(\frac{1}{R}\right) \tag{6}$$

where R is the lens radius of curvature. Using an auxiliary construction from Fig. 5, we obtain: $f\sin\alpha = f'\sin\beta$, for $\alpha,\beta<<1$, and from Snell law ($\gamma = \beta$), we obtain $\sin\alpha/\sin\beta = n_2/n_1$; thus the focusing power of aquatic lens, is ($n_1<n_2$),

$$\frac{1}{f'} = \frac{n_2}{n_1}\left(\frac{1}{f}\right) \tag{7}$$

i.e., n_2/n_1 – times smaller, and substituting Eq. (6) into Eq. (7), we obtain

$$\frac{1}{f'} = \left(\frac{n_2 - n_1}{n_2}\right)\left(\frac{1}{R}\right) \tag{8}$$

Therefore, the axial lens proposition (as in Fig. 5) does not work in an aquatic medium. As a result, Natural Engineering (NE) has selected a GRIN lens such as in Fig. 3, with higher focusing power. A typical aquatic lens, used by fish as well as cephalopods and marine mammals, has f# = 1.25, also known as Matthiessen's ratio (Land & Nilsson, 2002), in memory of Matthiessen's studies in 1880. In Refs. Jagger, 1992 & Nicol, 1989, a comprehensive review of aquatic eyes is provided.

3. A lobster eye as an advanced bug eye system

The surprising discovery of the seeing mechanism of a lobster eye in the 1970s (Vogt, 1980), "allowed shrimp to see," based on reflective optics rather than on more standard refractive optics. Since X-ray refractive optics has always been extremely difficult to achieve, the lobster eye solution has proven very convenient for (especially) hard X-ray optics. (This section is from Jannson, et al., 2007c.)

Bug-eyes are nonimaging systems with detectors located close to guiding channels. They are called *apposition eyes*, with no transparent (clear) zone allowing for imaging (Fig. 6(a)). In contrast, the **lobster eye** is an imaging system, due to the clear zone between the guiding channels and detector surface (Fig. 6(b)).

The lobster eye has interesting connections with Darwinian evolution. From 1955 to 1975 "shrimps could not see" (i.e., there was no explanation for their seeing mechanism). In 1975, Klaus Vogt, found the solution to this engima (full review in Land & Nilsson, 2002), in the form of two complementary focusing effects: (1) *central ray* one; (2) *skew ray* one. The first is described in Fig. 6(b); the second is based on corner retroreflection, combining two reflections of skew rays, that requires **quadratic** cross-section of the reflection (guiding) channels. Some animals have (1) but do not have (2) (a hexagonal cross-section). All *crustaceans* (shrimp, lobster, crayfish) have both. From an evolutionary point of view, it is interesting that larval stages of some shrimp, have *apposition* eyes, as in Fig. 6(a), with hexagonal facets that change at **metamorphosis** into *superposition* (imaging) eyes, as in Fig. 6(b), with square facets.

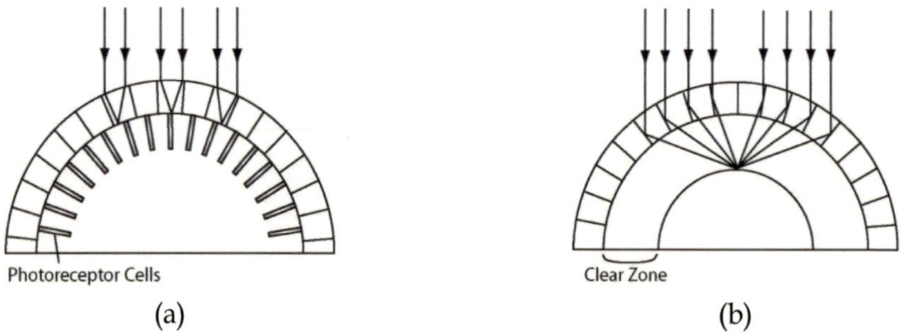

Fig. 6. Lobster eye as advanced bug eye system, including: (a) Bug eye nonimaging system: so-called apposition eye (no transparent (clear) zone); (b) Lobster eye imaging system: so-called superposition eye, with clear zone

The Lobster-eye lens is a transmission lens, based on reflective optics. Typical lenses are based on refractive optics and they are transmission versions. The biological *lobster-eye* lens (LEL) is for visible, or near-infrared (NIR) light, and the reflection channels are filled with material, based on *total internal reflection* (TIR) and Bragg diffraction. POC's LEL, shown in Fig. 7, is for X-rays, and the reflection channels are empty, based on *total external reflection* (TER).

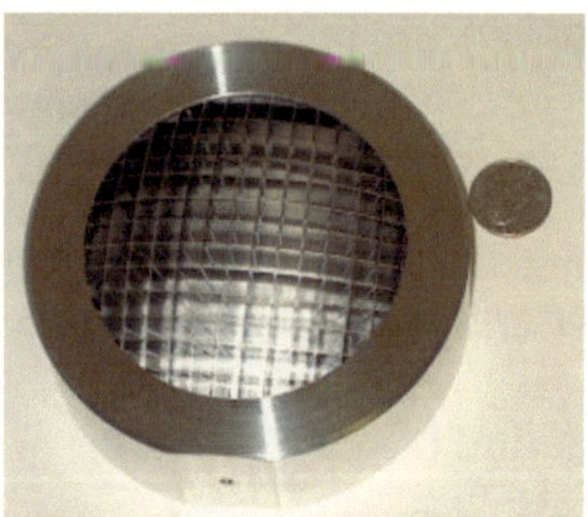

Fig. 7. Illustration of lobster eye, developed at Physical Optics Corporation. The biological lobster eye also has reflection channels with square-cross-sections

The two skew ray reflections from opposite walls of the square-cross-section of a reflection channel (as in Fig. 7) can be formally reduced to a single central reflection, as described in detail in Jannson & Gertsenshteyn, 2006b & Jannson et al., 2007a.

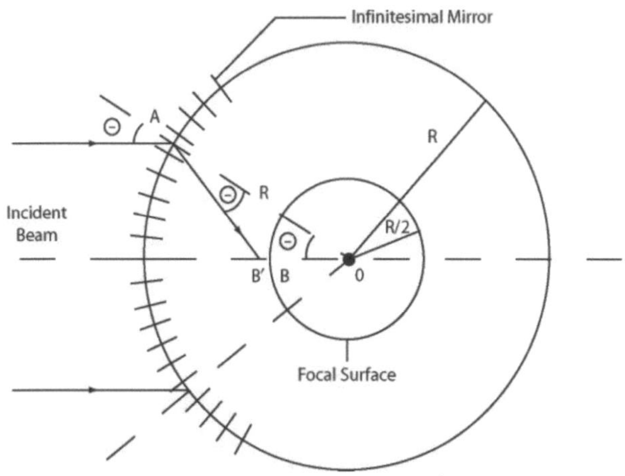

Fig. 8. Lobster-eye lens (LEL) geometry

Assume a continuum of radially directed infinitesimal mirrors located at the circle of radius, R. Then, any parallel (collimated) incident beam will focus at the point (focus), at the sphere of radius, R/2. The LEL geometry is shown in Fig. 8 (above). The essential feature is, that, because of three identical θ-angles, as in Fig. 8, the triangle AB′O has equal legs (AB′ = B′O); thus,

$$AB' = B'O = \frac{R}{2\cos\theta} \tag{9}$$

Since, for θ<<1 (paraxial approximation), we have:

$$B'O = BO \cong R/2 = f \tag{10a}$$

thus,

$$B' \rightarrow B \tag{10b}$$

and, the LEL system is indeed an imaging one. The lens equation has the form

$$\frac{1}{x} - \frac{1}{y} = -\frac{2}{R} = -\frac{1}{f}; \qquad f = R/2 \ , \tag{11}$$

and the effective aperture radius, a, is equal to $x\theta_c$, for f = ∞ where x, y are distances from an object to lens and image to lens, respectively; f is focal length, and θ_c is TER the critical angle (Gertsenshteyn et al., 2005; Jannson et al., 2007a & Gertsenshteyn et al., 2007); thus, it depends on image geometry. Eq. (11) is illustrated in Fig. 9.

From Eq. (11), we obtain the large x-distance of an object, and large y-distance of an image, as shown in Fig. 10. We see that lobster-eye spherical symmetry (Fig. 10) provides realization of the Luneburg lens, without a GRIN medium. In fact, from Eq. (11), for $x = \infty$, $y = f$, thus satisfying the Luneburg lens property of the focusing of any collimated beam.

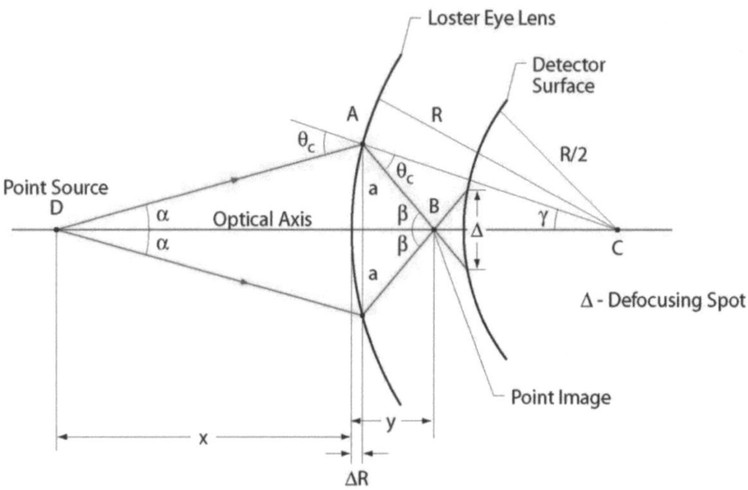

$$\frac{1}{x} - \frac{1}{y} = -\frac{2}{R} = -\frac{1}{f}; \quad f = \frac{R}{2}$$

2a - Effective Aperture

θ_c - Critical (Maximum) Angle (Grazing)

ΔR - Departure from Thin Lens Approximation

Fig. 9. Illustration of the LEL Eq. (11), with source point (D) and its image (B)

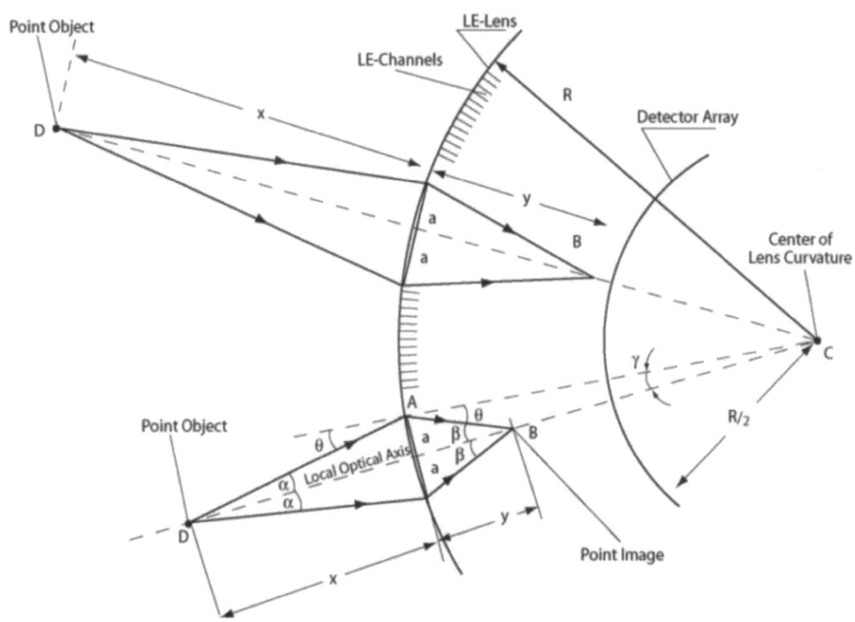

Fig. 10. Lobster-eye spherical symmetry

The ultimate goal of the military is to drop "sensor rocks" that will present a fully hemispheric field of view (FOV), such as bug eyes, or even better a lobster eye (see Fig. 11). The rocks will have natural camouflage, low cost, and disposability, and will work in the visible and IR regions (Grubsky et al., 2006).

Fig. 11. Camouflaged hemispheric lobster-eye awareness sensor, including: (1) IR target; (2), (3), (4), (7) lobster eyes; (5) remote solar panel that can be charged all day to provide electrical energy for all-night operation (in the stationary case); (6) power cable; (8), (12) local solar batteries; (9) metallic waveguide; (10) focal plane array (FPA); (11) sensor housing; (13), (14) sensor "rocks" dropped from the air

4. RGB artificial color vision and biological analogies

4.1 Prior art hyperspectral vs. RGB hyperspectral

The challenge is to combine the two essential features of hyperspectral cameras that are applicable to omnidirectional optical imaging: real-time or *ultrareal-time* (URT) operation, and effective hyperspectral imaging. *Real time* (RT) means 30 frames per second (fps), and *hyperspectral* means over 100 spectral channels (or *bins*) for each pixel during each frame time. This is related to the visible (and NIR), MIR (3-5 μm), or FIR (8-14 μm) spectral region. This is indeed a challenge, because "hyper" means a large number of spectral channels (N>100), and the more spectral channels, the fewer the photons that are available for each detection; so the sensitivity of classical hyperspectral cameras is low. On the other hand, if time-sequential *electro-optic* (EO) filters are used, the hyperspectral camera (Hyvarinen et al., 1998) is slow, far from RT operation. Therefore, in general, "high-speed cameras" and prior art "hyperspectral cameras" perform incompatible operations (this section is from Jannson et al., 2007c).

This dilemma is resolved by introducing the **RGB hyperspectral** camera, based on the novel "RGB vector" concept. In this concept, instead of N > 100 we have N = 2, 3, 4,….12, but, instead of **orthogonal** wavelength channels (as in the case of the classical hyperspectral camera), we have spectral *discriminants*, similar to "color pixels" in a CCD camera, or to color receptors (rods and cones) in the human retina. The novelty is in generalizing this concept to the IR region. The color pixel concept has recently been applied for digital video processing (Kostrzewski et al., 2001 & Jannson & Kostrzewski, 2006a). J. Caulfield is the inventor of the general concept of artificial color (Caulfield et al., 2004).

4.2 Design of color discriminants

The **color discriminants**, or color *primaries*, can be designed for specific object signatures. Those discriminants should discriminate *true targets* from *false targets* even when they have similar wavelength characteristics. Assume for a simplified example that we have five objects of interest: green pepper, snow peas, and carrots, as well as the plate and tablecloth, and that the true target is the green pepper and the remaining objects are false targets. We see that color discriminants can easily eliminate the carrot (orange), the plate (blue), and the tablecloth (white), but both the pepper and snow peas are green, so it is difficult to discriminate between them, so we need a further discriminant, increasing their number from N = 3 to N = 4. This illustrates the principle of how to discriminate targets of interest.
In the case of a **color signature**, or more generally, a *spectral signature*, we apply the generalization of the standard RGB (*red-green-blue*) scheme, represented in VGA video by 24 bpp (8 bpp per color). The RGB scheme can be generalized into similar multicolor schemes for IR (infrared) *multispectral* and *hyperspectral* sensors. Then, instead of comparing sample wavelength spectra with reference wavelength spectra, we compare the generalized RGB color components, which are defined in such a way that they accurately describe the sample *spectra of interest* (SOI). Then, **pixel-to-pixel intensity subtraction** (PIS) in the form of *Euclidean distance*, can be applied to the *color matching operation* (CMO) in the form of *3D pixel vectors*, similar to *speed pixel vectors*, as in *vector flow* analysis. *The color intensity ratio defines the vector direction, while the overall "white" intensity defines the vector module, or value.* Then the CMO is formalized by *color unit vector* (CUV) subtraction.

Let us consider the RGB intensity pixel vector $\vec{I}_{ij}$ (R_{ij}, G_{ij}, B_{ij}), where R_{ij}, G_{ij}, B_{ij} are red, green, and blue RGB color vector components in the form:

$$\mathbf{R}_{ij}^2 + \mathbf{G}_{ij}^2 + \mathbf{B}_{ij}^2 = \mathbf{I}_{ij}^2, \tag{12}$$

where R_{ij} is the ij-th pixel intensity for the red RGB component, and the same for the green and blue components, and

$$\left|\mathbf{I}_{ij}\right| = \sqrt{\mathbf{R}_{ij}^2 + \mathbf{G}_{ij}^2 + \mathbf{B}_{ij}^2} \tag{13}$$

is the overall intensity vector module. Thus, the CUV is

$$\vec{\mathbf{U}}_{ij} = \frac{\vec{\mathbf{I}}_{ij}}{\left|\mathbf{I}_{ij}\right|} = \frac{\left(\mathbf{R}_{ij}, \mathbf{G}_{ij}, \mathbf{B}_{ij}\right)}{\sqrt{\mathbf{R}_{ij}^2 + \mathbf{G}_{ij}^2 + \mathbf{B}_{ij}^2}}, \tag{14}$$

and $\left|\vec{U}_{ij}\right| = 1$. CUV subtraction is illustrated in Fig. 12, where $\vec{\mathbf{u}}_{ij}$ is a **sample** CUV and $\vec{\mathbf{U}}_{ij}$ is a **reference** CUV. This subtraction is in the form:

$$|\vec{\mathbf{u}}_{ij}-\vec{\mathbf{U}}_{ij}|=|\sqrt{(\mathbf{r'}_{ij}-\mathbf{R'}_{ij})^2+(\mathbf{g'}_{ij}-\mathbf{G'}_{ij})^2+(\mathbf{b'}_{ij}-\mathbf{B'}_{ij})^2}\ , \tag{15}$$

where the lower case u, r, g, and b denote the *sample* unit vector $\vec{\mathbf{u}}_{ij}$, while capital U, R, G, and B denote the *reference* unit vector U_{ij} (primes denote **unit** vector components).

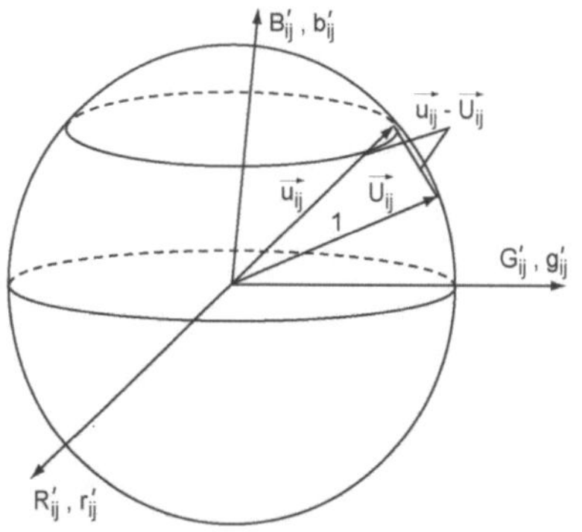

Fig. 12. Illustration of two color unit vector (CUV) subtraction, where $\vec{\mathbf{u}}_{ij}$ is a sample unit vector, and $\vec{\mathbf{U}}_{ij}$ is a reference unit vector. Cartesian coordinates are unit vector components $\mathbf{R}'_{ij}$, $\mathbf{G}'_{ij}$, **and** $\mathbf{B}'_{ij}$ for the reference unit vector, and $\mathbf{r}'_{ij}$, $\mathbf{g}'_{ij}$, **and** $\mathbf{b}'_{ij}$ for the sample unit vector, where: $|\vec{U}_{ij}|=|\vec{u}_{ij}|=\mathbf{1}$. Primes denote unit vector components

The **pixel-by-pixel** vector subtraction operation described above can consume computation time and bandwidth; thus, it is more useful for *automatic target recognition* (ATR). For that purpose we select those pixels for which the CUV subtraction value is below a threshold value, in the form:

$$|\vec{U}_{ij}-\vec{u}_i|\le \mathbf{T}\ , \tag{16}$$

where T is a predefined threshold value. The *spectral region* of *interest* (ROI) is defined by those pixel clusters that predominantly have CUV subtraction values below threshold value T. When the color signature has a dominant color component such as red, we can simplify this operation by applying the principle of "bright points," or **bright pixels**. Then, instead of Eq. (16), we can use the following relation:

$$\mathbf{R}_{ij} > \mathbf{T}_{\mathbf{B}}\ , \tag{17}$$

where $\mathbf{R}_{ij}$ is the absolute color intensity vector $\vec{\mathbf{I}}_{ij}$ component, and the same for green and blue. Then only "red-bright" pixels, which have a value higher than the predetermined threshold value T_B, will be selected. Then the T_B value must be normalized to an average color value to eliminate illumination background. The three RGB color primaries are shown in Fig. 13.

Procedure for finding color primaries in IR. They must be selected in such a way that all wavelength signatures of interest are within the color triangle. Also, to discriminate the specific region well, we need to place two primaries close to each other (for example, the x and y primaries in the 550-650 nm range are well discriminated). Also, some primaries should be expanded into all regions of interest, as the x primary is in the 400-680 nm range, as shown in Fig. 13.

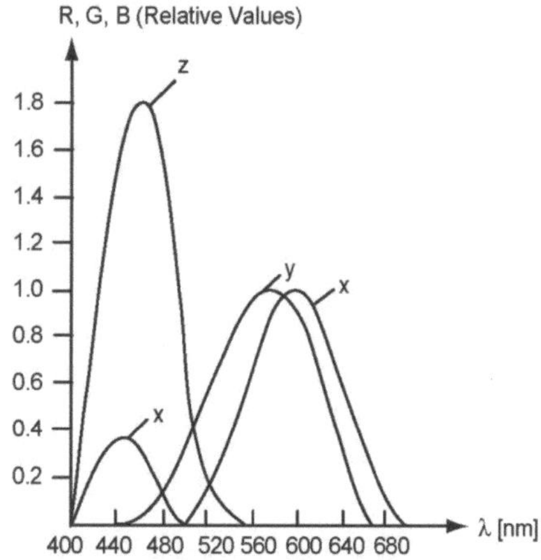

Fig. 13. Illustration of three RGB color primaries in wavelength domain, for human vision. We see that the x-primary is expanded into two hills, covering all regions of interest

4.3 Biological analogies

While human males almost always have three (RGB) color primaries, some women have four (Fu et al., 2004; Caufield et al., 2004 & Fu et al., 2005). Among animals, the *European starling* has four primaries. Other examples include the *mantis shrimp* (twelve primaries! Marshall & Oberwinkler, 1999), *honey bee* (three), and *bichromatic insects* (two). Furthermore, some women not only have four primaries, but also have rod sensitivity even in daylight.

All these biological analogies suggest that the number N of primaries and their related spectral profiles depend on specific tasks or CONOPS. In fact, N varies from two (bichromatic insect) to twelve (mantis shrimp). A specific spectral region of interest should be covered by a higher density of primaries, and the system sensitivity depends on their first differentiating wavelengths. Physically, the color primaries can be created by any of three methods:

- Dichroic beamsplitters
- Detector focal plane arrays (FPAs)
- Color filters directly on the pixels.

4.4 An example of natural engineering

An interesting example of *Natural Engineering* (NE) for aquatic vision is presented in Kröger et al., 1999 for shallow-water fish that have very good color vision, covering 250 nm range from UV to red (four cone types), while still preserving excellent resolution in this wide spectral range in spite of chromatic aberrations (shorter focal lengths for blue). This is due to chromatic aberration compensation by spherical aberration (shorter focal lengths for the inner zone). Then, red light from the inner zone focuses in the same location as the blue light from the outer zone.

5. Resolution and sensitivity in animal eyes

5.1 Resolution

Diffraction-limited imaging systems are those that achieve resolution limits, defined by diffraction rather than by (geometrical) aberrations. Such systems used to have photoreceptor ("pixel") sizes close to those limited by the *Rayleigh resolution criterion*, based on an Airy (intensity) pattern, in the form: $y = [2J_1(z)/z]^2$, where $J_1(z)$ is the *Bessel function* of the 1st kind and the 1st order, and

$$z = \pi D(\delta\Theta)/\lambda \quad (18)$$

where $\delta\Theta$ is the angular distance from the center of the Airy pattern (which is the point object response), D is the lens diameter, and λ is the optical wavelength (in air). The spatial distance, x, at focal plane, is

$$x = f(\delta\Theta) = \frac{z\lambda f}{\pi D} = \frac{z\lambda}{\pi} f\# \quad (19)$$

where f# = f/D. The Airy (circular) pattern is the diffraction one, with adjacent maxima and minima (rings), defined by the Bessel function, summarized in Table 1, for $\lambda = 0.5$ μm, and f# = 2.5 (easy lens).

Maximum/Minimum	z	x	y
1st maximum	0	0	1
1st minimum (1st ring)	1.22 π	1.52 μm	0
2nd maximum	1.635 π	2 μm	0.0175
2nd minimum(2nd ring)	2.233 π	2.79 μm	0

Table 1. Maxima and Minima of Airy Pattern (Analog Resolution), for $\lambda = 0.5$ μm and f# = 2.5

We see that, outside the 1st ring, the *Airy pattern* is almost flat, close to zero, since for the 2nd maximum, the y value is very low (only 0.0175). The energy fraction within the 1st ring is 84% (Born & Wolf, 1999).

The Rayleigh criterion, defining the analog resolution (valid also for animal eyes) is such that adjacent point objects are recognizable if the 1st maximum of the Airy pattern of the 1st object coincides with the first minimum of the 2nd one. According to Table 1, this is equivalent to $z = 1.22\pi$; thus, we obtain the following resolving angular element, $(\delta\Theta)^R$,

$$(\delta\Theta)^R = 1.22\,(\lambda/D) \quad (20)$$

and, the equivalent linear element $(\delta x)^R$, in the form:

$$(\delta x)^R = 1.22\,\lambda f\# \quad (21)$$

In contrast, the digital resolution (valid for *Human Engineering* (HE)), is defined by the so-called *Nyquist Criterion,* which states that two point objects are recognizable if they are located not closer that at the distance between two second pixels. Assuming, for illustration, that the size of each pixel is 4 μm, and the space between them is 1 μm, the *pitch* is 5 μm and the Nyquist resolving element, $(\delta x)^N$ = 10 μm, as shown in Fig. 14, where the Rayleigh resolving element: $(\delta x)^R$ = 1.52 μm, is also shown, for $\lambda = 0.5$ μm, and f# = 2.5.

The Nyquist criterion can also be applied to *Natural Engineering* (NE), if we identify the eye's photoreceptor size with pixel size. The HE-based video surveillance also uses the 3rd

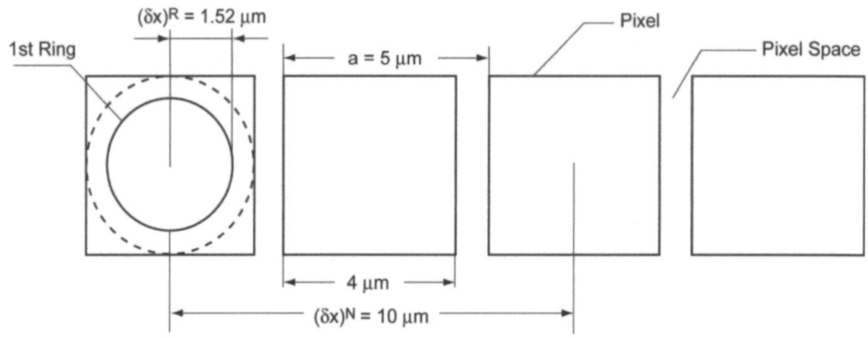

Fig. 14. Illustration of digital (Nyquist) resolution ($\delta x^{(N)} = 10$ μm), and analog (Rayleigh) resolution ($\delta x^{(R)} = 1.52$ μm)

resolution criterion, the so-called *Johnson criterion*, defined as a minimum number of pixels per object for: *detection* (D), *recognition* (R), and *identification* (I), as: 5, 10, and 15, respectively. For example, for an object (human) with a size of 1.8 m, the Johnson resolving elements are: 36 cm (D), 18 cm (R), and 12 cm (I), respectively.

Resolving Elements and Spatial Frequencies. In order to explain the role of the resolving element in animal eyes' resolution, consider the object detail, $\delta\ell$, to be observed at distance, r; then its angular size is $\delta\phi = \delta\ell/r$, and, assuming imaging system magnification, M = 1, the angular size of the image of this object detail, is also $\delta\phi$ (for, $M \neq 1$, we need to provide respective rescaling). The Rayleigh criterion defined by Eq. 20, determines the minimum recognizable angular size of such a detail.

The other important resolution quantity is *spatial frequency*, defined in Fourier optics (Goodman, 1968), by the so-called *Fourier transform* of 2D function U(x,y):

$$G(f_x, f_y) = \hat{F}\{U(x,y)\} = \int_{-\infty}^{+\infty}\int U(x,y)\exp\left[-j2\pi(f_x \cdot x + f_y \cdot y)\right]dxdy \tag{22}$$

where $\hat{F}\{...\}$ is the 2D Fourier transform of U(x,y) and (f_x, f_y) are 2D-spatial frequencies in the number of lines per mm. For example, for $f_x = 100\ell/\text{mm}$, the resolving element (spatial period) is: 10 μm = 10^{-2} mm.

In Land & Nilsson, 2002, spatial frequency is defined in a different way, namely, in a number of cycles per radian, as the *optical cut-off frequency*, ν_c, in the form:

$$\nu_c = D/\lambda \tag{23}$$

It can be shown that the equivalent Fourier cut-off frequency, f_c, is equal to $D/\lambda f$, for far-distant objects (see Goodman, 1968), *Frequency Analysis of Optical Imaging Systems,* for $d_i = f$), where the *Optical Transfer Function* (OTF) for noncoherent optical imaging systems reaches zero. This is equivalent to contrast ratio reaching zero for cut-off "spatial frequency," $\nu_c = D/\lambda$, Fig. 3-3, in Land & Nilsson, 2002.

The cut-off spatial frequency ν_c, as defined in Land & Nilsson, 2002, is a useful quantity in such a way that, according to Eq. (20), we have:

$$\nu_c = 0.82\,[(\delta\Theta)^R]^{-1} \tag{24}$$

i.e., it is approximately equal to the minimum recognizable angular object size, seeing at λ wavelength, with lens aperture diameter, D. The typical color wavelengths are: *red* (600-640 nm), *yellow* (570-600 nm), *green* (510-570 nm), and *blue* (450-510 nm). According to Schever & Kolb, 1987, the more subtle subcolors are: violet region (320-420 nm); blue region (420-500 nm); green-yellow region (520-580 nm); and orange-red region (590-610 nm). On the other hand, the mantis shrimp (*Neogonodactylus oerstedii*), a marine crustacean, has at least four color stimuli for UV light, at 315, 330, 340, and 380 nm (Marshall & Oberwinkler, 1999). Assuming D = 2 mm, and λ = 0.55 μm = 550 nm), we obtain ν_c = 3637 cycles/radian. According to Land & Nilsson, 2002, the highest ν_c value is 8022 cycles/radian for an *eagle*; a *man* (fovea) is *second* with ν_c = 4175 cycles/radian; then, the *octopus* (2632) and *jumping spider* (716); then, the *cat* (573), *goldfish* (409), and *dragonfly* (115); finally, with much lower resolution: *bee* (30), *crab* (19), *scallop* (18), *fly* (5.7), *nautilus* (*cephalopod:* 3.6), and *cirolane* (deep-sea *isopod*: 1.9).
The spatial visual *acuity* of the wedge-tailed eagle (*Aquila audex* (Raymond, 1985)) has been determined across a range of luminance, by applying behavioural (acuity) and anatomical (resolution) investigation (the eagle viewed test gratings and received a food reward if his grating resolution guess was right). The results were average acuity: from 138 c/deg (or, 7911 c/rad), for luminance of 2000 cd/m^2, to 34 c/deg (or 1948 c/rad), for luminance of 0.2 cd/m^2, corresponding to almost the same values of resolving power.

5.2 Sensitivity

Eye sensitivity is defined as the number of photons, N, received by a photoreceptor, with size, d, by a lens with an aperture diameter D, and a focal length, f, at a standard radiance (luminance) level, in the form (Land & Nilsson, 2002):

$$S = N / R = 0.62\,(d^2 / f\#^2)\,(\eta_{abs}) \tag{25}$$

where radiance, R, is in Watts/sr·m^2 (*objective* units), while luminance is in (cd/m^2, or nits (*subjective* units), f# = f/D, and η_{abs} is coefficient (fraction) of absorption. We see that *aquatic eyes* with very low f#-values are preferable here, while maximizing d-value (pixel size) also minimizes resolution. Of course, at very high luminance level, S-value can be low, but at very low ones, S-value should be high.
In Table 2, various luminance levels are presented, as summarized from various sources, especially including Land & Nilsson, 2002. We see that their range is very broad, from 10^{-8} nits (800 m - water depth), or even lower, to 10^4 nits (bright sunlight). At water depth, ℓ, the radiance (luminance) attenuates exponentially (according to Beer's law), as: $R = R_o e^{-\alpha\ell}$, where $\alpha = 0.032\ m^{-1}$.
Eye sensitivities are adjusted to specific light *habitat*. For example, for human light in daylight, s = 0.01 μm^2 sr (D = 2 mm, (d/f) = $1.2{\cdot}10^{-4}$ rad, and η_{abs} = 0.31; so, for d = 2.5 μm, we obtain f = 20.83 mm), while for the deep-sea *isopod* (*Crustacean Cirolana*), s = 4200 μm^2 sr (D = 150 μm, (d/f) = 0.78 rad, η_{abs} = 0.51; so, for f# = 1, f = D = 150 μm, and d = 117 μm; i.e., large size of photoreceptor).
Typical sensitivity levels for animal eyes are decreased with higher luminance levels (Land & Nilsson, 2002): *Cirolana* (marine *isopod* at deep sea): s = 4200 μm^2 sr; *Oplophorus* (*decapod* shrimp at deep sea): s = 3300 μm^2 sr; *Dinopis* (ogre-faced spider, nocturnal): s = 101 μm^2 sr; Moth *(nocturnal)* s = 38 μm^2 sr; *Man* (scotopic): s = 18 μm^2 sr; *Scallop* (coastal sea-floor):): s =

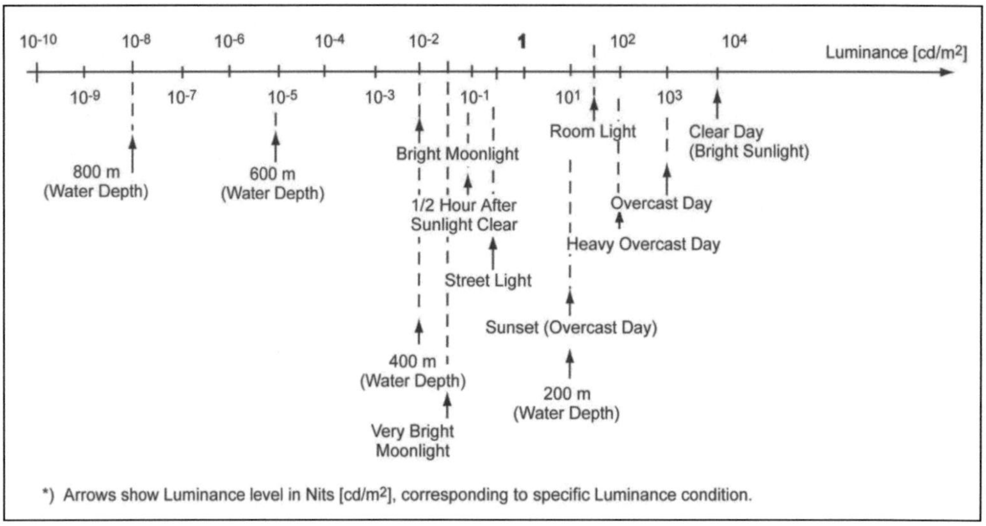

Table 2. Luminance Levels*)

4 μm² sr; *Crab* (diurnal):): s = 0.5 μm² sr; *Bee* (diurnal):): s = 0.32 μm² sr; *Jumping spider* (diurnal): s = 0.04 μm² sr; and Man (*fovea* in daylight):): s = 0.01 μm² sr.

5.3 Contrast and low photon numbers

Human eyes, as well as the majority of mammal eyes, have excellent sensitivity to low photon levels, even to single photons (Land and Nilsson, 2002), although the brain's "safety factor" (an equivalent of "decision threshold" in HE-photodetectors) is of about: N = 6. For such low photon numbers, N, the *quantum noise* occurs, guided by *Poisson statistics* (Margenau and Murphy, 1976). Its basic feature is such that the photon beam with statistical average, $\bar{N}$, fluctuates with dispersion, $\sqrt{N}$ (these fluctuations are of fundamental quantum nature, independent on measurement accuracy). This means that low contrast ratio levels (defined as light intensity relative variation: $C = \Delta I/2I$, where $\Delta I = I_{max} - I_{min}$) cannot be kept at low photon numbers. (The contrast is an important parameter of vision measuring "*spatial edges*" and "*object contours,*" or even "*temporal contours.*") Assuming $\Delta I = 2\sigma$, where σ is dispersion, we obtain

$$C = \frac{\Delta I}{2I} = \frac{\sigma}{I} = \frac{\sqrt{N}}{N} = \frac{1}{\sqrt{N}} \tag{26}$$

which is a generalized form of the so-called *Rose-deVries law*, studied by Hugo deVries and Albert Rose in the 1940s (Land and Nilsson, 2002).

This law shows that low contrast ratios, C, can be measured only at high photon levels. For example, for N = 10,000 = 10^4, $\sqrt{N} = 100$, and C = 1%. However, for N = 100, $\sqrt{N} = 10$, and C = 10%. In general, there is the rule that for nocturnal vision (equivalent to night vision in Human Engineering (HE)), we need to have animal eyes with high sensitivity (thus, with low resolution), in order to measure low contrast levels. This is the manifestation of general trade-offs between high *metrical information* capacity (or, high dynamic range and low contrast) and *high structural information* capacity (or, high resolution) (Jannson, 1980b and MacKay, 1950); simply speaking, we cannot have low contrast detectivity and high resolution at the same time, when photon levels are low. This general law is valid for any type of measurement noise, not only quantum noise.

To be complete, let us also discuss the so-called specific detectivity, or $D^* = \sqrt{AB}/(NEP)$, valid for HE-semi-conductor photodetectors, where A-detector surface, B-bandwidth, and NEP-equivalent noise power, in: $W^{-1}cm\ Hz^{1/2}$. Good D*-values are in the range of 10^{12} - 10^{13} $W^{-1}cm\ Hz^{1/2}$.

Let us consider the human eye with decision-threshold: N = 6 (against spontaneous *rhodopsin* activations (Land & Nilsson, 2002)). From X-Ray Data, 2001, we have: hc/1 eV = 1.2 μm, where h-Planck constant, c-speed of light; thus, hν = hc/λ = 1 eV, for λ = 1.24 μm, or hν = 2 eV, for λ = 0.62 μm (ν-photon frequency). Then, for λ = 0.62 μm, (red), (NEP) = (6) $(3.2)\cdot 10^{-17}$ J/sec = $19.2\cdot 10^{-17}$ W, assuming noise level (floor) for N = 6 during 1 sec-observation. Assuming retina's "pixel's size: d = $\sqrt{A} = 2.5\ \mu m$, we obtain: D* = ($2.5\cdot 10^{-4}$ cm) (1 $Hz^{1/2}$/($19.2\cdot 10^{-17}$ W) = $1.3\cdot 10^{13}$ $W^{-1}cmHz^{1/2}$; i.e., an excellent D*-value.

For (noise) fluctuation, based on Poisson statistics (or, in general, on Gaussian (normal) statistics) (Margenau & Murphy, 1976), it is useful to evaluate light-intensity variations in dispersion (σ) units. Then, we can easily determine probability, p, that a given N-value is located within the range: $N = \bar{N} \pm \varepsilon\sigma$, where ε is a number of σ-units, as shown in Table 3, based on the so-called *normal probability integral* (Dwight, 1961), related to *error-function*, tabulated in other sources.

ε	1.0	1.5	2.0	2.5	3.0	3.5	3.8
p	68.3%	86.6%	95%	98.8%	99.7%	99.35%	99.99%

Table 3. Probability P, of N-Number Location within: $N = \bar{N} \pm \varepsilon\sigma$, based on Normal Probability Integral

6. Animal mirrors and other natural optical elements

Animal mirrors cannot be **metallic** but rather **dielectric** ones. In such a case it is quite surprising that such a complex effect like *Bragg effect* has been discovered by the NE, including even *tunable interference filters* performing color changes in reflection (Lythgoe & Shand, 1989). This is because by changing the spatial period, Λ, due to mechanical shrinking effect, we can change resonant (Bragg) wavelength, λ_B, by the following Bragg resonance relation:

$$\Lambda = \frac{\lambda_B}{2\bar{n}} \tag{27}$$

where $\bar{n}$ is average refractive index, as shown in Fig. 15.

According to the *Bragg triangle* (Fig. 15(b)), we have: K/2k=cosα', or λ' = 2Λ cosα'; sinα = $\bar{n}$ sinα', the latter equation to be Snell law, while λ' = λ/ $\bar{n}$ (where λ' is in medium while λ is in air), and using Eq. (27), we obtain the following "blue-shift" relation (K = 2π/Λ, k = 2π/λ'):

$$\lambda' = \lambda_B \cos a\alpha'; \tag{28}$$

i.e., **Bragg wavelength shifts-into-blue** under slanted (α'>o) incidence (strictly speaking, any wavelength value and corresponding Bragg mirror efficiency value will be shifted under slanted incidence, according to Eq. (28)). This effect provides a good criterion for

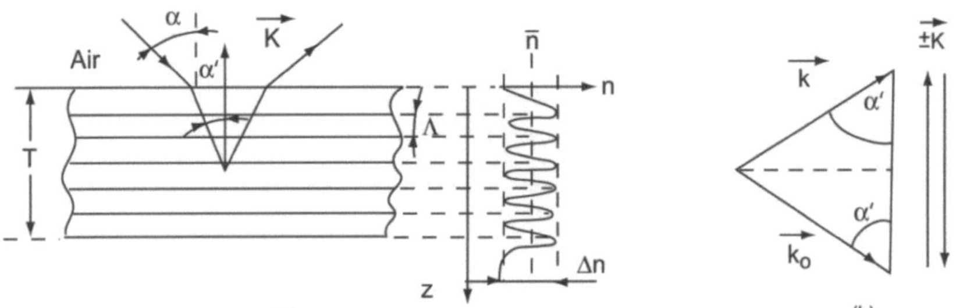

Fig. 15. Illustration of Bragg effect in sinusoidal Bragg grating, including: (a) Bragg reflection; (b) Bragg triangle

differentiation between metallic mirrors and Bragg mirrors. Still, the majority of *butterfly* wings have pigmentary (similar to metallic) mirrors. However, males of the genus *Morpho* have intensive blue wings based on constructive interference (Bragg effect in dielectric mirror).

The structural (Bragg) animal mirrors are based on *sinusoidal* index modulation (as in Fig. 15(a)) rather than on quadratic one, as in the case of HE-interference filters. Therefore, they are closer to *holographic Bragg mirrors,* such as those based on *dichromatic gelatin* (DCG) (Jannson et al., 1991), which is **volume holographic material, extracted from biologic tissues.** Then, Kogelnik's coupled-wave theory (Kogelnik, 2001) holds, with *coupling constant,* ν, defined as: $\nu = \pi\Delta n \cdot T/\lambda'$, where Δn is *index modulation* and T-grating thickness, as in Fig. 15(a). For $\nu = \pi$, the holographic (diffraction) efficiency reaches 99%; then, $\Delta n \cdot T/\lambda' = 1$, and required $\Delta n = \lambda/n \cdot T$. At the same time, the *Bragg grating linewidth,* Δλ, is defined by the relation: $\Delta n/\bar{n} = \Delta\lambda/\lambda$, and number of grating periods, M, is: $M = T/\Lambda = 2\bar{n}\,T/\lambda$; thus, combining all these relations, we obtain the following relation for Bragg linewidth, Δλ, preserving high (99%) diffraction efficiency,

$$\frac{\Delta\lambda}{\lambda} = \frac{2}{\bar{n}M}; \quad M = \frac{2\lambda}{\bar{n}\Delta\lambda} \tag{29}$$

For example, for λ = 600 nm, Δλ = 10 nm, and $\bar{n}$ = 1.45, we obtain M = 82; and, since: $T = M\lambda/2\bar{n}$, we obtain T = 17 μm, a very small mirror thickness (sufficient to obtain such high (99%) reflection). On the other hand, for α = 30° and λ_B = 600 nm, we obtain from Eq. (28), λ = 563 nm; i.e., the **blue-shift** is significant (36 nm).

Vignetting has been discussed in Section 1, as a vision effect discovered by the NE-based precursor of an eye (Fig. 1). In fact, such a primitive eye is still applied as *Nautilus* eye. Other *cephalopods* (*octopus, squid, cuttlefish*) have quite excellent eyes. This surprising NE-bottleneck can be explained by the fact that the Nautilus habitat is rather low risk. (Also, NE-moving into high-resolution small-pupil *pinhole* eyes would be impractical due to too-low sensitivity.)

Anti-Reflection (AR) Structures in the animal world are based on a pigment (like "black paint") material, rather than on the so-called *moth-eye AR-structures,* proposed by the HE, based on cone-like sub-wavelength microscopic structures, simulating GRIN-reflection, as shown in Fig. 16.

In such a case, in the intermediate ("GRIN") region: $0 \le z \le z_o$, the refractive index, n(z), changes as: $n = n_1 w + (1-w)\,n_2$, where w is a *weight factor:* $0 \le w \le 1$, in the form: $w = z/z_o$, which is illustrated in Fig. 16, for $n_2 = 1$ (air). This approximation is valid only if there is no "diffraction grating" effect, even for very large incidence angles; i.e., when $\Lambda < \lambda/2$. Since such solution (applied for HE-optical/microwave AR-structures) has not been discovered

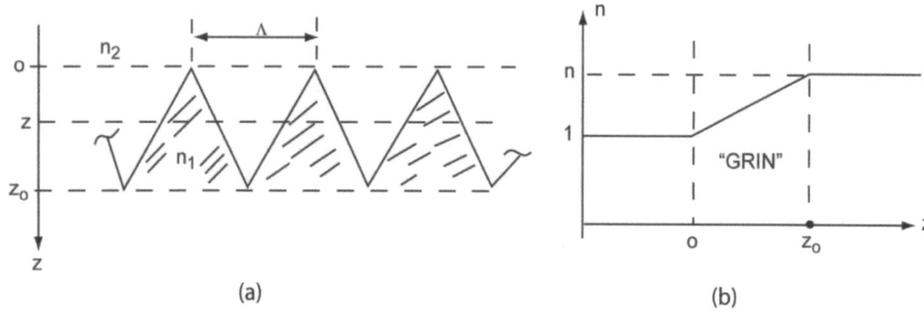

Fig. 16. Illustration of HE-"moth-eye" structure, simulating GRIN effect for $\Lambda<\lambda/2$, assuming $n_2 = 1$ (air), including: (a) Moth-eye AR-structure; (b) GRIN dependence: $n = n(z)$

by the NE, we need to call the "moth-eye" concept, as a kind of *Artificial Abstraction* (AA); see; also, non-Lambertian diffusers (Jannson et al., 2006c).

Total Internal Reflection (TIR) has been discovered by the NE in *superposition* eye of freshwater crayfish, *Cherax destructor*. Cherax is basically nocturnal and has a reflection superposition eye (see Section 3). In Bryceson & McIntyre, 1983, the TIR acceptance angles have been measured and average FOV curves were calculated to be within 5-10°, depending on light habitat. It should be noted that the TIR is much easier to achieve than the Bragg reflection (Fig. 15), as shown in Fig. 17, where the "mirage" phenomenon is also shown (such index profile can also be obtained in hot desert air environment).

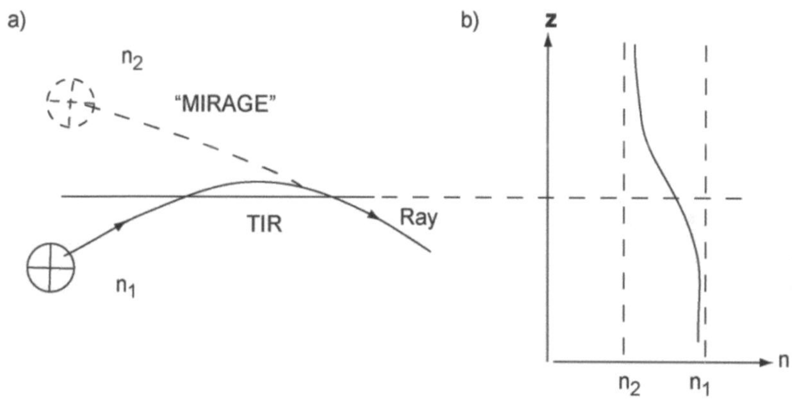

Fig. 17. Illustration of Total Internal Reflection (TIR) effect ("total" means 100%) in animal superposition eye optics; $n_1>n_2$, including: (a) "curved" ray reflection; (b) index profile

Reflecting Camouflage is applied by some fish such as *permits* (*trachinotus falcatus*). These are silver fish that apply a form of camouflage which in the open ocean makes their bodies very difficult to see (Denton & Nicol, 1965), because direct solar component becomes diffuse below the sea surface; so, the radiation becomes symmetrical around vertical axis. As a result, independently on sun light direction, a vertical mirror surface becomes invisible (light reflected from such a surface at any angle has the same intensity as the light passing through this surface). Therefore, by placing fins vertically (not parallel to the body surface) makes fish almost invisible. This effect works independently on color if the multi-layer (Bragg) mirrors are applied with proper color compensation (please see, Land & Nilsson,

2002, Section 6). It should be noted that a similar CONOPS (to that below sea surface) is under heavy canopy of rain forest.
Scotopic Nocturnal Vision is applied by primates and higher mammals, by applying two types of photoreceptors: *cones* and *rods*. In the case of **photopic** (diurnal) vision (field luminance not lower than 3nt (cdm^{-2})), we apply cones (after being dark adapted, the eye requires 2-3 minutes to become light adapted). In the case of **scotopic** (nocturnal), or night vision (field luminance not higher than $3{\cdot}10^{-5}$nt), we apply rods (dark adaption takes 45 min.). Retina's highest resolution area, *fovea*, contains only cones. The maximum photopic efficiency is at 555-nm wavelength, while the maximum scotopic efficiency is at 510 nm (*blue-shift*). The mixed (photopic/scotopic) light habitat is very frustrating for the human eye. Such habitat can be created, for example, by scattered street light, filling all the intermediate (10^{-5}-1 nt) region (see Table 2). This defect can be eliminated by LED illumination. Also, the change of sunlight spectrum (blue-shift for scotopic) can influence human sleep habit (level of melatonin is increasing in human blood under blue-shift of white light, simulating sunset conditions (Brainard et al., 2001)) which is broken under artificial lighting. This, again, can be regulated by LED illumination.
Infrared (IR) Vision has been applied to the detection of forest fires by the beetle *Melanophila accuminata* for mating purposes which usually takes place while the fire is still burning and females deposit eggs immediately after the flames have subsided (the larvae of Melanophila absolutely depend on wood of fresh fire-killed trees because they cannot cope with the defense reactions of a living tree). Forest fires emit IR radiation at 2.2 - 4 μm (assuming fire temperature between 500°C and 1000°C,) which is well transmitted through air due to atmospheric "window" ranging from 3 μm to 5 μm, at distances up to 80 km. In the experiments (Schmitz & Blackmann, 1998), all wavelengths shorter than 1.6 μm were excluded by a longpass IR filter.

7. Pseudo-apposition eyes

The apposition eyes of insects produce multiplicity of redundant identical images. This redundant imaging information is further lost through neuro-biological process. In this section, we propose a HE-based solution, called *pseudo-apposition eye*, which applies this imaging multiplicity information for spectral imaging purposes, as shown in Fig. 18. This *hyperspectral imaging* concept applies narrow band interference filters located in the front of each lens with different Bragg wavelengths λ_1, λ_2, λ_3, etc., representing different spectral bands. Each lens has its own camera with 2D photoreceptors (pixels). Since this system observes distant objects, at infinity, each so-called *world object point* is represented by certain plane wave with direction in spherical coordinates (Θ, ϕ). While every spectral band is represented, at normal incidence (Θ = 0), by its central (Bragg) wavelength λ_1, λ_2, λ_3, etc., this wavelength is <u>shifted</u> into shorter wavelengths for slanted angle incidence $(\Theta > 0;\ \theta \leq \pi/2)$, due to *Bragg wavelength shifts-into-blue* effect (see; Eq. (28)). Because this system monitors only plane waves, the lenses required have to produce only simple plane-wave-transformation-into-an-image-point, equivalent to Fourier transform, as in Eq. (22). The geometrical locii of these image points can be called an analog of Petzval's surface (Born and Wolf 1999), because this surface does not represent the same wavelength but rather Bragg wavelength distribution following Eq. (28). The optimum lens realizing this surface should be a kind of ball lens, with maximum number of degrees of freedom in order to maximize the optimization process (Kompaniets, 2010). Therefore, the ideal lens should be a

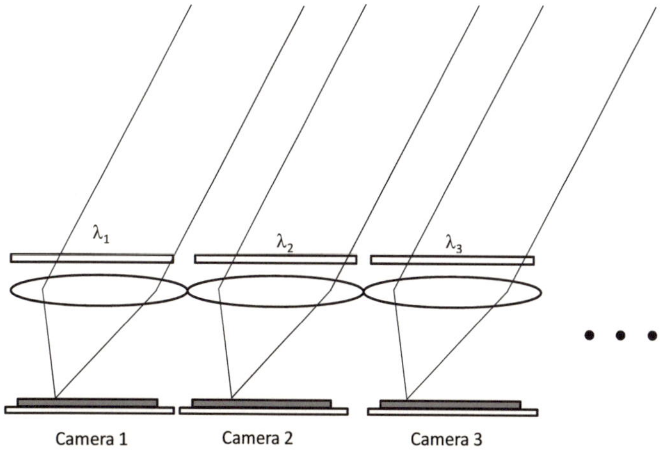

Fig. 18. A possible implementation of the hyperspectral imaging concept based on use of multi-aperture pseudo-apposition eye system. As shown above, multiple cameras observe the same scene at different spectral bands. Position of the object of interest in the so-called RGB color map can be determined by brightness of the relevant pixels in the multiple spectral bands

kind of GRIN lens, similar to that used in aquatic eyes, as in Section 2.3. Fig. 19 shows the photograph of object mapping with traces of TNT explosive (invisible to the naked eye), detected by the pseudo-apposition eye system.

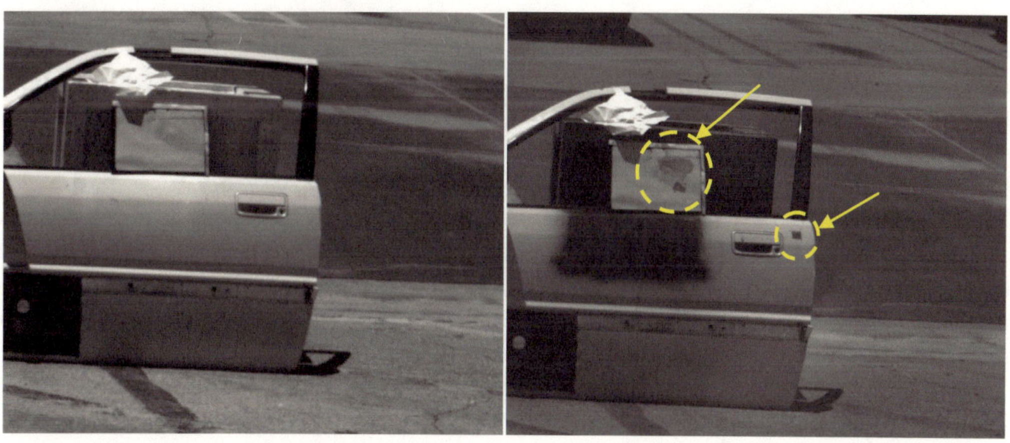

Fig. 19. Left - image captured using a regular monochrome camera that shows no traces of explosives. Right - Dashed yellow circles clearly show traces of explosives made visible through passive spectral imaging

8. Human eye, visual cortex and video imagery effects in primates' vision

8.1 Eye, retina and primary visual cortex

Analyzing human vision (or, more generally, primates' vision), in the context of video imagery, requires considering not only the eye but also the *primary visual cortex*. This, in turn, requires discussing not only human vision in a narrow sense (i.e., eye, including retina) but also the field of *central-nervous neurobiology*. In this section, we will present highly simplified (broader) view of human vision including NE-based temporal imaging effects related to **HE-based video surveillance**, based on excellent monography by Hubel (Hubel, 1988), a Nobel laureate with Wiesel in 1981). He refers to Ramon y Cajal and Golgi as fathers of *neuroanatomy* (Nobel prize in 1906). In Fig. 20, we show the topography of human brain emphasizing the eyes and primary visual cortex (Fig. 20(a)), including human left eye (Fig. 20 (b)), and microscopic view of eye's retina (Fig. 20(c)).

The **primary visual cortex** is located at the opposite side to the eyes (Fig. 20(a)). The second surprising fact is that the optic nerve bundles are reshuffled at *optic chasm* cross-roads: left-to-right and vice versa, at about 50/50-proportion ratio, while this ratio is different for lower mammals such as horses and mice (for more details, please see Hubel, 1988, Section 4). After passing cross-roads, the optic nerve bundle is distributed into broad so-called *optic radiation* channeling and then converged into a narrower channel leading to *primary visual cortex*.

As an *eye on a land* (terrestrial), the human eye has *cornea*, with some focusing power allowing to make homogeneous axial lens solution effective (in contrast to aquatic GRIN lenses). At the front of the lens there is *iris* (pupil), with its size tunable to various light habitats, while eye's accommodation (equivalent to camera's variable focal length) is provided by eye curvature change due to *ciliary muscles* (while *extraocular muscles* regulate the entire eye ball motion) as in Fig. 20(b). The light beam is focused into *fovea* which is a small part (about half millimeter in diameter) of *retina* (equivalent of CCD array).

Retina's photoreceptors (CCD pixel's equivalents) are both (scotopic) *rods* (which are far more numerous than cones) and (photopic) *cones*, totally about **125 million**, with fovea, a high-resolution spot, containing only cones. Behind photoreceptors, there is a back layer containing the *black pigment, melanin* (also found in skin), an equivalent of black paper inside a camera. It has also the second function: restoring functionality of photoreceptors after their bleaching by strong light beams. This is perhaps the reason that retina's thin (250 μm) semi-transparent neural cell structure (Fig. 20(c)) is placed into the front of light; thus, partially scattering (blocking) light beams, resulting in some obscuring of vision. This "*purposely mistaken*" NE-solution seems to be necessary compromise between eye optics and melanin's biochemical functionality needs. [Cones and rods, with 2-3 μm-diameter size, are terminated with "pixels;" their size is close to the diffraction (Rayleigh resolution) limit (~1.5 μm).] The light blurring, due to this compromise, would be disastrous in the fovea region, when high resolution demands are very stringent; thus, the NE provided a ring of thicker retina exposing the central cones of the fovea region, thus, avoiding its blocking (Hubel, 1988).

In Fig. 20(c), three retinal layers: *ganglion cells, bipolar cells* and rods/cones are shown; their total thickness is only 0.25 mm = 250 μm. We see that light needs to pass through two of them (ganglion and bipolar) before it gets to the rods and cones. Since the number of cells increases from left to right (from about 1 million to 125 million), two other in-parallel cells (*horizontal* and *amacrine* ones) provide the necessary fan-out.

Considering photoreceptor size of about 2.5 μm, and total number of cones/rods to be about 10^8, the retina size is about 25 mm, with semi-circular surface profile (Fig. 20(b)), to be reduced to about: 25 mm/(π/2) = 16 mm of straight-line length.

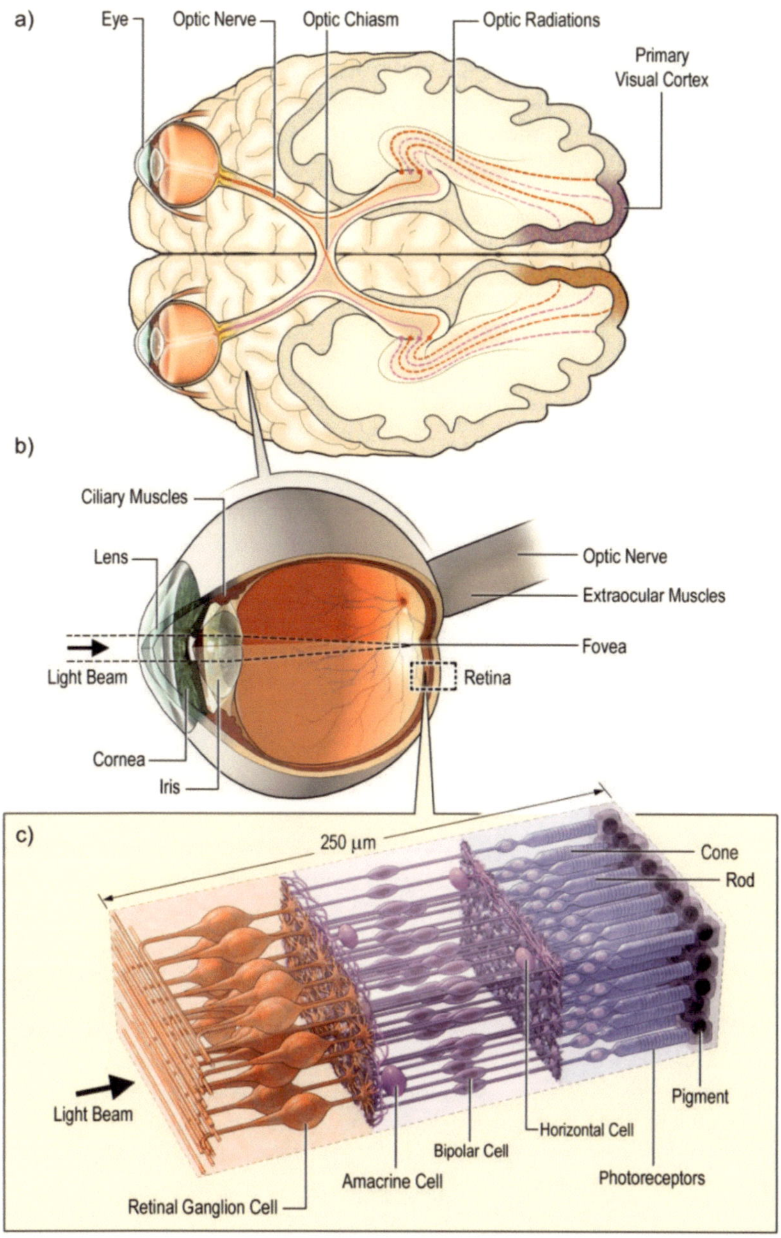

Fig. 20. General view of human brain emphasizing the eyes and primary visual cortex, including: (a) topography of brain; (b) an eye; (c) microscopic view of retina. It should be noted, based on Hubel 1998, that the entire retinal structure (c) is put in the front into the direction of light; so, light needs to go through this structure before it is detected by photoreceptors (retina's "pixels," by analogy to TV camera). It should also be noted that the retina structure is very thin (only 0.25 mm = 250 μm ≅ 10 mils); as in Fig.18(c). This figure is based on analysis in Hubel, 1988

8.2 Cortical neurons

The neural cells have approximately the same structures within retina as well as within cerebral cortex; the most complex of them, however, are *cortical* neurons.

Consider typical *cortical neurons* (Jannson et al., 2009) constituted of the *soma, axons, dendrites,* and *synapses,* in mammals or more generally in vertebrates, as discussed in general neurobiology (Fig. 21).

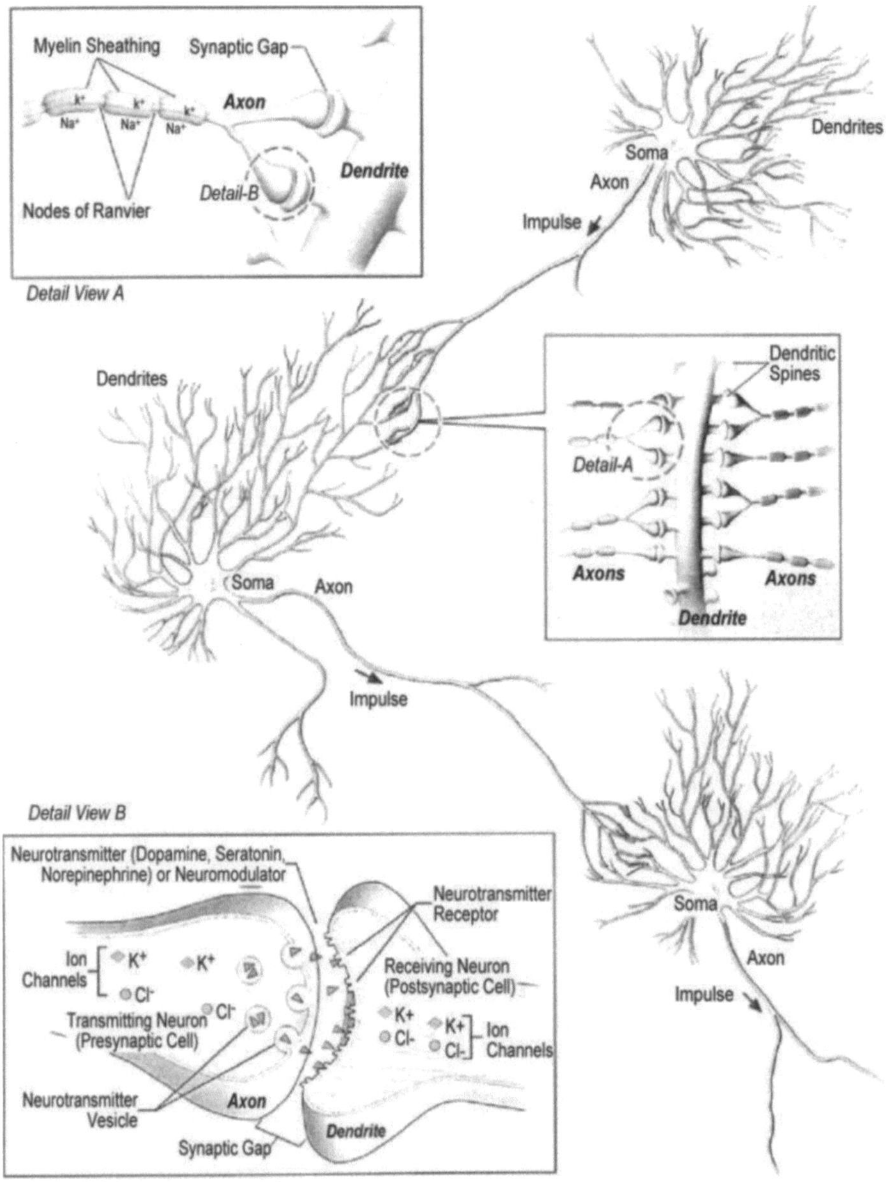

Fig. 21. Schematic of typical cortical neurons, constituted of the soma, axons, dendrites, and synapses, emphasizing the concept of synapse operation, as in Detail View B, from Jannson, et al., 2009

Fig. 21 shows a detailed general schematic of typical cortical neurons emphasizing the concept of operation of the *synapse* and its interconnectivity. More specifically, in Detail View B a synaptic gap between an *axon* and a *dendrite* is shown. We see that in an ion channel, a salt, KCl, is decomposed into positive K+ ions and negative Cl^- ions that are transmitted through those channels, which also activate *neurotransmitter vesicles*. These vesicles contain neurotransmitters such as *dopamine* and *serotonin*. Those neurotransmitters allow to preserve propagation of ion current through space (a synaptic gap) into neurotransmitter receptors and then through further ion channels. This ion current (according to Kirchhoff law) flows continuously perhaps as an electron current in a dendrite, which is a kind of wire, rather than a synapse which is an only a gap ("synaptic gap"). Therefore, as we see, typical HE-modeling of synapses analogs differs significantly from that of their natural (biological) equivalents, which are synapses presented as wires rather than gaps (as in Fig. 21), another example of the AA.

According to Fig. 21, the synapses' concept of operation, or CONOPS, is based on slowly varying (hours) **parametric** control of ionic current through a synaptic gap due to *neurotransmitters*, such as *dopamine* or *serotonin*. In other words, the ionic current **mobility** is parametrically controlled due to the presence of neurotransmitters. The physics of ionic current mobility, in general, is well described in Joos, 1986, in the chapter entitled *Electrolytic Conduction*. Assuming equilibrium, or constant-velocity movement, the electrical force: zeE, where z is the ion *valence* (here: z = 1), e is electron charge, and E is electric field intensity in volts cm^{-1}, is equal to *resistance force*, *f*, proportional to velocity in cm sec^{-1}. This force can be identified with *Stokes' law* (Joos, 1986), as

$$f = 6\pi\eta R_o v \tag{30}$$

where η is the viscosity coefficient, v is the ion velocity, and R_o is the radius of the *effective ion sphere*. Assuming that, in equilibrium, f = zeE, we obtain the formula for *ion mobility*, in the form (Joos, 1986):

$$u = \frac{v}{E} = \frac{ze}{6\pi\eta R_o} \tag{31}$$

If we measure these ion mobilities, we obtain, for K^+, the mobility value of $67.6 \cdot 10^{-5}$ cm sec^{-1}/volt cm^{-1}, which leads to an ionic radius of magnitude 10^{-8} cm = 10^{-4} μm ~1Å, which is the correct order of magnitude. We see, however, that the ionic radii decrease in order: Li-Na-K, rather than increase, according to well-founded results of atomic physics. The reason is that a small ion has a stronger surface force than a large one. This field causes the attachment of molecules of the solvent, thus, reducing mobility, equivalent to increasing effective radius, R_o, in Eq. (30).

In summary, the CONOPS of natural (biological) *mammalian synapses* has been discussed, within the visualization of natural *cortical neuron* connectivity, shown in Fig. 21, including ion current mobility as described by Eq. (31). In particular, the term of "synapse" should be considered in terms of synaptic gap (see Fig. 21), rather than as a kind of wire, the latter term being better fitted to dendrites of dendritic neurons, for example. In other words, a synapse, or rather a synaptic gap, is a basic connectivity element between different neurons, which constitute natural (NE) neural networks.

8.3 NE-based contour imaging

The *retinal ganglion* cells are the first cells performing a kind of *image processing*: responding, by firing of short (sub-milisecond) impulses (spikes) with variable frequency: *higher* if response is positive, lower if negative. (This type of cell's response is characteristic for all neural cells in the brain.) There are two types of retinal ganglion cells: *on-center* and *off-center* cells (Hubel, 1988); the first type responding positively to bright spots, while the second type responding positively to dark spots (their numbers are in 50/50 proportion, matching the natural habitat (dark objects are probably just as common as light ones (Hubel, 1988)). In general, no positive response has been observed for uniform diffuse light; only spatial edges with black/white contrast produce positive responses.
The role of neural *synapses* (see Section 8.2) and *neurotransmitters* is such that they are enabling high plasticity of *brain cortex*: synapses can be produced and also killed. Their transmittivity can be regulated by *neurotransmitters* such as *seratonin* (Fig. 21). Also, *inhibitory* synapses are about as plentiful as *excitatory* ones. (The excitatory synapses react positively to increasing some transmitter dose, while the same transmitter can react negatively in inhibitory synapses.) Also, the *amacrine* cells seem to be sensitive to motion (Hubel, 1988).
All the above specializations of ganglion cells lead to a kind of their collective response, emphasizing *contour* (edge/border detection of an object, both static and *on-the-move* (OTM)), including even *edge enhancement*. This tendency continues in the case of *cortical cells*, including a *famous experiment by Hubel and Wiesel in 1958, when, after comprehensive search to register cells' response into the artificial dot, they found, to their surprise, that the neural cells in question produced positive response not to this dot but rather to the sharp but faint shadow cast by the edge of the glass substrate used only for this experiment support.*
Further cell specialization is introduced by the cortical neural cells that respond to "*line*" *stimulus*, reacting positively to line's specific length and orientation. They are not only excitatory and inhibitory but also so-called *complex* and *simple* ones (Hubel, 1988). Their **collective** response can be summarized into positive response into not only specific line's length and orientation but also to its curvature and even its manifold surface topology, related to *catastrophe theory* (Ternovskiy et al., 2002).
The role of the *fovea* is emphasized by the spontaneous *saccadic* eye movement that performs random tiny so-called *microsaccades* that occur several times per second in order to detect any sharp contours (edges) and movements of objects within a given natural scene (Hubel, 1988).

8.4 Relations to HE-based video processing

Given the *NE-based contour imaging* (NECI), as in Section 8.3, we see the basic similarities and differences between the NECI and the HE-based video processing. The similarities are with *Artificial Retina* (Alteheld et al., 2007 & Cheng, 2008) **hard-wired HE-solutions**, simulating ganglion cells and some types of cortical cells, while software-defined pre-ATR HE-solutions (Jannson & Kostrzewski, 2006a) are entirely different, since they do not follow the idea of specialized neural cells. Rather, they are based on *wavelet transform pixel's clusterization* (decimation) (Jannson & Kostrzewski, 2006a), and pixel-by-pixel *Full-Frame-to-Frame Comparison* (FFTFC), as in Jannson, 2001, where also new electronic hardware, based on highly dedicated RISC (*Reduced Instruction Set Computer*) processor is applied.
In the FFTFC case, the *Novelty Filtering* (NF) has been introduced that provides object's *edge-enhancement* in both **temporal** and **spatial** domains. In the temporal domain, applicable to the OTM objects, two sequent video frames are compared by pixels' intensity subtraction, using high intensity *contrast* at object boundary (contour). This is *real-time* (RT) video processing in contrast to the previous ATR (*Automatic Target Recognition*), based on *Fourier transform* (Goodman, 1968), which is not real-time. The NF-operation can also be performed

at **spatial** domain, when frame translation is introduced in electronic domain (Jannson et al., 2007b) as in Fig. 22.
In contrast, in the HE-based hard-wired case, the response specificity is very high. In particular, in Hubel, 1988, Figure in p. 41, the *on-center* ganglion cells' response into small (optimum size) bright spot stimulus is presented, versus dark field (no stimulus). In the latter case (no stimulus) the firing pattern does exist but there is no changes ("no changes" - pattern, or "small changes" will also be in the case of non-optimum size spots (Hubel, 1988)). In the case of stimulus presence, the response is positive (random frequency of pulses increases). It should be emphasized that the positive response is only for the specific stimulus (an object) shape and, only, for small set of specialized ("on-center") ganglion cells. Therefore, indeed, the response specificity is very high. On the other hand, in the case of HE-based software-defined video processing (Fig. 20), the response specificity is low; i.e., the NF-effect is equally effective for widely different object contours, and it can work in both temporal and spatial domains.

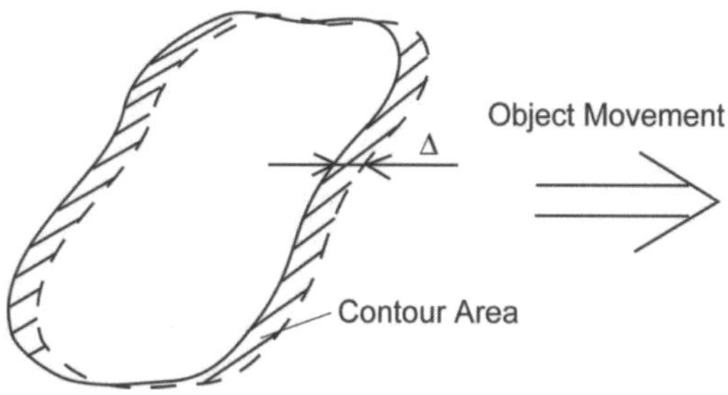

Fig. 22. Pixel-by-pixel subtraction of an object (continuous line), moving from left to right, translated (broken line) by Δ-value during frame-to-frame comparison. Amplified by Novelty Filtering (NF), the object contour area is visualized by the hatched lines

8.5 Holographic associative memory as an example of artificial abstraction

According to Goodman, 1968, the *cross- correlation theorem* has the form:

$$\hat{F}\{\iint U(x',y')V^*(x'-x,y'-y)dx'dy'\} = G(f_x,f_y)H^*(f_x,f_y) \quad (32)$$

where $\hat{F}\{\iint U(x,y)\} = G(f_x,f_y)$ and $\hat{F}\{V(x,y)\} = H(f_x,f_y)$ are 2D Fourier transforms (see: Eq. (22)). According to Gabor (Jannson et al., 1986), in the case of "noise-like" functions, U and V, that correlate sharply (or, only their fragments correlate sharply), the cross-correlation function takes the form of Dirac-delta function:

$$\iint U(x',y')V^*(x'-x,y'-y)dx'dy' = \delta(x,y) \quad (33)$$

Where

$$\delta(x,y) = \begin{cases} \infty, \text{ for } x=0,\ y=0 \\ 0, \text{ for } x\neq 0,\ y\neq 0 \end{cases} \quad (34)$$

The **cross-correlation** operation (32) takes place in the case of *holographic memory* with object function, U(x,y), stored during holographic recording process while the other object function, V(x,y), is applied during holographic reconstruction process (similar to Vander-Lugt filtering (Goodman 1968)). Therefore, if many $U_i(x,y)$-functions (pages) are stored, where: i = 1, 2, .., M; then, only those pages will be reconstructed which have the same *phrase* (graphical, or textual), as has V(x,y)-function. This is the basis of new highly parallel *query paradigm*, unknown in the

electronic domain, being possible base of future computer search engines with tremendous search capacity. Assume, for example M = 10^6, and 10^6-bits per holographic page. Then, if a given graphical/textual phrase is searched in the holographic domain, this phrase can be found, almost instantly (within, say, 10^{-4} sec), amongst: $10^6 x 10^6 = 10^{12}$ bits; i.e., the *search speed* of this new *computer search engine* will be: 10^{12} bits/10^{-4} sec = 10^{16} bits/sec (!).
Some authors have speculated (Jannson et al., 1986) that this kind of holographic associative memory, un-localized in nature (since the holographic storage is distributed all over the entire hologram volume) can be found in the human brain. However, in the view of hard-wired architecture of visual cortex (see Section 8.4), it would be hard to believe that this is a right guess (rather, such concept is closer to software-defined HE-based architectures; see Fig. 23, for comparison). Therefore, we can identify this AA as an indirect one (see Section 9).
The other AA, directly related to hard-wired NE-based architecture, is presented in Jannson et al., 2009. Based on (voltage) signal propagation in *dendritic neurons*, the proposed *neural lensing* follows, mathematically, Fourier heat conduction analysis, generalized by Lord Kelvin (1850) into cable theory, resulting in *descrete lens focusing principle*. It is too early to predict if it is possible to have this AA-concept to be confirmed by any neurobiological experiments. Nevertheless, this principle can explain such well-known neurobiological phenomenon as the criticality of some neurons in specific human face recognition, without the necessity of differentiating their biologic structure.

9. Conclusions

This paper is a kind of interdisciplinary essay discussing the relationships between animal eyes and relevant *human engineering* (HE), in the context of video surveillance. We purposely use engineering language rather than biologic one in order to make those relationships more familiar to video imagery scientists and engineers, including some necessary simplifications (and repetitions) which would be rather improper if addressed to neurobiological vision auditory. This paper is mostly based on two excellent monographics (Land and Nilsson, 2002, and Hubel 1988), as well as on a number of papers, representing work at Physical Optics Corporation (POC), especially including Jannson et al., 2007.
A number of basic conclusions can be made from this on-animal-eyes essay, namely, relationships between biologic evolution (called here: *Natural Engineering*, or NE), and *Human Engineering* (HE) are quite complex yet they can graphically be presented in the form of two crossing sets, as shown in Fig. 23, where the sets' cross-section is represented by a kind of *technology transfer*, called here *Artificial Abstraction* (AA) (which, obviously, can be only one way; this is why the set framework presented here makes sense). While still using this formal language, we can say that the AAs can be of two kinds: **direct** (with positive connotation) and **indirect** (with negative connotation). The first one is made by conclusion from direct observation of NE-process, with some possible HE-additions that can be made, however, only after direct NE-observation. The second one is made in inverse sequence; i.e., first to make the AA observation and then to find a proper biologic analogy. We hope that during the course of this essay, we have made clear why this indirect AA is usually unsuccessful (see, for example, Section 8.5). Briefly, this is because, while making the indirect AA, we are not able to predict some hidden biologic functions which, nevertheless, are essential for survival of biological organisms, yet they look unimportant for the HE-process.
The best example of this paradox is, perhaps, the role of **pigment** during 500 million years long evolution of animal eyes, from the "first" one (Fig. 1), to the "last" one (Fig. 20). We see that this role is so important (not only for protecting the interior of animal body against deadly UV photons, but also for restoring eye vision after eye's bleaching) that the pigment

entirely occupies one (internal) side of the retina; thus, leaving only the second (external) side available for other vision functions; thus, creating **blocking view** problem, which lingers on through the entire eye evolution.

The other important conclusion is light habitat's or CONOPS' influence on eye evolution, namely, *bifurcation* of *imaging eye* concept into **compound** (*superposition*) one and **elementary** (vertebrates) one, the first one dictated by the requirement of panoramic view (such as in lobster eye; see Section 3), while the second one dictated by the high resolution requirement.

Finally, in the context of moving objects' vision (related to video imagery), we should observe almost complete disparity between NE and HE, namely the NE-based *hard-wired* solution vs. HE-based *software-defined* solution, as discussed in Section 8.4.

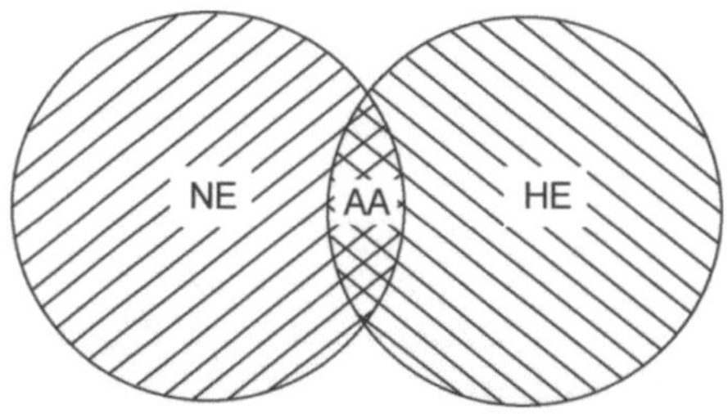

Fig. 23. Illustration of relationship between Natural Engineering (NE), Human Engineering (HE) and Artificial Abstraction (AA), the later one as sets cross-section

We believe this essay has shown the principal role of CONOPS (or, *light habitat*, using biologic language) in the animal eye designs, which, we hope will transfer to more efficient video designs in the future.

10. Acknowledgments

We gratefully acknowledge Joanna Jannson, Thomas Forrester and Kevin Degrood for their constant help during work on this paper. We would also like to thank Aparecida Mino, Sharon Peet and Robert Kim for their help in manuscript and figures' preparation.

11. References

Alteheld, N.; Roessler, G. & Walter, P. (2007). Towards the bionic eye - the retina implant: surgical, opthalmological, and histopathological perspectives, *Acta Neurochir. Suppl.*, Vol. 97 (Pt. 2), pp. 487-493.

Baker, S. & Nayar, S.K. (1999). A Theory of Single-Viewpoint Catadioptric Image Formation, *Int. J. Comp. Vision*, Vol. 35, No. 2, pp. 175-196.

Born, M. & Wolf, E. (1999). *Principles of Optics*, Cambridge University Press, ISBN: 0-5216-4222-1, Cambridge, UK.

Brainard, G.C.; Manifin, J.P.; Greeson, J.B.; Byrue, B.; Glickman, G.; Gerner, E. & Rollay, A.J. (2001). Action Spectrum for Melatonin Regulation in Humans: Evidence for a Novel Circadian Photoreceptor, *J. of Neuroscience*, Vol. 21, No. 16, August 2001, pp. 6405-6412.

Bryceson, K.P. & McIntyre, P. (1983). Image Quality and Acceptance Angle in a Reflecting Superposition Eye, *J. Comparative Physiology*, Vol. 151, No. 3, pp. 367-380.

Caulfield, J.; Fu, J. & Yoo, S.M. (2004). Artificial Color Image Logic, *Information Science*, Vol. 167, December 2004, pp. 1-7, ISSN: 0020-0255.

Cheng, J. (2008). Retinal Prosthesis: An Innovative Technology for Treating Blindness. *North American J. of Medicine and Science*, Vol. 1, No. 1, pp. 20-21.

Denton, E.J. & Nicol, J.A. (1965). Reflection of Light by External Surfaces of the Herring, *J. of the Marine Biological Association of the U.K.*, Vol. 45, pp. 711-738.

Dwight, H.B. (1961). *Tables of Integrals and Other Mathematical Data*, The MacMillan Co., Library of Congress Cat. #61-6419, New York.

Fu, J.; Caulfield, J. & Bond, J.J. (2005) Artificial and Biological Color Band Design as Spectral Compression, *Image and Vision Computing*, Vol. 23, No. 8, pp. 761-766, ISSN: 0262-8856.

Fu, J.; Caulfield, J. & Pulusani, S.R. (2004). Artificial Color Vision: a Preliminary Study, *J. Electronic-Imaging*, Vol. 3, No. 3, July 2004, pp. 553-558.

Gertsenshteyn, M.; Grubsky, V., Savant, G., & Jannson, T. (2007). Non-Scanning X-Ray Backscattering Inspection System Based on X-Ray Focusing, *Proceedings of SPIE*, ISSN: 0277-786X/09, April 2007, Bellingham, WA.

Gertsenshteyn, M.; Jannson, T., & Savant, G. (2005). Staring/Focusing Lobster-Eye Hard X-Ray Imaging for Non-Astronomical Objects, *Proceedings of SPIE*, ISSN: 0277-786X/05, Bellingham, WA.

Goodman, J.W. (1968). *Introduction to Fourier Optics*, McGraw-Hill, ISBN: 0-0702-3776-X, New York.

Grubsky, V.; Gertsenshteyn, M., & Jannson, T. (2006). Lobster-eye Infrared Focusing Optics, *Proceedings of SPIE*, ISSN: 0277-786X/06, Bellingham, WA.

Hubel, D.H. (1988). *Eye, Brain, and Vision*, Scientific American Library, ISBN 0-7167-6009-6 (pbk), New York.

Hyvarinen, T.S.; Herrala, E. & dall'Ava, A. (1998). Direct Sight Imaging Spectrograph: Unique Add-On Component Brings Spectral Imaging to Industrial Applications, *Proceedings of SPIE*, pp. 165-175, ISSN: 0277-786X, April 1998, Bellingham, WA.

Jagger, W. (1992). The Optics of Spherical Fish-Lens, *Vision Res.*, Vol. 32, No. 7, (July 1992) pp. 1271-1284.

Jannson, T. & Sochacki, J. (1980a). Primary Aberrations of Thin Phase Surface Lenses, *J. Opt. Soc. Am.*, Vol. 70, No. 9, pp. 1079-1085, ISSN: 0740-3232.

Jannson, T. (1980b). Shannon Number of an Image and Structural Information Capacity in Volume Holography, *Optica Acta*, Vol. 27, No. 9, pp. 1335-1344, ISSN: 0030-3909/80/2709.

Jannson, T.; Stoll, H.M. & Karaguleff, C. (1986). The Interconnectability of Neuro-Optic Process, *Proceedings of SPIE*, Vol. 698, pp. 157-169, ISSN: 0277-786X.

Jannson, T.; Tengara, I.; Qiao, Y. & Savant, G. (1991). Lippman-Bragg Broadband Holographic Mirrors, *JOSA A*, p. 371, in: "Fundamental Techniques in Holography," H.I. Bjelkhagen and H.J. Caulfield, (Eds.), *SPIE Milestone Series*, SPIE Press, ISBN 0-8194-4334-4, Bellingham, WA.

Jannson, T.P.; Kostrzewski, A.A., & Ternovskiy, I.V. (2001). Super-Fast Supercomputer Class On-Board Processing for Visual Sensor NMD Applications, *Proceedings of SPIE*, pp. 513-518, 2001, ISSN: 0277-786X/01, Bellingham, WA.

Jannson, T. & Kostrzewski, A. (2006a). Real-Time Pre-ATR Video Data Reduction in Wireless Networks, *Proceedings of SPIE,* pp. 6234 OM-1to 6234 OM-9, ISSN: 0277-786X/06, May 2006, Bellingham, WA.

Jannson, T. & Gertsenshteyn, M. (2006b). Hard X-ray Focusing Optics for Concealed Object Detection, *Proceedings of SPIE,* Vol. 6213, pp. 621302-1 to 621302-12, ISSN: 0277-786X/06, April, 2006, Bellingham, WA,

Jannson, T.; Arik, E.; Bennahmias, M.; Nathan, N.; Wang, S.; Lee, K.; Yu, K. & Poliakov, E. (2006c). Performance Metrics for Integrated Lighting Systems, *Proceedings of SPIE,* 6225B-53, pp. 6225E-1 to 6225E-19, April 2006, Bellingham, WA.

Jannson, T.; Kostrzewski, A. & Paki-Amouzou, P. (2007b). ATR for 3D Medical Imaging, *Proceedings of SPIE,* Vol. 6696-13, pp. 669606-1-11, ISSN: 0277-786X/07.

Jannson, T.; Gertsenshteyn, M.; Grubsky, V.; & Amouzou, P. (2007a). Through-the-Wall Sensor System Based on Hard X-Ray Imaging Optics, *Proceedings of SPIE,* Vol. 6538, pp. 65380A-1 to 65380A-9, ISSN: 0277-786X/07, Bellingham, WA.

Jannson, T.; Kostrzewski, A.; Gertsenshteyn, M.; Grubsky, V.; Shnitser, P.; Agurok, I.; Bennahmias, M.; Lee, K. & Savant, G. (2007c). Animal Eyes in Homeland Security Systems, *Proceedings of SPIE,* Vol. 6538-66, pp. 6538 1R-1 to -10, ISSN: 0277-786X/07.

Jannson, T.; Forrester, T., & Degrood, K. (2009). Wireless Synapses in Bio-Inspired Neural Networks, *Proceedings of SPIE,* Vol. 7347, pp. 73470T-1 to 73470T-13, ISSN: 0277-786X/09, Bellingham, WA.

Joos, G. (1986). *Theoretical Physics,* Dover Publications, ISBN: 0-4866-5227-0, Mineola, NY.

Kogelnik, H. (2001). Coupled Wave Theory for Thick Hologram Gratings, *BSTJ,* p. 44, in: *Fundamental Techniques in Holography,* H.J. Bjelkhagen and H.J. Caulfield, (Eds.), *SPIE Milestone Series,* SPIE Press, ISBN 0-8194-4334-4, Bellingham, WA.

Kompaniets, I. (2010). Private Communication, Physical Optics Corporation, Torrance, CA, October 2010.

Kostrzewski, A.A.; Jannson, T.J., & Kupiec, S.A. (2001). Soft Computing and Wireless Communication, (invited paper), *Proceedings of SPIE,* Vol. 4479, pp. 70-74, ISSN: 0277-786X/01, Bellingham, WA.

Kröger, R.H.; Campbell, M.; Fernald, R. & Wagner, H. (1999). Multifocal Lenses Compensate for Diomatic Defocus in Vertebrate Eyes, *J. Comparative Physiology A,* Vol. 184, pp. 361-369.

Land, M. F. & Nilsson, D. E.(2002). *Animal Eyes,* Oxford University Press, ISBN: 0-1985-0968-5, New York.

Luneburg, R. (1964). *Mathematical Theory of Optics,* University of California Berkeley Press, Library of Congress Card #64-19010, Berkeley, CA.

Lythgoe, J.N. & Shand, J. (1989). The Structural Basis for Videscent Colour Changes in Dermal and Corneal Iridophores in Fish, *J. of Experimental Biology,* Vol. 141, pp. 313-325.

MacKay, D.M., *Phil Mag.,* Vol. 41, p. 289, 1950.

Margenau, M. & Murphy, G.M. (1976). *The Mathematics of Physics and Chemistry,* Robert K. Krieger Publ. Co., ISBN 0-8827-5423-8, Huntington, New York.

Marshall J. & Oberwinkler, J. (1999). The Colorful World of the Mantis Shrimp, Brief Commentary, *Nature,* Vol. 401, p. 873, October 1999, ISSN 0028-0836.

Maxwell, J.C. (1854). *Cambridge and Dublin Math.,* J., Vol. 8, p. 188.

Nicol, J.A. (1989). *The Eyes of Fishes,* Clarendon Press, ISBN: 0-1985-7195-X, Oxford, U.K.

Raymond, L. (1985). Spatial Visual Acuity of the Eagle Aquila Audax: A Behavioral Optical and Anatomical Investigation, *Vision Research,* Vol. 25, No. 10, February 1985, pp. 1477-1491.

Schever, C. & Kolb, G. (1987). Behavioral Experiments on the Visual Stimuli in *Pieris Brassicae L.* (Lepidoptera)," *J. Comparative Physiology A,* Vol. 160, No. 5, pp. 645-656.

Schmitz, M. & Blackmann, M. (1998) The Photomechanic Infrared Receptor for the Detection of Forest Fires in the Beetle *Melanophila Acuminata* (Coleoptera: Buprestidue), *Journal Comparative Physiology A,* Vol. 182, pp. 647-657.

Ternovskiy, I.; Jannson, T. & Caulfield, J. (2002). Is Catastrophic Theory Analysis the Basis for Visual Perception? in: *Three-Dimensional Holographic Imaging,* C.J. Kuo and M.H. Tsai, (Eds.), Wiley, ISBN: 0-471-35894-0, New York.

Vogt, K. (1980). The Optical System of the Crayfish Eye, *J. Comparative Physiology,* Vol. 135, pp. 1-9.

X-ray Data Booklet, Lawrence Berkeley National Lab., 2001, Berkeley, California, USA.

23

Hot Topics in Video Fire Surveillance

Verstockt Steven[1,2], Van Hoecke Sofie[2], Tilley Nele[3], Merci Bart[3], Sette Bart[4], Lambert Peter[1], Hollemeersch Charles-Frederik[1] and Van De Walle Rik[1]
[1]*ELIS Department, Multimedia Lab, Ghent University – IBBT,*
[2]*ELIT Lab, University College West Flanders, Ghent University Association,*
[3]*Department of Flow, Heat and Combustion Mechanics, Ghent University,*
[4]*Warringtonfiregent (WFRGent NV),*
Belgium

1. Introduction

Fire is one of the most powerful forces of nature. Nowadays it is the leading hazard affecting everyday life around the world. The sooner the fire is detected, the better the chances are for survival. Today's fire alarm systems, such as smoke and heat sensors, however still pose many problems. They are generally limited to indoors; require a close proximity to the fire; and most of them cannot provide additional information about fire circumstances. In order to provide faster, more complete and more reliable information, video fire detection (VFD) is becoming more and more interesting.

Current research (Verstockt et al., 2009) shows that video-based fire detection promises fast detection and can be a viable alternative for the more traditional techniques. Especially in large and open spaces, such as shopping malls, parking lots, and airports, video fire detection can make the difference. The reason for this expected success is that the majority of detection systems that are used in these places today suffer with a lot of problems which VFD do not have, e.g., a transport- and threshold delay. As soon as smoke or flames occur in one of the camera views, fire can be detected. However, due to the variability of shape, motion, transparency, colors, and patterns of smoke and flames, existing approaches are still vulnerable to false alarms. On the other hand, video-based fire alarm systems mostly only detect the presence of fire. To understand the fire, however, detection is not enough. Effective response to fire requires accurate and timely information of its evolution. As an answer to both problems a multi-sensor fire detector and a multi-view fire analysis framework (Verstockt et al., 2010a) are proposed in this chapter, which can be seen as the first steps towards more valuable and accurate video fire detection.

Although different sensors can be used for multi-sensor fire detection, we believe that the added value of IR cameras in the long wave IR range (LWIR) will be the highest. Various facts support this idea. First of all, existing VFD algorithms have inherent limitations, such as the need for sufficient and specific lighting conditions. Thermal IR imaging sensors image emitted light, not reflected light, and do not have this limitation. Also, the further one goes in the IR spectrum the more the visual perceptibility decreases and the thermal perceptibility increases. As such, hot objects like flames will be best visible and less disturbed by other objects in the LWIR spectral range. By combining the thermal and visual characteristics of moving objects in registered LWIR, as well as visual images, more robust fire detection can be achieved. Since visual misdetections can be corrected by LWIR detections and vice versa, fewer false alarms will occur.

Due to the transparency of smoke in LWIR images, its absence can be used to distinguish between smoke and smoke-like moving objects. Since ordinary moving objects produce similar silhouettes in background-subtracted visual and thermal IR images, the coverage between these images is quasi constant. Smoke, contrarily, will only be detected in the visual images, and as such the coverage will start to decrease. Due to the dynamic character of the smoke, the visual silhouette will also show a high degree of disorder. By focusing on both coverage behaviors, smoke can be detected. On the basis of all these facts, the use of LWIR in combination with ordinary VFD is considered to be a win-win, as is confirmed by our experiments, in which the fused detectors perform better than either sensor alone.

In order to actually understand and interpret the fire, however, detection is not enough. It is also important to have a clear understanding of the fire development and the location. This information is essential for safety analysis and fire fighting/mitigation, and plays an important role in assessing the risk of escalation. Nevertheless, the majority of the detectors that are currently in use only detect the presence of fire, and are not able to model fire evolution. In order to accomplish more valuable fire analysis, the proposed video fire analysis framework fuses VFD results of multiple cameras by homographic projection onto multiple horizontal and vertical planes, which slice the scene. The crossings of these slices create a 3D grid of virtual sensor points. Using this grid, information about the location of the fire, its size and its propagation can be instantly extracted.

The remainder of this chapter is organized as follows: Section 2 presents the state-of-the-art detection methods in the visible and infrared spectral range, with a particular focus on the underlying features which can be of use in multi-sensor flame and smoke detection. Based on the analysis of the existing approaches, Section 3 proposes the novel multi-sensor flame and smoke detector. The multi-sensor detectors combine the multi-modal information of low-cost visual and thermal infrared detection results. Experiments on fire and non-fire multi-sensor sequences indicate that the combined detector yields more accurate results, with fewer false alarms, than either detector alone. Subsequently, Section 4 discusses the multi-view fire analysis framework (Verstockt et al., 2010a), which main goal is to overcome the lack in a video-based fire analysis tool to detect valuable fire characteristics at the early stage of the fire. Next, Section 5 gives suggestions on how the resulting fire progress information of the analysis framework can be used for video-driven fire spread forecasting. Finally, Section 6 lists the conclusions.

2. State-of-the-art in video fire detection (VFD)

2.1 VFD in visible light

The number of papers about fire detection in the computer vision literature is rather limited. As is, this relatively new subject in vision research has still a long way to go. Nevertheless, the results from existing work already seem very promising. The majority of the fire detection algorithms detects flames or smoke by analyzing one or more fire features in visible light. In the following, we will discuss the most widely used of these features.

Color was one of the first features used in VFD and is still by far the most popular (Celik & Demirel, 2008). The majority of the color-based approaches in VFD makes use of RGB color space, sometimes in combination with the saturation of HSI (Hue-Saturation-Intensity) color space (Chen et al., 2004; Qi & Ebert, 2009). The main reason for using RGB is the equality in RGB values of smoke pixels and the easily distinguishable red-yellow range of flames. Although the test results in the referenced work seems promising at first, the variability in color, density, lighting, and background do raise questions about the applicability of RGB in real world detection systems. In (Verstockt et al., 2009) the authors discuss the detection of chrominance decrease as a superior method.

Other frequently used fire features are flickering (Qi & Ebert, 2009; Marbach et al., 2006) and energy variation (Calderara et al., 2008; Toreyin et al., 2006). Both focus on the temporal behavior of flames and smoke. Flickering refers to the temporal behaviour with which pixels appear and disappear at the edges of turbulent flames. Energy variation refers to the temporal disorder of pixels in the high-pass components of the discrete wavelet transformed images of the camera. Fire also has the unique characteristic that it does not remain a steady color, i.e., the flames are composed of several varying colors within a small area. Spatial difference analysis (Qi & Ebert, 2009; Toreyin et al., 2005) focuses on this feature and analyses the spatial color variations in pixel values to eliminate ordinary fire-colored objects with a solid flame color.

Also an interesting feature for fire detection is the disorder of smoke and flame regions over time. Some examples of frequently used metrics to measure this disorder are randomness of area size (Borges et al., 2008), boundary roughness (Toreyin et al., 2006), and turbulence variance (Xiong et al, 2007). Although not directly related to fire characteristics, motion is also used in most VFD systems as a feature to simplify and improve the detection process, i.e., to eliminate the disturbance of stationary non-fire objects. In order to detect possible motion, possibly caused by the fire, the moving part in the current video frame is detected by means of motion segmentation (Calderara et al., 2008; Toreyin et al., 2006).

Based on the analysis of our own experiments (Verstockt et al., 2010b) and the discussed state-of-the-art, a low-cost flame detector is presented in (Fig. 1). The detector starts with a dynamic background subtraction, which extracts moving objects by subtracting the video frames with everything in the scene that remains constant over time, i.e. the estimated background. To avoid unnecessary computational work and to decrease the number of false alarms caused by noisy objects, a morphological opening, which filters out the noise, is performed after the dynamic background subtraction. Each of the remaining foreground (FG) objects in the video images is then further analyzed using a set of visual flame features. In case of a fire object, the selected features, i.e. spatial flame color disorder, principal orientation disorder and bounding box disorder, vary considerably over time. Due to this high degree of disorder, extrema analysis is chosen as a technique to easily distinguish between flames and other objects. For more detailed information the reader is referred to (Verstockt et al., 2010b).

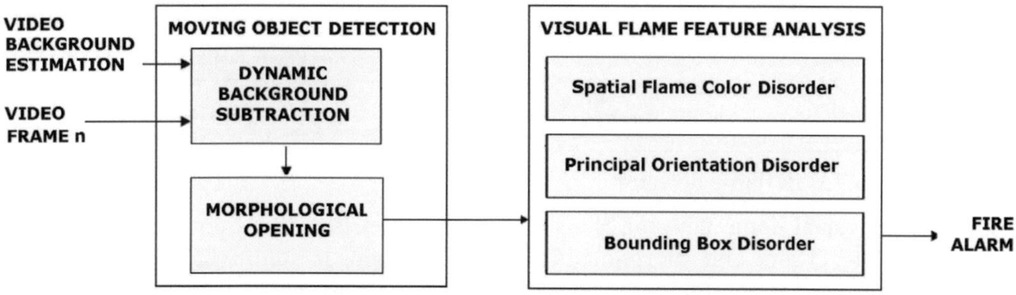

Fig. 1. Low-cost visual flame detector.

2.2 VFD in invisible light

Due to the fact that IR imaging is heading in the direction of higher resolution, increased sensitivity and higher speed, it is already used successfully as an alternative for ordinary video in many video surveillance applications, e.g., traffic safety, pedestrian detection, airport security, detection of elevated body temperature, and material inspection. As manufacturers ensure steady price-reduction, it is even expected that this number of IR imaging applications will increase significantly in the near future (Arrue et al., 2008).

Although the trend towards IR-based video analysis is noticeable, the number of papers about IR-based fire detection in the computer vision literature is still limited. As is, this relatively new subject in vision research has still a long way to go. Nevertheless, the results from existing work already seem very promising and ensure the feasibility of IR video in fire detection. (Owrutsky et al., 2005) work in the near infrared (NIR) spectral range and compare the global luminosity L, which is the sum of the pixel intensities of the current frame, to a reference luminosity L_b and a threshold L_{th}. If the number of consecutive frames where $L > L_b + L_{th}$ exceeds a persistence criterion, the system goes into alarm. Although this fairly simple algorithm seems to produce good results in the reported experiments its limited constraints do raise questions about its applicability in large and open uncontrolled public places with varying backgrounds and a lot of ordinary moving objects. (Toreyin et al., 2007) detect flames in infrared by searching for bright-looking moving objects with rapid time-varying contours. A wavelet domain analysis of the 1D-curve representation of the contours is used to detect the high frequency nature of the boundary of a fire region. In addition, the temporal behavior of the region is analyzed using a Hidden Markov Model. The combination of both temporal and spatial clues seems more appropriate than the luminosity approach and, according to Toreyin et al., greatly reduces false alarms caused by ordinary bright moving objects.

A similar combination of temporal and spatial features is also used by (Bosch et al., 2009). Hotspots, i.e., candidate flame regions, are detected by automatic histogram-based image thresholding. By analyzing the intensity, signature, and orientation of these resulting hot objects' regions, discrimination between flames and other objects is made. The IR-based fire detector (Fig. 2), proposed by the authors in (Verstockt et al., 2010c), mainly follows the latter feature-based strategy, but contrary to Bosch's work a dynamic background subtraction method is used which is more suitable to cope with the time-varying characteristics of dynamic scenes. Also, by changing the set of features and combining their probabilities into a global classifier, a decrease in computational complexity and execution time is achieved with no negative effect on the detection results.

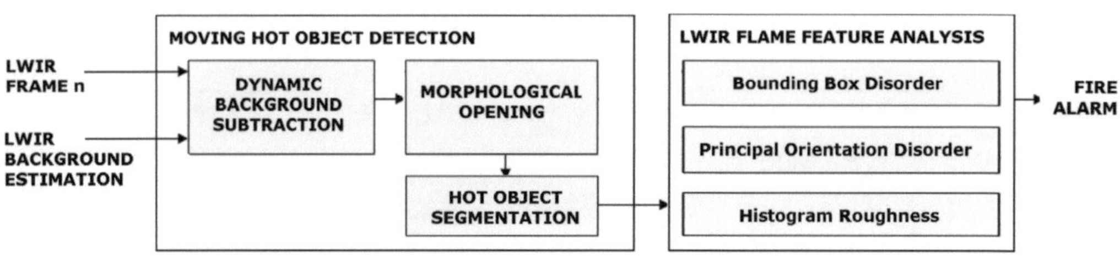

Fig. 2. Low-cost LWIR flame detector.

Similar to the visual flame detector, the LWIR detector starts with a dynamic background subtraction (Fig. 3 a-c) and morphological filtering. Then, it automatically extracts hot objects (Fig. 3 d) from the foreground thermal images by histogram-based segmentation, which is based on Otsu's method (Otsu, 1979).

Fig. 3. Therrnal filtering: moving hot object segmentation.

After this thermal filtering, only the relevant hot objects in the scene remain foreground. These objects are then further analyzed using a set of three LWIR fire features: bounding box disorder, principal orientation disorder, and histogram roughness. The set of features is based on the distinctive geometric, temporal and spatial disorder characteristics of bright flame regions, which are easily detectable in LWIR thermal images. By combining the probabilities of these fast retrievable local flame features we are able to detect the fire at an early stage. Experiments with different LWIR fire/non-fire sequences show already good results, as indicated in (Table 1) by the flame detection rate, i.e. the percentage of correctly detected fire frames, compared to the manually annotated ground truth (GT).

Video sequence	# frames	# fire frames (GT)	# detected fire frames	mean P(flames)	# false detections	Flame detection rate*
Attic (fire)	337	264	255	0,91	9	0,93
Attic (fire and moving people)	2123	1461	1296	0,86	34	0,86
Attic (moving people)	886	0	14	0,24	14	-
Lab (bunsen burner)	115	98	77	0,83	0	0,79
Corridor (moving person + hot object)	184	0	8	0,29	8	-

* Detection rate = (# detected fire frames - # false detections)/#fire frames

Table 1. Experimental results of LWIR-based video fire detection

3. Multi-sensor smoke and fire detection

Recently, the fusion of visible and infrared images is starting to be explored as a way to improve detection performance in video surveillance applications. The combination of both types of imagery yields information about the scene that is rich in color, motion and thermal detail, as can be seen by comparing the LWIR and visual objects in (Fig.4). Once the images are registered, i.e. aligned, such information can be used to successfully detect and analyze activity in the scene. To detect fire, one can also take advantage of this multi-sensor benefit. The proposed multi-sensor flame and smoke detection can be split up into two consecutive parts: the registration of the multi-modal images and the detection itself. In the following subsections each of these parts will be discussed more in detail.

3.1 Image registration

The image registration process (Fig. 5) detects the geometric parameters which are needed to overlay images of the same scene taken by different sensors. The registration starts with a moving object silhouette extraction (Chen & Varshney, 2002) to separate the calibration objects, i.e. the moving foreground, from the static background. Key components are the dynamic background (BG) subtraction, automatic thresholding and morphological filtering.

Then, 1D contour vectors are generated from the resulting IR/visual silhouettes using silhouette boundary extraction, cartesian to polar transform and radial vector analysis. Next, to retrieve the rotation angle (~ contour alignment) and the scale factor between the LWIR and visual image, the contours are mapped onto each other using circular cross correlation (Hamici, 2006) and contour scaling. Finally, the translation between the two images is calculated using maximization of binary correlation.

Fig. 4. Comparison of corresponding LWIR and visual objects.

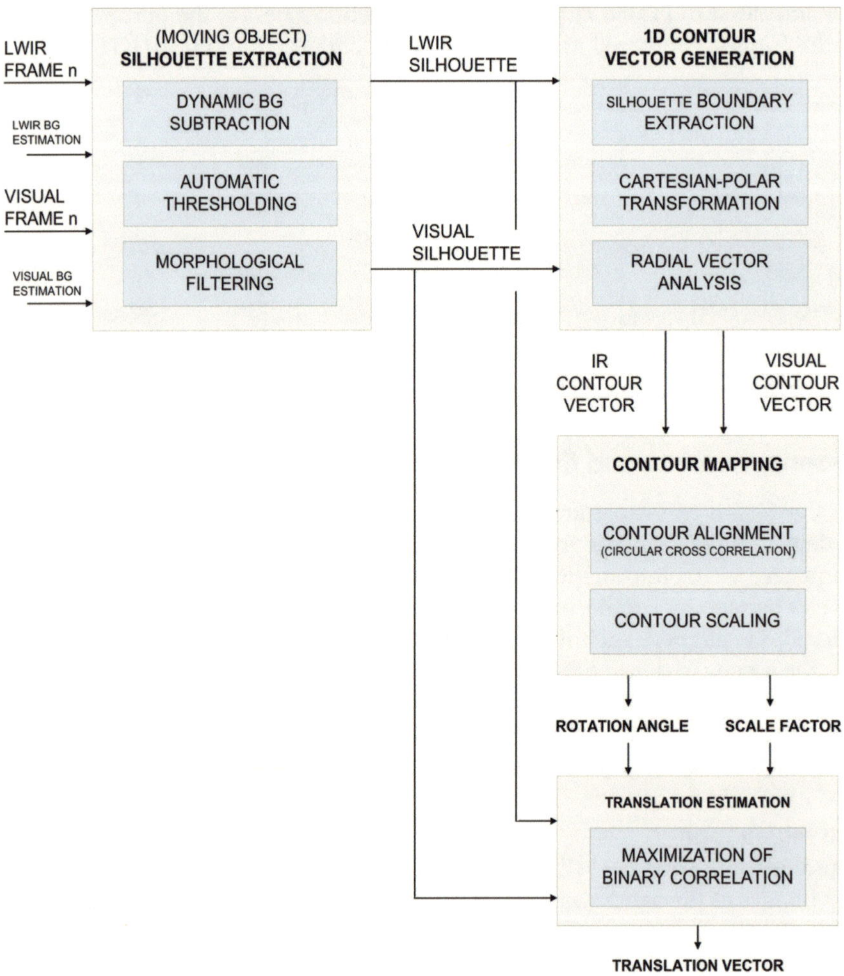

Fig. 5. LWIR-visual image registration.

3.2 Multi-sensor flame detection

The multi-sensor flame detection (Fig. 6) first searches for candidate flame objects in both LWIR and visual images by using moving object detection and flame feature analysis. These steps are already discussed in Section 2. Next, it uses the registration information, i.e. rotation angle, scale factor and translation vector, to map the LWIR and visual candidate flame objects on each other. Finally, the global classifier analyzes the probabilities of the mapped objects. In case objects are detected with a high combined multi-sensor probability, fire alarm is given.

As can be seen in (Table 2), the multi-sensor flame detector yields better results than the LWIR detector alone (~ Table 1). In particular for uncontrolled fires, a higher flame detection rate with fewer false alarms is achieved. Compared to the rather limited results of standalone visual flame detectors, the multi-sensor detection results are also more positive. As such, the combined detector is a win-win. As the experiments (Fig. 7) show, only objects which are detected as fire by both sensors do raise the fire alarm.

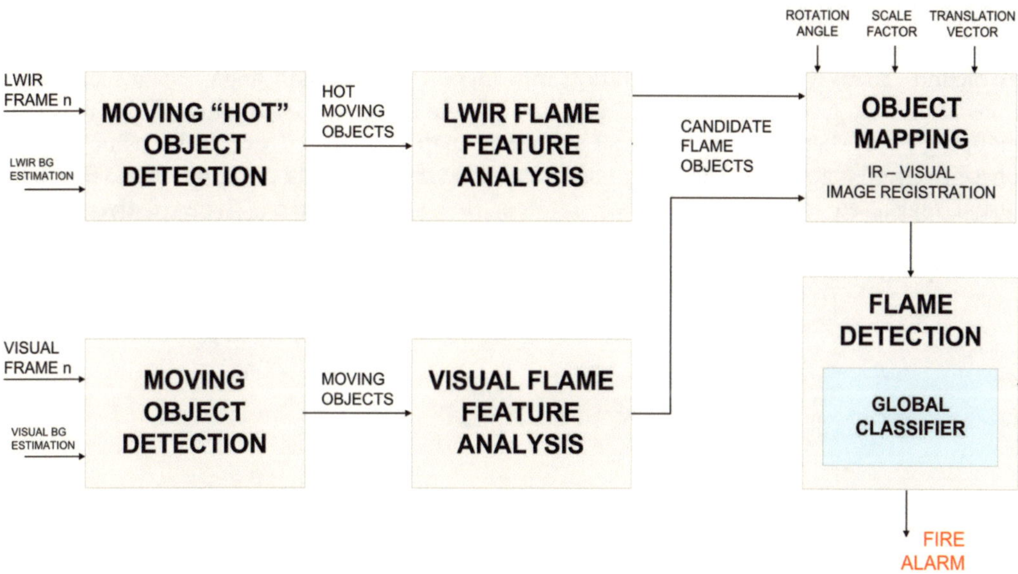

Fig. 6. Multi-sensor flame detection.

Video sequence	# frames	# fire frames	# detected fire frames	mean P(flames)	# false detections	Flame detection rate*
Attic (fire)	337	264	259	0.92	6	0.96
Attic (fire and moving people)	2123	1461	1352	0.84	19	0.91
Attic (moving people)	886	0	5	0.22	5	-
Lab (bunsen burner)	115	98	74	0.77	0	0.75
Corridor (moving person + hot object)	184	0	3	0.28	3	-

* Detection rate = (# detected fire frames - # false detections)/#fire frames

Table 2. Experimental results of multi-sensor video fire detection.

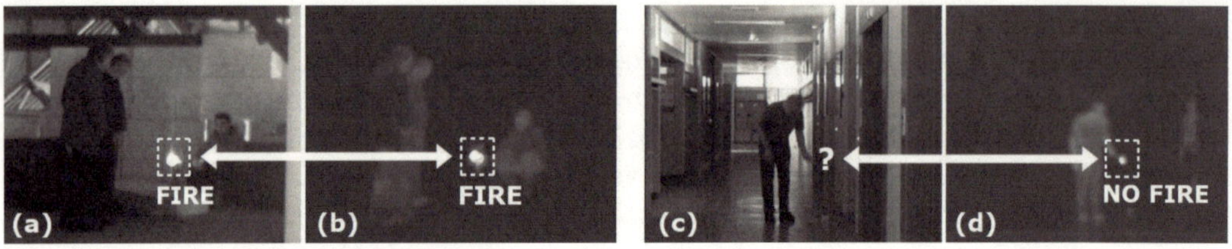

Fig. 7. LWIR fire detection experiments.

3.2 Multi-sensor smoke detection

The multi-sensor smoke detector makes use of the invisibility of smoke in LWIR. Smoke, contrarily to ordinary moving objects, is only detected in visual images. As such, the coverage of moving objects their LWIR and visual silhouettes starts to decrease in case of smoke. Due to the dynamic character of smoke, the visual smoke silhouette also shows a high degree of disorder. By focusing on both silhouette behaviors, the system is able to accurately detect the smoke.

The silhouette coverage analysis (Fig. 8) also starts with the moving object silhouette extraction. Then, it uses the registration information, i.e. rotation angle, scale factor and translation vector, to map the IR and visual silhouette images on each other. As soon as this mapping is finished, the LWIR-visual silhouette map is analyzed over time using a two-phase decision algorithm. The first phase focuses on the silhouette coverage of the thermal-visual registered images and gives a kind of first smoke warning when a decrease in

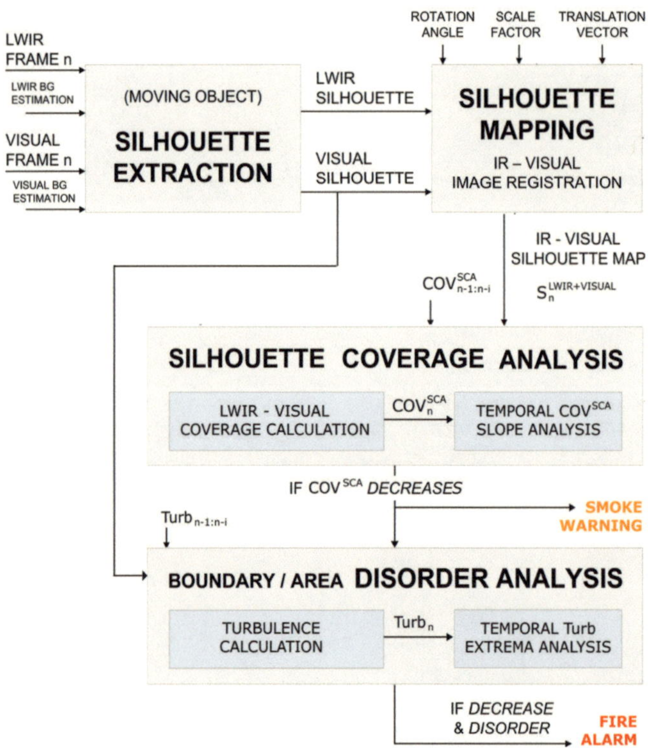

Fig. 8. Multi-sensor smoke detection.

silhouette coverage occurs. This decrease is detected using a sequence/scene independent technique based on slope analysis of the linear fit, i.e. trend line, over the most recent silhouette coverage values. If the slope of this trend line is negative and decreases continuously, smoke warning is given. In the second phase, which is only executed if a smoke warning is given, the visual silhouette is further investigated by temporal disorder analysis to distinguish true detections from false alarms, such as shadows. If this silhouette shows a high degree of turbulence disorder (Xiong et al., 2007), fire alarm is raised.

The silhouette maps in (Fig. 9) show that the proposed approach achieves good performance for image registration between color and thermal image sequences. The visual and IR silhouette of the person are coarsely mapped on each other. Due to the individual sensor limitations, such as shadows in visual images, thermal reflections and soft thermal boundaries in LWIR, small artifacts at the boundary of the merged silhouettes can be noticed. This is also the reason why the LWIR-visual silhouette coverage for ordinary moving objects is between 0.8 and 0.9, and not equal to 1.

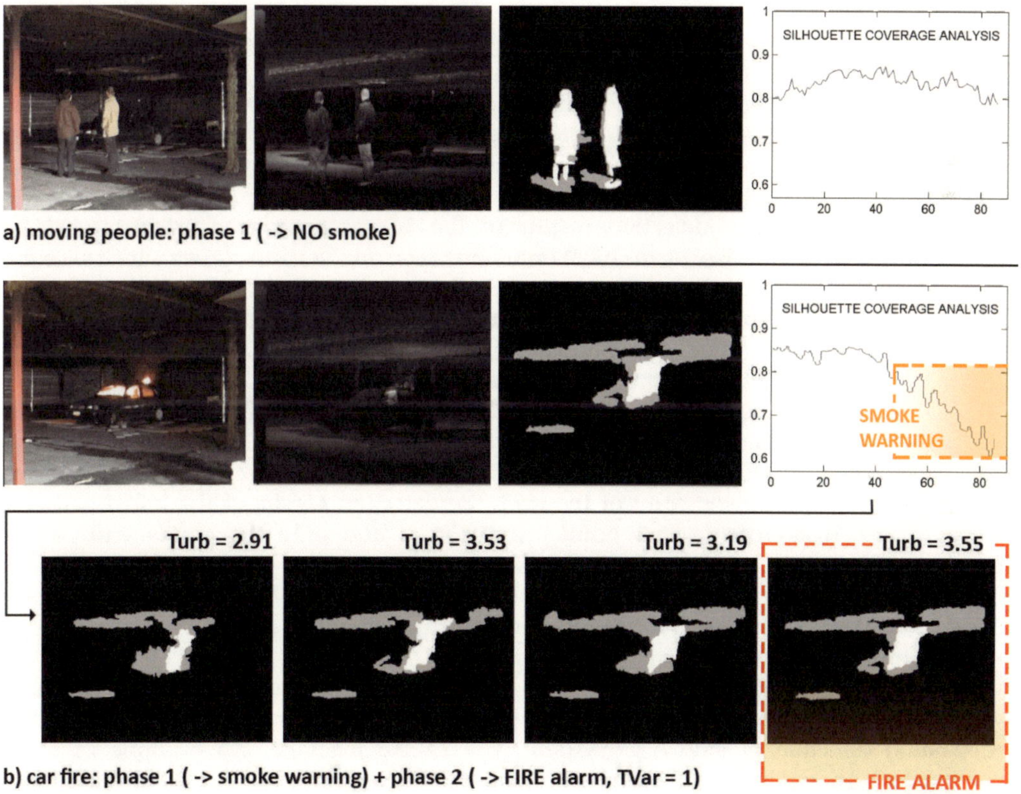

Fig. 9. Experimental results: silhouette coverage analysis.

As the results in (Fig. 9) show, the moving people sequence has a quasi constant silhouette coverage, and as such, no smoke warning is given and phase 2, i.e. the visual disorder analysis, is not performed. Contrarily, the silhouette coverage of the smoke sequence shows a high decrease after 45 frames, which activates the smoke warning. As a reaction to this warning, phase 2 of the detector is activated and analyzes the turbulence disorder of the visual silhouette objects. Since this disorder for the largest object is high, fire alarm is given.

Compared to the results of any individual visual or infrared detector, the proposed 2-phase multi-sensor detector is able to detect the smoke more accurate, i.e. with less misdetections and false alarms. Due to the low-cost of the silhouette coverage analysis and the visual turbulence disorder, which is only performed if smoke warning is given, the algorithm is also less computational expensive as many of the individual detectors.

4. Multi-view fire analysis

Only a few of the existing VFD systems (Yasmin, 2009; Akhloufi & Rossi, 2009) are capable of providing additional information on the fire circumstances, such as size and location. Despite the good performance reported in the papers, the results of these approaches are still limited and interpretation of the provided information is not straightforward. As such, one of the main goals of our work is to provide an easy-to-use and information-rich framework for video fire analysis, which is discussed briefly. For more details, readers are referred to (Verstockt et al., 2010a).

Using the localization framework shown in (Fig. 10), information about the fire location and (growing) size can be generated very accurately. First, the framework detects the fire, i.e. smoke and/or flames, in each single view. An appropriate single-view smoke or flame detector can be chosen out of the numerous approaches already proposed in Section 2. It is even possible to use the multi-sensor detectors. The only constraint is that the detector produces a binary image as output, in which white regions are fire/smoke FG regions and black regions are non-fire/non-smoke BG.

Secondly, the single-view detection results of the available cameras are projected by homography (Hartley & Zisserman, 2004) onto horizontal and vertical planes which slice the scene. For optimal performance it is assumed that the camera views overlap. Overlapping multi-camera views provide elements of redundancy, i.e., each point is seen by multiple cameras, that help to minimize ambiguities like occlusions, i.e. visual obstructions, and improve the accuracy in the determination of the position and size of the flames and smoke.

Next, the plane slicing algorithm accumulates, i.e. sums, the multi-view detection results in each of the horizontal and vertical planes. This step is a 3D extension of Arsic's work (Arsic et al., 2008). Then, a 3D grid of virtual multi-camera sensors is created at the crossings of these planes. At each sensor point of the grid, the detection results of the horizontal and vertical planes that cross in that point are analyzed and only the points with stable detections are further considered as candidate fire or smoke. Finally, 3D spatial and temporal filters clean up the grid and remove the remaining noise. The filtered grid can then be used to extract the smoke and fire location, information about the growing process and the direction of propagation.

In order to verify the proposed multi-view localization framework we performed smoke experiments in a car park. We tried to detect the location, the growing size and the propagation direction of smoke generated by a smoke machine. An example of these experiments is shown in (Fig. 11), where the upper (a-c) and the lower images (d-f) are three different camera views of the test sequences frame 4740 and 5040 respectively. Single-view fire detection results, i.e. the binary images which are the input for the homographic projection in our localization framework, were retrieved by using the chrominance-based smoke detection method proposed in (Verstockt et al., 2009). Since the framework is independent of the type of VFD, also other detectors can be used here. The only constraint is that the detector delivers a black and white binary image, as mentioned earlier. As such, it is even possible to integrate other types of sensors, such as IR-video based fire detectors or the proposed multi-sensor detectors.

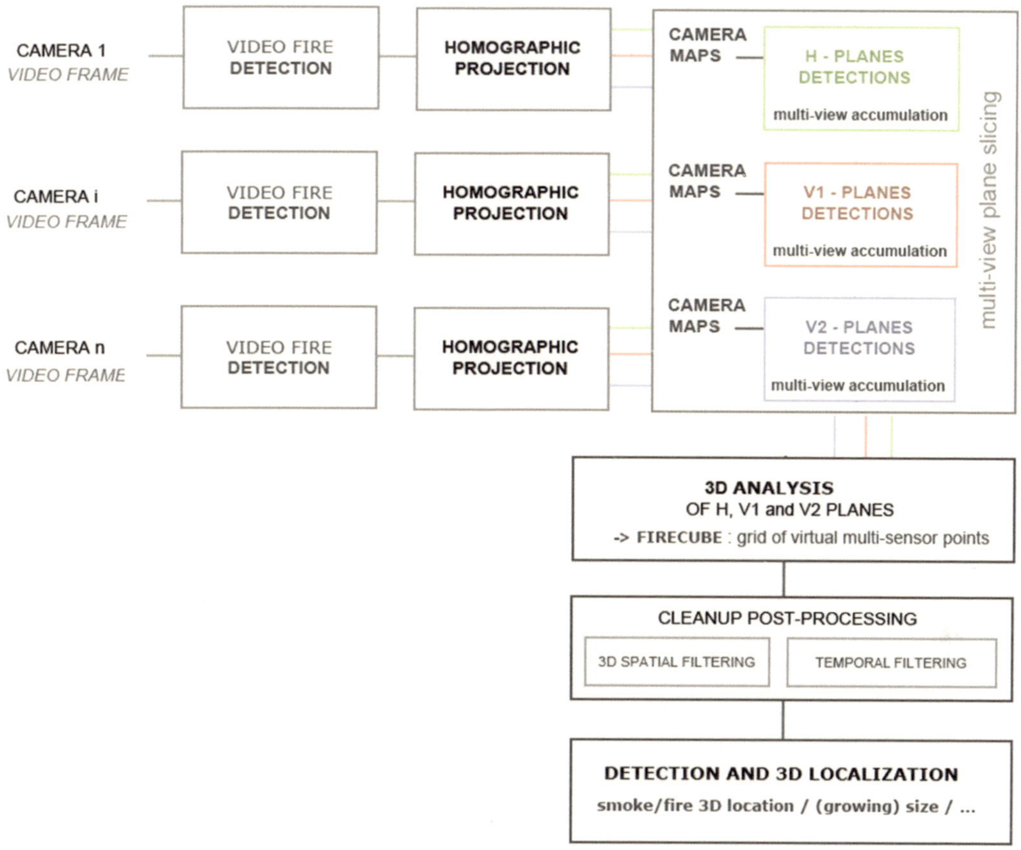

Fig. 10. Multi-view localization framework for 3D fire analysis.

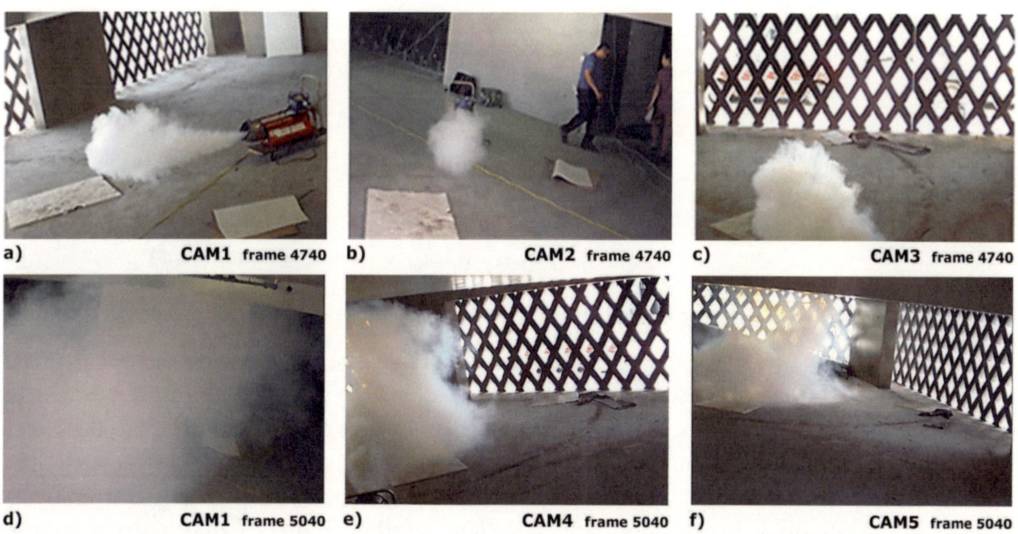

Fig. 11. Car park smoke experiments.

As can be seen in the 3D model in (Fig. 12) and in the back-projections of the 3D results in (Fig.13), the framework is able to detect the location and the dimension of the smoke regions. In (Fig. 12) the smoke regions are represented by the dark gray 3D boxes, which are bounded by the minimal and maximal horizontal and vertical FG slices. As a reference, also the bounding box of the smoking machine is visualized. Even if a camera view is partially or fully occluded by smoke, like for example in frame 5040 of CAM2 (Fig. 11 d), the framework localizes the smoke, as long as it is visible from the other views. Based on the detected 3D smoke boxes, the framework generates the spatial smoke characteristics, i.e., the height, width, length, centroid, and volume of the smoke region. By analyzing this information over time, the growing size and the propagation direction are also estimated. If LWIR-visual multi-sensor cameras, like the one proposed in this paper, are used, it is even possible to also analyze the temperature evolution of the detected regions. As such, for example, temperature-based levels of warnings can be given.

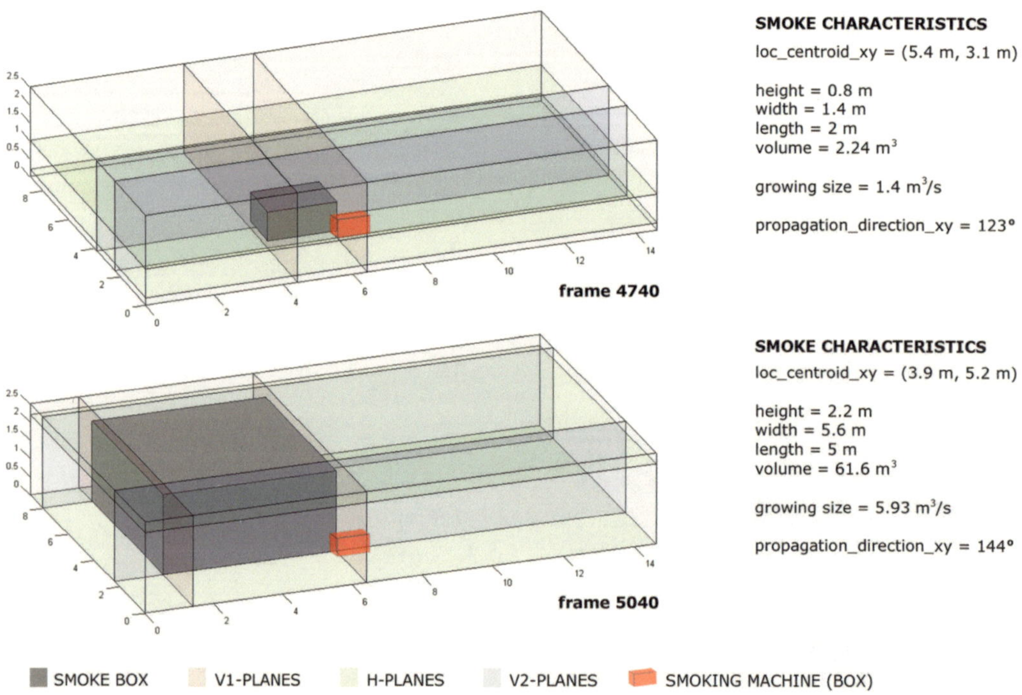

Fig. 12. Plane slicing-based smoke box localization.

The back-projections (Fig. 13) of the 3D smoke regions to the camera views show that the multi-view slicing approach produces acceptable results. Due to the fact that the number of (multi-view) video fire sequences is limited and the fact that no 3D ground truth data and widely "agree-upon" evaluation criteria of video-based fire tests are available yet, only this kind of visual validation is possible for the moment. Contrary to existing fire analysis approaches (Akhloufi & Rossi, 2009), which deliver a rather limited 3D reconstruction, the output contains valuable 3D information about the fire development.

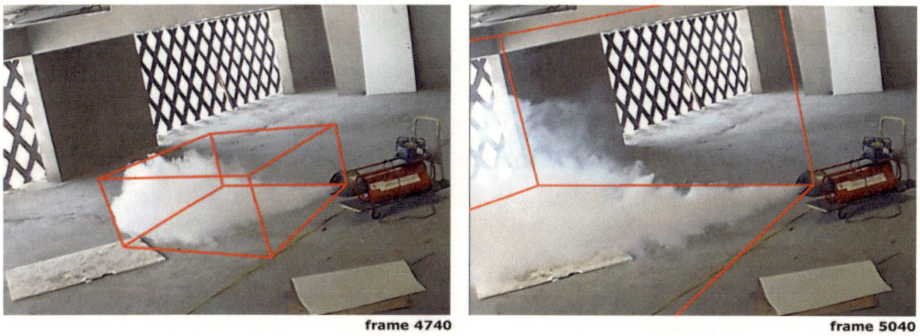

Fig. 13. Back-projection of 3D smoke box results into camera view CAM1.

5. Video-driven fire spread forecasting

Fire spread forecasting is about predicting the further evolution of a fire, in the event of the fire itself. In the world of fire research, not much experience exists on this topic (Rein et al., 2007). Based on their common use in fire modeling, CFD (Computational Fluid Dynamics; SFPE, 2002) calculations look interesting for fire forecasting at first sight. These are three-dimensional simulations where the rooms of interest are subdivided into a large amount of small cells (Fig. 14b). In each cell, the basic laws of fluid dynamics and thermodynamics (conservation of mass, total momentum and energy) are evaluated in time. These types of calculations result in quite accurate and detailed results, but they are costly, especially in calculation time. As such, CFD simulations do not seem to be the most suitable technique for fast fire forecasting. We believe, therefore, it is better to use zone models (SFPE, 2002). In a zone model, the environment is subdivided into two main zones. The smoke of the fire is in the hot zone. A cold air layer exists underneath this hot zone (Fig. 14a). The interface between these two zones is an essentially horizontal surface. The height of the interface (h_{int}) and the temperature of the hot (T_{hot}) and cold (T_{cold}) zones vary as function of time. These calculations are simple in nature. They rely on a set of experimentally derived equations for fire and smoke plumes. It usually takes between seconds and minutes to perform this kind of calculations, depending on the simulated time and the dimensions of the room or building. Therefore, it is much better suited for fire forecasting than CFD calculations.

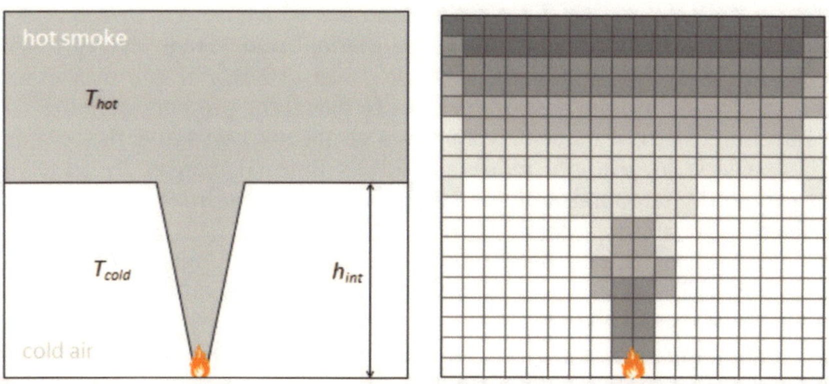

Fig. 14. Fire modeling techniques: a) zone model. b) Computational Fluid Dynamics (CFD).

The real aim of fire forecasting is to use measured data from the fire, e.g. obtained by sensors or video images in the room of interest, in order to replace or correct the model predictions (Welch et al, 2007; Jahn,2010). This process of data assimilation is illustrated in Fig. 15, which summarizes our future plans for video-driven fire forecasting. As can be seen in the graph, model predictions of smoke layer height (~ zone model interface h_{int}) are corrected at each correction point. This correction uses the measured smoke characteristics from our framework. The further we go in time, the closer the model matches the future measurements and the more accurate predictions of future smoke layer height become.
The proposed video-driven fire forecasting is a prime example of how video-based detectors will be able to do more than just generate alarms. Detectors can give information about the state of the environment, and using this information, zone model-based predictions of the future state can be improved and accelerated. By combining the information about the fire from models and real-time data we will be able to produce an estimate of the fire that is better than could be obtained from using the model or the data alone.

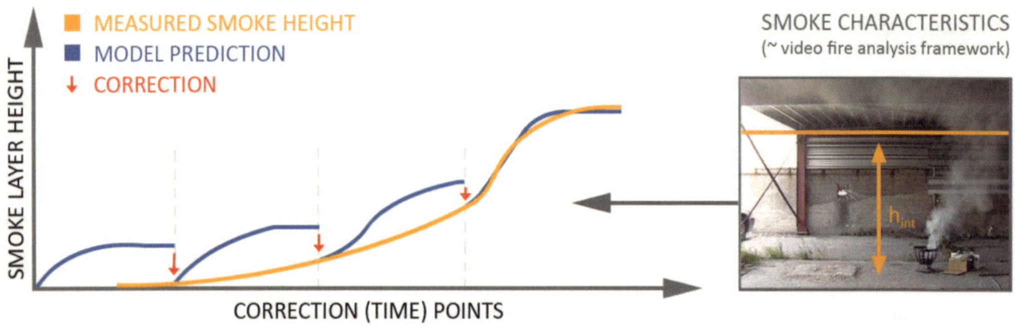

Fig. 14. Data assimilation: video-driven fire forecasting (~ Welch et al, 2007; Jahn, 2010).

6. Conclusions

To accomplish more valuable and more accurate video fire detection, this chapter has pointed out future directions and discussed first steps which are now being taken to improve the vision-based detection of smoke and flames.
Based on the analysis of existing approaches in visible and non-visible light and on our own experiments, a multi-sensor fire detector is presented which detects flames and smoke in LWIR and visual registered images. By using thermal and visual images to detect and recognize the fire, we can take advantage of the different kinds of information to improve the detection and to reduce the false alarm rate. To detect the presence of flames at an early stage, the novel multi-sensor flame detector fuses visual and non-visual flame features from moving (hot) objects in ordinary video and LWIR thermal images. By focusing on the distinctive geometric, temporal and spatial disorder characteristics of flame regions, the combined features are able to successfully detect flames.
The novel multi-sensor smoke detector, on the other hand, makes use of the smoke invisibility in LWIR. The smoke detector analyzes the silhouette coverage of moving objects in visual and LWIR registered images. In case of silhouette coverage reduction with a high degree of disorder, a fire alarm is given. Experiments on both fire and non-fire multi-sensor sequences indicate that the proposed algorithm can detect the presence of smoke and flames in most cases. Moreover, false alarms, one of the major problems of many other VFD techniques, are drastically reduced.

To provide more valuable information about the fire progress, we also present a multi-view fire analysis framework, which is mainly based on 3D extensions to homographic plane slicing. The framework merges single view VFD results of multiple cameras by homographic projection onto multiple horizontal and vertical planes which slice the scene under surveillance. At the crossings of these slices, we create a 3D grid of virtual sensor points. Using this grid, information about 3D location, size and propagation of the fire can be extracted from the video data. As prior experimental results show, this combined analysis from different viewpoints provides more valuable fire characteristics.

7. Acknowledgment

The research activities as described in this paper were funded by Ghent University, the Interdisciplinary Institute for Broadband Technology (IBBT), University College West Flanders, WarringtonFireGent, Xenics, the Institute for the Promotion of Innovation by Science and Technology in Flanders (IWT), the Fund for Scientific Research-Flanders (FWO-Flanders G.0060.09), the Belgian Federal Science Policy Office (BFSPO), and the EU.

8. References

Akhloufi, M., Rossi, L. (2009). Three-dimensional tracking for efficient fire fighting in complex situations, *SPIE Visual Information Processing* XVIII, http://dx.doi.org/10.1117/12.818270

Arrue, B. C., Ollero, A., de Dios, J. R. (2002). An Intelligent System for False Alarm Reduction in Infrared Forest-Fire Detection, *IEEE Intelligent Systems* 15:64-73, http://dx.doi.org/10.1109/5254.846287

Arsic, D., Hristov, E., Lehment, N., Hornler, B., Schuller, B., Rigoll, G. (2008). Applying multi layer homography for multi camera person tracking, *Proceedings of the 2nd ACM/IEEE International Conference on Distributed Smart Cameras*, pp 1-9.

Borges, P. V. K., Mayer, J., Izquierdo, E. (2008). Efficient visual fire detection applied for video retrieval, *European Signal Processing Conference (EUSIPCO)*.

Bosch, I., Gomez, S., Molina, R., Miralles, R. (2009). Object discrimination by infrared image processing, *Proceedings of the 3rd International Work-Conference on The Interplay Between Natural and Artificial Computation*, pp. 30-40.

Calderara, S., Piccinini, P., Cucchiara, R. (2008). Smoke detection in video surveillance: a MoG model in the wavelet domain, *International Conference on Computer Vision Systems*, pp. 119-128.

Celik, T., Demirel, H. (2008). Fire detection in video sequences using a generic color model, *Fire Safety Journal* 44(2): 147–158, http://dx.doi.org/10.1016/j.firesaf.2008.05.005

Chen, H.-M., Varshney, P.K. (2002). Automatic two-stage IR and MMW image registration algorithm for concealed weapons detection, *IEE Proc. of Vision Image Signal Processing* 148:209-216, http://dx.doi.org/10.1049/ip-vis:20010459

Chen, T.-H., Wu, P.-H., Chiou, Y.-C (2004). An early fire-detection method based on image processing, *International Conference on Image Processing*, pp. 1707-1710.

Hamici, Z. (2006). Real-Time Pattern Recognition using Circular Cross-Correlation: A Robot Vision System, International Journal of Robotics & Automation 21:174-183, http://dx.doi.org/10.2316/Journal.206.2006.3.206-2724

Hartley, R., Zisserman, A. (2004). *Multiple view geometry in computer vision*, 2nd edition, Cambridge University Press, Cambridge, pp. 87-131.

Jahn, W. (2010). *Inverse Modelling to Forecast Enclosure Fire Dynamics*, PhD, University of Edinburgh, Edinburgh, 2010, http://hdl.handle.net/1842/3418

Marbach, G., Loepfe, M., Brupbacher, T. (2006). An image processing technique for fire detection in video images, *Fire safety journal* 41:285-289, http://dx.doi.org/10.1016/j.firesaf.2006.02.001

Otsu, N. (1979). A threshold selection method from gray-level histograms, *IEEE Transactions on Systems, Man, and Cybernetics* 9: 62-66.

Owrutsky, J.C., Steinhurst, D.A., Minor, C.P., Rose-Pehrsson, S.L., Williams, F.W., Gottuk, D.T. (2005). Long Wavelength Video Detection of Fire in Ship Compartments, *Fire Safety Journal* 41:315-320, http://dx.doi.org/10.1016/j.firesaf.2005.11.011

Qi, X., Ebert, J. (2009) A computer vision based method for fire detection in color videos, *International Journal of Imaging* 2:22-34.

Rein, G., Empis, C.A., Carvel, R. (2007). *The Dalmarnock Fire Tests: Experiments and Modelling*, School of Engineering and Electronics, University of Edinburgh.

Society of Fire Protection Engineers, *The SFPE handbook of Fire Protection Engineering*, National Fire Protection Association, Quincy, 2002, p. 3/189-194.

Toreyin, B.U., Dedeoglu, Y., Güdükbay, U., Çetin, A.E. (2005). Computer vision based method for real-time fire and flame detection, *Pattern Recognition Letters* 27:49-58, http://dx.doi.org/10.1016/j.patrec.2005.06.015

Toreyin, B.U., Dedeoglu, Y., Çetin, A.E. (2006). Contour based smoke detection in video using wavelets, *European Signal Processing Conference (EUSIPCO)*, 2006.

Toreyin, B. U., Cinbis, R. G., Dedeoglu, Y., Cetin, A. E. (2007). Fire Detection in Infrared Video Using Wavelet Analysis, *SPIE Optical Engineering* 46:1-9, http://dx.doi.org/10.1117/1.2748752

Verstockt, S., Merci, B., Sette, B., Lambert, P., and Van de Walle, R. (2009). State of the art in vision-based fire and smoke detection, *AUBE'09 - Proceedings of the 14th International Conference on Automatic Fire Detection*, vol.2, pp. 285-292.

Verstockt, S., Van Hoecke, S., Tilley, N., Merci, B., Sette, B., Lambert, P., Hollemeersch, C., Van de Walle, R (2010). FireCube: a multi-view localization framework for 3D fire analysis, *(under review with) Fire Safety Journal*.

Verstockt, S., Vanoosthuyse, A., Van Hoecke, S., Lambert, P. & Van de Walle, R. (2010). Multi-sensor fire detection by fusing visual and non-visual flame features, *4th International Conference on Image and Signal Processing*, pp. 333-341, http://dx.doi.org/10.1007/978-3-642-13681-8_39

Verstockt, S., Dekeerschieter, R., Vanoosthuise, A., Merci, B., Sette, B., Lambert, P. & Van de Walle, R. (2010). Video fire detection using non-visible light, *6th International seminar on Fire and Explosion Hazards (FEH-6)*.

Welch, S., Usmani, A., Upadhyay, R., Berry, D., Potter, S., Torero, J.L., "Introduction to FireGrid," The Dalmarnock Fire Tests: Experiments and Modelling, School of Engineering and Electronics, University of Edinburgh, 2007.

Xiong, Z., Caballero, R., Wang, H., Finn, A.M., Lelic, M. A., Peng, P.-Y. (2007). Video-based smoke detection: possibilities, techniques, and challenges," *IFPA Fire Suppression and Detection Research and Applications – A Technical Working Conference (SUPDET)*.

Yasmin, R. (2009). Detection of smoke propagation direction using color video sequences, *International Journal of Soft Computing* 4:45-48, http://dx.doi.org/ijscomp.2009.45.48

24

Camera Placement for Surveillance Applications

Indu Sreedevi[1], Nikhil R Mittal[2], Santanu Chaudhury[3] and Asok Bhattacharyya[4]
[1,2]*Delhi Technological University, Delhi*
[3]*Indian Institute od Technology, Delhi*
[4]*Delhi Technological University, Delhi*
India

1. Introduction

Surveillance application is gaining research importance day by day. The application can be monitoring a production plant, an area for security reasons, industrial products etc. Visual sensor arrays form the backbone of any such surveillance applications. Proper placement of visual sensors (cameras) is an important issue as these systems, demand maximum coverage of sensitive areas with minimum cost and good quality of service. The quality of the images depend on the position and poses of the cameras. Depending on specific applications, the required view may vary, however, all vision based applications need a camera layout which assure acceptable quality of image. The main driving force of this work is to improve the off-line camera placement for surveillance applications. Camera placement depends on feasible location of cameras, obstacles present in sensitive areas, and the assigned priority of the area. Hence the placement problem becomes an optimization problem with inter related and competing constraints. Since, constrained discrete optimization problems do not have efficient algorithmic solution, evolutionary algorithm is used. A design tool for camera placement for surveillance apllication is presented in this chapter. This genetic algorithm based CAD tool is simple and efficient. Using this tool cameras can be placed for maximum coverage of the multiple sensitive areas defined by the user. The tool determines the position and poses of PTZ cameras for optimum coverage of user defined area. This tool can be used as camera placement planner for surveillance of large spaces with discrete priority areas like a hall with more than one entrance or many events happening at different locations in a hall etc. (Casino) or even a big sea port. As we are optimizing the parameters like pan, tilt, zoom and even the locations of the cameras, the images will provide maximum information with good resolution. Thus enhancing the QOS of the vision system.

Camera placement

The sensitive space is logically divided into cubical grids and probabilistic modelling of space is done for ensuring better coverage. The probability of occlusion by randomly moving objects is minimised by covering the priority areas by multiple sensors. The optimum camera locations with their respective poses are determined by mapping the camera model and space model into genetic algorithm. Many of the existing similar works S.Indu et al. (2008), Dunn & Olague (October 2006), Horster & Lienhart (2006) have kept zoom level constant, whereas we have developed a novel method for the same, with zoom level, as a constraint which will enhance the quality of the image. The proposed method do not require any synchronization and hence computationally light and can be easily used for large spaces using more number of cameras.

2. Related work

Visual sensor planning has been extensively researched by many researchers. In the initial stages the sensor planning is done based on occlusion pattern Maver & R.Bajcsy (1993). We can broadly classify the research in this field into 4 main categories. (1) No information about the surveillance field is known (2) the models of some set of information about the objects of the field are known. (3) Complete geometric information about the space is known (4) automatic placement of camera based on the information obtained from images and (5) Camera and light source placement for specific task. The work we carried out belongs to the third category. The Art Gallery Problem (AGP) was one among the initial research work similar to the current work, where minimum numbers of Guards are determined so that all points of the polygon can be observed for their static positions. The exact solution of the same is found to be NP-Hard, even though efficient algorithms exist giving a lower bound for AGPs with simple polygons Rourke (1987) Suzuki et al. (2001) Bose et al. (1997) Estivill-Castro et al. (1995). Current solutions to the AGP and its variants employ unrealistic assumptions about the cameras' capabilities like unlimited field of view, infinite depth of field, infinite servo precision and speed that make these algorithms unsuitable for most real world computer vision applications.

Camera calibration was extensively studied by many researchers such as (1) Christopher. R. Wren and et. al. for automatically retrieving contextual information from different camera images Wren et al. (n.d.), (2) Ioannis Rekleitis and et. al. for obtaining 3D pose of the cameras in a common reference frame using a mobile robot Rekleitis (n.d.), (3) E. Hoster and et. al. for automatic position calibration of visual sensors without synchronization Lienhart et al. (n.d.), (4) Marta Wilczkowiak and et. al. for 3D reconstruction Wilczkowiak & Sturn (2001), (5)Richard I Hartley did the self calibration of camera from different views taken from a point with different poses Hartley (1993). The camera calibration may be used along with camera placement for on line optimization of the camera poses which can be considered as an extension of our work.

some others developed vision systems based on image information. Mohan.M.Trivedi and et.al.Trivedi et al. (2005) developed a distributed interactive video array for both tracking people and identifying people, where as Huang Lee and et. al have addressed node and target localization Lee & Aghajan (n.d.). Ali Maleki Tabar and et. al. developed a smart home care sensor network using different types of sensor nodes for event detection Tabar et al. (n.d.). These three works are silent about camera placement. There are certain works in which the next optimal camera parameter was found out on the basis of the visual data history of the scene Rourke (1987) Bose et al. (1997) Suzuki et al. (2001) Krishnendu chakraborthy and et. al. Developed Grid based placement for Omni directional circular range sensors K.chakraborty et al. (2002). Sensor planning methods using more realistic model is given by Tarabanis K. et al. (1996). Siva Ram et.al in their work "selection and placement of sensors in multimedia surveillance systems" explained a real time control of PTZ cameras using cheap motion sensors Kankanhalli et al. (2006). They have addressed the placement of cameras using a performance index which is calculated on a trial and error basis. They have neither considered the quality of images and nor the optimization of pan angle and tilt angle of cameras.

Robot Bodor and et.al. in their work "multi camera human activity monitoring and Optimal camera placement for automated surveillance tasks" Fiore et al. (2008) Bodor et al. (2007) find out optimal locations of the camera after learning the activity. This method will be

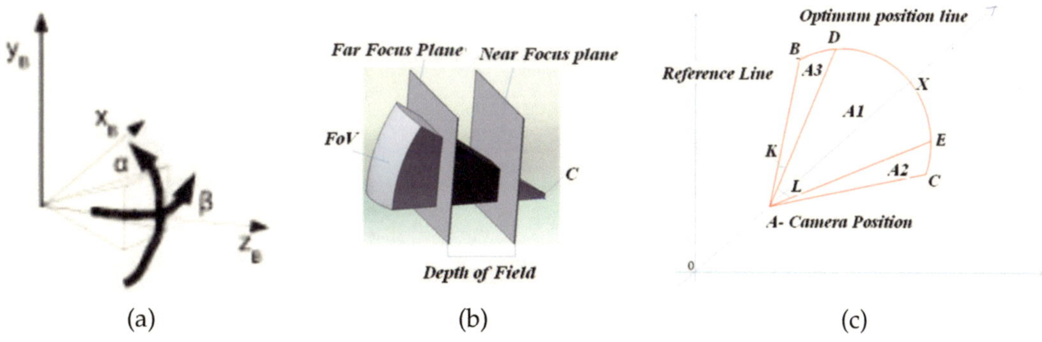

Fig. 1. (a) Camera Model (b) Depth Of Field (c) Extended FoV along optimum position axis

computationally intensive and will not be suitable for large space. The off line camera placement problem considering random occlusion was initially addressed by Xing chen Chen & Davis (1999) in their work "Camera placement considering occlusion for robust motion capture". Later on the same work was extended by Larry Davis and Anurag Mittal Mittal & Davis (2004). They used pinhole cameras. Anurag mittal A.Mittal & Davis (2008) have presented a camera placement algorithm using a probabilistic approach for 3D spaces considering occlusion due to randomly moving dynamic objects. They used a pin-hole camera in their design which again can be optimized by using PTZ cameras.

3. Camera placement problem

To determine optimal positions, poses and zoom levels of cameras which provide maximum coverage of the priority areas in a predefined surveillance space satisfying the task based constraints which may be static or dynamically varying according to the requirements.

Definitions

We first define terms that have been used in this paper. The crucial parameters for the cameras are:

- Field of View (FoV): the maximum volume visible from a camera. The FoV is determined by the apex angles (azimuth and latitude) of the visible pyramidal region emanating from the optical center of the camera. This pyramid is also known as the viewing frustum and can be skewed by oblique projection.
- Spatial Resolution: Spatial resolution of a camera is defined as the ratio between the total number of pixels on its imaging element excited by the projection of a real world object and the object's size. Higher spatial resolution captures more details and produces sharper images.
- Depth of Field (DoF): Depth of field is the amount of distance between the nearest and farthest objects that appear in acceptably sharp focus in an image.

The term floor plan denotes a physical three dimensional room which we aim to cover. A point is said to be covered if it is captured with a minimum required resolution. This constraint is satisfied if the point lies in the field of view of at least two cameras. We can divide the floor plan into different sections namely priority areas and non priority areas.

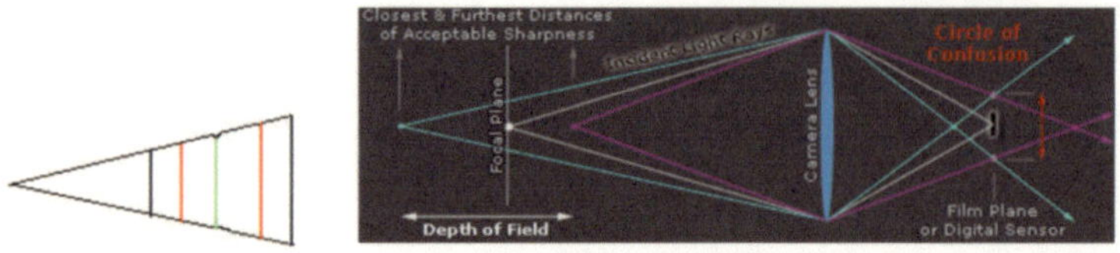

(a) (b)

Fig. 2. Showing the variation in zoom (a) Red vertical lines - higher zoom level, black vertical lines-lower zoom level and green vertical line- reference focal plane (b) Circle of confusion

Basic definitions and concepts related to Zoom

Zoom lenses are often described by the ratio of their longest to shortest focal lengths. For example a zoom lens with focal lengths from 100mm to 400mm may be described as a 4:1 or "4X" zoom. That is, the zoom level of a visual sensor is directly proportional to its focal length. There are two types of zoom, Digital zoom and optical zoom. The optical zoom is affected by camera parameters and hence this report will deal with optical zoom only. The perspective and depth of field will change with variation in zoom level. A change in perspective or angle of view means change in the dimensions of the viewing frustum of the visual sensor. As zoom level increases the focal length increases and thus the angle of view reduces. Field of View (FoV), the maximum volume visible from a camera, is determined by the apex angles (azimuth and latitude) of the visible pyramidal region (frustum) emanating from the optical centre of the camera. So reduction in angle of view reduces the field of view of the camera, as shown in fig. 3.

Depth of Field (DoF) is the amount of distance between the nearest and farthest objects that appear with acceptably sharp focus in an image. The nearest distance in focus is called near focus limit and the farthest distance is called far focus limit. These limits are represented by near focal and far focal planes. If the subject image size remains the same, then at any given aperture all lenses will give the same DoF i.e. DoF is independent of focal length of the visual sensor but depends on the magnification. For surveillance purposes the camera is fixed, so DoF changes with change in the zoom level as image size varies with zoom. Higher the zoom level, shallower will be the DoF and lesser will be the number of points in the viewing frustum. Thus the viewing frustum is the volume now bounded by the near focus and the far focus planes. Any point on focal plane is considered sharply in focus. With increase in zoom level, for the same focus distance, the near focal plane and the far focal plane move towards the focal plane as shown in fig. 2 (b)

The depth of field does not abruptly change from sharp to un-sharp, but it is a gradual transition. In fact, everything immediately in front of or in back of the focusing distance begins to lose sharpness, but this will not be perceived by our eyes or by the resolution of the camera. Since there is no critical point of transition, a more rigorous term called the "circle of confusion" (fig. 2 (a))is used to define how much a point needs to be blurred in order to be perceived as un-sharp. When the circle of confusion becomes perceptible to our eyes, this region is said to be outside the depth of field and thus no longer "acceptably sharp" .An acceptably sharp circle of confusion is loosely defined as one which would go unnoticed when enlarged to a standard 8x10 inch print, and observed from a standard viewing distance of about 1 foot.

Camera Model

The Figure.1(a) shows the model of a PTZ camera developed by E. HorsterHorster & Lienhart (2006). The pan and tilt motion of each PTZ camera is modelled as two idealized rotation around the origin along X-axis and Y-axis aligned with image plane and through camera's

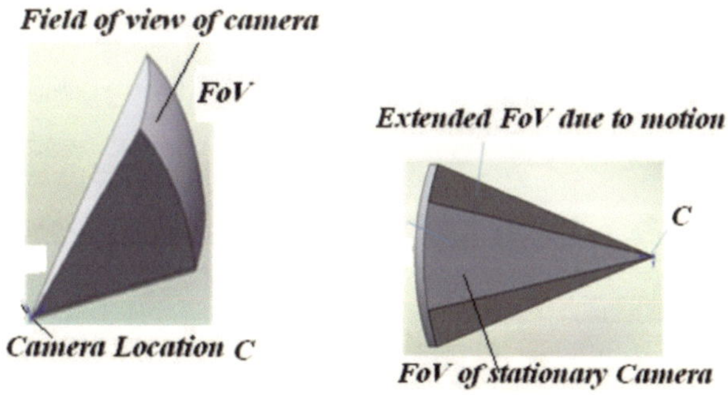

Fig. 3. (a) Field of view of camera (b) Extended Field of View

optical center. The field of view of the camera can be considered as a pyramid (fig.3 (a)). These cameras can be made to rotate $\pm\theta$ degrees about their optimum position along their pan and tilt axis so that they have an extended field of view as shown in Figure.3(b) and hence offer better coverage than pin hole cameras. For surveillance purposes the camera is fixed, so DoF changes with change in the zoom level as image size varies with zoom. Higher the zoom level, shallower will be the DoF and lesser will be the number of points in the viewing frustum. Thus the viewing frustum is now redefined as the volume bounded by the near focus and the far focus planes as shown in figure.1(b).

The zoom level of a visual sensor is considered proportional to its focal length. For a given zoom level of the optical sensor, multiple focal planes have been considered. The concept of multiple focal planes for a particular zoom level is similar to extended field of view. The effective area covered in this case is the union of grids covered by the sensor when focused at individual focal planes. As the problem cannot be solved for infinite values of poses and zoom levels (case of continuous sensor motion), we approximate the continuous case by sampling the poses and the zoom levels. While considering the covered area we considered the modified model of camera considering zoom as shown in figure.1(b). If a grid lies in the extended field of a certain no. of cameras say (n), the the grid is covered. The figure.4(c). shows the intersection of field of view of 2 cameras placed at C_1 and C_2. Any grid in the region II is covered by 2 (n = 2) cameras, and as 'n' increases the probability of occlusion due to randomly moving object reduces.

Probabilistic space model

The sensitive space to be monitored is logically divided into cubical grids (fig.5). The cameras are set to rotate along X and Y direction to enhance coverage. Because of these rotation, the space around the centre of the priority area will be covered for longer time than area near the edges as the most probable location of event will be the centre of the selected area. The probabilistic space model is explained as follows

1. Amount of time for which the space under consideration is covered

   As it can be seen from the Figure. 1(c), the space in the viewing frustum of the camera at the optimum position (centre of field of view) will be covered for the maximum period of time in course of camera motion. That is, the probability of the space at the centre of the field of view, being covered is more compared to the remaining portion of the priority area. A mathematical measure of the amount of relative time a space is under coverage, is

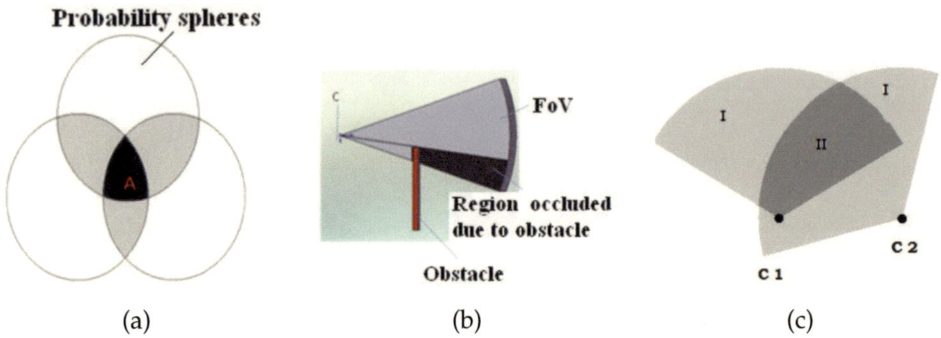

Fig. 4. (a) Region marked A is under the influence of three probability spheres and has the max. weightage compared to other regions (b) Field of view with obstacle (c) Intersection of Field of View

measured as "b " the average of "b_1" and "b_2" on a scale of 0 to 1, for α (pan angle) and β (tilt angle) using equations (1),(2) and(3) where α_{max} and β_{max} are the maximum pan angle and tilt anle respectively.

$$b_1 = 1 - \alpha/\alpha_{max} \tag{1}$$

$$b_2 = 1 - \beta/\beta_{max} \tag{2}$$

$$b = (b_1 + b_2)/2 \tag{3}$$

2. Identification of the high activity areas
   The probability of the presence of an object at the high active area of the priority area is more compared to that it being anywhere else. Hence more importance is given to the focal planes assigned to these high active areas.
3. Quality of image
   The resolution of the image of an object placed at space nearer to the focal plane will be more compared to that of an object placed at space farther from the focal plane. An appropriate distribution has been considered to accommodate this.
   The performance measure corresponding to the above two points, depends on the distance of the space with respect to the focal plane and is calculated as 'a ', a quantitative measure of the quality of the image.
   $$a = 1 - q/q_0 \tag{4}$$
   where q is the distance of point under consideration from the focal plane of the camera and q_0 is the maximum distance from the focal plane within the depth of field.
4. Probability of an image being at the centre of the priority area.
   Probability of an object being placed at the centre of the priority area will be more compared to that being on edges. This can be modelled by assuming a logical sphere of priority which decreases with distance surrounding the priority point. We have modelled the same using Gaussian function as shown in Figure.4(a). If W (eq: 5) is the net performance measure of a priority point under the influence of n Gaussian spheres, then
   $$W_i = W1_i + W2_i + W3_i + - - - - - - - - + Wn_i \tag{5}$$

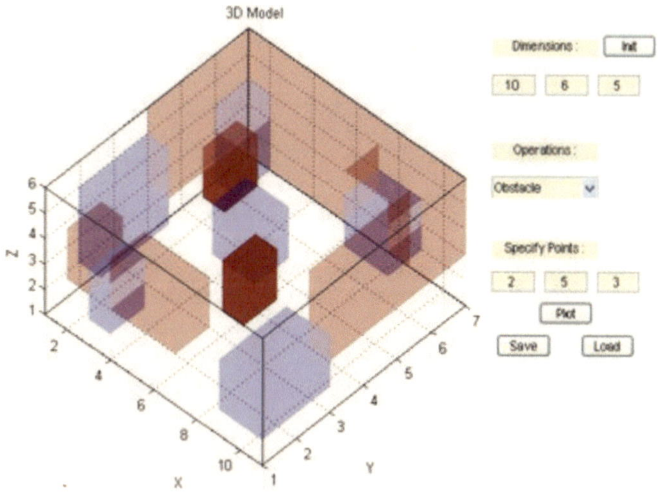

Fig. 5. GUI-Blue colored points represent the priority points, light Maroon colored points represent the feasible points and red colored points represent the obstacles

Where i represents the priority point under consideration, W_i, the performance measure of point i and W_{ji} is the effective performance measure considering the influence of jth on ith point, $1 \leq j \leq n$ for n priority points

Matrix P (eq: 6) denotes the location and performance measure of priority points and is defined as

$$P = P[i,j,k]_{(mXmXm)} \tag{6}$$

where

$$P[i,j,k] = \begin{cases} \Sigma exp(-((d)^2/constant)) & \text{if } d \leq r \\ 0 & \text{if } d > r \end{cases} \tag{7}$$

Where d is the distance of the point from all the priority points and r is the radius of influence that a particular priority point has. Thus P(i,j,k) (equation 7) is the value of the priority point based on the extent of influence of probability spheres affecting that particular priority point.

Floor plan model

The term floor plan denotes a physical three dimensional space which we aim to cover. Any point in space is said to be covered if it is captured with a minimum required resolution i.e. when it lies in the DoF and within the extended field of view of the camera. The feasible locations of camera, the size and shape of obstacles and the sensitive areas with assigned priority for each one can be fed as inputs to the system through GUI (fig.5). The concept of line of sight has been used to model the effect of obstacles on the coverage area of the sensors. Areas which come under the shadow of the obstacles from the line of sight have been removed from the covered area of that sensor as shown in Figure.4(b).These inputs are then converted to priority, feasible, visibility and obstacle matrices S.Indu et al. (2008) with dimension m*m*m, where m is the largest value of dimension among m, n and s of the floor plan so that the algorithm can handle cuboidal floor plan with cubical grids. All the objects and areas have a definite value.

3.1 Coverage metric

A coverage metric is formulated which incorporates all the above said constraints which is formulated based on following assumptions

- A simple, single lens element has been used to represent the optical sensor .
- Aperture of the lens of the optical sensor has been assumed to be constant throughout the algorithm.
- Effect of geometric distortion or blurring of objects has been neglected.

We approximate the continuous motion of cameras into discrete poses by sampling and hence cameras can adopt only those particular poses. The coverage metric is defined as in equation 8.

$$C = \alpha \sum_{priority(2-cam)} t_x + \sum_{non-priority} m_y + \sum_{priority(1-cam)} n_z \tag{8}$$

where

$$t_x = \begin{cases} performance\ measure\ of\ zoom+ \\ performance\ measure\ of\ priority\ points\ covered \\ by\ 2\ cameras + A(i,j,k) \end{cases} \tag{9}$$

$$n_z = \begin{cases} performance\ measure\ of\ zoom+ \\ performance\ measureof\ priority\ points\ covered \\ by\ 1\ camera + A(i,j,k) \end{cases} \tag{10}$$

$$m_y = \begin{cases} performance\ measure\ of\ zoom+ \\ A(i,j,k) \end{cases} \tag{11}$$

A (i,j,k) is the value of visibility matrix at the given point
In the total surveillance area some of the priority points will be covered by 2 cameras and some of them by only one camera and some of the non priority points also will be covered by cameras. The fitness function should be properly defined in such a way that the priority area covered by 2 cameras should be maximised and the covered non priority area be minimized. To increase the probability of covering maximum no. of priority points using 2 cameras we used a weightage factor α in the fitness function. Here t represents priority points covered by two cameras while m represents non priority points. α is the weightage to be given to the coverage of priority points by two cameras over priority points covered by one camera and all non priority points. With increasing value of α the probability of occlusion decreases. As zoom-level increases the DoF reduces and thus the number of points in the viewing frustum reduces. Better solutions will have a higher value of Coverage C. We used GA based optimization for maximising the coverage matric.
The user defined input is used to determine feasible matrix, obstacle matrix, location based priority matrix etc. as follows

$$\mathcal{F} = [f_{ijk}]_{mXmXm} \tag{12}$$

Where

$$f_{ijk} = \begin{cases} 1 & if\ i,j,k\ point\ is\ a\ feasible\ point \\ 0 & if\ i,j,k\ point\ is\ not\ a\ feasible\ point \end{cases}$$

And obstacle matrix as

$$\mathcal{O} = [o_{ijk}]_{mXmXm} \tag{13}$$

Where $o_{ijk} = \begin{cases} 1 & if\ i,j,k\ lies\ in\ obstacle\ region \\ 0 & if\ i,j,k\ does\ not\ \ lies\ in\ obstacle\ region \end{cases}$

Matrix P denotes the location based performance measure of priority points and is defined by equation 6 The visibility matrix generated from matrices F,O,P (equations 12, 13, 14) becomes 9 Dimensional which is very inconvenient to work with. To get a convenient dimension, we map every grid point, every pose and every zoom level to a particular number Erdem (2006) according to the mapping described by the equations (14, 15, 16)

$$position(i,j,k) = (j-1)*N*N+(i-1)*N+k \tag{14}$$

And every pose by

$$pose(\alpha,\beta) = M*(\alpha-1)+\beta \tag{15}$$

where M is the no of discrete pan or tilt angles the camera can assume. and

$$Zoom(z) = (highest\ zl - lowest\ zl)*z/zl \tag{16}$$

where zl is the no discrete zoom levels the camera can assume. The value of 'z' varies from 1 to zl. Now the visibility matrix (equation 17) is reduced to a 4 Dimensional matrix which can be expressed as

$$A = [a_{ijkz}]_{m^3XM^2Xm^3Xz1} \tag{17}$$

Where

$$a_{ijkz} = a + b \tag{18}$$

$0 < a < 1$, depending on the distance of the point under consideration from the focal plane.
$0 < b < 1$, depending on the offset of the pan and tilt angles from there optimum positions.
This visibility matrix along with the priority matrix is then used to calculate the coverage score of any set of cameras placed at different locations.

3.2 Genetic Algorithm Mapping

The first and the foremost step in a design using genetic algorithm is to select all the variables of the problem to be solved. This is a crucial point since other features of the algorithm depend on this selection. Each variable should represent size of the search space, efficiency of the genetic operators etc. The most natural way of representing solutions of the said problem would be a sequence of genes, each coding the actual position the pose and zoom level of individual camera.
Optimization criteria: max
A simple way of encoding would be through a binary bit string:
The Gene of a camera

$$(C(i)) = (X(i),Y(i),Z(i),\alpha(i),\beta(i),zoom[i]) \tag{19}$$

$1 \leq\ i\ \leq no.of camera$
where
$X(i) = \{\ a_1, a_2, ...a_k\}\ _{10}$
$Y(i) = \{\ b_1, b_2, ...b_k\}\ _{10}$

$Z(i)=\{\ c_1,c_2,......c_k\}\ _{10}$
$a_r\ ,b_r,\ c_r\ ,\ \varepsilon\ \{0,1\}\quad 1\le\ r\ \le\ k\quad k=\ log_2(N)\ .$
where coordinate feasible space is of dimension N^3 i.e. $0\le$ x[i],y[i],z[i] $\le$ N-1
$\alpha(i)=\{\ h_1,h_2,......h_s\}\ _{10}$
$\beta(i)=\{\ j_1,j_2,......j_s\}\ _{10}\quad h_t\ ,j_t,\ \varepsilon\ \{0,1\}\quad 1\le\ t\ \le\ s$
and s = $log_2(N_0)$ where pan-tilt space is of cardinality $(N_o)^2$
$N_0 \le \alpha$[i], β[i] $\le N_0$-1 and $zoom[i]=\{\ q_1,q_2,......q_v\}\ _{10}$
$q_b\epsilon\{0,1\}\ ,1\le b\le u$
$u=log_2(N_1)$ where zoom is of cardinality N_1 i.e. $0\le zoom[i]\le N_1-1\ \{\ ..,..,..\}\ _{10}$
is decimal representation of a binary bit string with left most bit as MSB. The gene of each camera C[i], is simply a concatenation of two bit strings. Alternatively speaking, the gene of camera is an abstraction of its location and orientation of its pose in the space. Being a collection of genes, a chromosome would therefore be a representation of an array of cameras belonging to the solution space. Hence problem is redefined to look into the solution space to choose the fittest among them. The fitness function (equation 8) very obviously is the coverage metric for each set of cameras.

3.3 Algorithm

1. An initial random population of N belonging to the search space (within the feasible region only) is chosen and encoded by the above procedure.
2. Next we evaluate the fitness value for each of the population using the matrices of coverage of priority and non priority points generated and a comparison is made regarding the optimality of the solution.
3. Then, we select a population of "good" networks by tournament selection method, two best individuals are simply passed on and we proceed for reproduction.
4. From this population we recombine the species using the following operations:
   a. Crossover with a probability of 0.8 using scattered crossover function.
   b. Mutation with a probability of 0.001 is essential to maintain diversity.
5. These operations yield a new population which replaces the existing one.
6. Steps 2, 3, 4 are repeated until the optimization criterion stabilizes.

All the above implementation has been achieved through the GA package (and toolbox) provided with MATLAB Version 7.0.

4. Validation of tool

Simulation

Both 2D and 3D simulations for camera placement are done and the results are as shown in fig. 9, fig. 10 fig. 11 and fig. 12. For simulation purposes, the floor plan is considered as a simple 10X10X10 cube. Also all the sides of the cube except the floor are being considered as a feasible camera location. The priority area is considered to be a smaller 4x4x4 cube with its center coinciding with the center of the floor plan fig. 11. An obstacle is considered as a pillar extending from grid points 3 to 5 in x, y directions from floor. We used of Genetic Algorithm to solve this optimization problem. The visibility matrix and the priority matrix help the Genetic Algorithm to evaluate the fitness function of various generations. All the coding and matrix representations have been implemented in Matlab. For the purpose of drawing 2-D spaces we have used the help of JAVA- 2D classes to visualize our task. In the case of 2D for simplicity

Pan angle	Tilt angle	Zoom Level	X	Y	Z
45	180	0	0	0	1
315	180	0	0	0	8
315	135	0	0	8	0
135	225	1	1	5	7
135	45	2	1	5	5
45	45	2	1	0	7

Table 1

we have considered the camera field of view to be an arc of variable subtended angle and feasible space containing the whole floor plan. while in case of 3D a simple cube has been considered.
The graph shown in Figure. 6(a) shows that we require only 4 cameras to cover the specified area and 6(b) shows the coverage variation by random placement of cameras and Placement using GA. Figure. 7 shows that the maximum value of α we can assume is 10. The positions and poses of camera when we use 3D model and 2D model are shown in Figure. 11, Figure. 12 and Figure. 9 and Figure. 10 respectively. Table 1 shows results of locations of 6 cameras with their corresponding pan angle, tilt angle, zoom level and coordinates x, y, z

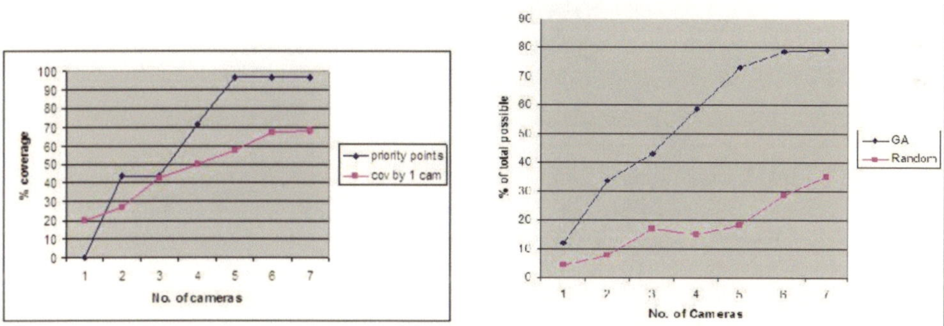

(a) (b)

Fig. 6. (a) No of cameras vs percentage Coverage (b) GA vs Random placement

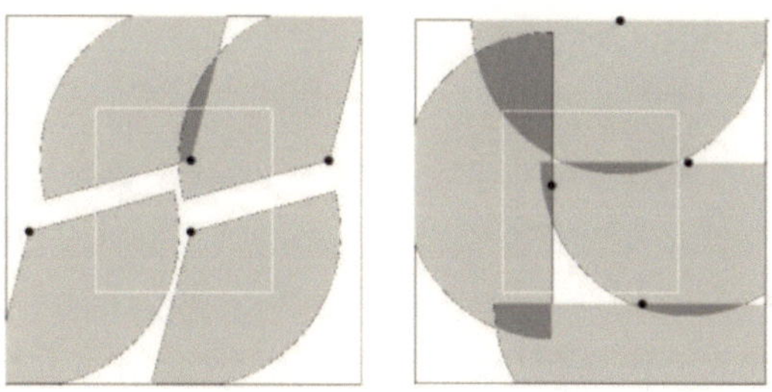

(a) (b)

Fig. 10. Shows the position and pose of the camera to cover an area, for (a) and (b) Equal priority for both inner and outer square

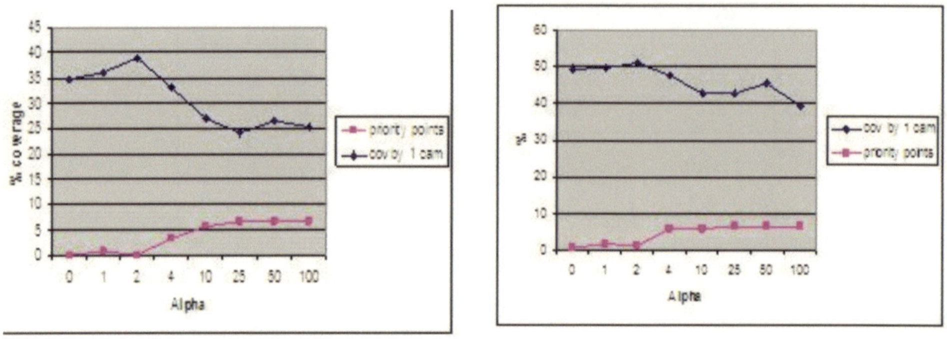

(a) (b)

Fig. 7. Effect of variation of α vs priority points covered by one camera or more than one camera

Fig. 8. Experimental set up with 3 cameras

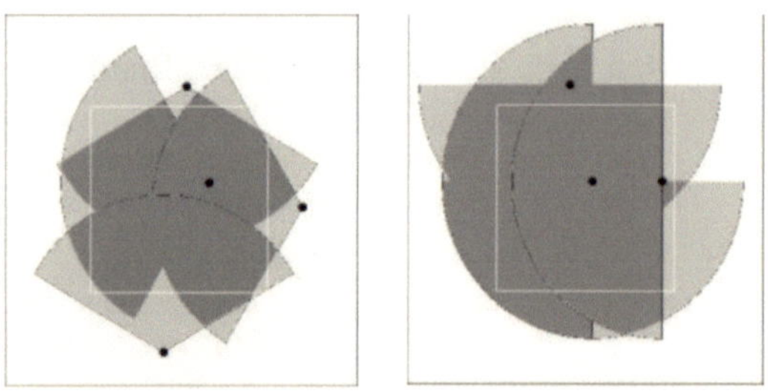

(a) (b)

Fig. 9. Shows the position and pose of the camera to cover an area, for (a) and (b) Inner square as the priority area and for

Experimental evaluation

We validated the proposed tool by placing 3 PTZ cameras. Six discrete clusters of priority points each with different number of points were randomly distributed throughout the space.

We have done the experiment in the digital lab of ECE Department of Delhi Technological

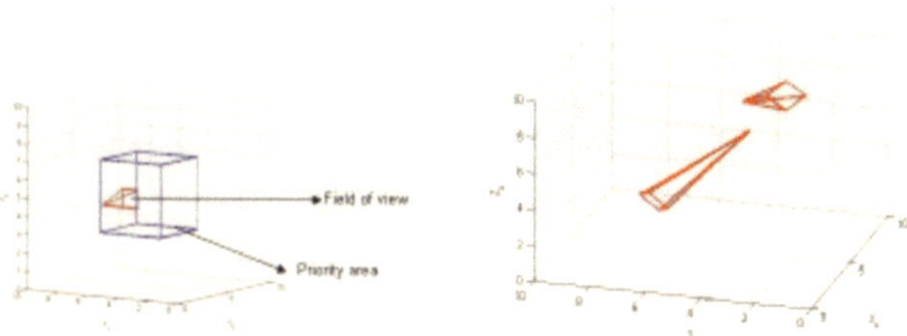

(a) (b)

Fig. 11. Shows the position and pose of the camera to cover a volume (a) using 1 camera (b) using 2 cameras

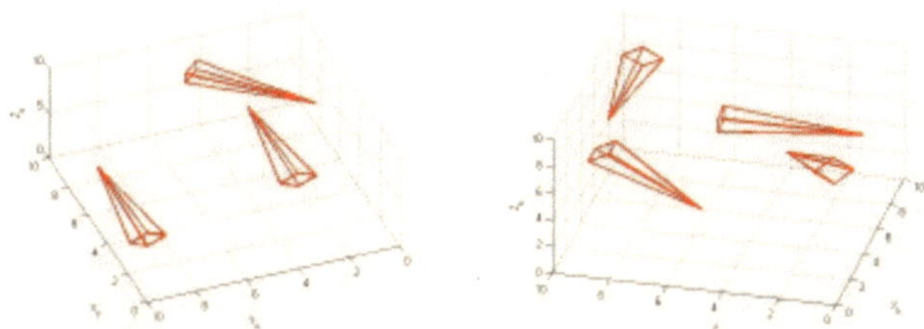

(a) (b)

Fig. 12. Shows the position and pose of the camera to cover a volume (a) using 2 camera (b) using 4 cameras

University, Delhi having the dimensions 60 feet x 30 feet x 10 feet and in the Multimedia lab of Indian Institute of Delhi with dimension 80 feet x 40 feet x 10 feet . Graphical user interface was used to model the lab. A total of 48 and 60 feasible points were identified respectively. Optimum positions, poses and zoom levels of the three cameras were determined using the proposed tool. The cameras were made to rotate 15 degrees about their optimum position along pan and tilt axes. Cameras were coordinated at the start so that their common coverage area is covered at different times to ensure maximum visibility. We observed that the zoom level of farthest area is smaller than nearby area so that we can have detailed information. Using camera locations, pan, tilt angles and zoom level, we can compute mean position corresponding to each camera which will be assigned highest priority as the probability of event at this location is more. Now using camera locations and mean positions the light source locations are determined using the proposed tool. The experimental set up in Digital Lab of Delhi College of Engineering is as shown in fig. 8.It has been observed that:

1. The priority area with largest number of priority points was covered by two cameras and the clusters with fewer number of priority points were covered by only one camera which validates our probabilistic framework.
2. The cameras that were focused at small distances as shown in Figure.14 (a) and Figure.15 (b) had a higher zoom level to capture a detailed image. By doing so it is reducing data redundancy by virtue of capturing fewer non priority points as the region under consideration had a low priority to non priority point ratio. Whereas the cameras focused at large distances as shown in Figure.13 (a) and Figure.14 (b) had a comparatively

lower zoom level to increase the number of points in its viewing frustum. By doing so it is increasing the coverage area to cover maximum priority points (as the region had higher priority to non priority points ratio) while maintaining the requisite resolution. Figure.13 (b) and Figure.15 (a) shows moderate zoom level.

3. The priority areas were covered for a larger time period during the camera motion than non priority areas. This is clear from the pictures shown below taken during camera motion.

   Thus all the six discrete priority areas were covered by the 3 cameras with satisfactory image quality. These observations clearly validate our probabilistic approach for optimization criterion. (Priority areas have been marked with a red boundary in the figures)

(a) (b)

Fig. 13. Shows the image taken by camera placed in IITD (a) camera1 (b) camera2

(a) (b)

Fig. 14. Shows the image taken by (a) camera3 at IITD (b) camera1 at Delhi College of Engineering

(a) (b)

Fig. 15. Shows the image taken by cameras placed in Delhi college of Engineering (a) camera2 (b) camera3

5. Conclusion

We have developed a novel tool for placement of cameras for surveillance applications. Apart from camera location, the tool provides optimum pan-tilt angles and zoom level. As the tool is based on extended field of view, it avoids redundancy in sensor placement. Unlike other placement methods, the proposed method calculates the optimum zoom level which improves the quality of service of the vision system . The tool is completely off line and do not depend on camera parameters or image parameters and hence computationally light. The experimental results validates the tool. The tool will be instrumental in designing camera locations for surveillance of a port or such bigger areas.

6. Acknowledgement

This work is funded by Naval Research Board, Govt. of India under the project "Vision based activity monitoring" with NRB project no. 73 in collaboration with Indian Institute of Technology Delhi. We are thankful to NRB in helping us to develop Computer Vision Lab in our institute, ie Delhi Technological University (Formerly Delhi College of Engineering).

7. References

A.Mittal & Davis, L. S. (2008). A general method for sensor planning in multisensor system: Extension to random occlusion , *International journal of Computer Vision* 76: 31 – 52.

Bodor, R., Drenner, A., Schrater, P. & Papanikolopaulos, N. (2007). Optimal camera placement for automated surveillance tasks, *Journal of Intelligent and Robotic Systems* 50: 257 – 295.

Bose, P., Guibas, L., Lubiw, A., Overmars, M. H., Souvaine, D. L. & Urrutia, J. (1997). The Flood Light Problem, *Int. J. Comp. Geom.* 1: 153 – 163.

Chen, X. & Davis, J. (1999). Cameraplacement considering occlusion for Robust motion Capture, *Standford Computer Science technical Report* .

Dunn, E. & Olague, G. (October 2006). Development of a practical Photogrammatic Network Design using Evolutionary Computing, *Photogrammatic Record* 17.

Erdem, U. M. (2006). Stan Sciaroff, Automated Camera layout to satisfy task specific and floor plan specific coverage requirements , *Computer Vision and Image Understanding* 103: 156 – 169.

Estivill-Castro, V., O'Rourke, J. & J. Urrutia, D. X. (1995). Illumination of polygons with vertex lights, *Information Process Letter 56* 1: 9 – 13.

Fiore, L., Fehr, D., Bodor, R., Drenner, A., Schrater, P. & Papanikolopaulos, N. (2008). Multi Camera Human Activity Monitoring, *Journal of Intelligent and Robotic Systems* 52: 5 – 43.

Hartley, R. . I. (1993). Self-Calibration from Multiple Views with a Rotating Camera, *MDA972-91-C-0053* .

Horster, E. & Lienhart, R. (2006). Illumination of polygons with vertex lights, *ACM Multimedia systems journal, Special issue on Multimedia Surveillance Systems* .

K., T., R., T. & A., K. (1996). Computing occlusion-free viewpoints , *PAMI* 18: 279 – 292.

Kankanhalli, M., Ramakrishnan, R. & Shivaram (2006). A design methodology for Selection and Placement of Sensors in multimedia systems, *Proceedins of VSSN-06* pp. 121 – 130.

K.chakraborty, S.S.Iyengar & H.Qi (2002). Grid Coverage for Surveillance and Target Location in Distributed sensor Networks, *Computer Vision and Image Understanding* 51(12): 1448 – 1453.

Lee, H. & Aghajan, H. (n.d.). Collaborative Node Localization in Surveillance Networks using Opportunistic Target Observations, *VSSNŠ06, October 27, 2006, Santa Barbara, California, USA* pp. 9 – 18.

Lienhart, R., Orster, E., Kellerman, W. & Bouget, J. Y. (n.d.). Calibration of Visual Sensors and Actuators in Distributed Computing Platforms , *VSSNŠ05, November 11, 2005, Singapore* pp. 19 – 28.

Maver, J. & R.Bajcsy (1993). Occlusions as a guide for automated surface aquisition , *IEEE Transactions on Pattern Anal. and Machine.* 15: 417 – 433.

Mittal, A. & Davis, L. S. (2004). Calibrating and optimizing Poses of Visual Sensors in Distributed Platforms , *European Conference on Computer Vision (ECCV).*

Rekleitis, G. (n.d.). Automated Calibration of a Camera Sensor Network , *VSSNŠ05, November 11, 2005, Singapore* .

Rourke, J. O. (1987). *Art Gallery Theorems and Algorithms*, Oxford University Press.

S.Indu, Chaudhury, S., Chaithaanya, Manoj & Bhattacharyya, A. (2008). Optimal Placement of visual sensors using Evolutionary algorithm, *Proceedings of NCVPRIPG* pp. 160 – 164.

Suzuki, I., Tazoe, Y. & Yamashita, M. (2001). Searching a polygonal region from the boundary, *Int. J. Comp. Geom.* 5: 529 – 553.

Tabar, A. M., Keshavarz, A. & Aghajan, H. (n.d.). Smart Home Care Network using Sensor Fusion and Distributed Vision-based Reasoning , *VSSNŠ06, October 27, 2006, Santa Barbara, California, USA* pp. 145 – 154.

Trivedi, M. M., Gandhi, T. L. & Huang, K. S. (2005). Distributed Interactive Video Arrays for Event Capture and Enhanced Situational Awareness, *IEEE 1541-1672/05* pp. 58 – 65.

Wilczkowiak, M. & Sturn, E. B. P. (2001). Camera Calibration and 3D Reconstruction from Single Images Using Parallelepipeds , *IEEE 0-7695-1143-0/01* pp. 142 – 148.

Wren, C. R., Erdem, U. M. & Azarbayejani, A. J. (n.d.). Automatic PanTiltZoom Calibration in the Presence of Hybrid Sensor Networks , *VSSNŠ05, November 11, 2005, Singapore* pp. 113 – 119.

25

Real-time Stereo Disparity Map for Continuous Distance Sensing Applications - A Method of Sparse Correspondence

Kunio Takaya
University of Saskatchewan
Canada

1. Introduction

The dense stereo disparity map, i.e. image based distance measurement has been developed for applications such as robotic vision and video surveillance. Two small video cameras embedded in the hand-held computer or game controller can be turned into a distance image sensor or a range finder. Electrical retina stimulation with the implanted 2D electrode array that has recently been reported is potentially capable for blind people to regain vision with the technology of BMI (Brain Machine Interface). The dense disparity map is definitely one important mode of artificial vision to sense the distance by vision, when such BMI is fully developed. The challenge is to perform frame-by-frame image processing fast enough to keep up with a video rate. (1) The objective of study is to develop a robust and fast stereo matching algorithm usable in the real time video environment.
To calculate and render the stereo disparity map in real time at a video rate is a challenging problem. In the approach to use two cameras posed to have their optical axes in parallel, typically local cross-correlations are measured from a point in the left image to that in the right image along the same raster scan line, then stereo correspondence is searched for every pixel by finding the maximum among the local cross-correlations. The time warp algorithm based on the dynamic programming (DP) optimizes the search for the entire raster scan line. To ensure the accuracy up to a pixel distance or even to a fractional distance, the pixel-to-pixel similarity matrix of size N^2 needs to be calculated for a raster length N. This imposes a large computational burden to calculate a dense stereo disparity map, and to keep up with a video rate such as 30 frames/sec.
The Dynamic Time Warp Algorithm (DTW), an implementation of Dynamic Programming (DP) is a well accepted method for the problem of stereo matching, because DTW has a time constraint that the sequence of data is retained when matching two sequences. In another word, a pixel in a sequence is matched to a pixel after the pixel following a previously matched pixel in the other sequence to be matched. Therefore, DTW is particularly useful to match two raster profiles which are basically a time sequence. Since the DTW matches all pixels in the raster according to the cost function to minimize, the stereo correspondence for all pixels in the raster is calculated as a result. However, the search for matching is exhaustively done for each and every pixel in the raster, thus the process is time consuming particularly to calculate

the N^2 similarity matrix which determines the correlation between a pixel in one raster and a pixel in the other matching raster.
To alleviate this computational burden, sampling sparsely the raster waveform (profile) can reduce the number of calculations N^2 as N becomes considerably smaller than the raster size. Down sampling is one approach, but this reduces the resolution of disparity measurement at the same time, thus defeats the ultimate goal of producing the dense disparity map. Alternative approach is to extract features common to the right and left image at the accuracy of the pixel distance. Those features must be sampled sequentially, so that the DTW can determine the correspondence among all extracted common features. For example, peak points and steep edges can be candidates for such a common feature.

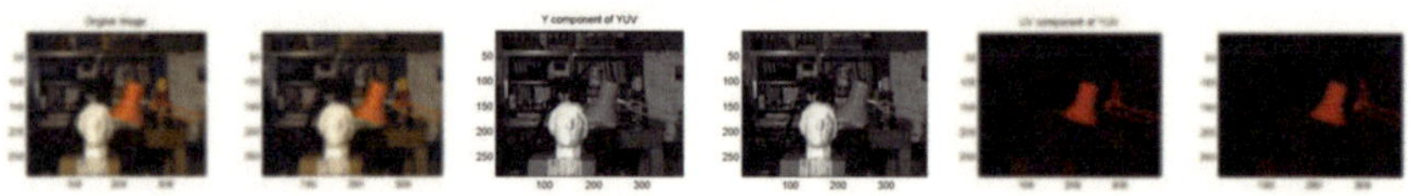

Fig. 1. A pair of original stereo images, Y and UV image pairs in YUV color space (or V and HS in HVS color space)

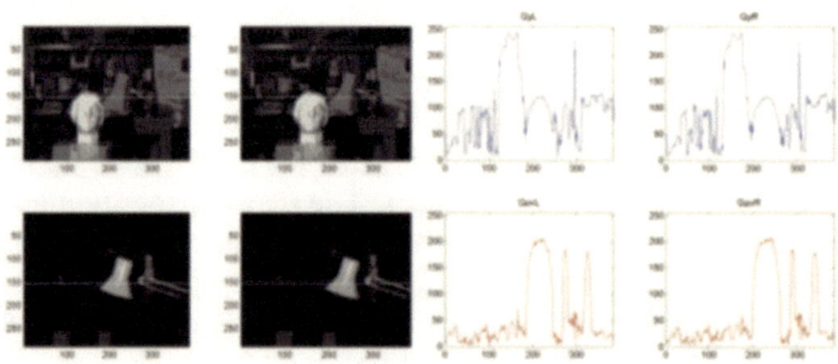

Fig. 2. Y (luma) image and UV (chroma) image of a pair of stereo images and raster waveforms sampled at the white horizontal line

Successful works in producing good quality dense disparity maps have rather used image processing (6) (5) (2) than digital signal processing (DSP) which is more advantageous for raster scanning video to gain the speed in time critical situations. Image based disparity maps adopt image segmentation to break down the whole image into many small patches often in terms of color. Then, the disparities among the segmented patches are calculated to produce a dense disparity map of the segmented image. In this paper, we do the image segmentation in terms of 1D raster image (waveform) to perform sparse sampling based on the 1D patches. We propose coarse qauntization applied to the luma image which is Y-component in the YUV color space or V-component in the HSV color space, and to the chroma image as well which is the UV-component in YUV or the HS component in HSV as shown in Fig. 1. Stereo matching can usually be performed well only with the luma image segmentation. But for some images dominated by color, color based image segmentation is better suited. The run-lengths at coarsely quantized levels are thought to be the 1D patch which is used as a feature to represent a given raster waveform. Thus, we can realize the sparse sampling to reduce the size of the similarity matrix, much smaller than N^2. We also consider humps observed in the denoised raster profiles by the median filter as a 1D patch similar to the 2D patches resulting from image segmentation. In this paper, we studied two methods of finding sparse correspondence for stereo matching, (1) run-lengths at the coarsely quantized raster waveform and (2) humps found in the denoised raster waveform. Typical raster waveforms observed in the Y and UV image are shown in Fig. 2 for a pair of the right and left image.

2. Dynamic Time Warp algorithm

Stereo matching in the binocular image pair is to find two corresponding feature points, one in the left image and the other in the right image. The distance between the corresponding points are referred to as stereo disparity that is inversely proportional to the distance to the point in the 3D space. Stereo matching is a problem of optimization to match all points in a raster scan line so that the error criterion that reflects the degree of mismatching is minimized. The time warp algorithm of the dynamic programming is one of the robust algorithms which is known to work even for the image having some occluded objects, meaning that an object is seen from a camera but not from the other. This method (7) called dynamic time warp algorithm (DTW) matches two sequences in the order of the sequence allowing multiple correspondence to a given point. This condition is regarded as a constraint imposed in the optimization. Therefore, the DTW is particularly useful to find stereo correspondence in the raster scanned 1D raster profiles (waveforms). There is another useful stereo matching method called Scott and Longuet-Higgins algorithm (8) that utilizes the singular decomposition method (SVD) applied to the proximity matrix **G**. The element of **G** is given by

$$G_{ij} = e^{-r_{ij}^2/2\sigma^2}, \quad i = 1, \cdots, m; \; j = 1, \cdots, n$$

where, **G** is Gaussian weighted distance between two features $I_i(i = 1, \ldots, m)$ and $J_j(j = 1, \ldots, n)$, and $r_{ij} = ||I_i - J_j||$. Unlike the DTW algorithm, this matching method is not constrained by the data sequence. Thus, the method is applicable to the 2D or multi-dimensional data. Since we chose to use 1D raster waveforms for stereo matching in order to reduce overall computation time to keep up with the video rate, we ruled out the SVD based Scott and Longuet-Higgins algorithm.

In the DTW algorithm (7), the similarity matrix **S** and the cost matrix **C** play the key role in the optimization process. The similarity matrix for two raster profiles I_ℓ and I_r of size N is given by

$$\mathbf{S} = \{s(n,m), \; n = 1, \cdots, N \text{ and } m = 1, \cdots, N\}$$

S indicates how similar the nth pixel point of the sequence I_ℓ is to the mth pixel point of I_r.

$$s(n,m) = \sum_{k=-L/2}^{L/2} |I_\ell(n+k) - I_r(m+k)|$$

for a window size $L+1$. Stereo matching is the problem to minimize the penalty to match dissimilar points to match all points in I_ℓ and I_r. Define the left pixel array up to the nth element, and the right pixel array up to the mth element as

$$X_{1\cdots n} = \{I_\ell(1), I_\ell(2), \cdots, I_\ell(i), \cdots, I_\ell(n)\}$$
$$Y_{1\cdots m} = \{I_r(1), I_r(2), \cdots, I_r(j), \cdots, I_r(m)\}$$

which is the sum of absolute difference (SAD) in correlation.

The element of the cost matrix **C** is given by

$$C(X_{1\cdots n}, Y_{1\cdots m}) =$$
$$s(n,m) + min \begin{cases} C(X_{1\cdots n-1}, Y_{1\cdots m-1}) \\ C(X_{1\cdots n}, Y_{1\cdots m-1}) \\ C(X_{1\cdots n-1}, Y_{1\cdots m}) \end{cases}$$

$C(X_{1\cdots n}, Y_{1\cdots m})$ is the minimum cost to match the nth pixel point of I_ℓ and the mth pixel point of I_r among all previous matches of $\leq n$ and $\leq m$. There are only three choices to match $I_\ell(n)$ and $I_r(m)$. Given the costs to match upto $I_\ell(n-1)$ and $I_r(m-1)$, $I_\ell(n-1)$ and $I_r(m)$, $I_\ell(n)$ and $I_r(m-1)$, the smallest of the three costs plus the similarity $s(n,m)$ is the cost to match $I_\ell(n)$ and $I_r(m)$. Back tracking the matrix **C** shown in Fig. 3 from the right most column or from the bottom most row yields the optimum path that defines the best matching of all pixels.

.	.	.	.	$I_\ell(n-1)$	$I_\ell(n)$
.	.	.	.	.	.
.	.	.	.	.	.
.	.	.	.	.	.
$I_r(m-1)$	.	.	.	$C(X_{1\cdots n-1}, Y_{1\cdots m-1})$	$C(X_{1\cdots n}, Y_{1\cdots m-1})$
$I_r(m)$	.	.	.	$C(X_{1\cdots n-1}, Y_{1\cdots m})$	$s(n,m)$ + min. of 3 neighbours
.	.	.	.	.	.

Fig. 3. Local decision making in the cost matrix **C** by the DTW dynamic programming

The size of a raster waveform is $N = 320$ for the CIF image. The size of the similarity matrix **S** and that of the cost matrix **C** is $N^2 = 102,400$. Furthermore, the window size is practically as large as $L = 10$. The required computation for **S** and **C** is about 1 million calculations, which substantially make the implementation of the DTW algorithm difficult in video applications.

3. DTW implementation for run-lengths in coarsely quantized Y and/or UV image

In Fig. 2, the gray scale image of the luma component Y and that of the chroma component UV combined (or V and HS in HVS color space) are shown along with the raster waveforms at the white position line of the left and right images. The luma image represents the light intensity of all wave lengths and the chroma image carries color information , hue at all saturation levels. The disparity measurement can be applied to either image or both depending on the objects of interest in the scene. In order to demonstrate the sparse feature extraction for the DTW algorithm to accomplish stereo matching, we use the luma Y image as an example to illustrate the steps of digital signal processing (DSP) illustrated in Fig. 4.

The raster waveform captured from a video camera is affected by various sources of noise such as photon noise, thermal noise, and electronic noise. The source video signal is, therefore, first filtered with the 1D median filter of a length of 5 or 7 to eliminate salt and pepper type noise which produces faulty break in a run-length. The denoised waveforms are then coarsely quantized to produced 4 non-zero quantization levels as shown in the top row of Fig. 4. Then run-lengths measured at each of the 4 quantized levels are calculated and shown in the middle and bottom row. Level 4 is the largest and level 1 is the smallest quantization level. The run-length traces in red is for the left image and blue is for the right image. Notice that the number of runs are not necessarily the same between the right and left, but similar in the numbers. The run at a coarsely quantized level means that the gray scale values within the run

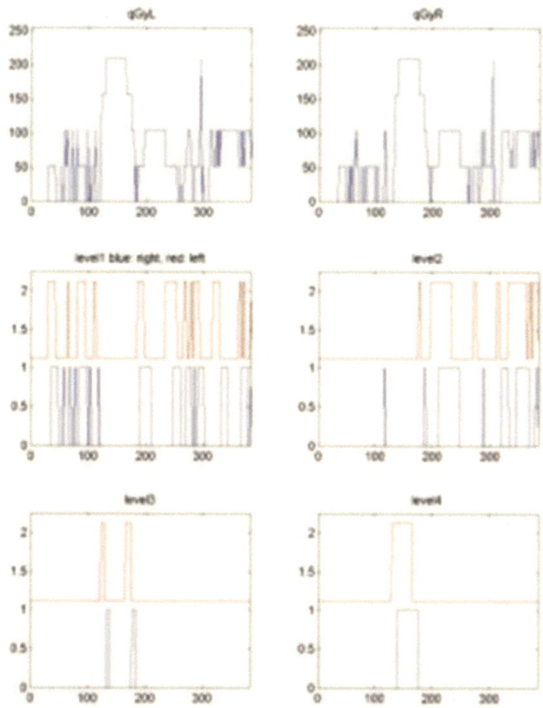

Fig. 4. Coarse quantization and run-lengths of level wise binary waveforms

fall in the range greater than the quantization level, but less than the next higher quantization level. We regard that such a run indicates a contiguous block of almost the same gray scale value, meaning a 1D patch of image segmentation. Such runs are generally a feature common to the left and right stereo images. Associated with the run-length, the position of centroid and the positions of edges constitutes the sparse samples for stereo matching. Since the number of runs found for all 4 levels are much smaller than the size of the raster waveform N, we can save the computational time to calculate $\mathbf{S}$ and $\mathbf{C}$.

The coarse quantization applied to the raster waveform produces four binary runs at the four levels of quantization, i.e. Level4 $>$ Level3 $>$ Level2 $>$ Level1, so that the higher the level number the more intense is the image object. The middle level such as Level3 and Level2 contains the transitions to a higher intensity. Let $r_L(i,k)$ denote the kth run-length of the left raster at the ith level. Let $r_R(j,\ell)$ denote the ℓth run-length of the right raster at the jth level. The indices k and ℓ are the sequential index to encompass all levels, $0 < k \leq N_L$ and $0 < \ell \leq N_R$ where N_L and N_R are the total number of runs found in the left and right raster, respectively. Let

$$q(i,j) = \begin{cases} 1 \text{ if } i \neq j \\ 0 \text{ if } i = j \end{cases}$$

The element of the similarity matrix $\mathbf{S}$ is defined as

$$s(k,\ell) = |r_L(i,k) - r_R(j,\ell)| + \alpha q(i,j)$$

to make $s(k,\ell)$ take a smaller value if the ℓth right run and the kth left run are similar in length and belong to the same quantization level. The size of the similarity matrix is $N_L \times N_R$.

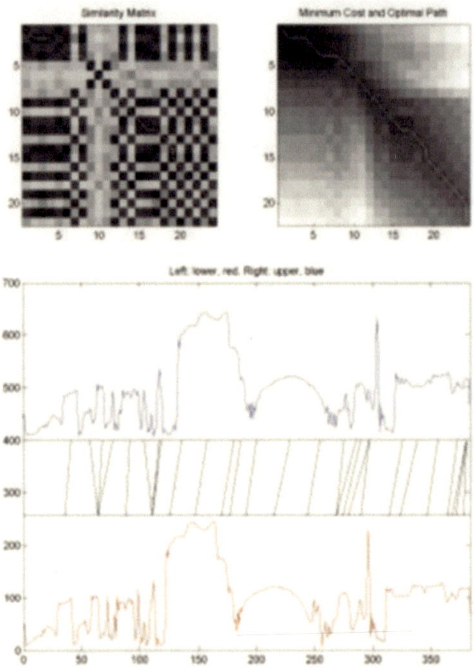

Fig. 5. The similarity matrix **S** and the cost matrix **C** of the DTW algorithm and stereo matching for the sparse feature points defined by the runs at coarse quantization levels

Where, α is the penalty to associate the runs in different levels. Another approach is to match runs with in the same quantization level. we define the similarity matrix **S** at level i as

$$s(k,\ell) = |r_L(i,k) - r_R(i,\ell)|$$

In this case, we deal with four similarity matrices of the size, $N_{L,i} \times N_{R,i}$ for $i = 1,2,3$ and 4. For the coarse quantization shown in Fig. 4, the size of the similarity matrix that considers all the runs in all 4 levels is $\mathbf{S}(23 \times 25) = 575$, whereas the sizes of the individual similarity matrices are of size $\mathbf{S}_1(13 \times 15) = 195$, $\mathbf{S}_2(7 \times 7) = 49$, $\mathbf{S}_3(2 \times 2) = 4$ and $\mathbf{S}_4(1 \times 1) = 1$. Thus, the total number of the elements is 249. The latter approach to match individually within a quantization level was resulted in a less number of calculations to evaluate the four similarity matrices compared to a single **S** in the former case.

The DTW algorithm is applied to the sparse features derived from the binary runs defined by the coarsely quantized raster waveform. The rising and trailing edge and the centroid of each run were used as sparse samples. The similarity matrix **S** and the cost matrix **C** for the combined runs of all 4 levels are shown in the upper images in Fig. 5, in which the minimum path (optimal solution) of matching is shown by the white zig-zag line. All correspondences between the sparse features in the left and those in the right are shown in the lower frame of Fig. 5. Matching with multiple points are resulted from the horizontal or vertical sliding of the minimum path in the cost matrix **C**. Multiple points matching with a single point generally means that those multiple points failed to find a better matching feature (partner) likely due to the occlusion that occurred in the image of the single corresponding point. The disparities

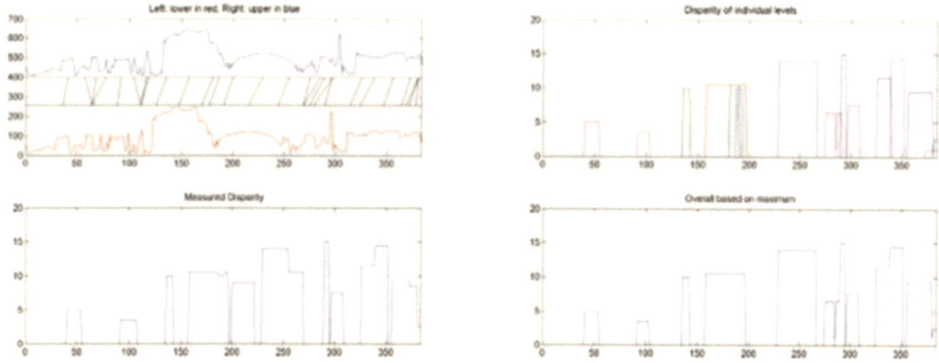

(a) by a combined **S** (b) by 4 **S**'s at 4 levels

Fig. 6. Bottom frames show the 1D disparity profiles determined (a) by the combined similarity matrix **S**, and (b) by the 4 **S**'s at 4 quantization levels

at the extracted sparse feature points are then calculated. Since the sparse feature is the run of a binary level, the disparity applies to the range of the run as shown in Fig. 6. The disparities found from the DTW individually applied for 4 different quantization levels are shown in the right column (b) in Fig. 6 which agrees well with the combined case in the left column (b) in Fig. 6.

4. Sparse correspondence based on major humps in the raster profile

Another approach to determine the sparse correspondence of features is to use major humps that exist in a raster waveform. The previous method approximated a raster waveform by a coarsely quantized step-wise waveform, then applied the measurement of runs at each of the quantization level in order to determine the sparsely sampled feature points. The approach to detect major humps involved in a raster waveform works equally well because those humps are generally the features representing the image in the raster scan line. The hump here means an upward convex shape defined by a sharp rising and a falling edge. Mathematically, a hump is defined for the waveform $f(t)$ for $t \in [t_1, t_2]$ with the condition that satisfies,

$$\frac{df(t_1)}{dt} > +\epsilon, \quad \frac{df(t_2)}{dt} < -\epsilon$$

ϵ specifies the steepness of the slope. Since the hump here is defined only in terms of the derivatives of the raster waveform, a hump is not necessarily a single modal hump, but it could have multiple modal points, or peaks in another word. We regard whatever the waveform that begins with a slope greater than $+\epsilon$ and ends with the slope less than $-\epsilon$ is a hump. Small wigglings that often exist in a major hump can be ignored and included in the big hump with an appropriate value of ϵ as the slopes of such wigglings are small when they appear minor profiles in the hump.

Since this hump detection uses the derivative waveforms, it is quite important to carefully denoise waveforms without altering major hump profiles in the waveform. The following digital signal processing procedure was adopted to successfully accomplish hump detection and extraction of sparse features.

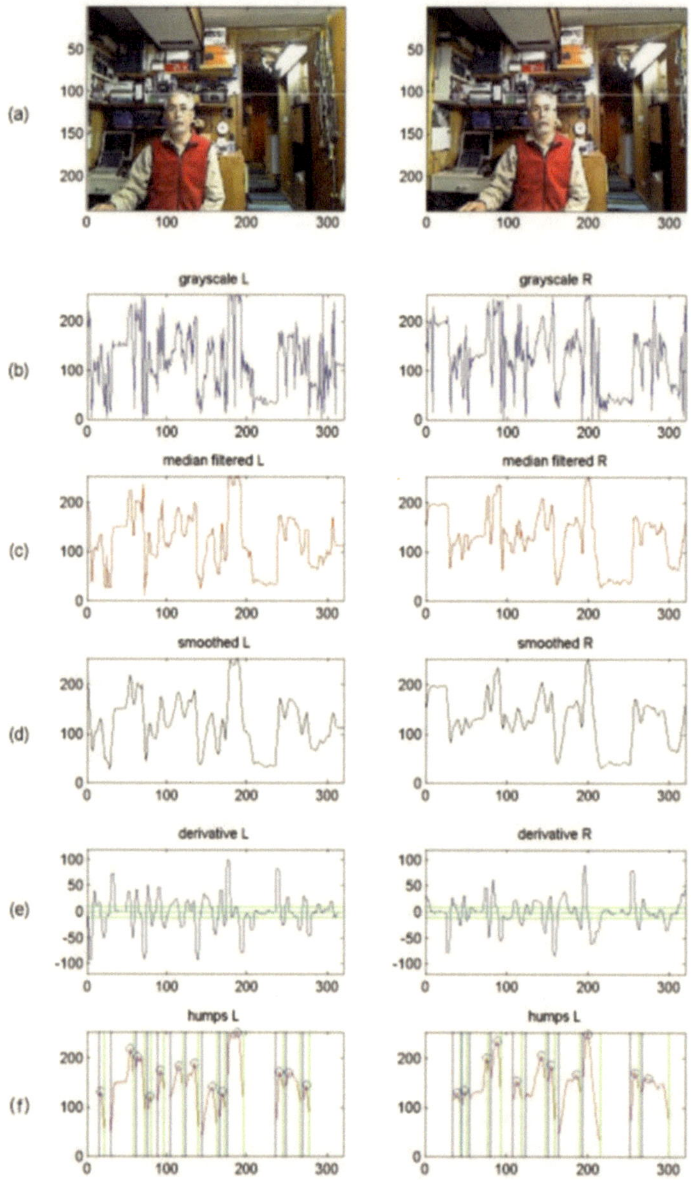

Fig. 7. Sequence of digital signal processings (DSP) for hump detection: (a) Original left and right image, (b) Raster waveforms at the cursor line of (a), (c) Processed by 7 point 1D median filter, (d) processed by 5 point FIR smoothing filter, (e) First derivative of waveforms in (d) and the threshold $\pm\epsilon$, (f) Detected humps indicated by a start line in black, a stop line in green, and a circle at the peak of the hump.

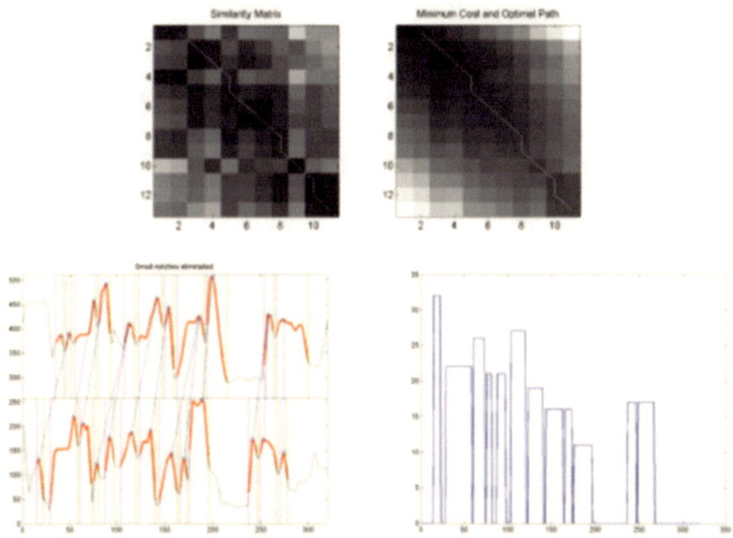

Fig. 8. The similarity matrix **S** and the cost matrix **C** of the DTW algorithm based on the major humps as sparse features (upper frame), correspondence of humps in the left and right waveforms, and the calculated disparities (lower frames) of the same waveforms as in Fig. 7.

1. Capture a pair of raster waveforms, left and right.
2. Apply a 7 point median filter to denoise the left and right waveforms.
3. Apply a 5 point symmetric smoothing FIR filter.
4. Differentiate the denoised and smoothed left and right waveforms.
5. Apply threshold ϵ to find the beginning and end of humps, and record the duration, peak position, peak value of each hump.

The sequence of digital signal processings (DSP) is illustrated in Fig. 7. The position of the raster scan line is indicated by a white line in (a) of Fig. 7. The humps found by this stream of DSP processings are shown in (f) of Fig. 7 for the left and right waveform. Features comparable between the left and right are seen in (f) of Fig. 7. Some detected humps have more than one peak, i.e. multi-modal. The threshold applied to waveforms of the first derivative, $\pm\epsilon$ are shown in (e) of Fig. 7.

For each hump detected, say ith hump of the left, duration $d_L(i)$ of the hump, peak value $v_L(i)$ are recorded. Similarly, duration $d_R(j)$ and peak value $v_R(j)$ are recorded for the jth hump of the right waveform. The element of the similarity matrix **S** is defined as

$$s(i,j) = \alpha|d_L(i) - d_R(j)| + \beta|v_L(i) - v_R(j)| + \gamma|i - j|$$

Fig. 8 shows the stereo matching with the DTW algorithm applied to the sparse features (humps). The numbers of humps found for this particular scan line are 11 for the left, and 13 for the right waveform. In this optimization, a set of parameters $(\alpha, \beta, \gamma) = (0, 0.67, 0.33)$ was used. Using the correspondence between the left and right humps, the disparities were calculated and shown in the lower panel of Fig. 8. The graph of the disparities indicates that images in Fig. 7 have relatively near background in the left edge of the image and far background in the left edge.

5. Experimental system and results

An experimental system that aims at the realization of real-time display of continuous changes of disparity maps at a video rate of 30 fps, was built for the Windows platform. The system is a software based system except that two USB CCD cameras (Webcam) were used. As two identical USB cameras are simultaneously used for video capturing, the driver has to be of type that recognizes different units of the same camera as separate units. Only a few USB cameras such as QuickCam Pro 4000, QuickCam Pro 9000, Watchport/V2 and Microsoft LifeCam VX-700 can be used in the multi-camera applications. The spacing between the two cameras is set between 6 cm to 10 cm. The programs were written in Visual C# 2008 Express (C language). XVideoOCX (Marvelsoft) was used to interface USB cameras to the programs, mainly utilizing its real-time video capturing capability. For video rate control of the developed programs, the timer interrupt caused by the end of frame was used.

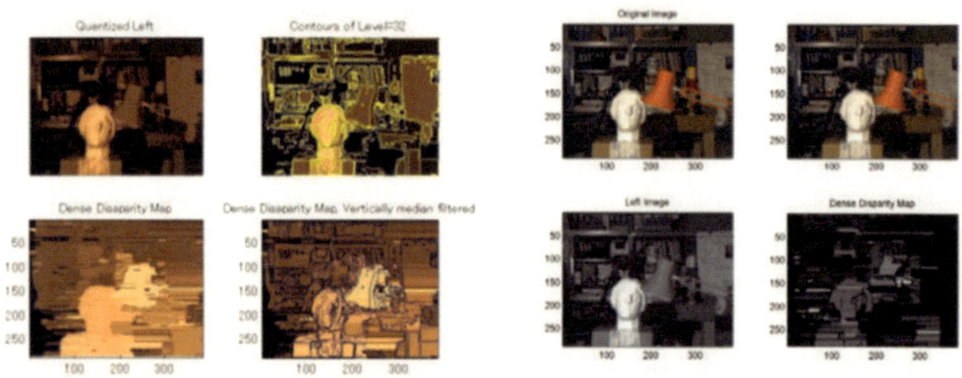

Fig. 9. Dense disparity map by the coarse quantization method (left), and dense disparity map by the hump detector method (right) are shown in the right-bottom frame for the data set "statue"

The proposed two methods, the coarse quantization method and the hump detector method, were applied to various stereo pair images, (Tsukuba database etc.) to find out what degree of reduction is possible for the size of the similarity matrix **S**. The major interest of this paper is to construct a compact similarity matrix **S** using sparse sampling of the features involved in a raster waveform of the image. The actual implementation of the proposed methods in an embedded system is in progress using the system mentioned above, however, it is beyond the scope of this paper. The DDM for the data set "statue" is shown in Fig. 9 (left) for the coarse quantization method, and in Fig. 9 (right) for the hump detector method. The DDM for another data set "buildings" is shown in Fig. 10. Figures for the coarse quantization methods, Fig. 9 and Fig. 10 (left), show the image of coarse quantization and the resulting DDM with and without contour lines superimposed. Figures for the hump detector method, Fig. 9 and Fig. 10 (right), show the original image and the resulting DDM in which borders are shown dark as no disparity is measured in between the adjacent humps. Dark border lines serve for the same purpose of contours. In DDM, the greater the disparity, the brighter is the pixel. The closer objects are shown by the brighter intensity. Vertically, the raster scan lines were down sampled by 4:1 for all DDM's shown here to further reduce computation time.

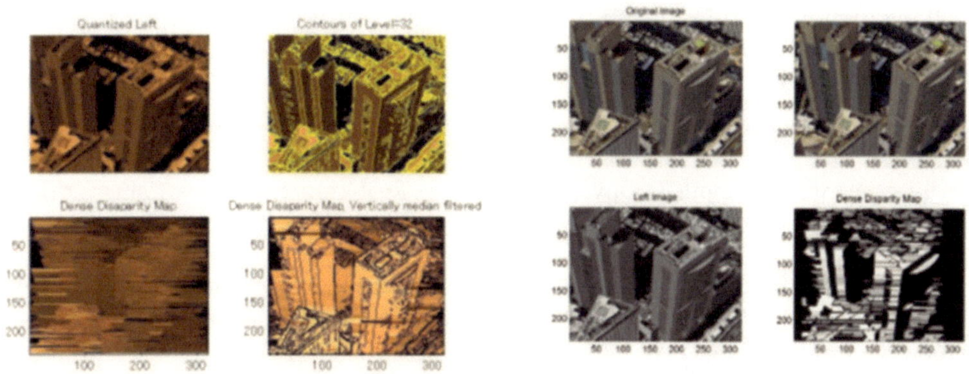

Fig. 10. Dense disparity map by the coarse quantization method (left), and dense disparity map by the hump detector method (right) are shown in the right-bottom frame for the data set "buildings"

6. Conclusive remarks

Dynamic dense disparity map showing the distance to the video objects in real-time at a video rate is a challenging problem. Raster based 1D stereo matching for the camera pose that the lens axes are in parallel is more straightforward and faster than the image based 2D matching. The dynamic time warp (DTW) algorithm of the dynamic programming is a well accepted robust optimization method for matching two 1D raster waveforms of the left and right image. This method requires the similarity matrix **S** of the size N^2 for the raster size N. The large size of **S**, N^2 is the obstacle to continuously display the disparity map, DDM at a video rate of 30 fps since the elements of **S** require local correlations amongst all points in the left image and all points in the right image. In order to realize real time display of the DDM, it is crucially important to reduce N down to a much smaller number of feature points. Thus, the computation time to calculate **S** can be dramatically reduced by the square of the size reduction. Down sampling to reduce N defeats the purpose of disparity measurement because the spatial resolution is also reduced resulting less accurate disparity measurement. Two methods to significantly reduce the size N to create the sparse feature samples without sacrificing the spatial resolution of stereo matching, are proposed and tested.

One approach is to use the binary runs at the levels of coarse quantization from the rising and falling edges and the centroids of the runs. The second method is to use major humps detected in the raster waveforms. The sparse feature points in this case are the starting and ending points and the peaks of humps. For the CIF image of 352×288, $N = 352$ and $N^2 = 123{,}904$. The size of the sparse set for the first method based on the binary runs is typically $N = 30$ and $N^2 = 900$. The second method based on the humps was around $N = 15$ and $N^2 = 225$. Roughly speaking, reduction is 10:1, whereas the second method of hump detector extracting 10∼20 humps gives a reduction of 20:1. In the previously developed system which performs the DTW algorithm for every pixel of the raster size $N = 352$, it took approximately 7 second to complete a dense disparity map. The raster scan lines are down sampled by the ratio of 4:1, so that the time for one raster waveform is 7000/72=97 ms. The reduction of the calculation time for **S** from $N^2 = 123{,}904$ down to $N^2 = 225$ is 550:1, and down to $N^2 = 900$ is 138:1. This means that the sparse feature points can be reduced to 0.176 ms per raster or 12.7 ms per frame if we use the hump detector. Including the overhead time to applly the 7 point median filter followed by the 5 point smoothing FIR filter, then the first derivatives, a frame time of the video rate 30 fps that is 33 ms, is sufficient to complete the digital signal processing (preprocessing) and the DTW algorithm to generate DDM.

7. References

[1] S. Forestmann, Y. Kanou, J. Ohya, S. Thuering, Real-Time Stereo by Using Dynamic Programming, Computer Vision and Pattern Recognition Workshop, vol. 27, issue 02 June 2004.

[2] A. Klaus, M. Sormann, K. Karner, Segment-Based Stereo Matching Using Belief Propagation and a Self-Adapting Dissimilarity Measure. ICPR 2006, Vol. 3, pp. 15-18, Hong Kong, Aug. 20-24, 2006.

[3] Christopher M. Christoudias, Bogdan Georgescu and Peter Meer, Synergism in Low Level Vision, Int. Conf. on Pattern Recognition. ICPR 2002, Vol. 4, p. 40150 Quebec City, Aug. 11-15, 2002

[4] S. Birchfield and C. Tomasi, Depth Discontinuity by Pixel-to-Pixel Stereo, The 6th IEEE Int. Conf. on Computer Vision, Bombay, Mumbai, India, pages 1073-1080, January 1998.

[5] M. Gong and Y-H Yang, Fast Stereo Matching Using Reliability-Based Dynamic Programming and Consistency Constraints, Proc. of the 9th Int. Conf. on Computer Vision (ICCV 2003) pp. 610-617. Nice, 2003.

[6] H. Hirschmuller, Stereo Vision in Structured Environments by Constistent Semi-Global Matching, IEEE Int. Conf. on Computer Vision and Pattern Recognition (CVPR 2006) New York, June, 2006.

[7] Dan Ellis, Dynamic Time Warp (DTW) in Matlab, http://labrosa.ee.columbia.edu/matlab/dtw/

[8] Maurizio Pilu, A Direct Method for Stereo Correspondence based on Singular Value Decomposition, In IEEE Conf. on Computer Vision and Pattern Recognition (CVPR 1997), pp.261-266, Puerto Rico June, 1997.